NORDIC FILM CULTURES AND CINEMAS OF ELSEWHERE

Traditions in World Cinema

General Editors
Linda Badley (Middle Tennessee State University)
R. Barton Palmer (Clemson University)

Founding Editor
Steven Jay Schneider (New York University)

Titles in the series include:

Traditions in World Cinema
Linda Badley, R. Barton Palmer, and Steven Jay Schneider (eds.)

Japanese Horror Cinema
Jay McRoy (ed.)

New Punk Cinema
Nicholas Rombes (ed.)

African Filmmaking
Roy Armes

Palestinian Cinema
Nurith Gertz and George Khleifi

Czech and Slovak Cinema
Peter Hames

The New Neapolitan Cinema
Alex Marlow-Mann

American Smart Cinema
Claire Perkins

The International Film Musical
Corey Creekmur and Linda Mokdad (eds.)

Italian Neorealist Cinema
Torunn Haaland

Magic Realist Cinema in East Central Europe
Aga Skrodzka

Italian Post-neorealist Cinema
Luca Barattoni

Spanish Horror Film
Antonio Lázaro-Reboll

Post-beur Cinema
Will Higbee

New Taiwanese Cinema in Focus
Flannery Wilson

International Noir
Homer B. Pettey and R. Barton Palmer (eds.)

Films on Ice
Scott MacKenzie and Anna Westerstahl Stenport (eds.)

Nordic Genre Film
Tommy Gustafsson and Pietari Kääpä (eds.)

Contemporary Japanese Cinema since Hana-Bi
Adam Bingham

Chinese Martial Arts Cinema (2nd edition)
Stephen Teo

Slow Cinema
Tiago de Luca and Nuno Barradas Jorge

Expressionism in Cinema
Olaf Brill and Gary D. Rhodes (eds.)

French Language Road Cinema
Michael Gott

Transnational Film Remakes
Iain Robert Smith and Constantine Verevis

Coming of Age in New Zealand
Alistair Fox

New Transnationalisms in Contemporary Latin American Cinemas
Dolores Tierney

Celluloid Singapore
Edna Lim

Short Films from a Small Nation
C. Claire Thomson

B-Movie Gothic
Justin D. Edwards and Johan Höglund (eds.)

Francophone Belgian Cinema
Jamie Steele

The New Romanian Cinema
Christina Stojanova (ed.) with the participation of Dana Duma

French Blockbusters
Charlie Michael

Nordic Film Cultures and Cinemas of Elsewhere
Anna Westerstahl Stenport and Arne Lunde (eds.)

edinburghuniversitypress.com/series/tiwc

NORDIC FILM CULTURES AND CINEMAS OF ELSEWHERE

Edited by Anna Westerstahl Stenport
and Arne Lunde

EDINBURGH
University Press

Edinburgh University Press is one of the leading university presses in the UK. We publish academic books and journals in our selected subject areas across the humanities and social sciences, combining cutting-edge scholarship with high editorial and production values to produce academic works of lasting importance. For more information visit our website: edinburghuniversitypress.com

© editorial matter and organisation Anna Westerstahl Stenport and Arne Lunde, 2019, 2021

© the chapters their several authors, 2019, 2021

Edinburgh University Press Ltd
The Tun—Holyrood Road
12 (2f) Jackson's Entry
Edinburgh EH8 8PJ

First published in hardback by Edinburgh University Press 2019

Typeset in 10/12.5 pt Sabon by
Servis Filmsetting Ltd, Stockport, Cheshire

A CIP record for this book is available from the British Library

ISBN 978 1 4744 3805 6 (hardback)
ISBN 978 1 4744 3806 3 (paperback)
ISBN 978 1 4744 3807 0 (webready PDF)
ISBN 978 1 4744 3808 7 (epub)

The right of the contributors to be identified as authors of this work has been asserted in accordance with the Copyright, Designs and Patents Act 1988 and the Copyright and Related Rights Regulations 2003 (SI No. 2498).

CONTENTS

List of Figures ix
Acknowledgments xii
List of Contributors xiv
Traditions in World Cinema xx

1. Introduction: Nordic Film Cultures and Cinemas of Elsewhere 1
   Patrick Ellis, Arne Lunde, and Anna Westerstahl Stenport

PART I. TRACES AND ERASURES

2. Mapping Cinema Ghosts: Reconstructing the Circulation of Nordic Silent Film in Australia 25
   Julie K. Allen

3. Charlie Chan's Last Mystery, or the Transcultural Disappearance of Warner Oland 42
   Kim Khavar Fahlstedt

4. Carin Fock-Göring's Gravestone: Tracing the Legacy of the Swedish First Lady of the Third Reich 53
   Patrick Wen

CONTENTS

5. Mobility and Marginalization: Arne Sucksdorff's Documentary Authorship in India and Brazil 67
   Emil Stjernholm

6. "Let's Get a Swede!": Peter Goldmann, The Beatles, and the Origins of the Music Video 76
   Scott MacKenzie

7. Out of the Margins of Feminist Filmmaking: Vibeke Løkkeberg, Norway, and the Film Cultures of 1970s West Berlin 85
   Ingrid S. Holtar

8. The Gothenburg International Exile Film Festival in Context 94
   Boel Ulfsdotter and Mats Björkin

PART II. INTERMEDIARIES

9. Opening up the Postwar World in Color: 1950s Geopolitics and Spectacular Nordic Colonialism in the Arctic and in Africa 105
   Anna Westerstahl Stenport

10. The Diasporic Cinemas of Ingrid Bergman 126
    Scott MacKenzie

11. "Here is My Home": Voiceover and Foreign-language Versions in Postwar Danish informational film 141
    C. Claire Thomson

12. A Sámi in Hollywood: Nils Gaup's Transnational and Generic Negotiations 157
    Gunnar Iversen

13. "There is no Elsewhere!": Stories of Race, Decolonization, and Global Connectivity in Göran Hugo Olsson's Documentaries 169
    Lill-Ann Körber

14. Aki Kaurismäki's Finno-French Connections and Other Transcultural Elsewheres 182
    Ana Bento Ribeiro

15. Nordic Noir as a Calling Card: The International Careers of Danish Film and Television Talent in the 2010s 190
    Eva N. Redvall

PART III. CONTACT ZONES

16. Paris Looks to the North: Swedish Silent Film and the Emergence of Cinephilia — 207
    Annie Fee

17. Celebrated, Contested, Criticized: Anita Ekberg, a Swedish Sex Goddess in Hollywood — 224
    Ann-Kristin Wallengren

18. The Finnish Cinema Colony in North America, 1938–1941 — 237
    Anneli Lehtisalo

19. The Transnational Politics of Lars von Trier's and Thomas Vinterberg's "Amerika" — 244
    Linda Badley

20. The Globalization of the Danish Documentary: Creative Collaboration and Modes of Global Documentaries — 261
    Ib Bondebjerg

21. Elsewheres of Healing: Trans-Indigenous Spaces in Elle-Máijá Apiniskim Tailfeathers' *Bihttoš* — 279
    Troy Storfjell (Sámi)

22. Denmark beyond Denmark: Soft Power, Talent Development, and Filmmaking in the Middle East — 287
    Mette Hjort

PART IV. REVISITATIONS

23. Dreyer's *Jeanne d'Arc* at the Cinéma d'Essai: Cinephiliac and Political Passions in 1950s Paris — 305
    Casper Tybjerg

24. *I Am Curious (Yellow)* as Sex Education in the USA — 319
    Saniya Lee Ghanoui

25. Transnational Cinefeminism of the 1970s and Mai Zetterling's Documentary Elsewheres — 327
    Mariah Larsson

26. *The Serpent's Egg*: Ingmar Bergman's Exilic Elsewheres in 1970s New German and New Hollywood Cinema — 341
    Anna Westerstahl Stenport and Arne Lunde

CONTENTS

27. Bridging Places, Media, and Traditions: Lasse Hallström's
    Chronotopes   360
    Lynn R. Wilkinson

28. Criminal Undertakings: Nicolas Winding Refn, European Film
    Aesthetics, and Hollywood Genre Cinema   370
    Björn Nordfjörd

29. The Cinematic Kon-Tiki Expeditions: Realism, Spectacle, and the
    Migration of Nordic Cinema   378
    Benjamin Bigelow

Index   386

FIGURES

2.1	Map tracing the three main circuits of the Australian circulation of *Temptations of a Great City* between 1911 and 1913	34
2.2	Map illustrating the movement of Swedish art films in Australia between 1919 and 1923	38
3.1	Oland and Chan playing hide and seek	46
5.1	Swedish posters for *The Flute and the Arrow* present two complementary messages	69
5.2	After facing criticism, Arne Sucksdorff addressed the public in the magazine *Idun veckojournalen*	73
6.1	Superimposition in *Strawberry Fields Forever*	79
6.2	Dream-like lens flare in *Penny Lane*	80
7.1	Frame grab from *Abortion*	88
8.1	Poster for the 10th International Exile Film Festival, in Gothenburg	95
9.1	*Qivitoq: The Mountain Wanderer* promotion poster	112
9.2	Cold War Arctic science fiction: *Terror in the Midnight Sun*	116
9.3	The welfare state and Swedish settler colonialism in *Make Way for Lila*	118
10.1	Ingrid Bergman as sacrificial star in *Casablanca*	131
10.2	Ingrid Bergman as Swedish-American ethnographer in *Swedes in America*	133

FIGURES

10.3	Ingrid Bergman: the problems faced by independent woman in *Europe '51*	136
11.1	Hospital Board members turn to look at the voiceover narrator in *Health for Denmark*	149
11.2	The Danish word for "eggs" situates the scene in Denmark in *The Pattern of Cooperation*	151
12.1	Mikkel Gaup in *Pathfinder*	159
12.2	Saying goodbye to the Indigenous people in *Shipwrecked*	160
12.3	The gorilla comforting Håkon in *Shipwrecked*	161
13.1	*The Black Power Mixtape, 1967–75*: a Swedish bus tour guide explains Harlem to Swedish tourists	172
13.2	*The Black Power Mixtape, 1967–75*: Swedish reporter Bo Holmström interviews Angela Davis during her detention at California State Prison	178
15.1	*The Bridge*: screenshot from the opening credits of the first episode	191
15.2	*Better Times*: screenshot from the opening credits of the first episode	196
16.1	The Ciné-Opéra advertises *Love's Crucible* in *La Publicité: journal technique des annonceurs*	218
17.1	Anita Ekberg in Stockholm 1955: her first visit to Sweden since she left for the USA	225
17.2	Anita Ekberg in Louella Parson's gossip column	229
19.1	*Dogville* was ultimately a critique of American capitalism, exceptionalism, post-9/11 vengeance, and "cowboy" politics	251
19.2	In *Dear Wendy*, Dick Dandelion poses with his beloved 6.6 5mm double-action revolver next to his heart	253
20.1	Basic modes or prototypes of documentary film as described by Bondebjerg	265
20.2	Frame grab from *Life Will Be Lived—Letters from a Mother*	268
20.3	Frame grab from *Look of Silence*	274
21.1	*Bihttoš* introduces Elle-Máijá's mother in an animated scene	281
21.2	Elle-Máijá and Áhčči open up to each other, in *Bihttoš*	282
22.1	Akram Al-Ashqar captures Nour's obsession with locks in *First Picture*	297
22.2	Laila Hotait depicts the imagination of the Palestinian artist Zuhdi Al-Adawi as a prisoner in Askalan	298
24.1	*I Am Curious (Yellow)* used real DDT on both actors in the scabies treatment scene	321
25.1	The weightlifter is dwarfed by the huge buildings of the Olympics in *Visions of Eight*	333

25.2	Mai Zetterling moves closer to capture the tension before the lift in *Visions of Eight*	334
26.1	Manuela (Liv Ullmann) and Abel (David Carradine) in a Berlin cabaret	343
26.2	Bergman(n)strasse at Bavaria Studios, as pictured in *The Serpent's Egg*	347
27.1	The Quoyles drag their house across the ice in *The Shipping News*	361
28.1	*Pusher III*: Milo hosts a Serbian birthday party for his daughter in Copenhagen	372
28.2	A typical shot in *Drive* (2011), expressing the isolation of its hero	374
29.1	Thor Heyerdahl trying to capture the *Kon-Tiki*'s encounter with a whale shark on film	383

ACKNOWLEDGMENTS

This book builds on over two decades of teaching and engagement with Scandinavian, Nordic, and Arctic cinema and media cultures at the University of California at Berkeley and Los Angeles, the University of Illinois at Urbana-Champaign, KTH Royal Institute in Stockholm, and the Georgia Institute of Technology in Atlanta. Years of ongoing intellectual exchange about the "elsewheres" that teaching and talking about these cinema cultures opened up to us, and the ways in which these never seemed to quite fit into national or transnational paradigms of cinema study, prompted us to quit wishing there were a book that addressed these matters and instead made us pursue making one happen. Following a number of productive conference presentations and conversations at the annual meetings of the Network for European Cinema Cultures (NECS), the Society for Media and Cinema Studies (SCMS), the Society for the Advancement of Scandinavian Study (SASS), and Visible Evidence (VizEv), we are grateful to all chapter authors for contributing the breadth, depth, range, and span of approaches, case studies, and perspectives to begin to do the topic justice. We are also extremely grateful to Linda Badley and Barton Palmer, who, as series editors, immediately saw the potential of the project and supported it from its inception. We hope this will be the first of many instances in which the concept of a cinematic "elsewhere" becomes productively mobilized in relation to small and large cinema and media cultures alike.

Funding and administrative support for the project has been allocated from the Scandinavian Section at UCLA, the School of Modern Languages and the

Ivan Allen College at Georgia Institute of Technology, the Social Sciences and Humanities Research Council of Canada, and the European Union Center's Jean Monnet Centre of Excellence and the College of Liberal Arts and Sciences Conrad Humanities Endowment at the University of Illinois at Urbana-Champaign. Archival footage and support in locating films and paracinematic records have been provided by the expert staff at the Danish and Swedish Film Institutes (DFI and SFI), the Norwegian National Library, the Finnish Film Foundation, the Margaret Herrick Library in Los Angeles, and the Royal Library in Stockholm. Thank you. We also wish to thank Patrick G. Ellis and Angela Anderson for their professional expertise in copy editing and manuscript compilation.

And, with that, we say, enjoy the journey to the elsewheres!

Anna Westerstahl Stenport and Arne Lunde, April 2019

CONTRIBUTORS

Julie K. Allen is Professor of Comparative Arts and Letters at Brigham Young University in Provo, Utah, and was formerly the Madsen Professor of Danish at the University of Wisconsin-Madison. Her work focuses on constructions of cultural identity in northern Europe through nineteenth- and early twentieth-century media. She is the author of *Icons of Danish Modernity: Georg Brandes and Asta Nielsen* (2012) and *Danish But Not Lutheran: The Impact of Mormonism on Danish Cultural Identity, 1850–1920* (2017).

Linda Badley, Professor Emerita at Middle Tennessee State University, is the author of *Lars von Trier* (2011), co-editor of *Indie Reframed: Women's Filmmaking and Contemporary American Independent Cinema* (Edinburgh University Press, 2016) and co-editor of *Nordic Noir Adaptation and Appropriation* (2020). With R. Barton Palmer, she co-edits Traditions in World Cinema and Traditions in American Cinema, companion series at Edinburgh University Press.

Benjamin Bigelow is an Assistant Professor of Scandinavian Studies at the University of Minnesota, Twin Cities. His research has focused on the intersections between media and literary studies, and he has authored articles on modern Nordic literature and film.

CONTRIBUTORS

Mats Björkin is Associate Professor of Film Studies at the Department of Cultural Sciences, University of Gothenburg. His research ranges from 1920s film production strategies to television history, industrial films, and historical television audiences, to the history and aesthetics of digital games.

Ib Bondebjerg is Professor Emeritus at the Department of Media, Cognition and Communication, University of Copenhagen. He was chairman of the Danish Film Institute 1997–2000, and has been co-directing major research projects, most recently *Mediating Cultural Encounters Through European Screens* (2013–16). His most recent authored and co-authored books are *Engaging with Reality. Documentary and Globalization* (2014) and *Transnational European Television Drama: Production Genres and Audiences* (2017).

Patrick Ellis holds a PhD from the University of California, Berkeley. He is a Brittain Postdoctoral Fellow in the School of Literature, Media, and Communication at the Georgia Institute of Technology. He has published in *Cinema Journal*, *Early Popular Visual Culture*, and *Imago Mundi*. His book project, *Aeroscopics: A Media Archaeology of the Bird's-Eye View*, provides a history of aerial vision in the era prior to commonplace flight.

Kim Khavar Fahlstedt holds a PhD in Cinema Studies from Stockholm University. He is a research fellow of American Studies at Uppsala University. His research interests include borderlands history, issues of cultural translation, and reception studies. He is completing his first monograph about the film culture in San Francisco's Chinatown in the early twentieth century.

Annie Fee is a Postdoctoral Research Fellow in the Department of Media and Communication at the University of Oslo. Her work has appeared in *Early Popular Visual Culture*, *Feminist Media Histories*, *Framework* and *The Blackwell Companion to D. W. Griffith*. She is currently developing an interactive historical map of 1920s Parisian cinema culture and working on a book manuscript dealing with the class and gender politics at play in the emergence of cinephilia in interwar France.

Saniya Lee Ghanoui is a PhD candidate in History at the University of Illinois at Urbana-Champaign. Her dissertation, "Hot-Blooded Teens and Silver Screens: Transnational Sex Education between the United States and Sweden, 1910–1960s," is a cultural history that investigates the development of sex education in the USA and Sweden in the first half of the twentieth century. She is also a producer for the podcast *Sexing History: The Past Made Intimate*.

CONTRIBUTORS

Mette Hjort is Chair Professor in Humanities and Dean of Arts at Hong Kong Baptist University, Affiliate Professor of Scandinavian Studies at the University of Washington, and Visiting Professor at the University of South Wales. Her books include *Small Nation, Global Cinema* (2005) and *Lone Scherfig's Italian for Beginners* (2015). Edited volumes include *African Cinema and Human Rights* (with Eva Jørholt) and *A Companion to Nordic Cinema* (with Ursula Lindqvist).

Ingrid S. Holtar is a PhD candidate in Film Studies at the Department of Art and Media Studies at the Norwegian University of Science and Technology (NTNU) in Trondheim. Her dissertation, "Cameras and Kitchens: Investigating the Norwegian Women's Cinema," examines women filmmakers and feminist filmmaking in the 1970s and early 1980s.

Gunnar Iversen is Professor of Film Studies at Carleton University in Ottawa, Canada, and former Professor of Film Studies at Norwegian University of Science and Technology (NTNU) in Trondheim, Norway. He has published more than twenty books and 200 articles, in eight different languages. He has co-written *Nordic National Cinemas* (1998) and *Historical Dictionary of Scandinavian Cinema* (2012) and co-edited *Beyond the Visual: Sound and Image in Ethnographic and Documentary Film* (2010) and *Unwatchable* (2019).

Lill-Ann Körber is Professor of Scandinavian Literature, Media and Culture at Aarhus University, Denmark. She has previously held positions at Humboldt-Universität zu Berlin, Germany, and at the University of Oslo and the University of Bergen, both in Norway. Recent publications include *The Postcolonial North Atlantic: Iceland, Greenland and the Faroe Islands*, co-edited with Ebbe Volquardsen (2014), and *Arctic Environmental Modernities. From the Age of Polar Exploration to the Era of the Anthropocene*, co-edited with Scott MacKenzie and Anna Westerstahl Stenport (2017).

Mariah Larsson is a Professor of Film Studies at Linnaeus University, Sweden, with previous appointments at Malmö University and Stockholm University. Her publications in English include *A Visual History of HIV/AIDS: Exploring the Face of AIDS Film Archive* (2019, co-edited with Elisabet Björklund) and *The Swedish Porn Scene: Exhibition Contexts, 8mm Pornography and the Sex Film* (2017). Her monograph on Mai Zetterling is forthcoming.

Anneli Lehtisalo is a research coordinator at Tampere University, Finland. She has also worked as a post-doctoral researcher in the project A Transnational History of Finnish Cinema (http://www.helsinki.fi/tfc/) at the University of Helsinki, Finland. Her research concerns issues of national cinema, relations between the past and cinema, cultural memory, genre, and the production and distribution of Finnish films.

Arne Lunde is Associate Professor in the Scandinavian Section and in Cinema and Media Studies at UCLA. His book *Nordic Exposures: Scandinavian Identities in Classical Hollywood Cinema* (2010) explores Scandinavian whiteness and ethnicity in Hollywood cinema between and during the two World Wars. He has published in *Journal of Scandinavian Cinema*, *Film International*, *Film Quarterly*, *The Moving Image*, *Scandinavian Studies*, *Scandinavica*, and *Comparative Literature*. His current research includes a book about Ingmar Bergman as auteur inside the Swedish studio system, 1944–60.

Scott MacKenzie is Associate Professor of Film and Media, Queen's University. His books include: *Cinema and Nation* (with Mette Hjort, 2000); *Purity and Provocation: Dogma '95* (with Mette Hjort, 2003); *Film Manifestos and Global Cinema Cultures* (2014); *Films on Ice: Cinemas of the Arctic* (with Anna Westerstahl Stenport, Edinburgh University Press, 2015); and *Arctic Cinemas and the Documentary Ethos* (with Lilya Kaganovsky and Anna Westerstahl Stenport, 2019).

Björn Nordfjörd is Visiting Associate Professor at St. Olaf College, Minnesota. He has edited a volume on world cinema in Icelandic, and published widely on Icelandic and Nordic cinemas in English, including a monograph on *Nói the Albino* (2010).

Eva N. Redvall is Associate Professor in Film and Media Studies at the University of Copenhagen. Her research focuses on film and television production, particularly screenwriting. She has published widely on Nordic film and television in books and journals, including the monograph *Writing and Producing Television Drama in Denmark: From The Kingdom to The Killing* (2013) and *The Danish Directors 3: Dialogues on the New Danish Documentary Cinema* (co-authored with Mette Hjort and Ib Bondebjerg, 2014).

Ana Bento Ribeiro holds a PhD in Film Studies from Paris Nanterre University, where she works on economic and sociological aspects of contemporary Romanian cinema. Her works have appeared in journals such as *Girlhood Studies*, *Afterimage* and *1895*.

Anna Westerstahl Stenport is Professor and Chair of the School of Modern Languages at Georgia Institute of Technology. She has written extensively about Nordic cinema, media, visual cultures, drama, and literature. She is the author of *Nordic Film Classics: Lukas Moodysson's "Show Me Love"* (2012) and co-editor of *Films on Ice: Cinemas of the Arctic* (with Scott MacKenzie, 2014) *Arctic Cinemas and the Documentary Ethos* (with Lilya Kaganovsky and Scott MacKenzie, 2019), and *August Strindberg and Visual Culture: The Emergence of Optical Modernity in Image, Text, and Theatre* (with Jonathan Schroeder and Eszter Szalczer, 2019). She has published on Nordic cinema and media in *Cinema Journal*, *Film History*, *The Moving Image*, *Convergence*, and the *Journal of Scandinavian Cinema*.

Emil Stjernholm holds a PhD in Film Studies from Lund University and currently works as a Senior Lecturer in Media and Communication Studies at Malmö University. His areas of research include documentary film, newsreels and propaganda studies. He has published articles in journals such as *Studies in European Cinema*, *BioScope: South Asian Screen Studies*, and *Journal of Media, Cognition and Communication*.

Troy Storfjell is Professor of Nordic Studies and Director of Native American and Indigenous Studies at Pacific Lutheran University. His research areas include Sámi and Norwegian literature, Nordic film, settler studies and trans-Indigenous studies. His current projects include work on Sámi ethics and aesthetics in the film *Sameblod* (*Sami Blood*, 2016).

C. Claire Thomson is Associate Professor of Scandinavian Film in the School of European Languages, Culture and Society at University College London. Her publications include *Short Films from a Small Nation: Danish Informational Cinema 1935–1965* (Edinburgh University Press, 2018), and *Thomas Vinterberg's Festen* (The Celebration) (2013). She is an editor of the journals *Scandinavica* and *Kosmorama*.

Casper Tybjerg is Associate Professor of Film Studies at the University of Copenhagen. His research interests include film historiography, the history of film style, and the relation between Danish and German filmmaking in the silent period. He has written extensively on Carl Th. Dreyer and Danish and Scandinavian silent cinema and has helped restore several Dreyer films.

Boel Ulfsdotter is Reader in Film at the Faculty of Arts and Humanities at the University of Gothenburg, Sweden. Her recent publications include the co-edited volumes *Female Authorship and the Documentary Image: Theory, Practice and Aesthetics*, and *Female Agency and Documentary Strategies: Subjectivities, Identity, and Activism* (both Edinburgh University Press, 2018).

Ann-Kristin Wallengren is Professor of Film Studies at Lund University, Sweden. Her research focuses on Swedish-American cinematic relations, celebrity, and film stars, as well as on film music. Her publications in English include the monograph *Welcome Home Mr Swanson. Swedish Emigrants and Swedishness in Film* (2014). With K. J. Donnelly she has edited *Today's Sounds for Yesterday's Films: Making Music for Silent Cinema* (2016).

Patrick Wen is a Continuing Lecturer in Scandinavian Studies in the Department of ELTS (European Languages and Transnational Cultures) at the University of California Los Angeles. His research interests include modern literary history, immigration, crime literature, comparative literature, Isak Dinesen, and film and television studies. His publications have appeared in *Lit: Literature Interpretation Theory* and *Studies in American Culture*. His current research projects include a study of John Steinbeck's influence on resistance movements in occupied Europe during World War II.

Lynn R. Wilkinson is Associate Professor of Germanic Studies and Comparative Literature at the University of Texas at Austin. She is the author of *The Dream of an Absolute Language: Emanuel Swedenborg and French Literary Culture* (1996), *Anne Charlotte Leffler and Modernist Drama: True Women and New Women on the Fin-de-siècle Scandinavian Stage* (2011), and numerous articles on European literature and film.

TRADITIONS IN WORLD CINEMA

General editors: **Linda Badley and R. Barton Palmer**
Founding editor: **Steven Jay Schneider**

Traditions in World Cinema is a series of textbooks and monographs devoted to the analysis of currently popular and previously underexamined or undervalued film movements from around the globe. Also intended for general interest readers, the textbooks in this series offer undergraduate- and graduate-level film students accessible and comprehensive introductions to diverse traditions in world cinema. The monographs open up for advanced academic study more specialised groups of films, including those that require theoretically-oriented approaches. Both textbooks and monographs provide thorough examinations of the industrial, cultural, and socio-historical conditions of production and reception.

The flagship textbook for the series includes chapters by noted scholars on traditions of acknowledged importance (the French New Wave, German Expressionism), recent and emergent traditions (New Iranian, post-Cinema Novo), and those whose rightful claim to recognition has yet to be established (the Israeli persecution film, global found footage cinema). Other volumes concentrate on individual national, regional or global cinema traditions. As the introductory chapter to each volume makes clear, the films under discussion form a coherent group on the basis of substantive and relatively transparent, if not always obvious, commonalities. These commonalities may be formal, stylistic or thematic, and the groupings may, although they need not, be popularly identified as genres, cycles or movements (Japanese horror, Chinese martial arts cinema, Italian Neorealism). Indeed, in cases in which a group of films is not already commonly identified as a tradition, one purpose of the volume is to establish its claim to importance and make it visible (East Central European Magical Realist cinema, Palestinian cinema).

Textbooks and monographs include:

- An introduction that clarifies the rationale for the grouping of films under examination
- A concise history of the regional, national, or transnational cinema in question
- A summary of previous published work on the tradition
- Contextual analysis of industrial, cultural and socio-historical conditions of production and reception
- Textual analysis of specific and notable films, with clear and judicious application of relevant film theoretical approaches
- Bibliograph(ies)/filmograph(ies)

Monographs may additionally include:

- Discussion of the dynamics of cross-cultural exchange in light of current research and thinking about cultural imperialism and globalisation, as well as issues of regional/national cinema or political/aesthetic movements (such as new waves, postmodernism, or identity politics)
- Interview(s) with key filmmakers working within the tradition.

1. INTRODUCTION: NORDIC FILM CULTURES AND CINEMAS OF ELSEWHERE

Patrick Ellis, Arne Lunde, and Anna Westerstahl Stenport

Nordic Film Cultures and Cinemas of Elsewhere proposes a new paradigm for Nordic film studies, as well as for other small national, transnational, and world cinema traditions. This book articulates Nordic cinemas as international, cosmopolitan, diasporic, hybrid, and traveling from their beginnings in the early silent period to their present dynamics more than a century later. It identifies and engages with a wide range of unknown, repressed, and overlooked forms and narratives that foreground movement, mobility, interaction, exploration, synthesis, resistance, loss, reclamation, and repatriation, inside and outside of established Nordic film traditions. *Nordic Film Cultures and Cinemas of Elsewhere* thereby introduces a new model of inquiry into a specific Scandinavian cultural lineage and into small-nation and pan-regional cinemas more generally. In this way, the book also speaks to a range of traditions in world cinema. The overarching goal is to breach entrenched structures and to invite more unexpected examinations. We advocate the intellectual and cultural ethos of "cinemas of elsewhere," coining a new term that expands on established interpretive traditions such as cinemas of diasporic, exilic, postcolonial, accented, and existential identities. It is therefore not a study of Nordic cinemas comfortably situated within national borders or self-enclosed brackets. Drawing on the specificities, dynamics, and ambitious reach and scope of Scandinavian cinema production, circulation, and influence for over a century, *Nordic Film Cultures and Cinemas of Elsewhere* navigates and narrates parallel and alternative histories.

What and Where is an Elsewhere?

Etymologically, an "elsewhere" is determined by what and where it is not. "At some other point; in some other place," offers the *Oxford English Dictionary* (1989). The "else" in the word was originally a synonym for "other." (You can still hear this in the German or Swedish equivalents, "anderswo" and "annanstans.") The historian of cartography J. B. Harley is known for emphasizing the "silences" on the map—those geographic features and civic sites the mapmaker conceals or neglects. A Nordic elsewhere is one such cartographic silence, terra incognita for film scholars.

Yet, if you were to plot the chapters of this book on a map, the Nordic elsewheres imagined would be global. Close your eyes, spin the globe, and point: there you find Nordic practitioners; there you find Nordic elsewheres. Elsewheres appear everywhere from Australasia to the Arctic, Newfoundland to Nigeria, as chapters in this book demonstrate. An elsewhere is thus as much a gateway to another place as it is a silence; it is an invitation to travel—physically, maybe; intellectually, certainly. To track an elsewhere leads one inevitably to accented cinemas, reception studies, transnational cinema, location substitution, production studies, world cinema, and other such place-based cinematic concepts that our authors engage with in this volume.

In that vein, *Nordic Film Cultures and Cinemas of Elsewhere* articulates models with which to re-think dominant categories of world film history, especially valuable for traditions that have been constituted as small, national, or regional. Any "national cinema" is potentially an international one, through the circulation of films themselves as well as through bodies, practitioners, stars, styles, criticism, and capital. This book foregrounds these kinds of circulation as a central part of Nordic film history and of the history of world cinema traditions.

Elsewhere as Cinematic Form

The cinematic elsewhere is multi-faceted. The birth of film was also the birth of a specific kind of visual exploration; cameras were brought to all corners of the world, circulating images of elsewheres understood as "remote," while bringing the "exotic" to the center. The cinema mediated elsewheres and it was a vehicle for elsewheres. A cinematic elsewhere is thus both spatial and metaphorical; it is lower-cased, not indicative of a proper place-name, but rather a generalized type of medial and mediated space, a cinematic epiphenomenon: itinerant, imaginary, diffuse. It can encompass the artifactual circulation of prints, the imaginaries of runaway productions, the creation of alternate worlds through CGI manipulation, programming and curation, or the expansion of public discourse through international film criticism.

The term itself is unanchored: one could easily imagine a Canadian elsewhere, a Filipino elsewhere, or any other elsewhere of a tradition in world cinema. We propose that the concept of a cinematic elsewhere may be especially valuable to "small" national cinemas, insofar as the elsewhere aids in conjuring up new cinematic and social spaces, and thus in looking beyond established categories of nationhood (see also Berry and Spigel 2009). All national cinemas are, at some level, cinemas of elsewhere.

Emphasizing the elsewhere fundamentally changes the map of Nordic film culture, modifying its scale, legend, and coordinates. In doing so, we move away from the material categories of national cinema (the base) to the intellectual circulation of Nordic elsewheres (superstructure); from the nominally stable category of the film strip to the layered categories of the palimpsest; from the canonical to the lacunal. We have aimed to strike a balance between the established auteurs of Nordic cinema and overlooked filmmakers, between the transit of key films and festivals of the overlooked.

Practitioner Mobility, Sites of Interaction, and Circulation

To examine the multiplicity of cinematic elsewheres, *Nordic Film Cultures and Cinemas of Elsewhere* foregrounds an analytical and interpretive strategy that emphasizes practitioner mobility, sites of interaction, and filmic circulation. The book shows how broader and more inclusive horizons reveal the self-imposed determinism, barriers, instability, and boundaries of the national cinema paradigm. Practitioner movements impact all aspects of the cinematic production chain—from script development, casting, and crew collectives, to filming, editing, post-production, branding, distribution, reception, and remediation. The book thus advocates the significance of an extra-national heterogeneity of film production, distribution, circulation, and reception, one parallel to and inscribed within multivalent migrations to (and periodic repatriations from) Nordic cinemas of elsewhere. These "elsewheric" vortexes of moving image indexicality and cultural historiography include (but are not limited to) Brazil, France, the Congo, India, Germany, Oceania, the UK, the circumpolar Arctic and Antarctic, Palestine and the Middle East, Hollywood, Russia and the Baltic, Northern Sub-Sahara and South Nigeria, Egypt, South Africa, and North America.

The focus on mobility, interaction, and circulation furthermore allows for rethinking the directorial canon and star personae of Scandinavian cinema (e.g. Victor Sjöström, Mauritz Stiller, Carl Th. Dreyer, Ingrid Bergman, Arne Sucksdorff, Anita Ekberg, Ingmar Bergman, Mai Zetterling, Lars von Trier, Thomas Vinterberg, Aki Kaurismäki, Lasse Hallström, Nils Gaup, Lukas Moodysson, and Nicolas Winding Refn, among others). The book thereby re-frames more recognized Nordic films and personae through less parochially defined and exclusionary approaches and perspectives. This mode includes exploring art cinema through paradigms beyond pantheistic auteurism and therefore via more inclusive materialist approaches (e.g. industrial systems and practices, genres, markets, colonialism, state funding, cinephilia, the archive, paraphernalia, etc.) and thus via the production, circulation, mediation, and artifacts of canonical and (heretofore at least) non-canonical and marginalized films, artists, and methods.

The Book's Organization: From Traces and Erasures to Intermediaries, Contact Zones, and Revisitations

The book favors thematic constellations so as to generate dialogue between chapters that—even when based in different periods, places, and languages—echo each other in surprising ways. We have identified four zones of elsewhere, and chapters placed within these zones are organized in loose chronological order.

Part One, "Traces and Erasures," asks, how are we to write about lost people, lost media, lost stories? Nordic elsewheres have more than their fair share of these lacunae. Episodes that transpire outside of the "here" often go undocumented. There are a variety of recovery strategies, and the chapters in this section embrace differing methodologies: following the breadcrumb trails of prints in circulation; closely attending to surviving extra-cinematic sources when the moving image is no more; mobilizing the fleeting archival trace. Elsewheres encourage media-archaeological digging—sometimes, even disinterment. The collection of chapters obliges the authors to do detective work, finding traces of those citizens of elsewhere who have been exiled, disappeared, or otherwise erased. This part starts with Julie K. Allen's recovery and reconstruction of the circulation of Danish and Swedish Golden Age cinema in 1910s and 1920s Australasia. Kim Khavar Fahlstedt discusses the mysterious disappearance of Swedish-American Hollywood actor Warner Oland (and his alter ego Charlie Chan) in the 1930s. In a subsequent chapter, Patrick Wen examines the haunting presence of Nazi cult figure Carin Fock, the late Swedish wife of Hermann Göring. Moving to the 1960s, Emil Stjernholm's chapter discusses Swedish documentarian Arne Sucksdorff's erasure from documentary film history when he began making films outside of Sweden and relocating to South Asia and South America. Scott MacKenzie's chapter finds the connections between European art cinema and the origins of the music video in 1967, the year in which Swedish director Peter Goldmann makes two of The Beatles' best-known experimental promo films. As an act of feminist interventionism locating film history's overlooked lacunae, Ingrid Holtar examines Norway's 1970s burgeoning feminist film culture in relation to the practices of West German women filmmakers of the time. This section concludes with the first scholarly presentation of a critical film festival that has been nearly erased from cinema studies, the International Exile Film Festival in Gothenburg, Sweden, which screens contemporary films made by and about immigrant, migrant, exiled, and diasporic filmmakers from around the world, especially the Middle East and North Africa.

Part Two, "Intermediaries," combines chapters that discuss how travel from "here" to "elsewhere" often requires mediating between two (or more) spaces, cultures, and languages. Nordic practitioners functioned sometimes as ambassadors, sometimes as scapegoats in this transaction. They serve as conduits between media industries, whether those of European co-production, contemporary television, or the Third Reich. For instance, Anna Westerstahl Stenport, in her chapter on 1950s spectacular cinema traditions, discusses how Nordic elsewheres mediated between different production and genre formats (widescreen, technicolor, 3D, and science fiction, for instance). Less materially—but just as importantly—Nordic elsewheres mediate between imaginaries: between, for instance, the idea of Hollywood and the idea of Scandinavia; or between the idea of the citizen and the idea of the exile. These topics are discussed by Scott MacKenzie in his chapter on Ingrid Bergman as a diasporic, polyglot actress. A "Nordic elsewhere" may even be too determinate a space for some, one which nation states have used for promotion or political purposes, a thematic that C. Claire Thomson examines in her chapter about language and voiceover in Danish governmental export films of the 1940s–60s. Other elsewheres are opened up when colonial practices are brought up for critique, which Gunnar Iversen addresses in his chapter on the international career of Sámi filmmaker Nils Gaup, and by Lill-Ann Körber in her chapter on race relations that triangulate Africa, North America, and Sweden in Göran Hugo Olsson's documentaries. A discussion of Aki Kaurismäki's French-connected films is analyzed through Ana Bento Ribeiro's compelling notion about "intermediary elsewheres." The section concludes with Eva Novrup Redvall's examination of Danish television directors as intermediaries between Scandinavia, the UK, and the USA.

Part Three, "Contact Zones," discusses both the points of contact between metaphorical and actual locations and interactions in the cultural marketplace, with a nod to Mary Louise Pratt's influential term about transculturation. There are a great many asymmetrical, transactional meetings taking place in the contact zone, as, for instance, Swedish cinema vitalizing Parisian audiences and French cinephilia in Annie Fee's chapter about the 1920s. Ann-Kristin Wallengren's inquiry into how star personae travel, bridging or challenging cultural assumptions, employs as a case study Swedish sex goddess Anita Ekberg as mediated in the 1950s American and European press. Anneli Lehtisalo's chapter recovers how exported Finnish cinema met Finnish immigrants in pre-World War II North America. Linda Badley illuminates how the USA is reimagined as an elsewhere of "Amerika" in Danish and Swedish studios by Lars von Trier and Thomas Vinterberg. Other chapters in this section examine how documentary practice, or films inspired by real events, construct contact zones where different cultural, social, and political assumptions meet, clash, converge, or diverge. For instance, Ib Bondebjerg's chapter traces the Danish documentary tradition's interventions into Africa and Southeast Asia as part of public funding initiatives, with Mette Hjort discussing Denmark's contributions to and interventions in education in the Middle East, especially Palestine; and Troy Storfjell (Sámi) discusses recent autobiographical Sámi documentary as transnational and trans-Indigenous, revealing a contact zone of interaction not usually accounted for in a national film history.

Part Four, "Revisitations," discusses how encountering an elsewhere often requires a return journey; sometimes more than one. Cinematic elsewheres are thus often sites of return, of remaking, of revisitation. For instance, Casper Tybjerg's chapter on 1950s French cinephilic culture's indebtedness to Carl Th. Dreyer's 1928 masterwork *La Passion de Jeanne d'Arc* considers how a film, embraced years after the fact, in another place, makes for a compelling elsewhere. In contrast, Saniya Lee Ghanoui examines how cinematic works, in this case *I Am Curious (Yellow)*, when revisited in another social or political context, can become catalysts for political change. Mariah Larsson's chapter inquires into how Mai Zetterling's 1970s films revisit and rearticulate notions of "Swedishness" when made in the UK or at the Munich Olympic Games. Anna Westerstahl Stenport and Arne Lunde discuss how Ingmar Bergman, self-exiled in Munich in the late 1970s, excavates Weimar and Nazi history while intervening in contemporaneous movements of New German Cinema and New Hollywood. The ways in which directors working abroad revisit and in the process construct imaginary, sometimes nostalgic, homelands are part of the following two chapters, Lynn R. Wilkinson's examination of Lasse Hallström's oeuvre in Hollywood and Björn Nordfjörd's discussion of Nicholas Winding Refn's journeys between the cinematic imaginaries of America, Denmark, and then back to America. The book's concluding chapter revisits a work critical to film history, the seminal documentary about Thor Heyerdahl's Kon-Tiki voyage, and how its legacy lives on, including when remade as part of a twenty-first-century global adventure film. The book's fourth and concluding section thus allows us to examine established works and revisit them and their place in the canon with an oblique eye, examining their odd and unexpected parameters, their leakages into other spheres and elsewheres.

Nordic Cinema Studies: Expanding the Scope, Diversity, and Inclusiveness of a Tradition

Nordic Film Cultures and Cinemas of Elsewhere builds on a range of important scholarship produced during the past two decades, and seeks to take this scholarship in new directions, as evidenced by the thematic organization of the book discussed above. The lion's share of twentieth-century historical surveys of Nordic cinema has valorized national narratives and certain periods and directors as high points. These include the Golden Ages of Danish and Swedish silent cinema in the 1910s and early 1920s, the re-emergence of the Swedish art cinema in the 1950s and 1960s, the revolutionary impact of the Danish Dogme 95 movement, individual auteur studies of major figures such as Dreyer, Bergman and von Trier, and so on. Although national framings have been convenient ways of historicizing this narrative, newer scholarship has forcefully countered with the argument that a great deal of Nordic cinema resists such categorizations and seeks to open up possibilities to tell complementary and alternative stories of Nordic cinemas of elsewhere. This trend is evident in recent historiographic narratives that move away from treating Nordic moving images as distinct and compartmentalized national cinemas of Denmark, Finland, Iceland, Norway, and Sweden.

While it is impossible to address every important and influential text, a partial list of English-language books that operate outside of the context of any one national tradition, genre, or auteur in chronological order would include *Transnational Cinema in a Global North: Nordic Cinema in Transition* (Nestingen and Elkington 2005); *Small Nation, Global Cinema* (Hjort 2005); *The Cinema of Scandinavia* (Soila 2005); *Nordic Constellations: New Readings in Nordic Cinema* (Thomson 2006); *Crime and Fantasy in Scandinavia* (Nestingen 2008); *Nordic Exposures: Scandinavian Identities in Classical Hollywood Cinema* (Lunde 2010); *Ecology and Contemporary Nordic Cinemas: From Nation-Building to Ecocosmopolitanism* (Kääpä 2014); *Films on Ice: Cinemas of the Arctic* (MacKenzie and Stenport 2014); *Popular Nordic Genre Film: Small Nation Film Cultures in the Global Marketplace* (Gustafsson and Käpää 2015); *Finnish Cinema: A Transnational Enterprise* (Bacon 2016); and *The Wiley-Blackwell Companion to Nordic Cinema* (Hjort and Lindqvist 2016). Departing from what may be, to an international audience (and partially also to domestic spectators), obvious "traditions" of the Nordic region, the authors in this book read against the grain of "the national" and reveal how significantly Scandinavian films and filmmakers transcend and transgress these national boundaries on myriad levels.

Nordic Film Cultures thereby re-thinks and re-formulates the images, legacies, and impacts of Nordic cinemas within far more dynamic and multi-directional global contexts. The book engages with lacunae in the transnational, extra-territorial history of Scandinavian and Nordic filmmaking from its early phases up to the present moment. And although our work intersects at moments with that of many of the scholars cited above, our quest is to re-imagine Nordic cinema outside the confines of national and even regional cinema brackets to an even further new degree and in locations often least expected.

The Book's Elsewhere Examples in Historical Context

Although the book's chapter organization is not one of temporal progress, there are insights to be gained by looking at this material chronologically, providing an "elsewhere history" of Nordic cinema culture. Considerable attention has been given to the silent Golden Ages of Danish cinema (1910–14) and Swedish film (1917–24) within Nordic national cinema contexts. Yet Scandinavian film directors, performers, and films circulated extensively abroad during the silent period, impacting European, American and world cinema in significant ways. Julie K. Allen's "Mapping Cinema's Ghosts: Reconstructing the Circulation of Nordic Silent Film in Australia" investigates how Scandinavian film prints traveled to the farthest side of the globe from their source of origin. Allen's chapter therefore ties into larger questions of circulation. For instance, Weimar Berlin became a magnet for the first European film star, Asta Nielsen ("Die Asta"), Danish directors Carl Th. Dreyer and Benjamin Christensen, and male stars Gösta Ekman, Einar Hansen, Nils Asther, and Valdemar Psilander. Given the smallness of the Scandinavian film cultures, postwar Berlin was akin to moving to a European Hollywood, with Babelsberg's vastly superior infrastructure, industrial capitalization, and artistic possibilities.

The aesthetic and intellectual impacts of Nordic cinema on France after World War I are explored in Annie Fee's "Paris Looks at the North: Swedish Silent Film and the Emergence of Cinephilia." Films of the Swedish Golden Age, as Fee demonstrates, made an impact in Paris, which also became a Nordic elsewhere of intellectual and creative ferment. Carl Th. Dreyer, the quintessential Danish director of the classic period, made seven of his fourteen feature films outside of his homeland, among them *La Passion de Jeanne d'Arc* (*The Passion of Joan of Arc*, France, 1928). Made in Paris entirely with French funding, this radical experiment drew from avant-garde poetics of French cine-impressionism and Russian montage. The film is emblematic of the internationalist fusion in late silent-era cinema art and constitutes an early example of Danish cinema wielding a global impact. In "Dreyer's *Jeanne d'Arc* at the Cinéma d'Essai: Cinephiliac and Political Passions in 1950s Paris," Casper Tybjerg examines the film's deep and lasting reverberations in French intellectual history a quarter century after its premiere. As early as the 1920s, one can identify the foundations of a globalizing film culture and industry, in which capital, craftspeople, technologies, style, and stars circulate between

Hollywood, Berlin, Paris, Rome, London, and other centers of production and reception. Los Angeles during the 1920s first experiences the kinds of massive population influxes, and oil and real-estate booms that would add economic fuel to the explosive growth of Hollywood as *the* film production epicenter of the world. Studios such as M-G-M, Paramount, Universal, and Warner Bros. engineered talent raids on their European studio competitors, attracting a stream of Nordic film émigrés, including three of Nordic cinema's greatest directors, Victor Sjöström, Mauritz Stiller, and Benjamin Christensen.

If one adds émigré stars Greta Garbo, Lars Hanson, Karin Molander, Einar Hansen, and Nils Asther to that list, Hollywood's Scandinavian colony essentially becomes an elsewhere for the Nordic silent art cinema in voluntary diaspora. Sjöström (renamed Seastrom) at M-G-M expands the nature lyricism and Lutheran guilt thematics of his Swedish works with *The Scarlet Letter* (1926), while also making the two most avant-garde and experimental films of his career, *He Who Gets Slapped* (1924) and *The Wind* (1928), the latter film a hellish, nihilist vision of American nature (shot in California's Mojave Desert).

The seismic shift of the talkie revolution (1927–31) and the en masse conversion to synchronized sound jettisoned the universal pictorial accessibility that silent cinema (and inexpensively added intertitles for any export language/market) had offered for a generation, making Danish and Swedish exports overnight far less international and far more provincially limited. The transitional 1930s and World War II years (1939–45) are captured in several chapters. In "Charlie Chan's Last Mystery, or the Transcultural Disappearance of Warner Oland," Kim Khavar Fahlstedt investigates the film career of Asian racial masquerade by this enigmatic Swedish-born actor, and his breakdown, return home, death, and funeral in Stockholm in 1938. Anneli Lehtisalo's "The Finnish Cinema Colony in North America, 1938–41" engages with the rich transatlantic circulation of Golden Age Finnish cinema within American and Canadian Finnish immigrant communities. World War II severely impacted the flow of Nordic talent and films abroad. In propaganda battles over importing and defining Nordicness, Third Reich cinema and Classic Hollywood both manipulated culturally-constructed imaginaries of a natural Nordic North—a landscape whose reigning hyperwhite tropes included mountains, snow, winter sports, ivory skin, and other essentialized markers of racial and moral virtue. Wartime anxieties and agendas also enlisted the biological fitness of the Scandinavian film diva. In Hollywood's imaginary these include Garbo, Ingrid Bergman and Sonja Henie. For Nazi Germany, Goebbels' propaganda machine mobilized ethnic Swedes in multiple ways. Patrick Wen's chapter "Carin Fock-Göring's Gravestone: Tracing the Legacy of the Swedish First Lady of the Third Reich" reveals the bizarre Nazi cult built around Hermann Göring's deceased Swedish wife and the ideological battles over her saint-like burial remains.

Scott MacKenzie further analyzes the transnational Swedish female star in his chapter on the "Nordic otherness" of Ingrid Bergman, which contextualizes her border crossings in stardom from Svensk Filmindustri in Stockholm to the Nazified UFA studio in Berlin in the late 1930s, to enormous popularity in Hollywood through the 1940s, and her teaming with Italian Neorealist Roberto Rossellini during 1949–57, including *Stromboli* (Italy, 1950), *Europe '51* (Italy, 1952), *Journey to Italy* (*Viaggio in Italia*, Italy, 1954), and *Fear* (*La paura*, Italy/West Germany, 1954). These films are reappraised through the lens of Ingrid Bergman as a transnational, polyglot persona, culminating in her return to Scandinavia as a "foreign" star in Ingmar Bergman's *Autumn Sonata* (*Höstsonaten*, West Germany/Sweden, 1978). Meantime, the Swedish sex-bomb siren as an international type only emerges in the 1950s with the female nudity and sexual freedom of the Swedish erotic summer film, most famously incarnated by Harriet Andersson in Ingmar Bergman's *Summer with Monika* (*Sommaren med Monika*, Sweden, 1953). This image partly reflects and refracts puritanical Eisenhower-era America's perception of Sweden as the essence of "sin, socialism, and suicide," with blonde bombshell Anita Ekberg's stardom as a Swedish sex goddess in fifties Hollywood as Exhibit A. Ann-Kristin Wallengren's chapter therefore interrogates the mediated constructions of Ekberg in the American and Swedish presses respectively, extending these accounts into Ekberg's subsequent Italian career, most iconically in Federico Fellini's *La Dolce Vita* (Italy, 1960).

Different elsewheres opened up Scandinavian film cultures globally during the decades following the end of World War II, as propelled by international developments in filmmaking, enhanced circulation of small national cinemas, and the rise of public funding and national film institutes. While standard film histories tell a story of the revival of Swedish art cinema during the period, often exemplified by Cannes Film Festival major awards in 1951 to Alf Sjöberg's *Miss Julie* (*Fröken Julie*) and in 1955 to Ingmar Bergman's *Smiles of a Summer Night* (*Sommarnattens leende*), an alternate and overlooked trajectory emerges when taking into account a number of Academy Award nominated or winning ethnographically inflected documentaries and feature films by Scandinavian filmmakers in the 1950s. Examples include the documentary *Kon-Tiki* (Thor Heyerdahl, Norway, 1950), addressed by Benjamin Bigelow in this volume, and Arne Sucksdorff's widescreen depictions of a remote tribe in India, *The Flute and the Arrow* (*En djungelsaga*, Sweden, 1957), examined in a chapter by Emil Stjernholm. C. Claire Thomson addresses the journeys abroad of the postwar Danish informational film, which conveyed the priorities of the Danish state as ones of democracy and prosperity to the world. Additional significant (but heretofore overlooked) examples that screened to international acclaim and that presented little-known aspects of Scandinavia, both to the world and to domestic audiences, include the color spectacles modeled on the widescreen "Hollywood International" phenomenon or subgenre of the 1950s, including the Danish Greenland films *Where Mountains Float* (*Hvor bjergene sejler*, Bjarne Henning-Jensen, Denmark, 1955) and the melodrama *Qivitoq: The Mountain Wanderer* (*Qivitoq: Fjeldgængeren*, Erik Balling, Denmark, 1956) as well as the romance *Make Way for Lila* (*Laila*, Rolf Husberg, Sweden, 1958) and the action drama *Gorilla Safari* (*Gorilla: En filmberättelse från Belgiska Kongo*, Lars-Henrik Ottoson, Sven Nykvist and Lorens Marmstedt, Sweden, 1956). As Anna Westerstahl Stenport examines in her chapter "Opening up the Postwar World in Color: 1950s Geopolitics and Spectacular Nordic Colonialism in the Arctic and in Africa," these films constitute an overlooked corpus of Scandinavian elsewheres in their portrayal of international or "exotic" locations, as well as Indigenous populations and practices, while also foregrounding the welfare state policies of Denmark and Sweden as those were being exported and marketed around the world at this time.

While French New Wave critics in the 1950s like François Truffaut and Jean-Luc Godard lauded Bergman's *Summer with Monika* as the greatest breakthrough art film of modern cinema, in America it was first released by producer Kroger Babb within the exploitation and grindhouse circuit as a bowdlerized, redubbed version entitled *Monika: The Story of a Bad Girl!* (USA, 1957). The established "sex and sin" image of Scandinavia, however, shifts through time, with welfare state egalitarianism and gender equality as a backdrop to subsequent films that made headlines abroad, including Vilgot Sjöman's *I Am Curious (Yellow)* (*Jag är nyfiken (gul)*, Sweden, 1967), explored in this volume by Sanyia Ghanoui. In the 1960s, Denmark and Sweden abroad connote a new kind of style—representing the Scandinavian Modern—in glamor, fashion, design, architecture, politics, and international humanitarianism. Some of this legacy, and its relationship to art cinema, is explored in Scott MacKenzie's chapter on The Beatles' Swedish connections through Peter Goldmann, who directed two of their more experimental promo films in 1967: *Strawberry Fields Forever* and *Penny Lane*. Paul McCartney stated that the group particularly sought a kind of Swedish art film aesthetic prevalent at the time as a gateway in their artistic evolution away from the Beatlemania mayhem of their live concert performances toward a more experimental, controlled, and mediated practice.

A different view of Nordic elsewheres emerges when analyzing responses in the 1960s to the near-collapse of a self-sustaining Scandinavian commercial film industry, mostly because of the competition from broadcast television. At the time, the state stepped in to save cinema through public film funding schemes and the promotion of "quality film," a particularly Scandinavian term that internationally became near-synonymous with art cinema. Part of this project also involved inviting the world to make films in Stockholm, which provides another elsewhere of Scandinavian cinema, with Bergman's first English-language film *The Touch* (Sweden/USA, 1971) funded by Hollywood's ABC Pictures and Susan Sontag's two shorts, *Duet for Cannibals* (Sweden, 1969) and *Brother Carl* (Sweden, 1971), shot at the invitation of the Swedish Film Institute's legendary founder and managing director Harry Schein. As Mariah Larsson argues in her chapter, women directors in the 1970s such as Mai Zetterling found it nearly impossible to finance and produce films in Sweden in this period, relocating instead to the UK as part of the cine-feminist movement there, producing material for the BBC, among other sponsors. Ingrid S. Holtar's chapter charts another little-known aspect of Scandinavian women's film history of the time, namely the connections between Norwegian women practitioners such as Vibeke Løkkeberg and the robust West German network of directors active in feminist filmmaking at the end of the 1970s.

Ingmar Bergman was at the zenith of his international reputation as a Swedish auteur when he went into a nearly five-year self-imposed exile over a tax scandal, settling in Munich, West Germany in 1976. Bergman's time abroad also leads to cinematic reinventions and attempts to work in new genres, languages, and production formats, making three films during this period: *The Serpent's Egg* (*Die Schlangerei*, West Germany/USA, 1977), *Autumn Sonata* (*Höstsonaten*, West Germany/Sweden, 1978), and *From the Life of the Marionettes* (*Aus dem Leben der Marionetten*, West Germany, 1980). The historically-underpinned suspense/mystery *The Serpent's Egg*, set in a hyper-inflationary Weimar Berlin of November 1923, foretells the chaos-fueled rise of German National Socialism, through an aesthetic inspired by German expressionism, constituting an intriguing set of elsewheres for the German, Swedish, and American cinemas of the 1970s. Anna Westerstahl Stenport and Arne Lunde examine the connections of *The Serpent's Egg* to New German Cinema and New Hollywood, arguing for the film's postmodern hybridity in its reconsiderations of the Nazi era as well as its contemporary context of a divided Cold War Europe. The chapter claims that *The Serpent's Egg* is Bergman's most interesting mobilization of history, politics, and aesthetics, with the opportunity of working outside of a national Swedish cinema context providing both opportunities and constraints.

Other Scandinavian directors also worked on marquee transnational productions in the 1970s, 1980s, and 1990s. Beyond the outsized shadow of Bergman, the trio of Jan Troell, Lasse Hallström, and Bille August were all established and recognized Scandinavian filmmakers within their home industries. All were Academy Award winners or nominees: Troell for *The Emigrants* (*Utvandrarna*, Sweden, 1971), Hallström for *My Life as a Dog* (*Mitt liv som hund*, Sweden, 1985), and August for *Pelle the Conqueror* (*Pelle erobreren*, Denmark, 1987). All left Sweden or Denmark with strong identities drawn from and pushing forward their respective national cinemas. They each entered into different kinds of production circumstances across transnational lines in the USA and in Europe. Traditional distinctions in the scholarship on this era that neatly compartmentalize between national cinemas, euro-puddings, and Hollywood tend to fracture when we look at the career dynamics of the three directors under consideration, as Lynn K. Wilkinson explores in her chapter about Lasse Hallström. Hallström carved out a long career niche in Hollywood projects that transcend hard and fast genre limits. Largely specializing in character-centered dramas adapted from popular fiction, Hallström forged an elegant, measured "European" style within larger-budget, star-driven Hollywood projects, including his work with Johnny Depp and Juliette Binoche in *Chocolat* (USA, 2000), Michael Caine in *The Cider House Rules* (USA, 1999), and Kevin Spacey and Julianne Moore in *The Shipping News* (USA, 2001), to name only a few. What may be most striking about Hallström's signature as a European director in America is his interest in exploring broader regional and international identities, not just those of New York and Los Angeles. The multifaceted and striated situations of all three filmmakers are also mirrored in the highly varied kinds of films that these displaced Scandinavian auteurs make when they leave their home countries, with films spanning a range of genres from historical costume epics, westerns, and disaster films to romantic comedies and family dramas. These films are shot on location in places as varied as Munich and Monterey, Tahiti and Newfoundland, Chile and the Caribbean.

As the 1990s seemed to further herald an accelerated process of globalization, a range of filmmakers and movements in Scandinavia continued pushing the envelope of what constituted "national cinemas." The most famous of these activist initiatives is Lars von Trier's performance-art stunt in Paris in 1995 (disrupting the respectful celebrations of the centennial of the French birth of the cinema, the Lumière Brothers, and their innovation of cinema practice as we know it), where Lars von Trier threw Marxist-red leaflets into the audience announcing the Dogme manifesto and its concomitant ten rules of chastity. It was his success internationally with English-language films *Europa/Zentropa* (Denmark, 1991) and *Breaking the Waves* (Denmark, 1996) that made the subsequent Dogme movement possible. In the past, a Danish director of equivalent stature might have seen himself forced to go abroad (as Dreyer did) to fully realize his potential. But von Trier has remained in Scandinavia thanks to changed production and funding mechanisms, making English-language films with name stars that have established him as a global, international art cinema filmmaker of enormous stature. As Linda Badley reveals in her chapter on Lars von Trier and Dogme 95 brother/director Thomas Vinterberg, these filmmakers have imported Hollywood and "Amerika" to Scandinavia. This process includes building sets at the Swedish Trollhättan and Danish Avedore studios while replicating and critiquing a violent, schizophrenic, and Kafkaesque "United States," as demonstrated by a range of films by von Trier (e.g. *Dancer in the Dark*, 2000; *Dogville*, 2003; *Manderlay*, 2005; *Antichrist*, 2009), subversively reversing Hollywood's dominant colonization of a global imaginary. In tandem with von Trier, Vinterberg's experimental eclecticism in the dystopian *It's All About Love* (2003) appears as a poisoned homage to both the studio system Hollywood cinema of the 1940s and 1950s and the New Hollywood of the 1970s, with its futurist and noir retro style, set design, costuming, and lighting that echo post-World War II America more than an imagined 2021. Badley thus engages with different aspects of von Trier and Vinterberg (beyond the aesthetics and influence of the Dogma movement) to interrogate another model of resistance to Hollywood hegemony. In these "Amerika" films, the Danish directors are the colonizers, not the colonized, reversing the usual "world according to Hollywood" projected onto the rest of the globe

Other directors of this time period mobilize different agendas of the globalization paradigm. Some of Aki Kaurismäki's films directly engage with American popular culture, such as *Leningrad Cowboys Go America* (Finland, 1989), with others linking to changing European industry and production circumstances, especially in terms of transnational funding and circulation. Ana Bento-Ribeiro's chapter examines Kaurismäki's longstanding French connections, including those with the production company Pyramide. Two of his French-language films, *La Vie de Bohème* (Finland, 1992) and *Le Havre* (Finland, 2011), engage diasporic dimensions of the new Europe emerging upon the expansion of the European Union, with migration and displacement thematized. Similar concerns form a part of Swedish filmmaker Lukas Moodysson's oeuvre, including the English-language *Mammoth* (*Mammut*, Sweden, 2009), set in three countries as a tale of globalization inequities.

The twenty-first-century breakthrough of Scandinavian documentaries shot outside of the region also addresses a range of critical issues pertaining to globalization. Several chapters in the book examine the production, funding, themes, and approaches of recent Scandinavian documentary practice. Ib Bondebjerg writes about Danish global documentaries and the work of Jon Bang Carlsen and Joshua Oppenheimer, identifying key aspects of international documentary work as a longstanding strength of Scandinavian cinema. For many, this wave of critically acclaimed work accelerated with the international reception of von Trier's and Jørgen Leth's *The Five Obstructions* (*De fem benspaend*, Denmark, 2003), shot in Cuba, Bombay, and Brussels. The von Trier/Leth film builds on tenets central to Dogma 95, including their philosophy of "obstacles," by which creativity and personal expression are best mobilized under clear constraints. This philosophy can be extended to describe pertinent aspects of the contemporary Scandinavian film industry, where funding and production circumstances of small national cinemas are creatively mobilized in the documentary genre in support of filmmakers who travel the world to tell stories of global significance. Related films include a range of award-winning documentaries that have had broad international circulation, while often mixing the personal with the political, and the subjective with the public. These include Janus Metz's *Armadillo* (Denmark, 2010) about Danish soldiers' experiences at a military base in Afghanistan, Erik Gandini's *Videocracy* (Sweden, 2009), about Silvio Berlusconi's media empire in Italy, and Fredrik Gertten's *Bananas!** (Sweden, 2009), about Dole workers in Nicaragua. This body of work has benefited from an expanded set of funding opportunities through regional film centers as well as through special programs by the national film institutes and national film schools. Mette Hjort's chapter about Danish support for filmmaking in Palestine provides a recent set of examples about capacity building, educational initiatives, and shared practitioner agency among documentary filmmakers in Europe and the Middle East. In a related vein, Lill-Ann Körber considers Göran Hugo Olsson's interventionism into Swedish national narratives of (neo)-colonialism and race that triangulate Europe, Africa, and North America. Oscar-awarded Malik Bendjelloul's *Waiting for Sugar Man* (Sweden, 2012) provides an intriguing elsewhere in terms of the rediscovery of US singer-songwriter Rodriguez and his significance for anti-apartheid movements in South Africa. Danish filmmaker Mads Brügger's documentaries and the recent *Cold Case Hammarskjöld* (Denmark, 2019) provide other angles on contested relationships between Scandinavia and Africa.

Filmmaking about contemporary Iran and cinematic cultures related to the Iranian–American diaspora has been strong in contemporary Scandinavia, with Nahid Persson Sarvestani's *The Queen and I* (Sweden, 2008) as a case in point, wherein the director and former Iranian empress Farah Pahlavi share recollections about the Iran that they had both fled. Some of these Iranian-Scandinavian exilic and émigré connections are also discussed in Boel Ulfsdotter's and Mats Björkin's chapter about the Gothenburg International Exile Film Festival in this volume. In sum, recent Scandinavian documentaries build on the strong foundations of non-fiction filmmaking in the region, bridging this practice with circulation and funding mechanisms of the "globalization" decades, where filmmakers from small nations, with small budgets, can tell stories that reach the world.

The last two decades have also seen a rise of Indigenous filmmaking in Scandinavia, with the first Greenlandic fiction feature film with international circulation produced in 2009 (*Nuummioq*, Torben Bech and Otto Rosing, Greenland), and the first documentary about Greenlandic history in 2014 (*Sumé: The Sound of a Revolution* (*Sumé: Mumisitsinerup nipaa*), Inuk Silis Hoegh, Greenland). To contextualize within a global perspective the rise of Indigenous filmmaking in the Nordic region, the International Sámi Film Institute (ISFI) is particularly important. Opening in Kautokeino/Guovdageaidnu, Norway, in 2007, the center has by now seen the production of over thirty films. Troy Storfjell discusses one of ISFI's international co-productions in his chapter "Elsewheres of Healing: Trans-Indigenous Spaces in Elle-Máijá Apiniskim Tailfeathers' *Bihttoš*" and Gunnar Iversen examines the oeuvre of internationally recognized Sámi filmmaker Nils Gaup in "A Sámi in Hollywood: Nils Gaup's Transnational and Generic Negotiations." An elsewhere of Nordic contemporary filmmaking is emerging across the nation states of Norway, Sweden, Finland, and Denmark/Greenland through a range of publicly funded initiatives, aimed at connecting with Indigenous film production globally. This includes facilitating screenings at film festivals around the world.

As is evident in Gaup's international career, Nordic Noir and a range of twenty-first-century film remakes in Hollywood have allowed Scandinavian cinema and television to travel globally as genre vehicles that emulate and reconfigure standard Hollywood conventions. Some of these remakes include the horror genre, as in Tomas Alfredson's *Let the Right One In* (*Låt den rätte komma in*, Sweden, 2008), remade by Matt Reeves into *Let Me In* (2010, USA), or crime dramas, such as David Fincher's 2011 remake of Niels Arden Oplev's 2009 *Girl with the Dragon Tattoo* (*Män som hatar kvinnor*). Police procedurals have been especially favored for remakes, including the Henning Mankell series *Wallander* (SVT 1994–2007) set and shot in Sweden, but later mutated into English language accessibility (while still filmed on location in Mankell's Swedish Skanian Ystad locale) by the BBC and Kenneth Branagh (*Wallander*, 2008–12). Other examples include the Danish-Swedish co-production *Broen/Bron* ("The Bridge," DR and SvT, 2011–13) about Danish and Swedish police cooperating to solve a murder in the middle of the Øresund bridge, which was remade by the US network FX in 2013 as *The Bridge* (for more on the Nordic remake in Hollywood, see Stenport 2016).

These and other remakes configure a set of Scandinavian elsewheres that are both connected to and dislodged from their points of origin. When television concepts and film genres travel as remakes (with changes in genre, location, language, narrative structures, aesthetics, and characterization), small film industries like those of the Nordic region benefit from the exposure and industry networks that remakes bring. Remakes often provide a "next step up" for access to star casts, bigger budgets, international exposure, and new technology. These developments have increased exposure of Scandinavia and Scandinavian film practitioners internationally and enhanced capacity-building for film and TV professionals who work in specific genre formats and go back and forth between their home countries and Hollywood or Hollywood-like production circumstances. Eva Novrup Redvall's chapter "Nordic Noir as a Calling Card: The International Careers of Danish Film and Television Talent in the 2010s" discusses how the circulation of Nordic Noir and other twenty-first-century remakes offer a viable vehicle toward transnational engagement, in ways that engage with how twenty-first-century globalization phenomena—commercial, geopolitical, pop-cultural—can be both visualized and challenged.

The past several decades have indeed seen an explosive acceleration of Nordic directors and performers working abroad in Hollywood and UK cinema and television. Not since the Scandinavian film diaspora of the silent period have there been as many Nordic directors and actors in Hollywood. Key forces behind this renaissance include a globalization of "Hollywood" popular genres within Nordic national cinemas that have in turn cultivated stylistically gifted genre directors attractive to English-language production and capital (just as was the case in the 1920s with Sjöström, Stiller, and Christensen). For instance, Danish director Nicolas Winding Refn, who Björn Nordfjörd considers in this volume, mastered the mean streets gangster film in Denmark through the *Pusher* trilogy (Denmark, 1996–2005), and his English-language projects abroad, such as *Drive* (USA, 2011) and *Only God Forgives* (Denmark/France, 2013), continue this approach. Transnational labor in the age of digital media appears to have accelerated the number of opportunities for Nordic practitioners to operate globally. The careers of Refn, Ole Bornedal, Susanne Bier, Lone Scherfig, and Nikolaj Arcel (all from Denmark), Renny Harlin (from Finland), Baltasar Kormakur (from Iceland), Nils Gaup, Erik Skjoldbjærg, Petter Næss, Bent Hamer, Tommy Wirkola, and Morten Tyldum (from Norway), and Mikael Håfström, Tomas Alfredson, and Daniel Espinosa (from Sweden), are all emblematic in this regard.

In addition, a cluster of Nordic directors have migrated to the UK as an alternative to Hollywood. Danish director Lone Scherfig, whose romantic comedy-drama *Italian for Beginners/Italiensk for begyndere* (Denmark, 2000) was the most commercially successful Dogme film, has virtually become a British director with *Wilbur Wants to Kill Himself* (UK, 2002), *An Education* (UK, 2009), *The Riot Club* (UK, 2014), and *Their Finest* (UK, 2016). Swedish filmmaker Tomas Alfredson's success with the vampire film *Let the Right One In* led to his British reboot of le Carré's *Tinker Tailor Soldier Spy* (UK, 2011). Morten Tyldum, who made *Headhunters* (Norway, 2011), the high-adrenaline Norwegian thriller adapted from Jo Nesbø's crime novel, directed *The Imitation Game* (UK, 2014) about English mathematician and World War II code-breaker Alan Turing, played by Benedict Cumberbatch. This growing cluster of Nordics in the UK represents another choice of an alternative to Hollywood genre filmmaking and ideally higher prestige and relative freedom compared to a more formulaic, corporate, and brutally monetarized tent-pole American cinema.

Nordic directors and performers adapting to Hollywood and UK cinema in the new millennium demonstrate the fluid notion of cinematic elsewheres. Each artist's experience can be fixed within a spectral continuum, one highly influenced by genre yet nuanced by a range of other factors. As elsewheres have become less fixed and defined by geographic location, as genres like action/ suspense, horror, sci-fi/fantasy, crime, and noir have become more globalized and international, Scandinavian talents have increasingly mastered film and television production expertise, efficiency, kinetic drive, and arresting poetics beyond the frame of the merely national. Exploring and historicizing more fully the transnational dynamism of Nordic cinema outside of its normative national borders reveal the substantive contributions of an increasing Nordic diaspora into the Hollywood–UK media apparatus and further recognition of its global reach and influence over the past century.

CONCLUSION: ABSENCES AND OMISSIONS

Nordic Film Cultures and Cinemas of Elsewhere is a revisionist project, seeking to reconfigure small national cinemas, especially, as inherently inter- and transnational, as diasporic and displaced, and as integrating a large variety of spatial, cultural, linguistic, and geopolitical considerations. This book is conceptualized in both a largely chronological and a historical sense, as the previous section illustrates, as well as thematically, as the four sub-groupings of book chapters indicate: From "Traces and Erasures" to "Intermediaries," "Contact Zones," and "Revisitations." A fifth category could well have been "Absences and Omissions." No book can cover everything, and as editors we have had to make choices. We have prioritized examples and phenomena that can be construed as integral to Scandinavian film history or that represent traditions of world cinema. These considerations necessarily mean that many important cinematic elsewheres could not be fully or even partially addressed. As a way of concluding this Introduction and setting the stage for the ensuing chapters, we put forward four different aspects that we would have wished to address more fully, and where we hope that others might well pick up the torch.

The experimental film tradition in Nordic cinema is not greatly emphasized in *Nordic Film Cultures and Cinemas of Elsewheres*, though it includes a long tradition of international influences and confluences. Viking Eggeling made his classic abstract film (the first known abstract film made) *Symphonie Diagonale* (*Diagonal-Symphonie*, 1924) in Germany, and the work went on to play in London, Paris and New York and greatly influence the rise of the Parisian and New York cinematic avant-gardes. Arne Sucksdorff's city film *Rhythm of a City* (*Människor i stad*, Sweden, 1947) played as an experimental work at Amos Vogel's Cinema 16 in the USA, and it won an Academy Award. Dreyer's *Thorvaldsen* (Denmark, 1949) is a poetic short on sculptor Bertel Thorvaldsen, which circulated widely on 16mm in universities and cine-clubs filled with budding experimental filmmakers in the USA. Danish filmmaker Jørgen Leth was influenced by, and was a member of, the Scandinavian Situationists and went on to make the classic experimental short *The Perfect Human* (*Det perfekte menneske*, Denmark, 1968), which gained an international audience both at the time of its release and again after the release of *The Five Obstructions* in 2003. Swedish filmmaker Gunvor Nelson emigrated to the USA, settling in California, and made a series of avant-garde films that were central to the establishment of American underground cinema. The global circulation of these works, and the concurrent patterns of migration, point to a thus untold story of the previously unrecognized influence of Nordic experimental elsewhere directors and artists.

Though the Nordic region is known for its policies promoting gender equality, feminist film practice has been understudied and underpromoted. Movements to change this are ongoing, with, for instance, Swedish Film Institute CEO Anna Serner's initiative 50/50 by 2020 garnering headlines around the world and generating similar priorities in other countries. Scholarship on Scandinavian women directors and producers working outside of national cinema cultures has also been scant. More can and should be done in terms of revisionist historiography in this regard. For instance, Susanne Bier occupies a nearly unique position in a Nordic and international feature film production context, with two Oscar nominations and one win and broad international distribution of her films. Yet substantive scholarship about the director and her body of work is only beginning to finally emerge (see Molloy et al. 2018). From an elsewheres perspective, many of Bier's films are especially relevant, given that they explicitly engage social issues pertaining to global conflicts and inequalities in Afghanistan, India, Africa, and the USA while situating these as also imbricated within contemporary Danish culture. This is evident in *Brothers* (*Brødre*, Denmark, 2004), *After the Wedding* (*Efter brylluppet*, Denmark, 2006), and *In a Better World* (*Hævnen*, Denmark, 2010). Yet several of her Hollywood productions, include *Things We Lost in the Fire* (USA, 2007, featuring Benicio Del Toro and Halle Berry) and *Serena* (USA, 2014 with Jennifer Lawrence and Bradley Cooper), have struggled to gain traction. The TV series *The Night Manager* (UK, 2016), on the other hand, has been sold to over 180 countries. Bier's career is profoundly transnational and has engaged in the juxtaposition of various elsewheres in ways no other contemporary Scandinavian filmmaker comes close to. Her regular, prolific, well-received, genre-driven productions are arguably the closest we get in contemporary Scandinavia to a "studio director" in terms of output that reaches audiences across Scandinavia and internationally.

A third category of absence in this book is the rich and varied tradition of immigrant, exilic, diasporic, accented, and refugee filmmaking and cinephilia cultures made inside the borders of the Nordic region or revisiting migration, cross-border, or asylum-seeking experiences. Though some examples are included, clearly much more work remains to be undertaken in this regard.

Postwar immigration from Hungary, Yugoslavia, Czechoslovakia, Italy, South America, and Africa has shaped Scandinavian cultures, but renditions of these experiences have been underrepresented in national support for film production. Not until the early 2000s, through the works of an emerging group of film practitioners with a background in the Middle East (notably Iran and Lebanon), such as Reza Bagher, Josef Fares, Susan Taslimi, and Reza Parsa, did "immigrant" film become a term in Scandinavian cinema (Wright 1998). Key recent fiction feature examples that have had international release include Milad Alami's *The Charmer* (*Charmøren*, Denmark, 2017) about an Iranian immigrant in Copenhagen and Rojda Sekersöz's film about a collective of young and rebellious *banlieue* women in *Beyond Dreams* (*Dröm vidare*, Sweden, 2017). Norwegian-born Rune Denstad Langlo's comedy *Welcome to Norway* (Norway, 2016) engages a diverse cast of polyglot immigrants, providing a new perspective on Norwegian diversity. Another important elsewhere film context in this regard concerns the large number of adoptees from Asia and South America who were brought to Scandinavia as infants from the late 1960s onward. For instance, there are more than 23 000 Korean adoptees in Scandinavia. This practice, now construed as a form of child abduction and trafficking, is garnering increasing political and media attention, with films such as the widely screened *Susanne Brink* (*Susan Brinkui arirang*, South Korea/Sweden, 1991) prompting international awareness and generating political pushback in South Korea and in Scandinavia about this history.

The fourth absence would be attention to films and cinematic practices that are literally and irrecoverably elsewhere, meaning they are lost or otherwise inaccessible. Case studies along these lines might attempt to excavate from surviving traces the multiple lost films of Sjöstrom/Seastrom, Stiller, and Benjamin Christensen in 1920s Hollywood. For instance, we have no way of seeing Seastrom's completely lost *The Tower of Lies* (MGM, 1925), adapted from the novel *The Emperor of Portugallia* by Nobel Prize-winner Selma Lagerlöf, or seeing Stiller's unfinished footage from *The Temptress* (MGM, 1926) starring Greta Garbo. Yet a methodology of archival vivisection of a sort (surviving production stills, candid photos, letters, contracts, script materials, etc.) can allow us to re-imagine if not reconstitute the missing objects of moving image art. There is also a rich wealth of material uncatalogued in archives or hidden from public view as part of individual collections, whether in the form of home movies, educational film, orphaned footage, salvaged off-prints, or private sector or industrial film, etc. This subset is usually absent from national film histories that emphasize productions that have had cinema or television release or that are locatable and accounted for in filmographies, on IMDB, or via related national services. Similarly, the moving image culture of our contemporary moment, which includes YouTube fare, gaming, virtual and immersive reality, and numerous other forms of digital media still in the future, cannot be extensively accounted for in this volume. These forms of para-cinematic expression clearly provide ample opportunity for considerations of elsewheres, just as an ongoing process of excavation of "lost" objects does.

References

Bacon, Henry, ed. 2016. *Finnish Cinema: A Transnational Enterprise*. London: Palgrave.
Berry, Chris and Lynn Spigel, eds. 2009. *Electronic Elsewheres: Media, Technology, and the Experience of Social Space*. Minneapolis: Minnesota University Press.
Harley, J. B. 2002. *The New Nature of Maps: Essays in the History of Cartography*. Baltimore: Johns Hopkins University Press.
Hjort, Mette. 2005. *Small Nation, Global Cinema: The New Danish Cinema*. Minneapolis: University of Minnesota Press.
Hjort, Mette and Ursula Lindqvist. 2016. *The Wiley-Blackwell Companion to Nordic Cinema*. Cambridge, MA: Wiley-Blackwell.
Kääpä, Pietari. 2014. *Ecology and Contemporary Nordic Cinemas: From Nation-Building to Ecocosmopolitanism*. London: Bloomsbury.
Lunde, Arne. 2010. *Nordic Exposures: Scandinavian Identities in Classical Hollywood Cinema*. Seattle: University of Washington Press.
MacKenzie, Scott and Anna Westerstahl Stenport, eds. 2014. *Films on Ice: Cinemas of the Arctic*. Edinburgh: Edinburgh University Press.
Nestingen, Andrew K. 2008. *Crime and Fantasy in Scandinavia: Fiction, Film, and Social Change*. Seattle; Copenhagen: University of Washington Press.
Nestingen, Andrew K. and Trevor G. Elkington. 2005. *Transnational Cinema in a Global North: Nordic Cinema in Transition*. Detroit: Wayne State University Press.
Oxford English Dictionary, 2nd edn. 1989. 20 vols. Oxford: Oxford University Press. Also available at <http://www.oed.com/>.
Pratt, Mary Louise. 1992 [2008]. *Imperial Eyes: Travel Writing and Transculturation*. New York: Routledge.
Soila, Tytti, ed. 2005. *The Cinema of Scandinavia*. New York: Wallflower Press.
Stenport, Anna Westerstahl. 2016. "Nordic Remakes: The North in Hollywood." In *The Companion to Nordic Cinema*, ed. Mette Hjort and Ursula Lindqvist. London: Wilcy Blackwell. 436–56.
Thomson, C. Claire. 2006. *Northern Constellations: New Readings in Nordic Cinema*. Norwich: Norvik Press.
Wright, Rochelle. 1998. *The Visible Wall: Jews and Other Ethnic Outsiders in Swedish Film*. Carbondale: Southern Illinois University Press.

PART I

TRACES AND ERASURES

2. MAPPING CINEMA GHOSTS: RECONSTRUCTING THE CIRCULATION OF NORDIC SILENT FILM IN AUSTRALIA

Julie K. Allen

Although Australia lies at the farthest geographical extreme from northern Europe, roughly 17000 kilometers from Copenhagen, high levels of cinema attendance in Australia in the early twentieth century made it an attractive market for silent films from the Nordic region. Few traces remain of the circulation of Nordic film in Australia, however, rendering it effectively invisible, a cinema ghost. Still, the cultural and economic exchanges between the Nordic region and Australia that silent film facilitated are worth mapping, if only, to borrow Giuliana Bruno's formulation, "as a metonymy of fragmentations ... a territory of subjugated popular knowledge" (1993, 4). Situated within the framework of the "new cinema history's preoccupations with the cinema as a commercial institution and with the socio-cultural history of its audiences" (Maltby 2011, 8), the circulation of Nordic silent film in Australia reveals an untold history of cinematic elsewheres that renders visible film's function as both a carrier of culture and a barometer for societal change in a country shaped by rapid modernization, contested settler colonialism, and escalating geopolitical tensions.

Methodological Considerations

Given the dearth of narrative sources, the history of Nordic silent film in Australia has to be reconstructed from scattered clues. The kinds of historical sources that would be most effective in exposing the conditions under which

Nordic silent film circulated in Australia simply don't exist any longer. Little tangible evidence remains from the early Australian film industry and cinema market—few company records, cinema logbooks, contracts, or publicity materials were preserved for Australian-made films, and even fewer for imported films. Denmark's Nordisk Films Kompagni (hereafter Nordisk) and Svensk Filmindustri (Swedish Film Industry, hereafter SF), which produced most of the Nordic films that could potentially have been screened in Australia in this period, maintained their own archives, but their records of exports outside of Europe in the silent era are fragmentary, consisting of a handful of lists, contracts, and letters.

The ephemerality of nitrate films as objects renders a traditional medium-specific film history approach impossible, since few of the films themselves have survived. As Australian film historian Richard Maltby explains, the early film industry was built on a model in which "motion pictures were understood to be consumables, viewed once, disposed of and replaced by a substitute providing a comparable experience" (2011, 7). Nitrate prints, usually just one or two of each film, were shipped to Australia and New Zealand and remained in circulation for months or years before being either shipped back or destroyed, with the result that few prints, if any, of Nordic silent films remained in Australasia. The new cinema history approach to the cinema as a site of social and cultural meaning-making offers a way out of this bind by using "quantitative information, articulated through the apparatus of databases, spatial analysis and geovisualisation, to advance a range of hypotheses about the relationship of cinemas to social groupings in the expectation that these hypotheses must be tested by other, qualitative means" (Maltby 2011, 8). Accordingly, this study pairs quantitative data about the circulation of Nordic film in Australia with qualitative contextual framing about the relevance of Nordic film to social developments.

Obtaining quantitative data about which Nordic silent films were shown in Australasia, where, how often, and for how long requires considerable detective work and a flexible approach. The most readily accessible source of raw information about Nordic silent film in Australia is the National Library of Australia's database Trove, which contains a text-searchable digital archive of more than 700 newspapers published in Australia between 1803 and 1957. Launched in 2009, this digital repository provides remote access to millions of Australian newspaper articles and ads, making it possible, by searching all mentions of the names of individual films, actors, and companies, to document screenings of Nordic films across Australia during the entirety of the silent era. This kind of research generates quantitative data that is useful for establishing hard facts about circulation patterns—which theaters in which towns tended to screen Nordic films, how long a given film stayed in a particular location, what kind of competition Nordic films faced from other films and different kinds of entertainment, how enthusiastically they were marketed, etc.—but it does not offer much insight into sociohistorical context.

Qualitative conclusions emerge in dialogue with information about the audiences for whom the films were screened, the state of the Australian film industry, and the global competition for cinema market share in the silent era. The pairing of quantitative and qualitative information can help answer such questions as "who would have been interested in importing Nordic films and why?" and "what kinds of aesthetic, social, economic, and cultural factors were involved in the distribution and exhibition of Nordic films?" The inclusion of narrative data, from fan magazines to personal memoirs to transcripts of governmental inquiries, transforms a catalogue of references to films and people into a dynamic web of connections and conversations both within Australasia and across the world. The circulation of Nordic silent film in Australia proves to be an intriguing part of a much larger but mostly forgotten story of cross-cultural contact, cooperation, and competition.

Scandinavian Silent Cinema in a Global Market

Denmark and Sweden were early adopters of film as a form of public entertainment and a vehicle for entrepreneurial ambitions. Among the many small production and exhibition companies that sprang up in the early 1910s, Copenhagen-based Nordisk and Swedish Biograph in Stockholm proved to be dominant in their respective countries. Although film exhibition was also popular in Norway and Finland, domestic film production was constrained by municipal control of local cinemas in Norway, which limited the availability of production capital, and by political tensions in Finland. Only seventeen feature films were made in Norway between 1906 and 1919, and none between 1913 and 1917. Similarly, the first Finnish feature film, *Salaviinanpolttajat* (*The Moonshiners*), was produced in 1907, but regular film production did not begin until the 1920s. This state of affairs resulted, according to Norwegian film historian Gunnar Iversen, in a "combination of uncertainty about the role of films in Norway and the massive drain of creative talent" to the Danish, Swedish, and German film industries (1999, 94). In comparison, Nordisk produced nearly 400 films between 1908 and 1910 alone, most of them short subjects, before reorienting its production toward multi-reel feature films, in particular the erotic melodramas for which it became world-famous.

Given their relatively small domestic markets, both Nordisk and SF were necessarily export-oriented. Nordisk was more successful in this endeavor in the pre-World War I era, while SF flourished in the early 1920s. Although film exhibition was state-regulated in both Denmark and Sweden, there was no governmental support for film production or distribution, in contrast to US State Department intervention on behalf of American producers in the interwar period and the quasi-governmental status of the German film company Ufa in the 1920s. As a result, Nordic film exports resulted solely from the efforts of the companies themselves, in cooperation with individual distributors and exhibitors in foreign countries. In the early 1910s, this approach was quite successful; Nordisk sent 98 percent of its films abroad (Thorsen 2006, 59), becoming the second largest exporter of films in the world in 1913 (Horak 2016, 457), behind the Paris-based Pathé Frères. Aware of the importance of navigating local regulations and exhibition networks, Nordisk established branch offices in London, Berlin, and Vienna, as well as a subsidiary company, Great Northern, in New York, to promote distribution of its films, in addition to acquiring an extensive network of cinemas in Germany for integrated distribution and exhibition.

Nordisk did not simply make films and ship them off to faraway markets in the hopes that they would appeal to foreign audiences. Instead, the company initially made a wide range of fairly generic films to please a variety of tastes—from travelogues about Siam and Norway to documentaries about stockfish and government rations. Nordisk tried to make films with universal thematic appeal and carefully non-specific locations, while also developing sophisticated strategies for targeting particular markets. In the title logbooks for Nordisk's early films, each film is given a title in as many as eight different languages, generally Danish, Swedish, French, German, Italian, Spanish, Portuguese, and English, along with the text for the associated intertitles. In many cases, the film's title is not simply translated from Danish, but is tailored for each country, often using name substitution. For example, the 1910 short *Jens ser levende Billeder* (which translates literally as "Jens sees living pictures") kept the same title in Swedish but was re-titled elsewhere, for example as *Willy Visits a Kinematograph Show* for English-speaking markets, *Hans im Kinematographen* for the crucial German market, *Bartolo va al cine* for Italian audiences, and *Calino au Cinématographe* for French ones. Both the name of the film's protagonist and the terminology for "living pictures" were tailored to particular national markets, with the French version referring to a popular comic character from a Gaumont series.

As both American and European film companies looked for new cinema markets along the path of colonial expansion, Australia became an increasingly important target. James Burns has documented how cinemas flourished in European colonies, from Bridgetown, Barbados to Dar es Salaam, Tanzania, and Mumbai, India to Capetown, South Africa (2013, 1), triggering fierce competition for a share of the most lucrative overseas markets, of which Australia was one of the largest. By 1913, there were roughly 650 permanent and several hundred more temporary cinema theaters across Australia, which had at that time a population of approximately 4.8 million people; by 1917 the number of cinemas had grown to 800. Australians were, as the Melbourne newspaper *Argus* declared on March 17, 1913, "as regular in attending picture shows as in having breakfast," with approximately 1/8th of the population of the entire country spending every Saturday night "at the pictures" (Collins 1987, 5). Such robust demand, paired with low domestic supply, meant that even small towns could support several different theaters and films could circulate on different circuits for years.

In the early silent period, Australian audiences had access to films from many different countries. Given the linguistic neutrality of silent film, audiences didn't seem to care where the films came from, as long as they were well-made. In 1913, slightly less than half of the films imported to Australia were American, 26.3 percent were British, and the remainder were European, including a significant number of films from Scandinavia (Mayer and Beattie 2007, 2). Quantitative data from Australian newspapers illustrates how the size and vigor of the Australasian cinema market allowed Nordic film to circulate far beyond its domestic markets and for much longer. Despite the fact that most cinemas changed their program once or twice a week, allowing each film a run of only a few days in a given city, the vastness of the Australian market gave rise to several different cinema circuits—first in metropolitan areas, then in smaller cities, and finally in tiny rural towns—which meant that Nordic films had potentially a much wider reach and longer exhibition life at the other end of the earth than they did at home.

Nordic Film in Australia, 1909–1918

Nordic film's path into the Australian market was paved by the French company Pathé Frères, which became the first European film company to establish a distribution agency in Australia when it opened an office in Melbourne in 1909 (Shirley and Adams 1983, 22). From this office, Pathé distributed gazettes, documentaries, and short historical, dramatic, and comedic features, including *La Tosca* (1909, France), *The Return of Ulysses* (*Le retour d'Ulysse*, 1909, France), and *Les Misérables* (1913, France). From 1909 to 1913, Pathé also operated cinemas in Alfred Hall in Ballarat and the Masonic Hall in Bendigo, Victoria, screening a mix of pictures from different countries, including the USA and Italy. After opening a branch office in Stockholm in 1912 and establishing cooperative endeavors with local filmmakers, Pathé agreed to distribute selected Swedish Biograph films internationally. Laura Horak reports that "Pathé distributed at least 13 Svenska Bio films, including six under the name Phoenix," between 1912 and the end of 1915 (2016, 459). According to Swedish Biograph records, the Swedish films sent to Australia in this period included *On the Fateful Roads of Life* (*På livets ödesvägar*, 1913, Sweden) and *The Stormy Petrel* (*Stormfågeln*, 1914, Sweden). However, the absence of Australian newspaper ads for these films in Trove makes it difficult to confirm whether any of them were ever delivered or screened there. By contrast, Nordisk handled its own distribution in Australia from at least 1909. Among the first Nordisk films screened in Australia were the Sherlock Holmes mystery *Cab Number 519* (*Droske 519*, 1909, Denmark) and the erotic melodrama *The White Slave Trade* (*Den hvide Slavehandel*, 1910, Denmark), which were followed by a steady stream of films between 1910 and 1914, including at least thirteen feature films in 1911 alone.

The circulation history of one of these early Nordisk imports, the three-reel Nordisk feature *Temptations of a Great City* (*Ved Fængslets Port*, 1911, Denmark), offers a useful case study of the reception of successful Nordic films in prewar Australia. Within four months of its premiere in Copenhagen on March 6, 1911, *Temptations of a Great City* was exported to Australia, either directly from Nordisk or through a British intermediary. As a high-quality feature film from an established production company, or "star picture," *Temptations of a Great City* offered businessmen a reliable source of revenue and audiences an exciting, entertaining picture. Newspaper ads reveal that the film was screened in Sydney, Hobart, Perth, Melbourne, Adelaide, and Brisbane during the summer of 1911, by different exhibitors. In-country distribution seems to have been handled initially by the Greater J. D. Williams Amusements Co. Williams supplied the film for screening at the Lyric Theatre in Sydney, one of two cinemas he controlled there, but also offered the film's exhibition rights outside of Sydney for sale or rent. In the Sydney trade journal *Referee* on July 12, 1911 Williams promises that, as a "dramatic production . . . produced on a scale of magnificence never before attempted," *Temptations of a Great City* would "be the talk of Australia" (16).

Newspaper ads like Williams' provide some insight into how the film was marketed. In keeping with Nordisk's policy at the time and general industry practice, no mention is made of any of the leading actor or actresses' names in any of the ads for the film, so the identity of the film's stars, Valdemar Psilander and Clara Wieth (later Pontoppidan), was not a factor in the film's anticipated financial success. This pattern held true for most Nordic films, with the exception of films featuring Asta Nielsen, which frequently included some mention of her name. Although the earliest ads for *Temptations of a Great City* do not mention Nordisk itself, subsequent ads, which often remind viewers of previously-screened Nordisk films, make it clear that Nordisk was becoming a recognizable brand associated with high-quality, socially-aware feature films. For example, an advertisement for *Temptations of a Great City* in the Melbourne paper *The Age* on August 12, 1911 notes that Nordisk had previously "presented the Famous Social Problem *In the Hands of Imposters*" (*Den hvide Slavehandels sidste Offer*, 1911, Denmark).

Nordic films were often promoted in terms of their relevance to Australian viewers' concerns. An ad that appeared on August 24, 1911 in the *Barrier*

Miner, the local paper for the fairly remote mining town of Broken Hill, NSW, describes a variety of hypothetical reactions to *Temptations of a Great City* in order to demonstrate its ability to appeal to many demographics:

> The man in the street says, "Have you seen the great winner, THE TEMPTATIONS OF A GREAT CITY?"
> The lady in her boudoir says, "My novels are tame in plot compared to THE TEMPTATIONS OF A GREAT CITY."
> The gay old spark says, "Well, I've had a good time in my youth, but I am beat by the doings in THE TEMPTATIONS OF A GREAT CITY."
> The lovers say, "Oh, we are shocked! We never spoon like those in THE TEMPTATIONS OF A GREAT CITY."
> Old Cent Per Cent says, "Mein gootness, the extravagance is awful in THE TEMPTATIONS OF A GREAT CITY."
> All the dear girls say, "Oh, I wish George would spoon like the nice, foolish boy in THE TEMPTATIONS OF A GREAT CITY."
> And the Wowser says, "It's dreadful but it points to a great moral, and I am going again and ALL SHOULD SEE THE TEMPTATIONS OF A GREAT CITY."

The ad makes it clear that the film is rather racy, with its depiction of lovers spooning and living it up, but suggests its scandalousness is legitimized by the film's moral lesson. It makes no reference to Nordisk or Denmark, but strikes instead a generic tone that underscores the film's universal attractiveness.

While the film's Danish origin was not emphasized in any of the ads, its association with European sophistication and culture lent it cachet. In the ad above, the German accent attributed to the viewer "Old Cent Per Cent," a somewhat derogatory term for a greedy or stingy person, underscores that Nordic silent films were marketed in Australia as an exclusive, luxury product with continental flair. Ads frequently mention how expensive it was to secure the exhibition rights for a particular Nordic film, attribute affiliation with continental (especially Parisian) theaters to the cast members, and reassure viewers (sometimes inaccurately) that the theater/distributor has exclusive rights to the picture. Two of the major film distributors in Australia in the early 1910s, J. D. Williams and T. J. West, were Britons who used their connections to import continental films, often through British companies. An ad for *Temptations of a Great City* in *The Daily News* (Perth) on September 7, 1911 boasted "a complete change of bill, the films having only arrived from the Old World by the last mailboat." A few days later, when West's Pictures in Sydney screened the Asta Nielsen–Valdemar Psilander drama *The Circus Girl* (*Den sorte drøm*, 1911, Denmark), West's ad in the *Sydney Morning Herald* on September 9 made a point of establishing Nielsen's alleged continental stage credentials:

> Mdlle. Asta Nielsen, of the Folies Bergères [sic], Paris, who plays the name-part in *The Circus Girl*, is one of the most fascinating ladies on the Continental stage. A woman of remarkable stage presence and exceeding beauty, she has long since become the idol of Parisian and Berlin audiences.

Australia might have been located at the end of the earth, as seen from Europe, but, as these kinds of ads underscore, silent film provided access to the best of European cultural sophistication. As Jill Julius Matthews argues, the promise of the modern world arrived in Sydney "from overseas not fully fledged and triumphant, but rather as a stream of amusing gadgets, scientific marvels and diverting ideas" (2005, 1), often conveyed on screen through film, that allowed Australians to see themselves as part of "the ceaseless international ebb and flow of commerce and ideas that underpinned cosmopolitan modernity" (8).

As a particularly successful example of a Nordic film circulating in prewar Australia, *Temptations of a Great City* illuminates the highly competitive nature of the Australian market. Australian newspaper coverage of the film reveals a pattern of aggressive promotion involving daily advertisements in local papers for days or weeks in advance of a screening, sometimes with two or more ads appearing on the same day in the same paper or in competing papers in the same town, or even in different towns at the same time. On August 7, 1911, while Williams was still showing *Temptations of a Great City* in Sydney and English Amusements Company was exhibiting it in Hobart, Tasmania, West's began screening it in Adelaide as an "exclusive attraction." Three days later, on August 10, *The Age* in Melbourne began advertising the film's exclusive August 12 premiere in Melbourne, at Tait's Pictures, offering the assurance that "this Great Interpretation of a Desperate Social Canker cannot possibly prove harmful to beholders. It is a true, honest representation of the terrible undertow which encompasses our young manhood in its relentless tentacles, and draws them down! down! down! into the fascinating vortex of oblivion" (12). Tait's seems to have been scooped by J. D. Williams, however, for on August 11, Williams' Melba Theatre added a 2:30 p.m. matinee, noting in *The Argus* that "we have much pleasure in submitting [it] to our patrons for the first time in Melbourne," a few hours before Tait's was to offer "the first presentation [of the film] in Melbourne."

While still making the rounds of major theaters in Australian metropolises, *Temptations of a Great City* entered the provincial cinema circuit. Parallel ads in the Sydney trade journal *Referee* on August 23, 1911 indicate that both J. D. Williams and the Clement Mason Ciné Co. were offering the film for hire; Mason also had *In the Hands of Imposters* on offer. Tait's Pictures' screening on August 11, 1911 at the Princess Theatre in Bendigo, 150 km north of Melbourne, was, as *The Bendigo Independent* reported, "crowded from gallery to stalls." On August 22, 1911, *Temptations of a Great City* was screened for the first time in the isolated mining town of Broken Hill, in the far west of outback New South Wales. Since Broken Hill, near the border of South Australia, is twice as close to Adelaide (500km) as to Sydney (1100km), it seems likely that the print shown at the Port Adelaide Empire Picture Palace until August 19 had then made its way north to Broken Hill. In Victoria, the Melbourne print was being screened in rural Colac, 150 km west-southwest of Melbourne, by August 28. In Queensland, the film traveled from Brisbane, where it had had a double run at West's New Olympia, to the brand-new custom-built Empire Theatre in Toowoomba, Queensland, approximately 150 km west of Brisbane, on September 9.

More than three years after the film's Danish premiere, *Temptations of a Great City* was still being screened in rural Australia, albeit in rather makeshift conditions. Following its run in a variety of provincial cinemas in 1911 and 1912 under the auspices of many different exhibitors, *Temptations of a Great City* was acquired by Miss Ettie Wilmott's traveling Wilmott Electric Picture Company. An initial one-night screening in Manila, New South Wales in April 1912 seems to have been successful enough to justify taking it on an extensive tour in the Australian hinterlands, with Wilmott bringing the film from town to town between May 1913 and June 1914 throughout rural South Australia and Victoria on a circuitous route. From reviews of these screenings, it seems that Wilmott, nicknamed "the lady with a man's voice" (*Pinaroo Country News*, September 12, 1913), paired screenings of the film with performances of operatic songs. From February through May 1914, Wilmott toured the film around Tasmania, including some places, like Launceston and Hobart, where it had been screened in picture palaces three years earlier. Wilmott's last documented screening of the film took place in Franklin, Tasmania, on May 20, 1914. Wilmott then seems to have handed the print off to a company called Souvenir Pictures, which screened the film for what appears to have been the last time in Australia on June 20, 1914, as the Saturday evening feature in Coleraine, Victoria, more than 335 km west of the state capital of Melbourne.

As this representative example illustrates, Nordic films were popular and apparently profitable on the Australian market in the early 1910s, but the outbreak of World War I had a devastating impact on European film exports, including those from Scandinavia. As products of neutral countries, Danish and Swedish films continued to circulate in Australia during the first few years of the war, until at least mid-1916. However, the disruption of global shipping, Australian tariffs on European films, and shortages of materials including film stock meant that far fewer films were sent abroad from European producers than in the prewar period.

Meanwhile, American film companies capitalized on American neutrality to target the Australian market, establishing local offices and making exclusive

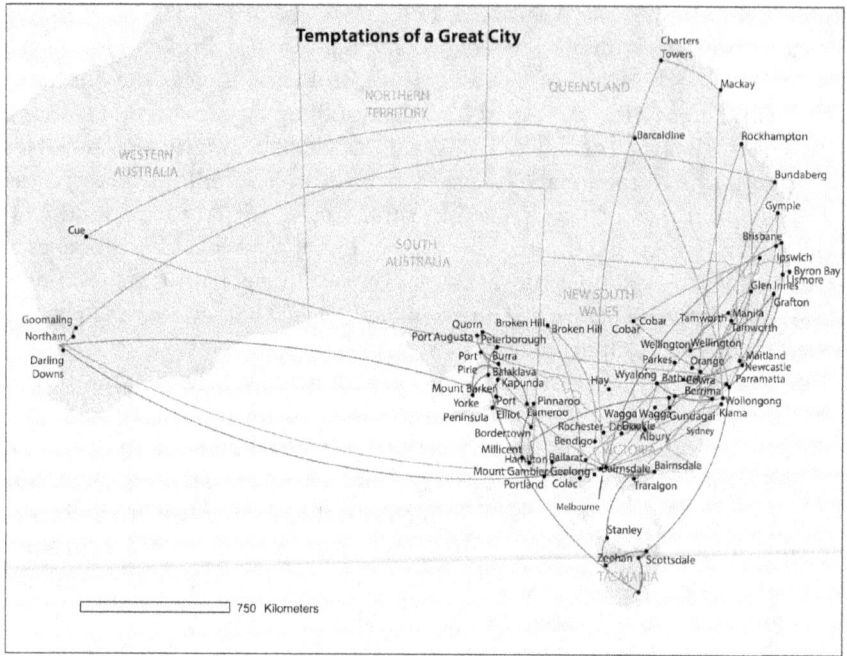

Figure 2.1 This map traces the three main circuits of the Australian circulation of *Temptations of a Great City* between 1911 and 1913. Graphic design by Julie K. Allen.

distribution agreements with the major Australian distributors and exhibitors that fundamentally changed distribution and exhibition conditions in Australia. A Thornton Fisher cartoon in the *Moving Picture World* on March 10, 1917 depicts the Hungarian-born president of Paramount Pictures, Adolph Zukor, scrawling "Paramount" across a map of Australia, with the caption "Zukor annexes Australia." In November 1917, the country's largest distributor, Australasian Films Ltd, joined the US-based First National Exhibitors' Circuit, and by December 1917, Australian cinema programs contained, on average, 95 percent American-made films (Thompson 1985, 81), a percentage that has remained largely stable for the past hundred years.

Nordic Film in Australia, 1919–1928

After World War I, when Nordic films regained access to Australian cinemas, the market was much tighter, due to the dominance of imported US films in both Australasia and Europe. Given their obligations to American producers, few Australian distributors were interested in importing Scandinavian films, but one exception to this rule was Mary Mason. Her husband Clement had been a film importer in the 1910s, one of J. D. Williams' competitors for *Temptations of a Great City*, and Mason's had grown, as the *Sunday Times* in Perth reported on September 5, 1915, "to a tremendous concern in the last five years," as Mason "knows the Australian public's demand to a degree." After her husband's death in June 1917, she went into the film business for herself as the head of Mason Super Films through which she began to carve out a niche for herself as the national supplier of exclusive, highbrow European films, particularly from Italy and Sweden.

Fortunately for Mrs. Mason's ambitions, the Swedish film industry had matured during the war, departing from its previous custom of copying Danish melodramas. Swedish production companies began to concentrate on making fewer, higher-budget films, often adaptations of Nordic literary works, such as Ibsen's narrative poem *Terje Vigen*. Swedish film scholar Tytti Soila explains that the goal was to "break new ground not only on a narrative level but . . . stylistically as well. A successful formula was to be found in topics that would appear familiar to the domestic audience, but which were conceived as exotic by the international audience" (Soila et al. 1998, 150). A merger of several small Swedish film companies in 1918 resulted in Filmindustri Inc. Skandia, which merged with Swedish Biograph in 1919 to create the massive AB Svensk Filmindustri (Swedish Film Industry, known as SF), which helped drive Swedish silent film production to its peak in 1919–21. The high-profile Swedish art films produced in this period seemed to offer real competition to lighter American fare. In contrast to the prewar period, when marketers and audiences seemed indifferent to the origin of the films on screen, branding films as Nordic now functioned as a marker of their quality and artistic seriousness.

The first Swedish film Mason introduced after the war was Mauritz Stiller's *The Flame of Life* (*Sången om den eldröda blomman*, 1919), based on a sensationalist novel by the Finnish author Johannes Linnankoski. The first mention of the film in the Australian press is a December 1, 1919 ad in *The Theatre Magazine* for a "Nordisk masterpiece" that had been enthusiastically received in London. Although it is possible that the film had been distributed to London (and thence to Australia) under Nordisk's auspices, it was described correctly as a Swedish film in the March 1, 1920 issue, accompanied by the description: "A fine film this, with a good story, beautiful old world scenery and some clever acting by Lars Larsen [sic], who among other things rides the rapids on a single log."

The circulation history of *The Flame of Life* illustrates the constrained conditions for the exhibition of Nordic films in Australia after World War I. It had been screened in London in August 1919, but it did not premiere in Australia until February 6, 1920, nearly a full year after its release in Sweden on April 14, 1919. It was screened first at the New Lyceum Theatre in Sydney for one week before moving on to Newcastle and Lithgow, New South Wales, in early March for a few days in each location. In April 1920, it was screened in Perth, Western Australia, whence it traveled to Ballarat, Victoria in June, and then on to Brisbane, Queensland, in August 1920, for one week. This itinerary, consisting of several multi-day screenings in far-distant cities with long gaps between screenings, suggests that only a single print of this seven-reel film had been imported to Australia to be exhibited in a single theater at a time. It apparently never appeared in theaters in Adelaide, Melbourne, Launceston or Hobart, all cities that had been enthusiastic in their reception of Nordic films a decade earlier, nor did it feature prominently on the provincial circuit, aside from the handful of screenings in Newcastle, Lithgow, and Ballarat.

Despite this constricted circulation, Mason Super Films continued importing Swedish films, touting both their artistry and their role as representative examples of the resurgence of the European film industry as competition for American films. In its initial description of *The Flame of Life*, the company described the film as a "brilliantly-acted ... REAL masterpiece," while an article in the January 1, 1920 issue of *The Theatre Magazine* connects Mrs. Mason's promotion of European films to "the determination that now exists on the part of [British] manufacturers to vie with Americans in the production of pictures." In July 1920, Mason Super Films justified its focus on importing Swedish art films, alongside Italian films from Itala and Caesar Film, in an article in *Film Weekly*, with the assertion that

> the Swedish and Norwegian group of manufacturers are making a bold bid for Continental supremacy in the output of films. Not long back the Swedish Biograph Co. increased its capital to 2 million pounds, with the result that it has in course of erection an entire film city at Rasund [sic]. The productions of this company that have already been seen are remarkable for the sincerity of the acting and the artistic presentation of the stories.

To prove this point, the company announced the imminent release of two additional Swedish films: *The Dawn of Love* (*Ingmarssönerna*, Sjöström, 1919) and *The Snows of Destiny* (Stiller, 1920). *The Dawn of Love* premiered at the Strand de Luxe Union Theatre in Brisbane on July 9, 1920, a month before *The Flame of Life* was screened at the Pavilion Theatre. In mid-August, *The Dawn of Love* was screened for a few days each in Launceston and Hobart, Tasmania, before finishing up at the Casino Theatre in Port Pirie, South Australia in December 1920, with a few encore screenings in Port Pirie in May 1921, as well as at Gilder's Pictures in Cairns, Queensland, in March 1922. Having two Swedish films in circulation in different cities at the same time increased the Australian public's exposure to this new, more literary-oriented incarnation of

Nordic films, a strategy that seems to have paid off for *The Snows of Destiny*, which ran (with gaps) from an initial March 4, 1921 screening in Perth to a final screening on July 8, 1924 in Cessnock, New South Wales. The prolonged circulation of this particular film, which was adapted from the novel *Sir Arne's Treasure* by the Nobel Prize-winning Swedish author Selma Lagerlöf, allowed it to be screened in nearly every Australian metropolitan area as well as in several towns on the provincial circuit. The prominence of Lagerlöf's name in reviews of and ads for the film suggests that her personal prestige helped earn the film a spot in many cinema programs.

Thanks to Mason's energetic efforts, at least six major Swedish feature films, almost all directed by Mauritz Stiller or Victor Sjöström, were screened in Australia between February 1920 and July 1924, with Stiller's *Erotikon* (Stiller, 1920) and two Sjöström films—*A Lover in Pawn* (*Mästerman*, 1920, Sweden), and *Thy Soul Shall Bear Witness* (*Körkarlen*, 1921, Sweden)—staying in circulation for seven months and two years, respectively. Two prints of *Thy Soul Shall Bear Witness* were shipped to Mason for exhibition on Australasian screens, suggesting confidence in their marketability. On the basis of the ads Mason ran for them, their appeal for Australian audiences lay in their exclusivity and artistic quality, in implicit contrast to frequently formulaic American productions. Mason also acquired the rights to several other films from SF Films, including *The Hell Ship* (*Eld ombord*, 1923, Sweden), *God's Way* (*Karin Ingmarsdotter*, 1920, Sweden), and *Fairy of Solbakken* (*Synnøve Solbakken*, 1919, Sweden), but many of these orders were never delivered, perhaps because of Mason Super Films' disappearance from the Australian market in late 1923. The company's sudden collapse suggests that, despite the artistic and sociopolitical merit of the films themselves, importing Nordic films was not profitable enough to compete, even on a very limited scale, with American conglomerates.

Danish film had a harder time than Swedish breaking back into the Australian market, due primarily to financial difficulties Nordisk encountered after the war and its lack of an Australian agent. When it was forced to sell its German operations in 1919 to the newly-formed, state-supported German film company Ufa, Nordisk suffered a major blow to its global distribution network, which led to Ole Olsen's resignation in 1924 and Nordisk's financial collapse in the mid-1920s. In contrast to the large numbers of Nordisk films circulating throughout Australia in the 1910s, only a handful of Nordisk productions were even made each year in the 1920s, let alone sent so far abroad. Even with such a reduced inventory, however, Nordisk contract records indicate sales to a few Australian distributors in this period, including Howe's Film Agency and Selznick Pictures, both located in Sydney. Nordisk seems to have paid particular attention to finding products geared to Australian tastes. The contracts specify that Nordisk must provide a sample copy of each "most

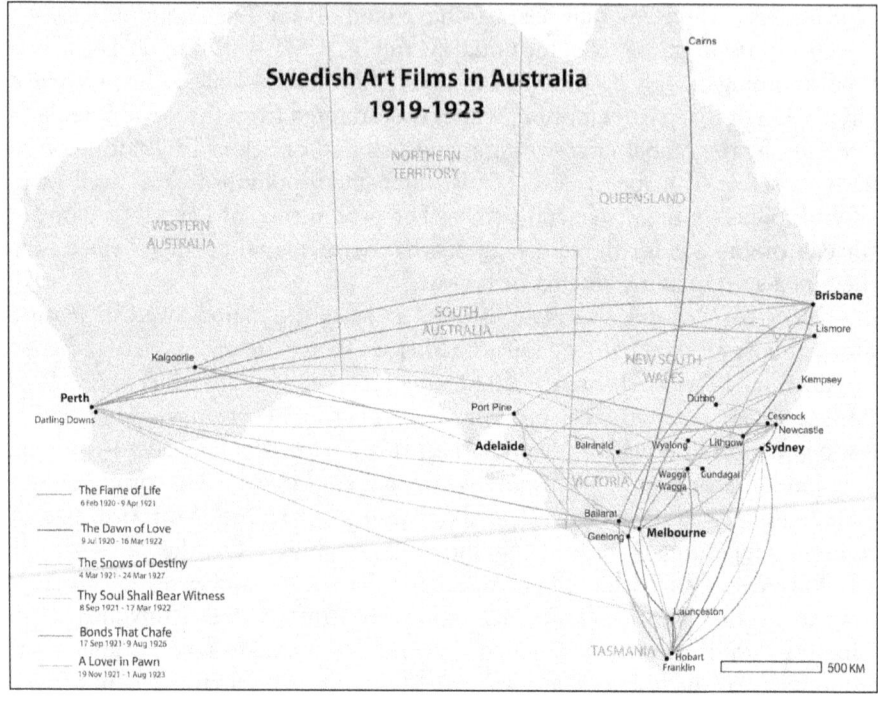

Figure 2.2   This map illustrates the movement of Swedish art films in Australia between 1919 and 1923. Graphic design by Julie K. Allen.

likely suitable film," which, if found "usable" on arrival in Sydney, would be purchased outright by the distributor, subject to a 50–50 profit-sharing agreement with Nordisk.

Although Nordisk only made four feature films in 1923 and six in 1924, it was able to export films from previous years that would have been new to Australian audiences. The films that Nordisk sent on trial to Howe's in 1923 included *Great Expectations* (*Store Forventninger*, A. W. Sandberg, 1922), *On the Stroke of Midnight* (*På Slaget 12*, Sandberg, 1923), *The Hill Park Mystery* (*Nedbrudte Nerver*, Sandberg, 1923), and *Mirrors of the Soul* (*Kan disse Øjne lyve?*, Sandberg, 1921), while those sent in 1924 featured *David Copperfield* (Sandberg, 1922), *Prometheus* (*Bonds of Hate*, August Blom, 1921), *Sealed Lips* (*Kærlighedens Almagt*, Sandberg, 1919), and *My Friend the Detective* (*Min Ven Privatdetektiven*, Sandberg, 1924). As the titles indicate, many of these films were adaptations of British novels, including two by Charles Dickens, and others were detective thrillers reminiscent of the crime fiction that has inspired today's Nordic Noir wave. Neither genre is particularly concerned with representing Danish culture and even the characteristically European literary adaptations of serious texts draw on familiar British narratives, which is consistent with the universalizing strategies Nordisk had employed in the prewar period for its export-oriented films.

The tighter circulation parameters in the interwar period meant that each Nordisk film that made it to Australia in the 1920s was individually more significant, in terms both of boosting Nordisk's vastly diminished exports and of exposing Australian audiences to Danish films, which presented an alternative, often quite sobering vision of modernity to the predominantly light-hearted American fare of the early 1920s and its correspondingly optimistic view of the modern world. All eight of the Nordisk films imported in 1924 and 1925 were screened widely around the country, but Nordisk's continued production difficulties prevented further Danish film exports in subsequent years, creating a gap that was quickly filled by German films.

As Nordisk declined, Ufa emerged as a leader in the European film market, in open competition with Hollywood. Ufa's rise illustrates how the character of European film production changed dramatically in the 1920s, becoming much more corporatized and somewhat more cooperative across national borders in order to compete more effectively with the American film industry. This development had some positive effects for Nordic film companies in terms of new possibilities of collaboration with other European producers. Andrew Higson and Richard Maltby note that the term "Film Europe" was used in this period to describe "the ideal of a vibrant pan-European cinema industry, making international co-productions for a massively enhanced 'domestic' market, and thereby in a position to challenge American distributors for control of that market," but concede that this ideal of European cooperation "always existed more as a set of principles than concrete practices" (1999, 2). "Film Europe" never coalesced into a coherent system on the scale of Hollywood, with the result that individual companies like Ufa made deals purely to their own advantage, while Hollywood companies poached individual European star actors and directors, like Sweden's Mauritz Stiller and Greta Garbo, further reducing the likelihood of blockbuster Nordic productions being produced, let alone making their way across the ocean to Australia.

By the time sound film was widely adopted at the end of the 1920s, the days when a Danish silent film like *Temptations of a Great City* could enjoy a three-year run in Australia, Nordisk could export thirteen feature films to Australia in a single year, or six Swedish films could be screened in rapid succession around the continent were ancient history, as was the viewing public's associated belief in Scandinavia's artistic and technical sophistication. Although some Australian film critics had expressed their pleasure in 1924 at the reappearance of high-quality Nordic pictures, audiences and critics alike at the end of the decade retained only a vague memory of Nordic film's popularity in prewar Australia and the prestige it had lent Nordic cultures and society. Sound film changed the parameters of global film circulation, boosting

American film's advantage and further limiting the access of Nordic films to English-speaking markets like Australia. The economic might of the American film industry had already effectively homogenized Australian cinema offerings, as the findings of the 1927 Royal Commission on the Moving Picture Industry in Australia confirmed (*Royal Commission* 1927), at the expense not only of European film but also of British imports and the domestic Australian film industry. All that remained of the once-dynamic circuits traveled by Nordic silent films across Australia and the acclaim the films received were ghostly traces on yellowing newsprint.

REFERENCES

"Advertising." 1911. *The Age* (Melbourne, Victoria), August 10, 12.
"Advertising." 1911. *The Argus* (Melbourne, Victoria), August 11, 12.
"Advertising." 1911. *Referee* (Sydney, NSW), July 12, 16.
"Advertising." 1911. *Referee* (Sydney, NSW), August 23, 16.
The Age (Melbourne, Victoria) 1913. March 7.
"Amusements." 1911. *The Age* (Melbourne, Victoria), August 11, 12.
The Bendigo Independent (Bendigo, Victoria) 1911, August 12, 4.
Bruno, Giuliana. 1993. *Streetwalking on a Ruined Map: Cultural Theory and the City Films of Elvira Notari*. Princeton: Princeton University Press.
Burns, James. 2013. *Cinema and Society in the British Empire, 1895–1940*. London: Palgrave Macmillan.
Collins, Diane. 1987. *Hollywood Down Under: Australians at the Movies: 1896 to the Present Day*. North Ryde, NSW: Angus & Robertson.
The Daily News (Perth, WA). 1911. September 7, 7.
Higson, Andrew and Richard Maltby, eds. 1999. *"Film Europe" and "Film America." Cinema, Commerce and Cultural Exchange 1920–1939*. Exeter: University of Exeter Press.
Horak, Laura. 2016. "The Global Distribution of Swedish Silent Film." In *A Companion to Nordic Cinema*, ed. Mette Hjort and Ursula Lindquist. Malden: John Wiley. 457–83.
Iversen, Gunnar. 1999. "Sisters of Cinema: Three Norwegian Actors and their German Film Company, 1917–1920." In *Nordic Explorations: Film Before 1930*, ed. John Fullerton and Jan Olsson. Stockholm Studies in Cinema. Sydney: John Libbey. 93–101.
Maltby, Richard. 2011. "New Cinema Histories." In *Explorations in New Cinema History: Approaches and Case Studies*. Malden, MA: Wiley-Blackwell. 1–40.
"Mason's Films." 1915. *Sunday Times* (Perth, WA), September 5, 12.
Matthews, Jill Julius. 2005. *Dance Hall & Picture Palace: Sydney's Romance with Modernity*. Sydney: Currency Press.
Mayer, Geoff and Keith Beattie, eds. 2007. *The Cinema of Australia and New Zealand*. London: Wallflower Press.
"Moving Picture World News Reel for February." 1917. *Moving Picture World* 31(10) (March 10): 1551.
Pinaroo Country News (SA). 1913. September 12, 4.
Royal Commission on the Motion Picture Industry in Australia. Minutes of Evidence. 1927.
Shirley, Graham and Brian Adams. 1983. *Australian Cinema: The First Eighty Years*. [Sydney]: Angus & Robertson.

Soila, Tytti, Astrid Söderbergh Widding, and Gunnar Iversen, eds. 1998. *Nordic National Cinemas*. New York: Routledge.
Theatre Magazine 1920. July 1, 26.
Thompson, Kristin. 1985. *Exporting Entertainment: America in the World Film Market 1907–34*. London: British Film Institute.
Thorsen, Isak. 2006. "The Rise and Fall of the Polar Bear." In *100 Years of Nordisk Film*, ed. Lisbeth Richter Larsen and Dan Nissen. Copenhagen: Danish Film Institute. 52–71.
"West's Pictures." 1911. *Sydney Morning Herald* (NSW), September 9, 13.

3. CHARLIE CHAN'S LAST MYSTERY, OR, THE TRANSCULTURAL DISAPPEARANCE OF WARNER OLAND

Kim Khavar Fahlstedt

"Charlie Chan is missing." On the morning of January 19, 1938, headlines in Stockholm's leading newspapers announced that Warner Oland, lead actor of the popular Charlie Chan film series, had walked off the set and vanished into thin air (*Stockholmstidningen* 1938a).[1] The irony was profound. As the Chinese-American detective Charlie Chan, the Swedish-American Oland had unknitted murder cases and solved mysteries all over the globe. Now the main actor himself was lost and missing. During the next days and months, newspapers and film magazines puzzled over the vanishing act. Reports on Oland's whereabouts soon tapped into a recurring discussion about Oland's ambiguous ethnic identity. The mystery would be Oland's last. In the end, he wound up dead in a Stockholm hospital bed.

Born Johan Värner Ölund in the small northern Swedish town of Bjurholm, Oland emigrated to the USA with his parents in the mid-1890s, a period in which the prospect of westward relocation was a tempting and viable alternative to an impoverished life in rural Sweden. Having started his career as a theater actor, Oland was smitten by the prospects of the emerging film industry in the early 1910s and soon became a frequently hired movie actor. Quite contrary to the photogeneity of other Scandinavian actors and starlets, Hollywood filmmakers had the large and stocky Swede perform a wide array of racialized characteristics. Most often, they cast Oland as a "screen oriental."

[1] All translations from Swedish to English are my own.

While Oland is mostly remembered for Charlie Chan, the role was preceded by a decade and a half of portraying exotic and foreign-looking villains, not least as the international master-criminal Dr. Fu Manchu. Alongside luminaries such as Anna Q. Nilsson and Greta Garbo, Warner Oland was one of Sweden's first and best-known stars of the silver screen. Oland's embodied villainy and sleuthing made him popular among film fans across the globe during the interwar years. Yet, the life, career, film production, and cultural impact of Warner Oland—an actor who transgressed common boundaries (geographic, cultural, and cinematic)—remains almost criminally understudied.

In this essay, the death of Warner Oland in 1938 provides an entry point to approaching the multitudes of his public persona. While Oland is still a marginal figure in standard Nordic film histories of this period, his career and practice of Asian racial masquerade have been explored by a few scholars of US film and popular culture (Wollstein 1994; Holmlund 2002; Lunde 2010; Mason 2012). In Arne Lunde's view, the film persona of Warner Oland countered "prevailing ideas in the American cultural imaginary of not only the Nordic body but of the Scandinavian ethnic as well" (Lunde 2010, 119). Chris Holmlund argued that Scandinavian actors working in the Hollywood studio system in the early 1930s were particularly likely to be cast as "screen-others" due to their racially "undefineable" characteristics (Holmlund 2002, 94). Lunde concluded that whether as Yellow Peril figures or the model minority-character of Charlie Chan, Oland always presented his version of Orientalism as geographically "unanchored" and "unlocatable" (Lunde 2010, 144). These conclusions serve well for analyses of representations of Swedishness (or the periodic lack of such a concept) in Hollywood. Moreover, some of Oland's onscreen ambiguity might, can, and should be attributed to the accumulated effects of Hollywood studios perpetuating the practice of "yellowface" (Lee 1999, 12–13). However, beyond the Hollywood manifestations of Orientalism, a parallel intermedial discourse continuously grappled with the task of solidifying Oland's ethnic fluidity in molds of national essentialism. Here, Oland's persona exemplifies what Russel Meeuf and Raphael Raphael have called "the impossibility of understanding stardom within the singular scale of the nation" (Meeuf and Raphael 2013, 1).

Scholars of stardom in the Classical Hollywood era generally agree that its star personae were discursively produced through intertextual negotiation between a variety of texts, such as film, interviews, and publicity photos (DeCordova 2001, 12; Miyao 2007, 136; Orgeron 2008, 8). Given the global circulation of Hollywood cinema during the interwar years, this production included regional and local appropriations that extended beyond the influence and agency of major US film studios (Maltby and Stokes 2004, 7; Xiao 2012, 91–4).

To approach the transnational, discursive production of Oland's persona, I find Mary Louise Pratt's notion of the "transcultural contact zone" particularly useful: those "spaces where disparate cultures meet, clash, and grapple with each other, often in highly asymmetrical relations of domination and subordination" (Pratt 1992, 4). I understand the notion of the contact zone as the study of transcultural interaction, encompassing both geographic and discursive space, reminiscent of Ed Soja's purposefully open-ended concept of thirdspace, attempting to capture "what is actually a constantly shifting and changing milieu of ideas, events, appearances, and meanings" (Soja 1996, 2). A similar approach has been championed by Meeuf and Raphael, who argue "the powerful images and narratives surrounding media celebrities are a key example of such contact zones" (Meeuf and Raphael 2013, 3). The notion of the transcultural contact zone, thus, in addressing a discursive realm where notions of the Scandinavian intermingled with popular notions of the Oriental and the American, provides a decentered entry point through which to approach the ways in which Oland's persona escaped contemporary tropes of Scandinavian identity and facilitated a site of cross-cultural interaction.

By addressing tentative descriptions of Oland's national and regional belonging in a variety of American, Swedish, and Swedish-American writings on the actor around the time of his disappearance, we can begin to understand the dialectics and historiographic transgressions of this contact zone. As the limitations of this essay do not allow for exhaustive comparative scrutiny of the uses and interpretations of Oland's star persona across a wide range of local and regional cultural locales, I will concentrate on addressing the borderlands spaces carved out for Oland to inhabit as he continued to elude common description. It is this "Nordic elsewhere" which this essay attempts to map out. More than pointing to Oland's importance as a transcultural node in Swedish film culture of the 1920s and 30s, this brief inquiry heeds calls for the accumulation of local and regional reception studies about the transcultural uses of particular star texts and cinematic exchange, as well as fleeting conceptualizations of national identity in transnational film culture during the interwar years.

Tracking Down the Elusive Oland with the Help of Charlie Chan

While Oland never portrayed a Swede on film, film magazines recurringly focused on his Swedish origins. Celebrity studies scholar Joshua Gamson has noted that during the Classical Hollywood era, stardom was often perceived as emanating from talents and qualities inherent in the actor (Gamson, 1994, 32). For example, an oft-regurgitated myth sought to explain Oland's ambiguous ethnicity by reference to a biological heritage. Another explanation could be found in a 1929 article in the *New Movie Magazine*. It read, "Warner Oland, a

Swede, is to blame for the Yellow Peril. His home was so close to Lapland that some of his ancestors were probably of the Mongolian type" (1931). While Oland himself often repeated versions of this story in interviews, there is no evidence in his family tree to suggest such lineage. Neither is there evidence to suggest that Oland was of Swedish Indigenous Sámi heritage, which would have been more plausible.

More commonly, Oland's ethnic ambiguity was discussed as if emanating from an internal battleground. In this scenario, cued by the familiar axiom of contemporary yellow peril—the Oriental "hive mind"'s inevitable overtaking of Western free society—Oland, through his continuous emulation of other ethnicities, risked losing touch with his own national heritage (Wu 1982, 1; Tchen and Yeats 2014, 30–4). The paradox of Oland's Swedish-American-Oriental identity was constantly reiterated, especially in relation to his Chan performance. An early example of this narrative can be found in a 1936 *Picture Play* article. "'Charlie Chan'—Warner Oland, I mean—is in danger of losing his identity because of his long association with the screen character which has made him famous" (Glass, 1936, 56). The article revealed that Oland had discovered his Oriental self in 1917, when preparing for the role of a Chinese general in the William Randolph Hearst-funded film serial, *Patria* (Jaccard, Wharton and Wharton 1917): "Oland discovered, to his surprise, that by contracting his the muscles of his eyelids in a certain fashion, and brushing the ends of his eyebrows up and the ends of his moustache down, his features and expression assumed a marked Oriental cast" (Glass 1936, 57). Before the Swedish premiere of *Charlie Chan at the Opera* (Humberstone 1936a), reports emerged that a fake Charlie Chan had been spotted on the streets of Stockholm (*Filmjournalen* 1937, 13). While the gathering crowd soon learned of the marketing coup staged by a Stockholm enterprise, the experience must have been augmented by previous reports that Oland himself often appeared as Chan in public settings (Huang 2011, 202–3, 252). "To speak with Warner Oland about Charlie Chan is like speaking to Charlie Chan about Warner Oland," wrote *Stockholmstidningen* in 1937, claiming that the Oriental character had subjugated Oland's Swedish nature. "Charlie Chan has really entirely entered into the bloodstream of the former Mr. Ölund from Sundsvall" (Piccolino 1937). Chan, the alter ego character, was given an agency of his own. As the Swede transformed into the Oriental, the lines separating the two in the public eye gradually converged. Oland was the host, Chan the occupant. The Oriental Chan was overtaking the westerner Oland.

When Oland disappeared in 1938, commentators in both Swedish and American newspapers returned to this dynamic, casting Oland's disappearance as a case of life imitating fiction. *Stockholmstidningen* wrote: "his disappearance seems to be an even bigger mystery than the kinds of mysteries which Charlie Chan solves with ease" (*Stockholmstidningen* 1938a). *Svenska Dagbladet* cited the *New York Times*, suggesting that Oland's continued transformation into Chan had brought on a disorientation severe enough for the actor to lose his sense of self. Ruling out China as a possible hiding place, *Svenska Dagbladet* quipped that it was the fictional character of Charlie Chan who had paid the studio's press office to finally get rid of Oland. A cartoon published in the same daily a week later further illustrated this theory. It showed Warner Oland in Chan-yellowface, dressed in a long coat and his trademark bowler hat, pulling away a curtain to reveal his doppelgänger, dressed in a tuxedo. The cartoon was accompanied by a poem, again casting Oland's vanishing act as a publicity stunt. In this scenario, it was the independent will of the Chan character that had located Oland and brought him back into the public eye (Lekholm 1938).

By repeatedly attempting and failing to define Oland's ethnicity through terminology based in national essentialism, newspaper and fan magazine discourse on Oland's public persona created a figurative space for Oland to inhabit. This space was seemingly organized by common boundaries of national, racial, and ethnic adherences, but still located elsewhere. As the news broke of Oland's disappearance, newspapers speculated that rather than being holed up in one of his known habitats, his home in Hollywood, his summer house in Southborough, Massachusetts, or his ancestral town of Bjurholm, Oland had disappeared to another space.

Figure 3.1 Oland and Chan playing hide and seek (Lekholm 1938). Courtesy of the Swedish Film Archive.

CRISES AND HOMECOMINGS

The circumstances surrounding Oland's disappearance were no mystery to those close to him. Oland's bouts with alcoholism had been known to studios for a number of years (Hanke 1990, 4). Yunte Huang has suggested that Oland's continuous yellowface performance went hand in hand with his drinking habits (Huang 2011, 203). But the drinks that might initially have helped Oland to fuse Swedish dialect, Orientalist makeup, and American film acting began to take their toll. During *Charlie Chan at the Race Track* (Humberstone 1936b), he kept nodding off in the middle of takes, and a nurse was assigned to him to make sure he stayed sober. These efforts were unsuccessful, and Oland's health deteriorated (Tuska 1978, 117).

There is a notable difference between the Hollywood film periodicals and the Swedish reportage on Oland's "illness." Oland's drinking was known in Hollywood, but these stories never seemed to reach across the Atlantic. Several Hollywood magazines and papers painted Oland as the culprit, and the *Motion Picture Herald* alluded to rumors that this was not the first time that Oland had wandered off set (*Motion Picture Herald* 1938). Swedish papers reported that Oland's absence was due to anxiety. *Svenska Dagbladet* speculated that his breakdown coincided with the finalization of his divorce from Edith Shearn (*Svenska Dagbladet* 1938a). While Oland's disappearance was not as much of a mystery to 20th Century Fox as it was in newspaper headlines, the incident demarcated an important transformation of his public persona. Up until that point, he had been portrayed as an unlikely, yet well-liked, movie star. The Oland who was found, drunk and confused, revealed a darker side to the public. The current Chan film was shelved by the studio, and Oland was given time off (Hanna 1938, 7). *Film Daily* reported that he was planning a trip to Europe, which would take him back to his ancestral home of Sweden (Wilk 1938). In early March of 1938, the Swedish-Californian ethnic newspaper *Vestkusten* confirmed that Oland was en route back home (*Vestkusten* 1938, 5).

Oland's trip was thus cast as a solution to his personal troubles; a homecoming that would rekindle a connection to his "roots" and reestablish an identity lost. But Charlie Chan was not far behind. Fox soon announced three new films with Oland as the lead to be filmed in 1938 (Schallert 1938a, 7). The first film would see the detective, much like Oland, embark on a trip back to his native origins. Production of *Charlie Chan in Honolulu* (Humberstone 1938) was to start after the summer (Schallert 1938b, 15).

Homecomings and Post-mortems

After a visit to southern Europe, Oland returned to Sweden for the first time since childhood. Stepping off the train in Malmö on June 14, 1938, he was eagerly anticipated. In the public eye, it was as if Oland was being repatriated, quickly regaining the Swedishness that had been lost during his years abroad. *Svenska Dagbladet* described him as "boy from Norrland" with "an American passport." His appearance was "the incarnation of the sly Chinese detective from the movies"; his moustache "Mongolian" (*Svenska Dagbladet* 1938b, 3). When Oland arrived in Stockholm the next day, it was as if the Swedishness had grown on him overnight. *Dagens Nyheter* wrote that his Swedish language skills were remarkable, given his long absence. Oland several times proclaimed himself to be "Swedish, despite that [American] passport of mine" (*Dagens Nyheter* 1938, 1).

In mid-July, Oland returned to his ancestral home of Bjurholm, Västerbotten for the first time since his emigration at age 12 in 1892 (*Västerbotten-kuriren* 1938). As Oland visited relatives, accompanying journalists wrote about the return of a lost son. "He remembers well how it looked here before he left this cottage, that rock, and that path in the woods," wrote local paper *Västerbotten-kuriren* (V. N. 1938). *Aftonbladet* assured that in Bjurholm there still lived "a good amount of older people who remember well the time when the Chinese detective still walked around in shorts and looked like an ordinary Swedish farm boy" (*Aftonbladet* 1938, 3).

Oland returned to Stockholm in late July in a bad condition. Despite assurances from the Fox studio physician that Oland was on the road to recovery, his condition worsened by the day. He contracted bronchial pneumonia and was sent to Beckomberga Hospital in Stockholm in late July. There, he remained bedridden until he succumbed to cirrhosis of the liver and died, on August 6 (*Bromma Församling* 1938).

As with Oland's disappearance seven months earlier, the news of his death traveled quickly around the world. The reactions inscribed Oland in what celebrity studies scholars Adrian Kear and Deborah Steinberg have called the "global community of mourning"; a transcultural interaction of post-mortems and obituaries encompassing "competing discursive constructions of 'the people,' 'the nation' and 'the international community'" (Kear and Steinberg 1999, x). In reporting Oland's death, the Swedish press continued its attempts at symbolic repatriation, placing emphasis on the characteristics that made him Swedish. *Svenska Dagbladet* wrote that Oland, even before Chan, held a very special place among fans of the film medium, especially with the Swedish audience: "he was a northerner [norrlänningen] who acted as an easterner with such impressive mimicry and gesture that his original nationality, to many, seemed almost improbable. We took pride in Warner

Oland from Umeå" (*Svenska Dagbladet* 1938c). *Stockholmstidningen* wrote: "Oland was never a friend of the beating on the drum of advertisement; and never really believed that Charlie Chan was as popular as people told him" (*Stockholmstidningen* 1938b). During his visit to Bjurholm, the regional paper *Västerbotten-kuriren* described him as "sincere and without airs [gemytlig och chosefri]" and "hearty and simple" [hjärtlig och enkel]," all qualities typically ascribed to people from the north of Sweden. (Svebe 1938; V. N. 1938). The regional context here suggests a connection between a set of personal characteristics and Oland's childhood hometown, characteristics which survived the actor's exile and ethnic transformation. As Richard Dyer noted, such claims to authenticity were universally valued assets in the economy of Hollywood stardom, often utilized to seek out separation between the distinguishing traits of performer and the performed (Dyer 1986, 9). However, such characteristics could, in the case of Oland, also be ascribed to Charlie Chan.

The cross-cultural tensions inherent in the actor's persona continued to manifest even after Oland's death. Henrik van Loon, an author and fellow European expat who had befriended Oland while lecturing at Cornell in the mid-1910s, wrote, "it is now too late to catch a glimpse of his slightly Oriental smile—over the years he came into the habit of seeing everything from the same viewpoint as old Charlie" (van Loon 1938). The *New York Times* wrote a long and detailed obituary, emphasizing the conundrum of Oland's national identity: "for so many years he had been identified with the Orient through his often sinister roles that Scandinavia, which produced Garbo, was rarely if ever credited with being the homeland of the man best known for his impersonation of Charlie Chan" (1938). Despite his final homecoming, the ghosts conjured by his exilic elsewhere continued to haunt Warner Oland beyond the grave. Darryl F. Zanuck, studio head at Fox, offered in sum that "Warner Oland and the screen portrayal were inseparable" (*LA Times* 1938: 2).

CONCLUSION

In this chapter, I have focused on the interplay of writing in Swedish and American publications in the period before Oland's death, in which Oland's persona appears as an unlikely blend between contemporary notions of Swedishness, Americanism, and Orientalism. While the constant public interchange between Oland's star persona and the Oriental film characters with which he was primarily connected in many respects served to reinforce Hollywood dissemination of a West-centric worldview, the ambiguity and fluidity of Oland's own ethnicity stubbornly contradicted attempts to organize humanity into neat categories of race, ethnicity, and nationality.

As the various public conceptions of Oland within a matter of months were subject of renegotiation and subsequently, eulogy, contemporary media commentators in both Sweden and the USA attempted to define, locate, and anchor his characteristics in common tropes of ethnicity, nationality, and regional adherence, only to conclude that his persona escaped such definition. Oland's "elsewhere" appears as a discursive space organized around its relation to, and negation of, stereotypes based on ideas of national and regional essentialism: a transcultural contact zone of geographic, cultural, and historical displacement, encompassing coordinates tied to popular perceptions of geo-cultural characteristics, such as San Francisco Chinatown villainy and West Bothnian unpretentiousness, Californian Yellow Peril-ism and northern Swedish terseness, provincial Stockholm cultural elitism, and glossy Hollywood commercialism.

Mary Louise Pratt based the idea of the transcultural contact zone on a concept introduced by Cuban ethnographer and folklorist Fernando Ortiz. Roughly around the same time as Oland's public identity was melding with those of his most iconic characters, Ortiz introduced the notion of transculturation to approach the formation of new cultural manifestations, placing an emphasis on the destruction both of cultures and of the creativity of cultural unions (Ortiz 1995 [1947], xvi). The import is thus: if one thinks of cultures as coherent structures, Oland's persona appears chaotic and ill-fitting. But if one regards cultures as open-ended nodes, Oland's persona is a heterogeneous construct which both facilitates and negates flows of transcultural interaction. It fuses into a potent, unruly cultural hybrid, ruminating in a borderland structured around, but not restricted by, popular conceptions of national and regional characteristics.

But in order to begin to understand these elsewheres, we must account for the flows as well as the communicative breakdowns involved in the processes of transcultural interaction in which they were formulated and produced. As the work of Stuart Hall continues to remind us, the study of mediated racial stereotypes and concepts of national identity should not only focus on their original transmission, but also account for their various reroutings and receptions (Hall 1980, 1994). Thus, Warner Oland and the uncharted space which he occupied present us with a complex and productive zone of transcultural refraction, holding the potential to reach a deeper understanding of the construction and transnational reception of racial stereotypes in the classical Hollywood narrative, but also challenging us to refocus historical inquiries into Nordic film cultures to explore further the multitudinous functions of transcultural exchange.

REFERENCES

Aftonbladet. 1938. "Charlie Chan känner sig riktigt hemma," July 15, 3.
Bromma Församling. 1938. "Jonas Wärner Oland," excerpt from *1938 års Död och Begravningsbok för Bromma församling i Stockholm*, August.

Dagens Nyheter. 1938. "Älskvärd filmbov i svensk kostym," June 15, 1.
DeCordova, Richard. 2001. *Picture Personalities: The Emergence of the Star System in America*. Urbana: University of Illinois Press.
Dyer, Richard. 1986. *Heavenly Bodies: Film Stars and Society*. Hoboken: Taylor & Francis.
Hanna, David J. 1938. "Hollywood." *Film Bulletin*, January 29, p. 7.
Filmjournalen. 1937. No. 12, p. 13.
Gamson, Joshua. 1994. *Claims to Fame: Celebrity in Contemporary America*. Berkeley; Los Angeles; London: University of California Press.
Glass, Madeleine. 1936. "Charlie Chan in person." *Picture Play*, August.
Hall, Stuart. 1980. "Encoding/Decoding." In *Culture, Media, Language: Working Papers in Cultural Studies, 1972–79*. Birmingham: Center for Contemporary Cultural Studies, University of Birmingham.
Hall, Stuart. 1994. "Reflections upon the Encoding/Decoding Model: An Interview with Stuart Hall." *Viewing, Reading, Listening: Audiences and Cultural Reception*, ed. Jon Cruz and Justin Lewis. Boulder: Westview Press. 253–74.
Hanke, Ken. 1990. *Charlie Chan at the Movies: History, Filmography, and Criticism*. Jefferson, NC: McFarland.
Holmlund, Chris. 2002. *Impossible Bodies: Femininity and Masculinity at the Movies*. London: Routledge.
Huang, Yunte. 2011. *Charlie Chan: The Untold Story of the Honorable Detective and His Rendezvous with American History*. Reprint edn. New York: Norton.
Kear, Adrian, and Deborah Lynn Steinberg, eds. 1999. *Mourning Diana: Nation, Culture and the Performance of Grief*. 1st edn. London; New York: Routledge.
LA Times. 1938. "Oland, Film 'Chan,' Dies in Sweden," August 7, 2.
Lee, Robert G. 1999. *Orientals: Asian Americans in Popular Culture*. Philadelphia: Temple University Press.
Lekholm. 1938. "Kinesiskt Kinotricks." *Svenska Dagbladet*, January 21.
van Loon, Henrik Willem. 1938. "Hela USA i tacksamhetsskuld." *Stockholmstidningen*, January 9.
Lunde, Arne. 2010. *Nordic Exposures: Scandinavian Identities in Classical Hollywood Cinema*. New Directions in Scandinavian Studies. Seattle: University of Washington Press.
Mason, Fran. 2012. "Ordering the World: The Uncompromising Logic of Charlie Chan and Mr Moto." In *Hollywood's Detectives*, 106–30. Springer.
Meeuf, Russell and Raphael Raphael, eds. 2013. *Transnational Stardom: International Celebrity in Film and Popular Culture*. New York: Palgrave Macmillan.
Miyao, Daisuke. 2007. *Sessue Hayakawa: Silent Cinema and Transnational Stardom*. Durham, NC: Duke University Press.
Motion Picture Herald. 1938. "20th-Fox Preparing Season's Final Ten," January 29.
New Movie Magazine. 1931. "The Hollywood Boulevardier," vol. 4, no. 1, July, 111.
New York Times. 1938. "Warner Oland, 57, Screen Star, Dies," August 7.
Orgeron, Marsha. 2008. *Hollywood Ambitions: Celebrity in the Movie Age*. Wesleyan Film. Middletown, CT: Wesleyan University Press.
Ortiz, Fernando. 1995 [1947]. *Cuban Counterpoint, Tobacco and Sugar*. Durham, NC: Duke University Press.
Piccolino. 1937. "Warner Oland är en lat figur säger Charlie Chan." *Stockholmstidningen*, July 18.
Pratt, Mary Louise. 1992. *Imperial Eyes: Travel Writing and Transculturation*. London; New York: Routledge.
Schallert, Edwin. 1938a."Oland to Achieve Spectacular Return." *LA Times*, March 5, 24.

Schallert, Edwin. 1938b. "Charlie Chan World Traveler." *LA Times*, July 18, 33.
Soja, Edward W. 1996. *Thirdspace: Journeys to Los Angeles and Other Real-and-Imagined Places*. Cambridge, MA: Blackwell.
Stockholmstidningen. 1938. "Charlie Chan försvunnen," January 19.
Stockholmstidningen. 1938. "Oland hyllas i Kina som stor kines," August 9.
Stokes, Melvyn and Richard Maltby. 2004. *Hollywood Abroad: Audiences and Cultural Exchange*. London: British Film Institute.
Svebe 1938. "'Very fine town,' sa W.O. om stan," *Västerbotten-kuriren*, July 18.
Svenska Dagbladet. 1938a. "Charlie Chan är spårlost försvunnen," January 12.
Svenska Dagbladet. 1938b. "'Charlie Chan' i Sverige efter 45 år," June 15.
Svenska Dagbladet. 1938c. "Charlie Chan ur tiden," August 7.
Tchen, John Kuo Wei and Dylan Yeats. 2014. *Yellow Peril!: An Archive of Anti-Asian Fear*. London: Verso.
Tuska, Jon. 1978. *The Detective in Hollywood: The Movie Careers of the Great Fictional Private Eyes and Their Creators*. 1st edn. Garden City, NY: Doubleday.
Vestkusten. 1938. "Warner Oland's svårigheter," March 3, p. 5.
V. N. 1938. "Warner Oland minns väl ungdomsåren i Bjurholm." *Västerbotten-kuriren*, July 14.
Västerbotten-kuriren. 1938. "Warner Oland anländ till födelsebygden," July 13, p. 4.
Wollstein, Hans J. 1994. *Strangers in Hollywood: The History of Scandinavian Actors in American Films from 1910 to World War II*, Vol. 43. Metuchen, NJ: Scarecrow Press.
Wilk, Ralph. 1938. "A 'Little' From the 'Lots'." *Film Daily*, March 3, p. 4.
Wu, William F. 1982. *The Yellow Peril: Chinese Americans in American Fiction, 1850–1940*. Hamden, CT: Archon Books.
Xiao, Zhiwei. 2012. "Translating Hollywood Film to Chinese Audience: The Role of Agency and Appropriation in Transnational Cultural Encounters." In *Transnational Asian Identities in Pan-Pacific Cinemas: The Reel Asian Exchange*, ed. Philippa Gates and Lisa Funnell. London: Routledge. 88–100.

4. CARIN FOCK-GÖRING'S GRAVESTONE: TRACING THE LEGACY OF THE SWEDISH FIRST LADY OF THE THIRD REICH

Patrick Wen

Throughout the prolonged trauma-spectacle of the Third Reich's rise and fall, various women, depending on the context, filled the role of symbolic First Lady of the Reich. The official party line, espoused by the Minister of Propaganda Josef Goebbels, was that "the Führer has no private life . . . He devotes himself to the German people day and night" (Sigmund 2000, 149). And while history has acknowledged the significant role played by Hitler's longtime paramour Eva Braun, her relationship with the Führer under the regime was effectively a state secret (Görtemaker 2011, 41–60). Goebbels' portrayal of Hitler as modern German messiah necessitated the deliberate fashioning of a First Lady of the Nazi State who embodied its ideal of femininity. Hitler would eventually call Leni Riefenstahl, the actress and film propagandist, his "perfect German woman" (Koonz 1987, 6), while Goebbels would lobby for his own wife Magda to be envisioned as First Lady (Meissner 1980).

In its formative years, however, the Nazi propaganda machine found its *first* First Lady and Patron Saint in the person of the Stockholm-born Carin Fock, whose aristocratic Nordic origins and marriage to Hermann Göring fulfilled the regime's requirements for publicly staging the master race. Moreover, her premature death was carefully exploited by Goebbels to elevate her image into that of a de facto Nazi saint, immortalized in the pageantry of a state funeral and a state-sanctioned, best-selling biography written by her sister. Much of the basis for Fock's sacred and iconic status within the Reich can be directly traced to her imagined Swedishness, which would have been heavily fetishized by the regime (Witoszek 2002, 51). The Nazis' documented occultist streak (Levenda 2006) appropriated fantasies of Nordic traditions that conformed to the propaganda pushing Aryan supremacy, while simultaneously being girded by legitimizing narratives of eugenicist anthropology by professors like Hans Günther and Eugen Fischer (Proctor 1988, 119). This chapter will show how Carin Fock's storyline dramatizes Nazi ideology's appropriation of Nordic femininity as a highly dynamic and effective propaganda tool within the broader spectacle of the regime's public face. Additionally, the chapter will show how the Fock persona has been mythologized in much the same way in the postwar era, hewing closely to the conventions of the new Nazi discourse.

The contours of the Fock narrative loosely conform to those of a fairy tale and a Romantic tale of ill-fated love, under a veneer of the prevailing visual culture of early German cinema. Born in Stockholm in 1888, Carin Axelina Hulda Fock was the fourth of five daughters in a prominent aristocratic Swedish family. Her father, Baron Carl Fock, was an army officer, as was her first husband, Baron Niels Gustav von Kantzow. Estranged from this inattentive husband, Fock assumes the role of Swedish damsel in distress, waiting to be rescued by a future soldier of the Reich. In 1920, long before he founded the Gestapo and rose to the top of the Nazi *Luftwaffe*, Hermann Göring was a decorated German war hero, but also a struggling, underemployed commercial airline pilot based out of Stockholm. The legend of their serendipitous meeting begins with Carin's globetrotting brother-in-law, Count Eric von Rosen, who needed a flight from Stockholm to his castle in the country during a major snowstorm. With trains canceled and all planes grounded at the airport, von Rosen attempted to charter a private plane from *Svensk Interkontinental Lufttrafik AB*, Göring's employer and one of the forerunners of SAS. After three pilots refused to shuttle the impatient count to his castle, citing dangerous weather conditions, it was only the bold and fearless German who had the courage to fly the plane. As the Goebbels propaganda machine would have it, destiny pulls our hero to his Nordic princess in her isolated castle, in a fairy tale that foreshadows the ascendancy of the Third Reich. Given that at least one source reports that the three Swedish pilots refused to shuttle the count home because they viewed it as "a suicide mission" (Sigmund 2000, 23), Göring's audacity in this tale can also be viewed as foreshadowing the fascist aesthetics to come in the telling of his romance with Fock. In this context, suicidal tendencies become a means of seduction. Susan Sontag argues that "fascist art glorifies surrender, it exalts madness, it glamorizes death" (Sontag 1980, 91), and this romantic anecdote of Göring the fearless and/or suicidal flying ace performs this glamorous and fascinating madness in the highly eroticized fashion that so unsettles Sontag. In much the same way as Sontag and others have viewed the larger constructed narrative of the Third Reich, so much of the Göring romance unfolds as an aesthetically pleasing, eroticized suicide mission.

After landing safely, Count von Rosen invites Göring into cozy Rockelstad Castle, where the tall, blonde Carin Fock von Kantzow appears at the top of the stately central staircase, an Aryan vision. In a letter to his mother-in-law, Göring writes that he believes Sweden is "home to the purest Germanic culture" and that Fock looked like a Nordic-German goddess, whose blue eyes "struck him like lightning" (Wilamowitz-Moellendorf 1942, 92). Not only does the love story offer the melodrama of Aryan love-at-first-sight, which strikes like lightning, it also provides the German hero with a Nordic kindred spirit and lifelong friend in the form of Count von Rosen, who shares Göring's Nazi fervor. It was at Rockelstad that Göring may have first seen the swastika symbol as a kind of decorative design in the chimney piece (Manvell and Fraenkel 2011, 39–41), and potentially have been taken with it. Count von Rosen had apparently started using the symbol while in school and subsequently adopted it as a family emblem (Manvell and Fraenkel 2011, 403). In this way, Rockelstad Castle operates as an exoticized and idealized sanctuary of Nordic purity, given that Carin's ascribed Swedishness qualifies her as racially pure and sexually desirable while Count von Rosen's fascist political purity signifies ideological brotherhood with the North. The love story presents a natural, inevitable, predestined attraction between German masculinity and Swedish femininity, with Germany in the role of knight in shining armor. The tableau of the pastoral grounds surrounding Rockelstad Castle here recalls the pervasive function of what Saul Friedlander calls "ancient legends and bucolic countrysides" (Friedlander 1993, 29) within the new discourse on Nazism. Postwar accountings of the Third Reich, in Friedlander's view, engage in the same kitschy tropes of the regime itself, which he characterizes as melodramatic representations of reality that stylize and aestheticize death and apocalypse (Friedlander 1993, 26). Retrospective narratives of Fock's legend carry the characteristic *frisson* of a romantic hold on the imagination bound up in "beauty and the order of things" (Friedlander 1993, 26) together with inevitable violence, death, and destruction.

Further contributing to Rockelstad Castle's iconic significance as a kitschy shrine to Nazi fantasies of the Nordic connection to Aryan supremacy would be Edelweiss Chapel and the larger Edelweiss Society. Founded by Fock's maternal grandmother, the Edelweiss Society was an esoteric sect that "awaited the appearance of a Nordic Messiah" (Ravenscroft 1982, 186). Fock, her sisters and mother were all devoted to the sect's mystical practices, meditating and holding séances in the specially commissioned Edelweiss Chapel in the Rockelstad Castle estate. Fock and Göring's moment spent together in this chapel cements their romantic bond within the love story narrative while simultaneously affirming a sense of the inevitability of the coming Third Reich. In one of his first love letters to Fock, Göring writes:

> I should like to thank you from my heart for the beautiful moment which I was allowed to spend in the Edelweiss Chapel. You have no idea how I felt in this wonderful atmosphere. It was so quiet, so lovely, that I forgot all the earthly noise, all worries, and felt as if in another world. I closed my eyes and absorbed the clean, celestial atmosphere which filled the whole room. I was like a swimmer resting on a lonely island to gather new strength before he throws himself once more into the raging stream of life. I thanked God, and sent up warm prayers. (Manvell and Fraenkel 2011, 42–3)

Framed within the structure of a fairy tale romance between Aryan icons, Edelweiss Chapel not only brings the two young lovers together, but also, more importantly, confers a mystical legitimacy upon their union. Even though Fock is already married with a young son and this burgeoning romance deviates from outward bourgeois morality, the air of destiny projected by Edelweiss Chapel purifies their union. Prostrating themselves before the inevitability of the coming Nordic messiah, everything is possible for the young couple, and disapproval expressed by both families toward the affair is, in Göring's view, mere "earthly" noise. The self-image of both Göring and Fock displayed in letters cleaves to deeply romantic, even Wagnerian impulses of nebulous longing and surrender. For example, in a letter to her sister Fanny Fock, Carin effuses about her passion for Göring: "he is the man of my dreams" (Mosley 1975, 40); "we are like Tristan and Isolde. We have tasted the potion of love and we are helpless, indeed ecstatically helpless under its influence" (Fontander 1990, 27). This brand of self-narration of a love story easily fulfills the later needs of Goebbels and others to present a fairy tale of supreme Aryan love to the German public that is equal parts tabloid and mysticism. In Fock, Goebbels had discovered his Swedish Isolde, a perfectly idealized first-lady legend that could be even more easily molded following her early death in 1931. In "Fascinating Fascism," Susan Sontag describes the continuing, almost visceral hold fascism has over us:

> National Socialism—more broadly, fascism— ... stands for an ideal or rather ideals that are persistent today under the other banners: the ideal of life as art, the cult of beauty, the fetishism of courage, the dissolution of alienation in ecstatic feelings of community; the repudiation of the intellect; the family of man (under the parenthood of leaders). (Sontag 1980, 96)

Most all of the components listed here by Sontag can be excavated within the mythology of the Fock–Göring love story by Goebbels, who will later present their surrender to love as a dress rehearsal for the submission of the German *volk* to their own glorified leaders.

In the absence of a Frau Hitler, Carin Fock fits very easily into the role of besieged First Lady through her ardent support not only of her new husband, but also of Hitler and the burgeoning Nazi party. Following their wedding in Stockholm, the Görings embark on an extended political confrontation with German authorities, in and out of exile, in and out of trial, in and out of armed conflict, bouncing between Bavaria, Austria, Berlin and Sweden. In their flamboyant show of loyalty to the Führer and the party, they establish their centrality to the origin mythology of the Nazi movement while also performing the eroticized drama of fascist political agitation-as-seduction. In Fanny Fock's posthumous biography of her sister, a creative combination of fervent letters home to Sweden about the struggles of the early Nazi party and outright fabricated anecdotes about Hitler memorialize and enshrine Carin Fock-Göring's place as a saint-like First Lady of the new Nazi regime. Her early demonstration of self-sacrifice and her fanatical adoption of Nazi anti-Semitism both function as powerful propaganda from Goebbels' point of view. Following the failed beer hall *putsch* in Munich, Fock writes a nonchalant letter home to her mother describing life under siege: "Our villa in Munich has been seized, our accounts frozen, the car confiscated . . . they have now issued a warrant for my arrest, as well . . . Still, everything is falling into place for Hitler and his work is progressing better than even before" (Sigmund 2000, 35). Fock's letter glorifies surrender to the messianic as the most natural of virtues in a deferential language that Goebbels fully appreciates. Her dogged loyalty to the Führer and the party's ideology becomes a kind of template for the ideal Nazi woman. This extends to her fealty to the categorical anti-Semitism of the Führer, her husband, and Nazi policy. In a letter to her sister Lily, Fock expresses admiration for her former chauffeur, who lost his job as a result of her own legal troubles:

> He is out of a job now, penniless. A Jew offered him a job as a chauffeur at his castle, but he rejected the offer saying, "anyone who has ever been privileged enough to serve Hitler or Göring must feel mortally insulted to be offered work by a Semite. It is a thousand times better to die of hunger than to work for a Jew." Strong, zealous, isn't he? But how proud, and wonderful from a poor man like him . . . tell Mama and Papa. (Sigmund 2000, 36)

Beaming with pride in her former charge, Fock's narration imbues quotidian anecdotes of the fascist infrastructure of terror with a style of messianic epochalism that Goebbels likely found irresistible. The voluntary surrender of agency epitomizes what Ernst Nolte calls the fascist tendency toward a "refusal of transcendence" (quoted in Friedlander 1993, 45). In another letter, Fock puts it more succinctly: "The individual is so powerless in view of all of this. The one and only person in whom I place all my hope is Hitler, once he takes the helm of this sinking ship" (Sigmund 2000, 43). Historian Saul Friedlander elaborates on this notion of negative transcendence, explaining that, under Nazism, "man and his world are dominated by a blind destiny that leads to inevitable destruction" (Friedlander 1993, 45). Fock's glorification of her chauffeur's ardent and self-punitive anti-Semitism and her own surrender to the prevailing currents of Nazism foreshadow her own eventual martyrdom for the honor of the Reich. Friedlander also elucidates the persistent theme of the hero and the martyr in Nazi propaganda: "The hero is the one who remains faithful to his destiny despite his lucid perception of destruction and of death. But here Nazism brings in 'the community of the saints': the dead continue to march with the living toward an inexorable destiny" (Friedlander 1993, 45). Fock's self-perception and self-narration as being among the Nazi elect prefigure the posthumous shaping of her legacy and legend by her sister Fanny as well as by the propaganda minister Josef Goebbels.

In many ways, Fock's image of her own place within the sweeping currents of destiny mirrors that of the dominant German visual culture of the 1920s and 1930s. Hitler's "perfect German woman," Leni Riefenstahl, got her start in cinema acting in several silent mountain films (*Bergfilme*), which Siegfried Kracauer called "a mixture of sparkling pick-axes and inflated sentiments" (Kracauer 1947, 111). The otherworldly, dehistoricized alpine mise-en-scène of these films arguably functions as a kind of metonym for the mythical Nordic homeland glorified by organizations such as the Edelweiss or Thule societies (Levenda 2006). Prior to directing her better-known Nazi propaganda documentaries such as *Triumph of the Will* (*Triumph des Willens*, 1935) and the *Olympia* (1938) films under the Hitler regime, Riefenstahl wrote and starred in her directorial debut, *The Blue Light* (*Das Blaue Licht*) in 1932. More precisely, Riefenstahl co-wrote and co-directed the film with Béla Balázs, the Jewish-Hungarian writer, film critic, and poet, whose originally-credited name was erased in the subsequent 1938 rerelease of the film under the Third Reich. In his careful study of the film, "Fatal Attractions: Leni Riefenstahl's 'The Blue Light,'" Eric Rentschler accentuates details that exemplify the German *zeitgeist*'s glorification of death and martyrdom, beginning with the opening images: "The prologue to the 'story without time and place' presents Riefenstahl in a close-up with her eyes shut, an image redolent of a death mask" (Rentschler 1989, 55). Rentschler engages in highly persuasive close readings of the film's protagonist Junta (played by Riefenstahl) that compare her ill-fated story to the biography of Riefenstahl as notoriously conspicuous Nazi auteur in early film history. Much of Rentschler's analysis of and many of his descriptors regarding Riefenstahl's filmic/biographical narrative trace the trajectory of Riefenstahl's public persona within the propaganda machinery of the Third Reich. In Rentschler's words, "*The Blue Light* recodes

Christian symbols in its secular religion of sacrifice, abandon and death" (Rentschler 1989, 59). Rentschler elucidates the many attractions, alluded to in his article's title, that the film's images hold for the Third Reich, enamoring many within the Hitler regime with Riefenstahl's dramatically epochal aesthetic outlook. Riefenstahl's own recollection of the film's impact on the Führer would support Rentschler's thesis bridging her aesthetic vision with the regime's propaganda strategy: "this film was pivotal in my life, not so much because it was my first successful effort as a producer and director, but because Hitler was so fascinated by this film that he insisted I make a documentary about the Party rally in Nuremberg. The result was *Triumph of the Will*" (Riefenstahl 1992, 210).

Das Blaue Licht had a mediocre box-office showing during its initial release in 1932 (Rentschler 1989). Following the rise of the Third Reich, and Riefenstahl's higher profile under the regime as artisanal curator of the party's cinematic image, Riefenstahl and German film critics blamed the film's poor performance on Jewish critics (Rentschler 1989, 66) and rereleased it in 1938, with the expectation that it would resonate in its new Nazi context. The new version erased all mention of any Jewish contributions to the film, including its producer Harry R. Sokal, scriptwriter Carl Mayer, and, most notably, its co-writer and co-director, Béla Balázs. In an incident reminiscent of Fock's proud letter home celebrating her anti-Semitic chauffeur, Riefenstahl bilks her Jewish colleague of his share of the film's profits in a performative fashion. In response to Balázs's financial claim on the film's new-found profitability, Riefenstahl replies with a "terse phrase signed in her hand on *Kaiserhof* (a favorite gathering place for Nazi luminaries) stationery: 'I grant to Herr Gauleiter Julius Streicher of Nuremberg—publisher of *Der Stürmer*—power of attorney in matters and claims of the Jew Béla Balázs on me" (quoted in Rentschler 1989, 66). Streicher's privately owned tabloid *Der Stürmer* became notorious for, among other things, its lurid and virulently anti-Semitic caricatures, its *Rassenschande* [racial defilement] reports (stories of Jewish men and Aryan women having illicit sex) and its "Letter Box" that encouraged citizen-reporting on suspected Jewish misbehavior (Koonz 2005, 230–1). As paragons of German femininity under Hitler, Riefenstahl and Fock surrendered to a comparable sense of destiny associated with the Third Reich in a way that necessitates a performative endorsement of anti-Semitism. Such performances would presumably have functioned as an ideological test of commitment to "racial purity" while simultaneously normalizing the process of dehumanizing Hitler's scapegoats. More broadly, their conformity to the propagandistic narrative of "Aryan purity" through vehicles such as the imaginary myth-making of the Edelweiss Society or *Das Blaue Licht* elides quite easily with the Third Reich's genocidal policies carried out under the pretext of "purification."

After Fock succumbed to tuberculosis and heart failure in 1931, the Nazi propaganda machine quickly capitalized on the situation by promoting the Fock–Göring legend for its own ends. As Anna Maria Sigmund notes:

> The romance of Carin and Hermann Goering served to establish a new type of reportage, in which the Nazi elite took the place of the crowned monarchs of the past. One of these publications, dripping with sentimentality, was called "Das Hohelied der Liebe: Deutsches Werden" [Song of Love: The Rise of Germany]. It was supposed to sway a politically uninterested readership ... and, at the same time, fill the void left by the vanished tabloids. The story of Carin and Hermann Goering filled a gap in the cleverly woven web of total indoctrination of the population. (Sigmund 2000, 42)

Publications like "Song of Love" and the Fock biography, together with the elaborate pageantry of Fock's funeral, serve to effectively "beatify" Carin Fock-Göring. The legend of Fock, painted as a monarch of the past no less than as a medieval saint, within the Reich serves as a powerful and iconic mosaic, eliding her ardent Nazism with imagined Nordic occult tradition.

Following Fock's interment in a small cemetery near the family's summer residence near Drottningholm west of Stockholm, the saga of her roving remains reflects a convoluted view of her body as sacred, saintly Nazi "relic." In his study of the cult of the saints, Peter Brown explains the significance of early Christian relics and martyrs' shrines in terms of physical and spiritual distance:

> By localizing the holy in this manner, late-antique Christianity could feed on the facts of distance and on the joys of proximity. This distance might be physical distance. For this, pilgrimage was the remedy ... But distance is there to be overcome; the experience of pilgrimage activates a yearning for intimate closeness. (Brown 1981, 86)

Göring's veneration of his late wife initially materializes as a perverse Nazi version of this sort of pilgrimage to Fock and all she represents, keeping as he did in close contact with her family and visiting her grave in Sweden often. In 1933, however, Göring lays a floral arrangement at her gravestone in the shape of a swastika, which is soon torn up and inscribed with a message that says: "we, a few Swedes, feel insulted by the desecration of this grave by the German Göring. May his former wife rest in peace but may he spare us German propaganda on her grave" (Fontander 1990, 171). Infuriated by what he sees as desecration of the sacred in the form of a swastika, Göring orders the first of several exhumations of Fock's remains. In what can best be described as a Nazi's pathological distortion of a martyr's shrine, Reichsmarshall Göring's infamous Carinhall hunting estate outside of Berlin in Schorfheide Forest not only bears Fock's name and multiple mini-shrines with her image within, but also includes a dedicated crypt for her newly-arrived "relics." Performing his own version of a "consecration," the Führer himself attends the ceremonial reinterring of her body, further establishing Fock's symbolic place in the Nazi elect and the fascist hagiophilia that surrounds her confected legend. Göring's saint-worship of his former wife continues past his second marriage, with further development of the elaborate Carinhall estate and crypt and the christening of his luxury yacht *Carin II*. In 1945, fearing the Red Army's approach and what that might mean for Fock's remains, Göring exhumes the "relics" yet again and reburies them in a nearby forest before transporting his looted artwork to safety and then ordering his troops to bomb the estate. The macabre legend of Carin Fock's "relics" assumes the shape and scope of the narrative of the theft of Saint Mark's relics and their long journey from Alexandria to Venice depicted in legends and in the mosaics of the presbytery and Zen chapel at Saint Mark's Basilica (Basilica San Marco, n.d.). When the Red Army arrives and desecrates the new grave at Carinhall, a faithful local forester exhumes what he believes to be Fock's remains, reinters them near his residence, and then informs Fock's relatives in Sweden. With East Germany now under communist control, the forester coordinates with Fanny Fock-Wilamowitz to smuggle the purported remains back to Sweden. After exhuming and bagging the body near his house outside the ruins of Carinhall, the forester brings the bag to Heribert Jansson, the Swedish pastor in Berlin. Jansson, in collaboration with Fanny Fock-Wilamowitz, has the unidentified body cremated under a false name and then smuggles the ashes to the family in Sweden, where the urn is buried in the original grave (Sigmund 2000, 44). The return of these cremains to their Nordic *loca santa* (Goodson 2014, 115) mirrors medieval European legends and other narratives of the power of relics being somehow interrelated with their surroundings, oftentimes with the original burial site holding the most sacredness.

The imagined sacredness of the Fock "relics" within a Nazi cosmos creates a twisted and disorienting refraction of many of the concerns of medieval Christian pilgrims. As Peter Brown points out in his study of ancient saint cults, for the pilgrim, there is significance not only in the journey to the shrine but also in the shrine and relics themselves:

> For the art of the shrine in late antiquity is an art of closed surfaces. Behind these surfaces, the holy lay, either totally hidden or glimpsed through narrow apertures. The opacity of the surfaces heightened an awareness of the ultimate unattainability in this life of the person [i.e. the saint] they had traveled over such wide spaces to touch. (Brown 1981, 86–7)

The Nazi/neo-Nazi legend of Carin Fock incorporates this vision of the significance of remains as "relics," both consciously and unconsciously. The remoteness, unattainability and mystery surrounding the life and legend of Carin Fock endure as a macabre, and what Friedlander might call kitschy, iteration of the morbid legacy of the Third Reich. The ruins of Carinhall outside Berlin continue to be a site of pilgrimage (or *loca santa*) for Nazi sympathizers as well as fertile ground for treasure hunters mining Göring's spoils of war. In 1991, a group of such pilgrims discovered an elaborate zinc sarcophagus containing a woman's body on the grounds of the former Carinhall estate. DNA testing conducted by Uppsala University in 2012 confirmed that these remains are those of Fock (Uppsala University 2012), and these have also now been reburied in the original plot in Sweden. This more recent forensic inquiry into the confounding question of which bones from which location may be genuine echoes the enormous *Inventio* mosaic page at Saint Mark's Basilica in Venice (Basilica San Marco, n.d.). This narrative image depicts the Venetian effort in 1094 of prayer and fasting to implore God to help locate the whereabouts of Saint Mark's long-lost remains and the subsequent miraculous extension of the saint's arm from a pillar, pointing out the exact location of the relics. The continued fascination with and excavation of Fock's legacy suggest that Brown's notion of "a yearning for intimate closeness" (Brown 1981, 86) with worshiped saints has not dimmed over the years and appears to perform many aspects of Friedlander's notion of a "new discourse" on Nazism.

Such a discourse extends to the analogy of the medieval Christian surge of interest in holy objects even tangentially associated with Jesus and his close disciples, such as the True Cross, the Shroud of Turin, the Veil of Veronica and the Crown of Thorns. Hermann Göring's pleasure yacht, *Carin II*, dedicated to and named for his late first wife, has functioned in an analogous way since its genesis in 1937, as equal parts Fock relic and modern totem of the new Nazi discourse. Unlike Göring's own palatial passion project Carinhall, *Carin II* originated as a gift-as-bribe by the German auto industry lobbyist Werft Hans Heidtmann. The 90-foot yacht, fitted with Burmese teak and Caucasian walnut, initially functioned as an ideal vessel of the Fock legend's legacy, performing as the preeminent floating spectacle of the Nazi elect. As propaganda, the boat broadcast German might, being the first of its size, scope, and cost, and Göring welcomed press coverage of his onboard soirées with Hitler, Hess, Goebbels, Himmler, and Heydrich. When not drinking cognac or shooting ducks from the specially constructed platform above the bow, Göring "would sit on the green leather sofa in the boat's splendid wood panelled salon – which remains unchanged to this day – and study Battle of Britain operational maps on the burr walnut table" ("Scramble begins" 2004). Armed with the perceived legitimacy conferred by its sanctified namesake, the ostentatious yacht and its hedonistic owner manufacture an aspirational image of the Reich worthy of a modern public relations campaign. Much in the way he does in his extravagant hunting lodge Carinhall, with *Carin* II Göring elides the sanctified legacy of Fock with state propaganda in the form of a bacchanal-as-communion. Military strategy aboard *Carin II* unfolds almost as a parlor game, with the conquest of Britain to be savored alongside cognac and *pâté de canard*. As mobile propaganda, the yacht trumpets Nazi expansion and conquest in the form of a booze cruise, motoring around the Baltic Sea, and even traveling up to a German-language performance of *Hamlet* at Kronborg Castle in Denmark, in an ominous prelude to invasion (Olsen 2016).

The postwar peregrinations of *Carin* II reflect the fraught accountings for the legacy of the boat and her namesake as metonym for Friedlander's formulation of absolute submission and total freedom, and even Sontag's notion of fascinating fascism. In 1945, when British Field Marshal Montgomery recognizes the yacht moored off Hamburg, he seizes *Carin II* as a spoil of war for King George VI, who then rechristens the vessel HMS *Royal Albert* ("Scramble begins" 2004). From 1945 until 1960, it was used as a privately owned holiday pleasure craft for the newly victorious British royal family, with high-profile visits from Princess Margaret, the Duke of Edinburgh, and the Prince of Wales ("Scramble begins" 2004). Upon the ascension of Queen Elizabeth II in 1952, the yacht was rechristened HMS *Prince of Wales* in honor of the four-year-old Charles ("Scramble begins" 2004). The postwar acquisition of this particular Nazi object only serves to cement an enduring conception of the power of Göring kitsch and its corollary, Fock kitsch. By 1960, perhaps because of an epiphany about the implications of vacationing aboard a Nazi relic, or perhaps because of an ongoing legal claim by Göring's widow (his second wife, the actress Emmy Sonnemann Göring), the Windsor family relinquishes its claim on the vessel, which has outlived its usefulness for them. Göring's widow quickly sells the yacht to a German printer, who renames it *Theresia* and holds onto it for twelve years, only to then hand it off to a notorious grifter and Nazi sympathizer.

The bizarre goings-on surrounding the yacht after its subsequent acquisition by one of postwar Germany's most infamous neo-Nazi hucksters only further amplifies the patina of kitsch that overlays the relic. Gerd Heidemann, a sometime journalist, is best known for the *Hitler Diaries* hoax of the 1980s in which he sold the publishing rights of fraudulent Hitler diaries to *Stern* magazine for 10 million deutschmarks (approximately US $6 million). At the time, Heidemann successfully duped not only *Stern*, but also the UK *Sunday Times*, as well as Oxford historian Hugh Trevor-Roper ("Scramble begins" 2004). One aspect of Heidemann's motivation for perpetrating the incredibly profitable hoax stemmed from the ongoing expenses of the upkeep of the deteriorating Göring yacht, which he rechristened *Carin II*. Having acquired the yacht and restored its original name, Heidemann appears to have attempted to resurrect the *Reichsmarschall*'s extravagant lifestyle, buying jewelry and other Nazi relics, and hosting flamboyant parties aboard the boat. Perhaps unwittingly invoking Friedlander's notion of Nazism's "community of the saints," Heidemann's guests aboard the vessel included unrepentant former Nazi SS generals Karl Wolff and Wilhelm Mohnke, along with Göring's daughter Edda, with whom Heidemann had a long affair (Wyden 2001, 173). Of these floating celebrations Heidemann recounts, "[w]e started to have long drinking evenings aboard ... I had always been a passionate reader of thrillers. Suddenly I was living a thriller" (Wyden 2001, 173). By 1984, Heidemann's *Hitler Diaries* hoax having been publicly exposed, the sometime journalist was tried and convicted, and *Carin II* was subsequently seized by Deutsche Bank to be auctioned off ("Scramble begins" 2004). The fascinating voyage of *Carin II* continued with its new owners, the Egyptian-born Mostafa Karim and his American-born wife Sandra Jean Simpson. During a journey in 1987 from Europe to Egypt, the couple were caught in a major storm and forced to seek refuge in Benghazi, Libya. Upon their arrival, Colonel Muammar Gaddafi seized *Carin II*, arrested the couple, and imprisoned them for four months of interrogation until the USA covertly negotiated their release ("Scramble begins" 2004). As with Carin Fock-Göring's remains, the at once sensational and unsettling odyssey of *Carin II* exemplifies Friedlander's formulation of Nazi kitsch-as-terror.

To conclude: the question of the continued yearning for intimate closeness with the legacy of Carin Fock-Göring encompasses all of the contradictions of what Friedlander has called the new discourse of Nazism. Ranging from the 1920s to the present, the arc of Fock's narrative trajectory evokes many of the oftentimes uncanny effects that arise from the process of mythologizing the banal. The contemporaneous crafting of Fock's persona by Goebbels' propaganda machine during the war, which was as effective as the more notorious imagery crafted by Riefenstahl, offers a noteworthy case study in image manipulation, and the ensuing memorializing of her legacy and remains after the war reflects the generalized anxiety of remembering and forgetting trauma. The fetishized relics of Fock evoke the frisson of fascinating fascism because of their oxymoronic status as equal parts terror and kitschy historical footnote. Friedlander puts it most succinctly when he describes this phenomenon as "on the one hand, an appeal to harmony, to emotional communion at the simplest and most immediate level; on the other, solitude and terror" (Friedlander 1993, 27). If kitsch and death are incompatible at the level of individual experience, the resurrection of the Fock-Göring legend simultaneously exposes the fascist ideology of surrender and enables it.

References

Basilica San Marco. n.d. "Mosaic Heritage." <https://www.basilicasanmarco.it/basilica/mosaici/il-patrimonio-musivo/storie-di-san-marco/?lang=en> (last accessed October 25, 2017).
Brown, Peter. 1981. *The Cult of the Saints: Its Rise and Function in Late Christianity*. Chicago: University of Chicago Press.
Fontander, Björn. 1990. *Carin Göring Skriver Hem*. Stockholm: Carlsson Bokförlag.
Friedlander, Saul. 1993. *Reflections of Nazism*. Bloomington and Indianapolis: IU Press.
Goodson, Caroline. 2014. "Archaeology and the cult of saints in the early Middle Ages: accessing the sacred." *Mélanges de l'École française de Rome: Moyen Âge*, 126 (1). <http://journals.openedition.org/mefrm/1818 >
Görtemaker, Heike B. 2011. *Eva Braun: Life with Hitler*. Trans. Damion Searls. New York: Vintage.
Koonz, Claudia. 1987. *Mothers in the Fatherland: Women, the Family and Nazi Politics*. New York: St. Martin's Press.
Koonz, Claudia. 2005. *The Nazi Conscience*. Cambridge, MA; London: Harvard University Press.
Kracauer, Siegfried. 1947. *From Caligari to Hitler: A Psychological History of the German Film*. Princeton: Princeton University Press.
Levenda, Peter. 2006. *Unholy Alliance: A History of Nazi Involvement with the Occult*. New York; London: Continuum.
Manvell, Roger and Heinrich Fraenkel. 2011. *Goering: The Rise and Fall of the Notorious Nazi Leader*. New York: Skyhorse.
Meissner, Hans-Otto. 1980. *Magda Goebbels: The First Lady of the Third Reich*. Trans. Gwendolyn Mary Keeble. New York: The Dial Press.
Mosley, Leonard. 1975. *The Reich Marshall: A Biography of Hermann Goering*. Munich: Dell.
Olsen, Jacob Steen 2016. "Hamlets århundrede." *Berlinske*, June 23. <https://www.berlingske.dk/navne/hamlets-aarhundrede>
Proctor, Robert N. 1988. *Racial Hygiene: Medicine under the Nazis*. Cambridge, MA and London: Harvard University Press.
Ravenscroft, Trevor. 1982. *The Spear of Destiny*. Boston; York Beach: Red Wheel/Weiser.
Rentschler, Eric. 1989. "Fatal attractions: Leni Riefenstahl's 'The Blue Light'." *October* 48 (spring): 46–68.
Riefenstahl, Leni. 1992. *The Sieve of Time: The Memoirs of Leni Riefenstahl*. London: Quartet.
"Scramble begins to own the last Nazi treasure." 2004. *The Scotsman*, February 14. <https://www.scotsman.com/news/world/scramble-begins-to-own-the-last-nazi-treasure-1-513865>
Sigmund, Anna Maria. 2000. *Women of the Third Reich*. Richmond Hill, ON: NDE.
Sontag, Susan. 1980. *Under the Sign of Saturn*. New York: Farrar, Straus & Giroux.
Uppsala University. 2012. "Carin Göring's remains identified by researchers at Uppsala University," December 21. <http://www.uu.se/en/media/news/article/?id=2257&area=2,16&typ=artikel&lang=en>
Wilamowitz-Moellendorf, Fanny. 1942. *Carin Göring*. Berlin: Gräfin.

Witoszek, Nina. 2002. "Moral Community and the Crisis of the Enlightenment: Sweden and Germany in the 1920s and 1930s." In *Culture and Crisis: The Case of Germany and Sweden*, ed. Nina Witoszek and Lars Trägårdh. New York; Oxford: Berghahn.

Wyden, Peter. 2001. *The Hitler Virus: The Insidious Legacy of Adolf Hitler*. New York: Arcade.

5. MOBILITY AND MARGINALIZATION: ARNE SUCKSDORFF'S DOCUMENTARY AUTHORSHIP IN INDIA AND BRAZIL

Emil Stjernholm

The Swedish filmmaker Arne Sucksdorff was recognized as an innovative documentary filmmaker in the 1940s and 1950s, but once his production moved internationally—first to India and then to Brazil—the authorial discourse on it changed dramatically. This chapter maps the transnational production and circulation of his feature-length documentaries *The Flute and the Arrow* (*En djungelsaga*, Sweden, 1957) and *My Home Is Copacabana* (*Mitt hem är Copacabana*, Sweden, 1965). The aim of the study is twofold: first, given that Sucksdorff occupied a privileged position within both Indian and Brazilian film culture during important transformative periods, I seek to examine any reciprocal influence between these film cultures and the established Swedish auteur; secondly, I analyze how and why these films seem to have marginalized Sucksdorff "at home," raising questions concerning his place within the Swedish national film canon.

Dubbed "the father of the Swedish documentary" (Jarl 2001), Arne Sucksdorff not only influenced generations of Swedish realist filmmakers but also gained significant international recognition. He became famous in the 1940s and '50s with a number of poetic nature documentaries that were hailed for their cinematography and their portrayal of land, sky, water, and animals. Working with short films under the auspices of the major Swedish film company Svensk Filmindustri (SF), Sucksdorff was gradually framed as an auteur with a personal vision. While these themes have been treated exhaustively in the scholarly works that have covered his career (e.g.

Edström 1968), less emphasis has been placed on the transnational dimension of his work.

Visions of Post-Independence India

Arne Sucksdorff had two extended stays in India. During the first, in 1950, he directed two short films, *Indian Village* (*Indisk by*, Sweden, 1951) and *The Wind and the River* (*Vinden och floden*, Sweden, 1953), on commission from the Swedish Cooperative Union and Wholesale Society (Kooperativa Förbundet) (Stjernholm 2017). During the second, he directed his second feature-length film *The Flute and the Arrow*, a film that was marketed as Sweden's most expensive to date.

Set in the Northern Indian province of Bastar, *The Flute and the Arrow* centers on a young boy called Chendru and the Muria tribe's struggle with the threatening wildlife around the village. *The Flute and the Arrow* features a score written by the Indian musician Ravi Shankar, who previously had made the music for Satyajit Ray's *Song of the Little Road* (*Pather Panchali*, India, 1955), the first part of the Apu trilogy. It was the first film that Sucksdorff made in the AgaScope widescreen format and in Technicolor. Drawing on Bill Nichols' well-known taxonomy of documentary film (Nichols 2001), we can describe the film as a "poetic documentary," combining aestheticized visions of village life with vivid depictions of the natural forces surrounding it. Moreover, one could argue that Sucksdorff's film features elements of the expository documentary mode, given that a narrator, who not only lends the film an air of ethnographical film but also situates the onlooker as a Westerner, firmly guides the story. These characteristics distinguish *The Flute and the Arrow* from much of the work done in post-independence India by other European auteurs, including Roberto Rossellini's *India: Matri Bhumi* (Italy/France, 1959) and Louis Malle's *Phantom India* (*L'Inde fantôme*, France, 1969) (cf. Garga 2005; Jhaveri 2009; Mulay 2010), which both bear a trace of the observational mode and cinema vérité-style filmmaking.

The Flute and the Arrow gained much attention in Sweden and internationally. In Sweden, the premiere was met with great enthusiasm, and some critics predicted that the film would lead to an international breakthrough (Tjerneld 1957). The cinematography, the expressive colors and the fact that the film was shot on location in a difficult setting was praised repeatedly. The Swedish press framed Sucksdorff as something of an Indophile with a longstanding interest in the country's religious practices, nature and wildlife. Moreover, several critics highlighted Sucksdorff's time in India as an important phase of his career, particularly because it was there that he began shifting focus from wild nature to human society (Lauritzen 1958). In this sense, the meeting with the Murias was interpreted as having a liberating effect on the director's perception of nature.

Figure 5.1 Swedish posters for *The Flute and the Arrow* present two complementary messages. The first promotes "Arne Sucksdorff's large India Film in Color and Agascope; A 'Fairytale' [saga] from the Jungle" and the second invites the audience to "Meet Chendru."

Meanwhile, not all critics were as positive. Some raised concerns about the ways in which Sucksdorff had interacted with the Murias and interpreted their traditions. The journalist Torgny Sommelius, who had traveled in the region depicted, questioned the authenticity of the film in Sweden's leading literary journal *BLM*, highlighting Sucksdorff's docudrama methods as faulty and dishonest. The author found Ravi Shankar's sitar music ill-fitting (given that this music had little to do with this region's traditions) and the decision to dress the Murias in festive garments on a daily occasion fraudulent: "He has depicted the Murias as more colorful than they appear, depicted them more romantically than they are, and exaggerated their noble traits and suppressed their less attractive qualities" (Sommelius 1958). Likewise, international reviewers zoomed in on this point of critique (Crowther 1960).

Sucksdorff's films also gained circulation in India. *The Flute and the Arrow* both screened in popular venues, such as the Excelsior in Old Delhi ("Excelsior" 1963), a movie hall primarily targeted at "the masses" ("New Delhi's Heritage Cinemas" 2011), and made an impression in "elite" Indian film societies (cf. Cherian 2017). While established Indian auteurs such as Ritwik Ghatak have expressed fond memories of the film (Ghatak 1987,

58), others, like the acclaimed Indian "neo-realist" Satyajit Ray (Majumdar 2013), have been more critical and have argued that Sucksdorff falls into the trap of being "too pictorial" (Cardullo 2007, 7). In this sense, Ray also touched upon discord between the picture painted by Sucksdorff and the Murias' actual life. Notably, these types of questions affected Sucksdorff's cinematic legacy in the country. For example, the 1996 documentary *Jungle Dreams* (*Pramod Mathur*, India/Germany, 1996) investigates the adult life of the child actor Chendru nearly forty years after *The Flute and the Arrow* was made. The 30-minute documentary tells Chendru's story of short-lived fame and highlights the impact the film had on his life with the Murias after the curtains were drawn. After traveling to Stockholm to attend the film's premiere, Chendru, who brought clothes, gadgets, and his experiences of Western life home, became somewhat of a curiosity in the eyes of his fellow Murias. This experience, according to the documentary, had a profoundly negative impact on Chendru's life. In this way, *Jungle Dreams* raises another set of ethical questions in considering Sucksdorff's film production.

Sucksdorff and the Brazilian New Wave

In the biographical histories surrounding Sucksdorff, the commercial failure of his next feature film, the Sweden-made *The Boy in the Tree* (*Pojken i trädet*, Sweden, 1961), emerges as one of the key reasons for his decision to leave the country. After a brief stint in southern Italy, Sucksdorff accepted a commission from the United Nations agency UNESCO to teach documentary film in Rio de Janeiro. Just as foreign filmmakers were attracted to India in the post-independence period, many prolific European filmmakers like François Truffaut, Roberto Rossellini, and John Grierson showcased an interest in Brazil in the late 1950s and early 1960s (Shaw and Dennison 2007, 87). This increased interest ran parallel to the emergence of the Brazilian New Wave, so-called "Cinema Novo," a film movement focusing on social equality which gained much international recognition during these years. In Brazil, Sucksdorff headed a seminar on documentary film, co-organized by the governmental Ministry of Foreign Relations and the Instituto Nacional de Cinema Educativo, teaching some of the filmmakers who were, or later would become, key figures in this movement, including Arnaldo Jabor, David Neves, and Nelson Pereira dos Santos. Notably, historian Fernão Pessoa Ramos marks the seminar as an important landmark in the history of Cinema Novo (2013, 223). Cinema Novo emerged in Brazil at a time when the country was plagued by social injustice and political instability. Drawing on the French New Wave and, perhaps foremost, Italian neorealism, the filmmakers associated with Cinema Novo worked with low budgets, outside of the film studios, and with a particular interest in the struggles of everyday life (Sarzynski 2013, 209). In particular, the underclass became the focal point of many films, set first in the cities and later on the countryside, and the movement gained much attention in Europe and elsewhere throughout the 1960s.

Although the UNESCO seminar put food on the table for Sucksdorff, it took him a long time to get the teaching equipment that he desired, such as an editing table and lightweight film equipment, in order to actually practice filmmaking with students. In the beginning, the course was mostly theoretical, featuring film analysis of both classic documentary films like Robert Flaherty's *Man of Aran* (Ireland, 1934) and current Brazilian films (Edström 1968, 110). Drawing on his experiences as a teacher for UNESCO, Sucksdorff solicited support to make a feature-length documentary about street children, the film later entitled *My Home Is Copacabana*. By this point, Sucksdorff had worked up a reputation within the Swedish film industry not only for being stubborn but also for making expensive films, having long pre-production processes, and shooting a lot of raw material. Indeed, Kenne Fant, head of SF, described contract negotiations with the filmmaker as "complicated" (Fant 1963). It was not until Sucksdorff had acquired one of the government body Statens Filmpremienämnd's "quality premiums" of 100 000 Swedish crowns that SF decided to back his project and started to seek the support of other investors, for instance from UNICEF (Stearns 1964).

Following the coup d'état in Brazil in 1964, the topic of social injustice in the country's capital became all the more controversial. As a UN representative wrote to SF: "The Brazilian Government has been made somewhat sensitive by past reportage and journalistic interpretation of their situation" (Edwards 1964). Although Swedish newspapers reported skirmishes with local police officers, Sucksdorff's connections with UNESCO afforded him a privileged position and he was able to complete the film, while many of the filmmakers of the Cinema Novo were branded left-wing rebels by the military dictatorship (King 2000, 111). Unlike the case in India, where most of the key film crew were Swedes, the production of *My Home Is Copacabana* was characterized by transnational creative exchange. Two of the Brazilian participants in the seminar, João Bethencourt and Flávio Migliacio, worked on the manuscript in cooperation with Sucksdorff, and other seminar participants were responsible for the lighting, set design, sound design, and other tasks. While some scholars describe the working relationship between the Swedish director and the students as an uncomplicated affair (Edström 1968), studies by the Brazilian scholar Ester Hamburger have noted that at times there were tensions (Hamburger 2013). Whereas Sucksdorff preferred more static cinematography, working with a tripod throughout his career, the young Brazilian filmmakers favored lightweight film equipment, a clash in film style that *My Home Is Copacabana* arguably reflects.

The documentary-style drama *My Home Is Copacabana*, which premiered in 1965, centers on a group of street children in the Brazilian capital Rio de Janeiro. The kids play, work, and steal, all in an effort to survive life in the slums. In Sweden, the film won critical acclaim. Critics labeled *My Home Is Copacabana* a great comeback and Sucksdorff also won a "Guldbagge," the principal Swedish film award, in the best director category. Even though the director was praised for the way that, with great care and humanism, he broached the subject of poverty, some critics begrudgingly labeled his idealistic, almost romantic, portrayal of these children's lives as out of touch, especially in relation to the current trends in Swedish art cinema (Eriksson 1965). *My Home Is Copacabana* features certain Cinema Novo characteristics, such as the way the camera tracks the main characters and the film's thematic focus on the experiences of poor outcasts from society. Meanwhile, Sucksdorff's approach to the topic contrasts heavily with the way in which this movement expressed its fury with the social and political system. In this case, film critics placed less emphasis on the question of authenticity. However, documentary ethics nonetheless became a topic of debate when Sucksdorff, just as he did with the Muria youngster Chendru, brought four of the Brazilian children to Sweden ahead of the premiere. Some critics labeled this a "publicity stunt" and questioned what the film company and Sucksdorff would do for these kids when the gala was over. Following this, Sucksdorff and his Brazilian wife Maria moved to the Pantanal region in Northern Brazil, where the former combined still photography with work as an environmental activist, making numerous failed attempts to finance feature film projects. His final major film and television project was the four-part documentary television series *On the Other Side of the Earth* (*På jordens baksida*, Sweden, 1972), which focuses on the tropical wetland in the Pantanal region.

Sucksdorff's Authorship Abroad

Despite the fact that Arne Sucksdorff's filmmaking made a strong international impact, the transnational dimension of his work has not been investigated in depth until recently. Transnational film practices tend to disrupt and unsettle national historiographies. In this case, the practitioner's mobility raises questions about reciprocal influence and cross-cultural confusion, perspectives that tend to be overlooked in a national cinema context. While Arne Sucksdorff had a personal affinity with both India and Brazil, he was more immersed in Brazilian film culture than he ever was in its Indian equivalent. As this chapter illustrates, *My Home Is Copacabana* showcases a hybridity both in production and film style. For example, the film crew mostly comprised students from Sucksdorff's UNESCO seminar and other Brazilian film workers. When comparing the receptions of *The Flute and the Arrow*

Figure 5.2 After facing criticism for having brought the Brazilian children who star in *My Home Is Copacabana* to Cannes and Stockholm, Arne Sucksdorff addressed the public in the magazine *Idun veckojournalen* (1965, issue 22). The headline reads: "What were they even doing here!?"

and *My Home Is Copacabana*, it is noteworthy that both films raised questions concerning documentary ethics related to the treatment of the local cultures. Looking more broadly at Sucksdorff's ventures to India and Brazil, one can further conclude that while the former journey gained much publicity, and the director was enthusiastically framed as something of an adventurer, Sucksdorff's relocation to Brazil essentially made him an outsider. He was seen as a demanding romantic, exceedingly out of touch with the cultural climate in Sweden. Throughout all the time Swedish critics praised *My Home Is Copacabana*, the director began to fall out of favor with key figures in Swedish film culture. This, in turn, contributed to his marginalization in the following decades, something which certainly affected his place within the national film canon.

References

Cardullo, Bert, ed. 2007. *Satyajit Ray: Interviews*. Jackson: University Press of Mississippi.
Cherian, V. K. 2017. *India's Film Society Movement: The Journey and its Impact*. New Delhi: SAGE Publications India.
Crowther, Bosley. 1960. "Screen: Sucksdorff with the Muria Tribe of India." *The New York Times*, October 11.
Edström, Mauritz. 1968. *Sucksdorff—Främlingen i hemmaskogen* [Sucksdorff—Stranger in the Home Terrain]. Stockholm: PAN/Norstedt.
Edwards, Paul B. 1964. "United Nations Children's Fund." Letter to Kenne Fant, 21 September.
Eriksson, Göran O. 1965. "Sucksdorff fortsätter söka ett förlorat paradis." *Expressen*, March 30.
"Excelsior." 1963. *The Times of India*, November 26.
Fant, Kenne. 1963. Letter to Arne Sucksdorff, August 26.
Garga, B. D. 2005. *The Making of Great Cinema: An Insider's Journey through Fifty Years of Film History*. New Delhi: Viking.
Ghatak, Ritwik. 1987. *Cinema and I*. Calcutta: Ritwik Memorial Trust.
Hamburger, Ester. 2013. "Fábula ou *Mitt hem är Copacabana* de Arne Sucksdorff." In *World Cinema: As Novas Cartografias do Cinema Mundial*, ed. Stephanie Dennison. Campinas: Papirus. 169–77.
Jhaveri, Shanay. 2009. *Outsider: Films on India, 1950–1990*. Mumbai: Shoestring.
King, John. 2000. *Magical Reels: A History of Cinema in Latin America*. New edn. New York: Verso.
Lauritzen, Bertil. 1958. "Saga utan slut: Några anteckningar om Arne Sucksdorff" [A Tale Without an End: Some Notes on Arne Sucksdorff]. In *Filmen* [Film], ed. Svenska filmsamfundet. Stockholm: Svenska filmsamfundet. 96–106,
Majumdar, Neepa. 2013. "Importing Neorealism, Exporting Cinema: Indian Cinema and Film Festivals in the 1950s." In *Global Neorealism: The Transnational History of a Film Style*, ed. Saverio Giovacchini and Robert Sklar. Jackson: University Press of Mississippi. 178–93.
Mulay, Vijay. 2010. *From Rajahs and Yogis to Gandhi and Beyond: Images of India in International Films of the Twentieth Century*. London: Seagull Books.
Nichols, Bill. 2001. *Introduction to Documentary*. Bloomington: Indiana University Press.

Pessoa Ramos, Fernão. 2013. "Cinema Novo." In *Encyclopedia of the Documentary Film 3-Volume Set*, ed. Ian Aitken. New York: Routledge. 222–4.
Sarzynski, Sarah. 2013. "Documenting the Social Reality of Brazil: Roberto Rossellini, the Paraíban Documentary School, and the Cinema Novistas." In *Global Neorealism: The Transnational History of a Film Style*, ed. Saverio Giovacchini and Robert Sklar. Jackson: University Press of Mississippi. 209–25.
Shaw, Lisa, and Stephanie Dennison. 2007. *Brazilian National Cinema*. Routledge.
Sommelius, Torgny. 1958. "En djungelsaga. Synpunkter på Arne Sucksdorffs film" [The Flute and the Arrow. Opinions on Arne Sucksdorff's Film.] *BLM: Bonniers Litterära Magasin* 2(2): 145–9.
Stearns, Monroe. 1964. Letter to Kenne Fant, May 5.
Stjernholm, Emil. 2017. "Visions of post-independence India in Arne Sucksdorff's documentaries." *BioScope: South Asian Screen Studies* 8(1): 1–20.
Tjerneld, Staffan. 1957. "En djungelsaga på Royal." *Expressen*, December 29.

6. "LET'S GET A SWEDE!": PETER GOLDMANN, THE BEATLES, AND THE ORIGINS OF THE MUSIC VIDEO

Scott MacKenzie

In 1966, Paul McCartney was sitting in The Scotch of St James, a club frequented by rock musicians in London, and began talking to Peter Goldmann, a director at SvT (Sveriges Television AB). McCartney, inspired by recent films by Ingmar Bergman and Jean-Luc Godard, was extolling the fact that the next Beatles' promotional films (which became a necessity after the group decided to abandon touring earlier in the year) ought to be in the emergent art cinema vein, breaking away from the *faux cinéma direct* of the group's two Richard Lester films, *A Hard Day's Night* (UK/USA, 1964) and *Help!* (UK/USA, 1965). Goldmann was also excited about this possibility and talked to McCartney about what kind of experimental films could be produced (even though he had, at that time, little to no experience with experimental cinema). McCartney thought that Goldmann ought to be hired to produce these works, and then told the band (perhaps apocryphally): "Let's get a Swede!" McCartney later stated: "We thought that kind of surrealist art film was very appropriate for the times . . . We were great admirers of Swedish art films—Ingmar Bergman and the like—and we'd met a Swedish director called Peter Goldmann in a club and said, 'Could you direct this?' And here we were going backwards and now running forwards and now running in slow motion" (The Beatles 2015, 5). Goldmann was a slightly known quantity in the UK music scene, as he had worked as a producer for Sveriges Television's *Popside*, which ran from 1966 to 1968, which featured UK-based bands such as Manfred Mann, The Troggs, The Who, and The Jimi Hendrix Experience. In their history of The Who,

Andy Neill and Matt Kent note that on June 3, 1966 "The Who spent most of the day rehearsing and taping six songs for Sverige [sic] Television's *Popside*, produced by Peter Goldmann, who went on to direct The Beatles' 'Penny Lane' and 'Strawberry Fields Forever' promotional films" (Neill and Kent 2002, 84). This taping eventually brought Goldmann to London; on October 11, 1966 he went there to shoot a documentary about The Who for SvT. The band "was filmed by producer Peter Goldmann ... The segment was part of a Sverige Television special, *My Generation—Popreportage från London*, broadcast in two 30 minute segments" (2002, 92). This may explain why he was sitting in The Scotch of St James, a bar frequented by both The Beatles and The Who. Another account claims that Manfred Mann bassist (and friend of The Beatles from their days in Hamburg) Klaus Voormann introduced them (Ingham 2003, 206; Lewisohn 2003, 242). By coincidence, it was The Beatles' own earlier work with Lester that inspired Goldmann to start directing pop groups for Swedish Television. In one of the few extant interviews with Goldmann, in the UK music paper *New Musical Express*, given while he was in London for The Beatles' shoot, he stated: "Originally, my enthusiasm for presenting English groups on TV in Sweden was fired by Dick Lester's fine film of The Beatles in *A Hard Day's Night*. I thought that was fantastic and wanted to try to present this music in an original and interesting manner on TV" (Altham 1967, 2).

Whatever the exact circumstances of Goldmann and The Beatles' first encounter, in late 1966 and early 1967 Goldmann directed the promo films for "Strawberry Fields Forever" and "Penny Lane." (Some filmographies also claim he went on to direct the promo for "A Day in the Life"—left unreleased for decades—though the most recent release of this work claims The Beatles themselves directed it. However, as the "A Day in the Life" promo was shot only three days after the completion of the shooting of the "Penny Lane" promo, one might presume Goldmann was involved [The Beatles 2015, 92].) These promo films represent the two works by a Swedish director quite probably seen by more viewers globally than any other—from their earliest global broadcasts in the 1960s, to the earliest days on MTV, to their recent release on digital platforms, including iTunes—and had a vast aesthetic influence that has gone unnoted by almost everyone writing on music videos or on Nordic cinemas. This chapter examines this history, and discusses these important promo films as representing a radical shift in The Beatles' visual aesthetic, a precursor to that of MTV, and a synthesis of avant-garde and popular culture forms.

The release of The Beatles' non-album tracks, the double "A" side 45 rpm of "Strawberry Fields Forever"/"Penny Lane" on February 13, 1967 (on the Capitol label) in the USA and February 17 (on Parlophone) in the UK marked a major turning point for the band, then already by far the most popular group in the world. Having quit touring on August 29, 1966 after their last concert at San Francisco's Candlestick Park, the band now found themselves free to experiment in the studio. The recording sessions for this double "A" side, and their subsequent album *Sgt. Pepper's Lonely Hearts Club Band*, released May 26, 1967, took over three months, or 700 studio hours, to record (see MacDonald 1997, 188–220). Originally, these two songs were to appear on the album, but were pulled off as singles at the behest of EMI (which their record producer George Martin once lamented was "a dreadful mistake" [The Beatles 2000, 239] and "the biggest mistake of my professional life" [Norman 2008, 484] as the two tracks could not then be part of *Sgt. Pepper's*). The absence of The Beatles from the live stage, and the demand to see them perform, led to the band commissioning Goldmann to direct these works. What the band required was something that was both visually interesting and that would not have them appear miming to their increasingly complex songs.

In their mid-20s, and living in what was considered at the time the most exciting city in Europe in terms of popular culture, the group immersed themselves in the rising multi-media phenomena taking place around them ("happenings," expanded cinema, hybrid performances, underground film imported from the States, and the recently launched London Film-makers' Co-op), in some ways begot by their own work. However, despite the centrality of London in the popular imaginary at the time, one area of the arts lagged far behind what was taking place on the continent, from Paris to Rome to Warsaw to Stockholm: the rise of art cinema auteurs. British cinema and theater were still very much ensconced in the realist traditions emerging from the "Angry Young Man" plays of John Osborne and realist, working-class "Kitchen Sink" films such as *A Taste of Honey* (Tony Richardson, UK, 1961), *A Kind of Loving* (John Schlesinger, UK, 1962), and *This Sporting Life* (Lindsay Anderson, UK, 1963)—modes of expression largely eschewed by The Beatles (except to some degree in *A Hard Day's Night*). Part of this disavowal (which was reflected in the band's backgrounds, as Harrison and Starr were from working-class families, McCartney's family was aspiring middle-class, and Lennon considered himself middle-class) came from a sea change in politics in Britain at the time around questions of class hierarchies and sexuality (see MacKenzie 2017). The band's interest in films by Bergman and Godard (the latter would later propose making a film with The Beatles, and subsequently did with The Rolling Stones with *1+1* [France, 1968]), reflected the fact that they saw themselves as internationalists, and were drawing on sources far removed from British music traditions (though those still ran through their work) in their music.

While Goldmann's two works reflect the international aesthetic being developed by The Beatles, they do not greatly resemble the works of Bergman in terms of cinematic aesthetics or those of contemporary Swedish experimental filmmakers (see Andersson et al. 2010, 100–21). Yet they do follow a Nordic (and perhaps continental) trend of exploring expressions of interiority in films such as Bergman's *Through a Glass Darkly* (*Såsom i en spegel*, Sweden, 1961)

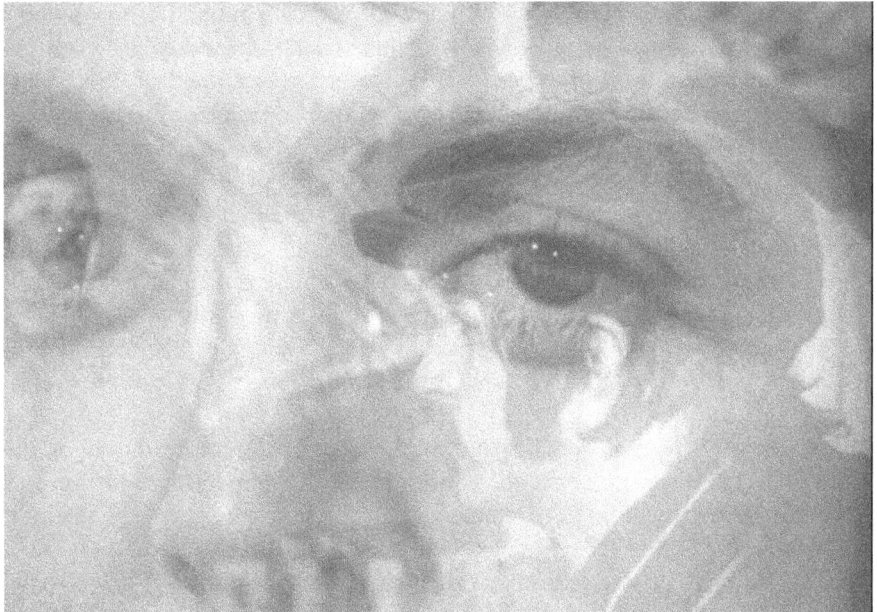

Figure 6.1 Superimposition in Goldmann's *Strawberry Fields Forever*.

and *Persona* (Sweden, 1966). As short works, the promos' closest cousins were the films coming out of the American underground movement, most notably those of Kenneth Anger, Bruce Baillie, and Stan Brakhage. Goldmann's works therefore form a potent synthesis of existential and philosophical issues coming out of European, and specifically Swedish, cinema with the free form aesthetic of the American underground.

This is not to imply that these works are in any way a form of pastiche; each of the two works also has its own distinctive characteristics. "Strawberry Fields Forever" is by far the more abstract of the two works, combining superimposition, reverse photography, an elliptical editing style, slow and fast motion, and solarization, as the four Beatles walk through Knole Park, Sevenoaks, Kent, climb a large, dead oak tree, and paint and destroy a piano in the field.

Shots alter between extreme close-ups of their faces, and wide shots of the four of them in the field. "Strawberry Fields Forever" has a hallucinatory feel, and if there were not a song on the soundtrack, and four famous faces onscreen, the work could fit well into the American avant-garde. (This is not to say that there was not cross-pollination, as Michael Snow used snippets of the song "Strawberry Fields Forever" in his seminal underground film *Wavelength* [Canada, 1967], and John Lennon would shortly start making experimental films in the American underground vein with Yoko Ono, who made Fluxus films in New York as part of a program with George Maciunas in 1966 including *Eyeblink (Fluxfilm no. 9)* [USA, 1966].) Goldmann's "Strawberry Fields Forever" does not function as an "illustration" of the song (the content of the song itself, lyrically speaking, can best be described as stream-of-consciousness). Michael Shore, in his history of the emergence of music videos, describes the promo film for "Strawberry Fields Forever" as follows:

> Richard Lester meets Kenneth Anger in the Twilight Zone, with surreal settings (mainly a cobwebbed upright piano in a meadow), chiaroscuro lighting, slow-and-backward motion, multiple overlapped images, and ominously slow dissolves to enigmatic closeups of the Beatles' faces. None of it made any sort of conventional sense; it was a nonliteral extrapolation of the song's disquieting *mood*. (Shore 1985, 36)

"Strawberry Fields Forever," then, can be seen as in the tradition of the American avant-garde cinema that Shore mentions, but the promo film has many intertexts, including earlier works of the avant-garde such as those of Mary Ellen Bute and Marie Menken, who sought to make synesthesia works.

"Penny Lane," on the other hand, depicts locales on the street Penny Lane in Liverpool, which was the basis of the song itself. These scenes are intercut with the four Beatles walking the streets and riding horses (these scenes were shot not in Liverpool but in London). While less abstract, Goldmann's "Penny

Figure 6.2   Dream-like lens flare in Goldmann's *Penny Lane*.

Lane" also deploys elliptical editing, slow motion, and the same contrast between extreme close-ups and long shots.

Significantly, The Beatles ride past their iconic stage gear on horses in a field, not stopping, leaving the old image of The Beatles behind. Implicitly, the temporality between past (the Penny Lane environs) and present (the Beatles walking through streets in the present, as if recalling the past) are juxtaposed, creating a location (past or present; reality or imagination) that is hard to firmly pin down. These two works by Goldmann were qualitatively different not only from previous promo films by The Beatles but from promo films from any other contemporaneous band, most of whom were still miming to their songs.

Goldmann's films are important, however, not simply because of their innovative aesthetic strategies, but also because they functioned as a global means to introduce vast audiences in Europe, North America, and Asia to experimental film forms through the imprimatur of The Beatles. What is also striking about these works by a Swede, which were seen all over the world, was that there is nothing in the scant biographical details that exist about Goldmann's life to suggest that he had any experience making experimental work, or that he was ever a particularly successful filmmaker. The records of his work that exist from Sweden, beyond his work on *Popside*, mostly concern his working on SvT documentaries such as editing *Secret Stockholm* (Edward Maze, 1963). Some obituaries say that he taught film at the Universities of Gothenburg and Lund, but this was long after his work with The Beatles. He spent the end of his life making documentaries in The Philippines, where he died in 2005. So, it was by chance that he made the two Swedish (or Swedish-British) films seen by a larger audience than films by any other Nordic filmmaker. And this was another principle that The Beatles were experimenting with in their music at the time: the possibilities of aleatoric art, or rather, chance. And while this chance encounter gave The Beatles a new visual vocabulary, as a migrant Goldmann also got the chance to experiment in a way that more rigid production systems, such as those he had experienced previously in Stockholm, would not allow.

Once the works were made, they were released internationally to keep audiences engaged while The Beatles worked on their forthcoming album. The reception the works received after being broadcast on *Top of the Pops* on February 16 and March 2 in the UK, on ABC's *The Hollywood Palace* on February 25, and *American Bandstand* on March 11 in the USA (Lewisohn 2003, 222, 242), *Beat Club* in Germany, and on *Popside* in Sweden was positive, even if audiences were a bit baffled by the surrealistic imagery. After the airing on *American Bandstand*, host Dick Clark polled the studio audience, who were "generally mystified" (Shore 1985, 36) by the two promo films. Keith Altham, a British rock critic, wrote about the works as both groundbreaking and beyond genre categorization at the time of their release (Altham 1967, 2). But the work of Goldmann with The Beatles also opened up another venue for them: that of multi-media art. If the elliptical surrealism of "Strawberry Fields Forever" and "Penny Lane" was compelling, when The Beatles attempted to make this kind of work on their own—such as *Magical Mystery Tour* (UK, 1967), which they directed collectively—the result was far less successful. Indeed, upon its release in the UK on BBC 1 on Boxing Day 1967, numerous critics found it to be incoherent. On December 27, for instance, The *Daily Mirror* ran a headline announcing: "Beatles' Mystery Tour Film Baffles Viewers" (Neaverson 1997, 71). Nonetheless, Goldmann provided the bridge between the cinéma vérité of Richard Lester and the avant-garde *Magical Mystery Tour*. And while the overall film was perhaps baffling, the four promo films embedded in the work—Lennon's "I Am the Walrus," Harrison's "Blue Jay Way," McCartney's "Your Mother Should Know," and, especially, "The Fool on The Hill"—were all highly evocative and quite surreal works, whose main influence can be seen as being Goldmann's promo films released just ten months earlier.

This points to another strength of Goldmann as a Nordic elsewhere film-maker: even without training in experimental film, he brought a certain ethos to his work that could be construed as positively European and Nordic. The difference between the farcical surrealism of *Magical Mystery Tour*—which could be seen as a precursor to Monty Python—and the claustrophobic atmos-phere created by the dream-like quality of his two surrealistic shorts for The Beatles is immense. Yet this feeling of claustrophobia was linked to two of the most popular songs of the 1960s; this aesthetic brought European and Swedish art cinema tropes about the exploration of interiority to audiences that would never think of going to a Bergman film. Moreover, given the time of release of the promo films, before the tsunami that was *Sgt. Pepper's Lonely Hearts Club Band* (while song cycles such as The Who's mini-opera "A Quick One, While He's Away" from December 1966, and The Mothers of Invention's *Freak Out*, released in June 1966, preceded The Beatles' album, theirs was the first that attempted to structure a complete album thematically, though Lennon stated that "it worked because we *said* it worked" [The Beatles 2000, 241]), it is his Swedish ex-pat aesthetic that introduced the world to the (now taken for granted as a cliché) image of The Beatles as psychedelic visionaries. The shift in their appearance from their last tour to these promos was, for audiences at that time, staggering. All bore mustaches, and brightly colored clothes. These attributes, combined with Goldmann's aesthetic choices, became the image of the 1960s that continues to this day.

There are other ways in which Goldmann's work was far-reaching. With the advent of MTV in 1981 (see Tannenbaum and Marks 2012), there were very few video promos around (Queen's "Bohemian Rhapsody" [Bruce Gowers,

UK, 1975] being one of the few near-contemporaneous works). As MTV looked for work to broadcast, and artists looked for models as to what kind of promos had already been made, Goldmann's aesthetic took on a new life, re-worked in videos by then-emerging artists like Duran Duran with "Rio" (Russell Mulcahy, USA, 1981) and Madonna with "Like a Virgin" (Mary Lambert, USA, 1984). Goldmann's works, then, defined not only the post-"mop top" image of The Beatles, but also the emergent language of the music video where words did not have to illustrate images, and images did not have to illustrate words.

What Goldmann's work with The Beatles illustrates, then, is not just a fortuitous moment that would most likely not be replicated today. It also functions as a means by which to trace the influence of Nordic filmmakers (ones that may not be auteurs), that vastly impacts not only the artists with which they work, but subsequent generations of artists in the same field, even if the contemporary artists in question have no idea who Peter Goldmann was. Moreover, it functions as an archeology of the ways in which certain aspects of Nordic cinema aesthetics have had a global impact based on what, in this case, was a chance encounter. Finally, it serves as a means to not overdetermine authorship: the influence of Goldmann—which synthesized modernist aesthetics from the opening montage of Bergman's *Persona* with the dream-like qualities of *Wild Strawberries* (*Smultronstället*, Ingmar Bergman, Sweden, 1957)—on The Beatles psychedelic image is mostly unknown, yet central as a part of the artistry of their own "authorship." Similarly, this same Nordic aesthetic, or its root in Goldmann's work with The Beatles, permeates music videos from the 1990s onwards. This aesthetic is wholly lacking in The Beatles' earlier films, or in the miming pop promos that dominated American and European television pop shows in the mid-1960s. While this may not make Peter Goldmann the most influential Scandinavian filmmaker ever, it does point to the fact that understanding the influence of transnational artists and aesthetics needs to move beyond the Great Man/Great Woman model of the auteur as a "visionary artist" and to explore the margins of cinema production, such as, in this particular case, rock and pop promo films and videos, to enable a better understanding of how mobility and elsewheres influence artistic practice globally.

REFERENCES

Altham, Keith. 1967. "Swedish Film Director Peter Goldmann Tells About TV-Filming with the Beatles." *New Musical Express* 1049: 2.

Andersson, Lars Gustaf, John Sundholm, and Astrid Söderbergh Widding. 2010. *A History of Swedish Experimental Film Culture: From Early Animation to Video Art*. London: John Libbey.

The Beatles. 2000. *The Beatles Anthology*. San Francisco: Chronicle Books.

The Beatles. 2015. Liner Notes. *1+*. London: Apple/Universal Music Group.
Ingham, Chris. 2003. *The Rough Guide to The Beatles*. London: Rough Guides.
Lewisohn, Mark. 2003. *The Complete Beatles Chronicle*. London: Hamlyn.
MacDonald, Ian. 1997. *Revolution in the Head: The Beatles' Records and the Sixties*, 2nd edn. London: Fourth Estate.
MacKenzie, Scott. 2017. "Kjærlighet, Klasse og Rock'n'Roll: Seksualpolitikk og det brittiske klassesystemet i *Lambert and Stamp*." *Z filmtidsskrift* 138: 54–63.
Neaverson, Bob. 1997. *The Beatles Movies*. London: Cassell.
Neill, Andy and Matt Kent. 2002. *Anyway Anyhow Anywhere: The Complete Chronicle of The Who 1958–1978*. London: Virgin.
Norman, Philip. 2008. *John Lennon: The Life*. New York: Ecco.
Shore, Michael. 1984. *The Rolling Stone Book of Rock Video*. New York: Quill.
Tannenbaum, Rob and Craig Marks. 2012. *I Want My MTV: The Uncensored Story of the Music Video Revolution*. New York: Plume.

7. OUT OF THE MARGINS OF FEMINIST FILMMAKING: VIBEKE LØKKEBERG, NORWAY, AND THE FILM CULTURE OF 1970s WEST BERLIN

Ingrid S. Holtar

Vibeke Løkkeberg has been and continues to be a pronounced feminist presence in Norwegian film, and is among the most controversial and outspoken directors to emerge in the Norwegian cinema of the 1970s and 1980s. This chapter restates her pioneering role as a feminist filmmaker by returning to the first film she directed, the overlooked short documentary *Abortion* (*Abort*, Norway, 1972) about Norwegian abortion legislation. In 1973, Løkkeberg traveled with the film to the First International Seminar on Women's Films in Berlin, a crucial event in the development of the vibrant feminist film culture in West Germany, and one of the earliest women's film festivals held in Europe. By moving Løkkeberg and *Abortion* to the geographical elsewhere of Berlin in 1973, I allow the concept to reflect not only a physical elsewhere outside of Norway, but also a conceptual elsewhere created by the nascent feminist film milieus of the 1970s. Through piecing together traces of Løkkeberg's participation at the Seminar on Women's Films and exploring *Abortion* as a feminist documentary against contexts of Norwegian cinema and international feminist film culture, I propose an elsewhere history of Løkkeberg and *Abortion* that asserts her early dedication to feminist activism and interest in exploring film language through modes of documentary realism.

An Uncompromising Auteur

For Vibeke Løkkeberg (b. 1945), the feminist mantra "The personal is political" has been a creative touchstone, and throughout her career she has combined her political dedication with her artistic practice. More than any other director of her generation, she has come to represent the director-writer, the auteur, in Norwegian film. She has written, directed, acted in, and produced nearly all of her films herself, with a significant partner in her husband, producer and long-time collaborator Terje Kristiansen. As Johanne Kielland Servoll has argued in her work on the Norwegian rendition of the concept of the auteur, Løkkeberg's film practice was from the beginning part of an existential and personal project (2014, 264). Before Løkkeberg started directing films, she was a well-known face from her modeling career for European fashion houses, and as an actor in the celebrated new wave films *Liv* (Norway, 1967) and *Exit* (Norway, 1970), directed by her first husband Pål Løkkeberg. *Liv* was conceived as a shared feminist project based on Løkkeberg's own experience of alienation from her work as a model, and even though she functioned as script-writer and co-producer in addition to playing the title character, the film seemed to solidify an image of her as an onscreen object of desire, and as her husband's creative muse. Her documentary practice in the early 1970s came to signify the starting point for her transition into a filmmaker in her own right, putting at stake a move from object to subject. Servoll summarized this as follows:

> After cutting off her long locks and putting her marriage behind her, Vibeke Løkkeberg went to the Norwegian Broadcasting Corporation's department for public information and got to make several social issues documentaries, some with clear gender perspectives, such as *Abortion* (1970), *Gypsies* (1973), and *A Child Needs a Father* (1974). (Servoll 2014, 265, my translation)

From this starting point, Løkkeberg developed a film career that has been uncompromisingly personal, decidedly political, and above all provocative. Løkkeberg has relentlessly explored issues of female sexuality, family relations, violence, and power through a style grounded in kitchen-sink realism imbued with visual imagery bordering on the surrealist and painterly. Her 1977 feature film debut, *The Revelation* (*Åpenbaringen*, Norway), is a devastating portrayal of the breakdown of a middle-aged woman who feels she no longer has a purpose in life. Løkkeberg's breakthrough followed in 1981 with the highly autobiographical *Kamilla* (*Løperjenten*, Norway), set in the immediate postwar Bergen of her childhood. *Kamilla* is still one of few Norwegian films with a theatrical release in the USA. Despite *Kamilla*'s success and the positive reception of the film, Løkkeberg found it increasingly difficult to obtain funding from the Norwegian State Film Fund during the 1980s and onward. *Vilde, the Wild One* (*Hud*, Norway, 1986) and *Seagulls* (*Måker*, Norway, 1991), both dealing with the historical oppression of women, received considerable backlash from critics. For her final film projects, Løkkeberg looked outside the border to engage in filmmaking elsewheres with the highly controversial anti-war films *Where Gods Are Dead* (*Der gudene er døde*, Norway, 1993), filmed in an active war zone in former Yugoslavia, and *The Tears of Gaza* (*Gazas tårer*, Norway, 2010), a documentary about children in occupied Palestine. Centering as they do on marginalized groups and drawing attention to silenced forms of abuse, such as incest in *Vilde, the Wild One* or marital rape in *Kamilla* and *The Revelation*, Løkkeberg's films can be understood as constituting elsewhere stories. Moving back to her early career and the narrative of growing political commitment and artistic ambition, *Abortion* figures as a locus for Løkkeberg's unapologetically personal and political filmmaking practice.

Abortion and Norwegian Women's Cinema

To begin within its Norwegian context, *Abortion* is a pioneering work in the development of a Norwegian women's cinema. With *Abortion*, Løkkeberg stated her subjectivity and her claim as a director by explicitly engaging in the struggle for legislative change on abortion. This was one of the major political achievements of the Norwegian women's liberation movement, culminating with the implementation of self-determined abortion in 1978 (Haukaa 1982). Løkkeberg started working on the film in the late 1960s, but due to funding issues she was only able to complete it around 1971 after receiving additional funding from the Ministry of Health. The film uses a frame story about sixteen-year-old Kirsten (Ege Askildsen), who must deal with an unwanted pregnancy and her experience of applying for an abortion to the Abortion Appeals Board (Abortnemnda). Other women supplement Kirsten's story through voiceovers, giving different perspectives on what an unplanned pregnancy and a rejected application for abortion could entail. These personal narratives are intercut with interviews with doctors who publicly supported women's right to abortion, as well as interviews with anti-abortion activists. The film ends with a montage showing Raphael's painting *Madonna with Child*, intercut with clips from Norwegian protests against EU membership, which, next to the fight for self-determined abortion, was the other defining political issue of the decade. The montage is set to a Norwegian rendition of Bertolt Brecht and Hanns Eisler's song *The Ballad of Paragraph 218* (*Lied vom Paragraphen 218*, 1929), also known as *Abortion Is Illegal*, sung by Løkkeberg herself. The film was shown on domestic television in 1972 without the closing montage in order to comply with the state-run Norwegian Broadcasting Corporation's policy

Figure 7.1 Frame grab from Løkkeberg's *Abortion* (*Abort*, Norway, 1972), depicting Ege Askildsen (right) as a young girl experiencing an unwanted pregnancy.

of neutral programming, a decision based on the contention that Løkkeberg's own opinion about self-determined abortion was too explicit in the sequence. Norwegian film societies and women's liberation groups organized events that screened the film in its entirety.

With the film's explicit ties to the women's liberation movement, *Abortion* can be read as part of the broad field of the emerging transnational feminist film culture of the 1970s known as cinefeminism (Rich 1998; White 2015, 205). In Scandinavia, Løkkeberg had contemporaries connected to cinefeminism in, for instance, Mai Zetterling in Sweden, or Jytte Rex and Mette Knudsen in Denmark. Zetterling's career in particular (for which see also Mariah Larsson's chapter in this volume) stands as an interesting point of comparison for Løkkeberg as an art house director who also made activist documentaries and realized her films by seeking possibilities elsewhere outside of Sweden and feature film-making (Larsson and Stenport 2015). In the case of cinefeminism in Norway, feminist concerns in film became most forcefully evident in the women's cinema that appeared in the latter half of the 1970s with the distinct (re)appearance of women directors in the mostly male-dominated film industry. So-called "women's films" (kvinnefilm) became a central genre designation, with a string of short and feature films by directors Laila Mikkelsen (*Weekend/Ukeslutt*, Norway, 1974), Anja Breien (*Wives/Hustruer*, Norway, 1975; *Games of Love and Loneliness/Den allvarsamma leken*, Norway/Sweden, 1977), Nicole Macé

(*The Guardians/Formynderne*, Norway, 1978), and Per Blom (*The Women/ Kvinnene*, Norway, 1979), in addition to the films made by Løkkeberg herself. Norwegian women's cinema did not break new ground solely by centering on women's stories and experiences. Films like Breien's seminal *Wives* and Løkkeberg's *The Revelation* represent the forefront of Norwegian social modernism. In this landscape, Løkkeberg's treatment of feminist issues in *Abortion* prior to the 1970s positions her as a forerunner of Norwegian feminist filmmaking. As Løkkeberg travels with the film to the First International Seminar on Women's Films in Berlin, her filmmaking practice finds its place within what I envision as the "feminist elsewhere" of the transnational feminist film culture.

The Feminist Elsewhere of the 1970s

"Women must challenge the managers of mass media: blatant male dominance in the whole of Western Europe and the USA" (Ramnefjell 1974, my translation). This was the headline of a short news story about Løkkeberg in the daily newspaper *Dagbladet*, where she was interviewed about her participation at the Seminar on Women's Films in Berlin. When I propose that the Seminar on Women's Films constitutes a feminist elsewhere for Løkkeberg's documentary practice, there is more at stake than discussion of a country that Løkkeberg traveled to and a venue where she screened her film. Rather, I am referring to a political space created for and by women who faced discrimination, marginalization or isolation in their work in film and television, who believed in the possibility of social change and an equal future, and who wanted to create new ways of seeing through filmmaking practices.

The Seminar on Women's Films in Berlin was a groundbreaking event precisely as a feminist meeting place for women working in film and television (Knight 1992, 102–3). The filmmakers Claudia von Alemann and Helke Sander, central if lesser-known figures in the male-dominated New German Cinema, initiated and organized the four-day event. It was held at the independent cinema Kino Arsenal, established in 1970 by the Friends of the German Film Archive (Freunde der Deutschen Kinemathek), which was also the seminar's main film distributor. The seminar screened 45 films by and about women from Germany, Norway, Denmark, France, Italy, the UK, and the USA, and included post-screening discussions and workshops. Julia Knight has argued that the Berlin seminar adopted a pioneering role in two ways which moved it beyond simply screening available works by women. Firstly, Sander and Alemann focused the program around an overt educational goal by screening films that would offer critical representations and analyses of women's situations. Secondly, with its more than 250 participants the seminar provided an invaluable elsewhere at a time when most women in film worked in isolation (Knight, 102–3).

The cultural significance of the women's film festivals as forums for the burgeoning feminist film culture is hard to overemphasize. In the words of B. Ruby Rich: "women's film festivals were experimental laboratories, producing new feminist cinematic consciousness while simultaneously putting into practice the political commitment behind the activity" (1998, 31). Not only did the festivals and similar events provide women and men with the opportunity to see and discuss the surge of new films made by women, they also contributed to the development of discourses on women and film. These were arenas of discovery and debate, a feminist elsewhere born out of the synergy between the political ideas and activism of the women's liberation movement and practices of cinema (Rich 1998, 65). While Løkkeberg was attending the seminar, she used the opportunity to record interviews with other women participants from the film and television sector in Europe and the USA for a film project she called *Women in Media* (*Kvinner i media*). The film was supposed to be a takedown of male domination in the sector, built around shared experiences among women across borders and across media, but it was never completed. Løkkeberg had funding from the Norwegian production company Centralfilm AS, which mainly produced short documentaries known as culture films, but according to Løkkeberg they lost interest in the project and most traces of the film have since disappeared. While we cannot access what Løkkeberg's lost film could have shown us about the encounters at the Berlin seminar, we can imagine—assume, even—the energy and sense of unity created through screenings, discussions, and sharing of experiences. If we allow some imaginative leeway, Løkkeberg's elusive film project attests to the political commitment and sense of community attaching to the time and space created by the feminist elsewhere, and to Løkkeberg's place within it.

Reclaiming Early Feminist Documentary

Lest we forget that cinefeminism began with films, I wish to return now to the film itself and to *Abortion* as a feminist documentary. Yet here we face a problem in writing film history elsewhere: that of finding what is not *here* and of coming to terms with the displacement itself. If elsewhere history can be understood as approaching the past through the lens of a different place or space outside the place from where the history is usually narrated, there is also at stake a historiographical question of access, removal, and recovery. While *Women in Media* is a lost project, *Abortion* is an obscure film. At the time of writing, the film is only available for viewing at the Norwegian National Library and thus is largely inaccessible save to dedicated researchers. This is a common situation. The hundreds of films that traversed the early women's film festival networks are mostly lost today, and only a few are available in digital formats. Shilyh Warren, in her work recovering the early feminist documentary in the USA, has termed this "the 'real' problem of the feminist film movement," where lack of access to early feminist films is mirrored in the marginalization of feminist documentary in the intellectual history of film feminism itself, still influenced by a bias toward formally experimental and avant-garde work by women developed in feminist film theory of the 1970s (Juhasz 1999; Waldman and Walker 1999; Warren 2008). However, most films made by women in these years were indeed documentaries, as it was difficult for women to gain access to the male-dominated structures of feature film production, but also seen as necessary to create alternative filmmaking practices outside of the mainstream in order to pursue new cinematic representations (Rich 1998). The development of 16mm cameras offered a relatively inexpensive and accessible way into filmmaking for women who wanted to make films as part of the political commitment of the women's liberation movement. In the tradition of direct cinema and cinéma vérité, the feminist documentaries centered on women's experiences and struggles, showing ordinary women as they had hardly ever been shown on any cinema or television screen before. Alexandra Juhasz has argued for both the plurality and sophistication of the early feminist documentary, and for the political project at stake in even the most "naively realist moments" of these films (1999). According to Warren, the feminist documentaries were radical, telling "stories that were supposed to be kept secret" (2008).

Løkkeberg's film *Abortion* was about such a secret tale, and the film itself and the Seminar on Women's Films in Berlin can constitute a European elsewhere for the continued reconsideration of feminist documentary, which has predominantly been approached from an Anglo-American perspective. Løkkeberg's film follows a trajectory of feminist documentary on abortion of telling rather than showing (Warren 2015). It is through spoken words in voiceover, interviews, and scripted dialogue that Løkkeberg makes her case for self-determined abortion. However, the film differs from the feminist documentaries in the USA discussed by Warren (2008) and Juhasz (1999) in its intermixing of different documentary strategies. Indeed, Alemann and Sander's use of the term "analytical documentary" (1974, 40) to categorize *Abortion* opens up a reading of Løkkeberg's documentary style as an attempt to develop an epistemological argument about women's right to self-determined abortion. The changing discourses and documentary modes of the film offer multiple and distinct cinematic realisms, through which Løkkeberg seems to suggest that only the pregnant woman herself knows her reality and her situation well enough to be able to decide whether she can have the child or not. With the film's particular focus on the socio-economical aspects of women's reproductive rights, this furthermore becomes a material argument. The women who share their stories of unplanned pregnancies do not tell us about their experience of the abortion procedure itself, or indeed about their experience of applying to the Abortion Appeals Board, but about their situation and their reasons for wanting the abortion. Løkkeberg introduces each woman by name, income, and family situation in voiceover, in this way pointing to both the concrete and the specific situation of each woman and to the class aspect of the legislation. The film ends with a closing montage that links myths of motherhood to the political economy, positioning the right to self-determined abortion as a political issue rather than an individual or medical one. This conclusion was too radical a statement in the public discussion in Norway, yet fully at home in the feminist elsewhere among filmmakers trying to find ways of using the film medium to develop a new feminist consciousness and new feminist analysis.

At Home, Elsewhere

This elsewhere history of Løkkeberg and her feminist documentary *Abortion* began with a geographical elsewhere: Løkkeberg's participation at the Seminar on Women's Film in Berlin in 1973. From this physical place, I envisioned a different kind of elsewhere as a conceptual space for community, political activism and the development of cinematic analysis. I argue that Løkkeberg found herself at home in this feminist elsewhere. Out of the margins of feminist filmmaking, Løkkeberg arrives as a pioneering Norwegian filmmaker committed to uniting her artistic ambition with her dedication to feminist politics.

References

Alemann, Claudia and Helke Sander. 1974. *Zur Situation der Frau. Modellseminar, Film- und Literaturverzeichnis*. Berlin: Freunde der Deutschen Kinematek eV.
Haukaa, Runa. 1982. *Bak slagordene: Den nye kvinnebevegelsen i Norge*. Oslo: Pax.
Juhasz, Alexandra. 1999. "They Said We Were Trying to Show Reality—All I Want to Show Is My Video: The Politics of the Realist Feminist Documentary." In *Collecting Visual Evidence*, ed. Jane M. Gaines and Michael Renov. Minneapolis: University of Minnesota Press. 190–215.
Knight, Julia. 1992. *Women and the New German Cinema*. London: Verso.
Larsson, Mariah and Anna Westerstahl Stenport. 2015. "Documentary filmmaking as colonialist propaganda and cinefeminist intervention: Mai Zetterling's *Of Seals and Men* (1979)." *Film History* 27(4): 106–29. doi: 10.2979/filmhistory.27.4.106.
Ramnefjell, Erling. 1974. "Kvinnene må utfordre sjefene i massemedia." *Dagbladet*, January 19.
Rich, B. Ruby. 1998. *Chick Flicks: Theories and Memories of the Feminist Film Movement*. Durham, NC: Duke University Press.
Servoll, Johanne Kielland. 2014. *Den norske auteuren. En begrepshistorisk analyse*. PhD dissertation, University of Oslo.
Waldman, Diane and Janet Walker. 1999. "Introduction." In *Feminism and Documentary*, ed. Diane Waldman and Janet Walker. Minneapolis: University of Minnesota Press.

Warren, Shilyh. 2008. "By, for and about. the 'real' problem in the feminist film movement." *Mediascape: The UCLA's Journal for Film and Media Studies* 4(2) (Fall). <http://www.tft.ucla.edu/mediascape/Fall08_Warren.html>

Warren, Shilyh. 2015. "Abortion, abortion, abortion, still: documentary show and tell." *The South Atlantic Quarterly* 114(4) (October): 755–79. <http://doi.org/10.1215/00382876-3157122>

White, Patricia. 2015. *Women's Cinema, World Cinema: Projecting Contemporary Feminisms*. Durham, NC: Duke University Press.

8. THE GOTHENBURG INTERNATIONAL EXILE FILM FESTIVAL IN CONTEXT

Boel Ulfsdotter and Mats Björkin

In 1993, two Iranian immigrants to Sweden, Hossein Mahini and Hassan Mahini, launched a film festival, Exilfilmfestivalen (The Exile Film Festival), in Sweden's second-largest city Gothenburg for films related to exile and refugee experiences. The first two editions focused on Iranian film in exile and screened a total of 122 films (64 and 58 respectively) made by Iranians living in exile in over a dozen countries. The festival has since been renamed and is now known as the "International Exile Film Festival" (IEFF), and has broadened its scope by including films from many countries as well as collaborating with similar ventures internationally. The programming of the festival thereby represents the large range of exilic, diasporic, ethnic, immigrant, and refugee communities that are part of the contemporary public sphere in Sweden and beyond. In this way, IEFF also constitutes an overlooked elsewhere of cinematic programming outside of the main commercial, art house, or mainstream film festivals. Under the tagline "The World Is My Home," the IEFF presents itself as a "free forum for filmmakers in exile to express themselves and screen their films—regardless of the filmmakers' national, ethnic or religious affiliation" (International Exile Film Festival n.d.), while also inviting "non-exile filmmakers to present [work] that features themes of exile, immigration, and democracy" (International Exile Film Festival n.d.).

IEFF is part of a local, national, and international ecosystem that circulates non-Western films in general, and exile or diaspora films in particular. Prominent examples include the Diaspora Film Festival in Toronto (see Jäckel

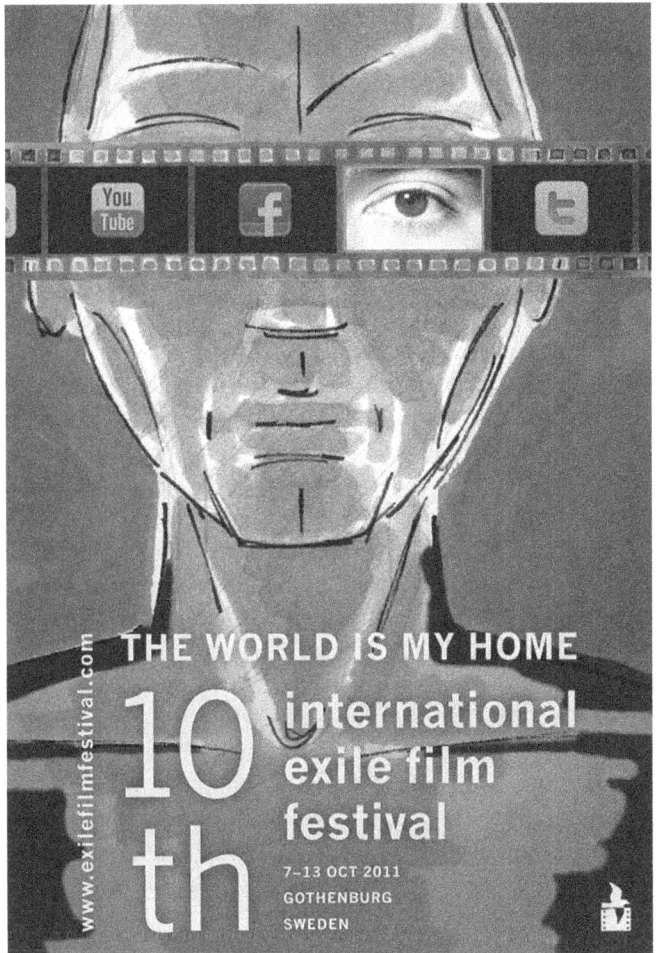

Figure 8.1 "The World is My Home." Poster for the 10th International Exile Film Festival, in Gothenburg, Sweden, 2011.

2010, 88; Naficy 2012, 408), which operates, like IEFF, in the broader context of film festivals that have, in the words of Thomas Elsaesser, "increasingly invested in upgrading the term 'world cinema' into a quality label" (2005, 504). The particulars of IEFF are striking, however, as this festival makes an intervention into Gothenburg suburbs that otherwise rarely see this kind of cinematic programming. This chapter examines both the local and the broader context and inquires into how to situate IEFF in local, national, and international contexts, especially in relation to influential film theory paradigms such as Fernando Solanas' and Octavio Getino's Third Cinema (1969), Hamid Naficy's "accented cinema" (2001), and Asuman Suner's concept of "accented cinema at large" (2006). The chapter also discusses the history of exilic cinephilia cultures in Sweden. By so doing, it introduces a range of cinematic elsewheres that are usually not included in a national film history.

Film Festivals in Sweden

Film festivals came late to Sweden. With the exception of a minor short film festival founded in Stockholm during the 1950s, it was not until the inauguration of the Gothenburg International Film Festival (GIFF) in 1979 that the festival circuit took off. GIFF has gradually become the largest public film festival in northern Europe and an important meeting point for the Nordic film and television drama industries, as well as a major popular event in the city of Gothenburg at the end of January each year. GIFF was followed, as a traditional, international art house film festival, by Umeå in 1986–2007 and Stockholm (1990–), the latter slightly more commercial in its selection of films. In 1996, acclaimed film director Bo Widerberg started a politically and aesthetically more critical, non-commercial alternative to the major festivals, the Lilla filmfestival [The Small Film Festival], in the summer resort of Båstad. After his death in 1997, it was taken over by documentary filmmaker Stefan Jarl. More thematic, or specialized, festivals followed suit, for example the Uppsala International Short Film Festival (1982–), the International Children and Young People's Film Festival in Malmö, BUFF [Barn-och ungdomsfilmfestivalen] (1984–), Lund International Fantastic Film Festival (1995–), and Tempo Documentary Festival (Stockholm 1998–). This proliferation indicates the role of festivals for key areas of Swedish cultural politics in terms of support of young filmmakers and films for children, the importance of participatory cultures (in this case fantasy and science fiction fans), and nonfiction film and television.

Exile or Diasporic Film Festivals

During the past two decades, a growing body of film festivals around the world have aimed to build identity by "addressing loyal audiences within the community or by trying to reach out and combat deeply ingrained prejudices and misconceptions" (Iordanova and Cheung 2010, 4). Two film festivals that started during the 1990s in Sweden were responses to political controversies and academic discourses. The Stockholm Jewish Film Festival (1992–) served as a response to the anti-Semitic right-wing tendency at the time, and the CinemAfrica Festival (Stockholm 1996–) emerged as an answer to the growing attention to postcolonial theory at Swedish universities and in the media. Both festivals explicitly addressed racism and prejudice against minorities, and were conceptualized, at least partly, to build and strengthen communities.

The more recent Malmö Arab Film Festival (2011–) may be connected to a stronger community-building function, seen in conjunction with the high levels of immigration from the Middle East since the beginning of the 2000s. Refugee groups arriving in Sweden from Latin America in the 1970s and 1980s neither started nor were the target audience of exile and diapora film festivals until the Panoramica Latin American Film Festival in Stockholm (2014–). The labor immigration from Finland, Italy, or the former Yugoslavia dating from the 1950s and 1960s has been even less represented or involved in nation- or ethno-specific film festivals. In the Swedish film festival context, there has thus been a difference between exilic communities representing labor immigrants and those representing refugees, as well as differences in region, location, and time period. Exile film festivals seem to be a contemporary phenomenon. Given the prominence of Latin American filmmakers and intellectuals in formulating a notion of Third Cinema (e.g. Solanas and Getino 2014 [1969]) and the fact that Latin America has been at the forefront of politically engaged filmmaking, both domestically and in exile, since the 1960s, this history cannot explain the lack of Latin American film festivals in Sweden. It is therefore reasonable to argue that the development of film festivals in Sweden is determined more by international film festival trends than by the structure of exile communities in Sweden. How, then, can we understand exile films in a Swedish film festival context?

Theorizing the International Exile Film Festival

Film scholar Hamid Naficy has referred to film festivals focusing on exile filmmakers as venues that argue for "comparative exilism and diasporism" (Naficy 2001, 85). In his discussion of IEFF, Naficy situates the festival as part of a social history of Iranian cinema that has broadened the notion of what "Iranian cinema" is, suggesting, though he does not use the concept, that IEFF constitutes an "elsewhere" of that country's film production and circulation. He writes that IEFF "added a diasporic dimension to Iranian filmic identity . . . mapping the global dispersion of Iranian diaspora communities" (2012, 409). Naficy has also argued that "exile is inexorably tied to homeland and to the possibility of return. However, the frustrating elusiveness of return makes it magically potent" (Naficy 1999, 3). IEFF's work functions as a bridge between these positions of exile.

IEFF's origin as a festival about Iranian exile has evolved to include a wide range of artistic expressions and audience desires. IEFF has also garnered international recognition for its approach to exilic filmmaking and for its contributions to broadening cinephilia culture in Sweden, with Mahini being invited to the USA to present his work (Domellöf-Wik 2017). The focus on "'exile' as a global question" (Naficy 2012, 409) is discernible in the programming of the

IEFF, which over the years has welcomed a broad range of cinematic expressions and filmmakers from diverse backgrounds. Several films by Swedish-Palestinian documentary filmmaker Mai Masri have been screened over the years, such as *Frontiers of Dreams and Fears* (2001) and *3000 Nights* (2015). Slovakia-based Sahraa Karimi's award-winning *Afghan Women Behind the Wheel* (2008) represents her debut as a documentary filmmaker. The film was immediately screened at the IEFF, which reflects the organizers' grounded expertise in the field as well as their stated emphasis on supporting women filmmakers and feminist films (Holmberg 2017). The popular films screened include productions in the comedy genre, such as the 2017 French opening film *Some Like It Veiled* (Sou Abadi, 2017)

IEFF's main focus, and the main section in the festival program, have been aimed at showing the works of filmmakers in exile. Many editions of the festival have also included supplementary programs, including films by "non-exiled film-makers about immigrants and people in exile" ("Long Shot | Another View," Program 2003), or another film program "about people's movements towards the globalization of social justice and democracy" ("Odyssey of Cinema—Freedom Odyssey," Program 2009). The festival also organizes discussions, concerts, and other events. Most screenings have taken place in art house cinemas in central Gothenburg, but also in cinemas, theaters, municipal libraries, community centers, and other public spaces in suburbs such as Angered and Lundby Hisingen, areas of Gothenburg that represent a diverse demographic of recent immigrants. The festival seems to have been reasonably successful in terms of box office. For example, in 2007, approximately 4000 tickets were sold to around 90 films (Cato and Domellöf-Wik 2009). Press coverage of the festival is mainly local and regional. Although the festival reaches out well in Gothenburg, it is rarely mentioned by the major newspapers in Stockholm. To Mahini, IEFF's artistic director, varied and accessible screening locations are central to the festival's ethos: "Since most of our films are about immigrants and their experiences, it is natural that we locate the festival in those suburbs of Gothenburg where most of the city's immigrants live" (Holmgren 2017; our translation). In comparison, the Gothenburg International Film Festival has, over the years, had few screening venues in these suburbs, focusing instead on the city center. The IEFF is therefore geographically and socially more diversely present in different parts of Gothenburg.

IEFF does not use an elaborate genre or stylistic categorization of films, focusing instead on foregrounding films with exilic themes. Basically, the main categories used are "fiction," "documentary," and "experimental" films. The overall aim and content of the festival, as well as its physical presence in areas where many people with exile experiences live, have been rather consistent over the years. It is more difficult to trace any aesthetic patterns in the festival's selection of films. If we use Naficy's concept of "accented cinema" as stemming from "what the filmmakers have in common: liminal subjectivity and interstitial location in society and the film industry" (Naficy 2001, 11), as well as the mode of production and funding of blockbusters around the world, it is hardly surprising that there are few big budget films at the festival. It is reasonable to argue that filmmakers in exile, who also want to tell stories about exile experiences, rarely get access to big production budgets. Naficy's understanding of accented cinema as a legacy of Third Cinema, because they "work independently, outside of the studio system or the mainstream film industries, using two chief modes of production: interstitial and collective" (Naficy 2010, 14), may be relevant for some of the experimental films screened at the festival, but is too narrow to explicate the general programming rationale.

Though Naficy's paradigm has been very influential for understanding exilic production and cinephilia cultures, Asuman Suner's concept of "accented cinema at large" (2006) may be more relevant in terms of critically describing the films programmed at the festival. To mitigate the risk of essentializing accented cinema, Suner introduces the concept "accented cinema at large" to underline practices and trends that cut across national and exilic or diaspora limits in filmmaking today. According to Suner, such a point of departure would still bring questions of belonging and identity to the fore, but not so much from the point of view of the exiled per se. Suner dismisses Naficy's narrow reading of accented cinema as a successor to the Third Cinema projects of the 1960s on the grounds that this ignores the multiplicity of experiences of exile and diaspora. It also turns the exilic position into an exotic point of view, leaving many forms of authorship to the side (Suner 2006, 377–8). Instead, the narratives would revolve around issues related to ethnicity, gender, and class in relation to the author's present situation as an immigrant in a new country (Suner 2006, 379). Suner's interpretation better describes the combination of films by exile filmmakers and films about exile in focus at the festival. For instance, François Verster's *The Dream of Sharazad* (South Africa, 2014) examines the Arab Spring political movement from a female storyteller's perspective, interweaving the legend of *A Thousand and One Nights* to argue that women of the Middle East have been struggling for independence for many hundreds of years. Shot in English and Arabic by a French director, and co-produced by a range of units in multiple countries and with funding from multiple countries, this film exemplifies Suner's expanded notion of accented cinema.

The International Exile Film Festival as an Art House Festival about Exile

The move from accented cinema to accented cinema at large is not only a theoretical dispute, but a way of describing the move from the films of Iranian exile filmmakers presented in the first edition of the Exile Film Festival to the diversity and multiplicity of perspectives showcased in the most recent editions. With regard to François Verster's film, *The Dream of Sharazad*, it is our contention that having a French director with no further connection to the diaspora or exile communities around the world lead such a multilingual and openly political film project in allegorical form, which is also of pivotal interest to any cinema audience, goes beyond Naficy's original matrix for accented cinema. We see a similar development in several recently programmed documentaries. Some of these focus on exile and human rights, such as *Gulistan, Land of Roses* (Zayne Akyol, Canada/Germany, 2016). This film exposes the hidden female, feminist face of a revolutionary Kurdish group united by a common vision of freedom. Similarly, *French Suburbe—A No-go Zone?* (Alexandre Stern, Switzerland, 2017) examines civic unrest in French cities during the election campaign in 2016. These films were part of IEFF's 2017 program and address political and transnational content while still being made by non-exilic filmmakers. As Hossein Mahini explains in an interview, a focus on feminist filmmakers, such as Zayne Akyol, is an important tool for defining the festival's socio-political and multicultural agenda (Holmberg 2017).

The unwavering political agency which characterizes the directorial approach in some of these documentaries places them in close vicinity to some of the iterations of Third Cinema, but hardly close to accented cinema. This, together with the observation that the most crowd-pleasing of the IEFF's films are screened at two well-known art house cinemas, Hagabion and Bio Roy in downtown Gothenburg, for maximal exposure, leads us to the conclusion that any nationally exilic mode of production represented by these films has become normalized, in particular, in European art house film production. A common characteristic of films screened at the festival is, therefore, rather, their conditions of production; they are produced on restricted budgets, and performed outside the mainstream commercial film industries. These films are therefore not likely to be picked up by the commercial entertainment cinemas, which is also the reason why they are presented as art house cinema fare by the festival. From a cultural studies perspective they are therefore indeed physically if not narratively exiled from mainstream cinema venues.

To conclude, the IEFF may represent a case where exile film festivals have run their course, given the ever-increasing impetus of globalization in the cultural spheres of every country today. Sweden's public sphere is increasingly shaped by multicultural and multiethnic priorities. The Swedish Film Institute (SFI), like Swedish Television (SVT), has for many years encouraged film projects reflecting a number of diverse viewpoints, backgrounds, and experiences. The notion of exilic, diasporic, and accented cinemas in relation to the International Exile Film Festival in Gothenburg thus merits further inquiry, especially given that the festival has been running for 25 years. This has been a period of paramount social change in Sweden, in terms of both its demography and its socio-cultural landscape. Could it be that the original purpose, showcasing films by directors in exile, is not enough to reflect the conditions of refugees or immigrants today? Should the festival rather be seen as a representative of a niche cinema veering toward art house film? Given the widespread aims of Hossein Mahini and Hassan Mahini as film festival producers, their international festival ambitions certainly represent rich research material for anyone interested in the notions of accented and exilic/diaspora cinema and Third Cinema, as well as transnational and minor cinemas, in relation to the genealogy used for film festival programming.

REFERENCES

Cato, Carl and Maria Domellöf-Wik. 2009. "Iran i fokus på årets Exilfilmfestival." *Göteborgs-Posten*, October 20. No pagination.

Domellöf-Wik, Maria. 2017. "Hossein Mahini hoppas få visa film i USA," *Göteborgs-Posten*, May. <http://www.gp.se/kultur/hossein-mahini-hoppas-f%C3%A5-visa-film-i-usa-1.4261085> (last accessed October 3, 2018).

Elsaesser, Thomas. 2005. *European Cinema: Face to Face with Hollywood*. Amsterdam: University of Amsterdam Press.

Holmgren, Tobias. 2017. "Dags för trettonde Exilfilmfestivalen i Göteborg." *Göteborgs-Posten*. November, 16. <http://www.gp.se/kultur/film/dags-f%C3%B6r-trettonde-exilfilmfestivalen-i-g%C3%B6teborg-1.4833752> (last accessed October 3, 2018).

International Exile Film Festival. n.d. "Manifesto: The world is my home | International Exile Film Festival." <http://exilefilmfestival.com/about/manifesto/> (last accessed May 27, 2018).

Iordanova, Dina and Ruby Cheung. 2010. "Introduction." In *Film Festival Yearbook 2: Film Festivals and Imagined Communities*, ed. Dina Iordanova and Ruby Cheung. St Andrews: St Andrews Film Studies. 1–10.

Jäckel, Anne. 2010. "State and Other Funding for Migrant, Diasporic, and World Cinemas in Europe." In *European Cinema in Motion: Migrant and Diasporic Film in Contemporary Europe*, ed. Daniela Berghahn and Claudia Sternberg. London: Palgrave Macmillan. 76–94.

Naficy, Hamid. 1999. "Introduction: Framing Exile from Homeland to Homepage." In *Home, Exile, Homeland: Film, Media, and the Politics of Place*, ed. Hamid Naficy. New York; London: Routledge. 1–13.

Naficy, Hamid. 2001. *An Accented Cinema: Exilic and Diasporic Filmmaking*. Princeton: Princeton University Press.

Naficy, Hamid. 2010. "Multiplicity and multiplexing in today's cinemas: Diasporic cinema, art cinema, and mainstream cinema." *Journal of Media Practice* 11(1): 11–20.

Naficy, Hamid. 2012. *A Social History of Iranian Cinema*, Vol. 4. Durham, NC: Duke University Press.
Solanas, Fernando and Octavio Getino. 2014 [1969]. "Toward a Third Cinema" ("Hacia un tercer cine"). In *Film Manifestos and Global Cinema Cultures: A Critical Anthology*, ed. Scott MacKenzie. Berkeley: University of California Press. 230–50.
Suner, Asuman. 2006. "Outside in: 'accented cinema' at large." *Inter-Asia Cultural Studies* 7(3): 363–82.

PART II

INTERMEDIARIES

9. OPENING UP THE POSTWAR WORLD IN COLOR: 1950s GEOPOLITICS AND SPECTACULAR NORDIC COLONIALISM IN THE ARCTIC AND IN AFRICA

Anna Westerstahl Stenport

This chapter examines the elsewheres that opened up Scandinavian film cultures globally in the 1950s. Reflecting international developments in genre, style, and mode of production, and the increased postwar mobility of people and technologies, the impact on Scandinavian film production and cinema cultures was transformative. This included: access to new shooting locations; lighter cameras and better on-site sound uptake; a motivation to film in color and in spectacular "-scopes" that could immerse cinemagoers in (exotic) scenery; reactions against television's small and monochromatic screens and domestic embeddedness; and the demise of the newsreel, which prompted a shift in representational technique from reporting to documentary. Locations closely tied to Scandinavia's long-standing colonial practices and their environments and cultures were mobilized in several visually spectacular films of the 1950s that were made for international circulation by major production companies. This chapter examines two of these regions, the Arctic and Africa, and their portrayal in spectacular 1950s cinema.

Big-budget spectacles had introduced "the Arctic" to audiences at home and abroad by the mid-1950s, as demonstrated by the documentary *Where Mountains Float* (*Hvor bjergene sejler*, Bjarne Henning-Jensen, Denmark, 1955), the melodrama *Qivitoq: The Mountain Wanderer* (*Qivitoq: Fjeldgængeren*, Erik Balling, Denmark, 1956), and the romance *Make Way for Lila* (*Laila*, Rolf Husberg, Sweden, 1958). At the same time, the action drama *Gorilla Safari* (*Gorilla: En filmberättelse från Belgiska Kongo*, Lars-Henrik

Ottoson, Sven Nykvist, and Lorens Marmstedt, Sweden, 1956) presented cultures and animal life of Central West Africa in sensationalist manner.

Undoubtedly colonial, ethnocentric, and also racist, these films convey a geopolitics that illustrates the international ramifications of the 1950s Nordic Model. This model stipulated a comprehensive, transparent, and efficiently organized welfare state with an extensive social safety net; a continuous balancing act to mitigate the tensions of the Cold War without large active-duty militaries; increasing secularism built on Lutheranism's emphasis on community; and public investments in education, health, and gender equality. These foundational ideologies of the Nordic Model were widely exported around the world, including as part of Dag Hammarskjöld's election in 1953 as Secretary-General of the United Nations, and through Foreign Aid projects in the developing world. Examining a little-known sub-genre of what I call the Scandinavian spectacular big-budget color film of the 1950s, this chapter addresses films made for international distribution and about regions that were deliberately construed as "elsewheres" for both domestic and international audiences. I analyze how these films illustrate the complex immediate postwar geopolitical context of the small nation states of Scandinavia.

Spectacular Cinema Cultures in 1950s Scandinavia

Most film historians understand 1950s American cinema production and culture as reactive, responding to the decline in cinema admissions after World War II and to the impact of television—the small, convenient box that brought both entertainment and news into the increasingly suburban home. McCarthyism was also to blame for the reactionary nature of the 1950s cinema landscape, with Republican attacks on leftist and liberal filmmakers and labor in Hollywood. While US cinema admissions rose between 1940 and 1946, ticket sales dropped quickly after World War II, and by 1956 attendance was down almost 50 percent from its 1946 peak (Lev 2003a, 7–8). This decline in cinema attendance is generally attributed to the rise of television. Developments in Scandinavia must be seen in relation to the US context because of Hollywood's pervasiveness, although the impact of television did not hit the Scandinavian film industry until almost a decade later (see Soila et al. 1998, 195 and 130).

In the 1950s, priorities in the USA and international film industry shifted toward color, widescreen, and "the motion picture's capacity for spectacle" (Lev 2003b, 107). For instance, the non-proprietary Eastman Color film was introduced in 1950 as a one-strip process that did not need special cameras, which facilitated filming in color in Hollywood and beyond, unseating the dominance of the Technicolor Corporation. Introduced in 1952, Cinerama never became mainstream. Its first film, *This Is Cinerama* (Merian C. Cooper; Gunther von Fritsch, USA, 1952), was a travel potpourri of Europe and the USA. A success with critics and audiences, *This is Cinerama* promoted adventure and "foreign" environments and cultures to a middle class poised to take advantage of the emergence of mass travel. Shortly thereafter, the CinemaScope format and other widescreen ratios (2.35:1) opened bigger windows to the world. In the Introduction to *Widescreen Worldwide*, John Belton, Sheldon Hall, and Steve Neale argue that these changes had a global significance far beyond technological innovation:

> The impact of the 1950s widescreen revolution on the cinema as an art and as an industry has been profound. It influenced the nature of the subject matter that was selected for production, the way in which films were staged, shot and edited, and the marketing, distribution and exhibition of motion pictures. Initially, epic stories, theatrical extravaganzas and narratives set in spectacular locations were sought to exploit the new dimensions of the screen. (Belton et al. 2010, 2)

The mainstreaming of 3-D technology around the same time further enhanced emphasis on the spectacular and immersive (Lev 2003b, 109–12).

In Scandinavia, few of these immersive and spectacular technologies were ever implemented on any grand scale, with the Academy ratio (1.37:1) standard in Scandinavian film production. It was simply too expensive to shoot in 3-D or widescreen, with a few and notable exceptions. But the immersive and spectacular aesthetics, themes, and screening infrastructure of the new cinema technologies, and industry investments of the 1950s, as well as Hollywood's outsourcing of film production to Europe and other locations in the 1950s gave rise to what Peter Lev calls "Hollywood International" (2003c, 147–68). These trends of Hollywood International impacted also Scandinavian film production, its critical assessment and reception, and audience priorities. Among several different outcomes, four stand out: (a) the travel documentary; (b) the priority on "quality film"; (c) the launch of international co-productions; and (d) the exotic spectacle feature film.

New developments in 1950s Scandinavian film production and circulation

The 1950s cinema documentaries about locations abroad differed from television news reporting, and in most cases from newsreels of the past. Notably, a variety of award-winning documentaries were produced about "exotic" locations, expeditions, and adventure endeavors, both in color and black and white. Notable examples include the Academy Award for Artfilm's *Kon-Tiki*

(Olle Nordemar, Sweden–Norway, 1950; see also Bigelow in this volume), or Hakon Mielche's color film *Jorden rundt på 80 minutter* (*Around the World in 80 Minutes*, Denmark, 1955) about a submarine traversing the seven seas. At least one Scandinavian widescreen documentary "scope" film was made in the 1950s, Arne Sucksdorff's highly regarded *The Flute and the Arrow* (*En djungelsaga*, Sweden, 1957; see also Stjernholm in this volume). The film was shot on location in India in Technicolor with AgaScope, a Swedish widescreen camera technology developed precisely to capture landscapes with clarity and acuity. *The Flute and the Arrow* was nominated for the Palme d'Or at Cannes in 1958. Danish travelogues of the time include expedition documentaries such as: Aage Krarup Nielsen's *Bali Everyday and in Holiday* (*Bali i hverdag og fest*, 1950); Jørgen Bitsch's *Safari* (1954) and *Amazonas* (1957); Peter Rasmussen's *African Wildlife* (*Afrikas Storvildt*, 1956); and Arne Falk Rønne's *Our Wondrous World* (*Vor vidunderlige verden*, 1957). Per Høst, Norway's primary mid-century documentarian, made many travel documentaries that brought foreign locations to domestic cinema audiences, including the popular *Another Look at the Jungle People* (*Gjensyn med jungelfolket*, Norway, 1950), shot in Panama, and *Galapagos* (Norway, 1955). Høst's most influential film of that time was about the Sámi, *The Laplanders* (*Same Jakki*, 1957). It was billed as a "storfilm," a common term in Scandinavian cinema that roughly corresponds to an amalgamation of high-budget, big production value, and expansiveness in theme, location, timespan, or scope. *The Laplanders* was in competition in Cannes in 1957. Sucksdorff, Høst, Bitsch, and other Scandinavian documentarians produced nature and ethnographically-inspired films that gave Scandinavian documentaries the reputation abroad of being high quality, balanced and non-sensationalist. Some of these films received European and US distribution as educational films through Encyclopedia Britannica, McGraw-Hill, 20th Century-Fox, or other publishing houses that provided 16mm copies for projection in schools and community centers.

The development, international distribution, and Scandinavian public funding of *kvalitetsfilm* [quality film] or art cinema became a way for small national cinemas to compete internationally, with this mode of film production designed to provide an antithesis to television productions and to gain recognition as part of the growing number of prestigious international film festivals. Exemplary films in this regard include Sucksdorff's *Symphony of a City*, aka *Rhythm of a City* (*Människor i en stad*, Sweden, 1947), which won an Academy Award in 1949; Alf Sjöberg's *Miss Julie* (*Fröken Julie*, Sweden, 1951), awarded the Grand Prix at Cannes in 1951; Arne Mattsson's *One Summer of Happiness* (*Hon dansade en sommar*, Sweden, 1951), awarded the Golden Bear at the new Berlin film festival in 1952; Ingmar Bergman's *Smiles of a Summer Night* (*Sommarnattens leende*, Sweden, 1955), a Palme d'Or nominee; Carl Th. Dreyer's *Ordet* (*The Word*, Denmark, 1955), winning the American Golden Globe at Venice; and Arne Skouen's World War II occupation drama film *Nine Lives* (*Ni Liv*, Norway, 1957), nominated for an Academy Award and entered into competition at Cannes. The emergence of an international circulation track for art cinema in the form of prestigious film festivals—in Europe and elsewhere—became a significant way for these small national cinemas to reach the world. The emphasis on quality film—and the subsequent national interest in supporting and promoting quality film—became the foundation for the mandate of the Scandinavian film institutes in the 1960s, specifically as a way for the nation state to support and market "quality film" to international audiences (see also Furhammar 1998, 202).

Many American cinemas needed additional material after the breakdown of the studio system's vertical integration in 1948 (the Supreme Court case *United States v. Paramount Pictures, Inc.*), retooling their repertoires for urban theaters. They turned to European art cinema as well as to exploitation flicks. This meant that some Scandinavian "quality film" circulated differently than intended. Some were re-cut and reedited as explicit sex and sin films. One of the most famous examples is the transformation of Ingmar Bergman's *Summer with Monika* (*Sommaren med Monika*, Sweden, 1953) by exploitation producer and distributor Kroger Babb into *Monika: The Story of a Bad Girl!* (USA/Sweden 1955; see also Ghanoui in this volume).

Another outcome of 1950s Scandinavian film culture responding to and integrating itself within new international modes is the emergence of co-productions. In Scandinavian film history, this is an overlooked trend in postwar filmmaking of the 1950s. Rune Waldekranz, then a producer at Sandrews, made the representative comment in 1950 that "Swedish cinema could no longer be limited only to the domestic market . . . to make Swedish quality film profitable in a time of increasing costs there was a need for a bigger market, a market outside the country's borders [with] new and unusual, audacious films" (cited in Söderbergh Widding 2005, 112). As a result of this re-orientation, at least eighteen international co-productions were made with Swedish involvement in the 1950s, including with countries such as Argentina, France, Italy, and the UK (Söderbergh Widding 2005, 112). One of these was the first four-country Nordic co-production *A Woman Behind Everything* (*Kvinnan bakom allt, Neljä rakkautta, Fyra gånger kärlek, Alt dette—og Island også*; Johan Jacobsen, Denmark, Finland, Norway, Sweden, 1951). This film had a cinema release in all four Nordic countries. The literary adaptations *Singoalla* (Christian-Jaque, UK, France, Sweden, 1949) and *The Firebird* (*Eldfågeln*, Hasse Ekman, Italy–Sweden, 1952) were major European co-productions with well-known actors and production houses behind them. While they achieved some cross-market success in Europe and the USA, there was little critical acclaim or audience appreciation, with "the critical reception of the 1950s . . . extremely hostile toward the attempts to international collaboration" (Söderbergh Widding 2005, 116). Other Scandinavian collaborations of note include the Cold War thriller *Escape from Terror* (*Flugten til Danmark*, Denmark; USA, 1955), which did not have extensive distribution or critical success. Though they were not technically co-productions, the Cinerama film *Windjammer* (Bill Colleran, USA, 1958) featured a Norwegian ship and a Norwegian crew sailing around the world, and the CinemaScope historical epic *The Vikings* (Richard Fleischer, USA 1958), starring Kirk Douglas and Tony Curtis, was partly filmed in Norway.

The Spectacular Elsewheres of the 1950s

The fourth major development in the 1950s Scandinavian film context was that of elsewheres—in terms of theme, content, technical innovation, aesthetics, industry context, circulation, and reception. This occurred at a time when Scandinavian welfare state practices and ideologies were being implemented and discursively positioned as models for the developing world, including as part of the growing decolonialization and national independence movements of the 1950s. Some of these postwar elsewheres can be situated historically and socially, in the context of the rise of the welfare state and Scandinavian geopolitics, and also of colonial histories during the Cold War.

The Arctic I: Danish Colonial Imaginaries of Greenland in Big-budget Color

Mainland Denmark's small size and small population have obscured its geopolitical centrality and impact, especially in the Arctic. Denmark's centuries-long rule over Greenland is a case in point. In 1953, notably, Greenland ceased to be labeled a "colony" and instead became Denmark's northernmost county. The result of decolonization trends in the early 1950s and the incorporation of Greenland into Denmark were geopolitically significant as the Cold War intensified. Denmark was a NATO country, and thus Greenland became one too. Straddling Cold War boundaries between East and West in the Arctic, Danish Greenland became a key US bulwark against the Soviet Union with the construction of the US Thule Airbase in the island's upper northwest. With the Indigenous Inuit population abruptly removed from their historical village, the Thule Airbase came to stand for the increasing militarization and politicization of the Arctic, concomitant with environmental destruction. The Thule Airbase localized the Cold War in a vast material structure in a largely unpopulated part of the world. It was a feat of engineering and planning initially envisioned as a vast underground city buried in snow and ice, turning the remoteness of the location into a key visual element of the militarization of the Arctic and Denmark's territorial investment in the Cold War (Doel et al. 2015). The very factors that marked the Arctic's isolation made it a central geopolitical player with the construction of the Thule Airbase. As indicated by films produced by the US Department of Defense, the Thule Airbase served clear goals of furthering the US agenda in the Cold War (see Stenport 2015 and MacKenzie and Stenport 2013).

At the same time as the construction of the Thule Airbase, Denmark produced a pair of remarkable Greenland films. These are noteworthy because they clearly signal a state-sponsored attempt to claim Greenland as "Danish" in the wake of World War II. Standard tropes of colonial and cultural appropriation appear in these films. Greenland was represented as a civilized, modern European welfare state, as if its Arctic Indigenous present and past were a mere afterthought (see Nielsen 2017). These two films, the documentary *Where Mountains Float* by Bjarne Henning-Jensen (1955) and the melodrama feature *Qivitoq: The Mountain Wanderer* by Erik Balling (1956), were produced by Danes with funding from the Danish Governmental Film Bureau. Both had international distribution and reach, and both were nominated for Academy Awards, though neither had regular cinema distribution in the USA. *Qivitoq*, moreover, was Denmark's first sound and Eastman color film, made to celebrate Nordisk Film's 50th anniversary, marking its status as the oldest continuously operating film company in the world (see also Allen's chapter on Nordisk silent films in Australasia in this volume).

Though the plots of *Where Mountains Float* and *Qivitoq* differ, the assumptions, worldviews, and aesthetics share similarities. The former is a dramatized documentary about a young Greenlandic boy learning to embrace the modernity of the Danish welfare state, having to leave his family and small settlement to receive treatment for tuberculosis in the local town. *Qivitoq* is a conventional "exotic" melodrama with a common set of characters and plot contrivances. A young teacher travels from the metropole (Copenhagen, in this case) to a colonial outpost (the fictional Fredriksminde), where she befriends a disgruntled rogue trader "gone native" in "the wilderness." Through heteronormative romance the two team up to bring education and enlightened modernity to the local Greenlandic population, whose transition from a sealing subsistence economy guided by environmental spirituality into industrialized cod-fishing, mass-scale processing, and welfare state regulation is an unacknowledged traumatic process of colonialism. Both films were well-received and *Qivitoq* was a box-office hit in Denmark, although it drew criticism from some reviewers, one remarking that the plot's contrived romantic rivalry between the Danes in the film presented a shallow and naïve understanding of Greenland and Greenlanders, especially in relation to Denmark, confirming that "Greenland is Danish: that is the story of this film" (*Dagens Nyheder* 1956).

Neither of these films directly addresses Greenland's significance in the geopolitical Cold War struggle over dominance in the Arctic, though by emphasizing Danish presence as bringing progress and prosperity in education, industry,

Figure 9.1 Danish colonial politics: a melodrama of modernizing Greenland: *Qivitoq: The Mountain Wanderer* (*Qivitoq: Fjeldgængeren*, Erik Balling, Denmark, 1956). Promotion poster.

and social services the films ostensibly fulfill several expectations for their Danish and international audiences. While Greenland might be perceived as "exotic" on a surface level, it is really an extension of the Danish democratic welfare state. In other words, Greenland is Western, not "Arctic" (e.g. a land of snow-houses and seal hunters). One Danish review affirms that *Where Mountains Float* will remind Americans, including Air Force sergeants based in Greenland, that Greenland is Danish (*Land og Folk* 1955). While it was well-received by most critics, some Danish reviews lambasted *Where Mountains Float* as state propaganda (*Jyllands-Posten* 1956), as naïve, or as an "official" production where no tension between Danes and Greenlanders could be expressed (*Land og Folk* 1955). But this was not how the film was received in the USA. *The New York Times* (1958) compares *Where Mountains Float* favorably to Robert Flaherty's *Louisiana Story* (USA, 1948) and praises its "simple, authentic serenity" and "pictorial magnificence of the wondrously-photographed backgrounds and vivid color."

Ostensibly eschewing larger geopolitical considerations of the circumpolar Arctic as a global arena for power struggles, popular internationally distributed Danish films about Greenland in the 1950s turned it into a domestic Danish affair on the level of plot and content, while the visual emphasis on ice-, sea-, and landscape continued the portrayal of the Arctic as spectacle. The opening sequence of *Qivitoq*, for example, follows the expedition form of many Greenland films and Arctic representations since the early 1800s (see also David 2000). The frame, filled with striking ice floes reflecting off the glaciers on each side, moves slightly up and down, while the camera, placed in the bow of a ship, records both the scenic spectacle of ravishing ice formations and the ship's own movement. The composition of the opening sequence is striking, transforming the audience into members of an expedition into the unknown, with the light reflecting and refracting off the ice This is a well-known trope of Greenland films made for domestic and international markets, including *Eskimo* (George Schnéevoigt, Norway, 1930), *The Wedding of Palo* (*Palos Brudefærd*, Friedrich Dalsheim with Knud Rasmussen, Denmark, 1934), and *S.O.S. Eisberg* (Arnold Fanck, Germany/USA, 1933) starring Leni Riefenstahl, produced in German and Hollywood versions, which explicitly uses the term "expedition" when describing the film crew and filming on location in the Arctic.

The conflation of nineteenth-century scientific and exploration expeditions with film crews visually capturing the scenery is prevalent. A second common trope is that of portraying the Arctic as an unpopulated empty space that westerners travel to. The landscape is one of spectacle, and the traveler as spectator takes it in as a diorama or a moving panorama. The seemingly endless, tiring journey, without the gratification of landmark discovery as in other colonial endeavors, is repeated in these films. The spectacle of empty space in these films served Denmark's immediate political need for full integration.

Both *Where Mountains Float* and *Qivitoq* are trite in terms of plot and content (which contemporary reviewers mostly recognize); they work primarily on the visual level, by constructing beautiful and captivating visual spectacles that remove content from focus, foregrounding the visual spectacle. In the case of *Qivitoq*, this is especially evident in the gorgeous colors, hues, and light gradations of the Eastman stock. As a "Post-card from Greenland" (*Dagens Nyheder* 1956), the film reinscribes a familiar story of Arctic representation: the emphasis on the visual as spectacle, which obscures the geopolitical potency underlying the very interest in capturing it visually. Henning-Jensen's approach was regarded as having international potential, and, building on the success of *Where Mountains Float*, he and his production partner Astrid Henning-Jensen pitched a major film about Lapland [sic] to New York financiers in 1957. Provisionally titled *A Trip to Myself*, it was intended to be widescreen and filmed in color, featuring extensive landscape photography. As the Henning-Jensens described it to *Variety*, the project had a broader significance: "'We, in Scandinavia, have a tendency to think too much in our own, limited geographical terms,' the producer-directors said. 'We never seem to want to worry about the rest of the world.'" (*Variety* 1957). Although never realized, the project signaled the potential of exotic, widescreen elsewheres for Scandinavian cinema of the 1950s.

The Arctic II: The Cinematic Imagination of Indigenous Sápmi and the Settler State

Like Greenland, the Nordic region's other Indigenous territory, Sápmi, also became a postwar spectacle, though not as part of the Henning-Jensens' proposed widescreen color spectacular representation. During the 1950s, the representation of Sámi peoples and the Sápmi region in visual culture took on distinct forms. This was because of geopolitical realities as well as the perceived need for Sámi integration into the Scandinavian welfare state, which was implemented differently in each national context. In Norway, the process of so-called Norwegianization had been underway for a century. In Sweden, the welfare state sought to modernize the Sámi—then known as Lapps—through two different and complementary processes that served to demonstrate that Northern Scandinavia was populated, a strategic aspect of Cold War Arctic politics. The first was the separatist policy called "Lapp shall be Lapp," which deemed the Sámi a wilderness people whose racial characteristics necessitated their living on the land as nomads; the second was an integration policy which positioned Sámi as Swedish national subjects, rather than as an Indigenous or colonized people with independent land claim rights (see Lundmark 2002, 63 and 2005, 14–15).

Eva Silvén (2014) has traced the representation of Sámi in visual cultures in several important articles, elucidating, for example, how the Nordic Museum's major Sámi–Lapp exhibit in the early 1950s prioritized reindeer herding, creating a Sámi hierarchy: A "good" Sámi was a nomadic reindeer herder who "remained" a Lapp but could also be domesticated through schooling, as opposed to Sámi who integrated into the Swedish welfare state as miners, loggers, settlers, or service workers. Amanda Kernell's much-lauded film *Sami Blood* (*Sameblod*, Sweden, 2016) tells part of this story.

Several Scandinavian Cold War films from the 1950s feature the north and Sámi populations, whether implicitly or explicitly. In the tradition of a spectacular elsewhere, the plot of Erik Blomberg's *White Reindeer* (*Valkoinen peura*, Finland, 1952) features a woman shape-shifter who functions as an allegory of exotic and otherized female sexuality, evoking the horror genre, not unlike Jacques Tourneur's B-movie *Cat People* (USA, 1942). *White Reindeer* won international prizes in Cannes (1953) and Karlovy Vary (1954), and after a limited release five years later in the USA it was awarded a Golden Globe Award for Best Foreign Film in 1957.

The production of science fiction films in the USA between 1948 and 1962 was astonishing, with over 500 features, many that responded directly to Cold War anxieties about nuclear annihilation, the bomb, or communist takeover (O'Donnell 2003, 169). The Arctic was a primary theater of Cold War tensions and one of the most militarized regions in the world at that time (Chaturvedi 2000). The B-movie *Space Invasion of Lapland / Terror in the Midnight Sun* (*Rymdinvasion i Lappland*, USA–Sweden, 1959), a Swedish–American co-production, exemplifies this trend in Scandinavia. Directed by American Virgil W. Vogel and co-produced by Gustaf Unger Films (Hollywood) and Fortuna Film (Stockholm), the film featured an American and Swedish C-list cast, a mostly Swedish crew, and a furry monster. When a meteor crashes in the remote Arctic, a herd of reindeer are mysteriously found dead. Scientists and military personnel are sent out to investigate, discovering that the meteor is a spaceship ferrying an alien creature who subsequently kidnaps the lone woman of the crew. The aliens destroy a Sámi village. London's *Monthly Film Bulletin* remarks positively on "the uncommonly distinguished monster, Lapp actors and finely photographed natural backgrounds," but slams the plot and acting, concluding that "even so, addicts will find the novelty of this American-Swedish item useful" (1960, 312). It is clear that *Space Invasion of Lapland* was positioned as part of a well-established genre (for "addicts"), sharing obvious similarities with Howard Hawks' and Christian Nyby's Arctic classic *The Thing from Another World* (USA, 1951), which featured the tropes of alien invader, military, science, and expedition. The conclusion to be drawn from these and other similar films was that what thaws or emerges in the Arctic is dangerous, but American technology, know-how, discipline, and ingenuity will save the world. For Swedish viewers, this sci-fi representation of Sámi and

Figure 9.2 Cold War Arctic science fiction: *Terror in the Midnight Sun* (*Rymdinvasion in Lappland*, Virgil W. Vogel, USA–Sweden, 1959).

northernmost Sweden was a novelty and an original elsewhere, but reviewers and audiences did not regard it positively.

In addition to the sci-fi schlock of *Space Invasion in Lapland*, two large-budget Swedish-produced films about the Sámi were made around this time. Ragnar Frisk's *Lapp Blood* (*Lappblod*, Sweden, 1948) was a "storfilm" Technicolor production. It was the second color film produced in Sweden and "a massive production in color, designated for a world market that showed itself entirely uninterested in a Swedish mountain romance," bankrupting the production company Filmo (Furhammar 1998: 210). The film is conventional in its depiction of Sápmi; it begins and ends with white snow-clad mountains and Sámi on skis, the plot a simplistic marriage tale with a herd of reindeer as dowry. The Sámi are portrayed in ethnic and racist stereotypes as "noble savages," with all "Sámi" characters played by Swedes.

In contrast to *Lappblod*, the next Swedish "storfilm" about the Sámi became an international success. Featuring stunning environmental cinematography by Sven Nykvist, Rolf Husberg's *Laila* (1958) mirrors Hollywood melodramas of the time, like those produced by Ross Hunter and directed by Douglas Sirk for Universal, such as *Imitation of Life* (about racial passing and miscegenation,

1959) and *All That Heaven Allows* (about class conflict and a younger man/ older woman romance, 1955). In *Laila*, two cultures are opposed, yet portrayed as stably separate. All actors are Swedish and speak Swedish without a Sámi-inflected accent. The protagonist Laila is an orphan, a white Swede who has been raised Sámi, making the film an allegory of miscegenation. Spending time outdoors in the first half of the film and indoors in the second, Laila is introduced as a complete and autonomous person. She is depicted as a free spirit, interested in education and competent in ways central to Sámi life, such as fishing, and reindeer herding and driving. There is no initial "lack" that needs to be narratively integrated into the plot, yet Laila's choices are later subsumed by patriarchal heteronormativity. Laila chooses the Swedish Anders as a groom, revolting against the patriarchal structure imposed by Sámi elders Aslaak and Mallet. The film posits the two cultures—like Hollywood 1950s melodramas about racial tensions and American politics—as "separate but equal," and sends the message that the two are incommensurable.

Laila normalizes the Swedish government's assimilation priorities of the preceding decades and celebrates the signs of "modernity" and progress that the settler state is bringing to the Indigenous communities, in the form of helicopters, motorcycles, radio, and education for office jobs. It posits that Sámi life is a way of the past, and even though the cultures are portrayed as fundamentally different, there is only one way for Sámis to survive, and that is to assimilate and to embrace technology and modernity, as well as to incorporate a more dynamic and nuanced patriarchy where heteronormativity is maintained, but where the woman can choose the "good" guy as a representative of the state, whereas the Indigenous Sámi love interest is a patriarchal villain. These narrative conventions echo the arguments in ethnographer and anthropologist Mary Douglas's *Purity and Danger* (1966), which charts power dynamics between outsider and insider in a range of cultures, focusing on the role played by cultural purity. Following Douglas's analysis, *Laila* situates the Indigenous Sámi as outsiders who will contaminate the purity of Swedish whiteness (Laila). *Laila* is undergirded by a well-known argument of normative whiteness: once released back into the dominant paradigm (the Swedish welfare state of the 1950s), Laila's transition will be wholly uncomplicated, conforming to an unacknowledged baseline of "standard" ethnicity. In *Laila*, the most successful indicator of the assimilation process is that her return to whiteness both as a cultural framework and a biological given is privileged in the film and faces no narrative opposition. Whiteness is the natural state, the untainted state, and Laila's assimilation back into being white is an easy one, echoing Hollywood conventions of the time, as articulated so well by Richard Dyer in his seminal work *White* (1997; see also Pallas 2011 and Wright 1998).

Laila had a broad international release as *Make Way for Lila*, its international title signaling an intrepid and plucky protagonist, garnering significant

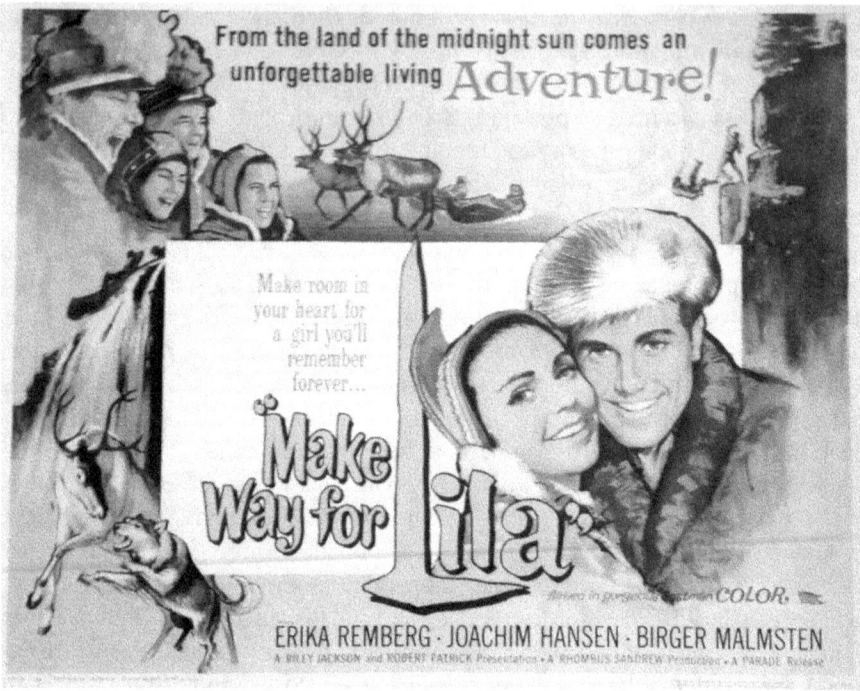

Figure 9.3 The welfare state and Swedish settler colonialism in *Make Way for Lila* (*Laila*, Rolf Husberg, 1958, Sweden and West Germany).

success in West Germany and France. It closely resembles 1950s melodramas that seek to bridge two different ethnicities, with the woman as a pawn or sometimes an agent in this cultural and ethnic transfer. Its majestic scenery, "exotic" depiction of reindeer, Indigenous customs, and wintry landscapes exported north Sweden as an elsewhere to international audiences, while maintaining a specific set of regional characteristics.

The Elsewheres of Equatorial Africa and Sweden's Colonial Connections to Congo

Laila's cinematographer Sven Nykvist began his career portraying Sweden's countryside and its characteristic light of extended dawn and dusk, later becoming known for his work with Ingmar Bergman in *Through a Glass Darkly* in 1961 (*Såsom i en spegel*), as well as with American and European art cinema directors of the 1970s and 1980s, including Woody Allen, Louis Malle, and Andrei Tarkovsky. In the late 1940s and early 1950s, Nykvist made a number of films in equatorial Africa, specifically Belgian and French Congo. These documentaries were motivated by Nykvist's desire to reconnect with the history of his parents, who had spent most of their adult lives in Africa as missionaries, with Sven and his siblings staying behind in Stockholm. Nykvist's Congo travels and travails when documenting local customs and practices are described in the photographic travelogue *The Journey to Lambarene* (*Resan till Lambarene*, 1959, co-written with Lars-Henrik Ottoson). This text demonstrates Nykvist's wonder at visiting the area and the people where his parents lived their entire lives, while paying close attention to local customs and the impact of Belgian and French colonial rule. The prose contains ample colonial and racial stereotypes, including Nykvist praising the Belgians as "competent colonizers" (1959, 11). The description of the journey up the Congo river and Nykvist's interactions with the Congolese bring to mind Joseph Conrad's novella *Heart of Darkness* (1899). Nykvist describes the difficulty of filming in Congo in detail, with equipment malfunctioning and supplies and travel arrangements being difficult to secure, sets of film destroyed in a plane crash on their way to Sandrews Studios in Stockholm, and people falling sick from malaria and exposure to other infectious diseases.

An important—although largely unacknowledged by Nykvist—geopolitical aspect is that Sweden and Scandinavia had a long colonial history, intertwined especially with King Leopold's brutal regime in Belgian Congo (Hochschild 1999). Nykvist's parents were part of the substantive group of missionaries who followed the influential Swedish evangelical missionary E. V. Sjöblom, who published highly critical eye-witness reports about the atrocities committed in Leopold's Congo in the name of "civilization." In the 1897 essay "Startling News from the Dark Congo," published in the USA and in Britain, as well as in letters, reports, and memoirs, Sjöblom referred extensively to the inhuman conditions of the rubber extraction industry and the violations committed by Belgian forces in the Congolese–Arab war in 1891–4 (see Stenport 2010, 170–84). At the end of the nineteenth century, Scandinavian seamen, traders, missionaries, and explorers were the third largest group present in Congo after Belgians and Italians (Reinius Gustafsson 2005, 11). Scandinavian skippers were so prominent on the river, sought after for dependability and expertise, that they were described in 1905 as the group of people that had made the Belgian conquest of Congo possible (Jenssen-Tusch 1902–5, 184). Sweden continued to have close ties to the Belgian Congo throughout the 1950s (the country became independent in 1960 as the Democratic Republic of Congo), with UN general secretary Dag Hammarkjöld taking an active role in defusing the Congo Crisis. He was later killed in Africa en route to cease-fire negotiations in 1961. Mads Brügger's recent documentary *Cold Case Hammarskjöld* (Denmark, 2019) tells part of this story.

There is thus a complex personal and political background to the body of work Nykvist shot in Africa between 1948 and 1965, which showed parts of Africa to European and American audiences that were rarely portrayed on film. One of these films, the color documentary *The Country Below the Equator* (*Landet under ekvatorn*, Sweden, 1950), was commissioned by the Mission Swedish Covenant Church (Svenska Missionsförbundet; see Nadi Tofighian, n.d.). Other films were made under the auspices of the production company Sandrews, where Nykvist had been a cinematographer since 1941. These included *Congo: A Short Report about Congo Then and Now* (*Bisi Congo: Ett litet reportage om Kongo förr och nu*, Sweden, 1950) about modernization processes in Congo, and the feature-length fiction film *Under the Southern Cross: A Film from French Equatorial Africa's Jungles, Based on Authentic Material, Taking Place at the Turn of the Century* (*Under södra korset: En film från Franska Ekvatorialafrikas urskogar, byggd på autentiska händelser, som utspelats kring sekelskiftet*, Sweden, 1952, co-directed with Olof Bergström), about a returning ethnographer reminiscing in an extended flashback about his travels in Congo around 1900. The actor and co-director Olof Bergström is the only white character in the film, which is unusual for cinematic representation of Africa at the time. *Reverence of Life: A Short Film About Albert Schweitzer* (*Vördnad för livet: En kortfilm om Albert Schweitzer*, Sweden 1952) is a collaboration with Svenska Missionsförbundet about the Swiss missionary, philosopher, and musician Albert Schweitzer and his hospital and missionary station at Lambarene.

The most ethnographic of these films, made for cinema release, is *I fetischmannens spår* (Sven Nykivst, Sweden, 1948). The film features a number of rituals captured by a camera that seems to be hidden (in the vein of visual anthropology), these rituals being in fact re-enacted and scripted for the camera to provide a dramatic contrast between "modern" medicine and "heathen" healing. Indeed, Nykvist describes that he sought to make more than a "documentary about an African people only by walking around in the bush and shooting pretty nature images and filling those out by an occasional portrait or glimpse of everyday village life," and that he would not shy away from orchestrating "something more substantial, something that provided a background to the story" (Nykvist 1959, 54). The production included bribes, subterfuge, threats, and manipulation of the village population, including putting them and the crew in danger by inciting conflict (Nykvist 1959, 38–57). *I fetischmannens spår* is a captivating and cinematographically sophisticated depiction of village life, though one that demonstrates the ethical and moral complexities of viewer implication in objectification through "third eye" ethnographic and colonial filmmaking, as described by Fatima Tobing Rony (1996, 1–16). The American company Cathedral Films turned this film into *The Footsteps of the Witch Doctor* (USA, 1950) for educational distribution in the USA, with a voiceover that exoticizes and sensationalizes the practices much more than Nykvist's original. This version of the film had relatively broad circulation, including screening as part of an

African-American education program in Chicago in 1962 (*Chicago Defender* 1962).

Nykvist's documentaries documented village and missionary life for Swedish and American audiences at a moment when few other films were made in this part of Africa, and especially not films intent on capturing rural life at a moment of political and social transition. As Femi Okiremuete Shaka (1999) and Glenn Reynolds (2015) show, domestic film production in West and Central Africa was intermittent and dispersed during the 1930s–50s. Hollywood's portrayal of the Congo during this period included installments of the ongoing *Tarzan* series (nearly one per year issued during the 1940s and 1950s), and the comedy drama *Congo Maisie* (H. C. Potter, USA, 1940), shot almost entirely in California. With postwar Hollywood expanding to international locations, and depicting them in spectacular color and sometimes in widescreen, films such as *The African Queen* (John Huston, USA, 1951), *Mogambo* (John Ford, USA, 1953), *White Witch Doctor* (Henry Hathaway, USA, 1953), and *The Roots of Heaven* (John Huston, USA, 1958) introduced environments of the Belgian Congo and French Equatorial Africa to new audiences as part of Hollywood International (see Lev 2003c, 150–2). These films maintained gendered and cinematic codes of the Hollywood genres that they were part of, especially those of the comedy–romance–action spectacle.

As that of a documentarian and fiction filmmaker working with documentary material, Nykvist's work from this period is unique. His body of work reflects the fact that the strong Swedish missionary presence in Belgian Congo was about to come to an end and that its legacy, and the cultures it had impacted, needed documenting, also, for a rapidly changing postwar Swedish society.

Absent from Nykvist's 1959 travelogue *Resan to Lambarene*, however, is any reference to the "storfilm" color and widescreen spectacle *Gorilla*, which Nykvist made in collaboration with director Lars-Henrik Ottoson and producer Lorens Marmstedt of Swedish Terrafilm in 1946. In his autobiography *Vördnad för ljuset* (*In Reverence of the Light*, 1997), Nykvist presents *Gorilla* as a despicable project, although he enjoyed, as he writes, shooting "my Africa" in color and AgaScope (78). Swedish film historian Lars Furhammar describes *Gorilla* as a "partially documentary Africa adventure" and a "dubious film" (1998, 218). Though Nykvist is credited only as the cinematographer, it is clear that his experience filming in Belgian Congo was a contributing factor to the launch of the project. Shot in three versions—English, French, and Swedish—the film was aimed for broad release and circulation. It failed both domestically and internationally, with Terrafilm going almost bankrupt as part of the project (Furhammar 1998, 218). It was the only large-budget Swedish film ("storfilm") made in Africa to date.

Inspired by CinemaScope, the Swedish industrial firm AGA developed the projection process AgaScope in 1955, a domestic widescreen format that Nykvist and co-director Lars-Henrik Ottoson used for filming *Gorilla*. The cinematographic qualities of *Gorilla* greatly inspired Arne Sucksdorff, who shot the documentary *The Flute and Arrow* in India with AgaScope, with Sucksdorff being one of few to find anything redeeming about *Gorilla* (Furhammar 1998: 218). Nykvist's color cinematography and the AgaScope technology created a beautiful aesthetic of quintessential sub-Saharan environments: glorious megafauna on the savannah, mysterious mountainous jungles, and marshland deltas with unpredictable rivers. The story appears copied from Hollywood International productions of the early 1950s, such as *The African Queen*, but its weak plot development signals its failure. A young blonde woman, a Swedish photo journalist from a "ladies'" periodical, is sent to Congo to write an "authentic" essay about local customs and the plight of large African animals during a time of increased bounty hunting. She brings a letter of recommendation to meet a Belgian colonial trapper, a killer of animals for profit, who is out to capture a gorilla which has threatened the local village. This part of *Gorilla*'s plot appears modeled on Nykvist's interactions with Congolese villagers and their concerns over an aggressive male gorilla threatening their settlement, as briefly portrayed in *I fetischmannens spår* (see also Nykvist 1959, 59–69).

The woman journalist reflects that the Congolese she meets "seem so civilized," conveying a benevolent Swedish colonial perspective on contemporary Africa. The film follows the standard Hollywood setup to ensure a successful romance between the two. The gorilla is shot in the end, and the Swedish photojournalist returns home. In this manner, *Gorilla* is like a Hollywood International spectacle, interjecting some identificatory cultural specificity with regard to the female protagonist for a Swedish and international viewership. The actress Gio Petré often played sensuous and seductive roles, providing a link between this African adventure and the Swedish sex and sin films that circulated on the international art cinema and exploitation circuit of the 1950s (see also Wallengren's chapter in this volume).

The fact that Nykvist does not mention this major film endeavor, which featured a US actor and a large crew, in his 1959 African travelogue is significant. (It is especially curious, given that *Gorilla*'s co-director Ottoson is a co-author of the travelogue.) Without access to additional sources, one can only guess that Nykvist was troubled by the depiction of Congolese practices and the reduction of the region's rich history to a playground for a foreign adventurer-expeditioner and a Swedish seductress photo-journalist. Up until now, scholarship on this period of Nykvist's career is nearly nonexistent, and few reflections on Sweden's filmmaking cultures in sub-Saharan Africa following decolonialization exist.

It appears that Nykvist sought to rectify *Gorilla*'s depiction of Congo. In 1965, Nykvist conceptualized, directed, and shot a smaller-scale art cinema family drama called *The Rope Bridge* (*Lianbron*). The script was originally based on his parents' marriage and life as missionaries in the Belgian Congo, but its realized version turns the missionaries into doctors, thus skewing the biographical connection. *Lianbron* moves between two time periods, the present featuring the medical researcher Johan Hedman, and a generation earlier featuring his parents, Mattias and his wife Ruth (played by Mai Zetterling). During the flashback scenes, Nykvist includes found footage from his documentary *I fetischmannens spår* and also what appear to be his own family's films and photographs. Notably, one of Nykvist's most important personal connections to his parents was the photographs they sent from Africa and the slide shows the family would enjoy together during the short periods they were at home in Sweden, which shaped Nykvist's image of Africa as "a wild land of adventure" (1959, 7). *Lianbron* thus appears to be an attempt at reconciliation, at re-telling the story of Sweden's relationship to Belgian Congo without the burden of making a film designed to compete with Hollywood big-budget "exotic" international co-productions. Nykvist's last film about Africa was the Swedish TV-film *The Calling* (*Kallelsen*), produced in 1974, based on his father's photographs, slides, and found footage narrow-gauge films (Nykvist 1997, 84–5).

Conclusion: Opening Up the World

The technological innovations of 1950s film production, the emphasis on spectacle through "Hollywood International" (Lev 2003c), and geopolitical changes in a postwar world that opened up travel and allowed for the portrayal of "foreign" cultures transformed global cinema cultures, including those of Scandinavia. But the stories told in this chapter are not necessarily ones that revel in success. Though designed for international reach and produced with large budgets, Danish and Swedish colonial elsewhere imaginaries failed to gain a great deal of traction outside the Nordic countries, even though some were nominated for major awards, and many did not garner great successes domestically either. However, the sheer number of 1950s films influenced by the norms of big screen spectacle and technological innovation (e.g. widescreen and color) point to a pressing need to reconceptualize Nordic cinema histories through the prism of elsewheres, in order to begin to chart how Scandinavian cinemas attempted to become popular beyond national borders and beyond the frame of art cinema. This alternative history not only sheds light on a neglected Nordic film genre, the "storfilm," but also points to now-neglected Nordic imaginaries of Denmark's and Sweden's place in the world—the worlds both of cinema and of geopolitics.

References

Belton, John, Sheldon Hall, and Steve Neale. 2002. "Introduction." In *Widescreen Worldwide*, ed. John Belton, Sheldon Hall, and Steve Neale. New Barnet: John Libbey. 1–4.
Chaturvedi, Sanjay. 2000. "Arctic geopolitics then and now." In *The Arctic: Environment, People, Policy*: 441–58.
Conrad, Joseph. 1899 [2016]. *Heart of Darkness*. New York: Norton.
David, Robert. 2000. *The Arctic in the British Imagination, 1818–1914*. Manchester: Manchester University Press.
Doel, Ronald, Kristine Harper, and Matthias Heymann. 2015. *Exploring Greenland: Cold War Science and Technology on Ice*. London: Palgrave Macmillan.
Douglas, Mary. 1966. *Purity and Danger: An Analysis of Concepts of Pollution and Taboo*. London: Routledge.
Dyer, Richard. 1997. *White: Essays on Race and Culture*. London: Routledge.
Furhammar, Leif. 1998. *Filmen i Sverige: en historia i tio kapitel*. Stockholm: Dialogos and Svenska Filminstitutet.
Hochschild, Adam. 1999. *King Leopold's Ghost: A Story of Greed, Terror, and Heroism in Colonial Africa*. New York: Mariner.
Jenssen-Tusch, Harald. 1902–5. *Skandinaver i Congo: svenske, norske, og danske Maends og kvinders verksomhed i den uafhenginge Congostat*. Copenhagen: Gyldendals.
Lev, Peter. 2003a. "Introduction." In *The Fifties: Transforming the Screen 1950–1959*, in the *History of the American Cinema*, ed. Peter Lev. New York: Thomson Gale. 1–6.
Lev, Peter.2003b. "Technology and Spectacle." In *The Fifties: Transforming the Screen 1950–1959*, in the *History of the American Cinema*, ed. Peter Lev. New York: Thomson Gale. 107–26.
Lev, Peter. 2003c. "Hollywood International." In *The Fifties: Transforming the Screen 1950–1959*, in the *History of the American Cinema*, ed. Peter Lev. New York: Thomson Gale. 127–46.
Lundmark, Lennart. 2002. *"Lappen är ombytlig, ostadig och obekväm": svenska statens samepolitik i rasismens tidevarv*. Umeå: Norrbottensakademiens skriftserie.
Lundmark, Lennart. 2005. "Sami Policy in the Shadow of Racism." In *The Sami: An Indigenous People in Sweden*. Stockholm: Ministry of Agriculture, Food and Consumer Affairs and the Sami Parliament.
MacKenzie, Scott and Anna Westerstahl Stenport. 2013. "All that's frozen melts into air: Arctic cinemas at the end of the world." *Public: Art Culture Ideas* 48: 81–91.
Nielsen, Kristian H. 2017. "Cod Society: The Technopolitics of Modern Greenland." In *Arctic Environmental Modernities: From the Age of the Explorers to the Era of the Anthropocene*, ed. Lill-Ann Körber, Scott MacKenzie, and Anna Westerstahl Stenport. London: Palgrave Macmillan. 71–85.
Nykvist, Sven and Lars-Henrik Ottoson. 1959. *Resan till Lambarene*. Stockholm: Gebers.
Nykvist, Sven and Bengt Forslund. 1997. *Vördnad för ljuset. Om film och människor i samtal med Bengt Forslund*. Stockholm: Albert Bonnier.
O'Donnell, Victoria. 2003. "Science Fiction Films and Cold War Anxiety." In *The Fifties: Transforming the Screen 1950–1959*, in the *History of the American Cinema*, ed. Peter Lev. New York: Thomson Gale. 169–98.
Pallas, Hynek. 2011. *Vithet i svensk spelfilm 1989–2010*. Göteborg: Filmkonst.

Reinius Gustafsson, Lotten. 2005. *Förfärliga och begärliga föremål. Om tingens roller på Stockholmsutställningen 1897 och Etnografiska missionsutställningen 1907*. Stockholm: Etnografiska museet.
Reynolds, Glenn. 2015. *Colonial Cinema in Africa: Origins, Images, Audiences*. London: McFarland.
Rony, Fatima Tobing. 1996. *The Third Eye: Race, Cinema, and Ethnographic Spectacle*. Durham, NC: Duke University Press.
Shaka, Femi Okiremuete. 1999. "Instructional cinema in colonial Africa: an historical reappraisal." *Ufahamu: A Journal of African Studies* 27(1–3): 27–47.
Silvén, Eva. 2014. "Constructing a Sami cultural heritage. essentialism and emancipation." *Ethnologia Scandinavica: A Journal for Nordic Ethnology* 44: 59–74.
Sjöblom, E. V. 1897. "Startling News from the Dark Congo." London: n.p.
Soila, Tytti, Astrid Söderbergh Widding, and Gunnar Iversen. 1998. *Nordic National Cinemas* London: Routledge.
Stenport, Anna Westerstahl. 2010. *Locating August Strindberg's Prose: Modernism, Transnationalism, and Setting*. Toronto: University of Toronto Press.
Stenport, Anna Westerstahl. 2015. "The Threat of the Thaw: The Cold War on the Screen." In *Films on Ice: Cinemas of the Arctic*, ed. Scott MacKenzie and Anna Westerstahl Stenport. Edinburgh: Edinburgh University Press. 163–77.
Tofighian, Nadi. n.d. "Svenska Missionsförbundet i utlandet." Svenska Filmarkivet. <http://www.filmarkivet.se/theme/svensk-mission-i-utlandet/> (last accessed October 8, 2018).
Wright, Rochelle. 1998. *The Visible Wall: Jews and Other Ethnic Outsiders in Swedish Film*. Carbondale: Southern Illinois University Press.

Newspaper articles

Chicago Defender. 1962. Chicago. May 6–12.
Dagens Nyheder. 1956. Copenhagen. November 7.
Jyllands-Posten. 1956. Denmark. February 27.
Land og Folk. 1955. Copenhagen. October 27.
Monthly Film Bulletin. 1960. London. Vol. 27: 312.
The New York Times. 1958. Howard Thompson. March 9. Page X 8.
Variety. 1957. "Kovner, Steinman Backing Danish Henning-Jensens; Four Features Planned." Los Angeles. November. Vol. 20.

10. THE DIASPORIC CINEMAS OF INGRID BERGMAN

Scott MacKenzie

This chapter examines the notion of Nordic otherness in the film work of Ingrid Bergman. Otherness, in this case, refers to the construction of Bergman as an outsider in films made in Hollywood, Italy, and, at the end of her career, Sweden itself. Otherness is related to, but different from, simply being an "outsider," as otherness, especially in Classical Hollywood, also had a quality of appeal and desire for difference. This difference can be understood as one that seemed both strange and yet compelling, and is part of a long history of Hollywood casting Europeans as compelling others.

From her works in Hollywood (1939–49) to her Italian period with Roberto Rossellini (1950–6), to her last film and her return to Swedish cinema in Ingmar Bergman's *Autumn Sonata* (*Höstsonaten*, Sweden/West Germany, 1978), I characterize Bergman's body of work through three interlinked themes: the role she played as a Swedish/European other; the working woman (i.e. a woman in the workforce), in terms both of the promotion of her career and of many of the roles themselves that are subject to forms of constraint (from marriage to martyrdom); and the role of the woman as a film artist in relation to what Mette Hjort has called "practitioner's agency" (Hjort 2010, 59–100), with a specific focus on Bergman as a woman who made non-traditional choices that challenged patriarchal norms of the time despite working for highly patriarchal men in the film industry. In what follows, I trace Bergman's transnational career, the roles she played, and how these intersected with the supposed controversies of her life. I do so to reclaim Bergman as an actress with a great deal of agency over her career, in her work from Classical Hollywood to art cinema, and to foreground how her Swedish/European otherness played a key role in this trajectory.

Bergman began her acting career in Stockholm, as a student at the Royal Dramatic Theatre School in 1933. By 1935, she had received her first onscreen credit in *The Count of the Old Town* (*Munkbrogreven*, Edvin Adolphson and Sigurd Wallén, Sweden, 1935). She went on to make eleven films in Sweden between 1935 and 1940, including *Intermezzo* (Gustaf Molander, Sweden, 1936), which was the film that brought her to the USA for a Hollywood remake, and *A Woman's Face* (*En kvinnas ansikte*, Gustaf Molander, Sweden, 1938), where she plays a disfigured woman criminal. *A Woman's Face* (George Cukor, USA, 1941) was re-made by M-G-M, with Joan Crawford; these remakes demonstrate the ways in which, post-Garbo, Sweden was looked upon as an elsewhere whose films could be re-imagined in Hollywood at a time characterized by a great deal of transnational cinematic mobility.

Most accounts of Bergman's star image position her as pure and virginal, and then argue that it was the upending of this image that led to the backlash against her. This, I argue, only tells part of the story. Bergman's image as ideal wife and mother (though she was, while in Hollywood, in a non-traditional long-distance relationship, with her husband as the primary care-taker of her child) drew attention away from another aspect of her life rooted in changes in Sweden in the 1930s: she was a woman in the labor force, and indeed the main provider for her family. Moreover, she placed her work above her supposed duties as mother and spouse; this is another aspect of her practitioner's agency. That Bergman put her career first was not necessarily radical in Scandinavia (see Hirdman 1998), but it certainly was in the USA, where, after World War II, women were released from the workforce to create space for returning soldiers. The fact that Bergman's Swedish/European otherness, once she arrived in Hollywood, was based on the heteronormative family structure and a sense of virginity functioned, for a while, to offset her very real Swedish/European otherness as a working woman in control of many aspects of her career (see Selznick 1972, 130–7 and Smit 2005 for how this patriarchal image was promoted).

Bergman as an Elsewhere "Star"

Bergman's European otherness in Hollywood, then, was not simply a trope propagated by producers such as David O. Selznick. Indeed, her status as Swedish runs through both the key biographies of Bergman (Steele 1959; Leamer 1986; Spoto 2001; Chandler 2007; Thomson 2009) and through her own autobiography (1980). These accounts of her otherness draw both on stereotypes and on her status as an independent woman. This otherness, then, was not simply a form of stereotyping, but something Bergman performed both on- and offscreen. The meta-narrative of her Swedishness is central to her autobiography, and her pan-Nordicness a recurring feature of the characters she played through the press and publicity machine so central to Classical Hollywood, it is not just possible but also necessary to read her works—those where she is expressly Nordic, those where this is ambiguous, and those where she is most definitely not—against the backdrop of her Swedish/European otherness, where her status functioned as a form of an imaginary elsewhere.

This otherness also manifested itself through her status as a polyglot, a rare attribute of Classical Hollywood stars, heightening her status as a European other. She made films in five languages (Swedish, German, English, Italian, and French), all of which she became fluent in, the latter three only learned after her mid-20s. From *The Four Companions* (*Die vier Gesellen*, Carl Froelich, Germany, 1938), her one UFA-produced film in prewar Nazi Germany (where her status as a Swedish elsewhere star took on a decidedly different connotation as Joseph Goebbels actively recruited Swedes to the Nazi screen; Adolf Hitler, after screening the film, however, referred to it as "not good" [Urwand, 2103, 12]), to *Elena and Her Men* (*Elene et les hommes*, France, 1956), made with Jean Renoir, Bergman had a long tradition as an elsewhere actress, where her status as other was either deployed diegetically in the film or, as often, used in promotional para-material. Her status as an other, then, was not limited to her best-known period of work in Classical Hollywood.

In his study of the star, Richard Dyer delineates various components of stardom. He writes: "stars are commodities that are produced by institutions"; "a star is a constructed image, represented across a range of media and mediums"; "stars represent and embody certain ideologies"; and "a star is an image not a real person that is constructed ... out of a range of materials (e.g. advertising magazines etc. as well as films and music)" (Dyer 1979, 14). To understand Bergman's star image as one partly constituted by Swedish otherness, then, is to understand her as a social text that extends beyond simply the roles she played. Moreover, it is to point to the fact that stars do not have total control over their images, not simply because of their constructed nature, but also because part of the meaning-making takes place by the publics consuming their works and images. Indeed, as Dyer notes, an actress's image as a star can be turned against the actress behind the image; the supposed scandal that enveloped Bergman is a key case in point: "attempts by a star may meet with box office failure—Ingrid Bergman is the locus classicus" (Dyer 1979, 110). This was the case when her positively constructed image as a Swedish/European other was turned against her in the 1950s.

This mapping of the star intersects with Umberto Eco's analysis of the cult film, in which he uses *Casablanca* (Michael Curtiz, USA, 1942) as an exemplar. For Eco, the cult film forms an intertext that extends beyond the single work. Perhaps more so than any other Classical Hollywood star, this is the case for

Bergman, as her personal history became embedded in her star image, whether the image constructed by Hollywood or that of her supposed fall when the Rossellini scandal broke. Eco writes: "I think that in order to transform a work into a cult object one must be able to break, dislocate, unhinge it so that one can only remember parts of it, irrespective of their original relationship with the whole" (1987, 198). This notion of fragmentation plays a central role in how Bergman's work was understood. Much is made of the fact that Bergman's image as "virginal" and "pure" greatly influenced the backlash against her, as the supposedly ideal mother and wife (the press made much of her marriage to Swedish dentist—and later neurosurgeon—Petter Lindström), and this image was retrospectively over-determined by her playing a Swedish-American nun in *The Bells of Saint Mary's* (Leo McCarey, USA, 1945). Yet many of Bergman's best-known roles were decidedly un-virginal, especially for Hollywood at the time: in *Dr. Jekyll and Mr. Hyde* (Victor Fleming, USA, 1941) she plays a sex-worker who is murdered; in Hitchcock's *Notorious* (Alfred Hitchcock, USA, 1946), she plays a woman (this time of German descent because Nazis were the Nordic villains during the war) who is forced into sex work at the behest of her lover on behalf of the American government, in part to "atone" for the crimes of her Nazi father. It is the fragmentation of her supposedly "pure" Nordic role as extra-diegetic wife in some of the most famous roles she played that led both to her star image and to its undoing. Bergman became an "archetype." As Eco notes: "The term 'archetype' ... serves only to indicate a preestablished and frequently repeating narrative situation, cited or in some way recycled by innumerable other texts and provoking in the addressee a sort of intense emotion accompanied by the vague feeling of a déjà vu that everybody yearns to see again" (Eco 1987, 200). While Eco is addressing the cult film, his notion of the "archetype" is equally applicable to Bergman's star image as Nordic other (with all the contradictions of how her roles and biography were understood). What both Dyer and Eco point to is that the star image is not a stable entity, but something that is re-imagined by various audiences over time. Eco's analysis of the cult film complements the particular questions raised by Dyer. Like Humphrey Bogart after *Casablanca*, Bergman became a cult image, endlessly recombinant: her star image was that of a cult figure, and her life, public and private, became as much of an intertext as her star image onscreen.

Bergman, Classical Hollywood, and the Purity Paradox

Bergman's star image of Swedish/European otherness was first codified in Hollywood. Looking to replace Garbo, Selznick screened the Swedish version of *Intermezzo* at home. Immediately afterwards, he ordered his story editor Katherine Brown to "take the next boat to Sweden and [do] not come home without a contract for Miss Bergman" (see Selznick 1972). Yet, as Selznick often did, he had doubts, and worried that it was not Bergman, but the "girl" Gösta Stevens, who was the star required. Working from the film's credits, and in an experience of Nordic otherness of a different kind, Selznick did not realize that Stevens was male, and the film's co-writer (Selznick 1972, 126). This confusion cleared up, Selznick remade *Intermezzo: A Love Story* (Gregory Ratoff, USA, 1939) in Hollywood. As noted in studio publicity and Selznick's memos, once Bergman was signed, he tried to "re-make" her in the traditional Hollywood, star-making fashion, by insisting on heavy onscreen makeup and a new name, as hers was "too German" (Selznick 1972, 130). Bergman refused both; Selznick took this in his stride, marketing her as a "natural beauty," "healthy," and in "love with nature" (Selznick 1972, 132).

This created one archetype of Bergman for American consumption: one of Nordic beauty and purity. As Arne Lunde notes: "Bergman's ... roles as a nun in *The Bells of St. Mary's* (1945) and as a saint in *Joan of Arc* (1948) contributed to her public image of almost virginal, sacred purity" (Lunde 2010, 163). Yet this reading in some ways limits the shifting signification of Bergman's roles in Classical Hollywood. In many of her films, her presumed pan-Nordic identity is put to other uses, becoming a shifting signifier of self-contained masochism, often mobilized in roles where Bergman was a working woman (which paralleled her own life as the family breadwinner), or an actual working woman martyr, as in *Joan of Arc* (Victor Fleming, USA, 1948) (which was publicized extensively, including a *Life* cover on November 15, 1948 and a comic book adaptation published in early 1949 by Magazine Enterprises, featuring her on the cover).

Bergman's first Hollywood film, then, sets the stage for her future role as a Swedish/European other. In Selznick's remake of *Intermezzo*, she plays (as in the original Swedish version) the Swedish piano teacher Anita Hoffman, who begins a love affair with her pupil's father, the violinist Holger Brandt. The affair for a time rips apart the family, but Brandt's sadness over losing access to his child leads to Hoffman sacrificing the relationship and allowing the nuclear family to survive. It is worth noting here that Bergman is playing an adultress (by no means the image of purity—and this is the role that made her a Hollywood star) and a woman who works, but the fact that her sacrifice becomes part of the narrative is what redeems her, both diegetically and within the confines of the Hollywood Production Code, where "Adultery, sometimes necessary plot material, must not be explicitly treated, or justified, or presented attractively" (MacKenzie 2014, 407). Like many negotiations with the Code, compromises were made: adultery in *Intermezzo* is explicitly treated, but the outcome becomes noble and not attractive.

Films such as *Casablanca*, *Spellbound* (Alfred Hitchcock, USA, 1945), and *Notorious* frame Bergman's otherness as a signifier of both desire and distance.

DIASPORIC CINEMAS OF INGRID BERGMAN

Figure 10.1 Ingrid Bergman as sacrificial star in *Casablanca* (Michael Curtiz, USA, 1942).

This image was also mobilized in a different manner as Bergman entertained troops during the war in places such as Alaska (Bergman and Burgess 1980, 127), and starred as a Red Cross nurse in Jacques Tourneur's little-known short fundraising trailer *Seeing Them Through* (USA, 1945) (see Lafond 2015), and played herself in a promotional film for The American Brotherhood of Christians and Jews in the short *The American Creed* (Robert Stevenson, USA, 1946).

In *Casablanca*, Bergman plays Ilsa Lund (a Norwegian) whose Nordic identity is defined by sacrifice for the greater good. This image of sacrifice was not only powerful for the audiences who flocked to the film, but also for the US Office of War Information, which noted: "The heroine and the man she loves sacrifice their personal happiness in order that each may carry on the fight in the most effective manner. They realise that they cannot steal happiness with the rest of the world enslaved" (cited in Urwand 2013, 226). This report from the OWI may have influenced its subsequent desire to make a film with Bergman.

In *Casablanca*, the sacrifice of Bergman's character is not simply a way to appease the Code, but to also engage her European elsewhere status as a means of wartime propaganda. In *Notorious*, Bergman plays Alicia Huberman, a woman of German descent, whose role is that of the self-hating, self-sacrificing, self-destructive masochist. In *Spellbound*, her unspecified Nordic heritage (signified by her last name Petersen) is codified as frigid and repressed, and with a great love of skiing (which helps her solve Gregory Peck's amnesia). In *Gaslight* (George Cukor, USA, 1944), her nondescript European character is forced to question her own sanity by her scheming husband, coining a now-accepted psychological term in the process. In a very different role, Bergman plays Sister Mary Benedict in *The Bells of St Mary's*, a film that in many ways resonates with the Hollywood publicity of her "goodness" and purity. But even in this film, her Nordic status (a Swedish-American from Minnesota, a Swedish elsewhere itself) is used to foreground her love of sports and the outdoors. And she is again punished, by contracting tuberculosis. In *Under Capricorn* (UK, 1949), her final film with Hitchcock, sacrifice again plays a central role, where Joseph Cotton takes responsibility for a murder committed by Bergman, leading to his exile in the Australian penal colony. In Bergman's major American films, then, her roles oscillate between a few that foreground an acceptable form of Swedish/European otherness (the pure Bergman), which, not coincidentally, is also the image of patriarchal desire, and a less acceptable form of otherness, that of the working woman (from sex worker, to rebel, to nun, to martyr), relatively free of the constraints of heteronormative patriarchal America. There are two sides to otherness, then: one that can be assimilated into the American melting pot, and one which ought to be excluded as challenging patriarchal norms. The shift from the former to the latter in Bergman's cult/star image leaves the screen and becomes actualized when she abandons Hollywood (and supposedly her child) for Italy, Europe, and art cinema.

The Star and Elsewhere Internationalism

In one film, however, Bergman's "Swedish-American" persona was put to use in what could be called "reversed elsewheres," through the propaganda film she made for the US Office of War Information, to explain the affinities between Sweden and America to Swedish audiences during the War: *Swedes in America* (*Svenskar i Amerika*, Irving Lerner, USA, 1943). As the war in Europe escalated, Bergman worried about how Sweden would be perceived in the USA. She wrote: "If Sweden should be overrun by the Nazis . . . I hope the people of America would not turn against my people. Sweden, like Switzerland, is surrounded, cut off, made helpless by the enemy. There is very little she could do. If the tragic moment of attack should come, I hope the people of America would not forget this" (cited in Spoto 2001, 140). So, when asked to make a film for Swedish audiences by the OWI, she accepted. In this propaganda short (made for distribution in Sweden in the first instance; both Swedish and English language versions were produced), Bergman offers a travelogue of the

Figure 10.2 Ingrid Bergman as Swedish-American ethnographer in *Swedes in America* (Irving Lerner, USA, 1942).

great Swedish-American accomplishments, while also helping out on a farm in Minnesota. The film plays a dual function: one the one hand, as a propagandistic means to keep Sweden neutral through outreach to Swedish audiences, and on the other, to embed the "bad" Nordics (neutral Sweden) into the sisterhood of "good" Nordics (occupied Denmark and Norway) for American audiences. Bergman discovered her own elsewhere in Minnesota: "this is the most wonderful trip you can ever imagine. I am crazy about the Swedes ... though I love Americans too ... I really feel as if I've come home here. People must also think I belong to them" (Bergman and Burgess 1980, 125–6).

The *New York Times* described the short as "an example of how minority groups are treated in this country ... The British are making their own prints ... and will exhibit the film in theatres throughout the United Kingdom. The short has also been sent to Sweden" ([anon] 1943, 14). Indeed, the film was positively reviewed in *Dagens Nyheters* (Jonsson 1943). In a longer review in the *Times*, the critic Bosley Crowther stated:

> With Ingrid Bergman as its charming narrator and participant in many of its scenes, it shows the simplicity and dignity and especially the cooperative spirit of American Swedes living in the Minnesota region. It was made primarily for showing in Sweden, with a Swedish narration by Miss Bergman, but it should be effective in other countries, for it has what

Mr. Riskin calls an "eavesdropping method of propaganda"—which is to say it looks in upon a particular phase of American life that is typical. (Crowther 1943, X3)

Swedes in America places the "real" Ingrid Bergman in front of the camera; yet this is also only another screen persona, and one that takes her Swedish/European otherness and subsumes it into America. Bergman also functioned as an elsewhere onscreen in Sweden as an expatriate: she both plays the role of the intrepid ethnographer of Swedish America and functions as a model of successful expatriate life. Yet, even this act of propagandistic assimilation was not enough to cement her star status as safe in America.

THE SACRIFICIAL STAR AND NEO-REALISM

In 1950, Bergman went to Italy to make what she thought would be one film with Roberto Rossellini. Because of the relationship that developed between them, her status as a Hollywood star changed drastically, and her status as a European other came to the forefront. She was perceived as having an anti-American moral sense because of the decisions she made about her career and her personal life. Perhaps because of this shift, the films Bergman made with Rossellini were perceived as failures upon release, rejected in both the USA and Italy. These transnational works challenged the image and acting style of Bergman as star in Classical Hollywood. Moreover, Bergman and Rossellini's works challenged the already canonized form that Italian neo-realism was supposed to take (non-actors, a quasi-documentary form, location shooting, at times meandering plots), heightening the role of melodrama to a far greater degree than earlier works. Rossellini saw Bergman as his chance to get Hollywood funding, since Bergman was perhaps the biggest female movie star in the world at that time. While most of Hollywood wanted to work with Bergman, very few wanted to work with Rossellini, with his contempt for Hollywood and his adamant desire not to write scripts (Gallagher 1988, 312–16; Spoto 2001, 259). Eventually, Bergman secured financing from Howard Hughes through his company RKO (Hughes did not care about the content of the proposed film, but wanted to work with Bergman). Bergman's first film with Rossellini, then, is not an Italian film per se, but an Italian-American co-production. In *Stromboli* (*Stromboli, terra di Dio*, Roberto Rossellini, Italy/USA, 1950), Bergman plays a woman locked in a displaced persons camp in Italy. To get out, she marries a fisherman from the remote island of Stromboli. When she arrives there, she immediately despises the place, feeling like an outsider and living in an elsewhere on an island from which its own inhabitants attempt to escape. She becomes pregnant (as Bergman herself did during the making of the film) and tries to make a life there. Frustrated, and at the end of her tether, she tries to escape by going over the island's volcano to a fishing village. Wandering overnight, she comes to a spiritual realization on the volcano. The film ends without the audience knowing if she will leave the island or return to the village.

Stromboli echoes developments in Bergman's life at the time. Her plan was not to be in Italy for the next six years, making films that were not successes and only working with Rossellini, but her pregnancy changed that trajectory, especially once it became public knowledge in the USA. While most accounts point to the undermining of Bergman's Nordic image of purity that led to the censure, it is also the case that her independence, and the value she put in her craft, were also part of the backlash that tied into larger debates in the USA at the time. Bergman was vilified in the US Senate by Edwin C. Jackson on March 14, 1950 for her extra-marital pregnancy:

> Mr. President, now that the stupid film about a pregnant woman and a volcano has exploited America with the usual finesse, to the mutual delight of RKO and the debased Rossellini, are we merely to yawn wearily, greatly relieved that this hideous thing is finished and then forget it? I hope not. A way must be found to protect the people in the future. When Rossellini the love pirate returned to Rome smirking over his conquest, it was not Mrs. Lindstrom's scalp which hung from the conquering hero's belt, it was her very soul. Now what is left of her has brought two children into the world—one has no mother; the other is illegitimate. Even in this modern age of surprise, it is upsetting to have our most popular but pregnant movie queen, her condition the result of an illicit affair, play the part of a cheap chiseling female to add spice to a silly story which lacks appeal. (cited in Stern 2015)

Here, Bergman's status as an outsider, framed through concepts of otherness, and her being from an elsewhere were now at odds. At a time in American geopolitics where foreign nationals of all stripes were looked upon with suspicion, the backlash against Bergman can be read through the prism of fear of various forms of European otherness. There is also a sense of betrayal in this response, as if the projections placed on the image of Bergman were being usurped by her personal life. Moreover, it was an implicit response to the fact that Bergman put her working career and personal life ahead of the moral frames that dominated the USA at the time. This censorious outcry was just the beginning of American witch hunts into supposed sex scandals by foreign nationals (Bergman never took out American citizenship). Charlie Chaplin (who had remained a citizen of the UK) was denied re-entry to the USA by the Attorney General on September 19, 1952. *Time* Magazine also published its infamous expose "Sin in Sweden" in April 1955. All three of these events were

Figure 10.3 Ingrid Bergman: the problems faced by independent woman in *Europe '51* (Roberto Rossellini, Italy, 1952).

tied to Cold War politics in the USA and to the archetype of Swedish/European otherness that Bergman became.

From *Stromboli* onwards, Bergman mostly plays Nordic/Swedish/European outsiders in Rossellini's films. In *Europe '51* (*Europa '51*, Italy, 1952), based on Rossellini's idea of what might happen to Francis Assisi were he to return to earth today, Bergman plays another Northern European bourgeois expatriate in Italy, transformed by the death of her son from complications following an attempted suicide, dedicating her life to helping the disenfranchised. She rejects both capitalism and communism, and follows a spiritual path. She ends up in an insane asylum, as martyred as Bergman's favorite anti-heroine Joan of Arc, within the confines of modern Europe.

In *Fear* (*La paura*, Italy/West Germany, 1954), based on a novella by Stefan Zweig, Bergman plays a highly successful woman trying to keep from her husband her recent affair in order to maintain the image, as she states, of the "perfect marriage." The ex-girlfriend of her lover blackmails her while she is wracked with guilt, only to find out that her husband knows of the affair and has used the girlfriend to blackmail her. She contemplates both murder and suicide as a remedy. In *Voyage to Italy* (*Viaggio in Italia*, Italy, 1954), Katherine Joyce (Bergman)'s marriage falls apart as she and her husband travel to Italy after the death of an uncle. Away from their bourgeois British social circle, the couple in this new land quickly realize that, without the British social structure, their relationship is empty and barren of emotion. Here, Bergman's Nordic/European status is seen as desiccated and ossified, compared to the lively and passionate Italians.

In these films, Bergman's character is changed by being in an elsewhere environment. This shift is not determined simply by the people she meets, but the elsewhere "objects" that populate her space. These "objects" (both material and philosophical) demarcate an interstitial space for her characters between their Northern European backgrounds and the elsewhere worlds they inhabit. As Slavoj Žižek notes: "we can specify the lure of Rossellini's Bergman films: they always contain some image of 'authentic,' substantial life, and it seems as if the heroine's salvation depends on her ability to immerge into this substantial 'authenticity'" (Žižek 1990: 40). In each work, the outsider character Bergman plays changes not because of human interactions, but, as Alain Bergala points out, because of things: whether the volcano in *Stromboli*, the statues in *Voyage to Italy*, or spirituality in *Europe '51* (Bergala 1984, 11). These things, however, anchor Bergman's characters to another part of the world; her relationship to these very Italian things is that of a Nordic outsider who changes through proximity to them.

The Italian press was displeased with neo-realism becoming a star vehicle for a (Swedish-) American actress (Gallagher 1988, 358–66). Many argued that Rossellini had "sold out" (358) by working with Bergman; her status as an other working in an elsewhere undercut the supposed purity of neo-realism. Yet, there was a transnational audience of critics for these works: the young French writers at *Cahiers du cinéma* thought these works were at the cutting edge of contemporary cinema, calling them the beginning of "modernist" cinema, and an inspiration for both the themes and the production practices of much of the soon-to-emerge *nouvelle vague*. Jacques Rivette called Rossellini, citing *Voyage to Italy*, the first modern filmmaker (Rivette 1985, 193). Eric Rohmer stated that "The term 'neo-realism' has become so debased that I would hesitate to use it in relation to *Viaggio in Italia* if Rossellini hadn't in fact claimed it himself" (Rohmer 1985, 205) and praised *Stromboli* and *Europe '51* for their use of documentary techniques (Rohmer 1985, 206). André Bazin wrote an open letter-cum-manifesto to the editor of the Italian film journal *Cinema Nuovo*, proclaiming that the French critics were right, and the Italian ones wrong, about the debasement of neo-realism, about Rossellini's works, and about those with Bergman in particular (Bazin 1971, 93–101). Of course, a key factor was that the French critics were more influenced by Hollywood than the Italians. What the French critics saw was not just a clash of styles, but Bergman playing a form of double otherness in her elsewhere roles: removed from Europe via America, and then removed from America via Europe. If Rossellini's films are the first modern films, prefiguring the work of Michelangelo Antonioni, they are so because of the kind of displaced acting and therefore screen presence Bergman brings to these films. The French critics were able to see the dual elsewheres playing out in these films: the displacement of some of the tenets of neo-realism through the presence of a Swedish American star, and the elsewhere roles played by Bergman as a cultural outsider in these works.

Bergman Does Bergman, or, Reverse Elsewheres

After years of making films in Hollywood and Europe, Bergman returned to Swedish cinema. By the time she did, her status as a Swedish star had changed, and was now far more identified with Hollywood and neo-realism than with her Swedish roots and early career. Yet, for many years, Bergman wished to make a film with Sweden's "other Bergman." As she did with Rossellini, she got Ingmar Bergman's attention through a note, this time slipped directly into his pocket (Bergman 1994, 327). It took a decade for Bergman to come up with a script, and in Bergman's first draft of the synopsis he states directly: "I must have Ingrid Bergman and Liv Ullman in the two roles, and no one else" (Bergman 1994, 326). The result, *Autumn Sonata*, tells the story of the highly successful, long-absent mother played by Bergman, who visits her daughter in a remote village in Norway after the death of her lover. Over a day and a half, the mother and daughter argue, the daughter condemning her mother for the abandonment of both her and her disabled sister. This film was also an elsewhere for Ingmar Bergman, who had been producing films in West Germany since his self-imposed tax exile in 1976.

Once filming began, the two Bergmans argued extensively, both about the story (which paralleled the "abandonment" both supposedly engaged in toward their children) and about acting. In what one might consider a "reversed Nordic otherness," Ingmar complained extensively about Ingrid's Classical Hollywood acting style, claiming that in the first rehearsals she was too staged and had been ruined by her time in Hollywood:

> The actual filming was draining. I did not have what one would call difficulties in my working relationship with Ingrid Bergman. Rather, it was a kind of a language barrier ... I discovered that she had rehearsed her entire part in front of a mirror, complete with intonations and self-conscious gestures. It was clear that she had a different approach to her profession than the rest of us. She was still living in the 1940s. (Bergman 1994, 329–32)

While he praises her work with Hitchcock, calling her performances in his films "always magnificent" (Bergman 1994, 332), the process of having Ingrid in an Ingmar film was, as he noted, taken by one French critic as "Bergman does Bergman" (Bergman 1994, 334), which led him to believe he was beginning to parody himself. But what the passage above is really about is the clash of two styles, and Ingrid Bergman coming back to Swedish cinema and acting in a manner deemed other to her own country. While Ingmar struggled with Ingrid's acting, and Ingrid struggled with Ingmar's direction, the coming together of these two traditions led to certain discoveries for both artists. Bergman writes: "Ingrid Bergman discovered a phenomenon she had never met before in her professional life. Between the many women in the whole troop, strong, independent, professionally and privately experienced women, there was a solidarity, a sisterhood" (Bergman 1988, 184). Ingmar also discusses Ingrid's home movies, which in part would form the basis of Stig Björkman's *Ingrid Bergman: In Her Own Words* (*Jag är Ingrid*, Sweden, 2015). He writes: "She kept some strips of film from her childhood and upbringing in a rusty tin she had taken with her all over the word ... Ingrid treasured her film and I, after some difficulty, was allowed to borrow it to make new negatives and new copies of the worn and dangerous nitrate strip" (1988, 184). These films point to a life very much lived on and mediated through screens, long before the advent of social media. Yet, like social media, perhaps Ingrid Bergman's films can be seen as a socially constructed account of aspects of her life as an elsewhere star. Some of this social construction is put forth by her, other parts stripped away and remediated by the public. In this light, *Autumn Sonata* functions as a summary of her highly conflicted star image, her position as a Swedish/European other, and her career as an elsewhere practitioner. Like Ingrid herself, her character in *Autumn Sonata* travels the world performing her art, at the cost of the supposed neglect of her family. As for Ingrid, the toll this takes is great: a loss of family, and a sense of displacement both at home and abroad. But what this journey also allows for is the Swedish other, the star persona and the person, to exist outside the constraints of either their home or their adopted countries. As Bergman's career progressed, her story became enmeshed with the characters she played; this became her "archetype," in Eco's sense. This also points to the fact that the image of sacrifice, so often attached to Bergman and to her characters, can be read, in the right Nordic light, as a story of emancipation through the practitioner's agency provided by the professional and personal choices she made just as much as it can be read as a story of the doomed victim with no control over her narrative trajectory.

References

[anon.]. 1943. "British to See OWI Short." *New York Times*, October 8, 43.
Bazin, André. 1971. "In Defense of Rossellini." In Bazin, *What is Cinema? Vol. II.* Berkeley: University of California Press. 93–101.
Bergala, Alain. 1984. "Celle par qui le scandale arrive." *Cahiers du cinéma* 856: 3–12.

Bergman, Ingmar. 1988. *Magic Lantern: An Autobiography*. New York: Viking.
Bergman, Ingmar. 1994. *Images: My Life in Film*. New York: Arcade.
Bergman, Ingrid and Alan Burgess. 1980. *My Story*. New York: Delacorte.
Chandler, Charlotte. 2007. *Ingrid Bergman: A Personal Biography*. New York: Applause.
Crowther, Bosley. 1943. "Destination Abroad: Something about the Pictures Which the OWI is Sending Overseas." *New York Times*, August 29, X3.
Dyer, Richard. 1979. *Stars*. London: British Film Institute.
Eco, Umberto. 1987. "*Casablanca*: Cult Movies and Intertextual Collage." In *Travels in Hyper-Reality: Essays*. London: Picador. 197–212.
Gallagher, Tag. 1988. *The Adventures of Roberto Rossellini: His Life and Films*. New York: Da Capo.
Hirdman, Yvonne. 1998. "Social Engineering and the Woman Question: Sweden in the Thirties." In Wallace Clement and Rianne Mahon, eds. *Swedish Social Democracy: A Model in Transition*. Toronto: Canadian Scholars' Press. 65–81.
Hjort, Mette. 2010. *Lone Scherfig's Italian for Beginners*. Seattle: University of Washington Press.
Jonsson, Thorsen. 1943. "Ingrid Bergman blev god guide i 'Svenskamerika'." *Dagens Nyheters* September 11: 5.
Lafond, Frank. 2015. "Un film réinventé." <http://debordements.fr/Un-film-reinvente>
Leamer, Laurence. 1986. *As Time Goes By: The Life of Ingrid Bergman*. New York: Harper & Row.
Lunde, Arne. 2010. *Nordic Exposures: Scandinavian Identities in Classical Hollywood Cinema*. Seattle: University of Washington Press.
MacKenzie, Scott. 2014. *Film Manifestos and Global Cinema Cultures*. Berkeley: University of California Press.
Rivette, Jacques. 1985. "Letter on Rossellini." In Jim Hillier, ed. *Cahiers du cinéma, The 1950s: Neo-Realism, Hollywood, New Wave*. Cambridge, MA: Harvard University Press. 192–204.
Rohmer, Eric. 1985. "The Land of Miracles." In Jim Hillier, ed. *Cahiers du cinéma, The 1950s: Neo-Realism, Hollywood, New Wave*. Cambridge, MA: Harvard University Press. 205–8.
Selznick, David O. 1972. *Memo from David O. Selznick* ed. Rudy Behlmer. New York: Viking.
Smit, David. W. 2005. "Marketing Ingrid Bergman." *Quarterly Review of Film and Video* 22: 237–50.
Spoto, Donald. 2001. *Notorious: The Life of Ingrid Bergman*. New York: Da Capo.
Stern, Marlow. 2015. "When Congress Slut-Shamed Ingrid Bergman." <https://www.thedailybeast.com/when-congress-slut-shamed-ingrid-bergman>
Steele, Joseph Henry. 1959. *Ingrid Bergman: An Intimate Portrait*. New York: David McKay.
Thomson, David. 2009. *Ingrid Bergman*. London: Faber.
Urwand, Ben. 2013. *The Collaboration: Hollywood's Pact with Hitler*. Cambridge, MA: Harvard University Press.
Žižek, Slavoj. 1990. "Rossellini: Woman as Symptom of Man," *October* 54: 18–44.

11. "HERE IS MY HOME": VOICEOVER AND FOREIGN-LANGUAGE VERSIONS IN POSTWAR DANISH INFORMATIONAL FILM

C. Claire Thomson

In 1948, the Central Film Library of the Danish Government (Statens Filmcentral) published an English-language brochure entitled *Documentary in Denmark: One Hundred Films of Facts* [sic] *in War, Occupation, Liberation, Peace, 1940–1948*. Its striking cover renders the "D" in "Documentary" as a teal-colored film strip upon which black stick figures re-live the recent German occupation. The cover design emphasizes the catalogue's diplomatic task: to market postwar Denmark overseas as a plucky, democratic nation emerging from foreign occupation.

The catalogue looks outwards to the world: its price is emblazoned on the back cover in shillings and dollars, and some of its entries list one or more languages in which the films are available alongside their length in feet, meters and minutes, and their gauge and stock. This was a catalogue for international distribution, paving the way for the worldwide trajectories of the films themselves. In multiple copies, in their canisters, they spread ideas and images of Denmark through established networks of distribution and exhibition, and sometimes via *ad hoc* acts of cultural diplomacy. Often, their paths followed or blazed a trail for other physical goods, from Danish bacon to Danish design.

Over the next two decades, *Documentary in Denmark* was superseded at intervals by catalogues advertising an updated selection of films: *117 Short Films from Denmark* (1960), and *236 Short Films from Denmark* (1971). Audiences at film festivals, trade fairs, in schools, clubs, libraries, and their own homes could learn about Danish social security in English, silverware and pottery in Spanish, or Copenhagen's architecture and parks in Japanese. The films were designed to present Denmark to the world as an elsewhere, often explicitly as a "little land" that was modern and democratic, with its own traditions, products and skills, and peaceful and progressive ambitions. To achieve this, the films had to quite literally speak the world's languages.

This chapter discusses a selection of foreign-language Danish informational films, giving an overview, firstly, of how the films traveled and in which languages. We then look more closely at a key principle in such filmmaking in Denmark: the use of voiceover, as opposed to subtitling or dubbing. This was a practice predicated on the medium-specific properties of film, as well as the networks of distribution and exhibition in play at the time. Voiceover was a practical necessity, but one which positioned the filmic narratives, and by extension Denmark, in spatio-temporal relation to the contexts of viewing. As Charles Wolfe has argued, mid-century documentary voiceover infers a spatial relationship to the onscreen world; voiceover, he comments, "comes from *else*where" (Wolfe 2016, 265, emphasis original). Examining a selection of typical and atypical films made between 1947 and 1960, I argue that voiceover, accent, and ambient sound often engender a delicate balance between "here" and "elsewhere." The chapter concludes with a discussion of *D...for Design!*, a 1956 short presenting Danish applied arts to a range of markets. *D...for Design!* was not unique in being later adapted for a domestic audience back in Denmark. However, its Danish title, *Her er mit hjem* ("Here is my Home"), unwittingly indexes the tensions inherent in constructing a voice that can present images of Denmark to the world as both immediate and other, here and elsewhere.

From Domestic Propaganda to Cultural Diplomacy

Denmark's postwar re-branding of itself through the medium of film was part of a burgeoning global network of documentary and what has been dubbed "useful cinema" (Acland and Wasson 2011): films made for purposes other than pure entertainment, such as education, propaganda and information. In Denmark, state-sponsored filmmaking started slowly in the mid-1930s, with the establishment of the semi-governmental agency Dansk Kulturfilm in 1932. In the late 1930s an emerging generation of filmmakers forged close links with the British Documentary Movement, set up their own companies, and made films worldwide, traveling, for example, with the Danish engineering firm Kampsax to shoot the construction of the trans-Persian railway (Boisen 1977).

During the German occupation of the country (1940–5), the Danish Government Film Committee (Ministeriernes Filmudvalg) was established to consolidate and rationalize state-sponsored filmmaking, initially with a focus on the war effort, such as employment and recycling of raw materials. Such films were often screened in cinemas as part of multimedia campaigns, but were also distributed on narrow gauge stock for use with portable projectors in a range of contexts. Increasingly, the Government Film Committee worked in tandem with Dansk Kulturfilm on commissioning and production, and the two organizations effectively functioned as one from 1946 (for a more detailed discussion of the period and these films, see Thomson 2018).

While production of informational shorts for domestic audiences continued after the Occupation, a large proportion of films produced from 1947 to around 1960 were designed for foreign audiences. The roots of this strategy can be discerned in committee minutes from the last year of the war; the Government Film Committee recognized that film would be a crucial tool of cultural diplomacy in the postwar world. From spring 1944, plans were laid to produce films that would tell the English-speaking world not just about the Resistance but also about Danish progress in a range of fields, particularly social security and key industries (Thomson 2018, 65–7). Immediately after the Liberation, Mogens Skot-Hansen, the head of the Film Committee, invited to Copenhagen an eminent British documentarian, Arthur Elton. Already enamored of the auteur Carl Th. Dreyer, Elton declared himself impressed by the Danish documentary filmmakers' "technical virtuosity, their humanity and their humour" (Elton 1948, 9). Initially tasked with reporting on the national documentary scene, Elton also agreed to oversee the production of a series of English-language films which would showcase Denmark's achievements in social security. A set of five short films was released in 1947 under the rubric *Social Denmark*. The four new films covered healthcare and education for children (*Denmark Grows Up*, dir. Hagen Hasselbalch, Astrid Henning-Jensen, Søren Melson), social care and pensions for the elderly (*The Seventh Age*, dir. Torben Anton Svendsen with screenplay by Carl Th. Dreyer), sickness insurance (*Health for Denmark*, dir. Torben Anton Svendsen with screenplay by Arthur Elton), and the holiday pay system (*People's Holiday*, dir. Søren Melson, with screenplay by renowned designer Poul Henningsen). A fifth film was a version of Carl Th. Dreyer's 1942 state-sponsored short about services for unmarried mothers (*Mødrehjælpen*, re-titled *Good Mothers*), with English voiceover. The inclusion of Dreyer's film seems to have been an attempt to use his international fame as a carrier wave for the rest of the set; indeed, several British reviews of *The Seventh Age* mention Dreyer's involvement in the script (Thomson 2018: 81–2).

This was a transformational project, in several ways. Firstly, it established Danish documentarians working on the international scene as filmmakers to watch. A second effect was to kick-start a postwar expansion of exchange of informational films between Danish and other national film libraries, and via a range of other developing international networks of exchange. Thirdly, during the production of the series a basic principle of Danish filmmaking for export crystalized: the use of voiceover, rather than dubbing or subtitling. In what follows, we consider the second and third of these in turn.

Versionizing and Distribution

Informational filmmaking for foreign audiences can be understood as a continuation of a longer tradition of public or cultural diplomacy, a political strategy in which the Nordic and Baltic nations, as small states, have participated at governmental and non-governmental levels since at least the early twentieth century (Clerc and Glover 2015). However, we must also pay attention to the medium-specific and historically specific ways in which film travels. Narrow-gauge film stock, portable projectors, national film libraries, exchange programs, and hungry audiences constituted the conditions of possibility for the international distribution and exhibition of informational films. As Zoë Druick observes, international circulation of such films tended to reiterate notions of national distinctiveness. Film festival programming framed documentary as reflective of national specificities, a focus which "reified culture as a form of national difference while simultaneously naturalizing the nation as a source of the traits of individuals" (Druick 2011, 84). The other side of the same coin was the growing film production under the auspices of bodies such as the United Nations Film Board, UNESCO, and the Marshall Plan, which were also exhibited at film festivals and used for education worldwide (Langlois 2016, 75; Fritsche 2018). Danish documentaries thus construct Denmark as an elsewhere not only through content but also through networks of distribution—themselves dependent on the materialities of film production and exhibition.

Attempts to trace the paths of films from Denmark out into the world encounter three main difficulties. Firstly, there was significant overlap between films for domestic and international markets. Many films for foreign audiences were eventually versionized into Danish, while some films originally in Danish were re-purposed for export. A second difficulty is the lack of a coherent and comprehensive record of where the majority of films traveled, who saw them, and how they were received. Statens Filmcentral's annual reports contain detailed data about domestic loans of films to schools, clubs, and libraries, and exchanges with foreign film libraries were often recorded. For example, the report for 1947–8 specifies that the rights to nine Danish documentaries had been given to the British Central Office of Information in return for eleven British Council films. This bundle included all the *Social Denmark* films, and up to twenty copies of each were distributed in the UK (SFC 1948, 2). The Press Bureau of the Danish Foreign Ministry (Udenrigsministeriets Pressebureau) coordinated foreign distribution of films, and diplomatic missions overseas were usually distribution nodes. The production files of a minority of films contain correspondence with the Press Bureau regarding circulation and viewing figures. Correspondence with a variety of organizations provided feedback on the reception of some films, and there are records of screenings at some film festivals. But overall, the picture is patchy, and international distribution seems often to have been reactive (e.g. responding to trade fairs or trends) rather than strategically proactive.

A third difficulty is the proliferation not just of language versions of films, but of different-length versions of the same film in different languages. Broadly speaking, the original commission for a film would specify its length, determined by two main factors: the budget, and the projected screening context(s). Films for projection in cinemas before the main feature (*forfilm*) or for general export would be around fifteen minutes at most. Films intended for Danish audiences, to provoke discussion in clubs and schools (*foreningsfilm*), might be as long as forty minutes. If a filmmaker was ambitious, renowned, or persuasive, budgets could expand, and organizations could request longer or shorter versions in one or more languages. New screening contexts emerged: the spread of television in North America from the early 1950s prompted seventeen-minute versions of films to fit commercial breaks (Thomson 2018, 178). There were so many versions in Danish, German, and English, longer and shorter, of *They Guide You Across*, Ingolf Boisen's 1949 film about the transatlantic air route, that Statens Filmcentral was unable to keep track and lost at least one booking (Thomson 2018, 98).

What we do know is which language versions were made of each film. *Social Denmark* was initially a bilateral Anglo-Danish collaboration, but plans were floated early on for more language versions; all five films were eventually versionized into French, and two of them (*The Seventh Age* and *Denmark Grows Up*) were made in German. As the data in successive catalogues suggest, this combination of languages—English, French, and German—was standard, with Spanish also fairly common, and Italian rarer. A handful of films were versionized into Japanese for a trade fair in Osaka in 1970 (Johansen 1968). Occasionally, governments or organizations would request permission to versionize films in their own languages. For example, the Belgian Co-operative Society asked permission to make a Flemish version of Theodor Christensen's *The Pattern of Cooperation* (1952) (Thomson and Hilson 2014). Perhaps the most exotic request was from the Danish Esperanto Society, which argued for an Esperanto version of Jørgen Roos' Oscar-nominated 1960 short *A City Called Copenhagen* (Svane 1959), a request that went unfulfilled.

Within the Nordic region, government policy was that Danish films were not versionized into other Scandinavian languages. A Finnish version of *A City Called Copenhagen* was made, however, and the policy was also relaxed for Theodor Christensen's anti-smoking film *Breathe!* (*Træk vejret!* 1958), which was versionized into Norwegian and Swedish to reach as wide an audience as possible. A selection of films was versionized into Greenlandic for use in what at the time was a Danish colony, including Theodor Christensen's *Enden på legen* (*The End of the Game*, 1961); Icelanders were expected to make do with Danish.

One filmmaker, Bent Barfod, decided on his own initiative to make *Somethin' about Scandinavia*, an English-language version of his film about Nordic political cooperation (*Noget om Norden*, 1956), and used children's voices with the aim of producing an engaging voiceover (MFU 1958). The experiment failed, at least in New York, where end-users complained that "our kids probably couldn't understand a word said ... Dialogue difficult due to accent" (Educational Film Library Association, Inc. n.d.). Normally, Dansk Kulturfilm kept a tight grip on foreign-language versions. Translators were carefully chosen, and translated scripts were checked by the Foreign Ministry. Given that the voiceover scripts had to calibrate with a standard cut of the film in question, there was little room for deviation from the source text.

Voiceover and Voice

Social Denmark established the use of voiceover as a key principle in Danish informational film for export. During pre-production, Elton had to school his Danish documentarian colleagues in this rule. Elton's response to a draft by Carl Th. Dreyer for *The Seventh Age* was blunt: "I found it long, dull and too detailed. I also think it unpractical because, *if you want to export the film, you should surely avoid synchronised dialogue*" (Elton 1946, my emphasis). Elton repeats the point in another commentary on an early draft of *People's Holiday*: "The present script appears to rely on dialogue. This is, of course, inadmissible unless we adopt the tiresome device of superimposed titles" (Elton n.d.). Films that would have to be versionized into foreign languages could not contain dialogue, except as ambient sound; all information had to be contained within the voiceover. Each language version would then replace the original voiceover wholesale.

The avoidance of synchronized dialogue was partly a response to a temporary technological limitation: the restrictions on sound mixing inherent in the available sound-on-film recording technique. Multiple language versions could not easily be edited in and out of a base recording in post-production. Audiences had quickly become accustomed to synchronized sound in the "talkies," and felt "cheated" if actors' mouths were not seen to produce the words heard; by the same token, there was little tolerance for glitches in "lip-synch" (Doane 1980, 34). Done badly, synchronization "carries with it the potential risk of exposing the material heterogeneity of the medium" and destroying the illusion of bodily presence (35). An experiment in the use of wire recording in a Danish informational film a couple of years after *Social*

Denmark, in *They Guide You Across* (1949), only demonstrated how clumsy dubbed speech mixed in during post-production could sound. But 1947 was, coincidentally, the year that Bing Crosby was famously recorded on magnetic tape, demonstrating the potential of the medium for fidelity and for the facilitation of sound mixing (McMurray 2017, 41), and leading to Hollywood's adoption of magnetic sound technology as standard by the early 1950s. In other words, the Golden Age of international exchange of informational films was founded on sound-on-film optical prints, a state of affairs which would not last long, but which had repercussions for how stories were told, and thus whose voices and languages were heard.

On the other hand, avoiding synchronized dialogue in films for export is a solution to a problem as old as sound film: dialogue in any language requires either dubbing or subtitling for foreign markets, and both practices are off-putting for (some) audiences. National preferences for dubbing versus subtitling had crystalized during the transition to sound (thus around fifteen years before the *Social Denmark* project), with France, Germany, Italy, and Spain generally dubbing foreign films, and subtitling being the preference elsewhere (O'Sullivan 2011, 10). In some contexts, voiceover functioned as a third form of audiovisual translation, that is, an alternative to dubbing or subtitling, as with the Polish "lektor" voice (O'Sullivan 2011, 94).

In documentary, voiceover is not (usually) for translation purposes, but a feature of the diegesis. It is usually crucial to (though not synonymous with) the "Voice-of-God" or "Voice-of-Authority" effect (Nichols 2010, 74–6). In its most calcified forms, such as the newsreel series *The March of Time*, this kind of voiceover can be "stentorian, aggressive, assuming a power to speak the truth of the filmic text" (Wolfe 2016, 264). From the late 1950s, movements such as Direct Cinema rebelled against the "Voice-of-God" model; in some quarters, this development was in turn critiqued for sacrificing "voice" (in the sense of clarity, opinion, point-of-view) along with the more problematically didactic elements of voiceover, and the complex and sophisticated experiments with voice by documentarians of the 1930s and 1940s have been belatedly recognized (Youdelman 1982; Wolfe 2016, 265). Many of the Danish films made for foreign markets aspire to, and achieve, the qualities ascribed by Youdelman to the best documentary voiceovers of the 1930s and 1940s: "strong, haunting, and lyrical ... rarely dull or detached," and functioning as "part of an orchestrated totality" with images, music, and other aspects of the film text (1982, 9). Furthermore, it would be reductive to assume that the "voice" of commissioned informational film emanated directly from the commissioning authorities. I have argued elsewhere (Thomson 2018) that the agendas of the funders and commissioners of informational films were often diluted, re-worked and complicated during the production process, and voiceover is certainly one of those battlegrounds.

Translational Narrating Voiceover

Wolfe poses the question of where a voiceover seems to come from. It does not, he ponders, emanate "from the image, nor from that surrounding diegetic space that images and sounds imply"; it can stem from a *post hoc* "place in time," or an undefined "extradiegetic register" (Wolfe 2016, 266). It can also resonate with the space and time of viewing in complex and self-referential ways (269). In the context under discussion, the implied cultural and/or geographical distance of the voiceover from the viewer and/or from the culture depicted is surprisingly varied. It is constructed using a variety of mechanisms, including accent and language variety, deixis, and self-referentiality. Underpinning all of these is the translation itself.

The adoption of voiceover in the films under discussion in this chapter is a combination of the practices outlined above: Voice-of-God as a narrative strategy, and as a translation of the entire film. O'Sullivan's term "translational narrating voiceover (TNV)" is pertinent here. This is a type of voiceover "which presents . . . a discourse which stands in a representational relationship to the heterolingual diegetic situation it overspeaks" (O'Sullivan 2011, 95–6). In other words, the English (or French, or Spanish, or Japanese) voiceover is commenting on a situation or lifeworld in which people are speaking Danish and engaged in the (Danish) activities with which the film is concerned. This is a productive tension which frames the foreignness of Danish language and culture as both here and elsewhere, both other and familiar.

This play with the tension between Danish as implicit vernacular and the foreign-language voiceover was already in evidence in the *Social Denmark* films. *Denmark Grows Up* features a voiceover dialogue between two women, one with an obvious Danish accent who refers to her country-people as "we" as she explains healthcare and education norms. In *The Seventh Age*, the sound of a national institution, Captain Jespersen's daily "Morgengymnastik" (Morning Gymnastics) broadcast, can be heard in Danish on an elderly resident's radio, much to his roommate's chagrin.

In *Health for Denmark*, the narrator describes how the citizens of the fictional town of Nordkøbing organize their own sickness club, with government subsidy. Twelve minutes into the film, there is a change of approach. Amid a meeting of the local hospital board, the voiceover suddenly interrupts the meeting: "Before they get down to business, I'd like to interrupt," he says. He asks the chairman to say something about the hospital. In Danish, the chair asks the other board members for permission, then switches to English to give an overview of the hospital's architecture, facilities, and plans. This shift in the voiceover to a thickly-accented "we" accompanies a montage of the latest medical treatments: x-rays, Mantoux tests for tuberculosis, heat and light treatments, isolation wards, nurses' quarters. After two minutes, the English

Figure 11.1 Hospital Board members turn to look at the voiceover narrator as he interrupts the meeting, in *Health for Denmark* (Torben Anton Svendsen, Denmark, 1947).

voiceover again interrupts and says "we've taken enough of your time," and the board meeting continues, in Danish. This play with levels of narration—a slippage between voiceover and "voice-off," or a variant on breaking the fourth wall—quite literally gives the local people a voice in the description of their achievements and future plans as regards social security and healthcare. It also serves as a surprising change of pace; retaining audience engagement is the holy grail for informational filmmaking. Flattering an audience by assuming its knowing complicity in a self-referential nod to the constructedness of documentary narrative is a variant on the theme. In this case, because this interlude in the manuscript highlights the difference between English and Danish language, the strategy reminds the audience that Denmark is indeed elsewhere, the kind of elsewhere that they have voluntarily come to the screening venue to learn more about. The technological restrictions on mixing dialogue and voiceover in films for export is exploited here to render the didactic effect of the informational films more subtle.

The *Social Denmark* films thus exemplify the kind of experimentation with voiceover which Wolfe tries to excavate from the much-maligned notion of "Voice-of-God." They illustrate, again in Wolfe's terms, "how accents, inflections, and forms of speech reverberate across and double back over fiction and non-fiction, film and radio, in the media dialect and dialogue of another era" (Wolfe 2016, 276).

Danish as Ambient Sound and Graphics

While foreign audiences demanded linguistic accessibility, the international circulation of films about aspects of national cultures was predicated on careful doses of otherness—the films depict a culture that is elsewhere. Put differently, the practice of versionizing films into a range of languages did not entail concealing the vernacular. Quite the contrary: Danish is often heard as untranslated ambient sound in versionized films, for instance, as background noise in meetings, on city streets, or in songs. In such cases, Danish is "an acoustic rather than verbal constituent of the soundscape" (O'Sullivan 2011: 72).

For example, in *They Guide You Across*, which details safety systems on the new transatlantic air routes, pilots and ground crew can be heard conversing in all three Scandinavian languages as well as English; the mix of languages underlines the regional cooperation on which Scandinavian Airline Systems was founded and the well-oiled collaboration of the staff, but its content is not directly translated by the voiceover. In *A City Called Copenhagen*, snippets of Danish are an integral part of the atmosphere of the city: the shouts of clowns at Bakken and Tivoli amusement parks, crowds of children screaming in response, the chant of soccer supporters, and the lyrics of folk songs performed in cellar bars. Danish viewers, though, have the amusing privilege of overhearing city councillors discuss funding for a new public toilet.

Just as the sound of Danish could be suppressed or integrated into the voiceover or soundtrack, so too could written Danish be strategically visible or invisible in the pro-filmic world. In *A City Called Copenhagen*, a sign brandished by a street preacher that warns "Jesus ved ALT om dig" (Jesus knows EVERYTHING about you) goes untranslated in the streetscape. Theodor Christensen's 1952 film *The Pattern of Cooperation* almost entirely suppresses the sounds of Danish, except for one short sequence which depicts the practice of collective song at a Co-operative Movement board meeting, with some of the meeting dialogue audible. However, the Danish language is regularly and markedly visible throughout the film, in the form of goods packaging. On the farm, the viewer sees boxes marked "ÆG" (eggs); in the local shop and on production lines, the Danish names of commodities—olive soap, oatmeal, coffee—stand out clearly; local place names are visible on trucks and street signs; and "DANMARK" is stamped on carcasses hung for bacon production. Given that this film's central concern and structuring logic is how commodities flow into and out of circuits of exchange, with Denmark as a hub, the graphi-

Figure 11.2 The Danish word for "eggs" situates the scene in Denmark in *The Pattern of Cooperation* (Theodor Christensen, Denmark, 1952).

cal presence of exotic Danish letters (æ, ø, å) in the pro-filmic world renders tangible the materiality and mobility of the goods—and thereby of the film and the culture it transports around the globe.

Accent and Language Varieties

The Pattern of Cooperation is also notable for the distinctive accented English of its voiceover. The West Country burr of BBC cricket and farming commentator John Arlott was felt to be just right for a film about the Cooperative Movement in agriculture (Thomson and Hilson 2014). In contrast, the voiceover of *Health for Denmark* (as well as *The Seventh Age* in the same series) features the authoritative upper-class tones of Arthur Elton's brother Ralph (the documentarist would inherit his father's baronetcy in 1951). Similarly, the English version of a well-traveled film about Danish design, *Shaped by Danish Hands* (Hagen Hasselbalch, 1948), uses the clipped, received pronunciation of Clive Bayliss, a voice again heard on the UK version of *A City Called Copenhagen* more than a decade later.

Shaped by Danish Hands was one of the most widely traveled Danish shorts, an artistically ambitious film which surveyed Denmark's traditions in pottery, silverware, furniture design, and other crafts. The film was not only screened to millions of viewers in the fast-growing television markets of North America, but also traveled across that continent with a major exhibition, "Scandinavian Design" (Thomson 2018, 146–55). The commissioning body, the Danish Association for Applied Arts (Landsforeningen Dansk Kunsthaandværk), was unhappy with how quickly it perceived the film to have aged within just a few years, and pressed for at least one more film. A key complaint was that narrator Clive Bayliss's very English accent in *Shaped by Danish Hands* had distracted North American audiences (Ekstrabladet 1953).

A new film about Danish design by the same director was therefore commissioned in the mid-1950s, with an American English voiceover specified in the remit (Johansen 1955). This film would be called *D...for Design!*. That the new film's voiceover was uppermost in Hasselbalch's mind when responding to this new commission is clear from the filmmaker's earliest draft. The voiceover, it is specified, should center on the "fiction" that the woman's home in which the film is set is not Danish, but could "easily be American, Canadian, English or Swiss" (Hasselbalch 1954, 1).

Most interestingly, the film's synopsis insists that "The voice is endearing and soft, and the language *is completely free of any accent*" (Hasselbalch 1954, 1, my translation and emphasis). This applied not just to the English version; special attention was paid to the suitability of the Spanish translation for use in South America, particularly Argentina. A Mrs. Cramer, an Argentinian who had married a Dane and had "fine and cultivated" Argentinian Spanish, was asked to record the voiceover (Hølaas 1955). The voiceover of the French version, *D...comme décoratif!*, was recorded by Danish filmmaker Gabriel Axel, who had spent part of his childhood and working life in France; his Franco-Danish credentials thus outweighed his gender, and the script was simply tweaked so that he as husband was commenting on his wife's choices for their common home (Dansk Kulturfilm n.d.).

While it can be argued that no speaker is "accent-free," what is revealing here is the logic of the ambition. In *D...for Design!*, the aim of eschewing accent is intrinsic to the film's construction of the space of enunciation of the voiceover. The same film, then, brings us back to Wolfe's maxim, that voiceover "comes from *else*where" (2016, 264).

Voice-off and Contiguous Space

The first-person voiceover in *D...for Design!* represents the perspective of a newlywed woman who has visited Denmark, interviewed its craftspeople, and selected furniture, dinnerware, and textiles to furnish her home. The nameless woman is placed at a distance from Denmark; the domestic artifacts over which the camera glides have been imported to whichever land corresponds to the language of the film version. Hasselbalch's script (1954) insists that the face and body of the narrating voice should never be seen, only glimpsed in reflections, but that her hands should occasionally be shown caressing a table, drapery, or fork.

Arguably, then, the woman's voice is not a voiceover but a sort of "voice-off," in that the narrating voice is implied to exist within the diegesis, "from a space contiguous to and a time continuous with the depicted action" (Wolfe 2016, 265). This voiceover's body is occasionally and obliquely glimpsed on screen; that it is only tentatively "anchored by a represented body" (Doane 1980, 40) eschews convention and draws attention to the voiceover's artificiality, causing a kind of "marginal anxiety" (41). This is one case where Denmark as elsewhere emerges in the plane of contact between the embodied voiceover narrator and the pro-filmic world she presents to the viewer. Put differently, she has been in Denmark and is now surrounded by its material craftworks, transported, like the film reel itself, to somewhere else; the undecidable location of her voice in tandem with her partially-glimpsed person creates a productive tension between the staged "home" of the mise-en-scène and the foreignness of its objects.

D...for Design! faced its greatest challenge when the script was translated back into Danish for use in Scandinavia, with the title *Her er mit hjem* ("Here Is My Home"). Here, the principle of pan-Scandinavian communication fell flat: the film had been appreciated by the students of Stockholm's Konstfackskolan (School of Arts), but even after four screenings the Rector could not grasp all of the Danish, he commented (Stavenow 1956). More importantly, the back-story, narrated by a woman who has visited Denmark and imported its applied arts to her own country, made little logical sense when the voice-off was enunciated in Danish from within Denmark.

The transformation of *D...for Design!* into "Here Is My Home" is an example of a *curiosum* of the history of postwar foreign-language informational film in Denmark: many of the films commissioned for foreign audiences were later versionized into Danish for domestic use. This was true of several of the films mentioned in this chapter.[1] Correspondence in the production files sometimes indicates that such decisions were made on the basis of perceived need or appetite for education about the relevant subject within Denmark, or sometimes facilitated by availability of funds or pressure from interest groups. Re-purposed international films were simply integrated into the available stocks of domestic informational films. Regardless of the intended or implied

---

[1] *Health for Denmark* became *Far bliver syg* (Dad Gets Ill), *The Seventh Age* became *De Gamle* (The Old Ones), *They Guide You Across* was re-worked as *Sikkerhed i luften* (Safety in the Air), and *Shaped by Danish Hands* was literally translated as *Skabt af danske hænder*. On the other hand, a mooted Danish version of *The Pattern of Cooperation* was never made, though the English-language version did circulate in Danish schools (Thomson and Hilson 2014).

audiences, the appetite for informational films in an age dominated by the portable projector rather than the television made the finer details of address irrelevant.

Conclusion

D...for Design! is a particularly complex, but not unique, illustration of the importance of the viewing context for audiences' understanding of Denmark as an elsewhere. In this case, the mobility of the film is baked into the narrative; the text is expressly designed to situate the voiceover in France, or the USA, or wherever "here" is. The deixis of the re-cast title in Danish protests too much: it cannot overcome the conceit of the narrative, that the speaking subject is somewhere else, by definition. Nonetheless, as a phrase, "Here Is My Home" aptly encapsulates the broader project of Dansk Kulturfilm and the Danish Government Film Committee: to present the nation, its culture and achievements to the rest of the world. By definition, the films present Denmark as an elsewhere, indexed in the pro-filmic world and its ambient sound. However, the films' voiceovers make a virtue out of a necessity. Pragmatically eschewing the narrative and technical risks associated with synchronized speech, the films exploit a range of possibilities inherent in foreign-language voiceover. They play with the tensions between voice-off and voiceover and between voiceover and ambient sound, and use poetic tropes, dialogue, and different accents and language varieties. The viewer, wherever he or she may be in the world, is thus moved between distance and intimacy, between the known and the unknown, between here and there, weaving "a complex spatial and temporal relation among commentator, spectator, and documented events" (Wolfe 2016, 275).

Apparent in some of the Danish press commentary on informational films for export is an ongoing fascination with the experience of "seeing ourselves as others see us"—that is, how Denmark would be seen abroad on the basis of the films. By the 1960 premiere of *A City Called Copenhagen*, journalists had a sophisticated take on how Danish culture could be mediated in film overseas:

> the foreign audience which the film targets will truly get the impression that humour is something we are very good at in the little land of Denmark. The film demonstrates in its own right that humour is related to wisdom; there is something fresh here that will make itself felt in the film's worldwide charm offensive. (V-r 1960)

In the recurring phrase "the little land of Denmark" there is a self-conscious modesty which echoes the tone of the inaugural international catalogue of a decade earlier, *Documentary in Denmark*. That publication modestly proffered the country's early documentary output to the world as "an experiment in post-war help and inspiration. Perhaps there are things to be found in Denmark which may be useful in other countries" (Anonymous 1948, 69). Somewhere between this outward-looking idealism and playful self-regard lies the elsewhere of mid-century Denmark on film.

Note. Most of the films discussed in this chapter can be viewed via the Danish Film Institute's streaming site, at https://filmcentralen.dk/museum/danmark-paa-film

REFERENCES

Acland, C. and H. Wasson, eds. 2011. *Useful Cinema.* Durham, NC: Duke University Press.
Anonymous. 1948. "1947." In *Documentary in Denmark: One Hundred Films of Fact in War, Occupation, Liberation, Peace 1940–1948.* Copenhagen: Statens Filmcentral. 69–70.
Boisen, I. (1977), *Klip fra en filmmands liv.* Copenhagen: Nyt Nordisk forlag/Arnold Busck.
Clerc, L., and N. Glover. 2015. "Representing the Small States of Northern Europe: Between Imagined and Imaged Communities." In *Histories of Public Diplomacy and Nation-Branding in the Nordic and Baltic Countries: Representing the Periphery*, ed. L. Clerc, N. Glover, and P. Jordan. Leiden: Brill. 3–22.
Dansk Kulturfilm. n.d. "D...comme décoratif!" Filmsager, SFC særsamling, DFI/Rigsarkivet.
Doane, M. A. 1980. "The voice in the cinema: the articulation of body and space." *Yale French Studies* 60: 33–50.
Druick, Z. 2011. "UNESCO, Film and Education: Mediating Postwar Paradigms of Communication." In *Useful Cinema*, ed. C. Acland and H. Wasson. Durham, NC: Duke University Press. 81–102.
Educational Film Library Association, Inc. n.d. "Comments on SOMETHING ABOUT THE NORTH from the Jurors of the American Film Festival." Noget om Norden—Versioner, Filmsager, SFC særsamling, DFI/Rigsarkivet.
Ekstrabladet. 1953. "Ny dansk film om kunsthåndværk?" *Ekstrabladet*, 8.12.
Elton, A. n.d. "Notes and terms of reference for the film on the Danish holiday system." People's Holiday, Socialfilmene, Filmsager, SFC særsamling, DFI/Rigsarkivet.
Elton, A. 1946. [memo on Dreyer's manuscript for The Seventh Age], The Seventh Age, Socialfilm (engelsk version), SFC særsamling, DFI/Rigsarkivet.
Elton, A. 1948. "Introduction." In *Documentary in Denmark: One Hundred Films of Facts in War, Occupation, Liberation, Peace 1940–1948.* Copenhagen: Statens Filmcentral. 5–11.
Fritsche, M. 2018. *The American Marshall Plan Film Campaign and the Europeans. A Captivated Audience?.* London; New York: Bloomsbury.
Hasselbalch, H. 1954. "Manuskript [27.6.1954]," D...for Design! Filmsager, SFC særsamling, DFI/Rigsarkivet.
Hølaas, A. 1955. [letter to Udenrigsministeriets Pressebureau, 3.10.1955], D...for Design!, Filmsager, SFC særsamling, DFI/Rigsarkivet.
Johansen, K. 1955. "Pressemeddelelse," 7.9.1955, D...for Design! Filmsager, SFC særsamling, DFI/Rigsarkivet.
Johansen, K. 1968. [letter to SFC, 18.12.1968], "Japansk version", *A City Called Copenhagen*, Filmsager, SFC, DFI.

Langlois, S. 2016. "And Action! UN and UNESCO Coordinating Information Films, 1945–51." In *A History of UNESCO: Global Actions and Impacts*, ed. P. Duedahl. Basingstoke: Palgrave Macmillan. 73–96.

McMurray, P. 2017. "Once upon a time: a superficial history of early tape." *Twentieth Century Music* 14(1): 25–48.

MFU. 1958. Mødereferat [udklip], 17.5.1958, Noget om Norden, Filmsager, SFC særsamling, DFI/Rigsarkivet.

Nichols, B. 2010. *Introduction to Documentary*, 2nd edn. Indianapolis: Indiana University Press.

O'Sullivan, C. 2011. *Translating Popular Film*. Basingstoke: Palgrave Macmillan.

SFC. 1948. *Beretning angaaende Finansaaret 1947–48*, Statens Filmcentral særsamling, Danish Film Institute.

Stavenow, Å. 1956. [letter to Kung. Danska Ambassaden, 6.4.1956], D...for Design! Filmsager, SFC særsamling, DFI/Rigsarkivet.

Svane, E. 1959. [letter to Københavns Rådhus, 13.1.1959], *A City Called Copenhagen*, Filmsager, SFC særsamling, DFI/Rigsarkivet.

Thomson, C. and Hilson, M. 2014. "Beauty in bacon: 'The Pattern of Co-operation' and the export of postwar Danish democracy." *Kosmorama* 255. <https://www.kosmorama.org/en/kosmorama/artikler/beauty-bacon-pattern-co-operation-and-export-postwar-danish-democracy>

Thomson, C. 2018. *Short Films from a Small Nation: Danish Informational Cinema 1935–1965*. Edinburgh: Edinburgh University Press.

V-r. 1960, "Københavns-filmen spræller af humør." *Aktuelt*, March 2.

Wolfe, C. 2016. "Historicizing the 'Voice of God': The Place of Voice-Over Commentary in Classical Documentary (1997)." In *The Documentary Film Reader*, ed. J. Kahana. New York: Oxford University Press. 264–80.

Youdelman, J. 1982. "Narration, invention, & history: a documentary dilemma." *Cinéaste* 12(2): 8–15.

12. A SÁMI IN HOLLYWOOD: NILS GAUP'S TRANSNATIONAL AND GENERIC NEGOTIATIONS

Gunnar Iversen

One of Norway's most internationally successful film directors, Nils Gaup is best known for his debut, *Pathfinder* (*Ofelaš/Veiviseren*, 1987). *Pathfinder*, the first feature made in a Sámi language, was nominated for an Academy Award for Best Foreign Language Film, and its international recognition launched Gaup's career. This chapter examines the director's international career and transnational negotiations, covering films made in the USA as well as international co-productions made in Scandinavia and demonstrating Gaup's unique position in recent Scandinavian film history. His films bridge and negotiate between traditions of Indigenous cinema, Hollywood paradigms, and production and circulation conventions of small national film cultures. They also highlight the international and transnational aspects of Scandinavian cinema, and its movement, mobility and interaction across borders and genres.

Gaup's international films exemplify many aspects of the circulation and appropriation of production contexts, genres, and themes circulating in inter- and transnational genre films of the late twentieth and early twenty-first centuries. For instance, the Norwegian-Swedish-American film *Shipwrecked* (*Håkon Håkonsen*, 1990)—co-produced by Walt Disney—melds Scandinavian content with the genre characteristics of the Hollywood adventure film. Similarly, the French-British-Norwegian-Italian co-production *Tashunga* (its European release title) / *North Star* (its North American title; 1996)—distributed by Warner Bros.—attempts to create a Euro-Hollywood production that reimagines the Western. Financed by a number of different production companies from different countries, *Shipwrecked* and *Tashunga / North Star* are Gaup's most ambitious attempts to negotiate international genre elements and aspects of Sámi and Norwegian culture. Perhaps less successful aesthetically and financially than *Pathfinder*, both films question the idea of national cinemas and explore the combination of American, European, and Indigenous concepts within genre cinema.

Similarly, Gaup's Norwegian feature films negotiate international genre elements and Sámi and Norwegian themes and motifs. These genres include the historical melodrama in *The Kautokeino Rebellion* (*Kautokeino-opprøret*, 2008) and *The Last King* (*Birkebeinerne*, 2016) and film noir in *Misery Harbour* (1999) and *The Glass Dolls* (*Glassdukkene*, 2014). Many of Gaup's Norwegian features integrate genre elements from American or transnational film culture to create counter-images of historical events and everyday life in the far north and among Indigenous communities. This chapter will address the cinematic elsewhere created by this kind of genre- and theme-blending.

Pathfinder is the first Scandinavian Indigenous feature film, retelling a local legend that Gaup had heard as a child growing up Sámi in Kautokeino (Guovdageaidnu) in northern Norway. The film is also a colonial allegory: a group of ferocious barbarian Tchudes—a fictional ethnic group—attacks a group of nomadic reindeer-herding Sámi. The community is saved by a young Sámi boy who tricks the invaders, leading them over a cliff to a violent death. Many of the actors in *Pathfinder* were part of the ensemble at Beaivváš Sámi Nasunálateáhter (The Sámi National Theatre), which Gaup co-founded in Kautokeino in 1981 after completing studies at the Norwegian Theater Academy. This is the only theater in Norway with Sámi as its performing language, and it has played a vital role in revitalizing Sámi art, culture, and film production. With its box-office success in Norway and Scandinavia, *Pathfinder* became the first Norwegian film to achieve wide distribution in the USA and England, breaking into territories regarded as unreachable for Norwegian films. The Oscar nomination and commercial success of the film inspired other Norwegian filmmakers, spawning international careers or success in distributing Norwegian features abroad, just as it inspired Indigenous filmmakers around the world.

Gaup has also directed comedies, such as the dark and absurd genre hybrid *Hodet over vannet* (*Head above water*, 1993). This comedy was a success at the box office in Norway, and was remade in Hollywood by Jim Wilson in 1996 as *Head Above Water*, starring Cameron Diaz and Harvey Keitel. Gaup has also made three television series for the Norwegian public broadcaster NRK. *Nini* (1998) and *Deadline Torp* (2005) were crime series. *Hjerterått* (*Heartless*, 2016), made with Grete Bøe-Waal, is a drama series for children that tries to counter stereotypical images and prejudices about the Indigenous Sámi population in Norway.

NILS GAUP'S TRANSNATIONAL AND GENERIC NEGOTIATIONS

Figure 12.1   Mikkel Gaup in Nils Gaup's *Pathfinder* (*Ofelaš*, Norway, 1987), the first feature film in a Sámi language.

A versatile director working in many different genres, Gaup has made a number of films that use different genre elements to create new images of Indigenous peoples in Norway, Alaska, and the Pacific, as well as of Norwegians. In Norway, *Pathfinder* and *The Kautokeino Rebellion* have played a particularly important role in the ongoing process of Sámi political and cultural revitalization. Gaup's films are always genre negotiations, films that use generic forms and genre elements in order to communicate with a broad audience and at the same time reimagine both the historical past and the present.

Shipwrecked: Adventures on the South Seas

Shipwrecked establishes a sharp contrast between Norway and the South Seas in terms of power, class, Indigeneity, and transnational travel. It posits that adventure is something that happens in the Big World and not in rural, remote Norway. *Shipwrecked* begins in London in 1859 but then moves quickly to Norway. The young Håkon Håkonsen (Stian Smestad) grows up on a small farm in the middle of Norway, but signs up as deckhand on a ship in order to pay the family's creditors. Norway is represented as a classed society where the main character Håkon and his poor family are threatened with expulsion from

Figure 12.2 Saying goodbye to the Indigenous people in Nils Gaup's *Shipwrecked* (USA, 1990).

their small farm. Only by escaping Norway is Håkon able to reimagine himself and his life, as well as save his family from the poorhouse. After run-ins with the British Navy and pirates, Håkon is shipwrecked on a small island in the South Seas. On the island, he finds the pirates' treasure and eventually escapes with it, returning to Norway as a wealthy man, able to become the owner of his childhood farm. Håkon also encounters the Indigenous population on a nearby island, that helps him and his friends beat the pirates.

Even though Håkon adapts both to life at sea and life on the small, uninhabited Pacific island where he is shipwrecked, he remains a typical example of a Norwegian "*askeladd*," a fairy-tale "ash-lad" who uses cunning, wit, and the odd things he finds on his travels to win the princess and half of the kingdom, as in many Norwegian folktales. In the beginning of the film, Håkon is always wearing a special red woolen cap, a "*nisselue*," or "goblin-cap," which emphasizes his Norwegianness, his youth, and rural identity. How the Indigenous people on the other island are depicted is especially striking. Although at first Håkon believes they are brutal savages, he soon discovers that they are peaceful helpers. They are superior navigators and have an advanced understanding of technology, well adapted to their environment. Their music, drumming, and dancing are presented as pleasant and harmonious, the opposite of the stereotypical "primitive" performance representation found in many Hollywood films. Gaup's focus on Indigeneity is one way of trying to redefine the adventure genre.

The unlikely presence of a big gorilla on the tiny uninhabited Pacific island where Håkon is shipwrecked is another example of Gaup's genre negotiations, and a nod to Hollywood conventions. The gorilla on the island is the opposite of a King Kong-like monster, and after their initial encounter, in which they are both equally scared of each other, the gorilla and Håkon seem to live

Figure 12.3   The gorilla comforting Håkon in Nils Gaup's *Shipwrecked* (USA, 1990).

peacefully together, looking upon each other with a certain respect and fondness. In this way, Gaup subverts the genre with a different depiction of both wildlife and the encounter between animal and human.

Gaup also plays with the genre of South Seas adventure stories. The interactions between the Indigenous people and the gorilla initially follow strict genre laws, especially how the Indigenous people dance and make music when Håkon first discovers them, but Gaup immediately subverts the genre conventions and expectations. In this way he creates positive images where most Hollywood films have created negative and threatening images. The real threat in the story is the evil British pirate, not the Indigenous people or the environment. The story of Håkon's adventures at sea and his shipwreck counteract a Norway divided by class. Håkon's father is a poor fisherman and brutally exploited by a merchant from the upper middle class. Gaup uses different genre elements to subvert the genre while creating new images of both Norway and the South Seas. Even though the film was received well in Norway and was released in many countries through the Disney connection, the film was not a big financial success.

Tashunga / *North Star*: A New Western

Tashunga / *North Star* is Gaup's least successful film at the box office. It is also the film over which he had the least artistic control. Yet it is an example of a re-imagination of the western genre in the 1990s. A French-British-Norwegian-Italian co-production distributed by Warner Bros., *Tashunga* / *North Star* reworks the pursuit narrative of *Pathfinder*, as well as its scenes, themes, and central dramatic elements, but fails to engage due to a lack of originality, as well as the problematic tensions and frictions inherent in the western genre itself.

The opening scene of *Tashunga / North Star* depicts a group of settler gold miners (all white men) hunting down the multiracial Hudson Santeek, played by French actor Christopher Lambert. Hudson has claimed the North Star area in Alaska to protect a sacred Indigenous cave from the miners. The white settlers interrupt an Indigenous ceremony, beat up the Indigenous men, and kill an elder on his deathbed. They then try to kill Hudson, unsuccessfully. Believing him dead, they assume they will have access to the gold in the sacred cave. In Nome, their leader Sean McLennon (James Caan) takes over the North Star claim. Through a number of plot contrivances familiar to the western, *Tashunga / North Star* depicts Indigenous cultures and practices as oppositional to white capitalist settler priorities, which are also aided by local law enforcement. Hudson and Sara (Sara McCormack), McLennon's white girlfriend, form an unwitting team to challenge the settlers. The military eventually declares martial law in Nome and announces that the US Congress will honor all claims, also by men who are not American citizens. McLennon is arrested but escapes after killing his captors. He also tries to kill Sara because she has testified against him, but Hudson rescues her and kills the rabid McLennon. In the last scene, Hudson returns alone to the snowy plains, and we hear his words: "My ancestors told me that you can't own land."

The central themes in *Tashunga / North Star* are questions of race and ownership of the land. The film starts with the attempt to kill the multiracial Hudson and with an emblematic scene of violence against Indigenous peoples. McLennon's hired hands are murderers who have no respect for their customs and traditions. With this, Gaup immediately sets the scene and shows that the Gold Rush was a violation of Indigenous people, their rights and traditions, and constituted theft of their land. The violence against Indigenous people is linked early on also to violence against the poorest settlers, who are not all American citizens. Although the family that Gaup uses to emphasize the violence in McLennon's scheme is of Nordic origin, with the names Bjørn and Anna, the theme of violence and aggression against immigrants has a larger resonance in contemporary American culture. *Tashunga / North Star* is a rather heavy-handed "drama of ideas" more than a smooth action film, and uses the historic past as a mirror for understanding contemporary issues in the USA.

The last part of the film creates tensions in the narrative, however, undermining the questions of colonialism and imperialism that are at the heart of the story. It is revealed that McLennon is also multiracial. He becomes Hudson's "evil twin" and not only a representative of the genocidal violence of the white settlers in Alaska and the USA. In this way, evil and violence are displaced or transferred away from the white settlers and the official authorities. At the very end of the film, Congress and the army become important saviors of both the

Indigenous people and the many immigrants in Nome. The messy complexities of race and class are solved by the US army and by the revelation that the most evil of all the thugs is also multiracial.

Gaup returns to many of the successful elements of *Pathfinder* in this film. McLennon's pursuit of Hudson is the dramatic core of the film. Even if some scenes seem to be lifted directly from *Pathfinder*, *Tashunga / North Star* has a different style. *Pathfinder* is set in a vague mythical past, about a thousand years ago, while *Tashunga / North Star* is set in Alaska in 1899. While anchored in an Alaskan cultural and natural landscape, it was filmed in Norway for financial reasons. The location substitution made the production less expensive, and it also generated European money that could not have been found had the film been made in Alaska or other parts of the USA. This is another illustration of "cinematic elsewheres," a physical location in one country standing in for a location in another, a type of location substitution that has a long history in Scandinavian cinema, going back to its very earliest years (Sandberg 2014). Where *Pathfinder* uses mostly close-ups and medium shots, with very few long shots of the stunning winter landscapes of the Norwegian North, the later film uses many long shots, creating a spectacular touristic representation of the landscape. The frequent use of non-diegetic traditional Western film music also downplays the Indigenous presence in the film and the landscape.

Pathfinder can be understood as a revisionist western, and one reason for its international success might be the revival of the western genre in the 1980s and 1990s (Iversen 2005, 2011; Solum 2010). Its national success in Norway might also be linked to the central role of the western in popular literature, especially the enormously popular Norwegian books about the US Marshal Morgan Kane (Dahl 1973, 1976; Gripsrud 1989). *Tashunga / North Star* is even more revisionist in that it recontextualizes familiar western genre elements and clichés, especially by telling the stories from the point of view of Native Americans (Neale 2002).

Even though Gaup's film has revisionist ambitions, especially in the retelling of the story of the Gold Rush as a theft of Indigenous land, it remains ambivalent and uncertain in its allegiances and story elements. Gaup was restrained by production circumstances, and the film does not take a clear political stance. It ends up only hinting at issues of colonialism, imperialism, and the genocide of Indigenous people. Instead of creating clear binary oppositions between the main characters (Hudson and McLennon), a more nuanced discussion of Native Americans in Alaska is undertaken, avoiding racial stereotypes and establishing a clear ethno-political dimension in the narrative. In the end, Gaup indicates that the story is a duel between two multiracial characters, and that the US cavalry and Congress guarantee law and order and fair treatment of all people, Indigenous as well as poor European immigrants. The omission of the precise status of the Indigenous people means that they become somehow "generically" Indigenous, falling into the old Hollywood pattern of grouping all "Native Americans" into one.

Tashunga / North Star is an example of a new Euro-western that clearly wants to re-imagine and recontextualize both the genre and the history of the American west, but it is only partly revisionist in its Indigenous perspective and emphasis on race and ownership of the land. In the end, Gaup's film becomes more of a neo-traditional western—a western that blends traditional elements with some updated attitudes, like the focus on Indigenous people.

Norwegian Historical Melodramas and Nordic Noir

Gaup's most popular Norwegian films after *Pathfinder* are the two historical melodramas *The Kautokeino Rebellion* from 2008 and *The Last King* from 2016. Most important is *The Kautokeino Rebellion*, which is based on historical events, namely the 1852 Sámi uprising in Kautokeino, when a group of Sámi rose up against oppressive Norwegian religious and national authorities. Gaup gives a Sámi perspective on what has been characterized as "the most traumatic and stigmatized event in the history of the Indigenous population of Sámi in Norway" (Christensen 2012: 57). In the opening scene of *The Kautokeino Rebellion*, a young Sámi boy watches from a distance as two of his relatives are about to be beheaded for their part in the rebellion. The events that lead to the executions are recounted by the boy's mother, Elen Skum (Anni-Kristiina Juuso), who has received a sentence of seventeen years' imprisonment. It is her perspective that we have on these tragic events, and she tells the story so that it can be understood and remembered by new generations.

The Kautokeino Rebellion explicitly rectifies misrepresentations of the 1852 Rebellion and the Sámi people in general, telling a Sámi version of the famous historical events and placing the responsibility for the violence on the Norwegian authorities and not on the Sámi people. The purpose of the film is both to give a new perspective on the actual rebellion and the tragic events that led to the execution of the two Sámi leaders Aslak Jacobsen Hætta and Mons Aslaksen Somby and to discuss misconceptions of the Sámi people in general. Pre-Christian religion played an important role in *Pathfinder*, but *The Kautokeino Rebellion* contrasts two forms of Christianity, namely the ecstatic Lutheran revival movement led by the Swedish priest Lars Levi Læstadius and the official Norwegian Protestant church. Many representations of the 1852 Rebellion have placed responsibility for the events on Sámi religious fanaticism or on the violence of the Sámi as a "nature people," they being more spiritual, irrational, primitive, and closer to nature than non-Sámi people (Christensen 2012, 2013; Dancus 2014). Gaup's film shows the opposite: how Læstadianism saves many Sámi from alcoholism, contributes to literacy, and gives the Sámi community more dignity and strength. Gaup's retelling of the historic events also places emphasis on economy and exploitation. Initially, the merchant Ruth becomes the main symbol of the brutal and violent colonial oppression and exploitation of Sámi people, and, even though he is killed, Gaup focuses on the systemic oppression and violence. Ruth and the other evil Norwegians become emblematic characters that symbolize the violence against the Sámi minority by a dominant Norwegian majority.

Even though *The Kautokeino Rebellion* is a Sámi version of actual historical events, is directed by Gaup, and uses many Sámi actors, it is not only a "Sámi film." It is a Norwegian-Swedish co-production, made possible with money from the Nordic Film & TV Fund, with actors from nearly all Nordic countries. Anni-Kristiina Juuso, who plays the main character Elen, is a Sámi from Finland. Its inter- and transnational negotiations are also obvious on the plot level. Gaup uses well-known genre elements of the historical melodrama, such as exotic costumes and beautiful landscapes, simple binary oppositions between good or evil, personifications of larger events and historical forces, victimization and idealization of the Sámi people, action-driven plot, and goal-oriented protagonists, in order to tell *his* specific story about the 1852 Rebellion.

Although *The Kautokeino Rebellion* generated heated discussions in Norway over historical accuracy, especially how Gaup downplayed the violence of the Sámi rebellion itself, the film is a convincing representation of the colonial oppression and humiliation of the Sámi people in the mid-1850s. The film has been called a powerful "call to audiences' post-colonial consciousness and conscience" (Christensen 2012: 62) and provides a substantive critique of the politics of assimilation in Norway. It is an insider's version of past events, told with all the tools of the inter- and transnational film industry. As a history lesson for the present and future, it reminds audiences that racialization has a long and dark history in Norway, and of the violent ethnic and cultural boundaries between the Norwegian majority and the Indigenous Sámi population.

The Kautokeino Rebellion is one of the most important and popular movies made in Norway in the last decade. Gaup's more recent historical melodrama, *The Last King*, was also a big box-office success, but failed to make the same impact as *The Kautokeino Rebellion*. *The Last King* depicts the historical events of 1204 when the old king of Norway died. Against the background of civil war between the North and the South, and internal struggles over power and the throne, Gaup tells the story of how two men guarded and saved the new infant king from a group of men backed by the Catholic Church.

The Last King is a Norwegian-Danish-Irish-Hungarian co-production, with additional financing from the EU through the Eurimages fund. Though it is a medieval national mythic story, it gives a different type of history lesson from *The Kautokeino Rebellion*. A simple action-filled story, built around Gaup's main dramatic elements such as escape, pursuit, and a flight to freedom, *The Last King* touches on familiar themes from his earlier films, including pursuit through a snowy landscape and the negative depiction of priests and official religion. From the brutal opening attack (similar to *Pathfinder*) to the dramatic last-minute rescue, Gaup's film is a genre film that re-imagines the national Norwegian past, while remaining too close to the action genre to be truly engaging as a more complex retelling of historical events. Resembling so many other action movies, Norway is somehow displaced as "elsewhere" in the film.

The historical melodrama is not the only genre Gaup has used to tell new stories about Sámi identity or Norwegian history in more recent years. Two of Gaup's lesser-known films use elements from film noir in order to tell their dramatic stories. The Norwegian-Canadian film *Misery Harbour* is an existential drama about how an innocent man is driven to murder through bullying. Based on a well-known novel by the Norwegian-Danish author Aksel Sandemose, the film also discusses the different oppressive structures in small towns and countries. Shown in a series of flashbacks, the author Espen Arnakke (Nikolaj Coster-Waldau) writes about his experiences in Newfoundland and tries to come to terms with his past and the act of killing a man who had tormented him. Set in the early 1930s, *Misery Harbour* is an existential noir period drama. The film does not have any Indigenous content and did not do well outside of Norway.

The Glass Dolls also uses elements from film noir, this time to tell the story of a Sámi detective and his hunt for a serial killer in the Arctic. The plot centers on the murder of a young woman, and the abduction of another young woman by a religious doctor who wants to punish girls with so-called loose morals. The Sámi detective Aslak Eira (Stig Henrik Hoff) manages to track down the killer and rescue the second woman, but the killer abducts Eira's own son Niilas, hoping this will give him free passage into Russia. When the killer makes Eira bring him gasoline for his car in a desolate mountain spot, Eira wounds him using his traditional Sámi knife, and rescues his son.

Gaup's film is most of all a drama about the idea of the modern family. Eira himself is Sámi, but exists somewhere between modernity and traditional life: a highly skilled modern detective, but at the same time a passionate outdoorsman who loves fishing and hunting. At the beginning of the film he has to leave nature in order to catch the fanatic killer in the city. Tromsø, a small town of only 75 000 inhabitants, is depicted as a noir-metropolis characterized by serial killers, modern alienation, and dark erotic desires.

The film deals with relations between the past and the present, traditional life versus modernity, and questions traditional images of Sámi identity, as well as the relationship between Sámi culture and Norwegian society. Gaup uses familiar elements from crime thrillers and noir films in order to create unconventional images of the North. He creates a film rooted in a regional culture, financially supported by the Norwegian government in order to create diversity while engaging transnationally with Hollywood genre movies.

Gaup deploys film noir to create a counter-image of modern Sámi identity, and new and unconventional images of the Arctic as a dark noir-universe, questioning traditional images of northern Norwegian and Sámi culture. The film also serves as a counterpoint to the "noir light" of *Insomnia* (Erik Skjoldbjærg, 1996), one of the best-known Northern Norwegian films. Most importantly, through the main character Eira, the film depicts a truly modern Sámi identity, a man who has one foot in traditional culture, and uses that as a police detective, and the other foot in the modern urban world. Instead of insisting on an identity only rooted in the past, Gaup creates a Sámi detective who exists in contemporary Norway. The genre connections, film noir in the case of *The Glass Dolls*, also works to create new ideas and images of contemporary Indigeneity, an identity using different pasts in order to create a more sustainable identity for the future.

Arctic Norwegian films have increasingly looked to genre elements from American film culture to create new counter-images of everyday life in the far north, Sámi culture, and the Arctic environment. A cinematic interest in the genres of the spy thriller and film noir is used to question different conceptions of modern Sámi identity. Even though *The Glass Dolls* was not a box-office success, it is one of the most compelling examples of Gaup's genre negotiations and of recent Arctic Norwegian cinema.

A Sámi in Hollywood

One of the best-known and most widely disseminated photographs of Gaup shows him just before the Academy Awards in Los Angeles in 1988, when *Pathfinder* was nominated for Best Foreign Language Film. The photograph shows Gaup, his producer John M. Jacobsen, and leading actor Mikkel Gaup on the red carpet. Mikkel Gaup wears his traditional Sámi clothes, while Gaup and the Norwegian producer wear black tuxedos. The photograph emblematically shows Gaup's position between Sámi tradition and international modernity. As a Sámi in Hollywood, Gaup has explored the combination of American, European, and Indigenous ideas, questioning the notion of national cinemas and re-imagining important elements of Sámi or Norwegian culture through transnational negotiations.

Gaup's cinema is truly heterogeneous. His oeuvre is extremely varied, inter- and transnational, trans-linguistic, trans-global and trans-cultural. Some of his films have been big artistic and economic successes, and others have been equally big failures. Two of Gaup's movies have been remade in Hollywood, most recently the disastrous *Pathfinder* (Marcus Nispel, 2007), and Gaup's own experiences with international co-productions have been very varied. His whole career can be seen as a series of frictions, successes, and failures. Genre elements in his films are narrative tools, as ways of reshaping and reinterpreting the past as well as the representations of the present. Gaup's transnational and genre negotiations function as a way of understanding characters and story elements, as a network of motifs, themes, stylistic elements, and ideas that can be used to tell stories that appeal to a global audience, or sometimes as a way of creating a Nordic elsewhere. They also create a network of understanding that links the fates of different Indigenous peoples together and questions aspects of local and national specificity. Gaup is truly a Sámi in Hollywood, working from within the commercial film industry, to create different images of Nordic or Indigenous identity.

REFERENCES

Christensen, Cato. 2012. "Reclaiming the past. On the history-making significance of the Sámi film *The Kautokeino Rebellion*." *Acta Borealia* 1: 56–76.
Christensen, Cato. 2013. *Religion som samisk identitetsmarkør. Fire studier av film.* Tromsø: Universitetet i Tromsø.
Dahl, Willy. 1973. *I kiosken og på skjermen*. Oslo: Gyldendal.
Dahl, Willy. 1976. *Morgan Kane fra Norge*. Bergen. Eide.
Dancus, Adriana Margareta. 2014. "Ghosts haunting the norwegian house: racialization in Norway and *The Kautokeino Rebellion*." *Framework* 1: 121–39.
Gripsrud, Jostein. 1989. "Masterson's Male Masterpiece: The Penetrating Story of a Norwegian Western (or Two)." In Michael Skovmand, ed., *Media Fictions*. Aarhus: Aarhus University Press. 135–48.
Iversen, Gunnar. 2005. "Learning from Genre: Genre Cycles in Modern Norwegian cinema." In *Transnational Cinema in a Global North: Nordic Cinema in Transition*, ed. Andrew Nestingen and Trevor G. Elkington. Detroit: Wayne State University Press. 261–77.
Iversen, Gunnar. 2011. *Norsk Filmhistorie: Spillefilmen 1911–2011*. Oslo: Universitetsforlaget.
Neale, Steve. 2002. "Westerns and Gangster Films since the 1970s." In *Genre and Contemporary Hollywood*. London: British Film Institute, 27–48.
Sandberg, Mark B. 2014. "Location, 'Location': On the Plausibility of Place Substitution." In *Silent Cinema and the Politics of Space*, ed. Jennifer M. Bean, Anupama Kapse, and Laura Horak. Bloomington: Indiana University Press. 23–46.
Solum, Ove. 2010. "En westernfilm fra sameland." In Gunnar Iversen and Ove Solum, *Den norske filmbølgen: Fra* Orions belte *til* Max Manus. Oslo: Universitetsforlaget. 76–93.

13. "THERE IS NO ELSEWHERE!": STORIES OF RACE, DECOLONIZATION, AND GLOBAL CONNECTIVITY IN GÖRAN HUGO OLSSON'S DOCUMENTARIES

Lill-Ann Körber

Born in 1965, Swedish director Göran Hugo Olsson started his career as a documentary filmmaker working for Swedish public television (SVT). He covered war-torn regions such as Yugoslavia, Israel and Palestine, and Chechnya. His documentary work has always been intertwined with political engagement. In his teens, he says, he raised money to support the struggle against apartheid in South Africa. The struggle against institutionalized racism and for social justice continues to be his main concern, which is also what connects the filmmakers and producers working for *Story AB*, the Stockholm-based documentary film company co-founded by Olsson.

I had the opportunity to meet with Olsson at *Story*'s main office in Stockholm in June 2017. This chapter is based on our conversation and foregrounds some of Olsson's films of the past decade, and his approach to documentary filmmaking, and to global decolonization. My aim is to contextualize Olsson's films with recent efforts to understand Sweden within transnational histories of colonial violence and their legacies. The production, distribution and reception processes of Olsson's films transcend the national framework, and their subject matter and cinematic techniques draw on a polyphony of transnational perspectives. The films thus offer apt material for a discussion of cinematic "elsewheres" beyond national or regional boundaries.

When I explained the publication context of this book and the chapter to Olsson, he exclaimed, "There is no Elsewhere!" I understand his instant refusal of the notion of "elsewheres" as a critique of the assumption of any essential difference between people, or between temporal and spatial entities. In the following pages, I will examine how his films insist on bridging such differences, on exploring and transcending the boundaries of "self" and "other," of "here" and "there," of "then" and "now." I argue that it is precisely this refusal to accept the existence of an "elsewhere," and the exploration of and insistence on fundamental connectedness, that make Olsson's documentaries a productive case study for this book.

Olsson's films are driven by an interwovenness of artistic and political concerns, in particular in the director's affinity with black music and black radical thought. His interest lies in emancipatory aesthetics and intellectual dimensions of the "Black Atlantic": the circum-Atlantic cultural realm with its shared history of enslavement, displacement, resistance, and hybridization, as theorized in Paul Gilroy's seminal book *The Black Atlantic: Modernity and Double Consciousness* (1993). The "Black Atlantic" is a transnational space per definition, characterized by movement, circulation, interaction, and by a consciousness of injustice and inequality. Olsson's films do not address these issues as if their relevance were limited to people and societies "elsewhere." Instead, they emphasize Europe's, and Sweden's, implication within these paradigms.

Olsson's films are part of a recent tendency in Scandinavian filmmaking to explore Scandinavia's status, and the status of (former) Scandinavian territories, as shaped by racial ideology and coloniality. Among other examples are the fiction feature *Sami Blood* (*Sameblod*, Amanda Kernell, Sweden, 2016), about racial discrimination against the Indigenous population of northern Scandinavia, the documentary *Sumé: The Sound of a Revolution*, about Greenlandic independence movements (*Sumé: Mumisitsinerup nipaa*, Inuk Silis-Høeg, Greenland, 2014), and the film installations and performances of Danish-Trinidadian artist Jeannette Ehlers. Olsson's approach is distinct not only in terms of style and artistic practice, but also in the self-reflexive and fundamental interrogation of territorial and identificatory boundaries. The films do acknowledge the situatedness of experience and knowledge, but his main interest is not in stories about places, but in stories about global connectedness.

FILMS, THEMES, AND TECHNIQUES

Olsson's *Am I Black Enough for You?* (2009) follows the aging soul singer Billy Paul (1934–2016) on tour, on stage, in interviews, and at home. Paul is perhaps best known for his 1972 #1 single "Me and Mrs. Jones." One of the film's most significant moments is Olsson's conversation with Billy Paul and his wife Blanche Williams about the follow-up single "Am I Black Enough for You?" (1972). The decision to release this track, with its clear political message related to the Black Power movement, as a sequel to the popular success of

"Me and Mrs. Jones" proved controversial. This is one of the rare occasions where Olsson's voice and persona appear in one of his films: he contradicts Paul's and Williams' judgment that the release had jeopardized Paul's promising mainstream career and white audience, and insists on the importance and relevance of the song's message for the struggle against racism and segregation. Paul's reaction—the realization that he perhaps has too vehemently distanced himself from the song and its cause—reflects what I see as the film's main concern: the pervasive influence of race on the production, distribution, and reception of art, but also the potential of art in the fight for social change.

Olsson's subsequent documentary *The Black Power Mixtape 1967–75* (2011) continues an investigation into the Black Power movement in the USA of the late 1960s and early 1970s, and its reflection in Swedish public culture. This found footage documentary compiles historical SVT segments about the Civil Rights Movement with statements by contemporary African-American musicians and intellectuals about the history and relevance of the Black Power movement. In our conversation, Olsson emphasized that the film should not be understood as a documentary about the Black Power movement itself, but "about how it was perceived in Sweden." The very first clip, from a TV documentary shot in Florida, sets the tone. The reporter explains, in voiceover, how the team, "fairskinned, maybe a bit naïve, and very Swedish ... disembarked on this shore 1972 to try to understand and portray America through sound and image as it really is" (my translation here and otherwise). In a later clip, we see white Swedish tourists on a guided bus tour in Harlem. The guide warns them to not go out on their own, because this is "undoubtedly the colored man's ghetto" and there is a risk they could be mugged (Fig. 13.1), while other clips show interviews of supportive Swedish journalists with black activists.

The Black Power Mixtape 1967–75 conveys an image of Sweden in the 1960s and 70s as a country that perceives itself to be innocent of racism, boasting governmental and grassroots support for liberation and decolonization movements in other parts of the world. The film shows how Swedish mainstream media were accused of anti-Americanism (this perception lives on, cf. Volquardsen 2014). For instance, the USA broke diplomatic ties with Sweden because of Prime Minister Olof Palme's sharp critique of the bombing of Hanoi during the Vietnam war.

The juxtaposition of found footage segments without additional voiceover reveals Olsson's agenda and method: the audience is invited to draw conclusions pertaining to Sweden's—or any nation's—status as "entangled" in global power structures based on exploitation and injustice, as well as in the struggle to change such structures or relieve their effects. This approach reflects recent historiographic thought that seeks to replace nation-centric historiographies with the recognition of shared, "entangled," and contested histories (Naum

Figure 13.1   Film still from *The Black Power Mixtape, 1967–75* © Göran Hugo Olsson/Story AB. A Swedish bus tour guide explains Harlem to Swedish tourists, 1973: "We're getting closer to the neighborhood known as Harlem. This is undoubtedly the colored man's ghetto. Large amounts of narcotics are circulating in Harlem. So you constantly have to raise money to get your fix, or whatever you call it. You might have read our welcome letter, where we inform you that we do not want anyone to visit Harlem for personal studies. That is because this neighborhood is only for colored people. Not even the 'better'—if I may use this wording—colored people visit this area because of the risk of being mugged."

and Nordin 2013; Rydén 2013; Conrad 2016). A consequential assumption of the entangled nature of the world would forgo its division into "here" and "elsewhere": *The Black Power Mixtape 1967–75* is neither about Harlem nor about Sweden, neither about Swedish journalism nor about the front figures of the Black Power movement, but about processes of reciprocal perception and conflicted, asymmetrical encounters. The compilation technique allows for investigations into relations over space and time, reflected by the repeated occurrence of issues of legacy and relevance in Olsson's films.

Concerning Violence (2014) is Olsson's most complex found footage compilation film. The film compiles footage from SVT's archive on liberation struggles and wars of decolonization in Africa in the 1960s and 70s. The history and aftermaths of colonialism are reflected on through Martinican psychiatrist and philosopher Frantz Fanon's 1961 book *The Wretched of the Earth* (*Les Damnés de la Terre*) (Fanon 2004). This seminal text—a radical critique of European imperialism and colonial violence—is reflected in *Concerning Violence* by the film's chapter structure, with a preface by literary scholar and postcolonial critic Gayatri Chakravorty Spivak, and by the text's visual representation on the screen and in the voiceover by singer and actress Lauryn Hill. In Olsson's words, "the film is all about the Fanon text. That was the cinematic task: how do we take this nonfiction book and turn it into a cinematic experience. To spread the word." The film provides new perspectives on the struggle against colonial power structures, emphasizing radical decolonial thought and scholarship. It furthermore explores Sweden's role in the history and legacy of European expansion.

Concerning Violence is an excellent example of a film that engages in various ways with cinematic "elsewheres," in the sense of transnational circulation and movement foregrounded in this book. The film transcends a national framework in terms of distribution and reception. It was screened and won awards at international film festivals. Among others, it won the "Cinema Fairbindet" prize at the Berlinale, and was nominated for the World Cinema Grand Jury Prize in the documentary section of Sundance Film Festival, both in 2014. It is seldom marketed or discussed as a Swedish film, but rather as a film dedicated to decolonization (Shringarpure 2014). It integrates Sweden and Swedish filmmaking into a global discussion of the repercussions of colonialism. The compilation montage technique allows for a transnational polyphony of voices and perspectives. Thus, the engagement with cinematic "elsewheres" in the case of *Concerning Violence* implies an interrogation of categories of territorial belonging, and of the common assumption that issues of decolonization are only marginally relevant in Sweden, or in the global North as a whole.

Olsson's subsequent documentary *Fonko* (co-directed with Lamin Daniel Jamada and Lars Lovén, 2016) examines the contemporary music scene in Angola, Nigeria, South Africa, Ghana, Burkina Faso, Senegal, Togo, and Benin. In the form of interviews with musicians and footage from their performances, the film presents the diversity of contemporary African urban club music in its respective artistic, political and social contexts. Like Olsson's other films, *Fonko* uses archival footage, this time in the form of the voice of late Nigerian Afrobeat musician Fela Kuti (1938–97) from the 1982 documentary *Music Is the Weapon* (Stéphane Tchal-Gadjieff and Jean-Jacques Flori). The combination of archival and original footage connects artistic and political issues over time: it explores the contemporary relevance of Pan-Africanism in its political and aesthetic dimensions as it was developed and advocated by Kuti in the 1970s and 80s. Through voiceover, the late Fela Kuti speaks to us from "elsewhere": from his residence in Lagos, Nigeria, from the early 1980s, and from beyond our world. However, this "elsewhere" is simultaneously "present," in that the film actualizes Kuti's aesthetic and musical heritage and political topicality.

About the Use of "Existing Material"

Göran Hugo Olsson prefers the term "existing [audio visual] material" to archival or found footage. "Existing material" does not limit the footage to the historical, but includes contemporary material. This reflects Olsson's desire to link past and present, and to emphasize relevance and continuity. Olsson's programmatic use of existing material has aesthetic, ethical, and political dimensions. He uses the notion of "recycling" to describe the re-use and recontextualization of past recordings. In *The Black Power Mixtape 1967–75*, for instance, we witness how political activist, academic, and author Angela Davis's appearance and voice have changed over time. In addition, Olsson says, "It also is as simple as that: brilliant people said those things, and nobody cared. We need to recycle this, because it's so good. It is so relevant today." Another aspect of Olsson's use of existing material is that it changes his role as a filmmaker from producing original material to a compilation practice (for a discussion of compilation and documentary, see Beattie 2004, 125–45). In that sense, he is able to create conversations between ideas and people, dead or alive, spanning temporal and geographical distances, to bridge "elsewheres." This approach can be said to reflect Bakhtin's notion of dialogism: a radical acknowledgment of the variety of voices, and perspectives, represented in a (in Bakhtin's case literary) narrative (Bakhtin 2002). Olsson adds that "the great thing about doing compilations or using existing material is that it is easier for people involved to talk about it. It is all laid out on the table. The question is then how to put it together. A more open process." The filmmaking process, then, is not only more open, but allows for a different kind of cooperation. "We are always a team," Olsson says, and within that team, due to the method, the border between people behind and in front of the camera seems to be blurred, foregrounding the common cause.

In the case of *Concerning Violence*, Olsson described the task as being "to take this super important non-fiction book and promote it." "Existing material" here comprises not only footage, but also critical theory in textual form. The existing audiovisual and textual material—Frantz Fanon's book and SVT footage from the decades following World War II, the era of the most intense decolonization struggles in Africa—is linked to the present through original footage and recordings, including an introduction to Fanon's *The Wretched of the Earth* by Professor Gayatri Spivak in her office at Columbia University, and Lauryn Hill's reading—or rather, performance—of Fanon's text as voiceover. Additionally, quotations from the text appear on screen in the typewriter-like Courier font. The letters and words appear as Hill speaks, giving the text an acute sense of presence, as if Fanon's writing were unfolding as we watch. Hill's performance amplifies the urgency of Fanon's decolonial manifesto, emphasized further by Hill's and Spivak's actual appearances in the film, linking the archival footage of African liberation struggles to postcolonial thought and contemporary black culture. In this sense, the film's complex interplay of image, sound, and text reflects the temporal continuum of anti-colonial struggles and the interwovenness of theory, politics, and the arts, in the context of those struggles.

The Practice of Documentary Filmmaking

Olsson's use of existing material also prompts questions of entitlement and relationality, which are central to his approach to documentary filmmaking. Who, he asks, owns the right to represent?:

> Documentary filmmaking is not a genre. It is a method. It is a process. Within that documentary process, you have to have a strong relation to, and access to, the subject of your films. If I use existing material, I can claim it, I can use it; I am not intruding. If it is on YouTube, it belongs to all of us. I do not even think that I have the right to film a house that I don't have a relation to. So all the still images I use are from hotel rooms, because they are "mine," I own them when I rent them, they are mine during those 24 hours.

In terms of a discussion of cinematic "elsewheres," Olsson thus cautions against the use, or appropriation, of an "elsewhere" for artistic or aesthetic purposes, if no reciprocal sense of connectivity or relationality is established and acknowledged. Olsson's films rarely present their issues as being "something different," or as occurring "somewhere else," or as being exotic or exciting in the sense of conveying "the foreign" to an audience in the global North.

His films forgo the ethnographic view, complicit with colonial appropriation, of other early or contemporary documentary films. In this context, Olsson considers one of the most influential documentaries in film history—Robert Flaherty's *Nanook of the North* (USA, 1922)—to be a

> totally patronizing film, but still a very important document. Today, you could never do a film like that. It is from another time. A total "from above" perspective that is outdated, both philosophically, economically, and technically.

Olsson furthermore emphasizes that he is "against anything that goes in the direction of 'exploring' and 'explaining' for an audience." When interviews are included in his films, only the interviewees are visible and audible. Olsson's films show, rather than tell, their stories. His intent is to let the protagonists speak for themselves.

Olsson explains that he used synchronized sound in *The Black Power Mixtape 1967–75* to let the audience "meet" Black Power activists such as Angela Davis and Stokely Carmichael (Kwame Ture), but he is also fascinated by the possibilities and effects of non-synchronized sound. In *Concerning Violence* and *Fonko*, multiple layers of sound, image, and graphic elements work together in a non-explanatory fashion, creating powerful effects. In

Concerning Violence, for instance, the Fanon text we hear and read has no direct reference to the specific events depicted in the footage. This waives any authoritative interpretation of particular wars, politicians, or resistance movements.

A recorded interview with musician and politician Fela Kuti—from the aforementioned documentary *Music Is the Weapon*—is used as voiceover in *Fonko*. Kuti explains the connection between music, politics, and black liberation that still proves relevant for the younger generation of African musicians interviewed and presented in *Fonko*. The assembling of archival material and original footage is yet another example of Olsson's compilation technique that allows it to span generations and continents. Olsson explains that Fela Kuti's voice was chosen because "he really is the prototype of the musicians, and he was so early, and he is relevant today, and he explains it in a great way."

Olsson seems to propose a temporal, spatial, and cultural interconnectedness of the "Black Atlantic," which he is intent on exposing and implementing in his films. The choice of Fela Kuti as narrator in *Fonko* recalls a passage in Gilroy's *The Black Atlantic* in which he describes a meeting between Kuti and African-American funk musician James Brown. In Gilroy's book, their recognition of mutual influences serves as an example for "the apparently magical processes of connectedness" between Africa and the African diasporas, shaping a hybrid transnational and transcontinental cultural realm based on a shared heritage (Gilroy 1993, 199).

The narrative technique in *Fonko* can be said to undermine the paternalism often associated with "voice-of-God" narration in Western documentary filmmaking. "Voice-of-God" narration has often been used to explain an "elsewhere" to an audience "at home," and in so doing exoticizes the "elsewhere." This can be illustrated by comparing *Fonko* to the original context of the Fela Kuti recording. The 1982 documentary *Music Is The Weapon* uses voice-of-God narration to introduce its subject to the audience; a male voice providing background information about Fela Kuti, his native Nigeria, and his connection to the Pan-Africanism and Black Power movements. *Fonko* is aimed at an audience outside the African continent too, but it waives such mediatory devices. Rather, the film is conceptualized as collaborative work between Olsson, Swedish-Gambian radio producer and presenter Lamin Daniel Jadama, Swedish journalist and filmmaker Lars Lovén, and contemporary African musicians. Regarding the cooperation with the musicians, Olsson says that "it's a meeting based on equality." He laughs, "They are super stars, and I'm just a filmmaker."

In the production of *Fonko*, which includes more original footage than *The Black Power Mixtape 1967–75* or *Concerning Violence*, Olsson deviated from a self-imposed rule, namely not to travel. Traveling from Sweden to Africa was limited, though, because many interviews were filmed in Sweden when the musicians toured there, and with local teams of friends on the trips to Africa. Other than such exceptions, Olsson says that "it makes no sense for anyone to travel anywhere":

> Since the 1990s, I have been of the opinion that no Swedish or European filmmaker should go to, let's say, Africa and make films there. There are great African filmmakers. I think that the time came 20 years ago for us to see their films. Back in the days, in the 1960s or 70s, there was a need for Swedes to go to America and explain for Swedes what America is like. That is not the case anymore.

He continues:

> We don't have to go there. We shouldn't go there. Thanks to internet and technology, they have the same cameras that we have. So there is no need for you or me to go and do some filming. There is no need for me to have a camera. There are millions of cameras in Stockholm alone.

Olsson's self-imposed constraint springs from a critical interrogation of practices of documentary filmmaking that imply traveling "elsewhere" with the goal of presenting and explaining the "elsewhere" to the audience "at home." This dominant pattern is deeply intertwined with global asymmetries related to the accessibility of production and distribution means and of a globalized market, and of opportunities of self-representation. In other words, the question is whether the common practice of "going there," of "going elsewhere," should be replaced by the "coming here" of those otherwise underrepresented, as a means of reaching equal representation and sovereignty of interpretation.

Sweden's Entanglements with Africa and the African Diaspora

Part of Olsson's project is to interrogate Sweden's role in the history of European overseas expansion and its aftermaths, of colonization, liberation movements, and postcolonial power structures. In our discussion of *The Black Power Mixtape 1967–75*, he described Sweden's position as "a very distinctive perspective." In *The Black Power Mixtape 1967–75*, Sweden literally opened the doors to the headquarters of the Black Power movement. From today's perspective, the Swedish TV journalists who knocked on the door of the Black Panther Party in the 1960s appear naïve but eager to understand and support the struggle. According to Olsson, the assumed innocence and ignorance of Swedish TV journalists was met with a politeness from the activists that they would not have expressed toward US media, making for unique footage.

Figure 13.2 Film still from *The Black Power Mixtape, 1967–75* © Göran Hugo Olsson/Story AB. Swedish reporter Bo Holmström interviews Angela Davis during her detention at California State Prison, 1972. Davis was charged as an accomplice to conspiracy, kidnapping, and homicide after guns that were registered in her name had been used in an armed attempt to obtain the release of three African-American prison inmates in 1970. She was found not guilty on all counts in her highly politicized trial in 1972. Observers assessed her prosecution as politically intended; she had previously been dismissed from her assistant professorship at the University of California, Los Angeles, because of her affiliation with the Communist Party and public "inflammatory speech."

One outstanding example in *The Black Power Mixtape 1967–75* is the coverage of Angela Davis's imprisonment in 1970 by journalist Bo Holmström (she was later acquitted of conspiracy charges). It includes a sensational interview with Davis: the first time a TV camera had been allowed to record a conversation in the basement of a courthouse outside of San Francisco. Davis sits facing the Swedish journalist, of whom we see only his back (Fig. 13.2). She appears calm, collected, and polite, yet flabbergasted when the interviewer asks her about her stance toward violent resistance:

> When somebody asks me about violence, I just find it incredible, because what it means is that the person who's asking the question has absolutely no idea what black people have gone through, what black people have experienced in this country since the time the first black person was kidnapped from the shores of Africa.

Interestingly, the clip has been re-published in several blogposts and YouTube channels since the film's release, and had the most views on YouTube shortly after *The Black Power Mixtape 1967–75* came out in 2011, with over 400 000 views. Most re-posts and comments point sympathetically to Davis's concise explanation of the resistance against anti-black violence, and celebrate her as a hero of the struggle of African-Americans past and present. *The Black Power Mixtape 1967–75* is often cited as the source of the clip, but what is lacking in most cases is any information about the film's director, and the name and origin of the person interviewing Davis in the clip.

Olsson's inclusion of this clip in *The Black Power Mixtape 1967–75* signifies the film's double, or self-reflexive, perspective: it investigates not only the Black Power movement's agenda and continuous relevance—represented by Angela Davis, who the camera is directed at, and whose retrospection we hear in voiceover—but also the Swedish journalist's position, whose gaze on Davis we share as viewers. This position is exposed by Davis's cited response, and is characterized by what Gloria Wekker (2016) has called "White Innocence": ignorance (however well-meaning), and privilege.

Olsson's films paint a complex and necessarily ambivalent picture of Sweden's position in relation to Africa and African diasporas. Sweden was and still is unmistakably part of an exploitative, asymmetrical, and inherently racist world order, while at the same time having fostered strong individual and collective bonds in the struggle for liberation and social justice. Our conversation about Sweden's connections with Africa and African-Americans spanned past and present, and friendly and hostile relations. Sweden's self-image seems to have emphasized narratives of innocence, benevolence, and solidarity, and to have downplayed involvement in oppressive and exploitative structures and undertakings. This self-image has been studied as an expression of Swedish, or Scandinavian, exceptionalism (Palmberg 2009; Jensen and Loftsdóttir 2012).

This can be further illustrated by recent discussions about how issues of race have been treated in Sweden. After World War II, Sweden adopted an official anti-racist image and policy supported by an ideology of "color-blindness" (e.g. the assertion that principles of equality, solidarity, and human rights are applied irrespective of race). Among the unfortunate consequences of this policy of "not seeing race" has been the unwillingness to address the Swedish history of race theory, ideology and related practices (e.g. the impact of botanist, physician and zoologist Carl Linnaeus' taxonomy on the development of theories of human races, or Swedish eugenics, centered at the State Institute for Racial Biology in the interwar period), or to attend to today's racial discrimination. In her article "Colonialism and Swedish History: Unthinkable Connections?" (2013), historian Gunlög Fur describes how any connection of Sweden to colonialism has long been dismissed as marginal, to the extent that the country has been able to represent itself as "untainted by colonialism's heritage" and, together with the other Scandinavian countries, has "successfully maintained positions as champions of minority rights and mediators in global politics" (Fur 2013, 18).

Olsson's documentary compilation technique proves an excellent tool to expose these evolving and contested self-images, with a focus on the decades from the 1960s to the 1980s, when Swedish grassroots movements and foreign politics were shaped in the spirit of global solidarity, anti-racism, and the critique of capitalism (The Nordic Documentation on the Liberation Struggle in Southern Africa Project, 2003–9). The SVT clips juxtaposed in *Concerning Violence*, for instance, reveal the eagerness with which Swedish journalists cover both the appalling racism of British farmers in Zimbabwe (at the time Rhodesia) and guerilla fighters' remote camps in the jungles of Mozambique, but also the unbearable ignorance of a Swedish missionary couple in Rhodesia about the very foundation and consequences of their actions.

Olsson grew up with and feels a strong connection with the tradition of Swedish support for liberation movements in Africa and the Civil Rights Movement in the USA. With outspoken racists of the right-wing Sweden Democrats party elected to the Swedish parliament in 2010 and again in both 2014 and 2018, he fears a massive backlash. It is against this backdrop that Olsson recognizes a renewed opportunity and necessity to, in his words, "recycle" anti-racist and anti-colonial thought and to mutually promote critical potential through cinematic arts, critical theory, and politics:

> I would do everything I can to make films that promote social justice. But in order to do that I have to make films that work as films. So I have to develop my skills as a filmmaker in the first place. [M]aybe some films could bring [Gayatri Spivak's works] to an audience that does not have a natural connection to [her] world. [Films could] be a link to the amazing insights of people [who] are not necessarily skilled to promote their ideas. This [the limited dissemination of critical thought] is tragic because there is so much knowledge that does take a long time before it will surface to common knowledge.

Thus, Olsson dedicates his filmmaking to the promotion of ideas and to consciousness raising: "If you have something, put it out there, with every accessible means." One way to achieve a broader reach and circulation, he notes, is through online platforms (the films are available on Vimeo). "I hope in the future that democracy will trickle down further in filmmaking. I think I have the right to do these films now, but I don't think I will have the right in the future." Perhaps Olsson's films and filmmaking practices and principles can contribute to a re-thinking of cinematic "elsewheres" with the suggestion of a new "anywhere": foregoing boundaries between "here" and "there," and foregrounding global solidarity and connectivity.

ACKNOWLEDGMENT

I would like to thank Göran Hugo Olsson for his time, sincerity, and generosity.

REFERENCES

Bakhtin, Mikhail. 2002 [1934–5]. "Discourse in the Novel." In *The Dialogic Imagination. Four Essays*, trans. Caryl Emerson and Michael Holquist, and ed. Michael Holquist. 14th printing. Austin: University of Texas Press. 259–422.
Beattie, Keith. 2004. *Documentary Screens: Non-Fiction Film and Television*. Basingstoke: Palgrave Macmillan.
Conrad, Sebastian. 2016. *What Is Global History?* Princeton: Princeton University Press.
Jensen, Lars and Kristín Loftsdóttir, eds. 2012. *Whiteness and Postcolonialism in the Nordic Region: Exceptionalism, Migrant Others and National Identities*. Farnham: Ashgate.
Fanon, Frantz. 2004. *The Wretched of the Earth*. Trans. Richard Philcox, with a foreword by Homi K. Bhabha and a preface by Jean-Paul Sartre. New York: Grove Press. Originally published as *Les Damnés de la Terre* (Paris: François Maspero, 1961).
Fur, Gunlög. 2013. "Colonialism and Swedish History: Unthinkable Connections?" In *Scandinavian Colonialism and the Rise of Modernity: Small Time Agents in a Global Arena*, ed. Magdalena Naum and Jonas M. Nordin. New York: Springer. 17–36.
Gilroy, Paul. 1993. *The Black Atlantic: Modernity and Double Consciousness*. London: Verso.
The Nordic Documentation on the Liberation Struggle in Southern Africa Project. 2003–9. Last modified October 15, 2012. <http://www.liberationafrica.se>
Naum, Magdalena and Jonas M. Nordin. 2013. *Scandinavian Colonialism and the Rise of Modernity: Small Time Agents in a Global Arena*. New York: Springer.
Palmberg, Mai. 2009. "The Nordic Colonial Mind." In *Complying with Colonialism: Gender, Race and Ethnicity in the Nordic Region*, ed. Suvi Keskinen, Salla Tuori, Sari Irni, and Diana Mulinari. Farnham: Ashgate. 35–50.
Rydén, Göran. 2013. *Sweden in the Eighteenth-century World: Provincial Cosmopolitans*. Farnham: Ashgate.
Shringarpure, Bhakti. 2014. "Fanon Documentary Confronts Fallacies about Anti-Colonial Philosopher," *The Guardian*, July 21. <https://www.theguardian.com/world/2014/jul/21/-sp-frantz-fanon-documentary-concerning-violence>
Volquardsen, Ebbe. 2014. "Scandinavia and 'the Land of UnSwedish Freedom': Jonathan Franzen, Susanne Bier and Self-conceptions of Exceptionalism in Crisis." In *Crisis in the Nordic Nations and Beyond: At the Intersection of Environment, Finance and Multiculturalism*, ed. Lars Jensen and Kristín Loftsdóttir. Farnham: Ashgate. 31–50.
Wekker, Gloria. 2016. *White Innocence: Paradoxes of Colonialism and Race*. Durham, NC: Duke University Press.

14. AKI KAURISMÄKI'S FINNO-FRENCH CONNECTIONS AND OTHER TRANSCULTURAL ELSEWHERES

Ana Bento Ribeiro

Aki Kaurismäki's cinema is based on transnational codes (Bacon 2016). He is mostly known for his unique style, and the national spaces in his films are seldom recognizable, referencing multiple cityscapes and cultures (Peden 2012, 14). Setting a number of films outside Finland, from *Leningrad Cowboys Go America* (Finland, 1989) to *Le Havre* (Finland, France, Germany, 2011), Kaurismäki successfully asserts his social commentary and affirms his aesthetic repertoire in different (trans)national backgrounds. The Kaurismäkian universe is mostly known for the employment of the road movie genre, the use of rockabilly music, the presence of Americana and vintage Soviet visual codes, and the location of narratives in major, yet almost unidentifiable cities. Thereby, the Finnish filmmaker builds a reputation as Finland's best-known film auteur through a prolific film production which, interestingly enough, sidesteps simple national readings. His transnational auteur profile, however, goes beyond narrative tropes, and surfaces in the economic makeup of his works.

With an institutional and industrial model that makes it the European hub for art house film production (Jäckel 1996; Creton et al., 2011), France, represented by its companies and institutions, has been a steady presence in Kaurismäki's films' credits. Starting in 1990 and emerging mostly from the decades-long collaboration with the French production and distribution company Pyramide, Kaurismäki's six French co-productions exemplify how economic and technical transnationalism contribute to the material existence and circulation success of art house films. Transnational production is not a rule for Kaurismäki's films, but, when this is the model at work, it is certainly relevant to the films' appeal to international audiences (Nestingen 2013; Bacon 2016).

An analysis of Kaurismäki's French co-productions brings to light the evolution of transnational film funding strategies and their relation to the films' circulation and reception. If *La Vie de Bohème* (*Boheemielämää*, Finland, France, 1992) and *Le Havre* are the only ones of these co-productions actually fully set in France, *The Man Without a Past* (*Mies vailla menneisyyttä*, Finland, 2002) had its domestic and worldwide success legitimated by the Grand Prix *cannois* and the Academy Awards nomination. In fact, being selected and awarded in Cannes remains a key factor for the legitimation of art house filmmakers, projecting them further in the international sphere, in terms both of prestige and of financial outcome (Turan 2002). Therefore, Kaurismäki is no exception when it comes to the recognition of Nordic cinemas via the French connection established by and at Cannes. The love story between the festival and Nordic auteurs is long-lasting. It can be traced from the constant presence of Ingmar Bergman's films, starting in the 1940s, through the recurrent selection of and awards for Lars von Trier's or Thomas Vinterberg's films, to the Palme d'Or for Ruben Östlund's Swedish, Danish, German, and French co-production *The Square* (2017). However, the transnational quality of Nordic films made within co-production schemes and translating into international distribution does not reside only in technicalities specific to the film industry. As Aki Kaurismäki's films exemplify, it also shapes films' narrative and aesthetics, making them appealing to an international niche audience (Nestingen 2013).

Within Kaurismäki's co-productions, the films (partially) "made in France" highlight the specificities of French film policies relating to foreign filmmakers. Second, they show how Kaurismäki secures these funding and circulation opportunities to make films that assert his societal views and aesthetic preferences while reaching the largest audience possible.

The French element first appears in Kaurismäki's filmography as a narrative resource attesting to his cinematic references as auteur. The Finnish filmmaker is a fan of French literary and cinematic canons, from Robert Bresson and Jacques Tati to Jean-Luc Godard. Honoring this tradition, he first collaborates with *Nouvelle Vague*'s fetish actor, Jean-Pierre Léaud, in *I Hired a Contract Killer* (1990), a multilateral European co-production, including Finnish, French, Swedish, British, and German inputs. Léaud's presence in Kaurismäki's films would continue in *La Vie de Bohème* and *Le Havre*.

If Kaurismäki seems to love French film culture, France's cinéphile milieu has an ambivalent standpoint on his works. The reception of his films by French critics hints at the different attitudes toward the transnational elements in his works. The first of Kaurismäki's films to be theatrically released in France was

Shadows in Paradise (*Varjoja paratiilsissa,* Finland, 1986), in 1988, followed by *Hamlet Goes Business* (*Hamlet liikemaailmassa,* Finland, 1987) that same year. The French general and cultural press reads both Finnish productions as expressions of a deeply ingrained Finnish character. Later, most notably since the release of *The Match Factory Girl* (*Tulitikkutehtaan tyttö,* Finland, 1990), French critics will multiply the comparisons between Kaurismäki's œuvre and other art house favorites, while still stressing its Finnish flavor: among the main references pointed out, we find Jim Jarmusch and Wim Wenders as well as René Clair, Luis Buñuel or even Woody Allen (Dunoyer 1999; Singh 1999). This referencing procedure facilitates the depicting of Kaurismäki's unique and multi-layered style to a foreign audience that is more familiar with the works of other, better-known film auteurs at the time.

Different from his previous Finland-set productions that were positively received by French critics, *Leningrad Cowboys Go America* is viewed mostly under a negative light. The relatively slow pace, particular humor and mixed (trans)national visual references do not seem to translate well among the French press. The second installment of Kaurismäki's international trilogy, *I Hired a Contract Killer*, distinguishes itself for the French audience especially for the casting of Jean-Pierre Léaud as the protagonist. The French press, Kartik Singh points out, "discusses much more the return of Léaud in a major role than the film itself" (1999, 81). Despite the problematic reception of his most transnational productions so far, Kaurismäki will situate the third part of this trilogy in Paris.

La Vie de Bohème is a Finnish-French-Swedish-German co-production. Although exhibiting identifiable Parisian cityscapes, the film was mostly shot in the suburbs of Malakoff, since Kaurismäki could not find the decors he identified with timeless, cinematic Frenchness in Paris itself (Kääpä, 2009). Made in 1992, the film indicates the tensions surrounding displacement and Europeanness at the time. The protagonists of the film are outsiders: Marcel (André Wilms) is a writer on the verge of being evicted from his flat. He meets two other outcasts, the Albanian artist Rodolfo (Matti Pellonpää) and the Irish composer Schaunard (Kari Väänänen). The film follows the budding friendship and love-lives of the trio, who try to remain committed to the arts despite their precarious living conditions. The protagonists speak French, with heavy accents in the case of Schaunard and Rodolfo—the latter, an illegal migrant, will be expelled from the country, only to make his way back.

The year 1992 fostered intense negotiations that would mark the evolution of the European Economic Community into the European Union the next year, furthering the bonds between its members beyond economic affairs. Finland, in its turn, would join the EU in 1995. Furthermore, the early 1990s entertained the opening of the former socialist bloc, favoring new flows of people beyond national borders, often illegally. These dynamics are ambiguous: while they strengthen transnational exchanges, especially in locations that particularly attract foreign populations, they also display the unequal conditions in which individuals of different nations join transnational movements. The three men in *La Vie de Bohème* find themselves trying to live the anachronistic lifestyle of the bohemian artist so deeply identified with an ideal of Frenchness, not to say "Parisianness." However, the actual scenario, while still promoting such cultural stereotypes, does not favor this way of life, either for foreigners or for French outcasts like Marcel.

Later on, French funding would be available for another four of Kaurismäki's feature films. *Leningrad Cowboys Meet Moses* (1994), *The Man Without a Past*, and *Lights in the Dusk* (*Laitakaupungin valot*, 2006)—and the aforementioned *Le Havre*—were Finnish, French, and German co-productions.

Starting in 1993, France's soft power reaches a new level in the realm of cultural policy. In order to protect its cultural sector—a key exponent of the French way of life—from the neoliberal competition promoted by the USA, France defends the principle of "cultural exception." Therefore, the cultural sector would be excluded from free-trade agreements and continue to welcome public funding, both from European institutions and national organizations. As a result, France, harboring a mature audiovisual sector and funding system, confirms its position as a leading agent for European co-productions. Moreover, the new perspectives opened by the EU would benefit multilateral co-production schemes, via the MEDIA support program, for instance.

Therefore, with a solid institutional model regulating, funding, and supporting the film industry (Forest 2001; Creton et al. 2011), France has an official position of taking pride in promoting its own cinema and supporting world cinemas ("Les domaines d'action de la diplomatie" 2017). Co-productions feed the French film economy while promoting its ties with foreign film industries. In numbers, this means that in the last few years French production has ranged between 203 and 300 films a year, the highest average in Europe (CNC France 2016). In the early 1990s, co-productions corresponded to almost half of the total of films produced in the country (Jäckel 1996, 85): a constant trend, since in 2016, the proportion of co-productions in the total of French-initiated films was 43 percent, with little fluctuation throughout the years (CNC France 2016). The complex and successful economic model of the French film industry has been influential for other national European film institutions and funding systems. Still, each of these operates according to social, historical, political, structural, and cultural specificities and corresponds to the availability of financial and technical resources.

The history of the funding of Kaurismäki's films reflects the diverse configurations of transnational film support. Aki Kaurismäki's first five feature films had modest budgets (Cowie 1990, 74) and full Finnish funding. The international collaboration started with Sweden in 1989 with *Leningrad Cowboys Go*

America (1989) and went on with *The Match Factory Girl* (1990). These films circulated in a number of international film festivals, a trend started with *Ariel* (1988). In the following years, between his Finnish-French-German collaborations, Kaurismäki still made films that were fully Finnish productions, like *Juha* (1999) and *Drifting Clouds* (1996), as well as Finnish-German features like *Take Care of Your Scarf, Tatiana* (1994) and *The Other Side of Hope* (2017).

In the Finnish film landscape, the international reach provided by festivals, critical acclaim, supranational programs such as MEDIA, Eurimages, and the Nordisk Film Fund, as well as the hard work of international sales agents (Nestingen 2013), is vital for covering expenses and prospecting profits for Finnish films. In spite of the remarkable domestic market share, Finnish admissions per capita and the country's population limit potential revenue. Moreover, despite being "the most visible Finnish cultural export" (Pantti 2005, 180) Aki Kaurismäki's films are not particularly popular with domestic audiences, who tend to concentrate their attention more on commercially-oriented Finnish productions, thus elevating the importance of the auteur's foreign reach (Nestingen, 2013).

The international market conquest, driven by festivals and critical acclaim, is tightly connected to funding schemes. After the successful career of *Ariel* in the international sphere, Kaurismäki's co-productions moved to new partner territories, with France playing a key role, participating in all his fiction-feature co-productions since *I Hired a Contract Killer*, with the exception of *Take Care of Your Scarf, Tatiana* (1994) and *The Other Side of Hope* (2017).

Co-production schemes certainly open the doors for new film markets. France, with its official policy of promoting world art house films and a particularly dynamic market for auteur cinema, is strategic for boosting audiences for niche films such as Kaurismäki's. According to statistics from the French National Film Center, 1.4 million people go on average at least once a week to the movies, while a further 11.1 million go at least once a month. Together, these populations acquire more than 73 million tickets per year (CNC France 2016). This is a well-informed, cinéphile audience that is particularly drawn to art house movies (Albert and Camilleri 2015, 63). To cater to such demand, France hosts numerous festivals and is home to several public-aided movie theaters around the country that welcome less known cinematic works. In addition, thanks to institutional incentives, Paris and its suburbs, where the population of steady filmgoers is locally concentrated, also accommodate a high number of theaters centering their activity on art house films, which makes the regular programming equivalent in diversity to a perpetual festival (Iordanova 2016).

The theatrical performance of Kaurismäki's films emphasizes the importance of the French market for their commercial success. According to Lumière

Database and CBO Box-Office, since the first wave of international recognition in the early 1990s, Kaurismäki's films have accumulated the following admission figures in France: *I Hired a Contract Killer* sold more than 71 000 tickets; *La Vie de Bohème* 58 074; *Take Care of Your Scarf, Tatiana* 31 443. *Leningrad Cowboys Meet Moses* had a meager 8756 spectators, *Juha* fewer than 28 000, while *Drifting Clouds* was a relative art house success with more than 134 000 admissions. After the critical, *cannois* phenomenon of *The Man Without a Past*, Kaurismäki's best-performing film reaching more than 176 000 viewers in Finland, 720 000 in France and a total of around 2 000 000 worldwide, his following features attained a whole new level of popularity, with the exception of *Lights in the Dusk* (around 60 000 tickets sold in France). *Le Havre* made more than 560 000 admissions, and *The Other Side of Hope* more than 250 000.

More important than absolute figures is the French participation in the total of worldwide admissions. France is the leading country in terms of number of admissions for Kaurismäki's post-1990 co-productions, except for *Lights in the Dusk* and *Juha*. Therefore, Kaurismäki's niche in foreign markets with larger film-going demographics can still be more profitable than the domestic space. In fact, since the gain in critical attention and in co-production involvement, Aki Kaurismäki's films have reached new territories. Since 1996, his works have entered between twelve and thirty international markets. This shows that transnational cooperation, often driven by France, brought his films to new *elsewheres*.

Le Havre is a Finnish, French, and German co-production, with an estimated budget of around 3 000 000 euros. It also exemplifies modern transnational film financing, being 41 percent French-, 49 percent Finnish-, and 10 percent German-funded. It was supported by the French CNC, the French regional fund Haute Normandie, the Finnish Film Center, and the Nordisk Film Fund, as well as the French TV channels Canal + and Cinécinéma, the Finnish channel YLE and the French-German Arte. This scheme seems to have paid off, since the film has reached 26 European markets.

Le Havre is an example of the potential of the French cinephile niche, that has made 41 percent of its worldwide admissions in France. The film itself expresses a new(er) set of conflicts regarding Europe and narratives of displacement. In fact, a plot portraying extra-European individuals in the continent replaces the intra-European scenario of *La Vie de Bohème*, two decades later. As the title indicates, the film is set in the harbor city of Le Havre, in northern France, a region of intense blue-collar past and current decadence. Actually, *Le Havre* is a continuation of *La Vie de Bohème*. Here, Marcel, again played by André Wilms, is an old shoe shiner. While living precariously and caring for his gravely ill wife, he comes across the young Idrissa (Blondin Miguel), an illegal, twelve-year-old Gabonese migrant smuggled in a container. Marcel will move heaven and earth to help Idrissa reach England, where he is supposed to meet relatives. Albeit serious and urgent in theme, *Le Havre* is a deeply optimistic film with an unlikely happy ending.

Released in 2011, *Le Havre* portrays the refugee crisis while criticizing its depiction in political discourses and the media. Set in a French region particularly concerned by the issue, the film shows how humanistic values may challenge the dominant view where (illegal) migration necessarily triggers violence and conflict. Like Paris in *La Vie de Bohème*, the city of Le Havre is presented as a mythic elsewhere displaced in time. In typical Kaurismäkian fashion, we see the visual codes of 1950s–1970s France in decors that evoke a long-lost proletarian lifestyle. This background functions as a reminder of forgotten values such as empathy and solidarity that seem to emerge more easily in tight(er)-knit communities. Instead of the foreigner being presented as a threat to these social bonds, the immigrants in Le Havre strengthen moral values such as compassion and mutual support. However, this does not result from a generalized, official standpoint but from the experiences of individuals facing different kinds of marginality. Marcel and his peers are examples of this *other* France: he is a poor shoe shiner, surrounded by owners of small neighborhood shops—the bakery, the grocery shop, the pub—that were once at the heart of French communities' daily life and are now disappearing.

Therefore, the city of Le Havre as shown through Marcel's entourage is positioned as an elsewhere opposed to Paris, the center of a political power that neglects subjective, human aspects of life. The orders for the special police forces to violently act upon refugees' arrivals and camps come from Paris. In another instance, Le Havre's police detective Monet (Jean-Pierre Darroussin) is obliged by the Ministry of Internal Affairs to track down Idrissa. However, Monet is a policeman from provincial France and an outsider himself: he uses his (small) power to help the boy leave for England. Le Havre is also where Chang (Quoc Dung Nguyen), an illegal Vietnamese immigrant, finds a new identity and a welcoming French-born community. Hence, the construction of a mythical Le Havre situates it as an intermedial elsewhere: for some, like Idrissa, it is a necessary site of passage where the humanistic values of its marginal inhabitants allow for the continuation of their journey. For others, like Chang, it is where these same rare values permit the making of a new identity.

Le Havre, then, challenges Manichean views of migrants as a threat and of France's working class as xenophobic. The film is itself *decentered*: this coproduction that deals with a French societal subject is directed by a knowledgeable outsider looking at France's margins. As in his other films, he focuses on overlooked social groups to build a hopeful view of contemporary society. In *Le Havre*, he goes further: he finds beauty and hope for the future in a spurned city, a marginal French elsewhere which is an exceptional place where individuals of any national and social background can be seen as equal. The French audience, that made the film an art house success, likely needed this fairy tale.

REFERENCES

Albert, Xavier and Jean-François Camilleri. 2015. *Le Marketing du Cinéma*. Paris: Dixit.
Bacon, Henry. 2016. *Finnish Cinema: a Transnational Enterprise*. London: Palgrave Macmillan.
Cowie, Peter. 1990. *Le cinéma des pays nordiques*. Paris: Centre Georges Pompidou.
CNC France. 2016. *Evolution du public dans les salles de cinéma*. Paris: CNC.
CNC France. 2017. *La Production cinématographique en 2016*. Paris: CNC.
Creton, Laurent *et al*. 2011. *Les producteurs: enjeux créatifs, enjeux financiers*. Paris: Nouveau Monde Éditions.
Dunoyer, Avril. 1999. "Aki Kaurismäki vu par les Cahiers du cinéma et Positif." *Contrebande*, 5/1999. Paris: Université Panthéon-Sorbonne. 97–104.
Forest, Claude. 2001. *Économies contemporaines du cinéma en Europe: L'improbable industrie*. Paris: CNRS.
Iordanova, Dina. 2016. "At the Cinema in Paris: The Privileged Outsider." In *Cinemas of Paris*, ed. Jean-Michel Frondon and Dina Iordanova. St Andrews: St Andrews Film Studies. 3–22.
Jäckel, Anne. 1996. "European Co-production Strategies: The Case of France and Britain." In *Film Policy: International, National and Regional Perspectives*, ed. Albert Moran. London: Routledge. 85–100.
Kääpä, Pietari. 2009. *The National and Beyond: The Globalisation of Finnish Cinema in the Films of Aki and Mika Kaurismäki*. Oxford: Peter Lang.
"Les domaines d'action de la diplomatie ... Exporter le cinéma français et soutenir les cinémas du monde." 12/05/2017. France diplomatie. <http://www.diplomatie.gouv.fr/article/exporter-le-cinema-francais-et-soutenir-les-cinemas-du-monde>
Nestingen, Andrew. 2013. *The Cinema of Aki Kaurismäki—Contrarian Stories*. New York: Columbia University Press.
Pantti, Mervi. 2005. "Art or Industry? Battles over Finnish Cinema during the 1990's." In *Transnational Cinema in a Global North: Nordic Cinema in Transition*, ed. Andrew Nestingen and Trevor G. Elkington. Detroit: Wayne University Press. 165–90.
Peden, Sana. 2012. "Directors: Aki Kaurismäki." In *Directory of World Cinema: Finland*, ed. Pietari Kääpä. Bristol: Intellect. 12–16.
Singh, Kartik. 1999. "L'accueil critique des films d'Aki Kaurismäki par la presse nationale quotidienne et hebdomadaire." *Contrebande*, 5/1999. Paris: Université Panthéon-Sorbonne. 75–86.
Turan, Kenneth. 2002. *Sundance to Sarajevo—Film Festivals and the World They Made*. London: University of California Press.

15. NORDIC NOIR AS A CALLING CARD: THE INTERNATIONAL CAREERS OF DANISH FILM AND TELEVISION TALENT IN THE 2010s

Eva N. Redvall

With the international success of serials such as *The Killing* (*Forbrydelsen*, 2007–12) and *Borgen* (2010–13), and the popularity of "Nordic Noir" drama, the Danish television production landscape enjoyed unprecedented international interest in the early 2010s. While these series found widespread circulation and sparked new discourses on the potential of subtitled content in the international market, the interest in what was perceived as a highly professional public service production culture simultaneously created new possibilities for Danish talent to launch A-list careers on the global television stage.

This chapter analyzes how the success of Danish television drama led to Danish talent being able to use their national television credits as a calling card for international film and television productions. It outlines how the Danish production culture of the 2000s was marked by so-called "cross-over" between the film and television industries that helped improve the quality of the domestic series and was helpful in training national talent for possible international careers.

Drawing from scholarship on careers in the creative media industries, the chapter discusses how the move from the national to the international realm aggravates many of the challenges that seem to be inherent in the "boundaryless" careers of the film and television industries (e.g. Jones 1996; Mathieu 2012). The concept of boundaryless careers comes from management studies, where it refers to careers marked by "mobility, flexibility, the development

Figure 15.1 Charlotte Sieling built an international career on the success of Hans Rosenfeldt's crime series *The Bridge* (*Bron*, 2011–18). Screenshot from the opening credits of the first episode. Cinematographer: Jørgen Johansson.

of knowledge and networks, and the taking of responsibility for one's own career" (Inkson 2008). The term "boundaryless" refers to moving across separate employers and breaking traditional organizational career boundaries, as well as potentially working across national borders in globalized work environments, as discussed in much of the literature on project-based media work in the cultural or creative industries (e.g. Hesmondhalgh and Baker 2011).

International interest in Danish television series has been helpful in terms of the "reputation work" that is an ongoing part of securing one's next job in film and television production (Zafirau 2007). This chapter analyzes the example of the Danish director Charlotte Sieling, who made an international boundaryless career for herself after being the conceptualizing director of the Swedish/Danish crime serial *The Bridge* (*Bron*, 2011–18). Sieling went on to direct episodes of high-end US serials such as *Homeland* (2011–) and *The Americans* (2013–18), as well as the pilot episode for *Queen of the South* (2016–).

The chapter combines a qualitative practitioner interview with Sieling with discussion of publications on other Danish directors working abroad to discuss the main challenges raised by practitioners in relation to boundaryless career work in the television industries, and their views about the reasons behind the recent international interest in Danish talent. The chapter closes with a discussion of how an initial enthusiasm for Danish talent gaining substantial ground abroad based on the Nordic Noir hype has gradually been combined with widespread criticism of domestic "talent drain." There is a general sense of pride in the industry and press when domestic talent launches successful careers elsewhere, but when this happens on a large scale, it can lead to a lack of experienced A-list directors in the national realm.

TELEVISION DRAMA AND FEATURE FILMS: ONE OR TWO ARENAS?

A number of Scandinavian directors have had successful careers abroad since the silent film era, as discussed by a range of film historians (e.g. Lunde 2015). Some managed to establish themselves when moving from Scandinavia to the USA, while others have been headhunted to try to bring a certain European touch to American productions. Danish directors describe encountering what they call the "euro trash" pile of screenplays when coming to Hollywood, referring to mediocre scripts looking for a European director who might take on the task of improving them and turning them into a decent film (see e.g. Kragh-Jacobsen and Kjeldsen 2017, 20). Several directors discuss this process as a tiresome rite of passage.

Historically, directing an award-winning feature film was the only way to get noticed outside of Denmark. Examples of Danish directors who have made international names for themselves based on their domestic feature films include Bille August, who launched an international career following his Oscar-winning historical drama *Pelle the Conqueror* (*Pelle Erobreren*, 1987); Lone Scherfig, who found attention with her popular Dogma film *Italian for Beginners* (*Italiensk for begyndere*, 2000); and Susanne Bier, whose national dramas such as the Oscar-nominated *After the Wedding* (*Efter brylluppet*, 2006) and the Oscar-winning *In a Better World* (*Hævnen*, 2010) paved the way for large-scale, international film and television productions such as the Emmy-winning mini-series *The Night Manager* (2016).

The 2010s brought about changes in the industry's "food chain" from national to international careers. While Oscars and other awards in the world of feature film are still excellent platforms for gaining an international reputation, there are now new ways to enter the international film and television landscape. For example, the Danish documentary filmmaker Janus Metz went from his award-winning and visually stunning war portrayal *Armadillo* (2010) to directing the third episode of the second season of *True Detective* (2014–15) before moving on to his international feature film *Borg* (2017) about Swedish tennis player Björn Borg.

Moving between documentary, television, and feature film, Metz has argued that he does not see major differences between directing factual and fiction content (Pilegaard 2016). However, it is still rare to see documentary filmmakers move into large-scale feature film production. Moreover, most documentary filmmakers seem to stay in Denmark, a fact which is often explained by the Danish documentary scene being quite well-funded, meaning that Danish directors are able to find financing for ideas without leaving the country (Kragh-Jacobsen and Kjeldsen 2017, 59).

As Lars von Trier has proven for a number of years, one does not have to leave Scandinavia to make major English-language productions with

Hollywood stars as long as the funding can be found in the region, although few directors have the name and opportunity to secure those kinds of feature film budgets without going abroad (see Badley, this volume). This situation gradually changed in the 2010s, when talented directors working in television drama were suddenly able to pursue international careers based on their credits from Danish serials. The national drama productions used to be watched primarily by Nordic audiences. When these serials started traveling, accompanied by the hype around Nordic Noir, working in television drama also became a calling card for bigger assignments abroad.

Traditionally, the worlds of film and television have been quite far apart, but the recent focus on what scholarly literature refers to as "high-end" television drama (Nelson 2007), "quality TV" (McCabe and Akass 2007), or "complex TV" (Mittell 2015) has meant that A-list talent now moves back and forth between what used to be regarded as the prestigious world of cinema and the less prestigious—and less artistically recognized—work for television. The power dynamics between film and television have changed, and the timing of the success of Danish television drama was perfect in terms of Danish talent having the opportunity to benefit and launch successful international careers, both behind and in front of the camera. Another advantage for Danish talent was that the domestic television production culture—contrary to the film and television industries in many other countries—had in fact been marked by so-called "cross-over" between the world of film and television for several years, with the Danish Broadcasting Corporation (DR) creating television drama with "cinematic" production value.

Danish Television Drama: From Training Ground to Calling Card

For many years, the production of expensive television drama for a country of only 5.7 million inhabitants almost only happened in the in-house drama unit of the main public service broadcaster, DR. This unit changed its approach to television drama in the mid-1990s, when criticism of "old-school" productions led DR to look to the international television market for new inspiration in content, style, and modes of production. An important approach, starting with the series *Taxa* (DR, 1997–9), was to produce high-end serial drama, comparable to international productions in terms of storytelling, acting, and production value (Redvall 2013a).

The DR drama unit strategically sought to make television drama productions attractive to the best talent from the National Film School of Denmark. DR thus entered into collaboration with the school, teaching writers and producers to create the kind of serials that it would like to realize (Redvall 2015). Its ambition was to have the best people from the Danish film industry working in Danish television, including actors and all the main positions behind the scenes (Redvall 2013b), referred to as "cross-over" between the film and television industries.

Transforming ingrained cultural and institutional frameworks to attract talent from Danish film was no easy task in a production culture where the film school's directors-in-training were taught to think of themselves as auteurs, aiming only for the cinema screen. But following Lars von Trier's hospital drama *Riget/The Kingdom* (DR, 1994), a new generation of directors began taking interest in television. *The Kingdom* proved that one could in fact create a unique work of art that appealed to both critics and mainstream audiences. Following *The Kingdom*, DR hired several young directors for their new flagship serial dramas, including Niels Arden Oplev as the conceptualizing director of *Taxa*, and episode directors such as Ole Christian Madsen, Per Fly, and Lone Scherfig, who all went on to become major names in Danish cinema.

These young directors embraced television directing from the perspective of entering someone else's vision, and gaining valuable experience of being on set and working with actors and crew. A well-known challenge for many small production cultures is that productions are often many years apart and directors thus have limited opportunity to consistently practice their filming craft. The many hours of serial drama provide the opportunity to gain such experience. Several directors who worked for DR early in their careers have stressed the importance of this experience. Ole Christian Madsen has called the early DR series a "boot camp" for young directors and emphasized its importance for the overall professionalization of Danish cinema (in Hjort et al. 2010, 169). Niels Arden Oplev has argued that TV series provide a chance to learn how to handle large teams and work at a fast pace (in Hjort et al. 2010, 212).

In the 2000s, young Danish filmmakers thus had the opportunity to practice their craft in television drama before moving on to feature film productions. The television credits were not regarded as impressive calling cards or as something that could open doors outside of Denmark, however. This gradually changed when foreign audiences took an interest in Danish series, and the writers, cast, and crew associated with national productions were deemed interesting, as they could bring some of the "Scandi" or Nordic Noir sensibility to the world.

THE NEW CIRCULATION OF DANISH TELEVISION DRAMA TALENT IN THE 2010S AND BEYOND

Building on this film and industry practice of the 2000s, Danish television drama began to launch international careers for both screenwriters and directors in the 2010s. A contributing factor to this success is the strong position of the head writers, or "showrunners," in the Danish television drama framework (Redvall 2013a). The "one vision" production framework for DR series has given head writers creative control and final cut, and this strong sense of authorial voice and vision has helped establish several head writers in the national as well as the international television landscape.

As a consequence, following the success of *Borgen* and *The Killing*, the series' creators Adam Price and Søren Sveistrup set up Sam Productions (together with producer Meta Louise Foldager), the first screenwriter-led company in Denmark. With French Studiocanal as co-founder, the company has had a strong international outlook from its inception.

Christian Torpe is another screenwriter who made it onto the international scene with the science fiction/horror thriller series *The Mist* (2017), following the Netflix distribution of his popular school teacher dramedy *Rita* (2012–). Other screenwriters such as Peter Thorsboe and Mai Brostrøm—the writers of Emmy-winning DR series such as *Unit One* (*Rejseholdet*, 2000–4), *The Eagle* (*Ørnen*, 2004–6), and *The Protectors* (*Livvagterne*, 2009–10)—have subsequently co-created European shows including *The Team* (2015–). The work of Danish screenwriters is thus not only transmitted through subtitling or remakes of their domestic work; they also create original work targeted specifically at international audiences.

TV series have also helped Danish actors gain recognition abroad. Serial drama provides the opportunity for audiences to relate to actors week after week. Actors can thus slowly build a star persona on foreign soil more efficiently than in one-off feature films. The female leads of *The Killing* and *Borgen* found dedicated international fan bases over the course of each series in different territories, and they both moved on to international roles. Sofie Gråbøl starred in the UK "Arctic Noir" *Fortitude* (2015–18) and the lead actress from *Borgen*, Sidse Babett Knudsen, acted in both Hollywood films (such as *Inferno*, 2016) and high-end television drama (*Westworld*, 2016–), as well as in French cinema.

One could list several other names, since an unprecedented number of Danish actors have secured major international roles in the 2010s. There has also been an interest in Danish talent behind the scenes, such as Danish cinematographer Eigil Bryld, who shot the first season of *House of Cards* (Netflix, 2013–18). Most of the cinematographers and technical crew working abroad (such as cinematographer Charlotte Bruus with her work for director Thomas Vinterberg) seem to have gotten their international work on the basis of their track record in cinema, however. Some also go abroad by accompanying Danish directors on their journeys to foreign production cultures, as will be discussed as part of the case study.

GETTING HIRED: *THE BRIDGE* AS THE LAUNCH OF AN INTERNATIONAL CAREER

Charlotte Sieling has had a nontraditional career path in Danish film and television. She has not gone through the traditional gatekeeping education in the

Figure 15.2   For five years Chalotte Sieling was the main director of DR's highly popular historical drama series *Better Times* (*Krøniken*, 2004–7, created by Stig Thorsboe), which portrayed Danish society from 1949 to the 1970s. Screenshot from the opening credits of the first episode. Cinematographer: Jørgen Johansson.

directing department of The National Film School of Denmark. Instead, she had an education as an actress from the Danish National School of Performing Arts. Following several years as an actress, she studied screenwriting at The National Film School. After graduating in 1995, she had a hard time getting her own projects funded and started directing commercials. This led to a call from DR producer Sven Clausen, who suggested she should try her hand at an episode of television drama for DR. She accepted the offer and directed some episodes of *Unit One* before spending five years as the main director of the historical drama *Better Times* (*Krøniken*, 2004–7), followed by four episodes of *The Killing*. Sieling describes those years in terms of her "gradually growing into the role of being a director." She had achieved an understanding of actors and storytelling from her acting and screenwriting background and had gradually mastered the various technical aspects of filmmaking through her close collaboration with cinematographer Jørgen Johansson (Sieling 2017).

Like the directors of *Taxa* in the 1990s, Sieling found that life after film school can be tough as a young director. It is hard to have just graduated and be expected to know everything and be a mature artist. She argues that television drama offers the opportunity to learn while being around extraordinarily skilled people, since—as an episode director—you enter a machine that is already up and running (Sieling 2017). For Sieling, this learning process happened in relative peace and quiet, since it wasn't until *The Killing* that foreign viewers started watching, creating a new interest in the people who were behind the successful productions.

When Sieling became conceptualizing director of *The Bridge*, US manager Ragna Nervik took an interest in her career. According to Sieling, Nervik was looking for interesting female directors and helped push her onto the international stage, stressing that it was another important turning point in her career. Scholarly literature on creativity and career-making points to how timing and luck are often issues in what is frequently described as the high-risk "nobody knows" film and television industries. As the creativity scholar Mihaly Csikszentmihalyi has stated, the recognition of one's work is related not only to talent or giftedness, but also to "chance, perseverance, or being at the right place at the right time" (Csikszentmihalyi 1988, 29). A strong track record and favorable trends, such as a global taste for Nordic Noir, are definitely helpful, but there are many circumstances to consider in relation to what is now often discussed as a "talent industry" of its own in relation to film and television (Boyle 2018).

Working with film and television in the multiplatform era is still marked by being hired from one project to the next in what are referred to as "Screen Idea Work Groups" (Macdonald 2013). Besides your track record, many factors come into play when being hired from one project to the next (Jones 1996). One study from the UK television industry (Stoyanovo and Grugulis 2012) points to being the best readily available candidate as an important factor, and research on careers in the creative industries stresses the importance of thinking of career management as also "relationship management" (Mathieu 2012).

While there are many scholarly studies on issues of class, ethnicity, gender, or age in the creative industries (see e.g. Leung et al. 2015 on women as "career scramblers" in UK film and television), Danish scholarly research, as well as the domestic production framework, paid very limited attention to such topics until the 2010s. Discourses about access, funding, and success in the Danish film and television industries have built on a general perception of a meritocracy where everyone has a fair chance of building a successful career. However, in the 2010s reports on ethnic representation in educational contexts, in production and on screen started challenging this notion, and the #MeToo movement generated a momentum for new gender discussions. Sieling's statements about her career development point to the importance of a manager actively scouting for strong female talent for the US context, but otherwise Sieling does not mention gender as a major issue in her career. Instead—like her male colleagues with experiences working abroad—she stresses how certain character traits and personal issues are crucial when selling oneself on the bigger stage.

In a special issue of the member magazine of the Danish Directors Guild focusing particularly on Danish directors working outside of Denmark, directors highlight "likeability," being "good in a room," and the ability to perform as crucial when presenting or pitching in foreign settings (Kragh-Jacobsen and Kjeldsen 2017, 11). Moreover, you need to have people on your side in what is described as a "go-to-business" (ibid.). In that regard, agents and managers are essential for an international career in a way that is different from small nation production cultures where most people know each other in advance and are aware of each other's work.

Project-based "portfolio career" industries are vulnerable to impediments such as working across multiple time zones or in creative constellations that continuously evolve, and where one has to maintain one's network and plan future projects while working full-time on another production. Danish director Ole Christian Madsen—who directed several episodes of the US action series *Banshee* (2013–16)—explains how networking in the US context requires being physically present on a regular basis to show your sincere interest in directing jobs. He has had to make strict rules for himself in terms of calls and travels since trying to work in two production cultures at once turned out to be too stressful (Kragh-Jacobsen and Kjeldsen 2017, 13). Maintaining good relationships and remaining on people's radar abroad is thus a major issue for Danish directors. Sieling stresses how the hype and buzz about the Danish production culture have created a widespread sense of wanting to work with that talent, across Europe as well as in the USA (Sieling 2017).

Several Danish directors emphasize that you never get a job solely on the basis of being Scandinavian, but there is a sense that as a Scandinavian director you bring something special to a production. Michael Noer—who went from directing Danish documentaries and feature films to the US production *Papillon* (2017)—argues that Danish directors are generally regarded as being good at working with actors (Iskov 2018). Sieling agrees. She regards her acting background as an asset and highlights working with actors as one of her particular directorial skills (Sieling 2017).

According to Madsen, another strength that is often ascribed to Scandinavian directors is being used to working within budgetary constraints (Kragh-Jacobsen and Kjeldsen 2017, 11). In his view, Danish directors are not only regarded as generally good at their job; they are also regarded as cost-efficient in the way they are accustomed to thinking about how best to intensify scenes with limited means. With little money, one often has to come up with original and efficient solutions, and there is a sense that Danish directors are capable of this, even when the big US production machine is up and running (ibid.). In Danish cinema, the Dogma 95 films were an extreme and successful example of cutting costs and working with creativity and constraints. On a smaller scale, the Danish television serials that traveled in the 2010s proved that one can create competitive, interesting content with high production value for certain niche audiences in the international market while spending only public service broadcasting budgets.

Several directors thus argue that Danish talent generally has a good reputation, but even with a strong "brand" one always has to sell oneself and be able to argue that one brings something particular to a production—even if it might be unclear to oneself what this "something special" is. For example, Sieling finds that one always has to convincingly sell visual ideas for the dramatic material at hand, even if still searching for their exact nature. In one case, she was hired on the basis of her explaining that she wanted to shoot a new series as "poetic noir." When she was asked what this meant in more detail, she truthfully answered that she wasn't quite sure but that she would like to explore this together with the team on the series. The decision-makers found this to be intriguing, and her Nordic Noir track record helped assure them that she would be able to lead a stylistic "poetic Noir investigation" (Sieling 2017).

As illustrated above, coming from a certain production culture and bringing a particular sensibility to a production is an important part of the many pieces that have to come together when being hired on major studio productions abroad. Danish directors had tailwind for many reasons when going abroad in the 2010s, but transitioning from a small nation production culture to major international productions is still far from an easy task.

Working with American versus Danish Television Drama

Once hired to work on non-domestic productions, Scandinavian directors meet a fundamentally different production culture in terms of size and speed of production. For Sieling, her work on *The Bridge* led to her directing two episodes of the French police series *Jo* (2013) with Jean Reno, before moving on to the USA as episode director of hit series such as *The Americans* and *Homeland* and being the conceptualizing director of *Queen of the South*. When comparing her work in the USA with her experience from Denmark, she highlights the big teams and the pace as the main difference (Sieling 2017).

In her view, one of the main tasks as director in the television drama "machine" is to make sure that the demanding daily schedules are met. Sieling describes how one has to create the sense that there is plenty of time even if the process must be expedited, and she argues that if all is working out with the main actors, you can control the rest. However, as an episode director you only have one day on set to show your worth; otherwise, the team "takes over the production." Accordingly, she argues that the work of the director calls for strong communicative skills as well as a directorial craft and an artistic vision (Sieling 2017).

The importance of interpersonal skills is often highlighted in studies of creative work, since good social and communicative skills are needed not only to secure jobs in a network- and project-based industry, but also to communicate in the ever-changing work constellations on different productions (e.g. Jones 1996). Sieling has not experienced major challenges in terms of language or cultural clashes. Part of the explanation for this is probably the widespread circulation of US content and high English language proficiency in the Nordic countries. The global flows of content ensure similar frames of reference, not least in a Scandinavian film and television culture where all foreign content is subtitled.

However, on a production level, Sieling describes remarkable differences entering big US productions compared to working on smaller serials in the national framework. The star-driven nature of the US film and television industries means that the right actors are essential for financing, and once a series is in production the actors are at the center of every episode, while directors come and go. As mentioned, Sieling regards her acting background as an asset. There can easily be conflicts around particular scenes or shots, and when entering an existing series as an episode director it helps to have a nuanced understanding of acting as a craft. Sieling admits to having had her share of disagreements on set—for instance, in front of the entire crew with Matt Dillon on the set of *Wayward Pines* (2015–16). She argues that as a director you have to be able to stand in the line of fire and tolerate conflicts and clashes, which takes a certain personality. This is always the case, but it can be even more terrifying on a big US production with powerful stars (Sieling 2017).

Sieling describes herself as a person who "has always hated when everyone has to agree." She doesn't mind disagreements, and she has gotten used to the fact that the level of conflict can be intense in the hectic framework of US productions. She knows that she will not always have it her way, but she will argue her case. Several other directors describe the decision-making processes on US productions as a major issue when coming from a production culture where directors are used to having final cut. Nikolaj Arcel describes the US production process as marked by a lot of "politics" when talking about films as "commodities," and as a director one has to be able to accept that (Iskov 2018).

It takes a certain personality to deal with that context, and Sieling argues that she has learnt to accept this, but notes how important it was for her to start her foreign career with the Danish cinematographer Jørgen Johansson by her side when shooting the French series *Jo*. It takes time to learn new production frameworks, and it felt secure moving onto the international stage alongside a long-term collaborator (Sieling 2017). Several other directors try to bring long-term collaborators with them when going abroad, such as Nikolaj Arcel, who worked with cinematographer Rasmus Videbæk on *The Dark Tower*. Building on previous successful work facilitates a sense of trust that is essential in creative work, and bringing a trusted partner in crime along can make the move to foreign productions less nerve-wracking.

Bringing a long-term collaborator can also help counter the loneliness that Sieling describes, working far away from family and friends and having massively long work days. This is not unique to the film and television industries, but it is a topic that is often foregrounded in studies of how to maintain successful careers in these industries where "the constant demands of performing quality work, seeking new projects, and maintaining a personal network of relations can consume the energies and lives of project-network participants" (Jones 1996, 67). The issue of balancing professional and personal life is an issue when working far away from home.

Several of Sieling's male colleagues similarly highlight the personal challenges of working abroad as difficult in the long run, together with a general sense that the US production culture is driven by an exhausting sense of performance anxiety and fear about how to secure the next job (e.g. Arcel 2007). The advantage of being a Nordic director in such a production culture is that you can actually leave. Contrary to directors who fled their home countries for political or other reasons, Danish directors have actively chosen to relocate, and they have the possibility of returning to Denmark, which many of them also do. Most directors of course prefer to be the ones making the decision of when to return—and they prefer to return to interesting projects.

Sieling finds the possibility of going back and forth between being a "hired gun" on major television productions and working on her own feature films in Denmark attractive, but it is always complicated by the timing and financing of projects. As discussed above, while the possibility of launching an international career based on the new interest in Danish television series offers many alluring possibilities, such as working with bigger budgets and international stars, the move from the national to the international arena contains a number of inherent challenges that call not only for talent and certain professional skills, but also for a certain personality and a willingness to adapt to foreign work ways.

Conclusion: A Story of Success—or of Talent Drain?

While there were many Nordic directors with successful international careers in the 2010s, there were also many directors who tried to go abroad and never made it—and many stories of directors who had a hard time in Hollywood, as reported in the Danish press by Susanne Bier regarding the making of her feature film *Serena* (2014), and by Christian E. Christiansen about his teenage thriller *The Room Mate* (2011) (Eriksen 2014). Several Danish directors have shared the stories of their failed attempts to negotiate deals or get projects off the ground. Before getting hired for *The Dark Tower*, Arcel wrote a tongue-in-cheek piece describing how he "wasted his life" having 50 meetings in Los Angeles over four weeks in 2007 that didn't amount to any concrete deals (Arcel 2007). However, Arcel also outlined why some directors keep trying: the thought of working with the big budgets, reaching big audiences, and working with the best people in the industry makes some Nordic talent continuously dream of Hollywood even if the process can be, in his words, a humiliating experience (ibid.).

As discussed in the literature on boundaryless careers, "persistence and high levels of motivation and commitment are critical due to the intense competition for opportunities" (Jones 1996, 63). This only intensifies when moving from the national to the international realm. The few people who manage to make it in the USA are normally hailed as success stories in the national press, but lately there have also been more critical stories about the experiences of Danish talent abroad. These can concern the creative compromises that are often related to entering major studio productions with many commercial stakeholders, such as the discussions around the production of Arcel's *The Dark Tower* (e.g. Bo 2017). Recently, press stories about Danish talent working abroad have also focused on the "brain drain" consequences for the Danish film and television industry.

From a political perspective, the export of Danish talent is not only regarded as a story of success. Outlining the main challenges of Danish feature film production in 2017, the Head of Film Funding at the Danish Film Institute, Claus Ladegaard, estimated that around fifteen Danish directors or writers were working abroad at any given point in time when they would otherwise have made Danish film and television (Ladegaard 2017). This may not seem like a huge number, but for a small-nation production culture with a limited feature film production and only a few high-end series produced every year it does make a difference, especially when a number of these writers and directors are what Ladegaard describes as "strong talent" (ibid.).

The discussions of how the state subsidies for film and television production should be spent question whether it is better to aim for larger production budgets to keep established talent working at home, or to develop new talent through low-budget initiatives. The debates in the press in 2017 about a challenged Danish cinema scene were ongoing, marked by directors leaving to make foreign films and television drama; a situation that, according to Ladegaard, was very hard to foresee just a few years ago (in Benner 2017).

As analyzed in this chapter, the interest in Danish television drama and Nordic Noir has meant that there are even more opportunities for Danish talent to be visible on the international stage. Television as well as film credits can now launch international careers, and directing episodes of TV series is not only about training new talent; being the director of a Danish series can now be an attractive calling card in its own right, and Danish television drama has created opportunities for many different kinds of talent, directors and screenwriters, as well as actors, cinematographers, and others. Charlotte Sieling built a successful international career based on *The Bridge*. However, as illustrated in the case study, an international career comes at a price when learning to navigate in a new production culture and trying to negotiate the balance between professional and private life in a boundaryless career.

Small-nation film cultures have always been challenged by their limited size and the lure of bigger budgets and audiences outside the national realm. With television now also in the mix, the talent exchange or export will most probably only grow. It is worthwhile for practitioners as well as scholars to investigate and discuss the nature of careers and creative collaborations in the global and digital film and television industries of today, and the consequences of this widespread traveling for small national film and television cultures.

ACKNOWLEDGMENTS

This chapter was written as part of the research project *What Makes Danish Television Drama Series Travel?* funded by the Danish Research Council (http://danishtvdrama.au.dk/). The author would like to thank the colleagues in the project for constructive ideas and input for this chapter, and Charlotte Sieling for her time and trust.

REFERENCES

Arcel, Nikolaj. 2007. "It's Hollywood, baby." Ekkofilm.dk, November 7. <http://www.ekkofilm.dk/artikler/its-hollywood-baby/>
Benner, Torben. 2017. "Dansk film fortsætter nedturen." *Politiken*, September 1.
Bo, Michael. 2017. "Den danske instruktør Nikolaj Arcel fik anmeldertæsk i USA: Nu har jeg nogle 'battle scars'." *Politiken*, August 5.
Boyle, Raymond. 2018. *The Talent Industry: Television, Cultural Intermediaries and New Digital Pathways*. Basingstoke: Palgrave Macmillan.
Csikszentmihalyi, Mihaly. 1988. "Society, Culture and Person: A System's View of Creativity." In *The Nature of Creativity*, ed. Robert J. Sternberg, Cambridge: Cambridge University Press. 325–39.
Eriksen, Jan. 2014. "Danske instruktører: Vores Hollywood-drøm blev et mareridt." BT, December 29. <http://www.bt.dk/film-og-tv/danske-instruktoerer-vores-hollywood-droem-blev-et-mareridt>
Hesmondhalgh, David and Sarah Baker. 2011. *Creative Labour: Media Work in Three Cultural Industries*. London: Routledge.
Hjort, Mette, Eva Jørholt, and Eva N. Redvall. 2010. *Danish Directors 2: Dialogues on the New Danish Fiction Cinema*. Bristol: Intellect Press.
Inkson, Kerr. 2008. "The Boundaryless Career." In *The Oxford Handbook of Personnel Psychology*, ed. Susan Cartwright and Cary L. Cooper. New York; Oxford: Oxford University Press.
Iskov, Brian. 2018. "Der er meget ego-fikseret angst i Hollywood." www.politiken.dk, April 8. <https://politiken.dk/kultur/filmogtv/art6417238/%C2%BBDer-er-meget-egofikseret-angst-i-Hollywood%C2%AB>
Jones, Candace. 1996. "Careers in Project Networks: The Case of the Film Industry." In *The Boundaryless Career: A New Employment Principle for a New Organizational Era*, ed. Michael B. Arthur and Denise M. Rousseau. New York; Oxford: Oxford University Press. 58–75.
Kragh-Jacobsen, Søren and Klaus Kjeldsen, eds. 2017. "Take off." Special issue of the journal *Take*, no. 72, July, published by The Danish Directors Guild.

Ladegaard, Claus. 2017. "Forsvar for spillefilmen." www.dfi.dk, June 14. <http://www.dfi.dk/Nyheder/FILMupdate/2017/juni/Claus-Ladegaards-tale-til-fiktionsdagen-2017.aspx>

Leung, Wing-Fai, Rosalind Gill, and Keith Randle. 2015. "Getting in, getting on, getting out? Women as career scramblers in the UK film and television industries." *The Sociological Review* 63(1): 50–65.

Lunde, Arne. 2015. "Going Hollywood: Nordic Directors in American Cinema." In *Nordic Genre Film: Small Nation Film Cultures in the Global Marketplace*, ed. Tommy Gustafsson and Pietari Kääpä. Edinburgh: Edinburgh University Press, 230–43.

Macdonald, Ian. 2013. *Screen Poetics and the Screen Idea*. Basingstoke: Palgrave Macmillan.

Mathieu, Chris, ed. 2012. *Careers in Creative Industries*. London: Routledge.

McCabe, Janet and Kim Akass, eds. 2007. *Quality TV: Contemporary American Television and Beyond*. London: I. B. Tauris.

Mittell, Jason. 2015. *Complex TV: The Poetics of Contemporary Television Storytelling*. New York: New York University Press.

Nelson, Robin. 2007. *State of Play: Contemporary "High-end" TV Drama*. Manchester and New York: Manchester University Press.

Pilegaard, Peter. 2016. "Bag om historiens største tennisduel." Ekkofilm.dk, October 4. <http://www.ekkofilm.dk/artikler/borg-vs-mcenroe/>

Redvall, Eva N. 2013a. *Writing and Producing Television Drama in Denmark: From The Kingdom to The Killing*. Basingstoke: Palgrave Macmillan.

Redvall, Eva N. 2013b. "Dogmas for television drama: the ideas of 'one vision,' 'double storytelling,' 'crossover' and 'producer's choice' in drama series from Danish public service broadcaster DR." *Journal of Popular Television* 1(2): 227–34.

Redvall, Eva N. 2015. "Craft, Creativity, Collaboration, and Connections: Educating Talent for Danish Television Drama Production." In *Production Studies, The Sequel!*, ed. Miranda Banks, Bridget Conor, and Vicki Mayer. Basingstoke: Palgrave Macmillan. 75–88.

Sieling, Charlotte. 2017. Interview by the author in Copenhagen, February 15.

Stoyanovo, Dimitrinka and Irina Grugulis. 2012. "Tournament Careers: Working in UK Television." In *Careers in Creative Industries*, ed. Chris Mathieu. London: Routledge. 88–106.

Zafirau, Stephen. 2007. "Reputation work in selling film and television: life in the Hollywood talent industry." *Qualitative Sociology* 31(2): 99–127.

All links last accessed May 16, 2017.

PART III
CONTACT ZONES

16. PARIS LOOKS TO THE NORTH: SWEDISH SILENT FILM AND THE EMERGENCE OF CINEPHILIA

Annie Fee

In 2016, the Cinémathèque Française marked the centennial of the Golden Age of Swedish Cinema at the *Toute la mémoire du monde* International Festival of Restored Film with a cycle of eight films from the archive of the Swedish Film Institute. French appreciation of Swedish art cinema is no coincidence, and recent homages to Victor Sjöström and Mauritz Stiller at the Cinémathèque Française illustrate an enduring relationship between the film cultures of Sweden and France.

The Cinémathèque is the public face of French cinephilia, an intellectual culture of film appreciation that emerged from the debris of World War I. Film critics, advocates, and filmmakers including Ricciotto Canudo, Louis Delluc, Émile Vuillermoz, Jean Epstein, and Léon Moussinac legitimized cinema as an art form recognized by the French state through new cinephile institutions, including the film press, ciné-clubs, and repertory theaters. In this chapter I investigate the curious synergy by which the emergence of cinephilia in early 1920s Paris resonated with the French release of landmark films of Swedish Golden Age cinema.

While scholars have noted the importance of Swedish cinema for early French film critics, they have yet to grasp the complex process through which individual cultural ambassadors and entrepreneurs working within a rapidly changing film industry and evolving exhibition network *construed* Swedish film as art cinema, simultaneously creating and shaping the uniquely French culture of cinephilia. In this chapter, I build on this work, as well as the scholarship of Bo Florin (1997) and Laura Horak (2016) on the French reception of Swedish

Golden Age cinema, to track the processes by which Swedish silent film gained the cultural legitimacy required to enter the cinephile canon, a process that began with the upheavals of the Great War and ended with the emergence of an alternative exhibition network in the late 1920s.

In doing so I illustrate how the city of Paris became a central elsewhere for Swedish cinema, a place where a handful of the world's first film critics embraced the films directed by Sjöström, Stiller, John W. Brunius, and Ivan Hedqvist in order to make their case for cinema's legitimacy as an art form worthy of recognition both by the state and by the Parisian cultural elite. In short, I argue that Swedish film production became an important catalyst for the emergence of cinephilia in France. In charting the rising esteem for Swedish film shown by Parisian critics, I mobilize a diverse range of historical materials, including fan magazines, advertisements, film programs, and newspapers to fill in a lost landscape of historical reception studies in film.

Art cinema is not a "natural" category; it had to be created. As David Andrews writes, art cinema is "an ongoing set of events impelled by an aspirational idea of cinema" (Andrews 2013, 22). In France, where the concept first emerged, it was cinephile critics who fought to reinforce the art cinema paradigm in the pages of their newly founded film magazines (*revues*) such as *Le Film*, *Ciné pour tous*, and *Cinéa*. They succeeded in launching a culture of intellectual cinema appreciation that we now call cinephilia, thanks in part to their early focus on Swedish film as exemplary art cinema. A striking example of their success in this process of legitimization can be read in critic Gilbert Bernard's review of Julien Duvivier's 1940 adaptation of *Körkarlen*, *La Charrette fantôme*:

> If there were a cinema department at the Sorbonne, the professor would tell students about *Sir Arne's Treasure* [*Herr Arnes pengar*, Stiller, 1919], *The Secret of the Monastery* [*Klostret i Sendomir*, Sjöström, 1920] and *The Phantom Carriage* [*Körkarlen*, Sjöström, 1921], works of the 1920s Swedish School which simultaneously revealed to us Nordic poetry in images, the art of superimpositions, dissolves, fades and soft-focus close ups. (*Le Matin*, March 5, 1940: 5)

This chapter examines how the films of the Golden Age of Swedish Cinema or the *école suédoise* became canonical for French cinephilia, simultaneously enabling its emergence and becoming incorporated into its core canon.

Cinephile Narratives: Critics Discover Sweden

Louis Delluc and other French critics connected to the young impressionist film movement Richard Abel calls "the narrative avant-garde" circulated their own version of film history in the first film magazines (Abel 1984, 279). The selection of films they collated, from Abel Gance's *J'accuse* (1919) and Marcel L'Herbier's *Rose-France* (1919) to L'Herbier's *Feu Mathias Pascal* (1925), was meant to restore France's reputation abroad. Behind the selection lay a very traditional mindset of a natural French superiority in the arts. They were to place France on the map as the country from which came Marcel Proust, Auguste Renoir, and now also Marcel L'Herbier and Abel Gance. If the French film industry could not contend with Hollywood in terms of quantity, it would stand out by the superior quality of its films and the discerning audience these films produced. French critics' success had an impact far beyond the cinema culture of their own day. By establishing magazines in which they authored film criticism and polemical texts about the state of French cinema appreciation, the cinephiles created a corpus of writing on which later cinema historiography was built, with Swedish films becoming a central part of this history.

In the summer of 1921, the editor of *Ciné pour tous*, Pierre Henry, asserted that there had been "three great dates in the history of cinema as it played out for French spectators." The first was at the beginning of the war in 1914 and 1915, with the release of Italian historical epics. Next came an influx of Hollywood productions between 1915 and 1917 from Thomas H. Ince and D. W. Griffith at the Triangle Film Corporation, along with William S. Hart westerns; and finally came the contemporaneous and "admirable series of vibrant Swedish visions," which included *A Man There Was* (*Terje Vigen*, 1917), *The Outlaw and His Wife* (*Berg-Ejvind och hans hustru*, Sjöström, 1918), *The Woman He Chose* (*Tösen från Stormyrtorpet*, Sjöström, 1917), *Sir Arne's Treasure*, *The Sons of Ingmar* (*Ingmarssönerna*, Sjöström, 1919), and *The Phantom Carriage* (*Ciné pour tous*, June 3, 1921: 4).

This historicization by early French film criticism has impacted the way we today understand these films to be landmarks of cinema history. Early critics mapped the webs of influence on their own thinking about art cinema while cinephile repertories of film classics were becoming commonplace thanks to their constant circulation in the film press. In his historical study of cinephilia, Christophe Gauthier describes how this "constitution of a system of references" led to the creation of a canon of film classics which would be screened in the first ciné-clubs and repertory cinemas (Gauthier 1999, 81–102). Within this canon, Swedish film was framed as a fixed genre or category; as Moussinac claimed, "in art cinema, the Swedes have created a genre unto themselves" (*Mercure de France*, September 1, 1922: 517). Swedish films released in Paris were marketed as exactly this genre of superior quality art cinema of exceptional interest to cinephile spectators.

Swedish Film during the Great War

During the war years (1914–18), French film production and exports came to a practical standstill while the industry mobilized for the war effort. In need of new highbrow films to feed their critical appetites, French film critics turned to Swedish releases. According to Delluc's personal cinephile narrative, the first film from Sweden to make an impact in Paris was *Wolo Czawienko* (*Balettprimadonnan*, Stiller, 1916). In a special issue of *Cinéa* on Swedish cinema, Delluc wrote, "Do you remember *Wolo*? It was the first Swedish film seen in France. It is by Mauritz Stiller. Jenny Hasselquist danced in the main role" (*Cinéa*, July 15, 1921: 6). The release of Swedish films coincided with the introduction of high-end cinemas in the wealthy neighborhoods of Paris. Stiller's film was one of the first to profit from the luxury surroundings of Ciné-Opéra when it screened there in March 1918. This 350-seat cinema, which opened in late 1917 on the Boulevard des Capucines, next door to the fashionable Café Américain, boasted a full orchestra led by Paul Fauchey. It was at Ciné-Opéra that Delluc "rediscovered Nordic cinema" with Sjöström's *The Kiss of Death* (*Dödskyssen*, 1916), released in France as *L'Étrange aventure de l'ingénieur Lebel* in April 1918 (*Le Film*, June 3, 1918: 14).

In part because of the turbulence of wartime Paris, then, many films from the film production company Svenska Bio appeared on Parisian screens. In addition to *Wolo Czawienko* and *The Kiss of Death*, Parisians also saw Sjöström's *Terje Vigen*, *Thérèse* (1916), *Ships That Meet* (*Skepp som mötas*, 1916), and *The Sea Vultures* (*Havsgamar*, 1916). Other Svenska Bio directors hailing from across Scandinavia saw their films released in the city, including Danish director Fritz Magnussen's dramatic features *At the Eleventh Hour* (*I elfte timmen*, 1916) and *His Father's Crime* (*Hans faders brott*, 1915), and Finnish director Konrad Tallroth's film *Professor Soriano's Serum* (*Sin egen slav*, 1917). One can imagine that the portrayals of Scandinavian rural idylls provided Parisians with a welcome escape from wartime trauma.

However, wartime conditions also presented obstacles to the distribution of Swedish film, and one major interruption to film production and exhibition—and a blow to Swedish film exports—came with a July 1917 decree banning film imports, including raw film stock (*Ciné-Journal*, August 25, 1917: 3–5). With film imports being stopped at the border, the critic Émile Vuillermoz, the writer Tristan Bernard, and respected industry figures Jules Demaria and Léon Gaumont successfully organized to overturn the decree in early September 1917 (*Hebdo-Film*, August 25, 1917: 6; September 1, 1917: 4). It was during this same period that Émile Paz, head of the film production company Films Paz, attempted to come to an agreement with Svenska Bio for distribution rights to its films in France. Negotiations soon fell through due to a rising climate of fear regarding the relationship of neutral countries to France's enemy, Germany, a context in which Swedish and Danish film appeared "extremely suspicious" (*Le Carnet de la Semaine*, August 12, 1917: 18). In the September 1917 edition of *Ciné-Journal*, Paz alluded to these suspicions without providing detail, claiming he simply ended the negotiations "due to recent events and the almost absolute impossibility of transactions with Scandinavian countries" (*Ciné-Journal*, September 15, 1917: 9). By "recent events" we can deduce that Paz was referring to the recent revelation by US Secretary of State Robert Lansing that the Swedish Foreign Ministry had illicitly transmitted encoded German diplomatic telegrams, thus undermining Swedish neutrality (Hobson 2012, 39). In her study "The Global Distribution of Swedish Film," Laura Horak shows the damage caused to Swedish films by their association with the Danish Nordisk Films Kompagni (2016, 464). Nordisk was blacklisted in October 1917 by the French Minister of Commerce Étienne Clémentel, accused of distributing German films in France and Switzerland (*Le Film*, October 22, 1917: 6; *La Cinématographie Française*, March 22, 1919: 23–5).

Under these difficult circumstances, Svenska Bio felt it necessary to have Swedish correspondents on the ground to represent Swedish cinema in Paris. One such figure was Folke Holmberg, who was assigned as exclusive agent of Svenska Bio, managing the company's film rental agency, which was strategically located close to the central boulevard entertainment district. Holmberg is an elusive figure who was nonetheless central to the burgeoning culture of cinephilia in Paris. His name is recurrent in the film press and on attendee lists of Ricciotto Canudo's early ciné-club meetings, the *Club des Amis du Septième Art* (CASA) (*Cinéa*, May 1, 1924: 28). He attended the very first ciné-club screenings "Vendredis du Septième Art," organized by and restricted to members of CASA in the spring of 1924, alongside avant-garde figures such as Germaine Dulac, Jean Epstein, and Ivan Mosjoukine.

It would appear that it was thanks to Holmberg that Svenska Bio was able to re-enter the French distribution market. Upon arriving in Paris, Holmberg quickly set to work on a charm offensive to win back French exhibitors for Svenska Bio. In a letter to the main Paris trade journal *Ciné-Journal*, Holmberg sought to remove any suspicion from Svenska Bio by casting aside rumors that it was a German company. Holmberg stated that Svenska Bio "works exclusively with Scandinavian capital and Scandinavian artists" and furthermore supports the allies by "screening English and French war films in all cinemas" (*Ciné-Journal*, October 13, 1917: 33). By all reports Holmberg was an extremely likeable figure and could always be seen at weekly press screenings shaking hands with Parisian exhibitors, directors, and journalists, leading Jean Tedesco to call him the "Swede from Paris" (*Comoedia*, September 21, 1923: 4; *Cinéma*, March 1932: n.p). His success was such that he remained the French representative for Svenska Bio, and from 1919 for its corporate successor Svensk Filmindustri (SF), for several decades (Olsson 2014, 265).

Holmberg's assimilation into the Parisian film industry was complete by the 1930s, when he was responsible for French film exports to Scandinavia.

Holmberg was not alone in ushering Swedish cinema into French cinephile circles. In 1919, Ture Dahlin, another Swedish film industry representative, arrived in Paris as a correspondent for the Swedish film magazine *Filmjournalen*. Just as Holmberg was a go-between for Svenska Bio and French distributors and exhibitors starting in 1917, Dahlin promoted Swedish film in the columns of *Cinéa*, the magazine founded and edited by Delluc (later by Jean Tedesco), alongside critics like Émile Vuillermoz, Léon Moussinac, Jean Epstein, Germaine Dulac, and Ricciotto Canudo. He also penned informative articles on Swedish cinema for the most widely circulated film magazine in France, *Cinémagazine*. Both figures, then, were at the center of the emergence of cinephilia in Paris. Like Holmberg, Dahlin was close to the emerging French avant-garde, a proximity revealed in his inclusion as an extra on Marcel L'Herbier and Jaque Catelain's film *La Galerie des monstres* (1924) (*Cinémagazine*, April 11, 1924: 77–8).

Dahlin's role cannot be overestimated, as it was his insider knowledge of the Swedish film industry that spurred public and critical interest in Swedish films, actors, and directors. The critic educated cinephile audiences about the history of the Swedish film industry with articles like "Le Film Suédois" (*Le Film*, November 1921: n.p.) and "Les studios cinégraphiques en Suède" (*Cinémagazine*, October 20, 1922: 87–90). He communicated insider information to the growing public of Paris cinephiles about which films were in production in Sweden and when French fans would be able to see favorite actors such as Jenny Hasselquist and Lars Hanson. He deftly catered to French national pride by emphasizing his country's respect for French art and literature. For example, he divulged to readers that Hanson—the most popular actor in Sweden—had become an actor after watching a stage performance of Jules Verne's novel *Around the World in Eighty Days*, and had discovered a passion for theater after watching French playwright Edmond Rostand's *Cyrano de Bergerac* (*Cinémagazine*, July 14, 1922: 41). In this way we can see Dahlin's role, like Holmberg's, as one of cultural diplomacy, flattering a sentiment of French national superiority in the arts as he aligns the two nations with a shared artistic and cultural heritage in a relationship unlike any other.

The Swedish Moment

After the war, French critics such as Delluc, Canudo, and Moussinac saw Sweden as a model for how French cinema could regain its prewar dominance, embracing a commercially successful art cinema with roots in noble theatrical and literary heritage. The branding of Swedish film as art cinema was aided by the phenomenal success of the Swedish Ballet (*Ballets Suédois*) at the Théâtre des Champs-Élysées in the autumn of 1920. The industrialist aristocrat Rolf de Maré created the Swedish Ballet in 1920 with Jean Börlin as principal dancer and choreographer, inspired by the success of the *Ballets Russes*. The Parisian elite was dazzled by the performances of Jenny Hasselquist, Carina Ari, and Clara Kjellblad, framed by sets designed by French artists Francis Picabia, Pierre Bonnard, Fernand Leger, and Blaise Cendrars, and compositions by Erik Satie, Darius Milhaud, and Arthur Honegger. The Swedish Ballet influenced how the first French film critics conceptualized film as an art form, leading Moussinac to conceive of Swedish cinema as part of a broader "magnificent evolution of Scandinavian art and of Swedish art in particular" (*Cinémagazine*, November 18, 1921: 8). Swedish cinema was aligned with other forms of Scandinavian high art, including the plays of Ibsen, the literature of Selma Lagerlöf and Bjørnstjerne Bjørnson, and the choreography of Jean Börlin.

The burgeoning film press also reinforced the crossover stardom of Swedish actors by reporting on both their dance and their film performances in their reviews. For example, in 1921, *Cinéa* announced that Clara Kjellblad, the actress who appeared in *The Windmill* (*Kvarnen*, Brunius, 1921), was in Paris for the Swedish Ballet ("Derrière l'écran," *Cinéa*, November 18, 1921: 10); and upon the Gaumont release of *Johan* (Stiller, 1921) the trade journal *La Cinématographie Française* wrote: "Miss. Jenny Hasselquist, so applauded in the Swedish Ballet, made the role of Mary an unforgettable creation" (*La Cinématographie Française*, August 20, 1921: 67). Jolanda Figoni, dancer in the Swedish Ballet, even graced the cover of *Cinéa* in July 1921, despite not having appeared in any films screened in Paris. This mobility of Swedish actors between stage and screen made Paris an exceptional "elsewhere" for the Golden Age of Swedish film. This cultural interchange developed further when French filmmakers sought to appropriate some of the cultural cachet of Swedish film by using Swedish actors in their own films. The year after Ivan Hedqvist appeared to French audiences in his hugely popular pastoral drama *In Quest of Happiness* (*Dunungen*, 1919), he starred in the French film *Rose de Nice* (Maurice Challiot, Alexandre Ryder, 1921) (*La Cinématographie Française*, August 20, 1921: 73). Advertisements for *Rose de Nice* sought to cash in on Hedqvist's Swedishness by including the line "the great Swedish actor Ivan Hedquist [sic]" (*La Cinématographie Française*, August 20, 1921: 62). An interesting go-between figure for Franco-Swedish film culture, he was praised in the press for his appreciation of French theater, called "a true friend of France" (*Le Gaulois*, April 27, 1920: 3), and even decorated with the title *Officier d'académie* in 1922 (*Cinéa*, July 21, 1922: 10).

With *Rose de Nice*, Challiot channeled a widespread feeling in the French film industry that directors needed to harness the full potential of French natural landscapes to convey a sense of nationhood. Critics saw Svenska Bio films as a continuation of a trend already apparent in Triangle films where natural landscapes played a central role. When Delluc saw *A Corner in Colleens* (Charles Miller, 1916) and *The Dividend* (Walter Edwards, Thomas H. Ince, 1916), he felt that the natural lighting and decor were reminiscent of the painters Alfred Sisley, Paul Cézanne, Auguste Renoir, and Claude Monet, creating a sense of *impressionisme cinégraphique* (*Le Film*, April 29, 1918: 30). The Swedes went even further, Delluc felt, with films like *The Outlaw and His Wife*, about which he wrote "the landscape is the star" (*Cinéa*, April 14, 1922: 12), avoiding the "elegant picture postcard" aesthetic of Italian cinema (Delluc 1920: 19). In their films, Swedish directors created semantic resonances between the characters and the natural environment (Tybjerg 2016, 274), providing a road map for French directors and for the emerging cinephile culture of spectators seeking out examples of film art to hold up to disbelievers who still considered cinema to be unworthy of intellectual attention.

Sjöström's literary adaptations, particularly of the Nobel Prize-winning Swedish author Selma Lagerlöf, were popular among the Parisian cultural elite, and aided Canudo, Delluc, and others in their ambitions for film to be recognized as an art form. They felt that French cinema could rise from the ashes of the Great War by drawing upon France's picturesque landscapes and rich cultural heritage, and bringing writers and playwrights to the cinema (*Le Film*, 7 January 1919: 22). By showcasing their assimilation of Hollywood advances in filmic language while staying true to a rich national artistic heritage, Swedish directors like Stiller and Sjöström demonstrated how literary material could be translated to the screen in what Delluc called a "truly cinematic" way, without relying upon numerous intertitles or theatrical staging. This became central to how French filmmakers conceived of the new direction cinema should take in the difficult postwar period (Abel 1988, 288).

In his discussion of Sjöström's film *Masterman* (*Mästerman*, 1920), Tom Gunning writes that Swedish film of the 1910s was a site of "convergence" of two styles of filmmaking: one dependent on editing, typically defined as American, and the single-shot tableau style, typically defined as European (Gunning 1999, 205–6). French critics praised the Swedes' ability to incorporate technical lessons learned from Hollywood while maintaining what they felt to be distinctly European good taste and delicacy. If French cinema followed their lead, critics thought, cinema would finally be recognized as an art form and receive the benediction of the Parisian elite of intellectuals, lawmakers, and educators.

In the tide of nationalist sentiment following the Great War, the idea of showing what critics construed as French national character on screen was intoxicating, and Swedish directors like Stiller and Sjöström made the task look achievable. While the French sought a model for "French film" that would not look like a copy of American film imports, Sweden showed them its model that used cinema to express its native landscapes, "Nordic" physiognomies, costumes, and national literature—without having recourse to literary or theatrical style. For Léon Moussinac, the joining together of the continuity editing style of filmmaking with tableau shots showcasing natural landscapes created a perfect balance of European "soul" with an American "discipline" and sense of "order" (*Mercure de France*, September 1, 1922: 514). He felt that Swedish directors took Scandinavian myth and legends and "transformed them through contact with their own souls" (*Mercure de France*, September 1, 1922: 514). Indeed, as Jan Olsson writes, "'soul' emerged as a key concept in the debate, setting a Swedish cinema of spiritual values apart from Hollywood's implied crass commercialism" (Olsson 2014, 245). American films might trump European films in their advanced editing, but for the Swedish critic Ture Dahlin, theirs was a "soulless technique" (*Le Film*, November 1921).

SWEDISH FILM SHARES THE BILL WITH THE FRENCH FIRST WAVE

Swedish films took on a particularly highbrow air when they were released in Paris as "Gaumont exclusivities" and were screened in the luxury Gaumont Palace cinema, the world's biggest cinema with a capacity of 5500 spectators (Meusy 2002, 288). The Gaumont Palace, as Jennifer Wild points out, "came to pompously stand out in the urban landscape as an authoritative symbol for a proud national film culture and its taste for quality" (Wild 2015, 171). Indeed, during the seasons 1919–20 and 1920–1, France's pride in its national film culture swelled at the Gaumont Palace with the release of key films of the narrative avant-garde, L'Herbier's *Man of the Sea* (*L'Homme du Large*, 1920), *Villa Destin* (1921), *El Dorado* (1921), and Abel Gance's *La Roue* (1920).

During the same seasons, the Gaumont Palace screened central films of Swedish Golden Age cinema: *In Quest of Happiness, God's Way* (*Karin Ingmarsdotter*, Sjöström, 1920), *A Norway Lass* (*Synnöve Solbakken*, John W. Brunius, 1919), Sjöström's *The Outlaw and His Wife, The Woman He Chose* (*Tösen från Stormyrtorpet*, 1917), and Stiller's *Song of the Scarlet Flower* (*Sången om den eldröda blomman*, 1919) and *Sir Arne's Treasure*. Refurbishments to the cinema in 1919 ensured that these films were screened in the upmost luxury with ornate orchestra lodges and a foyer decorated with works of French modern artists (*L'Écran*, September 27, 1919: 3). The musical acts brought further cultural status, with "the famous contralto" Alice de Swetska performing in the same program as *God's Way* in January 1921, and Gaumont's 60-piece orchestra accompanying several films (*Le Figaro*, January 7, 1921: 3). Advertisements for Svenska Bio films also became decidedly more highbrow as the decade progressed, with Gaumont advertising that Her Majesty the Queen Alexandra gave "a most flattering endorsement" of Stiller's film *Song of the Scarlet Flower* (1919) (*La Cinématographie Française*, March 6, 1920: 56).

The circulation of Svenska Bio films in this luxurious context fueled a vogue for Sweden that influenced the films of the narrative avant-garde. This influence is most striking in the case of Marcel L'Herbier. The male lead for many of L'Herbier's films, Jaque Catelain, had well-publicized "Swedish ancestry" and played Swedish characters in several of his films. In *El Dorado* (1921), he played a Swedish artist named Hedwick and reportedly spent much time researching to ensure the authenticity of his traditional costume (*Cinéa*, May 6, 1921: 23). In *L'Inhumaine* (1924), Catelain played a Swedish inventor Einar Norsen, in love with the singer Claire Lescot played by Georgette Leblanc. In the film, Lescot performs at the Théâtre des Champs-Élysées, where she appears on the same bill as the ballet *La Nuit de Saint-Jean*, performed by Jean Börlin and the rest of the Swedish Ballet troupe. First performed on the Swedish Ballet's opening night on October 25, 1920, at the same venue, this was one of the most "Swedish" of the troupe's performances in terms of theme—the national midsummer festivities with folk dancers in traditional costume—and in terms of collaboration, with painter Nils Dardel providing a folk-art backdrop and Swedish composer Hugo Alfvén the musical score (Garafola 1995, 68; 15).

We can see the "discovery" of Swedish cinema in Paris as a pivotal moment in French cinema history, in terms not only of the critical discourse on film, but also of the country's film production. Commentator Paul Ramain noted that Jaque Catelain and Marcel L'Herbier had both been "in complete awe" of *Love's Crucible* (*Vem dömer*, Sjöström, 1921), and that important parts of *Don Juan and Faust* (L'Herbier, 1922) were entirely indebted to Sjöström (*Cinémagazine*, March 12, 1926: 523). Marcel L'Herbier told the writer André Lang in 1923, at the height of his impressionist period, that Abel Gance is "A great director. But the Swedish film technique defeats his" (*Revue Hebdomadaire*, June 16, 1923: 334).

Franco-Swedish avant-garde collaborations would continue into the 1920s with the Swedish Ballet dancer Jean Börlin appearing in René Clair's films *L'Entr'acte* (1924) and *The Imaginary Voyage* (*Le voyage imaginaire*, 1926). This transnational connection reached an apex when in 1928 the Films Albatros production company entered co-production talks with Svensk Filmindustri, facilitated by the company's representative Folke Holmberg, leading to the Franco-Swedish co-production *Lèvres Closes* (*Förseglade läppar*, Gustaf Molander, 1927) (*Cinémagazine*, February 24, 1928: 342).

New Exhibition Practices: The Canonization of Swedish Film

The arrival of Swedish film in Paris coincided with the novel exhibition format of *exclusivités*. Rather than changing the program every Friday, several cinemas on the central boulevards of Paris began headlining one major film and kept it running for several weeks. The strategy of screening a film deemed to be of particular artistic or educational importance began during the Great War when the Théâtre du Vaudeville showed the Italian epics *Cabiria* (Giovanni Pastrone, 1914) and *Christus* (Giulio Antamoro, 1916). This practice continued after the war, with the luxury cinema Madeleine screening the adventure epic *L'Atlantide* (Jacques Feyder, 1921), and the Ciné-Opéra specializing in German Expressionist cinema, defying anti-German sentiment and screening *The Cabinet of Dr. Caligari* (*Das Cabinet des Dr. Caligari*, Robert Wiene, 1920). The Ciné-Opéra screened Sjöström's *Love's Crucible* as an *exclusivité* in December 1922.

Because Ciné-Opéra kept the film on the program for several weeks, the exhibitors decorated the cinema façade with lavish advertising. We know that this Sjöström film was one of the first to be advertised this way because, shortly after the film's run, Delluc remarked in the newspaper *Bonsoir* that "over the last few months, the grander boulevard cinemas have adopted the German-American advertising model of having huge images on their façade" ("Pellicules," *Bonsoir*, March 13, 1923, Fonds Louis Delluc 48 B4, CF). Passing Parisians would have seen a large sign over the entrance to the cinema and two signs on each side of the entrance reading "Le summum de l'art Suédois—*L'Épreuve du feu*."

By 1922, the designation "Swedish" marked a film as artistically superior and evoked expectations of serious art cinema. Lucien Doublon concurred that Swedish film was suited to an elite public when he wrote "So, it is only artists and the elite who look forward to soon seeing this film, which once more does honor to the great Swedish company Swenska [*sic*]" (June 23, 1922: 441) in *Cinémagazine*, after seeing *Love's Crucible*. Pierre Henry—who himself claimed to have seen *Sir Arne's Treasure* four times—argued that exhibitors should treat "beautiful" Swedish films with more respect by showing them as exclusivities (*Ciné pour tous*, July 15, 1921: 3).

However, the elevation of Swedish film to the level of film art in the eyes of intellectual critics did not automatically translate into wide distribution. Critics complained repeatedly in the film press about the difficulty of seeing certain Swedish productions in Paris cinemas. These films included Hedqvist's *In Quest of Happiness*, Stiller's *Chains* (*Fiskebyn*, 1920), and Sjöström's *The Sons of Ingmar*, which upon its release was screened at only one Parisian cinema—the Gaumont Théâtre (*Ciné pour tous*, February 11, 1921: 6). The nature of the exhibition landscape caused Delluc to conclude that "exhibitors don't like Swedish films" (*Cinéa*, July 21, 1922: 10).

The difficulty of watching art cinema in Paris led critics like Delluc to think about creating separate cinemas (*salles spécialisées*) for an elite, an idea that initially emerged in the wake of the cool reception of D. W. Griffith's 1919 film *Broken Blossoms*, released in Paris in 1920 (Fee 2018). The release of *The*

Figure 16.1 The Ciné-Opéra advertises Victor Sjöström's film *Love's Crucible* in *La Publicité: journal technique des annonceurs*, February 1923: 809. BnF.

Phantom Carriage at the Gaumont Palace the following year further prompted calls for the transformation of the Parisian exhibition landscape. *The Phantom Carriage* was hailed as "the most moving creation ever made by the great artist Victor Sjöström" (*Comœdia*, November 11, 1921: 4). The promotional campaign before the film's release was unlike any before, with the magazine *Ciné pour tous* creating suspense a year before the film's release with the announcement that *The Phantom Carriage* was set to "be a sensation" (*Ciné pour tous*, December 17, 1920: 13) and that it would have "a global impact" (*La Cinématographie Française*, January 8, 1921: 70). The Colisée cinema advertised the film as a *tragédie philosophique* (*Comœdia*, November 12, 1921: 3), and the Salle Marivaux described it as "an admirable Scandinavian film of a new and daring conception, a true artistic vision" (*Comœdia*, November 11, 1921: 4).

For Delluc, *The Phantom Carriage* represented the apex of Swedish cinema because it merged two tendencies: the superimpositions and dissolves used to evoke the supernatural in Stiller's *Sir Arne's Treasure*, an adaptation of a Lagerlöf novel, and Sjöström's human drama in *The Outlaw and His Wife* (*Cinéa*, October 14, 1921: 14). The cinematic rendering of Lagerlöf's novel brought technical innovation together with respected literature, and the highbrow framing of the film was reinforced when the respected publishing house Perrin released the French translation of *Körkarlen* in time for the film's release in cinemas (*Mercure de France*, November 1, 1921: n.p.). This intermedial synergy led Paul Ramain to call Sjöström's film "the highest pinnacle of cinema and the synthesis of Swedish Art" (*Cinéa-Ciné pour tous*, November 16, 1925: 288).

Cinephile critics saw *The Phantom Carriage* as a game changer, a film that would finally prove to Parisian audiences that film could be high art. After the press screening, Delluc announced: "Here is a film. And finally, certain people are beginning to see that cinema is an art" (*Cinéa*, October 14, 1921: 14). Yet Delluc was sorely disappointed when Sjöström's masterpiece was received with boos and whistles in many Parisian cinemas. Critics produced many reasons to explain the film's negative reception by Paris audiences, many placing the blame on the general public's lack of education and taste. Screenwriter André Legrand blamed the lowbrow cinema public, writing, "Nonsense films have distanced all elite minds, and even many average minds from our cinemas: their absence is proven by the fact that *The Phantom Carriage* and *El Dorado* were whistled down and nobody was offended" (*Comœdia*, December 30, 1921: 4). One reader of *Cinémagazine* echoed critics in his call for the creation of separate cinema venues for art cinema, writing, "As for the public, they will never understand *The Phantom Carriage* and *El Dorado*. It seems to me that we urgently need to set aside one or several cinemas for good films that would be reserved for true cinephiles. Because there are few cinemas that we can trust" (*Ciné pour tous*, December 30, 1921: 10).

The same week as the release of *The Phantom Carriage*, Ricciotto Canudo put his art cinema theory into practice and brought film into the art gallery for the first time. Indeed, a major turning point for Swedish cinema's institutionalization as art cinema was the screening of a selection of excerpts from films by Stiller and Sjöström at the annual art exhibition the Salon d'Automne in 1921, presided over by Frantz Jourdain. For Canudo, Swedish film provided the perfect example of film art for the Parisian elite attending the Salon. It was hoped that including films in a gallery space among the decorative arts, paintings, and architectural designs would, in the words of critic Pierre Landry, "contribute to putting silent art in its true place and no longer as a poor relation to the other arts" (*Le Petit Journal*, November 18, 1921: 4).

Canudo curated two screenings of film fragments at the exhibition venue the Grand Palais under the guise of the CASA ciné-club, including "A selection of fragments from French, Swedish, Italian and American films." The point of the presentation of filmic fragments, according to Canudo, was to open "a debate regarding the artistic essence of screen works, interspersed with examples chosen from the best films made up to this point." He told the crowd that "The Salon d'Automne will be famous for having proclaimed to the art world that cinema is an art form in its synthesis of science and art, and of all the arts" (Canudo 1995, 98). He felt that this was a solemn moment in which he was delivering a crucial "lesson" to Parisian intellectuals that "The Seventh Art is for artists" (Canudo 1995, 99). By removing Swedish film from the ordinary cinema circuit and placing it in the context of an art exhibition, Canudo presented a forceful argument for the cultural superiority of film. Frustrated with uncomprehending Parisian spectators and cinema exhibitors, he enforced a physical separation between popular and elite audiences, in the process reframing film as a form of expression whose artistry lay not in thrilling stories or sentimental drama but in the film medium itself.

Canudo must have been convincing, because a new and growing elite of artists, critics, and actors emerged from these annual screenings at the Salon d'Automne. They came together to watch film "classics" and listen to lectures by "the masters of the young cinema" such as Jean Epstein, Marcel L'Herbier, and Germaine Dulac at the "Vendredis du Septième Art" screenings organized by CASA in the spring of 1924, attended by the Svenska Bio representative Folke Holmberg. When Jean Tedesco converted the Théâtre du Vieux Colombier into the capital's first art cinema the same year, he included the *école scandinave* in his cinephile "repertory" of films to be screened there, with Gauthier calculating that Sjöström's films came second place in the repertory after those of Charlie Chaplin (Gauthier 1999, 282). Tedesco had been able to acquire a new and complete copy of *The Phantom Carriage* and held twelve screenings at the new art cinema venue, complete with an original score of modern Swedish music (*Cinéa-Ciné pour tous*, December 12, 1924: 488).

By the late 1920s, the idea that Swedish cinema was particularly suited to an intellectual elite seemed to be set in stone. In 1928, the height of the popularity of ciné-clubs in the French capital, Charles Léger of the Tribune libre du cinéma screened *The Outlaw and his Wife*, causing "passionate discussions from the audience" (*Le Petit Journal*, April 27, 1928: 4). One of the newly created repertory cinemas, priding itself as a *cinéma de l'élite*, was L'Oeil de Paris, where Swedish film was a regular feature in its program boasting "intelligent entertainment." At the new repertory cinemas, as at the Gaumont Palace earlier, Swedish film shared the bill with French avant-garde cinema. This tendency continued into the 1930s, when co-founders of the Cinémathèque Française Henri Langlois and Georges Franju showed *The Kiss of Death* in their ciné-club "le cercle du cinéma" in February 1936, and held a "festival" in honor of Victor Sjöström in January 1937, screening *The Outlaw and His Wife*, *The Secret of the Monastery* and *Walpurgis Night* (*Valborgsmässoafton*, Gustaf Edgren, 1935) (*L'Action Française*, February 20, 1936: 6; January 22, 1937: 6).

The opening of new repertory cinemas and the creation of the first ciné-clubs thus helped cement the reputation of Swedish film as suitable for a refined cinephile public. By the same token it provided French cinephiles with material with which they could argue that film should be treated like high art in terms of its cultural appreciation, financing and exhibition venues.

Conclusion

With the Gaumont Palace screening avant-garde works by Marcel L'Herbier and Abel Gance alongside Stiller and Sjöström, French directors assimilating Swedish film style, the first French ciné-club CASA incorporating Swedish film into a highbrow art event at the Salon d'Automne, and the repertory cinemas following suit, the 1920s became a decade of crystallization for Parisian cinephilia, in large part thanks to its assimilation of Swedish film.

Swedish films arrived in France at a time when the French industry was attempting to rebuild itself after the destruction of the Great War. Thanks to go-between figures Ture Dahlin and Folke Holmberg, Svenska Bio was able to navigate the obstacles of the turbulent wartime years. At the crucial moment when the French industry was debating the nature of "French film," the Swedes provided an example of a commercially successful and artistically accomplished national cinema, which was precisely the balance of art and commerce that the French had been seeking. Films directed by Victor Sjöström and Mauritz Stiller, among others, were immediately embraced as proof of cinema's artistic potential and its function as national propaganda. This made

Swedish film an attractive model for France as it sought to regain its stature as a great filmmaking nation with a long tradition in the fine arts, poetry, literature, and theater.

The task of normalizing Swedish cinema as art cinema was facilitated by the success of the Swedish Ballet and the already existing connections between Swedish art cinema and the avant-garde, as well as the screening of films in the luxury cinemas of Paris. Through screenings and lectures at repertory cinemas, Swedish Golden Age cinema found its place alongside Charlie Chaplin, D. W. Griffith, German Expressionism, and French avant-garde works in the canon at the heart of French cinephilia.

*Translations are my own unless otherwise noted.

References

Abel, Richard. 1984. *French Cinema: The First Wave, 1915–1929*. Princeton: Princeton University Press.

Abel, Richard, ed. 1988. *French Film Theory and Criticism*. Vol. 1. Princeton: Princeton University Press.

Andrews, David. 2013. *Theorizing Art Cinemas: Foreign, Cult, Avant-Garde, and Beyond*. Austin: University of Texas Press.

Canudo, Ricciotto. 1995. *L'Usine Aux Images*, ed. Jean-Paul Morel. Paris: Séguier; Arté Éditions.

Delluc, Louis. 1920. *Photogénie*. Paris: Maurice de Brunoff.

Fee, Annie. 2018. "Blossoms Breaking at the Dawn of Cinephilia: The Reception of D. W. Griffith in France." In *A Companion to D. W. Griffith*, ed. Charlie Keil. Hoboken: John Wiley. 510–32.

Florin, Bo. 1997. *Den nationella stilen: Studier i den svenska filmens guldålder*. Stockholm: Aura förlag.

Garafola, Lynn. 1995. "Rivals for the New: The Ballets Suédois and the Ballets Russes." In *Paris Modern: The Swedish Ballet, 1920–1925*, ed. Nancy Van Norman Baer. Fine Arts Museums of San Francisco. 66–85.

Gauthier, Christophe. 1999. *La passion du cinéma: cinéphiles, ciné-clubs et salles spécialisées à Paris de 1920 à 1929*. Paris: Association française de recherche sur l'histoire du cinéma; École des chartes.

Gunning, Tom. 1999. "'A Dangerous Pledge': Victor Sjöström's Unknown Masterpiece, *Mästerman*." In *Nordic Explorations: Film Before 1930*, ed. John Fullerton and Jan Olsson. London: John Libbey. 204–31.

Hobson, Rolf, Tom Kristiansen, Nils Arne Sørensen, and Gunnar Åselius. 2012. "Introduction." In *Scandinavia in the First World War*, ed. Claes Ahlund. Lund: Nordic Academic Press. 9–56.

Horak, Laura. 2016. "The Global Distribution of Swedish Silent Film." In *A Companion to Nordic Cinema*, ed. Mette Hjort and Ursula Lindqvist. Chichester: John Wiley. 457–83.

Meusy, Jean-Jacques. 2002. *Paris-Palaces ou Le temps des cinémas, 1894–1918*, 2nd edn. Paris: CNRS éditions.

Olsson, Jan. 2014. "National Soul/Cosmopolitan Skin: Swedish Cinema at a Crossroads." In *Silent Cinema and the Politics of Space*, ed. Jennifer M. Bean, Laura Horak, and Anupama Kapse. Bloomington: Indiana University Press. 245–69.

Tybjerg, Casper. 2016. "Searching for Art's Promised Land: Nordic Silent Cinema and the Swedish Example." In *A Companion to Nordic Cinema*, ed. Mette Hjort and Ursula Lindqvist. Chichester: John Wiley. 271–90.
Wild, Jennifer. 2015. *The Parisian Avant-Garde in the Age of Cinema, 1900–1923*. Oakland: University of California Press.

17. CELEBRATED, CONTESTED, CRITICIZED: ANITA EKBERG, A SWEDISH SEX GODDESS IN HOLLYWOOD

Ann-Kristin Wallengren

In September 1951, that year's Miss Sweden embarked on a SAS flight to New York to first visit the Miss America contest and then Hollywood, where Universal Studios, and later RKO and Paramount, contracted her. The young woman was Anita Ekberg, twenty years old, and newspapers and tabloids in Sweden invested much hope in her career in the USA and Hollywood, given that Greta Garbo had stopped making films and Ingrid Bergman had married Roberto Rossellini and moved to Italy. Other Swedish actresses who had tried to make their fortune in Hollywood included Signe Hasso and Viveca Lindfors, but no one had been able to take over from these former stars. Maybe Ekberg was the one, and several articles during her first year in Hollywood predicted a prosperous future, for instance calling her "Anita, a New Ingrid" (my translation, *Expressen*, August 31, 1951). The magazine *Life* published an article about Ekberg's appearance at the Miss America contest, and stated that she stole the attention from all the other girls ("Beautiful Maid from Malmo," *Life*, October 8, 1951). The article, however, mocks her deficient English and accentuates her short, blond hair, her blue eyes, and her figure as her most significant assets. Ekberg's body and figure will during the coming years be a focus in all coverage about her in the USA.

Ekberg arrived in a Hollywood imbued with a fascination with the hyperfeminine body and a vivid interest in films where a more or less explicit eroticism was portrayed, nourished not least by "the relaxation of cinema censorship in the face of competition from television" (Dyer 1979, 36).

ANITA EKBERG, A SWEDISH SEX GODDESS IN HOLLYWOOD

Figure 17.1 Anita Ekberg in Stockholm 1955: her first visit to Sweden since she left for the USA. (Photograph from ScanPix/Svenskt Pressfoto. Bilder i Syd.)

Marilyn Monroe had already become a star, personifying the blonde bombshell that since the 1930s had been a recurring type in the shifting figures of the American cinema (Kuhn and Radstone 1994). Other sex symbols were on their way to stardom, including Mamie van Doren and Jayne Mansfield. At the same time, a new kind of celebrity emerged in Hollywood, a celebrity that was not necessarily connected to significant accomplishments as a film actor but who was, in the words of Gaylyn Studlar, "dependent on the rise of mass media and urban life" (2015, 59). As for the 1950s, Studlar specifies that the film industry up until then had prevented scandals from circulating to the public, but all this changed radically when the magazine *Confidential*, considered pioneering in scandal and gossip journalism, started publication in 1952. With her voluptuous body and beautiful face, Ekberg fit perfectly into this new Hollywood era, which came to profit enormously from her assets. From 1953 onwards she appeared in films produced by Universal, Paramount, and John Wayne's company Batjac Productions, although with prominent parts only in about ten. For the most part, Ekberg was not greatly acclaimed in the reviews. Despite this, in a few years Anita Ekberg became one of the most written-about celebrities in Hollywood, and was on the covers of *Playboy*, *Life*, *Look*, and other magazines. Her celebrity arguably depended more on publicity than on prominent acting, though she appeared in films with many renowned actors. She became the first Swedish woman constructed as a sex goddess in Hollywood. Her decade-long career in the USA before she moved to Europe and Italy made her into a celebrity, which also influenced her roles and performances in later Italian films.

Ekberg was a woman in Hollywood coming from a Swedish elsewhere. This chapter explores how Hollywood used her origins to construct her "star image" as a Swedish sex symbol and a celebrity (Dyer 1979). She epitomized the concept of "Swedish sin" and contributed in substantial ways to how this idea was disseminated in American culture. She became a Nordic ambassador for an imaginary Sweden, but this ambassadorship was not particularly valued in Sweden itself. Ekberg had no considerable career in Sweden before she left for the USA, only minor modeling jobs. Her fame went global immediately. For Sweden on the other hand, Hollywood itself was an elsewhere, and the Swedish media opposed her star image created there. In this chapter, I will hence also discuss these cultural differences in the reception of Ekberg as celebrity.

Ekberg as Celebrity and Sex Goddess in the USA

Christine Geraghty examines the film star as a concept, and its relation to celebrity: "the term celebrity," she writes, "indicates someone whose fame rests overwhelmingly on what happens outside the sphere of their work and who is famous for having a lifestyle. The celebrity is thus constructed through gossip, press and television reports, magazine articles and public relations" (Geraghty 2000, 187). Hence, a celebrity can be famous for merely being a celebrity and the films in which the person appears can be insignificant: "This emphasis on the private sphere and the interaction with other forms of fame means that in the celebrity mode the films are relatively unimportant and a star can continue to command attention as a celebrity despite failures at the box office" (2000, 189). Relatedly, Studlar argues that scandal stories spread to the public with greater frequency at the beginning of the 1950s through the publication of the magazine *Confidential*. At the same time, a fundamental change in the road to stardom emerged. Instead of recruiting actors to film from the theater and other artistic arenas, beauty contests and modeling work created new kinds of film actresses. Ginette Vincendeau writes:

> A paradigm shift had occurred, in which the roots of stardom had been transplanted from the theatre to beauty contests, modeling, and photography. Crucially, female stardom was now intimately connected to the

erotic display and the mediatisation of private life, blond stars appearing as the epitome of the phenomenon ... This is in contrast to their acting talent, which was more often than not disparaged. (2016, 105)

Vincendau's statement connect to the way Ekberg became a celebrity. Her exterior characteristics such as blonde hair, attractive body, and sexual charisma were primary assets on the career path where beauty contests, modeling, and photography were decisive steps. Her behavior and her way of living constituted *gefundens fressen* for magazines and gossip columns which contributed to her otherness as coming from an exoticized elsewhere.

Above, I introduced the concept of "the star image" from Richard Dyer's book *Stars* (1979). Rooted in 1970s film theory, his definition remains useful. The star image is not "an exclusively visual sign but rather a complex configuration of visual, verbal and aural signs.... It is manifest not only in films but in all kinds of media text" (Dyer 1979, 38). The media texts that Dyer refers to are promotion, publicity, films, and criticism. The process for building up a star usually started with a "publicity buildup starting months or even years before the star is seen on the screen," and it was in the publicity material that Ekberg was most visible, at least during the first five years (Harris 1957, 46). Hence, the stars were and still are constructed through texts, or they "appear and circulate in public culture as mediated identities" (McDonald 2013, 14). Ekberg was deliberately created to become a Hollywood bombshell, and her star image was primarily constructed in magazines and gossip columns and through modeling in advertisements for cosmetics. Her film roles came later. She was assigned minor roles early on, and it was not until the mid-50s and her role as Helene Kuragina in *War and Peace* (*War and Peace*, USA/Italy 1956) that she had her breakthrough in film.

Nevertheless, it was not only the way to fame that had changed at the beginning of the 1950s; also, the female ideal had transformed. Body and sex were in focus in the cinematic discourse in the 1950s, as Marjorie Rosen outlines in her 1973 landmark book *Popcorn Venus: Women, Movies, and the American Dream*. Rosen argues that the cinematic discourse produced a popular culture that favored sex, breasts, and voluptuous female bodies. The general female ideal in the 1950s, according to Rosen, represented a backlash compared to the independent woman during the war; postwar women should marry, and, along with the men, return to their traditional gender roles. For women, this implied domesticity and housewifery. The societal pressure created a new, or returning, female ideal that focused on beauty and body: "mammary madness," as Rosen terms it (Rosen 1973, 267). "As box-office receipts plummeted during the decade, movies earnestly went about standardizing the desirable female. Enter the sex goddess" (1973, 269). Breasts were very much in focus, and bras got a new construction that lifted the breasts in a way not seen before. The sale of bras, girdles and "breast pads" rose enormously during the 1950s (Rosen 1973, 267). Other signs of this sexual fixation, Dyer argues, were the Kinsey report in 1953, the launching of the magazine *Playboy* in the same year, and perhaps the creation of the Barbie doll (Dyer 2004). Moreover, the films in this period oozed sexuality.

Ekberg was entirely appropriate for this type of female sex goddess ideal. She soon became a staple in the tabloids and magazines, supported by scandalous stories. She was photographed as a guest at parties, premières, and dinners, and was paired with a series of famous men in Hollywood—Frank Sinatra, Tyrone Power, Yul Brynner. Recurring rankings in the trade press of upcoming stars placed her high ("Stars of Tomorrow," *Motion Picture Herald*, September 15, 1956). She was often seen in advertisements for shampoo and other beauty products, and stories about her romances and shifting partners were common. Her outfits were commented upon, it usually being noted that dresses were tight around her body, perhaps too tight: "Anita Ekberg was bulging out of a low cut, figger-mauling [*sic*!] satin sheath two sizes too small for her obviously," as Sheila Graham in *Screenland Plus TV-land* expressed it (July 1956, 12). This kind of mild irony was often used when discussing Ekberg's scantily clad body. When writing about her role in *Paris Holiday* (Gerd Oswald, 1958, Switzerland/USA), one article emphasized it was a "rare opportunity—that of seeing Anita Ekberg fully clothed" ("National Pre-selling," *Motion Picture Daily*, August 23, 1957, 6). Few articles or news items avoid mention of her body or appearance. Readers often asked about her figure in advice columns, questions suitably chosen by the editors. The sexualized body was visualized on several film posters and pictures in magazines, with her pictured lying down, for example on the poster for the film *Zarak* (Terence Young, 1956, UK) (*Motion Picture Herald*, September 15, 1956). In the trailer for *War and Peace*, Ekberg is presented stretched out in bed with the voiceover stating that she is "perfectly cast as the sensuous Helene." In the film *Hollywood or Bust* (Frank Tashlin, 1956, USA) she plays herself, but her role epitomizes the most beautiful and sexy woman that Hollywood can present.

Within a few years, Ekberg had become one of the most renowned celebrities in Hollywood, "with a prominence quite out of proportion to her film career", as Vincendeau writes about Bardot (Vincendeau 2013, 18). *Modern Screen* reports from a charity ball in November 1955 that Anita is "probably our most popular girl" ("Louella Parsons in Hollywood," 15). In 1956 she was one of five winners of the Golden Globe, described as among the "most promising stars of tomorrow" ("Postkort från Carolyn," *Vestkusten*, March 1, 1956, 4). Merchandise was also produced that benefited from Ekberg's name: stockings in Sweden with the name "Anita;" in the USA a record called "Anita, My Love" with orchestral numbers reportedly inspired by Ekberg (*Bildjournalen*, no 10, 1956, 43; *Discogs*). Her hyper-feminine and

Figure 17.2 Anita Ekberg, "the Swedish beauty getting so much attention these days," in Louella Parson's gossip column. *Modern Screen*, August 1955, p. 10. (Source: Media History Digital Library.)

sexualized body stood in focus, which was one of the ingredients in her becoming a symbol for "Swedish sin." This also became one of the reasons for the devaluation of Ekberg in the Swedish press.

Ekberg herself had some influence over her celebrity construction. She appears to have mobilized the media in a conscious way, appearing to work according to her own judgment, and not that of others. Ekberg was known in Hollywood for behaving willfully, unconventionally, and obstinately. She was fired from the production of the television series *Sheena: Queen of the Jungle* (USA, 1955–6), reportedly the first person ever to be suspended from a television production ("1st Tele Suspension," *Variety*, September 8, 1954, 45). Earlier that year *Variety* reported that a couple of agencies also had dropped her because of her never showing up (Army Archerd, August 12, 1954). Her willful behavior suggests that Ekberg showed resistance to being objectified, and to some degree orchestrated what the press wrote about her. Jessica Jordan argues in *The Sex Goddess in American Film 1930–1965* (2009), in contrast to feminist film theories of the 1970s, that cinematic and media sex goddesses often manipulated coverage and publicity more than they were manipulated. Jordan also discusses how these actresses resisted objectification, or even objectified their audiences, and argues that they could have an empowering force in using their sexual attractiveness as a source of power. In the press, Ekberg often formulated herself as a person with progressive views on sexuality and relations, views that often were explained by her "Swedishness."

Accordingly, her Swedish origin came to be essential for her influence on the notion of Swedish sin.

THE NATIONAL BODY AND SWEDISH SIN

In 1956, the Swedish-American paper *Vestkusten* noticed that Ekberg, during her years in Hollywood, had been much publicized as "the Swedish blond bombshell" ("Anita Ekbergfilm på Golden Gateteatern,"*Vestkusten*, October 18, 1956, 1). In this coverage, her body was repeatedly related to her nationality. The Swedish evening tabloid *Aftonbladet* reports in 1958 that Ekberg has been a cover girl on *New York Daily News* and an article in the same paper described her as "an extravagant sample of a Swedish smorgasbord" ("Anita överdådigt prov," *Aftonbladet*, May 4, 13). Association of Ekberg with food, eating, and nationality also informs the title of an article about her in *Photoplay*, which is called "Swedish dish ... with Hollywood trimmings" (Mary Worthington, March 1956). In an article in *Modern Screen* from 1955, some stars are asked how they keep their bodies fit and slender. When it comes to Ekberg, her training, as well as her body, are essentially understood as depending on her exotified Swedish origin. The reader is reminded that Ekberg is a former Miss Sweden, and the article continues:

> She has a figure that moves even blasé actors and hardened studio crewmen to open admiration: "There must be something about that cold climate that produces sensational women," commented one cameraman the other day. "Actually," says Anita in her charming accent, "I don't do anything special to keep my figure. I swim. I cook Swedish foods and I walk." (Sally Simms, "How to keep glamor alive," *Modern Screen*, July 1955, 65–6)

Walking is regarded as eccentric in Hollywood; the writer has to explain that it is common in Sweden. Also, Ekberg's romantic life is coded as something decidedly strange and foreign. She is often interviewed about her views on relations with men. A December 1955 article in *Modern Screen* uses the headline "Ekberg Talks: Confessions of a Femme Fatale" to discuss what makes "the Scandinavian beauty ... such a temptress" (Alice Finletter, 27). The journalist concludes: "The obvious answer lies in Anita's obvious charms. She has more of everything than practically any other actress in Hollywood ... And her attitude toward men is enticingly inviting. Also Continental" (Finletter, 27). Another article in *Modern Screen* describes "Anita Ekberg's unusual ideas on love and marriage," calling her views on the same "at once shocking and stimulating" (September 1956, 64). The legendary Hollywood gossip writer Louella Parsons characterized Ekberg as "colorful, surprising, unusual" (*Modern Screen*, June, 1956, 24). In these articles and interviews, Ekberg is depicted as using men for her satisfaction in the same way as they use her. Ekberg appears provocative in breaking American gender codes of behavior in relation to men. Her otherness and "continentalness" were used as explanations for her transgressing the boundaries of what was allowed for American women. All this became important in terms of her effect on the idea of "Swedish sin."

The concept of Swedish sin and sexuality began to spread in the popular imagination in the USA in the 1950s, though the notion goes back to earlier in the twentieth century through sex education (see the chapter by Saniya Lee Ghanoui in this volume). The article "Sin in Sweden," written by Joe David Brown and published in *Time* in April 1955 (Brown 1955), is generally thought of as a key starting point (Hale 2003; Arnberg 2009; Arnberg and Marklund 2016). Two Swedish films are also regarded as influencing factors: *One Summer of Happiness* (*Hon dansade en sommar*, Arne Mattsson, 1951) and Ingmar Bergman's *Summer with Monika* (*Sommaren med Monika*, 1953). Both these films premiered in the USA in 1955, in March and September respectively, the same year as the *Time* article. Even more influential, perhaps, was the American version of Bergman's film, discussed in depth by Arne Lunde (Lunde 2016). American distributor Kroger Babb truncated and re-dubbed Bergman's *Summer with Monika* into a sexploitation flick, *Monika: The Story of a Bad Girl!*, giving it a new, sultry soundtrack, and marketed it as an erotic film (Lunde 2016). Ekberg's importance for the understanding and dissemination of the concept of Swedish sin has hitherto never been acknowledged, and considering that since the beginning of the 1950s she had been promoted as a Swedish sex goddess with unconventional relations to men, she must be regarded as crucial to the American fantasy of Swedish sexuality. The Swedish evening tabloid *Expressen* ordered a survey by the Associated Press in August 1955 (some months after the article in *Time*), in which people in the 48 states were asked what they thought of Sweden ("Vad tänker ni på," *Expressen*, August 6, 1955). Some mentioned the article in *Time*, but even more associated Sweden with Anita Ekberg, smorgasbord, and nude swimming, the latter probably inspired by the above-mentioned films. *Time* later published a story about Ekberg, reporting that her dress fell halfway off in the crowded foyer of a posh London hotel, revealing nothing underneath ("People," *Time* 1956). The same story was repeated in other magazines, with slight variations ("Anita Ekberg," *Vestkusten*, January 5, 1956). Swedish "immorality," as articulated by Brown in *Time*, was presumably, in the popular American imagination, to a considerable degree embodied by Ekberg and shaped by writings about her. The article in *Time* evoked a huge debate in Sweden, but so did Ekberg's celebrity and the way she used her body on her way to fame.

THE SWEDISH RECEPTION: EKBERG CRITICIZED AND CELEBRATED

The expectations regarding Ekberg's future career in Hollywood were, as mentioned, very high when she left Sweden in 1951. The Swedish press closely followed her life in the USA, and during the years 1951–3 articles and news were largely written in a positive vein. The papers reported about planned parts in films, publicity in American magazines, and how she prepared for upcoming roles with lessons in English and horse riding. Nevertheless, the papers soon revealed some impatience. In an article in 1954, the evening tabloid *Expressen* seems to be a little discontented when explaining that Ekberg has mostly been seen in gossip columns ("USA-cocktail: Anita Ekberg," July 20; see also "Filmögat" in *Filmjournalen* no. 49, 1953). However, the *Expressen* article conveys some hope in announcing that Ekberg was now awaiting a leading role with John Wayne, but later the same year the tabloid reports that Ekberg had been fired from the television production *Sheena: Queen of the Jungle* ("Anita fick sparken," September 4). The magazine *Bildjournalen*, in a short notice in 1955, expressed the hope that Ekberg would soon be seen in the cinemas in her most prominent part to date, in *Blood Alley* with John Wayne (William A. Wellman, 1955, USA; *Bildjournalen*, no. 30, 1955). Only some months later this turned into disappointment when the same magazine reported that she was hardly visible in the film (*Bildjournalen*, no. 41, 1955).

In 1954, the magazine *SE* launched an attack on Ekberg which is still remembered by many Swedes. The article was titled "Go home, Anita!" The Swedish journalist and screenwriter Rune Moberg did not hold back when reporting everything he thought Ekberg did wrong. She is, because of her reportedly bad behavior, a disgraceful representative for Sweden, he argues: she does not want to work and makes a fool of herself in a television show; she seems to love sensational dresses that show more than they hide; and she has no talent, no judgment, and no ambition. All this is of importance to all Swedes since, the author claims, it gives Swedes a bad reputation. He concludes the article: "Anita Ekberg still has got one chance. That is to become a girl in Malmö. A nice and decent Malmö girl. There are flights home every day, Anita Ekberg!" (my translation, Rune Moberg, *SE*, August 13–19, 1954, 12).

Critical attacks on Ekberg came swiftly from other papers, echoing almost the same views. She is not good PR for our kingdom, *Expressen* wrote in 1954 (Arne Thorén, October 24), noting that she was mostly seen in gossip columns and made her career by showing off her body. This kind of celebrity-formation seemed harder to digest for Swedish morality than for American. In the daily press, there was an abundance of notices about Ekberg from the years 1954 and onward that disparaged her in ironically formulated words. It was repeatedly accentuated in the media that she was vulgar, only cared about being seen in magazines and tabloids, and exploited her body in a sexual way. During the years 1955 and 1956, the reports on Ekberg peaked when she was assigned more significant roles. In 1955, Ekberg returned to Sweden and Stockholm for the first time since she had left for Hollywood four years earlier, for a short promotional visit hosted by Paramount. It was a triumphant return and she caused the biggest commotion in Stockholm in years (Bengt Olson, *Aftonbladet*, November 6, 1955). During the following years, when she visited her parents in Malmö in the south of Sweden, several police cars always guarded the house against fans and journalists. She caused an even bigger tumult in Stockholm when she visited for the Swedish première of *War and Peace* in 1958. *Dagens Nyheter* reported that around one thousand people crowded to get a glimpse of her, and they had to close some streets to cars ("Lugn Anita Ekberg," January 28, 1958). Perhaps the chaotic return in 1955 could, at least momentarily, be seen as a turning point and resurrection for Ekberg. There was no doubt that she was a notable celebrity in Sweden, perhaps one of the first in a new celebrity culture. After her return, there were also other voices in the media expressing a much more positive attitude toward her. These bifurcated views on Ekberg persisted during the years.

Ekberg never really forgave the Swedish press. Even after the positive reception in Stockholm in 1955, she was reportedly bitter and disappointed. Moberg's article may have poisoned her visit (*Aftonbladet*, November 16, 1955). She moved to Rome permanently in 1959 and returned to the USA only to make a couple of films; likewise, she returned to Sweden only now and then, to visit her family. After some years in Italy she gave an interview to *Tonawanda News*, stating: "I have returned to Sweden many times to visit my family and each time have been severely criticized and hounded by the press. I have taken the last abuse from them" ("Anita Ekberg to Become," October 15, 1964, 2).

The Contested Celebrities of Ekberg:
Reception in Sweden and America

Ekberg became known as a sex goddess and a film actress, and she was the perfect star in the American discourse of the 1950s. She was a celebrity in both Sweden and USA, but her celebrity status and its constituent parts were valued differently. For both nations, she was a star connected to an apprehension of elsewhere. Regarding the USA, she represented another culture that, among other things, implied foreign and "shocking" behavior; regarding Sweden, she made a career in another country with implications that were not really accepted in her homeland. The sexualized body was more prominent in American film and media culture than in Swedish. However, Ekberg was, in the American discourse, associated with Swedish nationality regarding her manners and unconventionality, which appeared to be gender-transgressive.

In the Swedish media, her success elsewhere was not regarded as something to be proud of, even if the attitude toward her was ambivalent. The pinup ideal was also widespread in Sweden, at least in magazines directed toward a younger generation where articles sometimes discussed the "leg and breast hype" (Olle Hellbom, *Filmjournalen*, no. 7, 1953, 17), and film posters could be as sexually exploitative as the American ones. There were also competitions for sexiest pinup girl ("Hon blev tusenskona," *Filmjournalen*, no. 16, 1953). However, the general ideal for female beauty in Sweden, harking back to the 1920s, was considerably more moderate and restrained than the ideal in Hollywood (Andersson 2006). Naturalness, in the meaning of simple hairstyle, no makeup and plain clothes, had long been guiding principles in the discourse of female gender in Sweden, together with disciplined behavior. This discourse is traceable in, for example, *Bildjournalen*, which was a popular magazine aimed at young female readers. Ekberg did not conform to these ideals. She was compared to other Swedish actresses in Hollywood, especially May-Britt Wilkens and Inger Stevens, who were said to make brilliant publicity for Sweden, unlike Ekberg ("Livet är underbart," *Bildjournalen*, no. 13–14, 1958). Wilkens especially was often portrayed in *Bildjournalen* with her naturalness always highlighted, and she explicitly stated that she did not want to be a "sex broad" (Kåge Sandell, *Bildjournalen*, no. 24, 1958, 6). In adopting a more glamorous outlook, Ekberg was regarded as more Americanized than her Swedish colleagues. All in all, the assets that made Ekberg a celebrity in Hollywood were not invested with the same significance and were not valued to the same degree in Sweden, if at all. Her influence on what was considered a negative American apprehension of Sweden made her an object for scorn and depreciation.

The celebrity culture per se was also something foreign to the Swedish media and public. The phenomenon was not at all unknown in Sweden, even if its *breakthrough* was later there, as in the rest of Europe (Vincendeau 2013). The politics of celebrity formation seemed, on the basis of the publicity, to be much more accepted in the USA than in Sweden, and even valued as good entrepreneurship. In the Swedish media discourse this was not regarded as *honest good work*; instead, writings about Ekberg formulated it as something shallow and unworthy.

Ekberg's class background may be of significance, too. Moberg's advice was that she should return to being an ordinary Malmö girl. According to Vincendeau (2013), Brigitte Bardot's high cultural milieu, her education and training as a ballet dancer, and her parents' network of contacts were vital for her path to stardom. Ekberg, meanwhile, came from a working-class family in the industrial town of Malmö, and it is possible that this background influenced how the media treated her. She came with no education, no training, and no cultural capital, which further nourished the Swedish press's view of her as uncultivated and, in their view, vulgar. The Swedish press prospered from her success, however, and she was often discussed in terms of being an export article. But even if exploiting Ekberg as a commodity themselves, the Swedish press did not consider her a "good old export article," but more a Hollywood product and a sex symbol produced elsewhere, and as such not a worthy ambassador for Sweden (Gunnar Nilsson, *Expressen*, October 25, 1955).

Gradually Ekberg herself became more negative toward being regarded as a sex object. She is said to have expressed the view that she was tired of sex and she criticized how sexuality was always connected to the body, not to love ("Morgondagens stjärna," *Bildjournalen*, no. 51–2, 1957); she also complained of the angles used by photographers, always accentuating her breasts or some other part of the body they wanted to show off ("Anita E. 'sårad'," *Expressen*, July 21, 1957).

After she moved to Italy things changed, even if she still was a sex symbol. Through her role in *La Dolce Vita* (Federico Fellini, Italy, 1960) and subsequent films, her casting and her performance differed from her American roles and she very soon became one of the most famous people in Rome and one of the most loved stars in Italy, and she was very productive in making films. The writings about her in the Swedish press continued with the same intensity. Her importance as the first Swedish sex goddess was significant, and how this was embraced and valued in Italian film and media culture will be the subject for further study.

References

Andersson, Therése. 2006. *Beauty Box: filmstjärnor och skönhetskultur i det tidiga 1900-talets Sverige*. Stockholm: Acta Universitatis Stockholmiensis.
Arnberg, Klara. 2009. "Synd på export. 1960-talets pornografiska press och den svenska synden." *Historisk Tidskrift* 129(3): 467–486.
Arnberg, Klara and Carl Marklund. 2016. "Illegally Blonde: Swedish Sin and Pornography in US and Swedish Imaginations, 1955–1971." In *Swedish Cinema and the Sexual Revolution. Critical Essays*, ed. Elisabet Björklund and Mariah Larsson. Jefferson, NC: McFarland. 185–201.
Brown, Joe David. 1955. "Sin and Sweden." *Time Magazine* 65(17).
Discogs. Roberto and his Orchestra. Anita My Love. <https://www.discogs.com/Roberto-And-His-Orchestra-Anita-My-Love/release/7905380> (last accessed July 4, 2018).
Dyer, Richard. 1979. *Stars*. London: BFI.
Dyer, Richard. 2004. *Heavenly Bodies: Film Stars and Society*, 2nd edn. London: Routledge.
Geraghty, Christine. 2000. "Re-Examining Stardom: Questions of Texts, Bodies and Performance." In *Reinventing Film Studies*, ed. Christine Gledhill and Linda Williams. London: Hodder Arnold. 183–201.
Hale, Frederick. 2003. "Time for sex in Sweden: enhancing the myth of the 'Swedish sin' in the 1950s." *Scandinavian Studies* 75(3): 351–74.

Harris, Thomas B. 1957. "The building of popular images: Grace Kelly and Marilyn Monroe." *Studies in Popular Communication* 1: 45–48.
Jordan, Jessica Hope. 2009. *The Sex Goddess in American Film 1930–1965: Jean Harlow, Mae West, Lana Turner, and Jayne Mansfield*. Amherst: Cambria Press.
Kuhn, Annette and Susannah Radstone, eds. 1994. *The Women's Companion to International Film*. Berkeley: University of California Press.
Lunde, Arne. 2016. "The Story of a Bad Girl! *Summer with Monika*, Sexploitation and the Selling of Erotic Bergman in America." In *Swedish Cinema and the Sexual Revolution. Critical Essays*, ed. Elisabet Björklund and Mariah Larsson, Jefferson, NC: McFarland. 11–21.
McDonald, Paul. 2013. *Hollywood Stardom*. Oxford: Wiley-Blackwell.
"People." 1956. *Time Magazine* 67(3).
Rosen, Marjorie. 1973. *Popcorn Venus: Women, Movies & the American Dream*. New York: Coward.
Studlar, Gaylyn. 2015. "The Changing Face of Celebrity and the Emergence of Motion Picture Stardom." In *A Companion to Celebrity*, ed. P. David Marshall and Sean Redmond. Chichester: John Wiley. 58–79.
Vincendeau, Ginette. 2013. *Brigitte Bardot*. Basingstoke: BFI/Palgrave Macmillan.
Vincendeau, Ginette. 2016. "And Bardot . . . became a blonde: hair, stardom and modernity in post-war France." *Celebrity Studies* 7(1): 98–112.

18. THE FINNISH CINEMA COLONY IN NORTH AMERICA, 1938–1941

Anneli Lehtisalo

Finnish cinema is not well known to international audiences. Only recently have a few productions from the small nation's film industry attracted international attention, mainly thanks to international film festivals and the success of a few auteurs. Therefore, it might surprise some to learn that the exporting of films has been part of the Finnish film business since at least the 1920s, following the establishment of the first major film company, Suomi-Filmi, in 1919. Between the mid-1930s and the early 1960s, Finnish films were produced using a studio-based system that was dominated by Suomi-Filmi and its competitor Suomen Filmiteollisuus (1933–65). These two companies, along with some other minor film producers, actively tried to expand their markets and were continuously exporting their productions (Lehtisalo 2016). More than two hundred Finnish films were distributed internationally during the studio period, mostly to the neighboring Nordic countries, to Central Europe during the exceptional circumstances of World War II, and to North America.

Considering the exclusivity of North American film markets, it might be perplexing that most exported films were distributed in the USA and Canada. Finnish films were not targeted at general audiences, however, but at the niche markets created by Finnish immigrants (Lehtisalo 2016, 120, 128–9). Nearly 400 000 Finns had migrated to North America between the 1870s and the early 1920s (Kero 2014, 41). At the beginning of the 1920s, the USA set new quotas limiting immigration to the country, which substantially decreased the number of incoming Finns (Kostiainen 2014, 14). However, during the first half of the twentieth century there were thriving Finnish communities, especially in Michigan, Minnesota, Massachusetts, and New York in the USA, and in Ontario in Canada (Nygård 1997, 9; Alanen 2014, 64).

Finnish films were imported and circulated within the immigrant communities during the entire studio period, but for a while these niche markets constituted a kind of extension of Finnish cinema: Finnish-born audiences were watching the same films as their cousins back home in Finland at almost the same time. This "Finnish cinema colony" existed for only a short period, from approximately 1938 to 1941. After that, World War II and the gradual decline of Finnish-speaking audiences changed the circumstances and the nature of film exhibitions.

This so-called colony was made possible by increasing studio production in Finland, on the one hand, and, on the other hand, by a growing interest in Finnish films from Finnish-American businessmen. These businessmen were already importing other Finnish cultural products, such as books and magazines, or they were actively operating in the Finnish-American cultural sphere, for example by publishing Finnish-American newspapers or working with Finnish-American theater groups (Nygård 1997, 27–9, 56, 59, 61). They may have had cultural interests, but it was mainly the import and distribution of Finnish films that promised them new, lucrative business opportunities (Nygård 1997, 102). Some had already imported a few Finnish films in the 1920s, but now there were more Finnish films to be circulated, and importantly, these Finnish-language sound films would give them a competitive edge within the Finnish-speaking immigrant communities. Consequently, the import and distribution of Finnish films started up on the Finnish Americans' initiative (Nygård 1997, 49, 50, 55). Finnish film companies did not have the resources to market their films themselves in North America (Lehtisalo 2016, 130), so they seized on the opportunity offered by these businessmen.

Finnish films were shown in different locales, such as the meeting halls of immigrant organizations, roadshows, and movie theaters (Nygård 1997, 75, 80–81). The film distributors preferred theaters, as they obviously guaranteed a more satisfying experience for the audience, and there was always also the possibility that the films would attract non-Finnish audiences. However, it was difficult to gain ground for the Finnish cinema colony. The owners of local movie theaters had to be convinced that it would be worth their while to screen a Finnish film.

During the spring of 1938, Carl H. Salminen, a Finnish-American businessman, editor, and owner of Finnish-American broadsheet newspaper *Päivälehti*, started to import films produced by Suomen Filmiteollisuus. Operating out of Duluth, Minnesota, he distributed the films particularly in Michigan and Minnesota (Wasastjerna 1957, 354–5, 376; Nygård 1997, 63). With the help of his newspaper, he aggressively promoted the films to his readers (e.g. "Joel

Rinne ja Laila Rihte" 1938; "Kuin Uni ja Varjo" 1938a; "Ester Toivonen" 1938; "Ansa Ikonen ja Jorma Nortimo" 1938). But promotional pictures and advertisements were not enough; in the premiere advertisement of *As Dream and Shadow* (*Kuin uni ja varjo*, 1937), Salminen directly appealed to the Finnish-American audience to ask local theater managers to show the film ("Kuin Uni ja Varjo" 1938b). In the fall, he renewed his appeal in a *Päivälehti* article: "Talk about this [screening a film] among yourselves and present your request to your local theatre . . . To everyone who one way or the other assists access of the film to a theatre, I will send something interesting to read in the evenings" (Salminen 1938b).*

Eventually, Salminen and other distributors managed to gain ground for their films in local theaters. Finnish films circulated actively within the Finnish communities noted above: Minnesota, Michigan, Massachusetts, New York City, and Ontario (Nygård 1997, 72, 73, 78). According to the film advertisements in the Finnish-American newspapers *Päivälehti, Raivaaja, Minnesotan Uutiset*, and *New Yorkin Uutiset*, there were at least thirteen film premieres during the cinema season of 1938–9, twelve during the 1939–40 season, and seven during the 1940–1 season. These were relatively high figures considering that the number of feature films produced in Finland annually fluctuated between thirteen and twenty-two. Some of the imported films were older, having been produced a couple of years earlier, but the time lag was generally quite short. During the 1939–40 cinema season, Finnish immigrants could see the films that had premiered in Finland in 1939. Thus, bearing in mind that films also circulated for a long time in Finland, Finnish immigrants could watch Finnish films at practically the same time as people in the old homeland.

Even the domestic competition between the major Finnish film production companies seemed to transfer to the Finnish cinema colony. Within the small film markets in Finland, Suomi-Filmi competed aggressively with Suomen Filmiteollisuus for audiences, popular film topics, and film professionals. On the other side of the Atlantic, Carl H. Salminen acted as a representative of Suomen Filmiteollisuus. He used the company's logo in film advertisements in *Päivälehti* and reminded the audience in a *Päivälehti* article that "Suomen Filmiteollisuus has nothing to do with Suomi-Filmi" (Salminen 1938a). Suomi-Filmi was represented in North America by other Finnish-Americans, George Koehsen and Werner Savela (Nygård 1997, 56–7, 59). In principle, these distributors competed with each other, but in practice the main actors also cooperated and made deals about ticket prices and exchanging films (Nygård 1997, 63–4). Moreover, Finnish-American audiences were probably more interested in the actual films than in the film producers.

The film repertoire of the Finnish cinema colony closely resembled the offerings in Finnish film theaters. These films were not typical exportable productions, nor were they nostalgic cinematic depictions that immigrant audiences used to prefer (Wallengren 2013, 147–8). It has been suggested that exportable films typically represented either Americanized popular culture or high culture rather than national or provincial culture (Higson and Maltby 1999, 20). National features, in particular provincial humor, have often proved too difficult to understand in a different cultural context. However, as Jean-Pierre Jeancolas (1995, 141–2) has noted, immigrant communities enjoyed even those parochial films that otherwise would be considered unexportable.

The specificity of immigrant audiences is highlighted in Ann-Kristin Wallengren's (2013) study on Swedish-American film culture. Swedish-American audiences preferred prestigious Swedish literary adaptions in the 1920s and popular Swedish comedies in the 1930s and 1940s (Wallengren 2013, 119, 127, 135). However, Wallengren (2013, 121–2, 130, 136, 144) stresses how all kinds of Swedish films were consistently interpreted from nostalgic and nationalist points of view, even when their reading in Sweden was totally different.

In comparison to Swedish Americans, Finnish immigrants seemed to be rather omnivorous during the late 1930s and the early 1940s. Finnish immigrants saw a wide variety of Finnish films ranging from contemporary farces to national historical dramas, from folk plays to high culture film adaptions of the works of Aleksis Kivi (1834–72), the national author of Finland. For instance, *As Dream and Shadow*, a rural melodrama set in a religious community, was followed by *The Old Bachelor's Love Troubles* (*Asessorin naishuolet*, 1937), a farce starring Finland's most popular comedian, Aku Korhonen (1892–1960). During the 1939–40 season, immigrant audiences could see more Korhonen comedies, as well as the pompous historical drama *The February Manifest* (*Helmikuun manifesti*, 1939) and an adaption of Kivi's renowned novel *Seven Brothers* (*Seitsemän veljestä*, 1939). In the 1940–1 season, the audience could enjoy the romantic comedies *The Man from Sysmä* (*Sysmäläinen*, 1938) and *Red Pants* (*Punahousut*, 1939). The repertoire even included melodramas addressing social issues, such as *And Below Was a Lake of Fire* (*Ja alla oli tulinen järvi*, 1937) and *Are They Guilty?* (*Syyllisiäkö?*, 1938), which were not typical of the usual productions by Suomi-Filmi and Suomen Filmiteollisuus.

The differences between Swedish-American and Finnish-American film culture can be explained by the robust state of Swedish cinema and the larger Swedish immigrant community. The Swedish film industry had established itself earlier than the Finnish one, and it was already stable in the 1920s. Accordingly, the import of Swedish films into North America had begun at the beginning of the 1920s (Wallengren 2013, 104). Thus, in the late 1930s, Swedish-American film culture had already matured, with the active import of films and public visibility in Swedish-American newspapers, whereas Finnish-American film culture was just taking shape. The Finnish cinema colony could be described as a test period when Finnish-American businessmen imported all kinds of films to see how audiences would respond. As for the Finnish immigrants, they might have been curious at first to see and hear all the Finnish-language films. Unfortunately, there were no regular film reviews in Finnish-American newspapers, nor comprehensive studies on Finnish-American film culture, so it is difficult to conclude which films Finnish immigrants preferred or how the films were interpreted. However, there are indications that the overall reception of Finnish films was not uniform. Among positive mentions in the newspapers there were also critical voices. For example, *Industrialisti*, a left-wing Finnish-American newspaper, criticized popular films of capitalist Finland for being unsuitable for working class audiences (Nygård 1997, 87–9, 92).

Despite the different views, for many Finnish immigrants Finnish-language films were significant as the films gave them an opportunity to hear their native language and to work through their relationship to the old homeland (on the importance of the language, see the film advertisements in *Päivälehti*). Finnish cinema was part of an active immigrant culture that flourished between the World Wars. There were numerous activities, including religious, temperance and political societies, sports clubs, choral groups, musical bands, and amateur dramatic societies. All these activities offered important means for Finnish immigrants to sustain and negotiate their national identities (see Virtanen 2014, 173, 187). In particular, Finnish-speaking entertainment, such as amateur theater and musical activities, fostered a sense of belonging. This was not only because participants could use their native language in their free time, but because amateur theaters and musical groups had close connections to the homeland and most of the plays and some of the music originated in Finland (Virtanen 2014, 180–1, 188, 190).

The importance of Finnish cinema started to increase just as amateur theater and musical activities passed their peak years of the 1920s and early 1930s (Virtanen 2014, 180, 190). Obviously, there were demographic reasons for the decline of such activities. For example, immigrants with families and the older members of the community might not have had the time or energy to take part in rehearsals and performances. Finnish sound films, instead, offered almost the same pleasures as Finnish-speaking entertainment and popular plays, but in a more convenient format. Thus, mediated ethnic culture started to replace cultural activities that were typical of Finnish social life at the beginning of the twentieth century. This change anticipated the diasporic cultural patterns of the latter part of the century when connections to the old homeland and a sense of belonging were sustained via satellite television, videos, and DVDs (cf. Iordanova 2010, 32–4).

World War II changed the circumstances for Finnish cinema in North America. It was no longer an extension of the cinema of the homeland; rather, Finnish immigrants formed a special audience. Although production actively continued in Finland during the war, the war impeded the distribution of films to North America, and the number of screenings decreased notably. The imports recommenced after the war, but the imported films represented only a fraction of the total film production of Finland. According to newspaper advertisements, only one to four Finnish films per cinema season were offered to immigrant audiences in the 1950s.

Finnish-American film culture dwindled. Activities turned more inwards, as films were typically screened on special occasions in Finnish-American immigrants' meeting places, not in local theaters. Distributors had increasing difficulties in finding screen time in local film theaters because Finnish-speaking audiences were gradually shrinking (Ramo 1954). Although some films had English subtitles (Nygård 1997, 64), it is probable that the younger generations were not interested in Finnish films made with poorer resources than American films.

The Finnish cinema colony evoked hopes for Finnish film producers and Finnish-American distributors to broaden film markets and create new business models. However, cinema was a vulnerable mode of business. Its existence was impeded by geopolitical circumstances, limited resources, and demographic changes. The Finnish-American immigrant community and the Finnish film industry did not have the economic power to sustain a flourishing immigrant film culture. Nevertheless, the significance of the Finnish cinema for immigrants should not be underestimated; this is indicated by the burst of interest in Finnish sound films in 1938–41 as well as the persistence of film imports during the 1950s. Finnish-American film culture is a much understudied area, and we know almost nothing about the expectations, cinematic experiences, or interpretations of Finnish immigrant audiences, nor how these aspects might have changed over time. Further studies could offer broader perspectives on the specificities of current mediated diasporic culture.

*Translations of Finnish quotations by the author.

References

Alanen, Arnold R. 2014. "Finnish Settlements in the United States." In *Finns in the United States*, ed. Auvo Kostiainen. East Lansing, MI: Michigan State University Press. 55–73.

"Ansa Ikonen ja Jorma Nortimo." 1938. *Päivälehti*, March 21.

"Ester Toivonen." 1938. *Päivälehti*, March 13.

Higson, Andrew and Richard Maltby. 1999. "'Film Europe' and 'Film America': An Introduction." In *"Film Europe" and "Film America". Cinema, Commerce and Cultural Exchange 1920–1939*, ed. Andrew Higson and Richard Maltby. Exeter: University of Exeter Press. 1–31.

Iordanova, Dina. 2010. "Rise of the Fringe. Global Cinema's Long Tail." In *Cinema at the Periphery*, ed. Dina Iordanova, David Martin-Jones, and Belén Vidal. Detroit: Wayne State University Press. 23–45.

Jeancolas, Jean-Pierre. 1995. "The Inexportable. The Case of French Cinema and Radio in the 1950s." In *Popular European Cinema*, ed. Richard Dyer and Ginette Vincendeau, trans. Peter Graham. London: Routledge. 141–8.

"Joel Rinne ja Laila Rihte." 1938. *Päivälehti*, March 17.

Kero, Reijo. 2014. "Migration from Finland to North America." In *Finns in the United States*, ed. Auvo Kostiainen. East Lansing, MI: Michigan State University Press. 41–53.

Kostiainen, Auvo. 2014. "Interest in the History of Finnish Americans." In *Finns in the United States*, ed. Auvo Kostiainen. East Lansing, MI: Michigan State University Press. 13–25.

"Kuin Uni ja Varjo." 1938a. Advertisement. *Päivälehti*, March 17.

"Kuin Uni ja Varjo." 1938b. Advertisement. *Päivälehti*, April 13.

Lehtisalo, Anneli. 2016. "Exporting Finnish Films." In *Finnish Cinema: A Transnational Enterprise*, ed. Henry Bacon. London: Palgrave Macmillan. 115–38.

Nygård, Mari. 1997. *Sähkökuvia siirtolaisille. Elokuva kulttuurisen harrastetoiminnan muotona 1920- ja 1930-luvuilla*. Masters thesis in history, University of Turku.

Ramo, H. 1954. "Suomalaiset elokuvat." *New Yorkin Uutiset*, December 10.

Salminen, Carl. 1938a. "Pohjalaisia." *Päivälehti*, October, 17.

Salminen, Carl. 1938b. "Taidefilmi 'Asessorin Naishuolet'." *Päivälehti*, October, 11.

Wallengren, Ann-Kristin. 2013. *Välkommen hem Mr. Swanson. Svenska emigranter och svenskhet på film*. Lund: Nordic Academic Press.

Wasastjerna, Hans R. 1957. *Minnesotan suomalaisten historia*. Duluth, MN: Minnesotan suomalais-amerikkalainen historiallinen seura.

Virtanen, Keijo. 2014. "Finnish Identity in Immigrant Culture." In *Finns in the United States* ed. Auvo Kostiainen. East Lansing, MI: Michigan State University Press. 173–203.

19. THE TRANSNATIONAL POLITICS OF LARS VON TRIER'S AND THOMAS VINTERBERG'S "AMERIKA"

Linda Badley

"All my films are set in the US," Lars von Trier asserted in reference to *Dear Wendy* (2004), directed by Thomas Vinterberg from Trier's script about a group of American western-style gun fetishists, and shot on a parking lot at Filmbyen, Trier's studio complex near Copenhagen ("Interview" 2004). This claim, like the film, was a cheeky provocation that turned out to be a prediction: beginning with *Dancer in the Dark* (2000), six (of eight) of his features have been set in an imaginary USA. Vinterberg, on the other hand, has been acclaimed for powerful Danish family dramas including *The Celebration* (*Dogme #1: Festen*, 1998), *The Hunt* (*Jagten*, 2012), and *The Commune* (*Kollektivet*, 2016). Vinterberg's *It's All About Love* (2003) and *Dear Wendy* are fascinating exceptions, however, in representing America through ideological and genre clichés.

Trier's penchant for patently faked American settings is often remarked upon (and frequently derided) but sidelined in recent Trier studies, whether film-philosophy (Sinnerbrink 2011), performance and cultural studies (Badley 2011), Lacanian approaches to the feminine (Butler and Denny 2017; Elbeshlawy 2017) or post-Brechtian "politics as form" (Koutsourakis 2013). Vinterberg's "American" films remain virtually forgotten. This chapter explores these auteurs' unabashed fascination with American mythologies and the transnational and cross-genre hybridities that compose it. I focus on the discursive play between their European locations and American settings, between European "art" cinema and American genres, to expose a counter-hegemonic politics.

Taking on Hollywood: Oppositional Transnationalism

From his first feature *The Element of Crime* (1981), an English-language neo-noir set in a vaguely German post-apocalyptic dystopia, Trier styled himself as a transnational auteur. *Element* led to the 1989 Film Act that denationalized the Danish industry by extending eligibility to any meritorious film produced by a Danish company (Hjort 2005, 12–13). Since 2008, Zentropa, Trier's production company founded in 1992 with Peter Aalbæk Jensen, has partnered with former rival Nordisk, allowing it to fund higher-risk projects and expand internationally, with companies in Sweden, Norway, Netherlands, Germany, France, Spain, and Belgium. Similarly, Dogme 95 became an international initiative for taking on Hollywood, aiming, as Vinterberg phrased it, to "put a mirror in front of [the movie industry] and say we can do it another way as well" (*The Name of This Film* 2000). Coinciding with the digital revolution and the consolidation of the European Union, Dogme created an oppositional form of globalization that allowed directors and small countries to compete (Hjort 2005, 155).

As Dogme co-founders and figureheads, Trier played the mastermind and the younger, extroverted Vinterberg was poster boy. This collaboration led to a nearly decade-long relationship in which Trier, Vinterberg, and "Dogme cinematographer" Anthony Dod Mantle worked from Filmbyen, the former military base where Zentropa, Nimbus, and over twenty production companies once made their home. In 2000 and 2003, Trier's *Dancer in the Dark* and Vinterberg's *It's All About Love* signaled an ambitious turn from Dogme's localized realism, minimalism, and "truth" to English-language "Europuddings" set in a faux America. While panning *Dancer*, Jonathan Rosenbaum articulated its logic well: together with "gimmicks" like the Dogme Manifesto, which "worked on the credulous American press" as planned, this switch was a survival strategy that exploited the international festival circuit (Durovičová and Rosenbaum 2003). Additionally, by taking on genres, issues, and themes that dominated the world stage while breaking a taboo against "foreign" criticism of America, Trier's and Vinterberg's films spoke *about* globalization and cultural imperialism.

Performing Exile: Amerikan "Accented" Cinema

To complain that Trier's and Vinterberg's settings are unconvincing is to miss the point. The Amerikan films are strategically "accented" in the sense in which Hamid Naficy has designated filmmakers marginalized in relation to globalized Hollywood entertainment norms, which pretend to be ideologically neutral, or lacking accent (Naficy 2001, 23). With alienation effects that foreground their transnational "foreignness" and displace what is seen and heard, they prevent international audiences from the immersive experience of either a Danish or a "Hollywood" film. All exhibit a tendency toward the conceptual and allegorical, announced in Trier's films by post-Brechtian devices such as chapter titles, narrators, or an obtrusive score, and in Vinterberg's *It's All About Love* through repeated dislocation and "weird" science, in which the behavior of natural phenomena defies Hollywood-style logic. For instance, the sarcastic voice of the USA Trilogy's narrator (British actor John Hurt) underlines cause and effect, linking characters and events to social, political, and historical contexts in a misanthropic and distinctively un-American tone. Then there is the literally accented dialogue spoken by international casts—an effect that Nataša Ďurovičová describes as "broken Hollywood English" (Ďurovičová and Rosenbaum 2003, 144), and in *Dancer in the Dark* the range of accents contributes to a theme of America as an ethnic mosaic. More often, however, as in the overtly staged USA Trilogy or the operatic and painterly *Antichrist* and *Melancholia*, the "broken" English reminds us that the film is a European, ideologically nuanced performance of Americanness and a politicized critique.

Trier's accented films have been inspired partly by Kafka's blackly humorous, unfinished *Amerika* (1927) and Brecht's five "American" theatrical productions from the 1920s, when American fashion, music, and manners were popular in Germany. The latter included the libretto *The Rise and Fall of the City of Mahagonny* (1927–9), which exploited a ready-made mythology of urban jungles, gangsters, and prostitutes, and the more Marxist-Leninist plays *St. Joan of the Stockyards* (1927–9) and *Seven Deadly Sins of the Bourgeois Class* (1933).

When accused of ignorance of the country he both aggrandized and mocked but had not then visited, Brecht responded with the poem "Understanding," which ends by asserting that "you understand me very well when I talk about America," the "best thing" about America being "that we understand it" (1976, 156). When challenged about his USA Trilogy, Trier retorted that the American entertainment industry has "standardized our culture in a most moronic fashion. Entering a country with troops is small change compared to the way we have allowed ourselves to be occupied" (Koster 2003). Claiming to be "60% American" (Higgins 2005) despite his refusal to set foot in the USA, he insinuated that it was not merely his right to make films about America, it was—in that "we" are all compulsory "Amerikans"—impossible to do otherwise. As Trier had earlier used postwar Germany to comment on Europe in the late 1980s, he and Vinterberg have used mythical American settings, often period backdrops such as the Old West or the Depression era, as a "common language" for provoking dialogue about immigration, capitalism, democracy, race, class, religion, and globalization.

Naficy is concerned primarily with "exilic" filmmakers whose exile may be internal (from facing oppression within their home countries) and/or external (2001: 11–12). Legendarily a homebody because of anxiety and flight phobia,

Trier has performed a sense of internal exile since his teenage years as the son of a Danish Jewish father and a mother who raised him to be a genius. His fascination with America was preceded by an obsession with Germany, the setting for his graduation film and Europe Trilogy (1981–91), which revisited the European heritage of the Holocaust. Rebelling against his parents' "cultural radicalism" and Danish culture, he shaved his head and adopted the German "von" to confer faux nobility while internationalizing his identity. Nevertheless, his Jewish heritage provided an identity marker, "a sense of belonging" (Björkman 2003, 9) that he lost after his mother's deathbed revelation that his real father, Fritz Michael Hartmann (whom his mother had selected for his "artistic" genes), had a German heritage. Thus Trier became an internal exile from the nationality and ethnicity he had assumed was his, neither Danish nor Jewish nor German. Worse, Hartmann refused to acknowledge his son. In retaliation, in *Europa* (1991) Trier gave the name "Max Hartmann" to a Nazi railroad magnate and war profiteer and took the role of a self-exiled "whitewashing" Jew employed by the Allies to exonerate him. This betrayal and loss, or lack, along with his original sense of entitlement and an acute awareness of the performed nature of identity, as I have previously argued (2011, 6–16), make Trier a textbook example of the postmodern subject-less, hence performative, subject—thus a permanent exile from any innate self or "home." His specious "Amerika" might therefore be seen as a self-conscious, performative introjection.

In contrast is the happily Danish, commune-nurtured Vinterberg's encounter with external exile, however temporary, as an international celebrity courted by Hollywood studios (who showered him with scripts and deals). Flying around the world, he became uprooted from home and family, demoralized, unable to write and lost in the non-space of global celebrity. Five years in the making, *It's All About Love*, which allegorized this experience, projects a synthetic New York City setting as its epicenter.

Immigrant Stories in Hollywood Frames: *Dancer in the Dark* and *It's All About Love*

Kafka's *Amerika: The Man Who Disappeared* was about the misadventures, in an America where the Statue of Liberty holds a sword instead of a torch, of a sixteen-year-old German émigré, who is bullied, raped, robbed, enslaved, and fired for crimes he did not commit. Similarly about "naïve" immigrants' brutal New World experiences, Trier's and Vinterberg's films from 2000 through 2003 deploy American genres as frames for European critique. A musical shot primarily in Sweden and Denmark, *Dancer in the Dark* is set in 1960s Washington State. Selma Jezkova (Björk), a Czechoslovakian immigrant going blind from a hereditary disease, works overtime in a metal press factory to afford her young son an operation to save him from the same fate. She is betrayed by her landlord, a policeman who steals her savings, and, in suicidal despair, forces herself to kill him to recover the money. As she is tried, found guilty, and executed, she turns to fantasies imagined as musical numbers.

Dancer alluded to the musical genre from its Hollywood heyday in the 1930s, 1940s and 1950s to its decline from the 1960s to the present. It featured the Icelandic composer and star Björk, French actress Catherine Deneuve, star of Jacques Demy's musicals *Les parapluies de Cherbourg* (*The Umbrellas of Cherbourg*, France, 1964) and *Les demoiselles de Rochefort* (*The Young Girls of Rouchefort*, France, 1967), and Joel Grey, sardonic Master of Ceremonies in *Cabaret* (USA, 1972). *Dancer* blends the upbeat Hollywood musical with the woman's melodrama styled as an opera, with a four-minute "Overture," musical numbers integrated fluidly into the narrative, emotional excess, and a protractedly tragic ending in which the heroine's final aria is cut off by a noose.

In the future Selma envisions for her son, America and the musical are conflated into a utopian, faux-Technicolor "land of opportunity" set against the real inequities of American capitalism accentuated by drab settings, melodramatic plotting, and hand-held realism. The film's USA lacks basic social nets (Selma commits her life savings to a single operation), and the middle classes are driven into debt and desperation. The film ends in a condemnation of the death penalty, an issue that had evoked anti-American sentiments throughout Europe. Selma's musical "daydreams" provoke or signal the downward-spiraling narrative, and Hollywoodized illusions seem responsible for her death (Woodgate 2007, 395–6).

Things are not that simple, however. Rather than being "anti-" *or* "pro-" Hollywood, *Dancer* is insistently international in its frame of reference and cast that includes Icelandic, French, French-Canadian, Swedish, English, Danish, and German actors, "denaturaliz[ing] the American provenance of the musical genre" (Martin 2003, 106). While working variations on the American Dream, Selma's fantasies lean, Trier has commented, "more toward the European traditions," resembling *The Umbrellas of Cherbourg* in social themes (Lumholdt 2003, 163) and (in "Cvalda" and "I've Seen It All") Soviet factory and "tractor" musicals of the late 1930s and 1940s that turned labor into choreographed collective pleasure (Ranga 2000). Czechoslovakia was chosen as a "counterweight to the USA" (Trier in Björkman 2003, 225), and the socialist realism of Soviet propaganda films modifies the capitalist American Dream. "Cvalda" cites a Soviet musical cliché that celebrates the mechanical, as proletarian-attired dancers perform the functions of a metal press machine.

Selma's fantasies merge American Dream landscapes and icons with communist kitsch and Eisensteinian didactic aesthetics. "I've Seen It All," which expresses Selma's resignation to blindness and refusal of desire, is a proletarian utopia in which tool-bearing laborers march on flatbed railway cars and rural couples dance over rolling hills. It recalls American Depression-era movies and 1950s–60s musicals, but draws equally on Soviet-era farm musicals. Instead of romantic love, Selma sings of common pleasures and the "New World" future generations will see, a subjectless proletarian heaven she chooses over a nuclear family. Both an idealized multicultural space and a challenge to Hollywood genres, Selma's "musical" demonstrates that dreams other than American ones did and still exist, while envisioning what the American Dream might have been had it been more "socialist."

Vinterberg's *It's All About Love* was also an Eastern European immigrant story and ambitious hybrid panned for its unconvincing settings and genre references. Shot on sound stages at Filmbyen and at Film i Väst in Trollhättan, with second-unit aerial and panorama footage in New York City, Venice, Paris, Oslo, Vancouver, and Kenya, it folded a melodramatic thriller into a science-fiction dystopia with allegorical pretentions, studio gloss, and Hollywood stars, and "report[ed] on the state of the world" (Said 2004). As Arne Lunde suggests, the film's "chilly 'no places' symbolically mirror the cultural emptiness" that Vinterberg experienced in the USA (2012, 28).

New York City, the epicenter of the world's malaise, deracination, is represented by an anonymous airport, a hotel, and repeated shots of three white stretch limousines gliding ominously down the streets. Joachin Phoenix's John Marczewcsi arrives with divorce papers for his wife, Elena (Claire Danes), an ice skating superstar (and Vinterberg stand-in) to sign between flights. They are Polish (translate: Danish) émigrés. When he discovers that Elena has a heart condition and her managers at Ice International plan to replace her with clones, their love rekindles too late. An elegy for the human—for family, home, and love—in an increasingly posthuman world, the film projects an image of our hyperglobalized condition through extreme close-ups of John's face disorientingly juxtaposed with flash panoramas of bizarre natural disturbances from around the world or uninhabitable snow-covered peaks.

A similar dislocation informs the film's mixture of genres, homages, modalities, voices, and tones. Noir thriller, retro sci-fi dystopia, and fairy tale romance jostle one another, with homages to Hitchcock, Kubrick, Polanski, Coppola, and Tarkovsky, and a production design suggesting the post-World War II era. In a reference to film noir, the film opens with Phoenix's posthumous voiceover ("I would like to tell you the story of the last seven days of my life"). Meanwhile, John's brother Marciello (Sean Penn, from some magic realist realm of perpetual flight) sends overwrought quasi-philosophical cellphone messages that break up or become lost from an airplane as he circles the globe. In a repeated news clip, Ugandan victims of an unexplained loss of gravity plead, "We are not angels. We are not meant to fly." The closing CGI shot of Ugandans tethered by ropes to prevent them from floating into space literalizes the concept and links the film's central narrative to the fate of Third World countries plagued by "cosmic disturbances."

Like Trier's *Melancholia*, *Love* abjures the action orientation and posthuman technophilia typical of Hollywood sci-fi from Ridley Scott's *Blade Runner* (USA, 1982) on, substituting a humanist (emotional, metaphorical) logic. Weakened human bonds have led to a dilution of identity from a literalization of the "frozen heart": people drop dead in the street so commonly that the living simply step over them. The family has been replaced by the corporation Ice International depicted in menacing large-group scenes reminiscent of *The Godfather* (USA, 1972, Francis Ford Coppola) and *Rosemary's Baby* (USA, 1968, Roman Polanski). In a reversal of global warming, Vinterberg predicts a New Ice Age of frozen hearts and frozen assets epitomized in the North American culture and landscape. Escaping, Elena and John freeze together in the Canadian Arctic, a winter wonderland that, recalling their idyllic past in Poland, yields to the hostile sublimity of a mountain range stretching to the horizon.

Brechtian Gangster Westerns: *Dogville* and *Dear Wendy*

Vinterberg's frozen, alienated nonlocations, as Lunde also observes, "eerily" correspond to the stark representations of emptiness in Trier's Amerikas, especially *Dogville* (2011: 28), which reveals a town laid out like a chalk map on a cavernous Trollhättan stage. The first film in the USA Trilogy, *Dogville* gazes through invisible walls and roofs, literalizing Brechtian distantiation, and represents identity in relation to a regulated community. Furnishing a petri-dish replica of the American imaginary constructed by the mass media (Peden 2005, 119), Trier deploys Hollywood genres to reveal the semantics and syntactical relations underlying "America" as seen from without, exposing their ideological underpinnings.

Like *Dancer* and *Love*, *Dogville* begins as a Kafkaesque immigrant tale in which Grace (Nicole Kidman) is exploited within an oppressive economic system. But *Dogville* is also a western, or rather, as *Variety*'s Peter DeBruge notes, a "deconstruction" of the genre (2014). Applying Rick Altman's terms, the western's semantic elements or "building blocks" (1999, 223) might include a frontier, a town, a sheriff, outlaws, horses, guns, and a climactic shootout. *Dogville*, set in the Rocky Mountains in a former frontier town with an abandoned silver mine, includes everything but cowboys and horses. In the syntactical relationships among these elements (Altman 1999, 222), a stranger seeks refuge in Dogville, her presence altering its socioeconomic and sexual dynamic while provoking terrorization by "outlaws" colluding with the sheriff to put up wanted posters with a price on her head. In a twist on the *High Noon* standoff, the town's representatives meet the outlaws to exchange her for the bounty, resulting in a one-sided shootout they least expect.

LARS VON TRIER'S AND THOMAS VINTERBERG'S "AMERIKA"

Figure 19.1 Ending as a bloody hybrid of the western and gangster genres, Lars von Trier's *Dogville* (Denmark, 2003) was ultimately a critique of American capitalism, exceptionalism, post-9/11 vengeance, and "cowboy" politics.

But instead of black hats on horseback, the town is threatened by Capone-era gangsters in menacing black automobiles who supply a more than adequate shoot-'em-up. Like Brecht, Trier deploys gangsters as metaphors for capitalism with its gloves off. As the film becomes a hybrid of western and gangster saga, with a *Godfather*-like boss (James Caan) and a two-generation family, *Dogville*'s "Amerika" takes on more layers of historicization. In a blackly comical turnaround, having been enslaved, dog-collared, chained to a grindstone, and raped by Dogville's males, Grace is revealed to be neither a victimized émigré nor a gun moll but the boss's petulant daughter seeking to get out from under Daddy's thumb. After lengthy discussion with the Big Man about ("arrogant") Christian forgiveness versus Old Testament justice, she orders his men to machine-gun and burn the town to the ground, topped off by her execution-style shooting of town "philosopher" Tom Edison, Jr. (Paul Bettany). The end-credit sequence with David Bowie's rollicking "Young Americans" over a montage of Depression-era Farm Security Administration photographs I interpret as an indictment of the ideological excess of Grace's western-style revenge. Trier builds indignation and suspense, tricking the audience into relishing the massacre, then to sit in stunned horror at the genocide they've been manipulated to desire (Badley 2011, 112–15). The film ends, as American westerns sometimes usefully do (in Fred Zinnemann's *High Noon* [USA, 1952] and John Ford's *The Searchers* [USA, 1956] for instance), by interrogating Old Testament (Mosaic Law) ethics of violence wielded in the name of justice but actually in revenge. Only Moses, indicated by an outline and labeled "DOG," is spared; in the film's final seconds he manifests in an image of frenzied, roaring fury.

Released in 2003, *Dogville* has since been interpreted by some as a critique of American capitalism, exceptionalism, post-9/11 vengeance and the "shoot first and ask questions later" "cowboy" politics exemplified in George W. Bush's Iraq War (Badley 2011, 114, 115, 116, 130). Released in 2004 as *Dogville*'s darkly absurdist addendum, *Dear Wendy*, set in a run-down 1960s West Virginia mining town, unfolds in a slightly more naturalized space, a Hollywood western-style town square constructed on a Filmbyen parking lot. Trier explains, "I wrote the film to be made here, like theatre" ("Interview" 2006). As in *Dogville*, the "West" is nowhere in sight, and in place of "outlaws" are offhand references to rumored but invisible "gangs"—other than the protagonists. The realism is thanks to a young, vibrant, primarily American cast and Vinterberg, whom Trier asked to bring life to his overly conceptual script. *Dear Wendy* is narrated (like *Dogville*) in mock-solemn voiceover by the (aptly named) protagonist Dick Dandelion (Jamie Bell) in a love letter to his 6.65mm double action revolver (Wendy). He relates the history of the "Dandies," a group of repressed adolescent misfits. Espousing pacifism, they bond (paradoxically) through their infatuation with antique handguns, dressing in outlandishly archaic long jackets, vests, and hats. In an abandoned mine dubbed the Temple, they shoot at targets, play gun-related games, study ballistics and instructional videos. Like Dogme brothers and Trier's idiots, they espouse rituals, rules, and prohibitions. Each chooses a gun ("partner") with a history, and names and "marries" it in a solemn ceremony. Revealing their partners outside the club is so taboo, however, that the word "killing," which contradicts their philosophy of pacifism with guns, is forbidden and is called "loving." When they actually shoot their weapons, they favor style over function (Dick shoots from the hip, and Susan prefers two guns and indirect hits with ricocheted bullets). In the streets, the Dandies' (concealed) partners provide "moral support" and sexual confidence, suggested in analogies with erections, masturbation, ejaculations, and breasts.

Dear Wendy predictably ends in a shootout between the Dandies and Marshal Krugsby (Bill Pullman) and deputies in an absurdist parody of *High Noon* by way of the Columbine school massacre, with "The Battle Hymn of the Republic" rising over the carnage like Bowie's "Young Americans" over *Dogville*'s end credits. Vinterberg "accented" the film further with animated MRI depictions of each bullet's internal trajectory until the Dandies, one by one, are stopped, but not before achieving consummation, as when the dying Dick looks reverently down at the exit wound that his former "partner" Wendy (wielded by his rival, Sebastian) has made through his heart.

When asked why he set the film in America, Trier quipped that the USA was one setting where many guns would seem natural, that *Dear Wendy* was merely "a study of people and guns" inspired by his own infatuation ("Interview"

Figure 19.2   In Thomas Vinterberg's *Dear Wendy* (Denmark, 2004), Dick Dandelion (Jamie Bell) poses with his beloved 6.6 5mm double-action revolver (Wendy) next to his heart.

2006)—despite or because of his Danish social-Democrat acculturation in which guns are taboo. Vinterberg similarly described ambivalent feelings of "aversion" and "power" while holding a gun. Shown surrounded by ballistics diagrams, both claim their fascination is with trajectories, "stopping power," entrance and exit wounds, and the "aftermath of the impact, [the fact] that you could actually die" ("Interview" 2006).

This fascination extended to the characterization of Sebastian (Danso Gordon), the last and only black Dandy, who is armed with street knowledge and sexual prowess. The "man of action," Vinterberg calls him, explaining that, in the same way as the Dandies treat Sebastian, "the film treats America ... [as] something we're somehow inferior to, and attracted to at the same time ... Lars does not want to be politically correct" (Aftab 2005).

Manderlay/Mandingo

From this angle, *Dear Wendy* is a bridge between *Dogville* and *Manderlay*, which proved even less "politically correct." As *Dogville*'s ending reveals, Grace is not the innocent she initially represented, or the gift of God connoted by her name; she is a female variant on Trier's rational humanist blinded by American ideological fervor and corrupted by systems in place. By *Manderlay*, she has shifted further in this direction. Discovering a plantation practicing slavery in the 1930s, invested with her father's power, she uses his military might to enforce freedom and democracy. Despite cross-cultural and racial miscommunications, natural disasters, and the recalcitrance of Manderlay's residents, they achieve a successful harvest, whereupon she pronounces them

"Americans"—a triumph that reverses abruptly in violence, darkness, and flames that allude back to *Dogville*'s conclusion. "We wasn't quite ready," the old house slave Willem (Danny Glover) explains, As in *Dogville*, viewers are left demoralized, forced to choose between two untenable positions, although *Manderlay* is heavily weighted. Its allusions to abuses of the Reconstruction and failures of the civil rights movement are filtered through Trier's view of the Bush administration's bungled attempts at nation building in Iraq to justify the option taken by the plantation's residents to resume slavery under "Mam's Law"—revealed to have been written by Willem as a blueprint for survival. Slavery is in this instance a relative good, whereas "freedom," imposed militantly and inexpertly, has brought on chaos and death.

Influenced by Danish socialist photographer Jacob Holdt (1986), *Manderlay* is "accented" to foreground elements of racist performativity. "Mam's Law," the tome that ranks the slaves by psychological types, corresponds with stereotypes perpetuated by the film and television industry (Doughty 2007) and alludes to the media heritage of the blackface minstrel show. The title is a probable composite of Kurt Weill's "Mandalay Song" from *Mahagonny* and *Happy End* (1929), "On the Road to Mandalay" (1907), the song based on Rudyard Kipling's colonialist orientalization of Burma, and the doomed estate (Manderley) of Hitchcock's adaptation of Daphne Du Maurier's *Rebecca* (1940). The film resonates with Southern plantation movies from D. W. Griffith's *Birth of a Nation* (USA, 1915) to Victor Fleming's *Gone with the Wind* (USA, 1939) as filtered through Brecht's "Alabama Song." In tone and affect, however, and at its pivotal moment, Grace's seduction just before the narrative reversal, *Manderlay* has a closer kinship with Richard Fleischer's *Mandingo* (USA, 1975), *Gone with the Wind*'s antithesis or parody, an explosive hybrid of exploitation, melodrama, and exposé of the economy of desire underlying slavery, central to which is the mythology surrounding the strength, nobility, and sexual prowess of the Mandingo warrior. Trier argues that underlying Grace's ideological fervor is a sadomasochistic lust for Timothy (Isaac Bancole), who is said to be a noble "Munsi," an association that explains his characterization until the ending where he reveals his true lights as a dissembling, seductive, thieving "Mansi."

Amerikan Puritanism and Superkitsch: *Antichrist* and *Melancholia*

Aborting *Wasington* [sic], projected as the third film in the USA Trilogy, Trier shifted to sharply focused genre experiments including *The Boss of It All* (*Direktøren for det hele*, 2006), an office comedy satirizing empty-suit capitalism (shot by a computerized "cinematographer" dubbed "Automavision") whose (nonexistent) title character resides in (where else?) America. In another shift, the first two films of his Depression Trilogy (2009–14), products of

Trier's clinical depression of 2006–7, took American settings and genres. Set near Seattle, Washington, to match its North Rhine–Westphalia location, *Antichrist* was announced as a horror film. The genre's inherent violence was perfect for Trier's aim: to transform personal trauma into Theatre of Cruelty.

The film begins as Bergmanesque family tragedy with a couple (Willem Dafoe and Charlotte Gainsbourg, "He" and "She") destroyed by the death of their child. The woman falls into despair; the man, a cognitive therapist, retreats into clinical detachment. Taking over her treatment, He forces her to confront her fears of "nature" by returning to their forest cabin, where she becomes increasingly volatile, and nature (external and internal) contributes to her, and eventually his, derangement. Opposed settings and characters drive the film while underscoring dialectical extremes inherent in the American landscape, ideology, and character. On one level, Trier has admitted, *Antichrist* "sarcastically" represents his experience of (American) cognitive exposure therapy (Fanning 2009). The chilly spaces of West Coast therapy and environmentalist culture, embodied in the Seattle hospital and modish but antiseptic apartment, are He's domain, and he views nature as placid and recuperative. Later, when he complains of having "crazy" dreams (of nature's true chaos), She quips "Dreams are of no interest in modern psychology. Freud is dead, isn't he?," siding with continental psychoanalysis. His stake in cognitive therapy identifies He as Trier's (American, male, rational) idealist whose adherence to system makes him defenseless against "nature." Sublimating his grief in her therapy (Sinnerbrink 2011, 172), he denies his wife's worsening condition and his own surreal experiences. With her violence begetting his, he repeats a misogynistic cycle.

At the other extreme is the woodland cabin redolent of colonial New England, the irrational, and witch persecution. Popular since *The Evil Dead* (Sam Rami, USA, 1981) and *The Blair Witch Project* (Daniel Myrick and Eduardo Sánchez, USA, 1999), cabin horror films resonate from a tradition going back to Charles Brockden Brown, who shifted the Gothic genre from the European castle to the American wilderness (Grant 2014; Whitaker 2017, 1–3). Although Heidi Laura, Trier's credited "misogyny" consultant, drew from the *Malleus Maleficarum* (1486) and other European sources (2009), and I have explored the film's rich Scandinavian heritage (Badley 2013), *Antichrist*'s American setting evokes the history of witch persecution handed down from American classics like Nathaniel Hawthorne's novel *The Scarlet Letter* and "Young Goodman Brown," Arthur Miller's drama *The Crucible*, and feminist accounts of "gynocide," lending veracity to Gainsbourg's sexualized performance of witch hysteria. Named "Eden" by the couple, the idyllic setting devolves into "Satan's church" to embody the dichotomous extremism with which nature has been regarded from the Puritan perspective. The unspoiled land evoked Eden before the Fall, yet the threat of "savage men, wild beasts, and still stranger creatures of the imagination" lurked within the forest darkness, and "civilized man . . . succumbing to the wildness of his surroundings" might revert "to savagery himself" (Nash 2001, 24). Accordingly, nature's death-dealing fecundity inspires Gainsbourg's increasingly vindictive sexuality, linking her to witchcraft, and the Three Beggars' successive revelations drive Dafoe to violence before the Beggar figures align magically with She's body, presenting as her familiars. "You should never have come here," She hisses; for the rational male, nature is hostile, female, pagan territory, as the film's final frames reveal.

Antichrist's dichotomous settings and ideologies deploy American puritanical extremism in a battle of the sexes that exposes a Western heritage of misogyny. *Melancholia*'s castle setting is harder to place (although the license plates identify Pennsylvania). A series of parallel contrasts, announced by title cards between parts named for its two heroines (Kirsten Dunst's unstable Justine and Charlotte Gainsbourg's stalwart Claire), two genres (the woman's film and apocalyptic science fiction/disaster), and tonalities (the social satire of the imploding wedding reception versus the Wagnerian sublime) are extended in tensions between the film's iconic location, Tjolöholms Slott, south of Göteborg overlooking Kungsbacka Fjord, and its ostentatious American setting. A Swedish national treasure, Tjolöholm embodies the film's Gothic–Romantic Sublime: an archive of aesthetic movements and architectural styles, it represents the summit of Western (European) culture doomed to extinction in a collision between Earth and a rogue gas planet ten times its size—on the one hand. Hence the overture's succession, in elegiac slow-motion, of allusions to a European tradition in music and art from Wagner to Pieter Brueghel's *Hunters in the Snow* (1565) to John Everett Millais' *Ophelia* (1851–2). On the other hand, as an American "tycoon's dream palace" (Claro 2013) it expresses the film's politics; it epitomizes Western modernization and globalization at its worst—the greed, excess, and empty materialism of late capitalism that Justine means when she asserts that life on Earth is "evil."

The late-nineteenth-century neo-Tudor castle (with interiors in Arts and Crafts style) is today an arty Swedish Disney World celebrated for its guided tours, holiday open houses, and lavish weddings. With Kiefer Sutherland's John, the self-made capitalist with no understanding of the heritage he has bought into, it represents modern global commodification of culture with an American neoliberal flourish. Congratulating himself on his eighteen-hole golf course, he bullies Justine into "enjoying" her (his) wedding. His pride in acquisition, technological prowess, and worship of science, of course doom him, and when his optimistic predictions fail he commits suicide, leaving his family to face catastrophe alone.

Like Disney World or Xanadu, Tjolöholm expressed power and capital by amalgamating past styles within a modern structure. "[S]uperkitsch!

Absolutely perfect!," Trier pronounced it; "a tremendously rustic box full of different styles" (Thorsen 2011, 386–7). For Adorno (2001), kitsch exemplifies the false consciousness inherent in capitalism, with "superkitsch" suggesting a post-postmodern awareness through which kitsch becomes provisionally "cool." Thus Justine is the unhappy art director of an advertising company whose latest design embodies her protest in a *Vogue*-style send-up of *The Land of Cockaigne* (1567), Brueghel's study of gluttony—art reduced to marketing.

Her melancholia stems not from trauma or loss but from having too much, as Abbas Ackbar (2013) has suggested. In the overture's clinging yarn and slow-motion sinking images, she is weighted down by the materialization of lack, expressed simultaneously by Wagner's "Tristan chord," which builds the tension of desire without resolution. Thus, in the overture, the image of the planet resembles a black hole into which the earth is sucked, a representation of nothing. *Melancholia*'s Tjolöholm stands for human aspiration, art, and culture doomed to extinction—but in the hugely diminished sense of "Amerikan" kitsch about to become space dust (or, more accurately, cyber dust). In the film's final moments, it is replaced by the simple eloquence of a teepee of stripped branches that speaks simultaneously of the emptiness of monuments, America's original inhabitants, and Earth before modernization.

Conclusion: Only in Amerika (*The House That Jack Built*)

Trier's and Vinterberg's "Amerika" reflects a mythologized history of violence and vivid extremes ripe for provocation and discourse, and it is no coincidence that Trier's most celebrated "American" films are claimed also by international Extreme Cinema, so designated for its deployment of sex, violence, and politicized provocation (Horeck and Kendall 2011; Frey 2016; Kerner and Knapp 2016). With similar reasoning, Canadian author Margaret Atwood chose New England, with its extremist theocratic Puritan heritage, as the setting for her gender dystopia *The Handmaid's Tale* (1985). Like Atwood, Kafka, and Brecht, Trier and Vinterberg employ the generic iconography of "Amerika" to "talk" about global issues that might otherwise stay under the radar. The USA offered a plausible setting for state-sponsored execution by hanging, a gangland massacre of genocidal proportions, climate change via global freezing, teenage gun fetishists, a plantation practicing slavery in the 1930s, witchcraft and witch burning, and the end of the world—and more.

Hence, Trier has summed up his 2018 serial killer film *The House That Jack Built*, set in Washington State, as "celebrat[ing] the idea that life is evil and soulless, which is sadly proven by the recent rise of the *Homo trumpus*—the rat king" (Shoard 2017). The statement was widely misquoted as saying that Donald Trump "inspired" the film—when the failed artist/architect Jack was by Trier's own admission a reflection of his own proclivities and obsessions, including the heritage and iconography of the Third Reich. Nevertheless, Jack's architectural efforts pointedly blight pristine lakeside forest settings, while references to American gun culture, and "a helluva country" in which screaming is futile because "nobody wants to help," are telling. "Incident 3" alone references mass/school shootings, MAGA hats, and hunting trophies, and Trier reimagines Dante's inferno as an inversion of the Mount St. Helens eruption. Above all, the serial killer is an *American* icon. Like Patrick Bateman in *American Psycho* (Bret Eston Ellis, 1991, Mary Harron, 2000), which proposed serial killing as a metaphor for 1980s Wall Street, Jack personifies Trier's darkening view of the Anthropocene as inherently destructive—and now epitomized in Trump's USA.

Acknowledgment

Brief references to Trier's background, Naficy's *An Accented Cinema*, Kafka and Brecht's influence, and parts of the section on *Dancer in the Dark* appeared in a different and expanded form in *Lars von Trier* (Badley 2011) and are reprinted with permission of the University of Illinois Press.

References

Aftab, Kaleem. 2005. "Film: The Mark of the Danes; Tomas Vinterberg's New Feature." *Independent*, August 5, 8.
Ackbar, Abbas. 2013. "Junk Space, 'Dogville,' and Poor Theory." Lecture. Film Theory and Visual Culture Seminar, Vanderbilt University, December 6.
Adorno, Theodor. 2001. *The Culture Industry: Selected Essays on Mass Culture*. New York: Routledge.
Altman, Rick. 1999. *Film/Genre*. London: BFI Publishing.
Atwood, Margaret. 1985. *The Handmaid's Tale*. Toronto: McClelland & Stewart.
Badley, Linda. 2011. *Lars von Trier*. Urbana; Chicago: University of Illinois Press.
Badley, Linda. 2013. "*Antichrist*, misogyny and witch burning: The Nordic cultural contexts." *Journal of Scandinavian Cinema* 3(10: 15–33.
Björkman, Stig. 2003. *Trier on von Trier*, trans. Neil Smith. London: Faber & Faber.
Brecht, Bertolt. 1976. *Poems 1913–1956*, ed. John Willett and Ralph Manheim. New York: Methuen.
Butler, Rex, and David Denny, eds. 2017. *Lars von Trier's Women*. London: Bloomsbury.
Claro, Manuel Alberto. 2013. Skype interview. November 22.
DeBruge, Peter. 2014. "Cannes Film Review: 'The Salvation.'" *Variety*, May 16. <https://variety.com/2014/film/festivals/cannes-film-review-the-salvation-1201182872/>
Doughty, Ruth. 2007. "*Manderlay* (2005): Lars von Trier's narrative of passing." *New Cinemas* 5(2): 153–61.
Durovičová, Nataša, and Jonathan Rosenbaum. 2003. "Movies Go Multilingual." In *Movie Mutations: The Changing Face of World Cinephilia*, ed. Jonathan Rosenbaum and Adrian Martin. London: British Film Institute. 141–9.

Elbeshlawy, Ahmed. 2017. *Woman in Lars von Trier's Cinema, 1996–2014*. London: Palgrave Macmillan.
Ellis, Bret Easton. 1991. *American Psycho*. New York: Vintage.
Fanning, Evan. 2009. "Antichrist Was Lars' 'Fun' Way of Treating Depression." *Independent*, July 26. <https://www.independent.ie/entertainment/movies/antichrist-was-lars-fun-way-of-treating-depression-26553823.html>
Frey, Mattias. 2016. *Extreme Cinema: The Transgressive Rhetoric of Today's Art Film Culture*. New Brunswick, NJ: Rutgers University Press.
Grant, Matthew. 2014. "The Cabin On the Screen: Defining The 'Cabin Horror' Film." *FilmMatters* 5(1): 5.
Higgins, Charlotte. 2005. "Lars von Trier Acts as a Slave to Controversy." *The Guardian*, May 17. <http://www.guardian.co.uk/>
Hjort, Mette. 2005. *Small Nation, Global Cinema: The New Danish Cinema*. Minneapolis: University of Minnesota Press.
Holdt, Jacob. 1986. *American Pictures: A Personal Journey through the American Underclass*. Copenhagen: American Pictures Foundation.
Horeck, Tanya and Tina Kendall, eds. 2011. *The New Extremism in Cinema: From France to Europe*. Edinburgh: University of Edinburgh Press.
"Interview with Thomas Vinterberg and Lars von Trier." 2006. *Dear Wendy*. Directed by Thomas Vinterberg. New York: Fox Lorber. DVD.
Kerner, Aaron Michael, and Jonathan L. Knapp. 2016. *Extreme Cinema: Affective Strategies in Transnational Media*. Edinburgh: Edinburgh University Press.
Koster, Ole. 2003. Interview with Lars von Trier. TV2. Cannes, May 23. *Dogville*. Disc 2. Nordisk. DVD.
Koutsourakis, Angelos. 2013. *Politics as Form in Lars von Trier: A Post-Brechtian Reading*. London: Bloomsbury.
Lumholdt, Jan. 2003. "There Will Be No Fun-Poking Today." Interview with Lars von Trier. *Filmhäftet* February 2000. In *Lars von Trier: Interviews*, ed. Jan Lumholdt. Jackson: University of Mississippi Press. 159–69.
Lunde, Arne. 2011. "After *The Celebration*: Thomas Vinterberg's *It's All About Love*. *Film International* 9(2): 20–9.
Martin, Adrian. 2003. "Musical Mutations: Before, Beyond and Against Hollywood." In *Movie Mutations: The Changing Face of World Cinephilia*, ed. Jonathan Rosenbaum and Adrian Martin. London: British Film Institute. 94–108.
The Name of This Film Is Dogme 95. 2000. Directed by Saul Metzstein, written by Richard Kelly. Minerva Pictures.
Peden, Knox. 2005. "The Threepenny Shot." *Critical Sense* Spring: 119–29.
Naficy, Hamid. 2001. *An Accented Cinema: Exilic and Diasporic Filmmaking*. Princeton: Princeton University Press,
Nash, Roderick. 2001. *Wilderness and the American Mind*. New Haven: Yale University Press.
Ranga, Dana, director. 2000. *East Side Story*. Kino International, 1997. Kino Video. DVD.
Said, S. F. 2004. "How I committed career suicide." *The Telegraph*, February 6. <http://www.telegraph.co.uk/culture/3611701/How-I-committed-career-suicide.html>
Shoard, Catherine. 2017. "Lars von Trier Inspired by Donald Trump for New Film." *Guardian*, February 14. <https://www.theguardian.com/film/2017/feb/14/lars-von-trier-donald-trump-the-house-that-jack-built>
Sinnerbrink, Robert. 2011. *New Philosophies of Film: Thinking Cinema*. London: BloomsburyAcademic.
Thorsen, Nils. 2011. *Geniet—Lars von Triers Liv, Film Og Fobier*. Copenhagen: Politiken.

Whitaker, Brandyn. 2016. "In the Wilderness 'Chaos Reigns': *Antichrist*, Cabin Horror, and the Puritan Perspective." Seminar paper for English 6760, Special Topics in Film Studies: Horror Cinema, Middle Tennessee State University.

Woodgate, Ken. 2007. "'Gotta Dance' (in the Dark): Lars von Trier's Critique of the Musical Genre." In *The Play within the Play: The Performance of Meta-Theatre and Self-Reflection*, ed. Gerhard Fischer and Bernhard Greiner. Amsterdam: Rodopi. 393–402.

20. THE GLOBALIZATION OF THE DANISH DOCUMENTARY: CREATIVE COLLABORATION AND MODES OF GLOBAL DOCUMENTARIES

Ib Bondebjerg

In Danish director Jon Bang Carlsen's autobiographical and poetic documentary *Life Will Be Lived—Letters from a Mother* (*Livet vil leves—breve fra en mor*, Denmark, 1994), several striking sequences and symbolic images address the relation between the emotional attachment to home and the longing for leaving and experiencing distant locations. This dichotomy is a well-known theme in documentary film, and in theories of nationality and globalization. With the increase in physical and digital mobility, and the mixing of images and experiences from global elsewheres with national cultures and imaginaries of home, this relation has become a central component of modernity (Anderson 1983; Morley and Robins 1995; Morley 2000). As David Morley formulates it: "Certainly, the traditional ideas of home, homeland and nation have been destabilized, both by new patterns of physical mobility and migration and by new communication technologies which routinely transgress the symbolic boundaries around both the private household and the nation state" (Morley 2000, 3).

In the following pages I will outline basic dimensions of globalization and basic documentary modes or genres, with special reference to Bill Nichols (2001), Carl Plantinga (1997), and Ib Bondebjerg (2014a). Within this theoretical context I will analyze different dimensions of the globalization through examples of Danish documentary, looking at production contexts, and the thematic, aesthetic, and formal modes. My cases represent different ways of addressing the global, and how documentary films use elements from different documentary modes.

The first example consists of the critical, authoritative documentary projects *Why Democracy* (2007) and *Why Poverty* (2012), transnational projects critically engaged in dialogue on fundamental global issues. The second example is a more subjective, poetically reflexive project by the Danish documentary filmmaker Jon Bang Carlsen, *Purity Beats Everything* (2007), in which the story of two Holocaust survivors is merged with the filmmaker's own childhood memories of ethnic conflict on the border between Denmark and Germany. The third example is Mads Brügger's film *The Ambassador* (*Ambassadøren*, 2011), a dramatized, investigative documentary about corruption in Africa and its links to Europe and other parts of the world. Finally, I discuss Joshua Oppenheimer films about the Indonesian genocide in 1965, *The Act of Killing* (2007) and *The Look of Silence* (2014), which have challenged the traditional understanding of documentary.

Dimensions of Globalization

Globalization is often construed as a modern phenomenon defined by economic, social, political and cultural interaction between nation states and regions, increasingly influenced by global technologies and communication media. However, even if this is true, and global interaction and mediated forms of communication have proliferated over the last two centuries, globalization has always been an important dynamic in all types of societies. The historic forms of globalization have changed, of course, but as David Held, Anthony McGrew, David Goldblatt, and Jonathan Perraton have pointed out in their seminal book on globalization, *Global Transformations. Politics, Economics and Culture* (1999, 27), globalization is not a condition but a continued set of processes that have historically influenced almost all areas of social life. Instead of trying to define globalization either as a process leading to domination, exploitation, and warfare or as one of free and creative exchange between nations and cultures, we might see it as a dynamic process that has many different outcomes and effects. Held et al. offer a descriptive definition:

> Globalization can be located on a continuum with the local, national and regional. At the one end of the continuum lie social and economic relations and networks, which are organized on a local/and or national basis; at the other end lie social and economic relations and networks which crystallize on the wider scale of regional and global interactions. Globalization can be taken to refer to those spatio-temporal processes of change which underpin a transformation in the organization of human affairs by linking together expanding human activity across regions and continents. (Held et al. 1999, 15)

The Danish documentary tradition incorporates characteristics of documentaries from the Nordic region, Europe and the USA. At the same time, in the history of Nordic documentary we see a shift from a more exotic interest in other cultures at the beginning of the twentieth century to a more critical, reflexive interest in global issues and problems in the late twentieth and early twenty-first century (see e.g. Barnouw 1993, 31f; Ellis and McLane 2006, 12f). With this shift came also the increase of Nordic-European-international co-productions, and directors from other countries making films in the Nordic region, or Nordic directors making films abroad (Bondebjerg and Bondebjerg 2017).

Globalization entails a dynamic interaction of the local, the national, and the regional. As Eviatar Zerubavel argues in his book *Social Mindscapes. An Invitation to Cognitive Sociology* (1997, 20f), our social and cultural imagination is linked to at least three different cognitive dimensions: *cognitive individualism*, a subjective, individual form of experience and history; *cognitive sociology*, understood as our inter-subjective experience and relations, in fact all those things that define our cultural and social identity with all its variations; and *cognitive universalism*, emotional and cognitive elements we all share as thinking and feeling human beings and as biological creatures with similar bodily functions. By telling stories that bring us close to individuals and groups from different parts of the world, documentary films have the possibility of bringing together these three dimensions in the minds of audiences around the world. Our globalized reality can make us aware of what we have in common, as well as the differences in our collective and individual realities.

Benedict Anderson coined the term "imagined communities" (1983) to describe how media, literature and history work to make us feel like citizens of a specific nation. National cultures and a feeling of belonging are still a very important part of our globalized world. The dynamics of globalization have always influenced what we see as our own culture, even though we may not be aware of the global influences. In this modern globalized world, it is more important than ever that we are confronted with global stories and images. As Zerubavel points out:

> Cognitive sociology tries to promote greater awareness of our *cognitive diversity* as social beings. The more we become aware of our *cognitive differences* as members of different thought communities, the less likely we are to follow the common ethnocentric tendency to regard the particular way in which we ourselves happen to process the world in our minds as based on some absolute standard of "logic." (Zerubavel 1997, 10)

Universalism thus doesn't exclude diversity, and as both Charles Taylor (2004) and Arjun Appadurai (1996) have pointed out, documentary stories are perhaps of special importance in the global flow of imaginaries with different social and cultural origins. Perhaps it is too optimistic to call this increased global collaboration and transnational flow of documentaries a new diasporic public sphere. However, in searching for and telling stories from a more multicultural and global reality, Nordic and Danish documentaries are trying to establish a common understanding of global issues, and in some cases also directly calling for audiences or politicians to see the global realities differently and to take action (see Bondebjerg 2014a, 2014c).

Basic Modes of Documentaries and Globalization

John Grierson's statement from around 1926, that documentary is a form of "creative treatment of actuality" (Aitken 1990), was one of the earliest definitions of documentary film. While other understandings of documentary tended to see it as a simple and direct documentation of reality, Grierson's statement pointed toward a broader aesthetic understanding of documentary, moving away from the understanding of documentary as educational and informational. The Danish documentary movement of the 1930s took up his ideas, and in 1938, the "Danish Grierson," Theodor Christensen, described documentary as "a realism, dramatizing modern life ... symbolic sounds, acoustic realism, contrasts between music and images ... reality, creatively arranged reality, reality in images, words, sound, music, creating together a narrative, a drama" (Christensen 1938; see also Bondebjerg 2014b).

In Eric Barnouw's book *Documentary. A History of the Non-Fiction Film* ([1974], 1993), he categorizes filmmakers according to their social and cultural roles: as explorers, reporters, advocates, poets, observers, prosecutors or catalysts. It was Bill Nichols who first suggested a more systematic and theoretical explanation of the different modes of documentary. In his seminal work *Representing Reality. Issues and Concepts in Documentary* (1991), he introduces four basic documentary modes. These are: *expository mode* (classic voice-of-God documentary); *observational mode* (minimizing the filmmaker's presence and "voice-of-God" rhetoric); *interactive mode* (where filmmaker and social actors interact directly); and *reflexive mode* (where the filmmaker put the film's form in focus). In his later book *Introduction to Documentary* (2001), Nichols added two new modes: the poetic mode and the performative mode.

In *Rhetoric and Representation in Nonfiction Film* (1997), his book on cognitive film theory, Plantinga argued for three basic documentary modes, which he called voices. By voices he meant "(1) the visual vantage point of the spectator or character, (2) the attitude of a character or a narrator toward projected world events, or (3) the attitude of the films discourse overall" (Plantinga 1997: 98–9). Acknowledging inspiration from Nichols, Plantinga asserts that argument, narration, and the use of rhetoric, together with a rich

Authoritative	Observational	Dramatized	Poetic-reflexive
Epistemic authority	Epistemic openness	Epistemic-hypothetical	Epistemic-aesthetic
Explanation-analysis	Observation-identification	Dramatization of factual reality	Reality seen through aesthetic form
Linearity, causality, rhetorical structure	Episodic, mosaic structure, everyday life	Reconstruction, narration, staging (drama-doc, doc-drama, mockumentary)	Symbolic montage, meta-levels, expressive, subjective form
Q & A, interview, witnesses, experts, Authoritative VO	Actor driven, human-institutional life world	Testing borders between reality and fiction	Form driven reality experience, the poetics of reality, framing reality
Information, critique, propaganda	Documentation of lived reality, social ethnology	Narrative drive, reality driven narrative. Media-reflexivity	Challenging reality concepts and traditional doc-forms

Figure 20.1 Basic modes or prototypes of documentary film as described by Bondebjerg 2014a.

palette of aesthetic and stylistic devices, can be found in different forms in documentary. Plantinga defines three basic voices. These are: *the formal voice* (this voice takes a position of epistemic authority toward the film's projected world and the actual world, making strong assertions about the world); *the open voice* (this voice is more about showing than explaining, exploring and provoking through the image of the world it shows us); and *the poetic voice* ("forgoes the epistemological function of the formal and open voices in favor of aesthetic representation, styling and structuring its subjects") (Plantinga 1997, 175).

In connection with the poetic voice, Plantinga discusses avant-garde nonfiction films, meta-documentaries, documentary parodies and highly reflexive forms of documentary. Neither Nichols nor Plantinga mentions the format docu-drama/drama-doc, a central and in some cases controversial forms of documentary (see e.g. Roscoe and Hight 2001).

In my book *Engaging with Reality. Documentary and Globalization* (2014a) I suggest four basic modes or prototypes of documentary, mostly inspired by Plantinga, but also acknowledging Nichols' work. Individual representations of these four basic modes fit the prototypes to a greater or lesser degree, and elements from one prototype are sometimes combined with elements from other modes, as my cases will demonstrate.

Documentaries and Cosmopolitan Dialogue: The Authoritative, Critical Global Documentary

In 2007 and 2012, the Danish broadcaster DR, the British BBC, and the NGO Steps International commissioned and financed two film and media projects, *Why Democracy?* (2007) and *Why Poverty?* (2012; see Bondebjerg 2016). These two projects are transnational co-productions where filmmakers from different countries were asked to address the issues of democracy and poverty from their individual points of view, in an attempt to produce a more cosmopolitan dialogue than individual global documentaries normally can. In the *Why Democracy* project, ten one-hour documentaries with very different takes on democracy were made by independent filmmakers in Denmark, Bolivia, China, Egypt, India, Japan, Liberia, Pakistan, Russia, and the USA. In the *Why Poverty?* project, eight documentary films and 34 short films were made on issues related to class and power from a national and global perspective.

Why Poverty?'s website describes the aims of the project as being the following:

- To produce narratives that contribute to reflection and broaden people's horizon.
- To involve the best filmmakers in the creation of bold and provocative factual films.
- To bring together broadcasters worldwide and engage with a wide and diverse audience through multiple media platforms.
- To create a global outreach campaign, supplementing the broadcasts.
- To engage with decision-makers and influencers to find solutions for change.

To achieve such ambitious goals, the organization collaborated with broadcasting partners and production companies from many parts of the world, including Al-Rasheed-Iraq, MBC Saudi Arabia, Al-Nahaar TV (Egypt), Namibian NBC, EG Ghana, RTHK Hong Kong, and many European, US, Canadian, and Latin American partners. The aim of this global alliance was to increase the global distribution and funding of the project, but the partners also created a network of newspapers and radio stations around the world to follow up on the films and create a global dialogue locally. The documentary films were launched simultaneously in 180 countries, and were made available on the project's website as well as for download on Vimeo. In parts of the world with poor distribution conditions, special screenings were arranged.

One of the films is Egyptian director Mona Eldaif and American Jehane Noujaim's documentary *Solar Mamas*, which focuses on women from the Arab world and Africa. In the film we follow Rafea, the second wife of her

Bedouin husband, as she is selected for a program to develop her technological skills in solar power and thus a newly independent and sustainable future. The film gives the viewer an insight into her particular form of life and family structure, and her many conflicts with her husband, family, and local community during the project. The film has an observational ethnographic dimension, but also presents an informational, didactic narrative which gives us a critical perspective on what it takes to change things in less developed parts of the world, especially for women. It exemplifies cosmopolitan dialogue and is an exemplary story of change and progress through collaboration (see other film cases analyzed in Bondebjerg 2016). The film is directly connected to the Why Foundation's special initiative *Why Women* (http://thewhy.dk/whywomen/).

It would be naïve to assume that film projects alone can change the world. However, films can perhaps reshape and challenge our global imaginaries and tell us how the world looks from diverse perspectives, and through the eyes of audiences and people in very different parts of the world. In an increasingly globalized world and media, where "the historical tie between nation, culture and citizenship is becoming increasingly decoupled" (Stevenson 2003, 35), there is a need for a new and more global, communicative society. This is exactly the position the Why Foundation and its partners are trying to fill, and it is not surprising that public service broadcasters in the UK and Denmark took this initiative together with NGO partners. Having always had an ethically engaged role in both national and global issues, the BBC and DR seem to embody what the late German sociology professor Ulrich Beck called "cosmopolitan realism" or "cosmopolitan common sense" in order to defend universal norms or a "universalistic minimum" (Beck 2006, 49). Later on the same page, he continues by saying that "realistic cosmopolitanism includes universal procedural norms, for they alone make it possible to regulate the treatment of difference in a cross-cultural manner."

HOLOCAUST IN DOUBLE PERSPECTIVE: JON BANG CARLSEN'S "PURITY BEATS EVERYTHING"

The films of Jon Bang Carlsen, one of the key figures in modern Danish documentary, often describe different places in the world where he has lived (e.g. America, South Africa, Ireland), but often in a reflexive context of home and abroad, of combining global and local memories. He is a poetically reflexive documentary filmmaker, and his films often have a strong subjective dimension:

> I was born five years after the end of the Second World War. The tall chimneys leading the ashes of the victims towards the Northern European sky weren't far away from the thatched farms where I grew up. As the chimneys stopped smoking in 1945, our parents would no longer face

Figure 20.2 Frame grab from Jon Bang Carlsen's autobiographical and poetic documentary *Life Will Be Lived—Letters from a Mother* (*Livet vil leves—breve fra en mor*, Denmark, 1994).

> the Germans . . . Ironically, Scandinavians were Hitler's favorite race and yet we blue eyed children of the fifties grew up hearing nothing about the romantic surge towards "purity." My main character's stories about being categorized as not pure in a time obsessed with purity fills the silence between the farms with pain. The times were different then and yet the times are still the same. The insanity of Adolf Hitler screamed out into the world is still reverberating throughout our present days, and echoes have a dangerous tendency to resurrect, disguised as the future. (Jon Bang Carlsen's voiceover at the beginning of *Purity Beats Everything*, translated for the DVD version)

As this passage from the director's opening voiceover indicates, in *Purity Beats Everything* the memories of holocaust survivors are merged with the director's own childhood memories of growing up in postwar Denmark. Visually, the film shifts between the director's present-day idyllic house in Denmark and South Africa, where the traces of apartheid are still visible, adding to the film's critical questioning of the current rise of nationalism, xenophobia, and the ideology of ethnic purity. History is used to teach us something about current societal tendencies around the world.

Purity Beats Everything is the last of four films, including *Addicted to Solitude* (Denmark, 1999), *Portrait of God* (Denmark, 2001), and *Blinded Angels* (Denmark, 2007), that Jon Bang Carlsen made in South Africa, where he lived with his family for many years. All the films deal with the cultural and social consequences of the apartheid system, which although formally removed is still very much present in people's minds as well as structurally. In his South African films, Jon Bang Carlsen uses the form and aesthetics he himself has called "staged documentary," a form of poetic-reflexive documentary in which he often uses landscapes and symbolic images to evoke mental landscapes of his main characters. He often involves himself, reflecting on how the film is made, and the strategies and considerations he has gone through to make the film (see the interview with Jon Bang Carlsen in Hjort and Bondebjerg 2001, 195ff). As a global documentary filmmaker, Jon Bang Carlsen invests himself in the reality behind his films, embodying the forms of life and realities everywhere in the films.

As global documentaries, Carlsen's films have a critical edge. His films about South Africa deal with race and class conflicts resulting from the terrible system of apartheid that was in place for decades. In *Addicted to Solitude* he portrays the white farmers and their loss of a privileged lifestyle, and their attempts to come to terms with the past and the present, but also the black population who now are at least formally free. His films deal with global and national social issues in a different way from more authoritative or observational critical documentaries. In his work, Carlsen tries to enter more subjective, mental spaces of both black and white people in South Africa. He uses his own encounters with people, and this mental and subjective dimension is present in all frames of the films. His films take the form of subjective, reflexive and poetic studies of social and cultural imaginaries. They become mental and mediated encounters with other parts of the world, seen through highly reflexive, subjective visual and narrative patterns (Bondebjerg 2012, 345f).

Purity Beats Everything exhibits this poetic, subjective, and reflexive documentary style, taking up the rise of Nazism, the Holocaust, apartheid and present-day tendencies of renewed national ethnic ideologies of purity. Speaking from his seemingly idyllic reality in Denmark, he scans history for evidence and experiences of the global phenomenon of xenophobia and ethnic conflict. The interviews with two Holocaust survivors in South Africa, which had just outlawed apartheid, and the director's reflections of his own reality, seem to indicate that the ideology of purity, against cultural and ethnic diversity, is not just a historical phenomenon. It is a global threat that keeps appearing in different forms in many countries around the world. One of the main messages of the film is that we need to look beyond manifest and institutionalized evil to ourselves, and understand how such ideologies can develop out of the lives and minds of seemingly ordinary people. As the director stated in an interview (Movin 2012: 481): "You cannot understand and enter the world and mind of others without projecting it back into your own mind and life. Therefore, in this film [as in all my films] I listen to the stories of my witnesses, and at the same time I look into my own micro cosmos" (my translation). The film only shows a few images from the Holocaust and the camps, instead entering the minds of the survivors and foregrounding the director's own memories and reflections.

Going Undercover in a Global World:
Mads Brügger's Dramatized Documentary *The Ambassador*

Having a background in both film studies and journalism, Mads Brügger has played with fiction and non-fiction throughout most of his film and TV career. He started making television for the main Danish public service broadcaster DR's youth department, known for its satirical play with reality. In one of his DR productions, the drama-doc series *Danes for Bush* (Denmark, 2004), the production team pretended to be a group of Danish George Bush fans. By expertly playing this role, they managed to get behind the scenes of the Republican presidential race. This kind of documentary strategy combines elements of Bill Nichols' interactive and performative modes. Brügger's films tend to involve intense interaction between the filmmaker and the characters, and an expressive and direct engagement in the represented reality (Nichols, 2001, 34). This style could also be described as dramatized documentary, in the sense that this format blurs the line between fiction and reality, and uses staging and role-playing to enter certain realities.

Entering closed worlds and institutions is a key issue in Brügger's films and TV series. In the documentary film *The Red Chapel* (Denmark, 2006), he uses two Danish comedians of Korean background to enter North Korea under the pretense of wanting to develop cultural cooperation and set up a Danish–North Korean TV show in Pyongyang. Although the film team worked under the rather restricted control of North Korean officials, the film nevertheless gives a unique insight into one of the most controlled societies in the world. In his next film *The Ambassador* (2011), Brügger played the completely fictional character Cortzen. With a fake diplomatic visa and the fake expressed intent of starting a match factory in Congo, he manages to get inside a circle of corrupt politicians and diplomats earning money from the illegal and secret sale of diamonds on the international market. Many of the scenes are shot with hidden cameras and the film portrays a critical image of a very corrupt African country run by white and black criminals. The strategy of dramatization used in this case seems to be the only feasible way for him to expose these hidden global structures of exploitation and corruption.

The Narratives, Fictions, and Fantasies We Tell About Ourselves:
The Films of Joshua Oppenheimer

The American documentary film director Joshua Oppenheimer also has a critical and activist agenda with his filmmaking. His films take the form of observational documentaries which employ strong reflexive and visual strategies inspired by the French *cinema verité*, and in particular Jean Rouch's way of involving subjects and creating a reflexive dimension while filming.

Oppenheimer's three films about Indonesia mobilize a critical approach to global issues: *The Globalization Tapes* (Indonesia, 2003), *The Act of Killing* (Denmark, 2012), and *The Look of Silence* (Denmark, 2014). The *critical globalization documentary* has many variations, and Oppenheimer's modus operandi has roots in the observational mode (Nichols, 1991; Bondebjerg, 2014a). His frequent use of re-enactment allows his subjects to play active roles in the filmmaking process. In *The Globalization Tapes*, a film about Indonesian plantation workers and their fight against global companies, Oppenheimer and his co-director Christine Cynn are only credited as producers, and the original film poster refers to it as "a film by workers, for workers." However, the way in which the directors lend the camera to their film subjects is quite different from in *The Act of Killing*, where perpetrators of the Indonesian holocaust re-enact their deeds in colorful skits. Oppenheimer's rather radical form of genocide documentary has divided critics and audiences, but key documentary film scholars have defended his method and approach (Nichols 2013; Bruzzi 2015; Nagib 2016), along with filmmakers like Werner Herzog and Errol Morris (Morris 2013). Both fervent admirers and detractors of *The Act of Killing* worldwide "would, however, agree that the film opens up uncharted territory on which to recast the tenets of documentary, world cinema and filmmaking in general" (Nagib 2016).

Oppenheimer has a universal moral agenda with his films, even though they deal with particular historical events and their contemporary aftermath. In an interview with the Danish newspaper *Politiken*, Oppenheimer addresses the question of a universal sense of morality, but also our tendency to run away from it or our inability to face the consequences of immoral and evil acts (Navne 2017). Even though humans have a universal moral compass, we often hide behind or live in different realities:

> There is no common experience of reality. We know our reality through the narratives, fictions and fantasies we tell about ourselves. And it is not always original stories, we construct by thinking deeply about the truth. They are often borrowed from television, social media and advertising: unconsciously—or just partly unconsciously. (Oppenheimer in Navne 2017, my translation)

With *The Act of Killing* and *The Look of Silence*, Oppenheimer is clearly on a mission to raise global moral consciousness about the Indonesian genocide of the 1960s, something Indonesia's ruling regime and the perpetrators still do not regret. Key to this project is the attempt to understand how people can do something like this and live with it, and even tell celebratory stories about what they did. Oppenheimer wants to get into the imaginations and minds of the perpetrators and their victims in order to inform us about how we use imagination and narratives to defend or negate what we have done. The innovative and shocking element in Oppenheimer's film is the extreme use of re-enactment orchestrated by the perpetrators themselves. As Nichols notes, the film deprives the spectator of the moral compass we find in other films like this provided by a dominant voiceover: "Oppenheimer's distinctive voice remains deeply but not entirely submerged beneath the visions and voices of his social actors ... the spectators must journey through a topsy-turvy landscape that redefines their grasp of historical reality and the sense of self that it sustains" (2013, 29).

What may seem to be a critique of the film is actually a statement of the film's ultimate originality and strength, as seen by Nichols. Others have supported this view, including Lucia Nagib (2016), who talks about the film's

> ethics of realism—[which] means in the first place a rejection of simplistic dualisms which place criminals as radical others to human beings, positioning instead filmmakers and film subjects as stakeholders in the same humanity capable of causing catastrophe as well as regeneration. (Nagib 2016, 218)

Stella Bruzzi has taken up the same point (Bruzzi 2015) from a different perspective, noting that Oppenheimer's strategy of re-enactment might function as an emotional wake-up call by letting audiences relive very painful past events or memories, including letting perpetrators relive their own evil deeds, despite their taking a heroic position. She writes:

> I would like to suggest here that it is extremely difficult, if not impossible, not to feel and relive the emotions and pain of a past trauma if what we are watching is a re-enactment, for as an event is being re-enacted, it appears to us as if in the present, as if incomplete and ongoing. We, its spectators, assume the place of the trauma's original audience. Re-enactments offer an especially emotionally charged form of déjà vu, an uncanny repetition or restaging of a historical action; even if it is not already familiar to those watching, it is summoning up events from the past into the present—and it is this temporal duality, this co-existence of past and present that renders it powerful. (Bruzzi 2015, 89ff)

Oppenheimer's films are about the darker sides of our global reality: oppression, genocide, exploitation of countries by global firms—just to mention a few things. At the same time they are about our shared universal moral norms, the human rights charter we try to uphold and how we stage our own imaginary reality. It is about how we seek to protect ourselves from the unbearable parts of the reality we live in and with. The message of the films is that we all have a global obligation to act against injustice in other parts of the world, but also that the line between the worst immoral acts and being a moral, just person is not unequivocal. In an interview with Oppenheimer in *Sight & Sound* (Bradshaw 2017), he pays homage to Jean Rouch as a filmmaker who "understood that every time you film anybody you're creating a reality with that person," continuing:

> I think in *cinema verité* [*sic*]... it was all about giving people the space to perform on camera, to imagine, to stage themselves on camera as a way of documenting how they see themselves and make sense of their world. In that sense I think *cinema verité* is trying to do something fundamentally more profound than Direct Cinema. I think Direct Cinema's trying to be insightful by looking at reality in a very close way, while in fact much more is staged than we like to think. In *cinema verité* it's about trying to make something invisible visible—the role of fantasy and imagination in everyday life. (Oppenheimer in Bradshaw 2017)

Oppenheimer originally wanted to tell the story of the victims, and he spent time with and talked to many of the survivors and their families. It turned out to be too difficult and dangerous to make a film about the survivors inside Indonesia, however, and it was the survivors who suggested to him that he should talk to the perpetrators, who were openly boasting about their past murders. Oppenheimer's interest in how people remember and how imagination plays a crucial role took a surreal and grotesque turn. The perpetrators were fascinated by Hollywood movies, and it turned out that one of the best ways to visualize their fantasies of the past and their glorification of genocide was to re-stage their acts and images of themselves in the form of musicals, gangster movies or other classical genres. The perpetrators even indicated that such movies had inspired their killings. Oppenheimer's intention was to provoke and challenge their understandings of what they had done, and their own imagination of themselves. Such a strategy also serves as a provocation for audiences. The fact that the imaginations of these perpetrators coincide with Hollywood imagery and genres brings these events scarily close to our own reality and media, because of the fact that Hollywood narratives are so pervasive in most parts of the world.

Although *The Act of Killing* and *The Look of Silence* are two sides of the same story, they are also radically different. *The Act of Killing* opens the door to an almost incredible world of evil by letting the perpetrators stage their own perverted fantasies as heroes in the official public of the present-day regime. In *The Look of Silence* we follow relatives of victims as they try to come to terms with the haunting image of the past and the perpetrators living among them. The main character, an optometrist by the name of Adi Rukun, whose

Figure 20.3 Frame grab from Joshua Oppenheimer's *Look of Silence* (Denmark, 2014).

brother was killed in the genocide, watches clips of the perpetrators from Oppenheimer's film or American news footage of the Indonesian genocide. Alongside this confrontation with the past, he asks his customers who are former perpetrators or victim's family members about the past. The film thus becomes a film about the victims that also confronts two different narratives about the past. The meeting between perpetrators and victims is in focus, and we get a strong feeling of what it means today that they are living side by side, that indoctrination and lies go on in the schools and in public media. Although the perpetrators speak openly about what they did, the full memory of what really happened and of the victims is buried by silence and negation.

In *The Look of Silence*, the thin wall between normality and madness becomes even more obvious through the seemingly "normal" everyday reality presented in this film. Unlike the gruesome perpetrator images in *The Act of Killing*, this film shows a reality where perpetrators and victims live side by side, although haunted by the past. But the images of the thin line between humanity, morality, and evil become almost tangible as the re-enactments of the perpetrators are played again and again. As Adi calmly and coolly intensifies his questioning of the former perpetrators—while taking care of their eye problems—this continuum from normality and everyday life to the surreal world of mass killings is spelled out loudly, despite the quiet style of the film. The sequences of children at home and at school also strongly contribute to the unmasking of the minds and memories of the perpetrators. That survivors and their family are still living with the guilty perpetrators as if nothing had happened reveals an almost surreal capacity of people to live with atrocities and without any clear remorse. In many ways, the film demonstrates why such documentaries are more important than ever. A documentary can make us reflect on moral issues outside our own national context, and thus discover the resemblance to moral issues in our own local and national reality. As Oppenheimer himself has said:

> Cinema has long shaped not only how political violence, from torture to warfare to genocide, is perceived, but also how it is performed. Today, when media coverage is central to terror campaigns, and newscasters serve as embedded journalists in the "war on terror'"s televisual front, understanding how the moving image is implicated in the imagination and actions of perpetrators and survivors of mass violence is all the more urgent. (Brink and Oppenheimer 2012, 1)

GLOBAL DOCUMENTARIES AND TRANSNATIONAL CREATIVE COLLABORATION: CONCLUSION

The documentary films with a global agenda analyzed here show the formal and aesthetic diversity of this type of documentary. The *Why Democracy* and *Why Poverty* projects represent the most authoritative position, and an activist intention of reaching a wide global audience and creating a dialogue for change. They do so via a multi-platform strategy (see Bondebjerg 2014c, 2016) using cinema, television, newspapers, and the Internet. While this is probably true for many documentary films, the forms and strategies vary. Jon Bang Carlsen addresses global issues, but he speaks with a more subjective and poetically reflexive voice, bringing us closer to people than issues as such. Mads Brügger is an activist and journalist with a critical, global message about authoritarian and corrupt regimes around the world, and he uses dramatized and staged strategies to get access to such regimes and to those in power and control. The films of Joshua Oppenheimer are unique examples of the globalization of documentaries produced in Denmark. He has fundamentally challenged the established forms of holocaust movies and transformed the way re-enactment can be used in observational films. His films have been extensively screened on the international film festival circuit (more than 225 times by 2017), and the international prizes he has received number more than fifty-five. The international reach of *The Act of Killing* and *The Look of Silence* exceeds that of the average Danish documentary, although Danish documentaries about global issues have generally increased their international reach and success since the 1990s.

An important factor behind this global reach is the transnational creative collaboration in the making of these documentaries. Oppenheimer's primary production company was the Danish company Final Cut for Real (FCR), and both films were made through an international network of production companies, private and public financial partners, and distributors. This is also the case with other film directors in this global wave. The core creative production companies behind most of these films are Scandinavian or European, including the Nordic Film & TV Fund and the European MEDIA Program, and European and Scandinavian public service broadcasters.

Signe Byrge Sørensen from Final Cut For Real (Sørensen 2017) explains that the development of co-production in Scandinavia and Europe actually started 25 years ago when the International Documentary Film Festival Amsterdam (IDFA) initiated the IDFA Forum. This systematically concentrated the way in which producers from Europe and elsewhere interacted with broadcasters and other funding bodies, creating a network of pitching films and establishing creative, international alliances. The format has now spread to almost all important film festivals.

The films analyzed in this article exemplify the two terms I introduced earlier in the article to describe the potential role of such documentaries for *mediated global cultural encounters* (Bondebjerg et al. 2017) and the creation of a *cosmopolitan dialogue*. Global documentaries are not just about the world out there, but are very much about our own world and how it is linked to a greater context, and about how the global is becoming a significant part of Scandinavian and European culture. Documentaries dealing with today's multicultural reality are high on the documentary agenda in Scandinavia now (see Bondebjerg 2014a, 197f; Bondebjerg and Bondebjerg 2017).

REFERENCES

Aitken, Ian. 1990. *Film and Reform. John Grierson and the Documentary Film Movement*. London: Routledge.

Anderson, Benedict. 1983. *Imagined Communities. Reflections on the Origin and Rise of Nationalism*, London: Verso.

Appadurai, Arjun.1996. *Modernity at Large: Cultural Dimensions of Globalization*, Minneapolis: University of Minnesota Press.

Barnouw, Eric [1974] 1993. *Documentary. A History of the Non-fiction Film*. Oxford: Oxford University Press.

Beck, Ulrich. 2006. *Cosmopolitan Vision*. London: Polity.

Bondebjerg, Ib. 2012. *Virkelighedsbilleder. Den moderne danske dokumentarfilm* [Images of Reality. Modern Danish Documentary Film]. Frederiksberg: Samfundslitteratur.

Bondebjerg, Ib. 2014a. *Engaging with Reality. Documentary and Globalization*. Chicago: Chicago University Press/Bristol: Intellect.

Bondebjerg, Ib. 2014b. "A Social Poetics of Documentary: Grierson and the Scandinavian Documentary Tradition." In *The Grierson Effect. Tracing Documentary's International Movement*, ed. Z. Druick and D. Williams. London: BFI. 79–93.

Bondebjerg, Ib. 2014c. "Cosmopolitan narratives, documentary and the global 'Other'." In *Defending Democracy. Nordic and Global Diversities in Media and*

Journalism, ed. H. Hornmoen and K. S. Orgeret. Special issue of *Nordicom Review* 35: 53–67.
Bondebjerg, Ib. 2016. "Documentary, Multi-platform Production, and Cosmopolitan Dialogues." In *Contemporary Documentary*, ed. D. Marcus and S. Kara. London: Routledge. 171–87.
Bondebjerg, Ib and Bondebjerg, Ulla. 2017. *Dansk film og kulturel globalisering* [Danish film and cultural globalization]. Frederiksberg: Samfundslitteratur.
Bondebjerg, Ib, Cecilie Astrupgaard, Rasmus Helles, Signe S. Lai, Eva Novrup Redvall, and Henrik Søndergaard. 2017. *Transnational European Television Drama: Production, Genres and Audiences*. Basingstoke: Palgrave Macmillan.
Bradshaw, Nick. 2017. "Build my gallows high: Joshua Oppenheimer on The Act of Killing." In *Sight and Sound*. <http://www.bfi.org.uk/news-opinion/sight-sound-magazine/interviews/build-my-gallows-high-joshua-oppenheimer-act-killing> (last accessed December 13, 2017).
Brink, Joram T. and Joshua Oppenheimer. 2012, eds, *Killer Images. Documentary Film, Memory and the Performance of Violence*. New York: Wallflower Press.
Bruzzi, Stella, 2015. "Re-enacting Trauma in Film and Television: Restaging History, Revisiting Pain." In *Therapy and Emotions in Film and Television*, ed. C. Wassmann. Basingstoke: Palgrave Macmillan. 89–99.
Christensen, Theodor, 1938. "Documentary—Hvad er det?," reprinted in *Theodor Christensen. En handling i billeder*, ed. John Ernst. København: Rhodos. 7–82.
Ellis, Jack C. and McLane, Betsy A. 2006. *A New History of Documentary Film*. New York: Continuum.
Held, Davis, McGrew, Anthony, Goldblatt, David, and Jonathan Perraton, 1999. *Global Transformations: Politics, Economics and Culture*. Stanford: Stanford University Press.
Hjort, Mette and Bondebjerg, Ib, eds. 2001. *The Danish Directors: Dialogues on a Contemporary National Cinema*. Bristol: Intellect.
Morley, David. 2000. *Home Territories. Media, Mobility and Identity*. London: Routledge.
Morley, David and Kevin Robins. 1995. *Spaces of Identity. Global Media, Electronic Landscapes and Cultural Boundaries*. London: Routledge.
Morris, Errol. 2013. "The Murders of Gonzago." *Slate*, July 10.
Movin, Lars. 2012. *Jeg ville først finde sandheden. Rejser med Jon Bang Carlsen*. København: Informations forlag.
Nagib, Lucia. 2016. "Regurgitated Bodies: Re-enactment as the Production of reality in *The Act of Killing*." In *The Routledge Companion to Film and Politics*, ed. Y. Tziomiakiss and C. Molloy. London: Routledge. 218–30.
Navne, Helene. 2017. "They Changed Reality in Order to Be Able to Live with Themselves." *Politiken*, July 5.
Nichols, Bill. 1991. *Representing Reality. Issues and Concepts in Documentary*, Bloomington; Indianapolis: Indiana University Press.
Nichols, Bill. 2001. *Introduction to Documentary*, Bloomington; Indianapolis: Indiana University Press.
Nichols, Bill. 2013. "Irony, cruelty and a wink in *The Act of Killing*." *Film Quarterly*, 67(2): 25–9.
Plantinga, Carl. 1997. *Rhetoric and Representation in Non-fiction Film*. Cambridge: Cambridge University Press.
Roscoe, Jane and Craig Height. 2001. *Mock-documentary and the Subversion of Factuality*. Manchester: Manchester University Press.
Stevenson, Nick. 2003. *Cultural Citizenship: Cosmopolitan Questions*. Maidenhead: Open University Press.

Sørensen, Signe Byrge. 2017. "Interview by Ib Bondebjerg, Final Cut for Real," November 27. Unpublished.
Taylor, Charles. 2004. *Modern Social Imaginaries*. Durham, NC; London: Duke University Press.
Zerubavel, Eviatar. 1997. *Social Mindscapes. An Invitation to Cognitive Sociology*, Cambridge, MA: Harvard University Press.

21. ELSEWHERES OF HEALING: TRANS-INDIGENOUS SPACES IN ELLE-MÁIJÁ APINISKIM TAILFEATHERS' *BIHTTOŠ*

Troy Storfjell (Sámi)

The short film *Bihttoš* (*Rebel*, Canada and Norway, 2014), by the Sámi and Kainai Blackfoot filmmaker Elle-Máijá Apiniskim Tailfeathers, is a cinematic invocation of multiple elsewheres. Set in the three settler states of Norway, the USA, and Canada, this film is not about those states. Instead, it narrates an Indigenous story situated elsewhere from the spheres of mainstream, settler culture that are often the presumed standards. In this sense, *Bihttoš* is not so much Canadian and Norwegian as it is Sámi and Kainai/First Nations—or, indeed, trans-Indigenous. The film's vision is divided between one colonized Indigenous space (the Blood Reserve) and a parallel but distinct experience of colonialism elsewhere (Sápmi), and the experimental documentary traces the ways in which these geographically disparate experiences inscribe themselves on the same individual: the Sámi/Blackfoot "Elle-Máijá." There are more elsewheres as well, elsewheres of language, of cinematic influence and context, and even of audience. And, although the themes of the film resonate with Sámi audiences, and are even treated by other Sámi films, *Bihttoš* emerges in direct dialogue not with them, but rather with First Nation films, especially *Suckerfish* (Lisa Jackson, Canada, 2004). Ultimately the strategic use of these many elsewheres, coupled with innovative use of lighting and experimental documentary techniques, results in a film that is eloquently trans-Indigenous, exploring the wounds of colonization while maintaining its focus on the agency and resilience of the colonized, instead of foregrounding the power of the colonizer.

Through a mixture of animation, archival photos, re-enacted scenes and some home video footage (see MacKenzie and Stenport 2016 for a fuller treatment of the film's experimental technical features), Tailfeathers uses *Bihttoš* to tell the story of her parents' marriage and divorce against the backdrop of a growing global Indigenous rights movement, and of Elle-Máijá's own journey toward understanding her father. It is a film about trauma and pain, but also about understanding, forgiveness, and triumph. Among other things, it is also very much a film honoring her father ("Áhčči"), Bjarne Store-Jakobsen, also known as Bihttoš Bierna (Rebel Bjarne) for his important leadership in the Sámi rights movement at a critical juncture in the late 1970s and early 1980s, at a time when the challenge brought by Indigenous activists on the Norwegian side to state plans for a large and disruptive hydroelectric plant on Guovdageaineadnu (the Kautokeino River) in Finnmárku was catalyzing a larger and longer-lasting process of decolonization.

Storytelling: Shedding Light on a Dark Place

The film opens with a close-up of feet in running shoes, lit as if by flashlight on an otherwise dark screen. They begin to run in slow motion, and the camera tracks right following them. A voiceover in North Sámi (by Tailfeathers) tells us that "When I was sixteen, my dad tried to kill himself." As the camera slowly zooms out to a full shot, following a dimly-lit teenage girl running through the dark, the voiceover continues, still in North Sámi: "How did we come to this dark place? Why couldn't our love guide us through the darkness?" Fade to black.

Throughout the rest of the film, lighting places a centrally important role. The first section, following the title screen, is a playfully animated sequence of viewfinder shots in which a North Sámi voiceover by Elle-Máijá as a young girl (performed by Máret Áile Gaup Beaska) tells the fairy-tale-like story of her parents meeting at a global Indigenous conference in Australia in 1981, and of their subsequent marriage. Archival family photos, animated in 2.5D, go on to illustrate Elle-Máijá's happy childhood in Sápmi, while pleasant music continues, punctuated by the sound of the viewfinder continuing to move from slide to slide, until the music abruptly turns ominous as the film makes a sudden switch to a largely dark screen and live action shots of Elle-Máijá as a teenager (played by Laura Wilson). An English-language voiceover tells of the family's move to North Dakota, where Elle-Máijá's mother had begun to study medicine. The interspersed archival photographs are well-lit, but the live action sequences, featuring Elle-Máijá, her Kainai mother Esther Tailfeathers (Mariel Belanger), and her father (Duncan Ollerenshaw), are all largely dark, with a dim spotlight on the actors. This visual contrast serves to build a tense sense of foreboding as the story moves through Áhčči's depression and on

Figure 21.1   Elle-Máijá Alpinskin Tailfeather's *Bihttoš* (2014) introduces Elle-Máijá's mother in an animated scene.

to the point where Elle-Máijá's mother decides to leave him after the family moves to Canada.

This is the point where the emotional nadir of the movie begins, showing us Áhčči's despair and his inconsolable binge drinking, and telling of his attempt to take his own life. The scenes in this portion of the film are very darkly lit, the visual murkiness underscoring the emotional tone while the directed lighting highlights the face or faces of the actors, drawing our attention to their pain. Finally, we hear the voice of Áhčči (performed by Ánde Somby) reading a Christmas card he had written to Elle-Máijá before he left his family and returned to Norway. Fade to black. Happier music and ample lighting mark a decided change in the next section, narrating Elle-Máijá's return to Sápmi as a twenty-five-year-old, and her reconnection and reconciliation with her father. In these scenes Elle-Máijá (played by Tailfeathers herself) and Áhčči (still played by Ollerenshaw) enjoy a road trip together, spending time at the Riddu Riđđu Indigenous Music Festival in Gáivuotna, sharing snacks in the car, and stopping to take in the dramatically beautiful, fjord-lined coastal scenery. Not only does Elle-Máijá gain a new appreciation of the importance her father holds for other Sámi in these brightly lit scenes, she also discovers a key to understanding his "dark place." During a shot of the old boarding school in Unjárga, cleverly shot through a car window so that Elle-Máijá's own reflection can be seen faintly superimposed over the image of the school, Tailfeathers' English-language voiceover tells us that "He opened up to me about a part of his childhood that he rarely spoke of—his time at boarding school. I heard things I wasn't prepared to hear, but for once, my childhood of Áhčči's ups and downs made sense."

The Sámi boarding schools, which were part of the colonial Norwegianization project of the nineteenth and twentieth centuries, are a topic frequently touched on in Sámi stories, featuring literary texts by such authors as Jovvna-Ánde Vest (1997), Kirsti Paltto (1971), and Aagot Vinterbo-Hohr (1987), and treated by such documentaries as Ellen-Astri Lundby's *Suddenly Sámi* (*Min Mors Hemmelighet*, Norway, 2009), the Norwegian National Broadcasting (NRK) television documentaries *Backlash: Tromsø and the Five Techniques of Domination* (*Tilbakeslaget: Tromsø og de fem hersketeknikkene*, Pål Hansen, 2012), *The Silent Struggle* (*Den stille kampen*, Rita Enstad-Karlsen and Tor Segelcke, 2013), and, more recently, in Amanda Kernell's 2016 *Sameblod* (*Sámi Blood*, Sweden). Yet Elle-Máijá's time in the USA and Canada has kept her isolated from that discourse, which means that it takes her father's revelation to bring the significance of that history for her own family to light.

Lighting functions as a visual metaphor for the healing change in Elle-Máijá's relationship with her father as the film comes to an end. The voiceover continues, as Elle-Máijá and Áhčči sit in dark silhouette in front of a seascape lit from behind by the low midnight sun. "I've witnessed the lasting and often painful impacts of the Indian residential school system on my Blackfoot family and community. But I had completely underestimated the damage that the Sámi boarding school system had on my father and our family." In contrast to

Figure 21.2   Elle-Máijá and Áhčči open up to each other, as the sun moves toward its destination between them in the concluding sequence of Tailfeather's *Bihttoš* (2014).

many of the earlier shots, the two people are dark and everything around them is light. The voiceover continues: "It was like someone had turned the lights on. I finally understood why his spirit was never at ease, and why he found true purpose fighting for the Sámi people. You see, it was a fight he could take out in the open, his own public cry for justice." The camera tracks left, and the sun appears to move between the two figures. Visually and metaphorically everything between them has been brought out into the light, and the trans-Indigenous perspective afforded to Elle-Máijá by her Kainai Blackfoot family leads to understanding and healing for her and her Sámi family.

Trans-Indigenous Juxtapositions

Bihttoš was part of the Embargo Collective II project, commissioned by the imagineNATIVE Film and Media Arts Festival in 2013. Seven Indigenous women filmmakers, inspired by the "creativity under constraints" of Lars Von Trier's film *The Five Obstructions* (*De fem benspænd*, Denmark, 2003), assigned a set of obstructions to each other while challenging each filmmaker to make a film in the style of one of the other participants. Tailfeathers was tasked with making a film in the style of Lisa Jackson (Anishinaabe), whose 2004 documentary *Suckerfish*, about the complex relationship between Jackson and her mother, had made a significant impression on Tailfeathers (Tailfeathers 2016, 278). All together, the obstructions assigned to Tailfeathers were:

1. The story had to be personal.
2. The film had to be inspired by Lisa Jackson's work and made in her style.
3. It had to have professional sound.
4. She had to use actual film.
5. The director had to operate the camera for at least some of the filming. (Tailfeathers 2018)

The transnational production of *Bihttoš*, and the international setting of the story it tells, only serve to highlight the trans-Indigenous space the film invokes. This Sámi story—about a well-known and respected Sámi activist and leader, and about the traumas inflicted by the boarding schools central to the colonial project of Norwegianization—emerges in a Canadian First Nations cinematic frame of reference. Embargo II is a First Nations endeavor, and *Suckerfish* is a First Nations film. Yet *Bihttoš* was partly funded by the International Sámi Film Institute (ISFI), based in Guovdageaidnu, and was included as one of seventeen Sámi short films on the BluRay collection *Sami Short Films* released by ISFI and the Norwegian Film Institute in 2015. One of its two spoken languages is North Sámi, used in the film's opening, in Beaska's voiceover performance as the young Elle-Máijá, and in Tailfeathers' voiceover just before the credits roll.

Staging a Sámi film within a Canadian First Nations framework foregrounds the ways in which Indigenous spaces operate as distinct elsewheres to settler majority spaces. When Elle-Máijá becomes aware of the parallels between the Indian residential school experiences of her mother's family and the Sámi boarding school experiences of her father, she is giving voice to a trans-Indigenous perspective. Chadwick Allen describes trans-Indigenous approaches as *"purposeful* Indigenous juxtapositions" (Allen 2012, xviii, original emphasis) that move past the comparative to view one Indigenous text or situation through the lens of another, to "provoke readings *across* various categories [to] enable interpretations of a broad range of texts and practices" (Allen 2012, xviii, original emphasis). Juxtaposing Sámi and Kainai Blackfoot (and more broadly, Canadian First Nations) experiences of the traumas of colonial residential and boarding schools serves to make the Sámi experience of Tailfeathers' father more understandable for her and her First Nation viewers, as well as for Indigenous viewers from the USA, Australia, and other Indigenous places with similar histories of colonial schooling. This is extremely important in bringing Elle-Máijá to the point where she can forgive both her father, for his emotional ups and downs, and her mother, for not being able to live with her father. It enables her to process the intergenerational, historical trauma so that she and her family can move into a healing space. The significance of this is not likely to be lost on Sámi or other Indigenous audiences, for whom the idea of moving into a healing space of understanding and forgiveness regarding intergenerational trauma may also be relevant.

But juxtaposing Sámi and First Nations experiences of colonial schooling also serves to help Sámi viewers make more sense of their own familial traumas. By highlighting similarities between what happened in Norway and what happened in Canada, *Bihttoš* helps Sámi viewers on the Norwegian side to put their own histories into a larger trans-Indigenous context. What happened to Indigenous people in Canada also happened to Indigenous people in Norway. And perhaps that recognition can help Norwegian Sámi to begin a process of healing too.

Interestingly enough, exactly what happened to Áhčči at the boarding school is one of the things Tailfeathers is routinely asked by settler audience members at film screenings. Sometimes questioners will persist in asking, even after she has given several diplomatic answers as to why it is better that the film does not go into explicit detail (Tailfeathers 2016, 282). Settlers' privilege includes, apparently, an assumption that personal privacy is something that need not interfere with their consumption of stories of Indigenous suffering. In contrast, Tailfeathers notes that "The Indigenous audience . . . has been really generous. They want to share their stories with me. After it opened at imagineNATIVE,

I got so many emails from people who told me they really identified with the story, that it resonated with them" (ibid.).

The differences in Indigenous and settler receptions illustrate the different spaces these two audiences occupy. And they show just how effective a transnational approach like this can be in articulating a trans-Indigenous elsewhere in which Sámi and First Nations viewers find more commonality in each other's viewings than between their viewings and those of their respective settler compatriots. This shared elsewhere of trans-Indigenous viewership, in turn, can illustrate the need for an elsewhere of critical visual sovereignty, a revision of Michelle Raheja's influential term (Raheja 2015) that amends it to indicate a space in which Indigenous critics and other viewers can interpret Indigenous films and other texts for themselves and their communities, without the expectation that they should relate everything they write to the colonial center of the settler state. Like Kernell's more recent *Sameblod*, *Bihttoš* screens stories that resonate with Sámi and other Indigenous audiences because of the experiences they share with its protagonist, while challenging settler audiences with the interweaving of the personal and the political in Indigenous lives.

Concluding: Love and Healing

In its love and understanding for Áhčči, and its celebration of his resilience and refusal to portray him only as victim, *Bihttoš* echoes *Suckerfish*'s compassionate exploration of its filmmaker's mother as not reducible to the role of broken Indian, as transcending her alcoholism to maintain her personhood (Tailfeathers 2016, 280). And in its use of experimental documentary techniques, *Bihttoš* expresses the ways in which Indigenous stories occupy an elsewhere distinct from the authoritative, patriarchal voice of traditional settler documentary. It is a therapeutic ceremony of Indigenous storywork (Archibald 2008, 15) that avoids the mistake of seeking to legitimize itself through colonial rubrics.

As the credits begin to roll, Áhčči/Bihttoš-Bierna/Bjarne Store-Jakobsen's presence is invoked as Ánde Somby performs his joik, the musical patterns and lyrics embodying his personhood and making this an integral part of the film, at least for a Sámi audience. The film *Bihttoš* is a tribute to Store-Jakobsen, but also to all of us who find ourselves enmeshed in colonial webs of historical trauma. It is a film about surviving and thriving despite the trauma, of moving through it to healing. And, for Indigenous audiences, for whom relating to intergenerational trauma caused by colonization is seldom a stretch, healing may be the best eleswhere. This is a film about that, for us.

References

Allen, Chadwick. 2012. *Trans-Indigenous: Methodologies for Global Native Literary Studies*. Minneapolis: University of Minnesota Press.
Archibald, Jo-ann/Q'um Q'um Xiiem. 2008. *Indigenous Storywork: Educating the Heart, Mind, Body, and Spirit*. Vancouver: University of British Columbia Press.
MacKenzie, Scott and Anna Westerstahl Stenport. 2016. "Contemporary experimental feminist Sámi documentary: the first person politics of Liselotte Wajstedt and Elle-Máijá Tailfeathers." *Journal of Scandinavian Cinema* 6 (2): 169–82.
Paltto, Kirsti. 1971. *Soagŋu*. Helsinki: Sámi cuvgetussearvvi doaimmatusat.
Raheja, Michelle H. 2015. "Visual Sovereignty." In *Native Studies Keywords*, ed. Stephanie Nohelani Teves, Andrea Smith, and Michelle H. Raheja. Tucson: University of Arizona Press. 25–34.
Tailfeathers, Elle-Máijá Apiniskim. 2016. "A Conversation with Helen Haig-Brown, Lisa Jackson, and Elle-Máijá Apiniskim Tailfeathers, with some thoughts to frame the conversation." *Biography* 39(3) (Summer): 277–306.
Tailfeathers, Elle-Máijá Apiniskim. 2018. Personal communication with chapter author.
Vest, Jovnna-Ánde. 1997. *Árbbolaččat*. Kárášjohka: Davvi Girji.
Vinterbo-Hohr, Aagot. 1987. *Palimpsest*. Kárášjohka: Davvi Media.

22. DENMARK BEYOND DENMARK: SOFT POWER, TALENT DEVELOPMENT, AND FILMMAKING IN THE MIDDLE EAST

Mette Hjort

In 1973, a manifesto outlining six objectives announced the creation of the Palestinian Cinema Association, which described itself as "an integral part of the institutions of the Palestinian revolution" (PCA 2014, 275). With an office at the Research Center of the Palestinian Liberation Organization, the PCA charted a new path for Arab cinema, one that would eschew stereotypical representations, moving images as a vehicle for facile entertainment, and "subjects having no connection to reality or dealing with it in a superficial manner" (PCA 2014, 273–4). Aspiring to replace Arab filmmaking that was "poorly developed" in terms of "content" and "always inadequate" in terms of form (PCA 2014, 274), the PCA called for the development of a "Palestinian cinema capable of supporting with dignity the struggle of our people, revealing the actual facts of our situation and describing the stages of our Arab and Palestinian struggle to liberate our land" (PCA 2014, 274). Last among the six objectives was a call for collaboration on a global basis. The aim, more specifically, was to "strengthen relations with revolutionary and progressive cinema groups throughout the world, participate in film festivals in the name of Palestine and facilitate work of all friendly groups working toward the realization of the objectives of the Palestinian revolution" (PCA 2014, 274).

Some forty-five years later, it is worth revisiting the aspirations of the PCA, including, especially, the evocation of a world-spanning network of supportive practitioners. The point here is not to chart the history of the PCA's affiliations over a period of many years, but to create a context for considering the goals, challenges, and contributions of Denmark's involvement in film-related institution building in the Middle East from around 2005 to the present. Denmark's contributions to filmmaking are typically discussed in terms of a range of questions having to do with the development of a successful national cinema, especially in a context marked by the constraints and opportunities of small nationhood (Hjort 2005). The role played by institution building, policymaking, and talent development is well recognized in this respect, yet what has been entirely overlooked is the extent to which Danish players have sought out opportunities to engage in similar undertakings beyond the borders of Denmark. Danish institutions, in short, are not just in the business of creating the conditions for a thriving national cinema but are also engaged in practices that have clear implications for the dynamics of world cinema and for the possibility of authentic expression on the part of marginalized groups.

The primary focus here is on two regionally-oriented institutions devoted to the development of professional film talent and a tradition for independent documentary filmmaking in the Middle East: the Arab Institute of Film (AIF) in Amman, Jordan (2006–8), and its successor institution, Screen Institute Beirut (SIB) in Lebanon (2009–). Reference will also be made to Denmark's most recent commitment to institution building in the region, namely FilmLab Palestine (2014–), in Ramallah, the capital of the Palestinian National Authority. The chapter builds on the author's personal involvement with FilmLab Palestine (during her time as a member of the Board of the Danish Film Institute) and on practitioner interviews with a significant number of program directors, policymakers, funders, and filmmakers.

With funding for the three initiatives identified above being sourced from the Danish state, Denmark's commitments to developing film cultures in the Middle East certainly raise political issues, but in a way that deviates from the PCA's stated aim of realizing "the objectives of the Palestinian revolution." Established in 2003, the Danish Arab Partnership Programme that underwrites Denmark's film-related initiatives in the Middle East is "a central pillar in Danish foreign policy in relation to the MENA-region." A central aim of the program is to support "processes of political reform and democratization" and to enhance "dialogue between Denmark and the Arab world." The policy document emphasizes the empowering of women, the strengthening of human rights, and enhanced freedom of expression. It also expresses a commitment to working within "areas of mutual interest" and to strengthening "Denmark's ties with the MENA-region" (DANIDA 2013, 3).

The thought that Denmark's film-related presence in the region may reflect strategies of soft power devised at the highest levels of government is by no means farfetched. Indeed, in response to a question about perceptions of the Arab Institute of Film in the region at the time of its creation, Lebanese filmmaker Mohammed Soueid points to the inevitability of suspicion: "Don't forget, here in the region, always something coming from the West, there will be the conspiracy theory" (Soueid 2017).

The timing of the Arab Institute of Film initiative was, he remarks, such that the usual suspicions were intensified. The Danish "cartoon crisis" occurred in 2005 and the Arab Institute of Film opened in Amman, Jordan in 2006. The AIF thus emerged at a time when Denmark's relation to Arab culture and the Arab world was a source of intense concern, not least for Danish businesses. In Saudi Arabia, for example, Danish products were removed from supermarket shelves and replaced with the sign "Danish products were here" (Arla 2006). In the incendiary environment created by the newspaper *Jyllands Posten*'s attempt to provoke debate about self-censorship through a series of intentionally offensive cartoons of the prophet Muhammad, Danish institution building in the region could easily be seen, not as a pursuit of mutual interests, but as an exercise in damage control with implications for foreign but also domestic affairs.

AIF, SIB, and FilmLab Palestine fall within the scope of Denmark's soft power policies and funding parameters. Is this a problem? Do the different instances of institution-building merit attitudes of skepticism as a result? Before attempting to answer these questions through institutional analysis, film analysis, and interviews with policymakers, film trainers, and filmmakers, we would do well to revisit Joseph S. Nye Jr.'s influential definition of soft power. In "Public Diplomacy and Soft Power," Nye situates his understanding of soft power in relation to the challenges of terrorism: "The current struggle against transnational terrorism is a struggle to win hearts and minds, and the current overreliance on hard power alone is not the path to success" (Nye 2008, 94). Unlike hard power, which involves coercion, soft power is a matter of *effecting* a convergence of desires: "If I can *get you to want to do what I want* [emphasis added], then I do not have to force you to do what you do *not* want" (Nye 2008, 95). Unlike hard power, soft power relies on "resources of culture, values and policies," on the "ability to affect others to obtain the outcomes one wants" (Nye 2008, 94). Especially interesting in the present context is the role that Nye imagines for nongovernmental organizations:

> postmodern publics are generally skeptical of authority, and governments are often mistrusted. Thus, it often behooves governments to keep in the background and to work with private actors. Some NGOs enjoy more trust than governments do, and though they are difficult to control, they can be useful channels of communication. (Nye 2008, 105)

Distrust regarding the workings of soft power has, it seems, to do with two aspects of Nye's conceptualization. First, there is the absence of mutuality, soft power being a matter, not of building on an already existing symmetry or convergence of desires, but of fostering, even instituting, desires in others, as a means of achieving strategic goals. *Our* desires are to become *your* desires, as this is how we secure optimal conditions for *our* culture, values, and pursuits. Second, there is the element of opacity. NGOs may, for example, be pursuing what is seen as a shared interest, across national and cultural boundaries, in independent documentary expression, local storytelling in an authentic voice, and cinematic art, without being focally aware of their actions' strategic role within a larger scheme of things. Strategic rationality is in play in both instances. In the first case, the strategic nature of the arrangement is well understood by those who wield soft power as a useful tool in the pursuit of interests that are very much theirs. In the second case, strategic rationality at a higher level of policy formation and political will is obscured at the lower level of frontline engagement where the intercultural interactions, often fueled by a strong sense of mutuality, actually take place.

Although initiatives such as the Arab Institute of Film, Screen Institute Beirut, and FilmLab Palestine are linked to soft power through policymaking and funding provisions, they should not be dismissed as illegitimate exercises in cooptation or strategic influencing. To characterize the relevant collaborative efforts on a North/South basis as straightforward examples of a Western state's attempt to enhance its power through cultural values and cinematic practices is to get this particular story of institution building deeply wrong. The challenge here is to explain why this is so and to articulate the implications for our understanding of soft power.

As we shall see, concepts of shared values, of local initiative, agency, and ownership, of voice and "direct speech" (Stoneman 2018), and of artistic quality help to pinpoint reasons why the relevant undertakings, however complicated and challenging, lie beyond the reach of tawdry power machinations. As for the implications for how we conceptualize soft power, the point to be made is this: soft power policies create funding regimes that enable shared projects based on genuinely overlapping or mutually supportive values and goals. Initiatives made possible by the frameworks of soft power can in fact escape the pressures and constraints of strategic rationality that are inherent in the very concept of power, be it soft or hard.

General policies aimed at influence and power cannot build institutions, this being something that people do, not policies. In the case of AIF, SIB, and FilmLab Palestine, the institution building has been decisively shaped by the values of the relevant Danish and Middle Eastern practitioners, all of them from the spheres of film and culture, who have created the relevant spaces of transnational collaboration. A significant number of these values have been seen as shared, or as mutually supportive and synergistic. Equally important is the issue of agency, of who initiates a given undertaking and takes ownership of it. As we shall see, Arab agency has been a driving force in the process of institution building. And then there is the question of outcomes. Speaking of the Beirut-based Arab Fund for Arts and Culture (AFAC), which is seen as exemplary in its achievement of independence from both Arab and Western designs on power, Mohammed Soueid points to the legitimating effect of desirable outcomes. AFAC has escaped skepticism and objections, he claims, "because they make good films, publish good books, and create good exhibitions. When you have a product that speaks for itself, it's safe" (Soueid 2017). Analysis of two films produced by the Arab Institute of Film (*First Picture* [Akram Al-Ashqar, Jordan, 2006] and *Full Bloom* [Sandra Madi, Jordan, 2006], both by directors with a history of being based in Amman, Jordan) and two films produced by Screen Institute Beirut (*Crayons of Askalan* [Laila Hotait, Lebanon, 2011] and *A World Not Ours* [Mahdi Fleifel, 2012, Lebanon]) serves to highlight the valuable qualities of the relevant institutions' outputs. Some of these qualities are stylistic and aesthetic, while others are cultural and historical. Whereas Hotait is a Spanish-Lebanese filmmaker who describes herself as "sympathetic to the Palestinian cause that I hold as mine" (Hotait 2017), Akram Al-Ashqar, Madi, and Fleifel are all Palestinian filmmakers. Politics in the films is typically a matter of historical memory and the documenting of lived experience as it was affected by the identity-based decision-making of individuals or groups, or by geopolitical forces.

The films' cultural qualities are intertwined with the memories, struggles, and aspirations of the Palestinian people, and this is typical of the vast majority of films produced through the AIF and SIB. While these institutional spaces cannot be said to be have been oriented toward the realization of the Palestinian revolution, as called for in the PCA's manifesto from 1973, the stories they have supported are compatible with the more cultural and historical elements in the PCA's vision, that is, with desires and aspirations originating from within the region. Transnational institution building on a North/South axis, but also on a small-nation basis, can, it would appear, be a hopeful undertaking. The dimension of small nationhood is no doubt significant here, since the central Western player, Denmark, is seen as disposing over far less "hard" power than a large nation such as the USA, and as having, also, a very different relationship to the state of Israel. With populations of approximately 9 million (Jordan), 4.8 million (Palestine), 5.8 million (Lebanon), and 5.7 million (Denmark), the nations that have been centrally involved in AIF, SIB, and FilmLab Palestine all count as small (Hjort and Petrie 2007, 1–19). Indeed, Palestine, which occupies such a significant place in this story of cultural collaboration through moving images, counts as doubly small, on account of a lack of statehood, a painful history of rule by non-co-nationals, and the dispersed existence of its people, including in refugee camps in Lebanon, Jordan, and Syria.

The Arab Institute of Film, Screen Institute Beirut, and FilmLab Palestine: The Dynamics of Institution Building

Established in Amman, Jordan, the Arab Institute of Film enrolled its first cohort of filmmakers in 2006. The institute was the initiative of four Arab filmmakers: Eliane Raheb, a Lebanese documentary filmmaker; Omar Amiralay, a FEMIS-trained Syrian documentary filmmaker and activist (Van de Peer 2013, 192); Hisham Bizri, a Lebanese filmmaker with substantial involvement in American academe, through program building and teaching at such institutions as MIT, University of California, Davis, New York University, and Boston University; and Nizar Hassan, a Beirut-based Palestinian director, producer, and screenwriter from Nazareth. Aware of the possibility of securing Danish monies in support of collaborative efforts between Denmark and the Arab world, these filmmakers approached International Media Support about their ideas for a regional film school. The consensus view emerging from a significant number of practitioner interviews is that internal conflict within the group led to Raheb and Hassan withdrawing from the project. Supportive of the aspiration to develop a regional film school in the Arab world, IMS granted the necessary funding and went on to collaborate with Amiralay and Bizri in developing the AIF's structure and program. Other figures who were centrally involved in the AIF initiative include: film trainer and IMS program manager for documentary film and twinning (an approach to talent development that involves the pairing of practitioners) Rasmus Steen; producer, talent developer, and at the time IMS consultant Jakob K. Høgel; Iraqi-born filmmaker Kais Al-Zubaidi, who currently lives in Berlin, where he is a responsible for a "national Palestine archive" (HKW 2016); Belgium-based Palestinian filmmaker Michel Khleifi; and Danish documentary filmmaker Anders Østergaard.

The AIF focused exclusively on documentary film training and talent development and sought to recruit talent at a semiprofessional level and on a regional basis (from Egypt, Palestine, Jordan, Lebanon, and Syria). Recruitment was through production houses in each of these locations, the relevant contacts being invited to select and recommend aspiring filmmakers to the AIF Board. The AIF adopted a project-based approach to talent development, the process having been structured by three distinct modules of activity, each lasting two months (Steen 2011). The first module was a pre-production phase, with students refining their filmmaking skills in conversation with visiting trainers, as well as with Omiralay and Bizri in Amman, Jordan, and then going on to develop and research the ideas for the documentary film project with which they had applied. The second module saw students return to their home contexts, for the purposes of shooting their films. The last module was dedicated to post-production, back in the AIF facilities in Amman.

During its short existence, the AIF produced fourteen films, many of which have "enjoyed a life on the festival circuit," where some have also been recognized with prizes (Steen 2011). Reflecting on the impact of the AIF's training program on the participating filmmakers' subsequent trajectories, Steen is unreservedly positive. The training itself and the concrete outcome of a well-developed film are seen as having provided significant stepping-stones toward ongoing and long-term involvement in professional filmmaking. Noting that the filmmakers remain part of the IMS family and network, Steen points out that "everyone is professionally involved with filmmaking," be it through teaching, as producers, or as directors of commercials, documentaries, or feature films (Steen 2011). Steen's assessment of the AIF's impact is in line with views held by Akram Al-Ashqar, Sandra Madi, and Majida Kabariti (director of *Torfa—Last of the Nomadic Bedouins*). Kabariti, for example, speaks of many "doors" having been opened, "on a professional level, a personal level, a mental level, an experience level, and a work level." She evokes the way in which the training effected "a beautiful mental transition" for her, a shift from a "TV outlook" to a "documentary-cinema outlook," one that she has been able to hold onto in all her subsequent work, even in the case of commissioned filmmaking (Kabariti 2012). The reference to TV norms, and to the AIF as having offered an alternative outlook and set of values, is striking. The AIF seems, in many ways, to have been an attempt to meet some of the needs that Palestinian scholar Edward Said (1997) identified a quarter of a century earlier and almost a decade after the manifesto by the Palestinian Cinema Association (in *Covering Islam: How the Media and the Experts Determine How We See the Rest of the World*, 1981/1997).

The Arab filmmakers are especially attuned to the opportunities, part of the vision throughout, that the AIF provided for Arab mentorship. Training arrangements based on Arab identity, as compared with the provision of Nordic training of Arab filmmakers, are seen as decisive when assessing the significance of the AIF. Such assessments foreground the filmmakers' enhanced skillsets, but also their personal growth as artists, and the value of a supportive Arab network with links extending well beyond the Middle East. Statements by Sandra Madi and Akram Al-Ashqar corroborate views expressed by Palestinian filmmaker Alia Arasoughly with reference to the establishing of Shashat in Ramallah for the purposes of creating "Palestinian-Palestinian" talent development and film training provisions (Arasoughly 2013, 111). More specifically, the two AIF filmmakers identify ethnicity and local knowledge as being decisive, in terms of assessing the AIF's most significant contributions:

> I can tell you something, honestly, I prefer to work with a master, with a filmmaker, with an expert, who is from my region ... The language thing is really very important. We were very happy doing the exercises and

the analysis. But if you ask me, this very intimate talk and opening up and discussing what is happening with me, you know, during a process of creating, or trying to, I did it with Omar and Hisham and Michel; they understand us better. *An expert from our region is very important* [emphasis added]. Because we have a lot of stories and they are all very dramatic and a lot of them go under the same title. If you say "Palestine" you have endless topics. (Madi 2007)

Talking about the two persons that you mentioned before, Omar and Hisham, we kind of lived together in one place for a long time. Spending day and night together, eating together, cooking sometimes together, going outside together for this period of time. It was important for us, for me personally I can say, because Omar has experience as a filmmaker working in Syria. The situation is very hard for a documentarian who wants to criticize the society and government and all that. So it was helpful to talk about this. I think in both ways. Sometimes Omar was asking me lots of questions about the situation in Palestine ... and I was asking him about Syria ... In terms of filmmaking it was very important, because we watched the films that Omar did, five or six movies, we talked about every one of them, the story behind it ... how he changed the political point of view from one side to another. (Al-Ashqar 2017)

These statements by Madi and Akram Al-Ashqar are not merely personal articulations of the AIF's place in the life stories of two Palestinian filmmakers. They are also poignant evocations of the need for, and promise of, a regional film school in the Middle East, one creating the conditions for professional friendships on a transnational basis, for support for independent voices and creative documentary filmmaking, and for the telling of meaningful stories, many of them linked to Palestine, that are embedded in the history of the region.

Interestingly, in the Danish context, where funding for the AIF was sourced, support for the project of building a regional film school shows little evidence of strategic thinking aimed at an expansion of power. Evoking such organizations as the Nordic Film & TV Fund, Steen (at International Media Support) recalls being "drawn to the idea of collaborating across countries, across borders, and to the thought that this might strengthen the film milieus in those countries." He remarks that the hoped-for gains were ones that had indeed emerged "here at home, in the Nordic countries" (Steen 2011). Recollecting his motives for becoming involved in institution building in the Middle East, Høgel foregrounds three elements. First was the ethnic and geographic provenance of the originating intentions ("It was really important to me, that the starting point wasn't a Danish initiative, that there were other people who wanted to do something, and that we could make a difference by supporting their ideas" [Høgel 2013]). Second was the regional, as opposed to the narrowly national, outlook driving the project ("Their mission was pan-Arabic, not national. There was an idea of a cultured Arab world, one that was completely uninterested in narrow national politics, rising to a higher level and creating an actual film academy for the region" [Høgel 2013]). Third was the welcome opportunity to counteract outdated policy thinking at odds with the realities of an increasingly globalized world ("In Europe we've built the whole world of film on national entities . . . But these national entities, they're really not the reality we operate in . . . So the least we can do is to collaborate in all possible ways beyond national borders, so that those filmmakers who are 'betwixt and between' can feel more at home somehow" [Høgel 2013]).

As an institution the AIF had a short life span. After a few years and following assessment of its operations and longer-term prospects by former CEO of the Danish Film Institute and Executive Director of the European Think Tank on Film and Film Policy Henning Camre, the IMS made the decision to close the AIF. The decision was prompted by difficulties relating, among other things, to the actual location of the school (in a high-security neighborhood making it problematic for students to use their cameras in the immediate vicinity), failures of administrative oversight at the local level of the school's operations, and long-brewing conflicts between Amiralay and Bizri that came to a head at a dramatic board meeting. IMS did, however, remain committed to the original idea of offering documentary film training in the Middle East on a regional basis. Funding was thus allocated for a successor institution in Beirut, the mandate of the new Screen Institute Beirut being "to support and strengthen creative documentary filmmaking in the Middle East and North Africa (MENA) region with the aim of promoting freedom of expression and furthering film's role socially and culturally thereby contributing to the progress of those communities and to further regional and inter-cultural understanding" (SIB 2017).

Factors influencing the decision to establish the AIF's successor institution in Beirut included a "greater openness to the West" (Camre 2015), the existence of a relatively well-developed sector with relevant skill sets, and the hope that local funds allowing for autonomy and the (gradual) withdrawal of IMS could be accessed in due course. Drawing on legal expertise at the American University in Beirut, Henning Camre, chairman of the Board of Governors, ensured that SIB was registered as a Lebanese non-profit association. As such, the institution's governance is predominantly local, Board membership by nonlocals, including Camre, being limited to 25 percent. The original aim was to establish a genuine film academy, with a two-year program devoted to independent documentary filmmaking. Difficulties with local fundraising, a stronger dollar, and changing political winds in Denmark all combined to create insurmountable obstacles for the new Beirut-based institution. Seeking an alternative model, the SIB Board now emphasizes three elements: a dedicated site with filmmaking equipment that documentary filmmakers can access (modeled on the influential Danish "workshops"); short courses for local and regional filmmakers, typically in groups of six to eight; and production support through the SIB fund. A priority for the future is to find a solution to issues of distribution, films emerging from the region having to compete with hundreds of satellite channels, and to negotiate a difficult environment shaped by rival religious affiliations (Camre 2015). In spite of the many challenges faced by SIB, the nonprofit organization has been able to support some fifty films, most of them feature-length works. As Camre sees it, these films have a very important role to play, inasmuch as they foster a tradition of independent documentary filmmaking while also countering the "very limited image" of the region that circulates through the mainstream media (Camre 2015). As in the case of the AIF, there are echoes here of Said's critique of Western representations of the Arab world, as well as of the Palestinian scholar's hopes for a solution through, in part, historically grounded, authentic image-making from the region.

The final example of Denmark's involvement in institution building in the Middle East is FilmLab Palestine. Hanna Atallah, founder of FilmLab Palestine, points to the "personal experience" of "empowering Palestinian youths in refugee camps in Jordan" and identifies the "sole purpose" of the initiative as being the revitalization of the "culture of film in Palestine," a goal that also involves a process of liberation "from the grasp of conventional European filmmaking industries and Hollywood" (FLP 2017). FilmLab Palestine's core partners are the Danish House in Palestine (based in Ramallah, and with Lone Bildsøe Lassen serving as director for many years) and the Children & Youth section at the Danish Film Institute (DFI) in Copenhagen (developed and overseen by Charlotte Giese and Claus Hjorth). In 2017, FilmLab Palestine, the Danish House in Palestine, and the Children & Youth section at the DFI commissioned a report with the aim of identifying existing media literacy and filmmaking provisions (in Palestine) for children and young people in three age groups, from 4 to 18. Khulood Badawi, a Ramallah-based researcher, worked with Hjort at the University of Copenhagen to produce the report, the central findings of which were presented to stakeholders in Ramallah during Days of Cinema in October 2017. Badawi, Giese, and Hjort also presented the report to the Minister of Culture and to the Minister of Education and Higher Education in Ramallah. It is expected that the findings of the report will provide the basis for the further development of FilmLab Palestine, and for the sourcing of relevant funds. The strong commitment, now and in the future, is to enable children and young people in the West Bank, East Jerusalem, and Gaza to tell their *own* stories.

FILMMAKING IN THE MIDDLE EAST

FOUR REPRESENTATIVE FILMS: *FIRST PICTURE* (2006), *FULL BLOOM* (2006), *CRAYONS OF ASKALAN* (2011), AND *A WORLD NOT OURS* (2012)

Akram Al-Ashqar's AIF film, *First Picture*, is motivated throughout by the desire to tell a story from Tulkarem, the director's home town, and to do this in a way that deviates from the sensationalist approach of the mainstream media. *First Picture* is about the two-year-old Nour, who was born to a Palestinian mother, Manal Ghanem, in prison. As a result of an Israeli court order, Nour is forcibly released to a family he does not know at the age of two, in spite of objections from his mother and her fellow prisoners. Akram Al-Ashqar recalls traveling to the Tulkarem camp to meet Nour and his family. He found journalists in the process of treating the young boy as a mere "object": "They put the camera in front of him, took a photo or video of him, and then left. From then on I was thinking about how to work with this kid, about how to develop a relation with him, and about how to film him in a different way" (Al-Ashqar 2017).

The title of the film refers to the prisoners' efforts to create some kind of continuity between infancy within and outside the prison walls, by making sure that the infant Nour, like most other children, would have a baby picture of himself. The film captures Nour's difficulties in adjusting to life outside the prison, his fascination with locks and keys, and his persistent searching, especially evident in the concluding moments of the film, for his mother.

A quiet, gentle film that is the result of the filmmaker's development of a trusting relationship with Nour over a period of months, *First Picture* is also a

Figure 22.1 Akram Al-Ashqar captures Nour's obsession with locks after the young boy's release from an Israeli prison (*First Picture*, 2006).

297

Figure 22.2 Laila Hotait depicts the imagination of the Palestinian artist Zuhdi Al-Adawi as a prisoner in Askalan (*Crayons of Askalan*, 2011).

deeply political work: "I found personally that the story of Nour summarizes the story of Palestinians in a way. If you are not living in a prison, the building itself, then you are living in the West Bank or the Gaza strip, and you are living in a prison, even if you are at home . . . It's a kind of symbolism of the whole situation" (Al-Ashqar 2017).

Sandra Madi's *Full Bloom* is similarly anchored in a strong sense of Palestinian identity. As Madi puts it, in an interview about the film and her professional trajectory in the wake of her AIF experience, "Over half the population in Jordan is Palestinian. My mother is Palestinian. My father is Palestinian. My heart and soul are Palestinian" (Madi 2017). Filmed in an observational manner, *Full Bloom* tells the story of Faraj Darwish, a young boxer from the Baqa'a refugee camp in Jordan, just north of Amman, where the AIF was located. Winner of the Arab boxing championship in 2004, Darwish was subsequently banned by the Jordanian boxing federation for life because of his refusal to compete against an Israeli in 2006. An especially moving aspect of Madi's film is her evocation of boxing as a means of accessing a world beyond the camp and as a potential source of strength, community, dignity, and recognition. The tragedy depicted in *Full Bloom* extends beyond the story of Darwish, with Madi weaving the fate of an older generation of gifted boxers from the Al Baqa'a camp into her narrative. What emerges through Madi's observational approach is a detailed picture of hope and commitment, but also disappointment and injustice across generations.

Supported by Screen Institute Beirut, but also by the Arab Fund for Arts and Culture, the Sundance Documentary Institute, the Berlinale Talent Campus, and Dox Box Damascus, *Crayons of Askalan* by Laila Hotait offers yet another example of how Danish involvement in institution building in the Middle East is creating the conditions of possibility for Palestinian storytelling. *Crayons of Askalan* tells the story of the Palestinian artist Zuhdi Al-Adawi, who completed nearly a hundred illegal drawings while imprisoned in the high-security Israeli jail, Askalan.

The film concludes with an exchange with Zuhdi Al-Adawi, years after he was "released in an exchange of 1500 Palestinians for two Israeli soldiers." Living in the Yarmouk refugee camp in Jordan, the artist reflects movingly on how the experience of imprisonment transformed young Palestinians into poets, philosophers, and artists. Hotait's documentary is a work of considerable visual and conceptual ingenuity, the filmmaker having devised compelling strategies for capturing how imprisonment and solitary confinement, a strong sense of Palestinian identity and group belonging, and solidarity, both within and beyond the prison walls, ended up fueling the prisoner's considerable creative energy and artistic talent.

It is worth noting that Hotait's involvement with SIB was not her first encounter with Danish efforts at talent development on a transnational basis. More specifically, Hotait participated in CPH:DOX's talent development Lab in 2011–12, where she was "twinned" with Rania M. Tawfik, an Iraqi-Lebanese graduate of the National Film School of Denmark. With Tawfik representing Denmark and Hotait Lebanon in the twinning process, the filmmakers co-directed *From a Distance*, a film about "Rania and Laila," both of them "daughters of the Arab diaspora," as they explore "shattered memories of childhood, swimming pools, war and diaspora" (CPH:DOX).

A World Not Ours by Palestinian Mahdi Fleifel offers yet another example of how SIB is helping to create the conditions of possibility for Palestinian storytelling. An autobiographical work that "borrows its title from a novel by the author and activist Ghassan Kanafani" (Bradshaw 2014), Fleifel's documentary is set in the Palestinian refugee camp of Ein el-Helweh in Southern Lebanon. Fleifel, who was born in the camp and lived there for years before moving to Dubai and eventually Denmark, continues to think of it as a site of considerable belonging. Drawing on his many visits to the camp to see family and friends, Fleifel makes vivid the extraordinary complexity of feeling at home (Hedetoft and Hjort 2002) with reference to displacement and the loss of an originary homeland. Drawing on the archive of video material that he built up over the years, Fleifel's film is, as Peter Bradshaw aptly puts it, "a very watchable study of a stateless community, subsisting on dreams and memories of a lost homeland, and a generation of young men who have no prospects, sometimes drawn to jihadism out of sheer personal frustration; yet . . . often quite as critical of the Palestinian leadership as everything else" (Bradshaw 2014).

A Living Archive of Deeply Personal Stories

It is clear that Danish efforts at talent development in the Middle East, all of them traceable to and made possible by policies of soft power, are facilitating practices that are at least continuous with many of the aspirations expressed in the Palestinian Cinema Association's manifesto. With its stunning audiovisual language, Hotait's film echoes, for example, the goal of creating a "new aesthetic." The PCA hoped to "create a film archive" that would "gather film and still photograph material on the struggle of the Palestinian people in order to retrace its stages" (PCA 2014, 273–5). As documentaries with a focus on the lived experience of Palestinians in various sites in the Middle East, films such as *First Picture*, *Full Bloom*, *Crayons of Askalan*, and *A World Not Ours* are research-based contributions to what is essentially becoming a living archive of deeply personal stories that are firmly rooted in the political complexities and struggles associated with Palestine. The PCA sought to produce films that would "present the Palestinian cause to the whole world," and here too there are elements of continuity. *First Picture* and *Crayons of Askalan* explore the self-understandings and actions of Palestinians who were imprisoned for their commitment to "the cause." Finally, the PCA's hopes for participation in a global network and for a strengthening of "relations with . . . progressive cinema groups" (PCA 2014, 274) appear to be entirely synergistic with the regional, and more generally transnational, outlook of institutions such as AIF, SIB, and FilmLab Palestine.

The continuities between the PCA's aspirations and Danish institution-building in the Middle East exist not only at the level of storytelling, but also in the involvement of specific film practitioners. Sandra Madi, for example, speaks movingly of just how important the support of Kais Al-Zubaidi was during her time at the AIF, but also subsequently; his efforts on behalf of her film, *Full Bloom*, were crucial, she points out, in terms of her ability to access the all-important international film festival circuit (Madi 2017). Kais Al-Zubaidi, interestingly, is someone who figures centrally in Annemarie Jacir's reflections on Palestinian cinema in *The Electronic Intifada*. Writing in her capacity as artistic director of the "Dreams of a Nation film festival in Palestine in 2003," Jacir foregrounds the efforts, in the late 1960s, of "a group of young Arab women and men" who chose to "contribute to the resistance through filmmaking." As founders of the initiative Jacir names Mustafa Abu Ali, Sulafa Jadallah, and Hani Jawhariya, but she also refers to Khadija Abu Ali, Ismael Shammout, Rafiq Jijjar, Nabia Lutfi, Fuad Zentut, Jean Chamoun, and Samir Nimr, most of them "refugees, exiled from their homes in Palestine," and, significant in the present context, to Kais Al-Zubaidi, "who was part of the group of filmmakers, and now lives in Berlin" (Jacir 2007).

With its focus on reform and democratization, and on dialogue and collaboration, Danish soft power, as framed by the Danish Arab Partnership Programme, is facilitating new forms of "direct speech" in the Middle East. Particularly significant in this regard is the work of small-scale institutions such as the AIF and SIB, and, more recently, FilmLab Palestine (Ministry of Foreign Affairs of Denmark n.d., 67). Especially striking is the fact that many of the filmmakers who are gaining support for their independent documentary projects are deeply committed, as Sandra Madi puts it, to telling some of the "dramatic stories" that "go under the same title," under "Palestine." Soft power, it appears, is not a matter in this case of instituting certain desires and values, but of creating the conditions under which an already existing desire to articulate stories of deep personal significance can be realized, and this within an independent space offering scope for a whole range of values, including, especially, cultural and artistic ones. Soft power, in this case, would appear to be a rather hopeful phenomenon.

References

Arla. 2006. "Press Release: Arla Affected by Cartoons of Muhammed." January 21. <https://www.arla.com/company/news-and-press/2006/pressrelease/arla-affected-by-cartoons-of-muhammed-760044/> (last accessed August 15, 2017).

Arasoughly, Alia. 2013. "Film Education in Palestine Post-Oslo: The Experience of Shashat." In *The Education of the Filmmaker in Africa, the Middle East, and the Americas*, ed. Mette Hjort. New York: Palgrave Macmillan. 99–123.

Bradshaw, Peter. 2014. "A World Not Ours—Review." <https://www.theguardian.com/film/2014/feb/20/a-world-not-ours-review> (last accessed August 29, 2017).

CPH:DOX. "Rania M. Tawfik & Laila Hotait—From a Distance." <http://cphlab.dk/teams20112012/rania-m-tawfik-laila-hotait> (last accessed August 29, 2017).

DANIDA. 2013. "Danish Arab Partnership Programme 2013–2016. Strategic Framework Document." Copenhagen: Ministry of Foreign Affairs of Denmark.

FLP (FilmLab Palestine). 2017. "About FLP." http://flp.ps/flp/about-us (last accessed August 21, 2017).

Hedetoft, Ulf and Mette Hjort, eds. 2002. *The Postnational Self*. Minneapolis: University of Minnesota Press.

Hjort, Mette. 2005. *Small Nation, Global Cinema*. Minneapolis: University of Minnesota Press.

Hjort, Mette and Duncan Petrie, eds. 2007. *The Cinema of Small Nations*. Edinburgh: Edinburgh University Press.

HKW. 2016. "Screening and talk with Kais al-Zubaidi (Director)." <https://www.hkw.de/en/programm/projekte/veranstaltung/p_126515.php> (last accessed August 17, 2017).

Jacir, Annemarie. 2007. "Coming Home: Palestinian Cinema." *The Electronic Intifada*. February 27. <https://electronicintifada.net/content/coming-home-palestinian-cinema/6780> (last accessed August 29, 2017).

Nye, Joseph S., Jr. 2008. "Public diplomacy and soft power." *The Annals of the American Academy of Political and Social Science* 616: 94–109.

Ministry of Foreign Affairs of Denmark. n.d. "Danish Arab Partnership Programme 2017–2021." Copenhagen, file nr. 2016-11680.

PCA (Palestinian Cinema Association) 1973 [2014]. "Manifesto of the Palestinian Cinema Group." In *Film Manifestos and Global Cinema Cultures: A Critical Anthology*, ed. Scott MacKenzie. Oakland: University of California Press. 273–5.

Said, Edward. 1997. *Covering Islam: How the Media and the Experts Determine How We See the Rest of the World*, revised edn. New York: Vintage.

SIB. 2017. "About Us." <http://www.screeninstitutebeirut.org/about.html> (last accessed August 21, 2017).

Stoneman, Rod. 2018. "African Cinema: Perspective Correction." In *African Cinema and Human Rights*, ed. Mette Hjort and Eva Jørholt. Bloomington, IN: Indiana University Press. 39–59.

Van de Peer, Stefanie. 2013. "The Moderation of Creative Dissidence in Syria: Reem Ali's Documentary *Zabad*." In *Arab Cultural Studies: History, Politics and the Popular*, ed. Anastasia Valassopoulos. London: Routledge. 190–210.

Interviews

Al-Ashqar, Akram. 2017. Interview by Mette Hjort (Skype). Amman/Copenhagen.
Camre, Henning. 2015. Interview by Mette Hjort. Copenhagen, Tranquebar.
Hotait, Laila. 2017. Interview by Mette Hjort (email). Mexico/Copenhagen.
Høgel, Jakob K. 2013. Interview by Mette Hjort. Copenhagen, Danish Film House.
Kabariti, Majida. 2012. Interview by Mette Hjort (email). Amman/Hong Kong.
Madi, Sandra. 2017. Interview by Mette Hjort (Skype). Amman/Copenhagen.
Soueid, Mohammed. 2017. Interview by Mette Hjort (Skype). Beirut/Copenhagen.
Steen, Rasmus. 2011. Interview by Mette Hjort. Copenhagen, International Media Support.

PART IV

REVISITATIONS

23. DREYER'S *JEANNE D'ARC* AT THE CINÉMA D'ESSAI: CINEPHILIAC AND POLITICAL PASSIONS IN 1950s PARIS

Casper Tybjerg

In 1953, the Italian film journal *Cinema nuovo* ran an article with the title "52,000 hanno visto Giovanna" (52000 people have seen Joan [of Arc]) (Lo Duca 1953). Written by the Italian-born cinephilia promoter and organizer Lo Duca, the article described his remarkably successful revival of Carl Th. Dreyer's 1928 film *The Passion of Joan of Arc* (*La Passion de Jeanne d'Arc*) at his Parisian art cinema, the Cinéma d'Essai. This 1952 reissue is a relevant case to study if we want to investigate the process by which certain films become canonized as key works of film history, which is what the present chapter sets out to do. No film by a Nordic director appears as often on lists of the "best films of all time" as *The Passion of Joan of Arc*. Examining the reception and canonization of *The Passion of Joan of Arc* is particularly relevant in the context of this volume: the process of film canon formation is one that depends on institutions and tastemakers located "elsewhere" (Paris being important here), and the film itself was made by a Nordic director working outside Scandinavia.

Although Carl Th. Dreyer's most famous sound films (*Day of Wrath*, 1943; *Ordet*, 1955; *Gertrud*, 1964) were made in Denmark, his silent film career was conspicuously international; of his nine silent features, only four were made in his native Denmark. The success in France of his 1925 film *Master of the House* gave him the opportunity to make a big-budget historical film there: *The Passion of Joan of Arc*. Boldly, he chose to make a highly stylized film rejecting all the usual trappings of the historical spectacular, its oddly angled shots offering only brief glimpses of the massive, expensive sets, exploring instead the naked faces of the actors with unprecedented intensity. *The Passion of Joan of Arc* was hailed as a masterpiece by critics, but it was not a commercial success. Soon after its premiere, European cinemas converted to sound, brusquely pushing the great works of the late silent cinema off their screens.

While *The Passion of Joan of Arc* continued to have a high reputation among the *cognoscenti* in the 1930s and 1940s, Lo Duca's reissue increased its visibility considerably; its successful run at the Cinéma d'Essai convinced Gaumont to make new prints available for rental, making it much easier for art cinemas and ciné-clubs to program the film. The version of the film distributed by Gaumont until the mid-1980s had been shaped by Lo Duca in a number of ways (pre-recorded musical score, framing, intertitles) that Dreyer scholars have denounced (more about this in the second section of this chapter). Following the rediscovery in the early 1980s of an original print (one of the two prints sent to Copenhagen in April 1928 for the world premiere of the film), this has entirely eclipsed the problematic Lo Duca version, but the role of the latter in the film's critical fortunes remains significant.

Today, *The Passion of Joan of Arc* seems firmly ensconced in the film-historical canon, but what happens if we look historically at the esteem in which such a film is held? The prominent Shakespeare scholar Gary Taylor has argued that no cultural artifact that escapes oblivion and becomes part of "cultural memory" is able to do so without the work of people other than its makers, who have "recontextualized, reproduced, restored, or resituated it" (Taylor 1996, 123). Taylor calls such people "editors," a broad term that includes reviewers, film historians, art cinema programmers, and silent film accompanists. Their activities have a crucial influence on what gets remembered and what gets forgotten, and they are not necessarily part of the same national context as the films or other artworks in question.

To investigate the history of how Dreyer's film achieved its preeminent status, we must look to France, not because it is a French-made film (some auteurist critics, as we shall see, labeled it a Danish film of sorts) but because of the importance of French cinephilia in the construction of what David Bordwell has called the "Standard Version" of the history of film style (see Bordwell 1997, 12–45). The French film scholar Laurent Jullier has been quite sharp in insisting that the canon of taste embodied in the "Standard Version" is a very particular one; he writes of his realization that "the history of styles that I had been taught was just another 'Grand Recit' in the postmodern sense" (Jullier 2009, 203). Jullier has examined the international critics' poll of the greatest films of all time held by *Sight & Sound* every decade since 1952, discussing the aesthetic priorities the votes seem to reveal. In the most recent poll in 2012, *The Passion of Joan of Arc* came in at number nine (full disclosure: I cast one of 65 votes that elevated *Passion* to this eminent position). Jullier implies that this elevated status reflects a certain tradition of highbrow cinephilia that is formalist and elitist in its approach. In France, the standard-bearers of this tradition are Parisian cinephiles clustered around *Cahiers du cinéma* and certain other institutions. Lo Duca was a co-founder and editor of *Cahiers*, and the Cinéma d'Essai, where he was the manager, was one of the leading art houses in Paris. He thus occupied an important place within French cinephile culture.

Jullier identifies three different paradigms of cinephilia. In the first section of this chapter, I will argue that the paradigm that encompasses "highbrow" cinephilia describes Lo Duca's activities very well. In the second section, I will focus on Lo Duca's version of *The Passion of Joan of Arc* and its initial presentation in February 1952, where Dreyer's film was placed in a framework that was strongly cinephiliac, but also drew attention to the director's Danish nationality. However, neither of these interpretive frameworks (cinephiliac and national/auteurist) was mentioned in the reviews and press reactions. Instead, as we shall see in the third section, the reviewers emphasized Falconetti's performance in the role of Jeanne and claimed the film for whichever side of Cold War cultural politics they favored. This shows that there exists a broad range of reasons for considering *The Passion of Joan of Arc* a great film. Its canonization, as I will argue in conclusion, cannot therefore be regarded as evidence for the entrenchment of a particular set of cinephile or national preferences.

Highbrow Cinephilia in Context

Laurent Jullier and Jean-Marc Leveratto have done a great deal of thoughtful work on cinephilia and the evaluation of films. They are critical of a traditional French (even "Parisian") cinephilia, which they regard as overly elitist and dismissive both of more commonplace film fandom and of more sociological, industry-oriented scholarship (Jullier and Leveratto 2010). While their critique is focused on France, Jullier also argues (referring to David Bordwell's work on the history of film history in Bordwell 1997) that the same assumptions have colored "'official' histories of cinema" internationally:

> Everyone can see today that the "History of Cinema" (with a capital H), such as is taught in French high schools, is more an artificial construction based on the subjective tastes of the *Cahiers du cinéma* than a scientific analysis of all films produced. (Jullier 2009, 203)

Jullier objects to this construction of film history because it is auteurist, focused narrowly on genius directors, and because it is art-for-art's-sake-ist, focused exclusively on formalist pleasures. He calls it "modernist" since it relies, "on the one hand, on the celebration of insurgents, outlaws, and the singularity of artworks; on the other, on the cult of novelty" (Jullier 2015a, 62).

Lo Duca was an important contributor to this construction, a figure at once obscure and central to the history of French cinephilia. Born Giuseppe Maria Lo Duca in Milan in 1910, he moved to France in the mid-1930s and frenchified his given names to Joseph-Marie, although he usually used only his last name. He published a number of books on cinema, including a short 136-page *Histoire du cinéma* for the pocket-sized paperback series *Que sais-je*, which was reprinted in new editions no fewer than seven times (Lo Duca 1947).

This *Histoire du cinéma*, first published in 1942, shows that the auteurism Jullier and Leveratto regard as characteristic of highbrow cinephilia is integral to Lo Duca's work. The book is illustrated with line drawings, most of them portraits of great directors, their faces surrounded by little stars. Jullier and Leveratto write: "modern cinephilia maintains a cult of the auteur which differs only in name from the cult of the star" (Jullier and Leveratto 2010, 130). Lo Duca's *Histoire* is palpable evidence of this.

As co-founder of *Cahiers du cinéma* (a name he claimed he came up with; Gili 2007, 1), Lo Duca formed part of the editorial committee with André Bazin and Jacques Doniol-Valcroze until 1955. He was largely responsible for the magazine's look and layout, and he was also a frequent contributor. In his writings, Lo Duca often comes across as combative and opinionated. He had little respect for the film industry, decrying its regular output and repeatedly praising filmmakers unwilling to kowtow to commercial interests. He reserved special vitriol for moralistic figures like Will Hays: "Hypocrisy finally had its grand pontiff, His Holiness Preventive Censorship" (Lo Duca 1947, 42).

According to Jullier and Leveratto, antinomian, "modernist" preferences are characteristic of highbrow cinephilia: "Relying on the rhetoric of artistic critique, it valorizes 'sexual and aesthetic transgression,' which makes it oppose 'the moralism and the aesthetic classicism' of the popular audience" (Jullier and Leveratto 2010, 137, quoting Boltanski and Chiapello 1999, 84–5). These preferences were certainly shared by Lo Duca. After leaving *Cahiers* in 1957, he devoted himself to erotica, publishing a series of books under the collective title *De Erotica*, including four volumes on *L'Érotisme au cinéma* (1957–68). Most of these were published by Jean-Jacques Pauvert, for whom Lo Duca also oversaw the sexological book series *Bibliothèque international d'érotologie*. Pauvert issued the first non-clandestine edition of the works of the Marquis de Sade in 1947 (resulting in his prosecution in 1956), and published *The Story of O* in 1954. Lo Duca's example supports Jullier and Leveratto's contention that in modern highbrow cinephilia, "pornographic representation and the celebration of Sadeian motifs" are compatible with an overarching "concern for Form" (with a capital "F"; Jullier and Leveratto 2010, 127).

The concern for Form is particularly apparent in one of the three "'cinephile paradigms'" Jullier identifies in his article on the *Sight & Sound* critics' poll. He suggests that these three "manners of apprehending, interpreting, and utilizing films" delineate "the three principal manners of speaking publically about films" (Jullier 2015b, 156). These three manners are identified with the three founding fathers of philosophical aesthetics, Baumgarten, Kant, and Hegel (Jullier cites Cohn 2007 as his inspiration). As Jullier explains it, the Baumgarten principle sees art as providing *Bildung*, life lessons; a good artwork or film is one that teaches us something important about how to live. Jullier's own contribution to the critics' poll explicitly adopts this criterion (BFI 2012). The Kantian principle of disinterested appreciation is "the touchstone of orthodox, educated cinephilia—at least in France" (Jullier 2015b, 161). Jullier links it to the modernist ideals of Clive Bell and the emphasis on "significant form," arguing that the replacement in 2012 of *Citizen Kane* by *Vertigo* in the poll's top spot is evidence of the growing importance of this approach. The third tendency, the Hegelian one, consists of "meta-aesthetic and metahistorical" approaches, where films are appreciated through their relations to other films and artworks (Jullier 2015b, 165–6). I would give these approaches more descriptive names, referring to the "Baumgartian" approach as meliorist, the "Kantian" as own-sakist, and the "Hegelian" as meta-aesthetic.

Jullier mentions *The Passion of Joan of Arc* only in passing, but he clearly implies that its place in the top ten owes much to the strength of the "Kantian" or own-sakist approach. He mentions the film in the context of a discussion of the way own-sakist critics have no interest in the often absurd and problematic storylines of their favorite films: "Neither the misogynist inanity of the screenplay of *Sunrise* nor the UFOlogical and anti-Darwinian farrago of *2001* bothers their defenders, whose admiration relates to other characteristics" (Jullier 2015b, 163). Jullier continues: "Similarly, no 'Kantian' cinephile is expected to tarry over the eye-rollings and grimaces of the actors playing the judges in *The Passion of Joan of Arc*" (Jullier 2015b, 163). But "Kantian" film lovers have not been alone in finding greatness in Dreyer's film, even if its 1952 presentation was framed by an almost caricatural own-sakism.

THE 1952 RE-RELEASE OF *THE PASSION OF JOAN OF ARC*

In the reception history of *The Passion of Joan of Arc*, Lo Duca usually appears as a villain; his re-release version stands as an exemplar of excessive and disrespectful intervention in a silent classic. In his 1985 article "Jeanne d'Arc livrée au bourreaux" (Joan of Arc delivered to the executioners), Dreyer's biographer Maurice Drouzy accuses the Gaumont-distributed Lo Duca version of "betraying" Dreyer's work: "when you have watched the Gaumont print, you have not seen Dreyer's *Joan of Arc*. In reality, you have watched a fake!" (Drouzy 1985, 66).

Lo Duca's version used an original negative from 1928. While this was a negative different from the one used to make the prints for the world premiere in April 1928, using the second-best takes of each shot (the first negative was destroyed in a lab fire), that was not the reason Drouzy rejected Lo Duca's version. Rather, the way he made the prints, using equipment for sound films, interfered with the film's aesthetic properties, because the images of Dreyer's film were cropped on one side to make room for the sound track, ruining their careful compositions. Furthermore, instead of using stark backgrounds for the intertitles, Lo Duca printed them on images of medieval stained-glass windows that clash with the austere look of the film's images, muddling up the visuals. Finally, Lo Duca had chosen a prerecorded musical accompaniment felt by many (including Dreyer) to be entirely inappropriate for the film (for more details on Lo Duca's version, see Pipolo 1988, Tybjerg 2012).

I have no intention of defending Lo Duca's ham-fisted treatment of the film. It must be recognized, however, that his reissue and promotion of *The Passion of Joan of Arc* certainly helped make it more visible among the tastemakers of the time. The revival was a big success. On April 2, 1952, Lo Duca wrote to Dreyer that nearly 26 000 people had come to see *The Passion of Joan of Arc* (DFI/D II A: 1659). The Cinéma d'Essai had sixteen shows per week (twice daily on weekdays, three on Saturdays and Sundays), giving an average of 270 spectators per show. Even if every show was not sold out (the cinema apparently had 476 seats as per CinemaTour, n.d.), it still seems very impressive.

In late 1949, a year after the Cinématheque Française opened its first 60-seat screening room in Paris, the Association of French Film Critics (*Association française de la critique de cinéma*, AFCC) decided to set up a cinema to present overlooked films that had not found commercial distribution. The initiative received support from the government, and Lo Duca was put in charge of the Cinéma d'Essai, as it was called (Thomas 2007, 13). It was located in the former cinema Les Reflets, on Avenue des Ternes no. 27 in Paris, in the 17th arrondissement just west of the Place Étoile. The programs consisted not only of a feature film, but also of a series of shorts including "a scientific film, an amateur film, an exceptional documentary, an animated cartoon or a retrospective short" (Cinéma d'Essai program pamphlet, 1952, DFI/D I, A: Passion de Jeanne d'Arc, La, 2).

The Cinéma d'Essai opened in early 1950. Two years later, a gala celebrating its second anniversary was held with Lo Duca's new print of *The Passion of Joan of Arc* as the main attraction. It was preceded by a program of short films: (1) a selection of old Gaumont newsreels; (2) the short animation film *Rêve d'un garçon de café* (Émile Cohl, 1910), better known as *Le Songe du garçon de café*, which mixes live action and hallucinatory line drawings; (3) the silent color film *Rites sauvages* ("Savage Rites," Régine Le Henaff, 1948), shot in French Equatorial Africa and showing a "grand gathering of witch doctors" (Le Henaff n.d.); (4) *La légende cruelle* ("The Cruel Legend," Alexandre Arcady and Gabriel Pommerand, 1951), an art documentary about the paintings of the

Italian-Argentinian surrealist Léonor Fini; and (5) *Shakespeare og Kronborg* (Jørgen Roos, 1950), a Danish short—scripted by Dreyer—re-enacting the possible visit of Shakespeare to Denmark in 1587.

All in all, a highly eclectic program, and one which would have primed spectators to see *The Passion of Joan of Arc* in an avant-garde context, a cabinet-of-curiosities-type aesthetic seeking to decontextualize artworks and foster admiration for their most abstract qualities. Spectators at organized artistic events will tend to look for coherence and pattern, and the presence on the program of a short film scripted by the director of the main feature has an obvious auteurist logic to it, suggesting that the other films were not randomly chosen either. However, the juxtaposition of *The Passion of Joan of Arc* with Fini's sensual sphinxes and vaguely unsettling portraiture, Cohl's delirious fancies, and African sorcery is hard to make sense of except as presenting a palette of purely artistic pleasures, a gourmet meal for the discerning and even jaded palates of highbrow cinephiles.

The musical accompaniment can also be regarded as reflective of a cinephiliac attitude, both in the choice of music and the reasoning behind it. After the film's run at the Cinéma d'Essai, Lo Duca prepared a sonorized version for Gaumont, which had its premiere on the closing night of the Venice Film Festival, September 12, 1952 (Drouzy 1987, 4); it was submitted by Lo Duca to the CNC for authorization on October 10 and passed on October 27 (CNC, Dossiers de censure, Bois d'Arcy: no. 13431). For this sonorized version, Lo Duca chose music by Johann Sebastian Bach, Alessandro Scarlatti, Albinoni, Vivaldi, Geminiani, Torelli, and Sammartini. Years later, Lo Duca wrote about his choice of music: "Following the example of Dreyer's images, we sought to be *timeless* [*hors du temps*]" (Lo Duca 1978, 26; original emphasis). At the time, he described the eighteenth-century composers he used as "the young men of the future" and objected to the term "restoration" for his presentation of the film (Lo Duca 1953, 212). For the original presentation in February 1952, Lo Duca had used music from gramophone records played on a wire recorder (Lo Duca, letter to Dreyer, February 8, 1952). This was his normal practice for silent film shows. Lo Duca scoffed at Henri Langlois' practice of showing silent films without any accompaniment:

> Anyway, I do not understand the museum mentality. When Langlois shows silent movies in silence in the screening room on Avenue de Messine, that's making a museum, that is, filmic necrophilia. When the Cinéma d'Essai presents the same silent film with sound accompaniment, that's doing and serving cinema. (Lo Duca 1953, 212)

This attack is revealing. Watching films for their historical importance, to get a fuller understanding of the development of the art form, is for Lo Duca the equivalent of having sex with a corpse. Only the aesthetic impact in the present moment counts. This strongly "own-sakist" view has also marked the Cinémathèque française itself. Its permanent exhibition, opened in 2005, seemingly embraces Lo Duca's presentism in order to refute his old charge: a caption at the end of the display claims that the institution's support for living filmmakers, particularly those of the avant-garde, "rescues the Cinémathèque from cinephiliac necrophilia" ("Les avant-gardes," caption, Collection Henri Langlois 2–8).

The presentation at the Cinéma d'Essai offered another possible approach for spectators besides the cinephile one: to take the presence of the Danish ambassador at the gala and the presentation of *Shakespeare og Kronborg* as cues to watch *The Passion of Joan of Arc* as the work of a Dane. This would not only mean taking the auteurist position of regarding the film as a direct product of the director's personality, but adding the ethno-determinist notion that that personality is likely to be a reflection of national character and cultural specificity. Such ethno-determinist notions are commonplace in pre-1950 film histories and critical writings, but the reception of the Cinéma d'Essai presentation by contemporary reviewers does not reflect either this kind of approach or a highbrow formalism. Instead, most of the reviews focused on the film as a drama, with those from Catholic newspapers emphasizing Joan's saintliness, the Communist ones comparing her to heroic party members martyred by the Nazis.

The Reviewers' Reactions

Except for Bazin's review, reprinted in *The Cinema of Cruelty*, my discussion of the initial reception of Lo Duca's presentation of *The Passion of Joan of Arc* is based on clippings from the newspapers *Le Figaro*, *Le Monde*, *La Croix*, *France-Soir*, and *L'Humanité*, and from the magazines *Arts*, *L'Écran français*, and *Les nouvelles littéraires*, all kept in Dreyer's personal files—they were collected by the Danish embassy in Paris and sent to him by the cultural attaché, Helge Wamberg (DFI/D I, A: Passion de Jeanne d'Arc, La, 6).

Lo Duca took advantage of his editorial position at *Cahiers du cinéma* and wrote a piece entitled "Trilogie mystique de Dreyer" in place of a review. The supposed "trilogy" consists of *La Passion* and Dreyer's following two films, *Vampyr* (1932) and *Day of Wrath*, but Lo Duca's rambling text offers little discussion of what unites the three films beyond the title's claim that they are "mystical," dealing with faith, the supernatural, and magical beliefs (Lo Duca 1952, 61). He quotes a passage on *The Passion of Joan of Arc* from *Der Geist des Films* by Béla Balázs, which had not been translated into French at the time, emphasizing the power of the camera to expose inner reality: "Behind the face shown to the world, it exposes the face we truly possess, the face we can neither change nor control" (Balázs 2010, 103). The passage was re-quoted by both Bazin and Nino Frank in their reviews.

Nino Frank belonged to the older generation of critics born around the turn of the century, whose formative experiences were the silent cinema of the twenties and the transition to sound, and who remembered seeing *The Passion of Joan of Arc* when it first came out (for more on Frank, see Holmes 2016). Writing in the weekly *Arts*, Frank used the Balázs quotation to emphasize the similarity between Dreyer and the greatest painters and sculptors, masters of human portraiture like Verrocchio and Zurbarán (*Arts*, February 22, 1952). Frank's approach is clearly own-sakist; so is that of Georges Charensol, another member of what the young Turks of *Cahiers du cinéma* dismissively referred to as "the old guard" (de Baecque 2003, 104).

Charensol had written about cinema since the early 1920s and discussed *The Passion of Joan of Arc* in his pioneering survey of film history, *Panorama du cinéma*, where he placed it in the section on Scandinavian film because its director was a Dane, and its virtues were his:

> Even if *The Passion of Joan of Arc* is the noblest, worthiest, and most moving film that France has produced, in reality it owes nothing to our country. The same hard, astringent accent as in *Master of the House* resonates in *The Passion*, the same systematic mind reveals itself here in even greater fullness. (Charensol 1930, 139)

Charensol's review is particularly interesting from the point of view of Jullier's typology, because he explicitly contrasts *The Passion of Joan of Arc* with another film, a new French film that appeared a week before the revival at the Cinéma d'Essai: *La Vérité sur Bébé Donge* (*The Truth of Our Marriage*), a film Jullier suggests could have been among the top fifty of all time if a "Baumgartian," meliorist approach were dominant. Its virtues are described by Geneviève Sellier and Noël Burch: "In the whole history of French cinema, this is probably the film that displays the keenest psychological acuity and social insight in laying bare the battle of the sexes in the well-guarded milieu of the grand bourgeois patriarchy, which it does with a stylistic starkness worthy of Robert Bresson" (Burch and Sellier 2013, 328). Directed by Henri Decoin, *La Vérité sur Bébé Donge* tells the story (through elaborate flashbacks) of a callous, womanizing businessman (Jean Gabin) who is poisoned by his wife (Danielle Darrieux). While Charensol praised it as "happily breaking with the ambient conformism" of present-day filmmaking (*Les nouvelles litteraires*, February 28, 1952), it is clear that he regarded it as mediocre in comparison with Dreyer's film. In particular, its virtues resided in Darrieux's performance rather than Decoin's direction; Charensol describes film actors as "most often merely instruments in the director's hands." But while Charensol's strongly auteurist approach may not be the one best suited to appreciate the virtues of *La Vérité sur Bébé Donge*, this does not mean that it is the only one suited to appreciate *The Passion of Joan of Arc*.

André Bazin's review in the Catholic weekly *Radio-Cinéma-Télévision* (renamed *Télérama* in 1960) may seem superficially similar to Nino Frank's; it makes the same comparison with the art of the past—"A Dreyer is the equal of the great painters of the Italian Renaissance or Flemish school" (Bazin 1982, 21)—and uses the same quotation from Balázs. Bazin, however, quotes Balázs in support of a larger theoretical argument: that the cinema, through its capacity to capture the visible world as it really is, may reveal the spiritual side of it as well. Bazin writes: "Herein lies the rich paradox and inexhaustible lesson of this film: that the extreme spiritual purification is freed through the scrupulous realism of the camera as microscope" (Bazin 1982, 20). Bazin, born in 1918, was still a child when the talkies came in, and his theory regarded the sound film as an aesthetic advance over silent cinema. The review directly reflects this, claiming (without foundation) that Dreyer "so regretted" not being able to make the film with sound, but that it was so great that it was "already virtually speaking" (Bazin 1982, 21). Bazin's discussion of *The Passion of Joan of Arc* thus very evidently takes a meta-aesthetic, "Hegelian" approach; his praise for the film is tied up with his larger commitment to realism.

The reviewers in the daily newspapers focus less on Dreyer and more on the palpable intensity and stark candor of Falconetti's performance in the role of Joan of Arc. Indeed, Jean Rochereau, writing for the Catholic paper *La Croix*, sees it as undermining the auteurism reflected in some of the other reviews: "The heroine and the actress are so perfectly identified that it is just as valid to speak of Falconetti's JOAN as of *The Passion of Joan of Arc* by Dreyer" (*La Croix*, February 23, 1952). Rochereau goes on to describe the emotional progression of Falconetti's performance as "An entirely interior adventure, without the aid even of the inflexions of the voice, but all the more enriching a spectacle." The notion that the spectator is "enriched" suggests that the review takes a meliorist approach.

This is underscored by Rochereau's next sentence: "How better to sum it up than in the words of Pius X: prayer surrounded by beauty [*prière sur de la beauté*]." The critic invokes a famous saying by a pope who was a leading liturgical reformer, bent on purifying church music of profane and "theatrical" influences "in order that through it the faithful may be the more easily moved to devotion and better disposed for the reception of the fruits of grace belonging to the celebration of the most holy mysteries" (Pius X 1903). Stylistic differences aside, this is surprisingly similar to Jullier's description of the meliorist stance: "Far from providing escape, fiction becomes the underpinning for thought experiments directed at preparing its users to make good decisions when the moment comes to make choices that concern their whole existence" (Jullier 2015b, 157).

In 1952, the PCF (French Communist Party) exerted a powerful influence in French cultural life (see de Baecque 2003, chap. 2). In an even more evident fashion than their Catholic colleagues, the communist critics responding to *The Passion of Joan of Arc* described it as offering a model for making "good decisions." Pol Gaillard, the critic for the PCF daily *L'Humanité*, celebrated Jeanne's proletarian origins and compared her bravery to that of (implicitly communist) World War II resistance fighters: "The girl of the people who knows neither to read nor to write responds with all her good sense and all her power to the kollaborators [*kollaborateurs*] presiding under the protection of enemy troops ... What a resonance this admirable life has today!" (*L'Humanité*, February 23, 1952). Normally, the word "collaborateurs" is spelled with a C, but is here Germanized by being spelled with a K.

The weekly film paper *L'Écran français* marked the revival of *The Passion of Joan of Arc* with full-page coverage, including a gallery of quotations from earlier tributes to the film (*L'Écran français*, undated clipping, DFI/D I, A: Passion de Jeanne d'Arc, La, 6). One of these was written by the author Elsa Triolet, wife of Louis Aragon and the mouthpiece of PCF's campaign for evaluating literature on strictly ideological grounds (see Lazar 1986). Triolet writes of the appropriateness of showing extracts from *The Passion of Joan of Arc* at an event in 1951 held to commemorate the communist militant Danielle Casanova, who was arrested for resistance activities in 1942 and deported to Auschwitz, where she died of disease.

For the same issue of *L'Ecran français*, Georges Sadoul, the most authoritative communist critic, wrote a more detailed appreciation of the film where he not only echoes Triolet's invocation of Danielle Casanova, but also likens Jeanne to other communist martyr-heroes: André Marty (who was court-martialed as a ringleader of a naval munity in 1919 and subsequently became a leading figure in the French communist party and the Komintern), Henri Martin (a seaman sentenced to five years' imprisonment in 1950 for propaganda against France's war in Indochina), and Nikos Beloyannis (a leader of the Greek communist party, who was on trial at the time and executed on March 30, 1952). It is somewhat jarring to see Dreyer's Jeanne likened to a Stalinist thug like Marty, who supposedly bragged about having ordered the execution of hundreds of comrades during the Spanish Civil War (Beevor 2007, 181); but it is clear that Sadoul regarded Jeanne's unshakable commitment to her beliefs before the tribunal of a ruthless, oppressive power as furnishing an appropriate life lesson for fellow communists.

Conclusion

We have found a considerable variety of critical approaches in the contemporary reviews of Lo Duca's successful revival of *The Passion of Joan of Arc* at the Cinéma d'Essai in February 1952. While the program, the musical accompaniment, and Lo Duca's overall approach might have encouraged a highbrow cinephiliac reception of the film, the reviews were more diverse. A veteran reviewer like Georges Charensol might still—on the basis of an ethno-determinist auteurism that regards films as the creations of their directors and directors as imbued with the spirits of their nations—regard *The Passion of Joan of Arc* as a "Nordic" film, but most of the other reviewers did not regard this as significant, even if the program, with its Danish, Dreyer-scripted short, also lent implicit support to such an approach.

The variety of reactions is significant, not least because Laurent Jullier has argued that some films only look good from one of the three critical perspectives he describes (which I have called meliorist, own-sakist, and meta-aesthetic): "Any film can be appreciated according to any of the three tendencies we have described; one may nevertheless observe that certain films occasion (undoubtedly because they lend themselves better to it) a preponderance of public analyses that reflect only one of these tendencies" (Jullier 2015b, 160). Jullier may regard *The Passion of Joan of Arc* as such a film; his brief remarks about it imply that (like *Sunrise* or *2001*) it is a film that only an own-sakist can really admire. However, the critical response to it in 1952 demonstrated that this is not the case: Dreyer's film invites appreciation as a masterpiece from a very broad range of perspectives. Even so, Jullier's model is useful for examining the history of critical responses to a given film, the way a particular film has been treated by its "editors" (in Gary Taylor's expanded sense). Taking the work of these "editors" into account is necessary if we want to have a full view of the historical importance of a film like *Le Passion de Jeanne d'Arc*, and we can only do so properly if we recognize that while the influence of "editors" and their critical perspectives is sometimes a very local matter, it will often reach across national borders. The making of film history is never an exclusively national affair.

References

*Unless a translated version is cited, all translations are mine.

References to the Dreyer archive at the Danish Film Institute are given as (DFI/D).

Balázs, Béla. 2010. *Béla Balázs' Early Film Theory: Visible Man and the Spirit of Film*. New York: Berghahn.
Bazin, André. 1982. *The Cinema of Cruelty: From Buñuel to Hitchcock*. Trans. Sabine d'Estrée. New York: Seaver.

Beevor, Antony. 2007. *The Battle for Spain: The Spanish Civil War 1936–1939*. London: Phoenix.
Boltanski, Luc and Eve Chiapello. 1999. *Le nouvel esprit du capitalisme*. Paris: Gallimard.
Bordwell, David. 1997. *On the History of Film Style*. Cambridge, MA: Harvard University Press.
Burch, Noël and Geneviève Sellier. 2013. *The Battle of the Sexes in French Cinema, 1930–1956*. Durham, NC: Duke University Press.
Charensol, Georges. 1930. *Panorama du cinéma*. Paris: Éditions Kra.
CinemaTour. n.d. <www.cinematour.com/tour/fo/4662.html> (last accessed July 2, 2018).
Cohn, Danièle. 2007. "Quand et comment naît l'esthetique?" In *Dictionnaire d'esthétique et de philosophie de l'art*, ed. Roger Pouivet and Jacques Morizot. Paris: Armand Colin. 168–71.
de Baecque, Antoine. 2003. *La Cinéphilie: Invention d'un regard, histoire d'une culture (1944–1968)*. Paris: Fayard.
Drouzy, Maurice. 1985. "Jeanne d'Arc livrée aux bourreaux." *Cinématographe* 111: 62–7.
Drouzy, Maurice. 1987. "A qui appartient la *Jeanne d'Arc* de Dreyer?" *1895: Bulletin de l'association française de recherche sur l'historie du cinéma* 3: 3–6.
Gili, Jean A. 2007. "Lo Duca, de Milan à Samois-sur-Seine." *Archives* (Institut Jean Vigo) 100: 1–3.
Holmes, M. E. 2016. "Nino Frank, from Dada to Film Noir." <http://www.rememberninofrank.org> (last accessed May 31, 2017).
Jullier, Laurent. 2009. "Dossier: Cinephilia: Philistines and Cinephiles: The New Deal." *Framework* 50(1–2): 202–5.
Jullier, Laurent. 2015a. "Cinéma, l'histoire des styles reste à faire." *Positif* 647: 61–4.
Jullier, Laurent. 2015b. "Les 'meilleurs' films de tous les temps. À propos du palmarès décennal de *Sight & Sound*." In *Les films à voir cette semaine. Stratégies de la critique de cinéma*, ed. Laurent Jullier. Paris: L'Harmattan. 149–72.
Jullier, Laurent and Jean-Marc Leveratto. 2010. *Cinéphiles et cinéphilies: une histoire de la qualité cinématographique*. Paris: Armand Colin.
Lazar, Marc. 1986. "Les 'Batailles du livre' du parti communiste Français (1950–1952)." *Vingtième siecle: revue d'histoire* 10(1): 37–49.
Le Henaff, Régine. n.d. "*Rites sauvages*, résumé." <http://www.cinematheque-bretagne.fr/Base-documentaire-Rites-sauvages-426-10054-0-102.html?ref=> (last accessed May 12, 2017).
Lo Duca, Joseph-Marie. 1947. *Historie du cinéma*, 3rd edn. Que sais-je? Paris: Presses universitaires de France. Original edition, 1942.
Lo Duca, Joseph-Marie. 1952. "Trilogie mystique de Dreyer." *Cahiers du cinéma* 9: 60–3.
Lo Duca, Joseph-Marie. 1953. "52.000 hanno visto Giovanna." *Cinema nuovo* 2(20): 212.
Lo Duca, Joseph-Marie. 1957–68. *L'Érotisme au cinéma*. Vol. 1–4. Paris: Jean-Jacques Pauvert.
Lo Duca, Joseph-Marie. 1978. "Les films vieillissent-ils?" *Cinématographe* 36: 25–7.
Pipolo, Tony. 1988. "The spectre of *Joan of Arc*: Textual Variations in the Key Prints of Carl Dreyer's Film." *Film History* 2(4): 301–24.
Pius X. 1903. "*Tra Le Sollecitudini* Instruction on Sacred Music." <https://adoremus.org/1903/11/22/tra-le-sollecitudini/> (last accessed May 31, 2017).
Taylor, Gary. 1996. *Cultural Selection: Why Some Achievements Survive the Test of*

Time—and Others Don't. New York: Basic Books.
Thomas, Magali. 2007. "Joseph-Marie Lo Duca 1910–2004." *Archives* (Institut Jean Vigo) 100: 4–20.
Tybjerg, Casper. 2012. "Two Passions—One Film?" In *The Passion of Joan of Arc*. Blu-Ray/DVD Edition. London: Eureka/Masters of Cinema.

24. I AM CURIOUS (YELLOW) AS SEX EDUCATION IN THE USA

Saniya Lee Ghanoui

In 1969, a movie theater in Houston, Texas burned to the ground; fire officials said it had the hallmarks of arson. The theater manager, identified in the *New York Times* as Mrs. John Scott, said, "someone probably burned this place down in the name of decency." These "moral vigilantes," as Mrs. Scott called the culprits, started the fire to protest the showing of the Swedish film *I Am Curious (Yellow)* (*Jag är nyfiken—en film i gult*) (*New York Times* 1969). Mrs. Scott based her response on the barrage of protests—including picketing by a church group and numerous telephone calls by people conveying bomb threats—that had started since the theater, which she owned with her husband, had begun showing the film. Yet the theater owner did not apologize for playing the film and countered that she needed to do so for financial reasons: "We ran family movies for nine years and almost went broke," Mrs. Scott said angrily, according to the *Los Angeles Times* (Chriss 1969). Three years before the bombing, the theater began exhibiting pornographic movies and had been doing better financially. Even though the theater had been showing pornographic movies for three years, it was *I Am Curious (Yellow)*—the presence of a Swedish film in the American South—that caused the most controversy.

The plot of *I Am Curious (Yellow)* challenges standard description as it employs elements of documentary film, while also drawing from late-1960s art house cinema. Art house films of that decade often adopted "realism and authorial expressivity," according to film scholar David Bordwell, as a motivator for narrative (1979, 57). It is these two characteristics that give *I Am*

Curious (Yellow) space to function as a documentary film, even if it is a piece of fiction. The film also contains characteristics of the "participatory mode" of documentary film, a term coined by film theoretician Bill Nichols. In the participatory mode of documentary, filmmakers interact with their subjects and interviewees, and meaning is created from these collaborations (Nichols 1991).

I Am Curious (Yellow) tells the story of Lena (played by Lena Nyman), a socially conscious young woman whose political and sexual exploits with her lover Börje (played by Börje Ahlstedt) are recorded by her director-boyfriend Vilgot Sjöman, the real director of the film. For the film within the film, Lena walks around Stockholm interviewing random people about different problems affecting Swedish society—class structure, gender equality, and conscientious objection—before she goes to the countryside to learn about nonviolent political protests. Lena also begins a tumultuous relationship with Börje—their sex life is graphically shown throughout the film—that ends with both of them seeking scabies treatment. At the same time, the audience sees Vilgot and Lena's relationship deteriorate, and at the film's conclusion Vilgot meets another young woman. Intercut throughout the film are Vilgot's interviews with civil rights activist Martin Luther King, Jr. and the then-Minister of Communications and future Swedish Prime Minister Olof Palme.

Previous scholarship on *I Am Curious (Yellow)* has examined the film from two broad angles: the legal ramifications of the film in the USA, and the critical and audience reception. In 1968, US Customs officials seized the film for obscenity when it entered the country. The film advanced through the US court system, and in November 1968 the Second Circuit Court of Appeals, in *United States v. A Motion Picture Film Entitled "I Am Curious—Yellow"*, declared "the showing of the picture cannot be inhibited" (404 F. 2d 196 (2d Cir. 1968)). This ruling meant the film could enter the USA; however, different state governments still had the power to decide whether or not to show the film (Björk 2012, 2016). Reception of the film revealed how critics focused on four issues: the legal problems with the film, whether the film was pornographic, the film's dullness, and the physical appearance of actress Nyman (Heffernan 2014).

Yet these approaches largely neglect exploration of why the film received such a diverse set of criticism prompted by its release in the USA. Critical responses ranged from those who thought it was boring to those who thought it pornographic, or as one critic said, it "may well be one of the most important films of our time" (Smith 1969, 42).

The response the film received in the USA, I argue, demonstrated that it functioned as a form of non-normative sex education. Documentary film intends to inform or educate; as such the documentary endeavor of *I Am Curious (Yellow)* presented the film as a piece of historical record, and thus educational. Both film critics and the legal system grappled to identify the film's

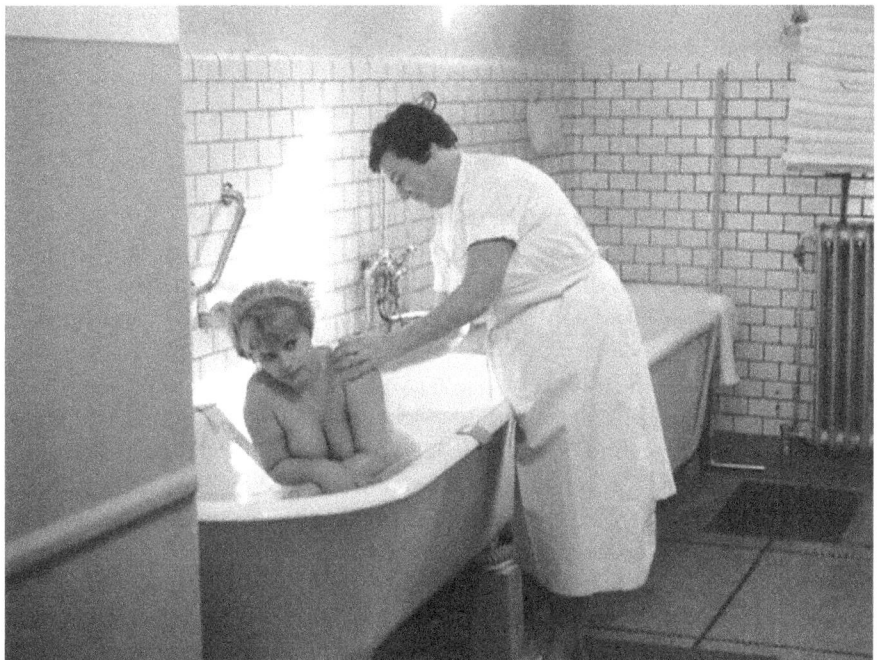

Figure 24.1 *I Am Curious (Yellow)* used real DDT on both actors in the scabies treatment scene. Director Vilgot Sjöman later commented that he never considered faking it, as he was so absorbed in the documentary genre.

genre; even if the US Court did not view the film as pornographic, it struggled to identify the film as anything else. How could a film that graphically showed sex not be pornographic? The film pushed the definitions of what was and was not documentary and educational film through its portrayal, and questioning, of real issues—class, gender equality, and sex—through a fictional storyline. The film's documentary style "link[ed] the film's overarching concern with sex to larger social issues" (Heffernan 2014, 112). Sjöman became so embedded in creating a documentary film that he forgot that *I Am Curious (Yellow)* was fictional. In the DVD commentary, Sjöman spoke about filming the scabies scene: "venereal diseases, like scabies, were treated at Sankt Göran Hospital, so we filmed the bath in that hospital in a documentary way." As the standard practice at the time was to treat scabies with the insecticide DDT, Sjöman used DDT in the scene, a chemical that stung actress Nyman. Sjöman reflected that it never occurred to him not to use DDT, even if the chemical never showed in the film, as "that's what happens when you film so much in the documentary way" (Sjöman 2003).

To be clear, I do not contend that the filmmakers intended *I Am Curious (Yellow)* to be educational, but it nonetheless functioned as such. The evolution of sex education films means that there is no one way to define normative sex education, but there are trends that have transformed as these films became more prevalent. In the USA, theatrically released sex education films tended to focus on venereal disease control; those made specifically for school use turned more toward issues of biology and reproduction (Eberwein 1999; Schaefer 1999).

In the 1960s, the modern conservative movement in the USA mobilized and targeted sex education as a problem; this transpired at the same time as "sexual revolutions" occurred throughout the USA and Europe (Allyn 2000). Evangelical churches and conservative social activists in the USA became more vocal against sex education; they viewed it as a threat to the heteronormative nuclear family (Luker 2006; Petrzela 2015). Conversely, in Sweden sex education had been a requirement in public schools since 1955. As the country's sexual norms changed in the late 1960s, Sweden experienced economic expansion that influenced "a major transformation" in the Swedish film industry that brought with it the loosening of censorship (Björklund 2012, 154). The reform that began in Sweden in the 1960s hit the USA in the 1970s in what film historian Kevin Heffernan calls "an unprecedented (and since unequaled) level of sexual frankness to the public exhibition of motion pictures," (Heffernan 2014, 105). *I Am Curious (Yellow)* served as a transnational flashpoint during a moment of contentious national debate over sex and society in the USA.

Social and political commentary informs audiences and challenges them to question the assumptions of their ordinary social interactions. By having Nyman's body at the forefront of her own sexual experience, and not that of her male partner, Sjöman educated audiences as to the sexuality of the female body. It seems plausible to suggest that Sjöman knew the kind of reviews *I Am Curious (Yellow)* would receive and knew that Nyman's body would be central to those critical reviews—and that is precisely the point. The audience's education revolved around sex and sexuality, but also on the impact of outside social forces on the female body.

As *I Am Curious (Yellow)* moved through the US court system, Sjöman testified that his intentions were to "make a portrait of Sweden right now in the late '60s" (Sjöman 1968, 235). Sjöman described how he made Lena the center of the film, even if her storyline was fictional, to elucidate the larger educational, non-fictional issues he wanted to address: "If you are going to make a portrait of your own country, what is going on, you are making documentaries, interviewing people. Then if you don't have a focus for that theme, somebody who is trying to understand this won't get any feeling for it" (Sjöman 1968, 236–7). Three years later, at an American Film Institute seminar held in Beverly Hills, California, Sjöman nodded to the fact that he intentionally made the film for an international audience, saying he initially wanted to go further by doing "propaganda pieces" on the political climate in

Sweden. He concluded that he "wasn't the kind of guy" who would be able to do that, but he still felt *I Am Curious (Yellow)*'s political impact was more important than its artistic contributions (Sjöman 1971, 10).

Sjöman's use of Lena as the focal point disrupts the film within a film and speaks to larger implications of sex, relationships, and even social healthcare, particularly in the DDT scene. After Lena confronts Börje and tells him that she has scabies, they go to a clinic together for treatment. Lena and Börje's relationship is tainted not only emotionally, but physically as well. Vilgot films the process in which Lena and Börje are scrubbed, washed, and disinfected, and he himself is involved in the scene: the audience sees the film crew waiting around for the clinicians to finish. This scene halts the film within the film to show the consequences of Lena and Börje's sex life. As with many theatrically released sex education films, the results of sex, particularly pregnancy and infections, are often included as a means of education. Sjöman used that educational tool to comment on how sex in other films often did not portray realistic sex. When testifying in the USA on behalf of his film, Assistant US Attorney Lawrence W. Schilling asked Sjöman if his intention behind the sex scenes was "to show things as they actually happened." Sjöman responded: "Yes, to break away from the ordinary way of presenting very arranged love scenes, and to approach reality and reconstruct reality, and to give the audience the feeling that this is more likely to be the real behavior than what is shown in many other films" (Sjöman 1969, 242–3).

The portrayal of sex in *I Am Curious (Yellow)* confounded film critics and the US Courts because the sex did not fit into a specific category of sex education or pornography, documentary or fiction. Specifically, in *United States v. A Motion Picture Film Entitled "I Am Curious—Yellow"*, the Court focused on "prurient interests" and if the film appealed to only those interests. Judge Paul R. Hays acknowledged that "sexual conduct is undeniably an important aspect of the picture and may be thought of as constituting one of its principal themes"; however, the central subject of the film "is certainly not sex" (404 F. 2d 196 (2d Cir. 1968)). Even though Hays did not explicitly say what the dominant theme of the film was, by recognizing the important, but decentralized, place of sex in the film, he turned the film away from obscene and pornographic themes and reified its documentary status.

Additionally, Hays characterized the "sexual theme" as "subordinate" and "handled in such a way as to make it at least extremely doubtful that interest in it should be characterized as 'prurient.'" By not confining the film to one specific genre, Hays equated the representation of sex with "redeeming social value" that labeled the film as a tool for fulfilling a social need (404 F. 2d 196 (2d Cir. 1968)). The sex, then, became informational through its ability to be used as a social tool when there was not one; Hays' use of "redeeming" indicated that the sex put forth a compensatory quality that contributed to the public importance of ideas and the dissemination of those concepts. The film as an entire piece of work, as measured by the Court, played off the film within the film framing. This allowed it to function as a documentary with an educational rationale for its treatment of sex.

Film critics also saw the film as being beyond contemporary understandings of obscenity, as the editor for *Film Quarterly* put it. Films like *I Am Curious (Yellow)* and Andy Warhol's *Blue Movie* (1969, also called *Fuck*), the editor wrote, "ought to be run as a required sex-education film in high schools, thus turning off millions of hot-blooded teen-agers" (Editor's Notebook 1969, 2). In *Film Quarterly*'s review of the film, critic Clyde B. Smith equated the documentary scenes of Lena with "that of social documentaries such as we see on US network public programming" (1969, 38). Sjöman's goal of creating a portrait of Sweden succeeded in the USA as the film mirrored the style often seen in public broadcasting documentaries. *I Am Curious (Yellow)*, then, served as a familiar and yet disruptive vehicle for contemporary Swedish cinema in the US market. Furthermore, Smith noted that there were no distinct lines between the non-fictional and fictional parts of the films, and that by the time the audience was well into the film, "Sjöman is weaving together at least three major elements on the first level of perception: direct social comment and two sets of emotional relationships. And by this time his social comment is both direct and indirect" (1969, 38). Many critics viewed the film not only as the opposite of erotic, but rather as "anti-erotic," including Roger Ebert of the *Chicago Sun-Times*. He noted that, "this movie will drive thoughts of sex out of your mind for weeks. See the picture and buy twin beds," indicating that couples would be so turned off by this picture that they would never sleep in the same bed again (Ebert 1969).

Social understandings of sex education films separate them from pornography in their themes—pregnancy, sexually transmitted infections, or reproduction, for example—and their intentional inability to excite their audience. These concepts have been socially understood as educational, and thus helped *I Am Curious (Yellow)* escape the label of pornography. Sjöman's outspokenness about his desire to showcase an index of Swedish society at that time rejected the old understanding of social relations; for example, we see this in Lena's questions about a classless society. While the sex scenes and nudity may have been the central issue for the US courts and film critics, in Sweden Sjöman's approach to political issues caused the most controversy. As film historian Peter Cowie noted, in the DVD commentary of the film, the debate in Sweden around *I Am Curious (Yellow)* centered on the "complacency of many Swedes" towards their social environment (Cowie 2003). Sjöman's film also advocated for a rethinking of the "so-called new morality" while also "making a powerful argument for sexual equality for women" (Smith 1969, 38). The boringness of the film, which both the US courts and many film critics recorded, challenged the social and legal understandings of a pornographic film.

The USA had seen sex on film before. For instance, Times Square in New York City housed many pornographic theaters and sex shops, and similar businesses dotted the nation—but *I Am Curious (Yellow)* was different. The film did not portray sex as a sensual experience as depicted in mainstream Hollywood films. Nor did it present the sterile and methodical sex that people saw in pornography from the USA. Rather, it showed sex in full spectrum; it flaunted natural bodies in ways not yet seen in popular American film. It is in this way, then, that the film actually served to educate American audiences on the difference, in sex, between sensual Hollywood romance and stale pornographic depictions. *I Am Curious (Yellow)* conveyed a sense of elsewhere that was, at once, both startlingly familiar and defiantly foreign. The film's critique of Swedish social democracy served to educate American audiences on the reality of sexuality in politically charged ways at a moment of change the world over.

Acknowledgments

I gratefully acknowledge Anna Westerstahl Stenport and Arne Lunde for their thoughtful feedback on this chapter. I presented an earlier version of it at the Entangled Media Histories conference at Lund University and I thank the audience for its questions and comments.

References

Allyn, David. 2000. *Make Love, Not War: The Sexual Revolution: An Unfettered History*. Boston: Little, Brown.
Björk, Ulf Jonas. 2012. "Tricky Film: The Critical and Legal Reception of *I Am Curious (Yellow)* in America." *American Studies in Scandinavia* 44, no 2: 113–34.
Björk, Ulf Jonas. 2016. "A Modicum of Social Value? The Critical and Legal Discussion of *I Am Curious (Yellow)* in America." In *Swedish Cinema and the Sexual Revolution*, ed. Elisabet Björklund and Mariah Larsson. Jefferson, NC: McFarland. 201–15.
Björklund, Elisabet. 2012. "The Most Delicate Subject: A History of Sex Education Films in Sweden." PhD dissertation, Lund University.
Bordwell, David. 1979. "The Art Cinema as a Mode of Film Practice." *Film Criticism* 4, no. 1 (Fall): 56–64.
Chriss, Nicholas C. 1969. "Arson Suspected After Houston Theater Burns." *Los Angeles Times*, June 7.
Cowie, Peter. "The Battle for *I Am Curious (Yellow)*." Disc 1. *I Am Curious (Yellow)*, DVD. Directed by Vilgot Sjöman. New York: Criterion Collection, 2003.
Ebert, Roger. 1969. "I Am Curious (Yellow)." <https://www.rogerebert.com/reviews/i-am-curious-yellow-1969> (last accessed March 24, 2018).
Eberwein, Robert. 1999. *Sex Ed: Film, Video, and the Framework of Desire*. New Brunswick, NJ: Rutgers University Press.

Editor's Notebook. 1969. "End of the foreplay flick?" *Film Quarterly* 22, no. 4 (Summer): 1–2.

Heffernan, Kevin. 2014. "Prurient (Dis)Interest: The American Release and Reception of *I Am Curious (Yellow)*." In *Sex Scene*, ed. Eric Schaefer. Durham, NC: Duke University Press. 105–25.

Luker, Kristin. 2006. *When Sex Goes to School: Warring Views on Sex—and Sex Education—since the Sixties*. New York: Norton.

New York Times. 1969. "'I Am Curious' in Flames." June 7.

Nichols, Bill. 1991. *Representing Reality: Issues and Concepts in Documentary*. Bloomington: Indiana University Press.

Petrzela, Natalia Mehlman. 2015. *Classroom Wars: Language, Sex, and the Making of Modern Political Culture*. New York: Oxford University Press.

Schaefer, Eric. 1999. *Bold! Daring! Shocking! True: A History of Exploitation Films, 1919–1959*. Durham, NC: Duke University Press.

Sjöman, Vilgot. 1968. *I Am Curious (Yellow): The Complete Scenario of the Film by Vilgot Sjöman with over 250 Illustrations*. New York: Grove Press.

Sjöman, Vilgot. 1971. "American Film Institute Seminar with Vilgot Sjöman." Seminar, American Film Institute: Center for Advanced Film Studies, Beverly Hills, CA, May 4.

Sjöman, Vilgot. "Director's Diary." Disc 1. *I Am Curious (Yellow)*, DVD. Directed by Vilgot Sjöman. New York: Criterion Collection, 2003.

Smith, Clyde B. 1969. "I Am Curious (Yellow)," *Film Quarterly* 22, no. 4 (Summer): 37–45.

25. TRANSNATIONAL CINEFEMINISM OF THE 1970s AND MAI ZETTERLING'S DOCUMENTARY ELSEWHERES

Mariah Larsson

Often thought of and described as a Swedish woman film director, Mai Zetterling was nonetheless active as a filmmaker in several different countries. After her first documentaries, which were shot in Sweden, France, and Iceland, but backed by the BBC and broadcast first and foremost in Great Britain, Zetterling made films in Sweden, Denmark, France, Canada, Greenland, and the UK. Although she would recurrently be associated with the country of Ingmar Bergman, her career was independent of national borders. In fact, already during her time as an actress, after concluding her work in Bergman's *Music in Darkness* (*Musik i mörker*, 1948), in December 1947 she emigrated from Sweden to England, where she would live for much of the rest of her life. From the mid-1960s onwards she divided her time between London and southern France. She never moved back to Sweden, although she made her first feature-length fiction films within the Swedish film industry in the 1960s. Later, however, when refused funding in Sweden, she did not hesitate to seek opportunities elsewhere. In the 1970s, Zetterling made a virtue of necessity, looking actively outside of traditional, national feature film production contexts in order to find financial backing for her projects.

Accordingly, rather than pinning her into a particular national cinema, it makes sense to conceive of Zetterling as a transnational filmmaker. Undoubtedly, those of her films produced by Sandrews, or by Sandrews in collaboration with the Swedish Film Institute, belong within the Swedish art cinema institution: *Loving Couples* (*Älskande par*, 1964), *Night Games* (*Nattlek*, 1966), *The*

Girls (*Flickorna*, 1968), and *Amorosa* (1986). These feature-length fiction films are produced by a Swedish production company, are sometimes based on Swedish material or take place during a tour of Sweden, and obviously display Swedish actors and actresses. Nonetheless, a case could be made that even these films carry with them something "un-Swedish" or even "anti-Swedish" (see e.g. Axelsson 1968; Bergström 1968; Schein 1977; for a further discussion see Larsson 2006). For the rest of her career, moreover, Zetterling worked outside of a strictly defined national cinema. If we look beyond her traditional feature-length fiction film production, Zetterling emerges as a remarkably transnational film director—in her choice of topics and locations, at the level of financial backing and production, and in the contexts in which she made her films. At the same time, however, her nationality, like her gender, is always in the foreground, emphasized in the production context, by her reception, and also, to some extent, by herself.

In this chapter, the aim is to explore how Zetterling negotiated her own (trans)nationality in order to find opportunities for filmmaking in three documentary films, *The Prosperity Race* (1962), "The Strongest" (a segment of *Visions of Eight*, 1973), and *Concrete Grandma* (*Betongmormor*, 1986). *The Prosperity Race* was the third of four documentaries Zetterling made for the BBC. When deciding to become a film director, Zetterling took it upon herself to learn filmmaking by beginning with small-crew documentaries. Like the other three, *The Prosperity Race* is a black and white, half-hour long documentary with an explanatory voiceover by Zetterling. As the film's narrator, she is also present in several shots. "The Strongest" is one of eight segments that make up the Olympic Games omnibus documentary of the Munich Games in 1972. Approximately eleven minutes long, it portrays weightlifters, in color and without explanatory voiceover except in the brief introduction. Finally, *Concrete Grandma* was made for the Swedish construction company Skanska's hundredth anniversary. Twenty-six minutes long, it is shot on video and has a fictional narrative as a framework for the showcasing of Skanska's various construction projects. Zetterling features prominently in the film as the titular grandmother.

These three films will be used as case studies to demonstrate Zetterling's complex and sometimes paradoxical relation to geographic and symbolic space. This relationship is paradoxical because, on the one hand, she seems to project herself as a citizen of the world while, on the other, she needs to negotiate as well as exploit various expectations placed on her due to both her national and her gender identity. In some of these cases, it is precisely due to her nationality that she is given the opportunity to make the film. And often, because of her gender, she is anticipated as making certain choices or as providing a "woman's perspective." Although made in different decades, with different technology, in different conditions, with different narrative strategies, and for different purposes, the films all share the particular trait of a careful balance of proximity and detachment. Zetterling both distances herself from and is deeply involved in her subjects at the same time, something which is sometimes expressed in the narrative, voiceover and tone of her films and sometimes in shot size (close-up, medium shot, long shot).

A National/Transnational Auteur?

As film scholars have come to regard transnationalism as, in Mette Hjort's words, "a welcome demise of ideologically suspect nation-states and the cinematic arrangements to which they gave rise" (Hjort 2009, 13–14), it may seem a given to regard Zetterling's transnationalism as something positive. Nonetheless, there are many reasons why films are made across national borders, and several of them have to do with conditions for production, economic circumstances, or simply opportunity. As Hjort argues in "On the Plurality of Cinematic Transnationalism," transnationalism is the "new virtue term of film studies" (Hjort 2009, 13), and associating Zetterling with it means that the director would thereby also be associated with qualities of ideological goodness, among them the end of nationalism. However, as the discussion below of the films demonstrates, the nation-state may be more markedly brought to the fore in a transnational situation than in a national one, because the expectations of a perceived particular national belonging become more pronounced. Although—or perhaps because—Zetterling frequently worked outside Sweden, she would never be able to shed the spectre of "Swedishness." Rather, it seems as if her nationality was enhanced and became more marked by her election to work abroad.

Moreover, on the one hand, Zetterling's transnationalism can be described as a romantic choice. A significant part of her self-crafted image and biographical legend construed her as cosmopolitan and as a citizen of the world (Larsson 2006). On the other hand, however, these characteristics were also born out of her expulsion from the Swedish film industry due to the commercial and critical failures of her 1960s feature films. For eighteen years, between *The Girls* and *Amorosa*, Zetterling did not make one single feature-length fiction film in her native country. This time period in Zetterling's life and career has, from a strictly national perspective, previously been regarded as a forced exile or even as a long slump in her artistic output (Jordahl 1999; Åhlund 1996; Larsson 2006, 10). Nonetheless, being a modernist in exile seems to have been Zetterling's preferred state, and those eighteen years were remarkably productive. No fewer than four documentaries, two feature-length fiction films, one short TV-production, three episodes of an omnibus film, and episodes of a TV-series called *The Hitchhiker* (France, Canada, USA, 1983–91), as well as four works of written fiction and one autobiography, were made during this "slump." Although there is no question that Zetterling did feel ostracized by the Swedish filmmaking community and unfairly treated by Göran Lindgren, the producer at Sandrews (Zetterling 1985), most likely the narrative of her slump was made in hindsight. Between 1986 and her death from pancreatic cancer in 1994, Zetterling repeatedly made unsuccessful attempts to make a film adaptation of Swedish cleaning woman and author Maja Ekelöf's *Rapport från en skurhink* (1970, "Report from a Wash Bucket"), a struggle which shaped the narrative of Zetterling's career in Sweden. During this time period, Zetterling's biographical legend became focused on themes of conflict, marginalization, being misunderstood, and even bitterness.

Moreover, earlier forms of film historiography would focus on theatrically released films, fiction or documentary, and make use of a more or less narrow conceptualization of national cinema. Consequently, Zetterling's eighteen years outside of the Swedish art cinema institution, productive as they were, have been overlooked. Although feminist film scholars are well aware of the conditions under which women filmmakers have worked, the paradigms of national cinema and art cinema, respectively and in conjunction, have traditionally been strong within film studies. On the one hand, trying to draw attention to and gain respect for women filmmakers includes conforming to an existing paradigm and elevating them into the "pantheon" of national auteurs (cf. Staiger 1985). On the other hand, women filmmakers have been overlooked because of their work in what have been regarded as "minor" genres and "minor" formats, concepts which are reinforced by conforming to a traditional paradigm. Nevertheless, more recent approaches to film history propose a wider definition of film and—as the endeavor of this book demonstrates—attempt to look beyond the national, thereby opening new ways of finding connections, causal relations, and complementary historiographical narratives.

Considering the way Zetterling negotiated her own transnationality in order to attract funding to her different projects, one can see how she creatively navigated among potential financial backers, making a virtue out of necessity due to harsh economic constraints. For instance, for her Greenland documentary *Of Seals and Men* (1979), the initial impetus to film on Greenland came from well-known explorer Wally Herbert, who wanted a TV series documenting his circumferential travel of the remote island. When that expedition had to be cancelled, Zetterling tapped into the Greenlandic seal hunt debate—partly initiated by Brigitte Bardot—and thereby secured the means needed to make a 30-minute documentary on seal hunting funded by the Royal Greenlandic Trade Department (see Larsson and Stenport 2015). Another such creative navigation, albeit one which never came to fruition, was her proposal for a seven-part TV series on Simone de Beauvoir's *The Second Sex* (*Le Deuxième Sexe*, 1949). The seven one-hour episodes were to take place around the globe, featuring a different woman in the lead and a different country in each episode and mainly using a voiceover, to facilitate dubbing or subtitling with the aim of international release (Mai Zetterling collection A1.6.2 vol 3; see also Larsson, forthcoming).

Zetterling's various efforts at making herself transnational in order to attract funding were perhaps especially prominent and successful with respect to her documentary production, which bracketed her years of feature-length fiction film production in the 1960s. These years ended with the disastrous reception, in terms of both box-office and critical assessment, of her eventually most famous film, *The Girls*. In many ways, it seems as though documentary filmmaking was a kind of "safe space" for Zetterling, a genre in which she could try out ideas, experiment, or hone her skills. In the early 1960s, the explicit intention was to learn the "ABC of film making" (Zetterling 1985), whereas in the 1970s, documentaries became a refuge after she had been snubbed by Swedish art cinema institutions.

The Prosperity Race

Already in Zetterling's first ventures as a film director, the four documentaries she made in collaboration with the BBC, her tone, and her choice of subjects bespoke her fascination with people and cultures outside of mainstream Western culture. *The Polite Invasion* (1960) dealt with the Sámi people in Jokkmokk; *Lords of Little Egypt* (1961) took place among the Roma people in southern France; and *The Do-It-Yourself Democracy* (1963) portrayed Iceland and the Icelanders. The documentaries are unequivocally ethnographic, with Zetterling as a curious guide who conveys information as she finds answers to her questions. However, in *The Prosperity Race*, Zetterling turned her inquisitive and ethnographic gaze toward Sweden and the Swedes, her "own" people, one could say, which led to controversy among Swedes living in the UK.

The controversy arose out of Zetterling's representation of Sweden. At that point in time, the image of Sweden as a middle way between the USA and the Soviet Union, between capitalism and communism, had become highly charged and symbolic. There were several elements to this image of the "Swedish model" (see e.g. Marklund and Petersen 2013). One had to do with sexuality and the introduction of mandatory sex education in schools in 1955. Another one had to do with suicide statistics, misconstruing suicide rates in Sweden as the highest in the world. Both of these came out of the idea of a nation-state where the reach of government had taken control over and colonized all individual privacy and intimate life, where the welfare state killed any spontaneity, passion, and joy in life by providing too much comfort, protecting its citizens "from the cradle to the grave" (see Lennerhed

1994; Marklund 2009; Arnberg and Marklund 2016). When Zetterling was interviewed in a Swedish women's journal, she claimed to be interested in dismantling the myth of Sweden, and the interview concluded on a positive note, affirming that such an ambassador was just what Sweden needed (Edvardsson 1961; Larsson 2006, 48).

However, when the film was broadcast in Great Britain, UK-based Swedes complained to Swedish media. "The usual old hogwash," was the angry verdict (Nilsson 1962, translation mine), because Zetterling depicted the Swedes as lonely and welfared to death, with loveless sex lives, alcoholism, juvenile crime, and, yes, suicides. "Swedes do not drink more than Americans," Zetterling's voiceover explained, to the images of a man reeling along a sidewalk, "but the way they drink . . ." At the end of the film, Zetterling is shown at the top of the Katarina-elevator in Stockholm, looking out over the beautiful cityscape and then into the camera. "Swedes are for themselves," she stated into the camera, "alone." The Swedish evening newspaper *Aftonbladet* accused Zetterling of opportunism. In the words of the newspaper's London correspondent: "Mai Zetterling knows very well that Sweden is not like the nation she has described in her film. She knows—very well, all too well—that the misconception sells. It works with the general public, it makes its participants popular. Consequently, she has acted out of pure opportunism, against better knowledge. You give people what they want, even if it harms your own old home country" (Nilsson, 1962, translation mine).

Nationality is, quite obviously, in the foreground in this controversy. As an expatriate Swedish star, Zetterling had for many years been regarded as an ambassador of Sweden abroad, as someone who represented Swedish people and, in particular, Swedish women (Larsson 2006: 48–50). Simultaneously, there was an expectation that she would remain the same, uncorrupted by the foreign influences she experienced by living abroad. Several articles and interviews in the popular press in the 1940s and 1950s emphasized that Zetterling had not picked up outlandish ways, that she was in no way a star diva, but still an unassuming Swede. For the Brits, on the other hand, Zetterling's familiar unfamiliarity—her respective status as a film and theater star and as a Swede living in the UK—was instrumental in paving the way for the documentaries, in particular the ones dealing with Sweden (Larsson 2006, 48–50).

Zetterling defended her film by stating that even a welfare society could not be without its problems and that it was not right to deny their existence (Anthal 1962). Nonetheless, her film can quite neatly be compared to other Sweden-bashing films, for instance Luigi Scattini's Italian mondo-documentary *Sweden—Heaven and Hell* (*Svezia, inferno e paradiso*) from 1968, but since she was Swedish (*our* Mai Zetterling, *our* star), her representation of Sweden was considered a betrayal. She should have known better, because she is one of us, was the idea, although Zetterling had lived abroad for fifteen years.

"THE STRONGEST"

The 1972 Summer Olympics in Munich became tragically marked by the events of the Munich massacre, the terrorist act in which eleven Israeli hostages were killed. Of the eight directors contracted to create the Olympics documentary *Visions of Eight* (1973), only one had not completed the shooting of his segment when the terrorists struck. John Schlesinger's "The Longest," about the marathon runner Ron Hill, thus became the only part of the Munich Olympics documentary that included something of the hostage taking (Diffrient 2005). Accordingly, the result is an omnibus documentary which seems to downplay the tragedy and instead focus on sports. The idea behind the film, however, was to showcase directors from different nations, much like the Games were supposed to be a friendly competition between athletes representing different countries (Diffrient 2005).

Each of the eight segments is introduced with still black-and-white images of the respective director at work, with the sound of a shutter going off accompanying the director's brief comment on their chosen topic on the voiceover. Zetterling's episode focused on the weightlifters. In her introduction to the segment, Zetterling explained "I am not interested in sports, but I am interested in obsessions." Her segment juxtaposes the big, heavy weightlifters with images from the preparation of food for the thousands of athletes in the Olympic village.

The film begins with a lone figure, outdoors in the Olympic village, rehearsing the weightlifting moves again and again while the camera zooms out to

Figure 25.1 The weightlifter is dwarfed by the huge buildings of the Olympics in *Visions of Eight* (prod. David L. Wolper, 1973), segment "The Strongest", dir. Mai Zetterling.

show him as a small, lonely dot in the park. Abruptly, the segment cuts to a close-up of a heavy barbell, hitting the ground with a loud clanking sound. Again, we are shown a lone weightlifter, frog-jumping through the training hall with only the surrounding equipment as company. As the hall begins to fill up with weightlifters warming up and exercising, the soundtrack begins to list things necessary for such a huge arrangement as the Olympics. Mattresses, pillows, even curtain rings, but most especially, food: 1 350 kilos of porridge, 120 000 bread rolls, 140 000 litres of orange juice, and so on. In a montage, we are shown the preparation of these masses of food, interspersed with images of the weightlifters, somehow pointing to the sheer physicality and corporeality of sports and athletes, and the bloatedness of both weightlifters and the Olympic Games. As film scholar David Scott Diffrient has pointed out, the segment seems "critical of the kind of nationalistic pageantry that had earlier been associated with the Berlin Games of 1936" (Diffrient 2005, 22). This far into the segment, Zetterling has presented us with a detached distance, both in shot size (the zoom-out to show the lone figure in the first shot) and in her mechanical listing of the items of the Olympics' machinery.

However, as the competitive event begins, Zetterling's segment enters into a different mood. There is still a fascination with the bizarrely huge bodies, but her camera also captures the concentration, apprehension, and hesitation experienced by these enormous men as they approach the bar-bell as if it were a wild beast, succeeding or failing at lifting it above the head. "In a moment like that, we begin to understand something of the difficulties of the weightlifter," Roger Ebert wrote in his review of *Visions of Eight* (Ebert 1973).

Figure 25.2 Mai Zetterling moves closer to capture the tension before the lift in *Visions of Eight* (prod. David L. Wolper, 1973), segment "The Strongest", dir. Mai Zetterling

The humoristic detachment of the earlier part of the episode transforms into something more like awe and respect, but also a kind of identification and understanding. Her camera zooms in on these giant weightlifters, and instead of bizarre inhuman bodies incorporated into the machinery of the Olympics, they become deeply human and, in spite of their looks, their gender, and their choice of sports, not so different from the director herself.

At the end of the segment, Zetterling displays the deconstruction of the weightlifters' podium after the competition is over. It takes five men to carry the bar-bell from the podium. Although her segment thematizes loneliness and obsession, it also seems to want to demonstrate how the few moments of the weightlifter's lift are dependent on large machinery, involving many workers and much planning. The concluding shot comically shows one of the weightlifters and his much smaller coach from behind as they leave the training hall.

The 1972 Olympic Games in Munich were planned with a focus on creating an event that could positively replace the ugly memory of the 1936 Berlin Olympics in Nazi Germany (Young 2005). Perhaps because of this, the documentary intended to commemorate the Games consisted of eight different directors' visions, rather than the unified and highly personal single aesthetic vision of Leni Riefenstahl's famous *Olympia* (1938). The omnibus result does form a multi-focal perspective on the Olympics. Moreover, it can be described as an example of what Hjort calls "auteurist transnationalism" (Hjort 2009, 22–4). All the directors invited were famous auteurs: Schlesinger, Michael Pfleghar, Milos Forman, Kon Ichikawa, Claude Lelouch, Yuri Ozerov, Arthur Penn, and Zetterling, with each representing a different national cinema and nationality.

Accordingly, in *Visions of Eight*, nationality and auteur status took precedence over gender. While Zetterling was the single woman among the directors, she was not there to represent women but to represent Sweden, actually replacing Ingmar Bergman, who was busy elsewhere and declined to participate in the film (Diffrient 2005, 21). The women athletes were covered by German director Pfleghar, after Zetterling had elected to dedicate her part of the film to the weightlifters. A juxtaposition of Pfleghar's and Zetterling's respective contributions to the film is revealing, in that Pfleghar's "cast a decidedly male gaze" (Diffrient 2005, 23) on the women athletes, with "leering close-ups and fragmented editing" (Diffrient 2005, 23). In contrast, Zetterling's gaze at the male weightlifters begins as a detached, almost humorous, observational gaze, only to continue into intense, empathetic identification, moving from distance to proximity.

Nevertheless, although each of the directors represented a country, their respective episodes did not necessarily reflect that country's athletes or sports. Rather, it was a gathering of nationalities, mirroring the Olympic Games, in friendly competition (Diffrient 2005). As that of a national auteur, Zetterling's perspective on the Olympics was (somewhat like her co-directors') almost nation-less in its close study of the weightlifters' loneliness and obsession.

A CONCRETE GRANDMA?

In 1986, Mai Zetterling made a commissioned film for the construction company Skanska. *Concrete Grandma* (*Betongmormor*) was a 26-minute film detailing the various international and national construction projects with which Skanska was involved. Produced by AB Förberg film, which specialized in industrial film, *Concrete Grandma* is the only such film Zetterling ever made. Although she had made commissioned films before, *Concrete Grandma* falls squarely into the category of industrial film. As Patrick Vonderau and Vinzenz Hediger point out in their introduction to *Films That Work*, "industrial and utility films have to be understood in terms of their specific, usually organizational, purpose, and in the very context of power and organizational practice in which they appear" (Hediger and Vonderau 2009, 10). Therefore, industrial films have not been regarded as "self-sufficient entities for aesthetic analysis" (10). Nonetheless, it can easily be argued that in the commissioned industrial film, artistry and commerce might very well meet and compete for space (cf. Stjernholm 2018, 24–6), in particular when a more or less established auteur is enlisted to make the film.

Zetterling further reinforces her own presence in the film by placing herself in the lead role as the titular "grandmother." *Concrete Grandma* has a fictional narrative that frames the documentary images and soundtrack detailing Skanska's various projects. Zetterling plays a woman who, having driven her grandchild to a job interview at Skanska, falls asleep in the lobby while waiting for the interview to finish. She dreams that she is followed around by corporate spies, who want to know the secret of Skanska's success. In various costumes, such as dungarees and hard hat, Viennese traditional dress, and a well-tailored man's suit, Zetterling takes them around the globe and demonstrates that no one does construction better than Skanska. To a cheesy 1980s synthesizer soundtrack, she drives trucks and helicopters, rides construction site elevators, and serves ice cream cones, while spouting aphorisms in a tongue-in-cheek declamatory tone.

The film was made in relation to Skanska's upcoming hundredth anniversary. Beginning as Skånska Cementgjuteriet in 1887, Skanska developed into one of the leading construction companies in Sweden during the twentieth century, specializing in large-scale construction: power stations, freeways, bridges, and tunnels. From the mid-1960s to the early 1970s, it built much of the so-called "million dwelling program" (Miljonprogrammet, 1965–75), a large-scale housing project all over Sweden, via which the social democratic government aimed to provide cheap apartment housing for large portions of the population. This was in no small part due to the fact that it specialized in the prefabricated concrete components which were used to build the apartment complexes. The million-dwelling program was at the time, and has continued to be, heavily criticized (see e.g. Svensson 1996).

In the 1970s, Skanska began to branch out internationally. This more prestigious international reach, rather than the million-dwelling program, was heavily emphasized in Zetterling's film—from Indonesia to New York, from Greenland to Algeria—and one can only imagine Zetterling's enthusiasm for having an excuse to travel to these remote locations. From the sources available to me there is no way of discerning why Zetterling was chosen for this project. However, the juxtaposition of an outspoken feminist filmmaker whose most recent film (*Amorosa*) was based on the life of an esteemed and notorious female writer known for her boldness in depicting sexuality, but also for her symbol-filled lyricism, and a construction company whose fortune came from reinforced concrete is confounding as well as fascinating. The sturdy practicalities of construction contrast with the poetic and fragile strength of Agnes von Krusenstjerna, just as the domesticated image of the frumpy but kind grandmother, knitting in a rocking chair and serving home-made pie, contrasts with the adventurous explorer-grandmother showing off Skanska's international projects.

By promoting Skanska, this film also has the implicit purpose of promoting Sweden, not least because construction performed a significant role in the Swedish welfare state. Construction was the means by which the welfare society would become truly modern and progressive, especially in the 1960s and early 1970s. Eventually, it became the welfare state's reach out into the world, both as a growth industry and as foreign development aid, especially in the 1970s and 1980s. Skanska's success story is reflected in its name—from the local ("Skånska" in Skånska cementgjuteriet referring to the southernmost part of Sweden, Skåne/Scania) to the global. The company had by this time dropped the diacritical circle over the A to become international in spelling and pronunciation.

The film plays on Zetterling's early star persona by placing her centrally in almost every scene. She is in her sixties, but moves and acts, in relation to the corporate spies, like the diva she never was, providing a self-humoristic performance which adds an ambiguous resonance to what might have been just another glossy promotion film. She drives her grandson in a sporty car, and has an air of superiority in relation to the petty issues of important businessmen, thereby creating an ironic distance from the very company she is endorsing. Furthermore, Zetterling's persona at this time, as a strident woman filmmaker and outspoken feminist, contrasts with the very masculine business of concrete and construction. Except for some young students at the school in Algeria, she is the only woman present in the film.

In *Concrete Grandma*, Zetterling seems to make a film that subtly mocks the seriousness of large, multinational construction business, while still carrying out the task in hand—showcasing Skanska's prestige projects around the world. She constructs a persona which allows her to juxtapose the role of grandmother, performed self-ironically, with the role of explorer, performed in earnest. As several of her previous documentaries—such as the BBC films from the early 1960s and the Greenland film from 1979—as well as her autobiography demonstrate, Zetterling was obsessively interested in exploring and traveling (Zetterling 1985). The Skanska film gave her ample opportunity to do just that. By using the grandmother role, Zetterling simultaneously challenged a clichéd perception of knitting, kitten-loving, rocking-chair grandmas and gave herself a space in the film to explore, to film, and to be both an auteur and a star.

CONCLUSION

Elsewheres in Zetterling's documentary aesthetics can be anywhere: in her native country, on a podium or in a training hall at an Olympic event, or in remote corners of the world. The "other places" are defined by her own position in relation to what she depicts, and she approaches them with a mix of, on the one hand, proximity and identification, and on the other distance and detachment. Interestingly, although only one of these films is commissioned and paid for by any kind of Swedish institution, Zetterling's own national position plays an important role in each of the films. In the BBC documentary, she is, for the British audience, a Swede who can explain Swedes, whereas for the Swedish audience she is an expatriate Swede who "should know better" (Nilsson 1962). For the Olympics omnibus film, she represents Sweden like the Swedish athletes in the Games do and like the other invited auteurs represent their respective countries, and in *Concrete Grandma* she is a Swedish female globetrotter who promotes Swedish Skanska to the world.

Although Zetterling is not visible in front of the camera all the time in these films—in "The Strongest" she only appears in the black-and-white still images that introduce her segment—her presence is nevertheless tangible in all films, through the authorial director's mode of presentation. In all three films, Zetterling makes use of an oscillation between her own Otherness and her affinity with the subjects she portrays, between her distance and her proximity. In *The Prosperity Race*, she is simultaneously familiar and strange to both Brits and Swedes, which is why she can take on the role of ethnographer and detachedly regard her own former home country and explain it to the British audience. Her slight, almost unnoticeable accent reminds viewers of her strangeness (and perhaps also of her very first beloved role in the UK, as the German girl in Basil Dearden's *Frieda*, 1947), but at the same time, the voice, the accent, and the face are well-known to a population who have not only seen her on the screen but also heard her on the radio. For the Swedes, however, her very expatriate Swedishness is what makes the betrayal worse—the betrayal being that a Swedish woman would go on British television and tell the world that the welfare state is full of problems.

The distance with which the weightlifters are portrayed in "The Strongest" as grotesque, almost comical figures is juxtaposed with the intimate way in which the moment of hesitation before approaching the barbell is captured. She detaches herself from her subject by stating, frankly, "I am not interested in sports," but draws near in sympathy and fascination to the obsession of the weightlifter. The fears and uncertainty plaguing him before he must exert his strength and prove himself are presented closely and intimately. Sports, and the mechanisms behind the Olympics, the amounts of food and mattresses necessary, become a mere backdrop to that single moment of obsession.

In the Skanska film, Zetterling's ironic and self-parodying performance seems to shrewdly undermine the purpose of the film. The ease with which she travels across the globe and handles heavy machinery contrasts with expectations of gender as well as of age, something which is further emphasized by her masquerade in types of clothing particular to a region (veil and all-covering dress in Algeria, dirndls in Vienna) or to a certain kind of work (dungarees and hard hat), or in cross-dressing. The resulting impression of transience is antithetical to the steadfastness of concrete and construction, to the stability that Skanska is supposed to stand for and the strength of its buildings, tunnels, and power plants. At the same time, her immersion in the different countries and workplaces of Skanska also indicates a sense of nearness to her subject.

By looking at three short documentary films, produced at different points in Zetterling's career, one can note that her transnationality is always entwined with her nationality. It may be an "opportunistic transnationality" (Hjort 2009), a compromise made out of economic necessity, but within that compromise, the Swedishness of Zetterling is always significant, for better or for worse. Although one virtue of transnationalism might be—ought to be?—the dissolution of the boundaries of the nation-state, national identity seems to matter more when borders are being crossed.

References

Åhlund, Jannike. 1996. "Mai Zetterling—kvinna och filmregissör." In *I rollerna tre, Filmkonst no 38*. Gothenburg: Gothenburg Film Festival, 80–9.

Anthal, Jussi. 1962. "Jag tycker om framsteg och är själv socialist." *Expressen*, April 23.

Arnberg, Klara and Carl Marklund. 2016. "Illegally Blonde: Swedish Sin and Pornography in US and Swedish Imaginations 1955–1971." In *Swedish Cinema and the Sexual Revolution: Critical Essays*, ed. Elisabet Björklund and Mariah Larsson. Jefferson, NC: McFarland. 185–200.

Axelsson, Sun. 1968. Review of *The Girls*, *Chaplin* 85(8): 312–13.

Bergström, Lasse. 1968. "Osvensk kvickhet om tre kvinnor." *Expressen*, September 17.

de Beauvoir, Simone. 1949. *Le Deuxième Sexe*, Paris: Gallimard.

Diffrient, David Scott. 2005. "An Olympic omnibus: international competition, cooperation, and politics in *Visions of Eight*." *Film & History* 35(2): 19–28.

Ebert, Roger. 1973. Review, *Visions of Eight, Chicago Sun-Times*, August 20.

Edvardsson, Cordelia. 1961. "Jag har behållit mina ideal—säg gärna att det är naivt!." *Damernas värld* 33: 8–9, 61.

Ekelöf, Maja. 1970. *Rapport från en skurhink*, Stockholm: Rabén & Sjögren.

Hediger, Vinzenz and Patrick Vonderau. 2009. *Films That Work: Industrial Film and the Productivity of Media*. Amsterdam: Amsterdam University Press.

Hjort, Mette. 2009. "On the Plurality of Cinematic Transnationalism." In *World Cinema, Transnational Perspectives*, ed. Nataša Ďurovičová and Kathleen Newman. New York and London: Routledge.

Jordahl, Annelie. 1999. "Trevlighetsfascismen släckte nyfikenheten." In *Vi som inte var med—en orättvis betraktelse över sextiotalet*, ed. Per Wirtén. Stockholm: Atlas. 15–25.

Larsson, Mariah. 2006. *Skenet som bedrog: Mai Zetterling och det svenska sextiotalet*. Lund: Sekel bokförlag.

Larsson, Mariah. Forthcoming. *A Cinema of Obsession: The Life and Work of Mai Zetterling*. Madison: University of Wisconsin Press.

Larsson, Mariah and Anna Stenport. 2015. "Documentary filmmaking as colonialist propaganda and cinefeminist intervention: Mai Zetterling's *Of Seals and Men* (1979)." *Film History* 27(4): 106–29.

Lennerhed, Lena. 1994. *Frihet att njuta: sexualdebatten i Sverige på 1960-talet*. Stockholm: Norstedts.

Mai Zetterling collection, Swedish Film Institute, A1.6.2 vol 3 (proposal for TV series on The Second Sex).

Marklund, Carl. 2009. "The social laboratory, the middle way and the Swedish model: three frames for the image of Sweden." *Scandinavian Journal of History* 34(3): 264–85.

Marklund, Carl and Petersen, Klaus. 2013. "Return to sender: American images of the Nordic welfare states and Nordic welfare state branding." *European Journal of Scandinavian Studies* 43(2): 245–57. <http://urn.kb.se/resolve?urn=urn:nbn:se:sh:diva-19897>

Nilsson, Ulf. 1962. "Aftonbladet visar de första bilderna ur Mai Zetterlings skandalfilm om Sverige," *Aftonbladet*, April 21.

Schein, Harry. 1977. "Det hände på 60-talet." In *Svensk filmografi 6: 1960–1969*, ed. Jörn Donner, Nils-Hugo Geber, Staffan Grönberg, Berit Nordin, Gösta Werner, and Sven G. Winquist. Stockholm: Svenska filminstitutet. 9–31.

Staiger, Janet. 1985. "The Politics of Film Canons." *Cinema Journal* 24(3): 4–23.

Stjernholm, Emil. 2018. *Gösta Werner och filmen som konst och propaganda*. Lund: Mediehistoriskt arkiv.

Svensson, Per. 1996. *Storstugan eller när förorten kom till byn*. Stockholm: Bonnier Alba.

Young, Christopher. 2005. "Munich 1972: Re-presenting the Nation." In *National Identity and Global Sports Events: Culture, Politics, and Spectacle in the Olympics and the Football World Cup*, ed. Alan Tomlinson and Christopher Young. Albany: SUNY Press. 117–32.

Zetterling, Mai. 1985. *All Those Tomorrows*. London: Jonathan Cape.

26. *THE SERPENT'S EGG*: INGMAR BERGMAN'S EXILIC ELSEWHERES IN 1970s NEW GERMAN AND NEW HOLLYWOOD CINEMA

Anna Westerstahl Stenport and Arne Lunde

In 1976, at the zenith of his international reputation as a Swedish auteur, Ingmar Bergman went into self-imposed exile in Munich, West Germany, for almost five years, after a taxation scandal. There he worked primarily as a director at the Residenz Theater, staging more than twelve productions, many of them to high acclaim. For instance, his 1977 production of August Strindberg's *A Dream Play* (*Ett drömspel*, 1901) was lauded by *The New York Times* as "exciting," "complex," and "fascinating," with the critic praising the actors' "vivid performances" and the "elaborate, ingenious sets" and commenting on Bergman's apparent joy in reinventing the classic Swedish play in a new context (Popkin 1977). Bergman's time abroad also led to cinematic reinvention and attempts to work in new genres, languages, and production formats. Bergman made three films outside of Sweden during this time: *The Serpent's Egg* (*Die Schlangerei*, West Germany/USA, 1977), *Autumn Sonata* (*Höstsonaten*, West Germany/Sweden, 1978), and *From the Life of the Marionettes* (*Aus dem Leben der Marionetten*, West Germany, 1980).

The historical drama *The Serpent's Egg* is set during the hyper-inflation of Weimar Berlin in November 1923 and retells the rise of German Nazism. The aesthetics of German expressionism run through the film, connecting New German Cinema's rearticulation of the past with New Hollywood's interest in psychological interiority. This chapter examines *The Serpent's Egg* against the backdrop of German expressionism and its multiple articulations in subsequent German and American cinema, emphasizing the film as a nexus of elsewheres for both 1970s New German Cinema and New Hollywood. Filmed entirely in English with a multi-national and multilingual cast, and a mostly German crew, in Munich's Bavaria Studios, and co-produced by Rialto Film of West Germany and Hollywood-based Italian producer Dino de Laurentiis, *The Serpent's Egg* is the auteur's most international and least markedly "Scandinavian" project. Aimed at American audiences, the film was unusually large and complex for Bergman, with a budget of $3 266 000 USD (Cowie 1982, 313–14). The shoot was over fifteen weeks long, with 35mm color cinematography by Bergman's long-time collaborator Sven Nykvist. The elaborate sets of 1920s Berlin streetscapes by Rolf Zehetbauer consumed most of the budget, and were later re-used for Rainer Werner Fassbinder's television serial *Berlin Alexanderplatz* (West Germany, 1980). *The Serpent's Egg* should be understood, we argue in this chapter, as a rich fusion film that plays off past and present, sincerity and pastiche, theatricality and meta-cinematic formalism, divergent national and stylistic traditions, competing industry paradigms, and experimental new directions for big-budget multinational co-produced fiction features (for a related interpretation, see Elsaesser 2008).

The plot of *The Serpent's Egg* combines personal drama of poverty and traumatic loss, the rise of Nazism, a criminal investigation, and an analysis of torturous psychological research. The film opens in 1923 Weimar Berlin with former circus acrobat Abel Rosenberg (David Carradine) discovering his brother's body after an apparent gun suicide. He tracks down his brother's wife Manuela (Liv Ullmann) working as a cabaret singer-dancer in a decadent Weimar-era nightclub. Backstage at the cabaret he also meets an old acquaintance and ex-lover of Manuela, Dr. Vergerus (Heinz Bennent). While being continually hounded by Berlin police commissar Bauer (Gert Froebe), Abel pursues the murder-mystery of his brother (and a number of other victims) through a dreary, Kakfaesque urban labyrinth where destitution becomes the backdrop to violent rallies by National Socialist thugs. Ultimately, Abel and the police discover that the series of mysterious killings is the result of Dr. Vergerus' diabolical experiments on human subjects, who are filmed without permission and driven to suicide. With Manuela dead, the doctor commits suicide by cyanide, and Abel, released by the police, disappears into the Berlin night and (the voiceover narrator tells us) is never heard from again. The film ends with a black and white montage of anonymous faces in a large crowd, implying the rise of totalitarianism, and the rejection of human agency and annihilation of democracy.

The Serpent's Egg was not successful, with critics or audiences, although the reception in some quarters could be seen as ambivalent. The first of two reviews in *The New York Times* is especially damning, with Vincent Canby calling the film a melodrama that on the whole is "dead," while criticizing the "peculiar sense of dislocation within [Bergman's] English-language screen-

Figure 26.1   Manuela (Liv Ullmann) and Abel (David Carradine) in a Berlin cabaret.

play" and the "beautifully photographed weather and handsome period sets and costumes that encase characters who remain as anonymous as the bodies in a morgue (1978a, C8). The next day Canby wrote another review called "Bergman's Baffling 'Serpent's Egg'," which contextualizes the film within Bergman's oeuvre to date and concludes by emphasizing that although the film is boring it is "not a failure" (1978b, D17). Swedish critics saw similar issues with the film, although they were more positive.

The Serpent's Egg remains a problematic film—perhaps even a failure—if judged by European art cinema standards that prioritize narrative arc, stylistic cohesion, realistic plot development, and credible psychological drama conveyed by ensemble actors, such as the works of François Truffaut or Margarethe von Trotta. Instead, the film's strategies belong to another tendency within European art cinema which includes Brechtian fragmentation, dispersed subjectivity, and interest in challenging normative and dominant historiography. These include works by Jean-Luc Godard, Helke Sander, or Rainer Werner Fassbinder, or New Hollywood films by Martin Scorsese, Woody Allen, and Brian De Palma, where narrative cohesion is challenged by exposing the cinematic apparatus. The Serpent's Egg straddles both realms without fully accomplishing either, which speaks to the productive hybridity of the film. Specifically, its combined genres (historical, epic, psychological, horror, retro noir), stilted performances (no actors seem comfortable or convincing in their roles and many appear uncomfortable with the English-language dialogue), problematic scenography (e.g. fake-looking movie sets that nevertheless consumed the production budget), and self-reflexive interrogation make it hard to place it firmly in either New German Cinema or New Hollywood.

In Munich, Bergman became immersed in 1970s West German public discourse around the rise and legacy of Nazism, including reading Joachim Fest's controversial *Hitler: Eine Biographie*, published in 1973, which was the first postwar biography of the Führer written in German. It became an international bestseller and was later made into the documentary *Hitler: A Career* (*Hitler: Eine Karriere*, Joachim Fest and Christian Herrendoerfer, West Germany 1977; the biography was also translated into Swedish in 1974). Bergman writes in his own autobiography, *Laterna Magica*, that he had strong memories of having as a teenager spent a summer with a pro-Nazi German family in 1935, which led to a fascination with National Socialism's pageantry and enthusiastic crowds (1986, 146–7; see Ohlin 2009 for an extensive treatment of the longstanding controversies surrounding Bergman and Nazism). By engaging historic and current German and American elsewheres, *The Serpent's Egg* furthermore combines meta-cinematic Hollywood spectacle, critical historiography of Weimar Germany, and mediated Cold War European trauma and displacement that informed West German cinema of the 1970s. *The Serpent's Egg* is largely disregarded by scholars—unjustly so, we contend—because of its hybrid nature. This chapter examines the film's rich historiographic, aesthetic, and cultural complexity as a cinematic elsewhere, situating it outside of the national auteur and Swedish art cinema frameworks that have dominated Bergman scholarship.

New German Cinema, West German Historiography about Nazi Berlin, and Imaginaries of a Divided Cold War City

Integrating *The Serpent's Egg* into the canon of New German Cinema of the 1970s requires some explanation. Thomas Elsaesser has argued throughout a rich series of work, including the seminal tomes *New German Cinema: A History* (1989) and *Fassbinder's Germany: History, Identity, Subject* (1996), that a mediated historical revisionism about the Nazi era by West German filmmakers was a constitutive element of the movement:

> A good deal of the interest aroused by the so-called New German Cinema in the 1970s and 1980s was generated by the impression—as well as the expectation—that the films of Werner Herzog, Rainer Werner Fassbinder, Hans-Jürgen Syberberg, Wim Wenders, and others were not just another European new wave but would show the world how Germany intended to come to terms with, or move out of, the shadows cast by its disastrous history. Especially in the late 1970s, an image-composite emerged of the recent past [which] directly or indirectly, re-assessed West Germany's self-understanding in relation to the Nazi legacy. (Elsaesser 2012: 72)

Elsaesser also outlines the strategies of spectacle, exoticism, popular culture entertainment, and anachronism that are part of what he calls a 1970s sub-genre of retro-fashion, including films such as Bob Fosse's *Cabaret* (USA, 1972)—a

Liza Minnelli vehicle—or *The Serpent's Egg*. He defines retro-fashion films as ones that "broke many of the previously held taboos about the representation of the Nazi period, not least by acknowledging the ambiguous fascination of fascism. Yet by doing so in terms of spectacle, glamour and erotic perversion" (Elsaesser 2008, 167). *The Serpent's Egg*'s production designer Rolf Zehetbauer and costume designer Charlotte Flemming had both won awards for their creation of 1930s Berlin in Fosse's multi-Oscared *Cabaret*, based on Christopher Isherwood's 1939 memoir *Goodbye to Berlin*. There is little doubt that Bergman's film, released five years after *Cabaret*, borrows freely from its decadent underground trappings, gender-bending guises, and politicized meta-musical performances.

In Munich, Bergman likely encountered a younger generation who explicitly challenged their parents' support of Nazi ideology and the political amnesia about the Holocaust that was pervasive in German culture in the 1970s. Depicting Germany of the 1920s and 1930s constituted a diegetic elsewhere for a director like Bergman, while his relocation to West Germany in the 1970s, as the trauma of the Nazi years was beginning to be represented on screen, provided a productive vantage point. Indirectly, his relocation and the integration of German expressionist modes into *The Serpent's Egg* echoed the displacement of German and Austrian Jewish directors to Hollywood during the Nazi era, with both *The Serpent's Egg* and *Cabaret* referencing a Hollywood pre- and postwar tradition of musical and performance spectacle designed for popular consumption in the American market.

Bergman shared his experience of displacement with a number of New German Cinema directors, such as Wim Wenders for example, who began to make films outside of West Germany in 1977. *The Serpent's Egg* is made by a director displaced *to* West Germany, who inscribes exile through his protagonist who has relocated to Berlin from North America and through a plot that thematizes being lost, not understanding cultural codes, and being under constant surveillance as an alien. The plot and characterization of *The Serpent's Egg* seem to mirror Bergman's own sense of entrapment within a big-budget film made far from his familiar circumstances and in a foreign language.

The Serpent's Egg thus aligns with the way New German Cinema anachronized history or conveyed it as spectacle, "whose emergence in the space of less than a decade was indicative of a profound shift in the understanding of history itself, [and] amounted to a series of displacements of postwar paradigms" (Elsaesser, 1989, 253). The displacement of these postwar historiographic paradigms occurred at least partly through New German Cinema's explicit attention to mediation. Elsaesser writes: the "fact that the German fascism has left a more complete account, in sight and sound, in visual records and staged celebrations, of itself and its version of history than any previous regime ... amounts to a particularly heavy moral and aesthetic legacy on the history of cinema" (1996, 135). Nazism, under the auspices of Joseph Goebbels, was made for the cinema and it spectacular powers. This is integrated into *The Serpent's Egg*'s historiographic project in ways that both align with the emergent tradition of New German Cinema and also diverge from it, especially in terms of strategies of cinematic experimentation.

The final third of *The Serpent's Egg* leaves the Berlin cityscape to focus on the experimentation on human subjects at the Saint Anna Klinik, a hospital, archive, and labor camp. This space is accessed when Abel smashes a mirror in his apartment, realizing that the whirring sound comes from cameras recording his and Manuela's actions. The camera, the film strip, and the projection of moving images, as in Bergman's *Persona* (Sweden, 1966), are made apparent to us in this pivotal scene. Climbing through the broken mirror, Abel ends up running through the clinic's stairwells, archives, and examination rooms in a series of expertly shot labyrinthine and Kafkaesque spaces, at risk of capture by anonymous authorities. He finally arrives at Dr. Vergerus's lab, which doubles as a film production studio and cinema. This is also where Dr. Vergerus kills himself while watching his own death in a mirror. The experiments conducted and recorded in his lab are supposed to test the limits of human ethical behavior, revealing stretchable morals when people are submitting to authoritarian contexts with the power to anonymously inflict pain and suffering on others (the example is a nurse killing an infant when the infant will not stop crying). The scene evokes imagery of Nazi experiments on human subjects and the atrocities committed in the name of science.

The Serpent's Egg appears also to reference Yale University's Milgram project, which controversially recorded the behavior of participants without prior consent, and is detailed in the monograph *Obedience to Authority: An Experimental View* (Milgram 1974) and the made-for-television film *The Tenth Level* (Chales S. Dubin USA, 1976). Notably, *The Serpent's Egg* was originally titled "The Experiment," which signals Bergman's likely awareness of the Milgram project. There are also Bergman-related nods, both to *Persona*'s meta-cinematic references and to his sixth film (*Fängelse*, Sweden, 1949), made on a shoestring budget but with complete artistic freedom. In *Prison*, Bergman exposed and deconstructed the film studio's tricks, illusions, and sleights of hand, providing a commentary on film production.

The Serpent's Egg thus becomes a metaphorical mise-en-abyme through its meta-cinematic references and nods to German expressionism, yet one whose materiality—its mise-en-scène and its references to concurrent political and current events—constitutes an amalgamation of German elsewheres, past and present. Later self-reflexive cinematic mediations on German history, such as Quentin Tarantino's *Inglorius Basterds* (USA, 2009), come to mind here, too. When Abel exposes the cinematic apparatus, it would be easy to suggest an auteurist reading, where Bergman reminds the audience that he has been conducting an experiment on us as well, presumably keeping us captivated and enthralled with his reproduction of Berlin in 1923.

Instead, what *The Serpent's Egg* creates is a cinematically-mediated effect of striking alienation, along the lines of quintessential German expressionist classics such as Robert Wiene's *The Cabinet of Dr. Caligari* (*Das Cabinet des Dr. Caligari*, Germany, 1920). Dr. Vergerus turns out to be both a film director and criminal mastermind, a stand-in for Bergman's own master puppeteer of the project. *The Serpent's Egg* emphasizes the power of film and the significance of the cinematic apparatus in shaping twentieth-century history. In this sense, German fascism could be presented as a subset of Bergman's drive to construe therapeutic films that engage a philosophy about the form and function of film as a medium: an auteur gesture if ever there was one. Indeed, the final scenes of *The Serpent's Egg* return us to an anonymous Berlin street crowd, which Dr. Vergerus shows us through a black and white film strip, whose message of anonymity is echoed as Abel disappears into the masses, never to be heard of again.

Cinematic depictions of prewar Berlin were prevalent in German cinema of the 1970s, and Hollywood treatments such as *Cabaret* had familiarized the era and location for mainstream US audiences. For Sabine Hake, Berlin is a privileged topography in German cinema for the negotiation of class and national identity: "Weimar Berlin has played—and continues to play—a key role in organizing these symbolic investments and allegorical readings and in defining the terms under which architecture has emerged as one of the most

Figure 26.2   Bergman(n)strasse at Bavaria Studios, as pictured in Ingmar Bergman's *The Serpent's Egg* (1977). Frame grab.

347

powerful tropes of mass society and what mass discourse sought to contain: the crisis of traditional class society" (Hake 2008, 2). The class-striated urban architecture of an imagined and imaginary Berlin of the 1920s—its apartment buildings, restaurants, bars and cabarets, and police stations and hospitals—forms privileged locations in *The Serpent's Egg*. Indeed, as noted above, most of the film's budget went toward constructing a massive Berlin streetscape on the sound-stage at Bavaria Studios in Munich.

Bergman's re-imagined Berlin has a disorienting and paranoiac spatiality. It's a nightmarish city, difficult to navigate, with myriad claustrophobic interiors and darkly-lit exteriors in random, unidentifiable locations. Domestic interiors look like "Old Europe" in the Kaiser Wilhelm style of the late 1800s: dreary yet extensively decorated, with wallpaper in floral patterns, dark furniture, and heavy curtains in saturated colors. The exteriors emphasize crowded street scenes or narrow courtyards and alleys with little natural light. In both *Cabaret* and *The Serpent's Egg*, Weimar Berlin's surface glamor and escapism is always hollow and garish, and undermined by decadence and seediness.

Indeed, *The Serpent's Egg* emphasizes the ways in which architecture functions as ideology, as Hake notes about Berlin films. The film's streetscape is called "Bergmannstrasse" and has a complex origin. Bergman notes in *Images: My Life in Film* (1990, 202) that he was looking for a Berlin environment to copy, but he could not find one, and instead found an appropriate imaginary from an illustration in the journal *Simplicissimus* from 1923, which happened to be an image of Bergmannstrasse in West Berlin's Kreuzberg. This Bergman(n)strasse—the irony of its name is indeed pronounced—was subsequently recreated at Bavaria Studios.

The 1970s Cold War reality of a divided Berlin and a bifurcated German culture is a critical subtext of *The Serpent's Egg*. The working-class Berlin environments depicted in the film would have been located largely in East Berlin, behind the Iron Curtain. This space—a particular topography of class in Sabine Hake's terminology—thus needed to be recreated on a set in Bavaria Studios in Munich. Babelsberg Studios, Germany's and Berlin's great studio of expressionist film of the 1920s (where *Metropolis* and other classics were shot), was located in Potsdam outside Berlin and ended up in the Soviet-occupied and later the East German zone. UFA became DEFA after the war, one of Europe's greatest film studios serving the interests of the GDR (German Democratic Republic). German cinema was itself bifurcated from 1945 up until 1990. Similarly, the historical moment onscreen is actually a simulation of history, or perhaps a dialectical image of it. November 1923 appears as an anachronistic condensation of the following fifty years of the representation of fascism, historiographically and cinematographically, reengaged through New German Cinema with the historical trauma of divided Berlin as a focal point.

FASSBINDER'S REIMAGINATION OF BERGMAN(N)STRASSE:
DESPAIR AND *BERLIN ALEXANDERPLATZ*

The Bergman(n)strasse set remained at Bavaria Studios for decades, serving as a displaced prewar Berlin that could be mobilized for film production during the Cold War. As a convenient site for a number of West German film productions set in Berlin, the production design of films such as *Berlin Alexanderplatz* and *The Tin Drum* (*Die Blechtrommel*, Volker Schlöndorff, West Germany, 1979) became a phantasmagorical elsewhere for many West German films (see Fassbinder and Baer 1980, 510–15). As such, it is like an obverse of the ending of *The Serpent's Egg*, in which the cinematographic apparatus is revealed in all its cruelty and the fantasy of immersion is revealed as false. Indeed, Zehetbauer's elaborate and largely historically accurate set from *The Serpent's Egg* serves as a nodal point for New German Cinema, with several connections to one of that movement's most important directors: Rainer Werner Fassbinder. As head of production design for Bavaria Studios, Zehetbauer worked with Fassbinder on two productions shot on Bergman(n)strasse, including the TV series *Berlin Alexanderplatz* (West Germany, 1980) and the English-language film *Despair* (*Eine Reise ins Licht*, West Germany/USA 1978). Set in 1929–30 in Berlin, "with the gradual, perceptible-imperceptible rise of Nazism very much in evidence" (Elsasesser 1996, 76), *Despair* is based on Vladimir Nabokov's novel, with a script by Tom Stoppard. Dirk Bogarde played the lead and "the sawdust and tinsel glamour" of Fassbinder's previous films took a step up with this international production that cost ten times more than his other films (Elsaesser 1996, 73). *Berlin Alexanderplatz*, on the other hand, is a fifteen-and-a-half-hour TV series based on Alfred Döblin's classic 1929 novel set in the Weimar Republic. Shot on 16mm, and co-produced by the West German WDR, Bavaria Film Gmbh and the Italian TV network RAI, it was primarily intended for a domestic German TV audience and featured an almost exclusively West German cast and crew.

These productions helped shape each director's legacy in different ways, with *The Serpent's Egg* generally portrayed as one of Bergman's worst films which failed to reach audiences in North America or Europe, and *Berlin Alexanderplatz* as one of Fassbinder's best productions (with *Despair* largely disregarded). *Berlin Alexanderplatz* helped establish Fassbinder's cult status in the USA, with movie theaters screening two episodes per night and PBS airing it in 1983. As with Bergman's production, finding a location in Berlin to shoot *Berlin Alexanderplatz* proved impossible for financial and geopolitical reasons (Fassbinder and Baer 1980). Like the downtrodden areas of *The Serpent's Egg*, those in Fassbinder's film would have been off-limits because they were located in East Berlin. *Berlin Alexanderplatz* production manager Dieter Minx notes, almost as an aside, that the *platz* is in the Eastern sector, but there are concrete buildings and a TV-tower in the way and a large waste-land between the wall and center city of East Berlin (Fassbinder and Baer 1980, 383; see also Ladd 1997 on traces of the past in the Berlin landscape)

Bergmannstrasse at Bavaria Studios emerged as a fortuitous alternative—with nearly all exterior urban scenes from *Berlin Alexanderplatz* shot here. While Bergman emphasizes the material location and includes a number of street scenes in *Serpent's Egg*, Fassbinder shuns most street representation. There are a number of episodes with no street scenes at all, even when a transition shot could have been logically motivated, such as when the main character Franz Biberkopf moves from his rented room to a bar or restaurant. Yet Fassbinder focuses on interiors, which can be seen as a concession to the smaller-screen television format of the 1970s, where epic scale and vistas are lost in transference. But there appears to be more at stake with Fassbinder largely excluding Berlin streetscapes. The trauma of a bifurcated Germany is evident in the absence of Berlin in this series developed from *Berlin Alexanderplatz*, one of German expressionism's most important literary works. There is one striking street scene in episode seven, when Biberkopf visits Strasse Babylon, the red light district and prostitution alley. Fassbinder reuses the same perspective and street segment for the scene as Bergman did in Abel's visit to a prostitute. When Biberkopf exits the barred-off enclave, we see the sign "Pension Holle"; this is the boarding house where Abel and Manuela reside.

These concrete remnants of Bergman and of Bergmannstrasse in Fassbinder's *Berlin Alexanderplatz* are intriguing. They signal how Bergman and Fassbinder relate differently to the potential and pitfalls of opulent production design and to the status of Berlin in relation to German expressionism of the 1920s and the contemporary divided Cold War cityscape of the late 1970s. For Bergman, the street scenes and the opulent interiors are anchors to history and serve as conceits of authenticity that can only be broken meta-cinematically, as when Abel discovers the hidden cameras, leaves the streetscape, and enters into the Saint Anna Klinik and its laboratories of filmed human subject research. Fassbinder's *Berlin Alexanderplatz* does not suffer from an authenticity conceit in terms of production design—historical and geographical references are established in the montage of images in the opening credits (some of which evoke the sketch Bergman used for his 1923 Berlin street reproduction)—but rather in its insistence on creating an elsewhere of largely invisible production design to mask the absences of the "real" Berlin inaccessible behind a wall. The sets are re-used and already mediated; they are salvaged and re-cycled, and did not consume as large a portion of the budget as they did for Bergman. Nor are they made from scratch to fit a particular director's imagination of the past. Fassbinder's sets are postmodern; they reference the centrality of Berlin for German expressionism. In fact, the only on-location shooting in Berlin was at the U-Bahn station Deutsches Oper, which was meant to represent several different metro stations, including Untergrundbahn Potzdammer Platz, then located in the Eastern sector (Fassbinder and Bauer 1980, 500). Warehouse locations and the slaughterhouse were shot in the Munich vicinity. Other landscape shots were filmed at the edge of the Bavaria Studios backlot or in the outskirts of Munich. The fact remains, however, that in Fassbinder's *Berlin Alexanderplatz*, there is not a single shot of Berlin's Alexanderplatz, despite the novel being set largely in the *Scheunenviertel*. Geographical and historical references are instead made with the help of documentary and news media footage inserted into the montage, emphasizing the mediated aspect of historiography.

Berlin Alexanderplatz references a canonical German expressionist novel with which Fassbinder had a deeply personal relationship, as he indicates in his autobiographical writing. The novel, he writes, transformed his life (Fassbinder 2007, 42). Fassbinder is interested in exploring the limits of TV production, the mass-market medium of the 1970s. *Berlin Alexanderplatz*, though experimental, is a production based in the conventions of literary adaptation, not in the "original screenplay" and "original production design," but in Fassbinder's mediation and adaptation of the narrative, which is explicit and acknowledged in the epilogue of the first episode as his own creative reassessment of the novel. The reception indicates that what Fassbinder does to his national literary and cinematic traditions is problematic and contentious. He is reimagining his own national tradition, yet the location in which that representation of a national literary tradition is set remains off-limits in East Berlin, while the material basis for its production design stems at least partly from a Swedish director's attempts at reinterpreting Berlin for an international audience.

The material connections between Bergman and Fassbinder through the echo of German expressionism reflect an increasing interest in the production design of 1970s German film, which acknowledges that any seemingly historically accurate representation of Berlin is a construction. This is seen in works such as Wim Wenders' *Wings of Desire* (*Der Himmel über Berlin*, West Germany/France, 1987) or the current Tom Tykwer series *Berlin Babylon* (Tom Tykwer, Hendrik Handloegten, and Achim von Borries, Germany, 2017–), with Tykwer stressing how Fassbinder's *Berlin Alexanderplatz* has influenced his work (2007, 19–38). Berlin continued to be what it had been during the twentieth century—a litmus test of tensions in German history, from the Weimar Republic through the division of the city into the Eastern and Western sectors. This status, as Sabine Hake notes, became a privileged topography for German identity, culture, and history. Bergman, who had remained largely unconcerned with World War II and the Holocaust in his films made in Sweden during previous decades, thus contributes quite deliberately to the cinematic and historiographic attempts of the first wave of 1970s New German Cinema to come to terms with the concrete specificity of the Nazi legacy. For Fassbinder in *Berlin Alexanderplatz*, that authenticity conceit is negated on every level, arguably even to edge any overt sense of foreboding out of the picture.

WEIMAR REDUX, GERMAN EXPRESSIONISM, AND NEO-NOIR

As Elsaesser has identified within the concept of "retro-fashion," a number of non-German European filmmakers of the 1970s appropriated Third Reich history and aesthetics for their own purposes, among them Luchino Visconti, Bernardo Bertolucci, Pier Paulo Pasolini, François Truffaut, Louis Malle, and Joseph Losey (2008, 161). These films cover a range of approaches in terms of plot, characterization, style, and aesthetics. Bergman's *The Serpent's Egg* ranks as perhaps the brutally darkest and most nihilistic of the subgenre, a gloriously expensive project made to look ugly, hopeless, dreary, and unappealing. In *The Serpent's Egg* there is no aesthetic or entertainment redemption possible in this history of the rise of fascism, even in the production or costume design; there is nothing prettified; there is nothing about fascism, German expressionism, or Berlin in the 1920s that looks appealing or guiltily pleasurable. Elsaesser has also catalogued the many Weimar cinema intertextual citations coursing through *The Serpent's Egg*, including Fritz Lang's *Metropolis* (1927), *Spies* (*Spione*, 1928), and Josef von Sternberg's *The Blue Angel* (*Der blaue Engel*, 1930) among others. Bergman, working and living in Germany, mines and dissects Weimar film history, venturing toward the heart of a reclaimed—if not recycled—German Expressionist film aesthetic for a 1970s international audience. Bergman's mentor during the mid-'40s at Svensk Filmindustri in Stockholm, Alf Sjöberg, had likewise borrowed German silent expressionist techniques for *Hets/Torment* (Sweden, 1944), based on Bergman's first produced screenplay, with Bergman on set during the entire filming as a kind of glorified assistant director in training.

One under-investigated aspect of *The Serpent's Egg* is the German–American connection between noir, jazz, and urban cultures. Many films made by Bergman in the mid-1940s to early 1950s evidence a Hollywood-inspired film noir vein. Tropes of these films include the loneliness, angst, and oppression of the big city. American-style jazz represents a subversive imported music of youth and rebellion, with scenes portrayed in chiaroscuro expressionist lighting modeled after Hollywood cinematographers like John Alton. Several key films directed by Bergman during this time period show evidence of Hollywood noir inspiration, including *Crisis* (*Kris*, 1946), *Port of Call* (*Hamnstad*, 1948), *Prison* (*Fängelse*, 1949), and the Hitchcockian Cold War thriller *This Can't Happen Here* (*Sånt händer inte här*, 1950). Bergman's stylistics and aesthetics integrated multiple aspects of film noir, borrowing as freely from postwar Hollywood as from European cinema.

Classic American film noir (1944–58) was largely created by German-speaking auteur exiles in Hollywood such as Fritz Lang, Billy Wilder, Robert Siodmak, and Otto Preminger, as well as German and Austrian émigré cinematographers, screenwriters, and other behind-the-camera collaborators. Hollywood noir and the sordid underbelly and corruption of postwar America are in many ways an elsewhere for what remained of the Nazi-purged German film industry under Goebbels and its subsequently divided East/West postwar aftermath. Such transnational and intertextual references are key to *The Serpent's Egg*, which has a number of elements that would classify it as neo-noir *avant la lettre*, such as the male voiceover, a city of dark rain, a nightmarish labyrinth for a doomed male protagonist, expressionist lighting, and indigo shadows. As much as it evokes Weimar-era Berlin, the film is also very much a classic Hollywood-infused big city crime story and police procedural.

Sven Nykvist, Bergman's steady cinematographer starting in 1960 with *The Virgin Spring (Jungfrukällan)*, photographed *The Serpent's Egg* in Munich. Nykvist was a master of simulating and capturing natural light, and Bergman's general preference had been for on-location shooting of exteriors during the 1960s and early 1970s in Sweden. In *The Serpent's Egg*, Nykvist's cinematography channels a byzantine noir-ish style quite unusual for him, emphasizing shots of dark courtyards, crowded streets, views through barred windows, fences, and barriers and vertical shafts, as well as a tendency to visually trap Abel in frames (à la Fritz Lang). The Berlin of *The Serpent's Egg* in fact blatantly appears like a set—elaborate, but obviously fake. This approach relinquishes the naturalistic, realistic, and nature-dominated aesthetic of Scandinavian film history in favor of a spatial aesthetics that harks back to the interior studio aesthetics of Weimar and Classical Hollywood. Indeed, few other Nykvist-shot films are as indebted to a Germanic/Hollywood studio aesthetic as *The Serpent's Egg*.

Bergman's Ambivalent Courtship with 1970s New Hollywood

The Serpent's Egg became not only an elsewhere of Bergman's production in New German Cinema, but also an elsewhere of New Hollywood. That includes its implicit references to American popular culture in 1920s Germany (especially jazz and cabaret performance) and in the West Germany of the mid-1970s (particularly the looming presence of US military troops stationed there to prevent a possible WW III). Distributed by Paramount, *The Serpent's Egg* is also part of a rich circulation history of European films in North America during the 1970s. Although Bergman had received and rejected offers to work in Hollywood ever since his rise to international prominence in the late 1950s, his courting by Hollywood studios is another 1970s elsewhere that this chapter explores. As a lifelong cinephile, Bergman had admired the dazzling, star-driven Hollywood studio system, whose products dominated Stockholm cinemas and Swedish film magazines from at least the early 1920s and onward. Although he declined to work in America, his push–pull flirtations with Hollywood offers of money, prestige, and clout dominated much of Bergman's transcultural identity in the 1970s, especially when commercial misfires of late 1960s, such as *Shame* (*Skammen*, 1968), had lost money and made financing in Sweden much more challenging.

Bergman's first English-language film, *The Touch*, from 1971, is a direct outcome of these setbacks and engagements. Rather than filming in California, however, Bergman brought New Hollywood to Stockholm, utilizing the transnational star power of Bibi Andersson and Max von Sydow. ABC Pictures in Hollywood provided the funding, with the stipulation that an American movie star had to appear in the film alongside the Swedish actors, with that role ultimately going to *M*A*S*H* breakout star Elliott Gould (Meryman 1971). Around the same time, Roger Corman, best known as a B-movie/exploitation director and producer of the 1950s and 1960s, distributed *Cries and Whispers* (*Viskningar och rop*, Sweden, 1972) through his new foreign art cinema boutique brand New World Pictures, which would later become the primary North American distributor of European and world cinema (Tapper 2017, 31). These events situated Bergman at least on the margins of New Hollywood.

The Touch did not do well at the box office, but despite this, one scholar writes, "Hollywood's cheque book was still wide open to Bergman" (Tapper 2017, 30). Visiting Hollywood twice within the span of a few months in the mid-'70s, he was actively making inroads. He toured Universal studios in October 1975. In January 1976, after having left Sweden for Germany, Bergman again flew to Los Angeles at invitation of de Laurentiis and Paul Kohner, his agent, to meet with studio executives, directors, and actors and shore up support for *The Serpent's Egg* (Bryson 1975). The project was actually first announced at a press conference held at one of the most iconic industry sites, the high-end Beverly Wilshire Hotel, on April 25, 1976 (Cowie 1982, 310). De Laurentiis as producer-distributor-matchmaker arguably made Bergman's dream of a big-budget epic film a reality, by securing funding from Hollywood sources and articulating the project as designated for an American market, accompanied by the appropriate media fanfare.

As with *The Touch*, De Laurentiis's financing of *The Serpent's Egg* depended on casting an Anglo-American film star. The zeitgeist of New Hollywood was one greatly inspired by the idea of independence as re-defined by European art film directors (many of whose films had been distributed by Corman), which effectively provided a window during the mid-1970s of Hollywood supporting new auteurist freedom and risk-taking in the wake of a collapsing studio system. The old moguls were on their way out and production companies were looking to exploit the emergent cinema tastes. That meant that both filmmakers and studio heads envisioned (at least partially) a European model of auteurist freedom, where lower budgets with socially, politically, and historically engaged films could play to a range of audiences. *The Serpent's Egg* came to represent these virtues and Bergman got the chance to do the project, though not on a California studio backlot, but in Munich.

The grim downbeat nihilism of *The Serpent's Egg* was by no means necessarily unfashionable or uncommercial vis-à-vis the New American cinema of the 1970s. For a brief period in the wake of Vietnam and Watergate, dark, paranoid narratives and bleak endings were highly commercial. New Hollywood works such as Milos Forman's *One Flew Over the Cuckoo's Nest* (USA, 1974), Alan J. Pakula's *The Parallax View* (USA, 1974), and Roman Polanski's *Chinatown* (USA, 1974) share affinities with and interest in German expressionism and the interiority of psychological states, which are central to *The Serpent's Egg*. For instance, Martin Scorsese's *Taxi Driver* (1976) is no doubt influenced by German expressionism: set in New York, with a protagonist seemingly lost within it and with narrative inconsistencies unexplained. *Taxi Driver*'s final scene parallels the final sequence in *The Serpent's Egg* in an explosion of madness: the relationship between what the audience sees and what it means is in *Taxi Driver*, as in *The Serpent's Egg*, up for consideration, as both include acts of murder that may or may not have happened outside of the protagonist's imagination.

The topics and aesthetics of Bergman's films may well have helped audiences prepare for this turn. For instance, Scorsese looked at European cinema as a means not simply of making films for entertainment, but also, as he writes, "to think about. That means being moved by it or repulsed by it at times. To leave the theater saying, you know what, that is a very interesting point of view ... Seeing Ingmar Bergman's *Seventh Seal* and *The Virgin Spring* and practically every Bergman film that came out every six or ten months" was transformative for Scorsese at the start of his career (Schickel 2011, 371). Though technically not a "New Hollywood" director but a New York-based auteur, Woody Allen has consistently remarked on the enormous significance of Bergman's films for his own career (Allen 2011, 3–7). Allen's *Interiors* (USA, 1978) is a direct homage to Bergman's intimate, torturous chamber dramas, while conveying priorities of the new American cinema in terms of aesthetics, narrative, and characterization. Similarly, Paul Mazursky's *An Unmarried Woman* (USA, 1978) is virtually a set-in-Manhattan remake of Bergman's *Scenes from a Marriage* (*Scener ur ett äktenskap*, Sweden, 1973). Though only briefly operative within an American cinema production context, one of the elsewheres of Bergman's career is his constitutive connection to New Hollywood and new American independent cinema.

The Serpent's Egg furthermore integrates German expressionism with numerous references to American popular culture, some of which resonated with New Hollywood's attention to socio-political, racial, and class tensions. Jazz is one such example. The final credits of *The Serpent's Egg* give a nod to Fritz Lang's subterranean worker slaves in *Metropolis* (1927), with black and white images of slow-motion faces of a proletariat crowd advancing forward in deathly silence, intercut with the credits accompanied by an upbeat Twenties jazz score that seems taken not only from German expressionism, but also as a nod to the significance of the American jazz age and the legacy of the Harlem Renaissance in Europe.

Historiographies of German–American Relations

While *The Serpent's Egg* functions as Bergman's imaginary of a Weimar Germany of the 1920s, it also critiques and reflects West Germany's relationship to the USA in the 1970s. The film's elsewheres contain a richer exchange than the historical surface indicates. It provides an American imaginary inside Cold War Germany and Europe. The film's postmodern pastiche and intertextual references speak to American culture and the *Pax Americana* presence in postwar Germany and the ongoing military occupation within West Germany during the Cold War, consisting of a racially diverse US Army of tens of thousands of soldiers maintaining the bifurcation of Germany into West and East.

This connection between *The Serpents Egg*'s amalgamation of Cold War geopolitical context, bifurcated East and West German cultures, nods toward German expressionism, and engagement with New Hollywood provides yet another connection with a Fassbinder film. *The Marriage of Maria Braun* (*Die Ehe der Maria Braun*, West Germany, 1979) also situates West Germany as an American elsewhere through its African-American GI who enters into a mutually exploitative relationship with the title character. *The Serpent's Egg* notably includes an expat African-American character named Monroe (Glynn Turman). Monroe's brief role in a bordello scene together with several female German prostitutes and Abel has multiple registers, including in its Fassbinderesque aesthetics. Monroe can be read possibly as an ex-Doughboy from the American Expeditionary Force of World War I, who has remained in a conquered Germany after the Armistice or else has returned to Europe after re-encountering Jim Crow America. The jazz and cabaret scenes in which the character appears also resonate with the European imaginary of the Harlem Renaissance, as conveyed through Josephine Baker's La Revue Nègre tour in Berlin in 1925 or even *The Jazz Singer* (Alan Crosland, USA, 1927). Black actors appear in only a handful of Bergman films. In his homage to Rossellini in *Port of Call* (1948), Bergman inserts an African-American character named Joe (Bill Houston) playing jazz on the piano while a Swedish sailor has an alcohol-fueled lost weekend with a Gothenburg prostitute. On the wall behind Joe is a poster advertising Parlophone Rhythm Records ("rhythm" signaling "race records"), with the caricature of a saxophone-playing black musician on it, to further reinforce the point.

Perhaps more relevantly, Monroe appears to signal the political controversy surrounding the presence of American GIs liberating Axis Europe during World War II and occupying Cold War West Germany, US troops being abundant in and around Munich. Monroe's frustrations at the sexual tauntings of prostitutes and his own impotence under pressure link race, sexuality, brothels, and jazz in ambivalent ways. Monroe's black male sexuality in the Berlin brothel sequence furthermore intersects intriguingly with macho empowerment and coolness in the 1970s Blaxploitation Hollywood subgenre, as well as those mobilized in Fassbinder films. Yet Monroe's own desperate performance anxiety about his sexual prowess undermines the stereotype. Male blackness as racial performance is further explored in the film's staging of a technically dazzling dance-hall overhead tracking shot. Abel makes his way through a crowded gauntlet of dancers up to the bar where nearby, white German jazz musicians perform on the bandstand in blackface (a practice of racial masquerade and burlesque with a very long history in Europe as well as in the USA).

Conclusion: The Elsewheres of *The Serpent's Egg*

The Serpent's Egg was an ambitious exercise in citation and influence for Bergman, with German expressionism as a consistent undergirding in topic, theme, and aesthetics. But the film also demonstrates its indebtedness to Hollywood film noir and the crime film. Bergman furthermore experiments bravely with postmodern pastiche, not least his recycling of *The Blue Angel* and *Cabaret* as decadence-soaked Weimar musicals and deterministic tragedies before the fall of Weimar and rise of Nazism, *à la* Kurt Weill, Bertolt Brecht and *The Threepenny Opera* (*Die Dreigroschenoper*, 1928). In addition, *The Serpent's Egg* made interventions into two major cinematic movements of the 1970s. For New German Cinema, the film provided a striking approach to revisionist historiography by an outsider director who chooses, seemingly of his own volition, to rewrite an especially complex aspect of German history. In addition, by virtue of its production context, *The Serpent's Egg* makes an intervention into New Hollywood, by referencing and presaging a number of prevalent tropes and strategies of that movement, many of which were influenced by German expressionism of the 1920s, as well as by German exiled directors in Hollywood in the 1930s and 1940s. Upon concluding his stay in West Germany, Bergman returned to his homeland in critical and commercial triumph with a nostalgic and celebratory ode to the fin-de-siècle extended family universe of his parents and grandparents through *Fanny and Alexander*

(*Fanny och Alexander*, Sweden, 1982). On the surface, *Fanny and Alexander* seems far removed from any suggestion of expressionism, critical historiography, postmodern pastiche, or political commentary. Yet the thematic fascination with historical enactment of a personal and political imaginary and the use of lavish sets in *The Serpent's Egg* shares many similarities with *Fanny and Alexander*. As we have argued throughout this chapter, Bergman's self-imposed German exile period in the late 1970s should not be understood as years in an artistic wasteland simply because works were not made in Sweden. *The Serpent's Egg* not only reveals fascinating new elsewheres of American and German film history, but also rewrites Swedish film history as one whose legacy integrates a range of cinematic elsewheres, including those by its primary auteur: Ingmar Bergman.

References

Allen, Woody. 2011. "Introduction. The Man Who Asked Hard Questions." In Ingmar Bergman, *Images: My Life in Film*. Trans. Marianne Ruth. New York: Arcade. 3–7.
Bergman, Ingmar. 1990 [2011]. *Images: My Life in Film*. Trans. Marianne Ruth. New York: Arcade.
Bergman, Ingmar. 1986. *Laterna Magica*. Stockholm: Norstedts.
Bryson, John. 1975. "Ingmar Meets Bruce, Hollywood Meets Ingmar: It Could Only Happen in Tinseltown," *People Magazine*, November 17.
Canby, Vincent. 1978a. "Screen: Slouching Toward Berlin: Made in Exile," *The New York Times*, January 28. C 8.
Canby, Vincent. 1978b. "Film View: Bergman's Baffling 'Serpent's Egg'," *The New Times*, January 29. D 17.
Cowie, Peter. 1982. *Ingmar Bergman: A Critical Biography*. New York: Scribner.
Fest, Joachim. 1973. *Hitler: Eine Biographie*. Hamburg: Spiegel.
Elsasesser, Thomas. 1996. *Fassbinder's Germany: History, Identity, Subject*.
Elsasesser, Thomas. 2008. "Ingmar Bergman's *The Serpent's Egg*. Reflections on Reflections of Retro-Fashion." In *Ingmar Bergman Revisited: Performance, Cinema, and the Arts*, ed. Maaret Koskinen. New York: Wallflower Press. 161–79.
Elsasesser, Thomas. 1989. *New German Cinema: A History*. Amsterdam: Amsterdam University Press.
Elsaesser Thomas. 2012. "*Our Hitler*: A Film by Hans-Jürgen Syberberg." In *Hitler—Films from Germany. The Holocaust and Its Contexts*, ed. K Machtans and M. A. Ruehl. London: Palgrave Macmillan. 72–96.
Fassbinder, Rainer Werner. 2017. "The Cities of Humanity and the Human Soul: Some Unorganized Thoughts on Alfred Döblin's Novel *Berlin Alexanderplatz*. In *Berlin Alexanderplatz*. DVD box set booklet. New York: Criterion Collection. 42–68.
Fassbinder, Rainer Werner and Harry Baer. 1980. *Der Film "Berlin Alexanderplatz": Ein Arbeitsjournal*. Frankfurt Am Main: Zweitausendeins.
Hake, Sabine. 2008. *Topographies of Class: Modern Architecture and Mass Society in Weimar Berlin*. Ann Arbor: University of Michigan Press.
Ladd, Brian. 1997. *The Ghosts of Berlin: Confronting German History in the Urban Landscape*. Chicago: University of Chicago Press.
Milgram, Stanley. 1974. *Obedience to Authority: An Experimental View*. New York: Harper Perennial.

Ohlin, Peter. 2009. "Bergman's Nazi past." *Scandinavian Studies* 81(4): 437–74.
Meryman Richard. 1971. "I live at the edge of a very strange country." *Life Magazine*, October 15, 60–73.
Popkin, Henry. 1977. "Ingmar Bergman Lights Up The Munich Stage." *The New York Times*. June 5. D 3; D 28.
Schickel, Richard. 2011. *Conversations with Scorsese*. New York: Knopf.
Tapper, Michael. 2017. *Ingmar Bergman's Face to Face*. New York: Wallflower Press.
Tykwer, Tom. 2007. "He Who Lives in a Human Skin." In *Berlin Alexanderplatz*. DVD box set booklet. New York: Criterion Collection.

27. BRIDGING PLACES, MEDIA, AND TRADITIONS: LASSE HALLSTRÖM'S CHRONOTOPES

Lynn R. Wilkinson

One of Lasse Hallström's signatures as a European director in America is his interest in exploring regional identities, not just New York City and Los Angeles. Hallström's post-Sweden films are collectively set in distinct places, not generic "anywheres" but specific sites with their own regional markings and diversity. His Hollywood career could be described as cinematic traveling. *What's Eating Gilbert Grape* (1993) is set in Iowa but shot in Texas; *Once Around* (1991) is shot in Boston and the Caribbean; *Something to Talk About* (1995) is set in the American South, *The Shipping News* (2001) in Newfoundland, *The Cider House Rules* (1999) in Maine in 1943, *Chocolat* (2000) in France, *Casanova* (2005) in eighteenth-century Venice, *Salmon Fishing in the Yemen* (2011) in the Middle East; and *The Hundred-Foot Journey* (2014) is a tale of Indian culture in a small French village. Even *ABBA: The Movie* (1977) is a documentary concert film shot in Australia. As an auteur, Hallström employs a more classical, almost "invisible" narrative style which is not particularly showy or attention-seeking. Most of his films are literary adaptations that reveal an enormous curiosity not only about the connectivity between literary and audio-visual moving image storytelling, but also about places and spaces at the margins and their specific grain of the rural, the local, the regional, the multicultural, and the global. This chapter attempts to trace in some detail these interconnections in Hallström's auteurship, which bridges the literary and the cinematic, to argue for the consideration of a provocative set of "elsewheres" as constitutive of his oeuvre. For this discussion,

I draw on Mikhail Bakhtin's concept of the chronotope and Hamid Naficy's arguments about accented cinema (Naficy 2001) to examine a range of film adaptations made throughout Hallström's career. I begin with an illustrative example from *The Shipping News*.

Haunted Connections in Time and Place

In a remarkable dream sequence in Hallström's *The Shipping News* (2001), the protagonist envisions the scene in which his ancestors drag their house across the ice, to the jeers of the townspeople who will no longer tolerate the Quoyles' presence among them. The contemporary Quoyle and his family have been living in this house, the witness and the symbol of the crimes of the past. Returning to the family home, they have made it livable again, after many years of absence, but as Quoyle, his aunt, and his daughter, Bunny, make new lives for themselves in Newfoundland, they gradually come to terms with and liberate themselves from the family's gruesome past. They do not mourn when the house literally blows away at the end of the film.

Quoyle's discovery of his family's dark past also plays a central role in E. Annie Proulx's 1993 prize-winning novel, as does the representation of Newfoundland as an ambivalent place, a harsh northern landscape at the edge of North America that both fosters unspeakable crimes and offers some individuals a chance to make new lives worth living. Proulx herself loved the place and made her home there for a time. (Cooke 2013). The Newfoundland of Hallström's film, however, is a place of multiple beginnings and settlements, the new home not only of the disgraced Quoyles as well as the protagonist and his family, but also of the first settlers, the Vikings, who for a time inhabited L'Anse aux Meadows. In *The Shipping News*, Newfoundland is Nordic, as

Figure 27.1 The Quoyles drag their house across the ice in Lasse Hallström's *The Shipping News* (2001).

well as Canadian, and the overlap is nowhere more in evidence than in the dream sequence in which Quoyle sees his ancestors drag their house over the ice.

This dream sequence harks back to one of the most iconic in Swedish film history, the scene in Mauritz Stiller's 1919 adaptation of Selma Lagerlöf's *Herr Arnes penningar (Sir Arne's Treasure)* (1903) that shows the funeral procession of Elsalill, the innocent victim of robbers, as it moves across the ice, a scene that immediately precedes a thaw and the restoration of order in the world of the film. Hallström's film thus embeds itself in North American tradition by reworking Proulx's Pulitzer Prize-winning novel, while also situating itself in the history of Scandinavian and European film. Moreover, the overlap between traditions also suggests a kind of global North, in which international boundaries are fluid, as well as contested. Filmed on the island of Newfoundland and Labrador by a Swedish director living mostly in the USA, *The Shipping News* reflects the increasingly globalized world of film production and its complex images the perspectives of mobile filmmakers and viewers, for whom home is everywhere and nowhere.

Indeed, the Quoyle house, in most of the film tied down to prevent it from moving again, represents an ambiguous homecoming for the filmmaker, as well as Quoyle and his aunt, who was raped nearby. While the characters travel to a place at the easternmost edge of North America where they thrive at the same time as they confront their family history, Hallström moves closer to Scandinavia and Scandinavian film. In both cases, the house is haunted, as well as fragile. It is one of many such structures in Hallström's films, in which the history and potential of characters are given spatial form as imperfect, sometimes transient, buildings or places that offer the characters enough warmth, solidarity, and even pleasure that they can look forward to a future that includes some kind of human happiness. In both the novel and the film, Newfoundland and, especially, the small town where the office of the eponymous newspaper is located embody this second nurturing space that allows Quoyle and his family to flourish. Both spaces are intimately bound up with the development of these characters and thus represent what Mikhail Bakhtin called "chronotopes" or, in his terms, "the organizing centers for the fundamental narrative events of the novel ... the place where the knots of narrative are tied and untied ... Time becomes, in effect, palpable and visible; the chronotope makes narrative events concrete, makes them take on flesh, causes blood to flow in their veins" (Bakhtin 1981, 250). In Bakhtin's essay, chronotopes range from the spaces lovers must travel through between their meeting and their marriage in Greek romance, to the roads, horses, and vehicles of picaresque narratives, to interiors that suggest imprisonment or the uncertain boundary between public and private in the nineteenth-century European novel. In Hallström's films, chronotopes of buildings and places that are either safe or unsafe havens figure prominently, suggesting an ambiguous quest for a home and a future in the face of the rapid changes and uncertainties of globalization in the twentieth and twenty-first centuries.

Bakhtin's essay offers examples of chronotopes drawn exclusively from literature and folklore, although his focus on narrative and visuality offers fertile ground for the analysis of fictional films. In fact, the notion of the chronotope is central for Hamid Naficy's study of a kind of filmmaking he calls "accented cinema," films made by exiled and displaced filmmakers that also echo the situation of their directors. According to Naficy, accented films are often the work of directors working outside their home traditions; their plots often emphasize communication between different locations or communities and the contrast between locations, or in Naficy's terms, chronotopes of exile and chronotopes of imagined homelands. According to Naficy, the chronotopes of such films weave together time and space, registering not only the changes that occur in a single place but also the links between locations perceived by readers and spectators, as well as fictional characters. As "accented cinema," then, *The Shipping News* offers Newfoundland as a chronotope that is at once a fiercely beautiful part of Canada, the home of the Quoyles who had emigrated from Europe, and the site of a very early Scandinavian settlement.

An adaptation of a novel, Hallström's film translates the literary chronotopes of Proulx's text into images and sounds that are arguably far more vivid than their linguistic counterparts. At the same time, his version of *The Shipping News* becomes itself a chronotope related to the autobiographical journeys taken by writers and filmmakers who attempt to account for their own development. Like the Newfoundland of the film, Hallström's *The Shipping News* suggests the presence of a filmmaker who works at the crossroads between North American, European, and, in the past decade, world cultures.

Literary Origins and Cinematic Elsewheres

The fact that *The Shipping News* is a literary adaptation also situates the film in the tradition of the Swedish art film, which emerged in the second and third decades of the twentieth century with a series of films by Victor Sjöström and Mauritz Stiller that were based on narratives by Selma Lagerlöf, including Stiller's *Sir Arne's Treasure*. Lagerlöf was a highly regarded writer who won the Nobel Prize for Literature in 1909, and her name conferred prestige and the aura of art both on the adaptations and on their directors. Since the end of World War II, however, the status of adaptations in the history of film in the West has been more vexed. As is well-known, the French filmmaker and critic François Truffaut associated at least one kind of film adaptation with the tired and cliché-ridden "cinéma de Papa" (Daddy's cinema) (Truffaut 1954). Thus, for Truffaut and many other theorists and historians, adaptations of literary works are opposed to the notion of the cinematic auteur, the director who exerted a high degree of control over his or her film, which was, in turn, conceived of as a work of art.

Hallström is recognized as a film director in Sweden and elsewhere, and his films are marketed as his work, but he has given relatively few interviews about his films and filmmaking and, in general, seemed unconcerned with his status as the creator of art films or even his status as an auteur. Does that mean that his films are merely sold as the products of a European director branded as an auteur? Or has Hallström, a filmmaker who was born in Sweden and lived and worked there until he was nearly forty, become a new kind of cinematic auteur, a filmmaker whose work, like its author, is concerned with the multiple locations of production, with the role of filmmaking in a globalized world? Hallström is one of many filmmakers who, since 1989 at least, have made films outside the countries where they were born. However, unlike the displacement of the directors Naficy discusses, Hallström's move to the USA was not caused by war, famine, or a request for political asylum. In contrast, he seems to have been free to follow the money, to take advantage of the funding, as well as the appeal to large audiences, offered by Hollywood and the USA in general. But like other cinematic exiles, Hallström's films register the ambiguities and growing pains of an increasingly globalized world. In the sense that all of his films since 1991 are concerned with globalization, mobility, and the plight of the vulnerable, Hallström is a global auteur, as the term is used by Jeong and Szaniawski and Elsaesser (Elsaesser 2016; Jeong and Szaniawiski 2016).

Connecting Sweden to the World

Hallström has been able to make films in the USA because his film *My Life as a Dog* (*Mitt liv som hund*, 1985) received international recognition; he is one of a distinguished tradition of Scandinavian filmmakers—most notably Sjöström in the 1920s—who were able to make films in Hollywood. Although Sjöström made several masterpieces in the USA, he remained in the country for just seven years. Hallström's first American film was released in 1991 and since then he has worked primarily in the USA, making him the most prolific and successful Scandinavian filmmaker who has worked abroad.

Hallström made his first film, a short concerning the Swedish pop group The Mascots, in 1965, and made eleven feature films, one documentary, and various shorts and episodes for television series in Sweden between 1973 and 1988. He also made around thirty music videos of the Swedish pop group ABBA, as well as the longer *ABBA: The Movie* (1977). During this time, he often wrote the scripts for the films he made, sometimes also serving as cinematographer or editor, although several of his feature films, including *My Life as a Dog* and those based on Astrid Lindgren's series about children who live in Byllerbyn or Noisy Village, are adaptations of novels. From 1969 to 1979, he was also employed by SVT2, the second channel of Swedish television. Despite the mixed nature of his production, Hallström was able to exert a high degree of control over the films he made in Sweden, which makes it possible to view him as an auteur during these years.

Since 1991, however, when he began making films in the USA, all of Hallström's feature films have been adaptations of novels, including *Hypnotisören* (*The Hypnotist*), based on Lars Kepler's novel of the same name (Kepler 2009), which he made in Sweden in 2012. Hallström, however, has emphasized the care he takes in choosing scripts, noting that he prefers those which focus on character, rather than action (Jordahl and Lahger 47–8). Moreover, it will not do to exaggerate the differences between his Swedish and American films. Although perspectives shift through time, all of Hallström's films show a concern with several interrelated questions. How do ordinary people navigate the ambiguities of changing gender relationships? What kinds of places foster happiness and allow people, even the most marginalized, to thrive? How do we treat the most vulnerable among us, including not only children but also animals? Finally, how do cultural clashes lead to enrichment, rather than violence? The exploration of these issues links all of Hallström's feature films as parts of a single oeuvre. Further, Hallström's films emphasize movement and change. Thus it makes sense to view his production as part of the same global flow of film production that also includes the first- and second-generation migrant filmmakers that are the focus of Naficy's study.

The protagonist of Hallström's *My Life as a Dog*, an unwanted child whose mother dies in the course of the film, is able to survive because he is taken in by an uncle who lives in the Swedish province of Småland, where he works in the local glass works and enjoys the company of an understanding wife and many warm and generous neighbors and coworkers. It seems, then, that little Ingemar has come to one of those places that allow vulnerable outsiders to survive and even thrive. But nothing is stable even in this idyllic village. New workers from Southern Europe arrive and take over a floor in the uncle's house, forcing Ingemar to move in with an old woman who had also been obliged to find new lodgings. And Swedish viewers in the mid-1980s would have known that the industry and community portrayed in the film were both threatened; in 2012, Orrefors was the last glass factory in Småland to close its doors, but the decline of production in the region had begun much earlier. *My Life as a Dog* offers several chronotopes that register the changes brought about by migration and in Ingemar's life. Again, a house plays a central role. During Ingemar's first stay in Småland, his uncle and aunt have the entire first floor and a retired factory worker and his wife live below, but when he returns the old man has died and a large family from Greece has moved in so that Ingemar has to go and live with the old widow elsewhere. His uncle builds a summer pavilion that represents a masculine space where he and his nephew can bond, and it is here that Ingemar finally realizes that his dog is dead and his mother did not want him. Finally, the village in *My Life as a Dog* is a chronotope that represents a kind of safe haven where Ingemar can thrive despite his past and the changes brought about through mobility and migration.

It should also be noted that Småland is depicted as a quintessentially "Swedish" province, including its landscape of deep dark woods dotted with white-trimmed red farmers' cottages. It was also one of the provinces the saw the highest rate of emigration to the USA in the late 1800s, which fundamentally changed its demography. The most direct echo of a chronotopic representation of Småland in Hallström's American production occurs in his masterful adaptation of John Irving's 1985 novel, *The Cider House Rules*, released in 1999. Both the film and the novel are set in rural Maine, in an area that features an orphanage run by a doctor who also performs abortions and apple orchards that are picked by migrant workers who arrive every autumn and live in a bunkhouse known as the Cider House. Both the bunkhouse and the orphanage are structures designed to house transients, although the migrant workers return every year and many of the orphans remain in the orphanage until adulthood. Both also exist in a problematic relationship to conventional morality. Dr. Larch both cares for the abandoned children housed in the orphanage and at the same time takes measures to ensure that fewer unwanted children arrive in the world. The black migrant workers in the Cider House also have few reasons to obey the list of rules posted in their lodgings by the white owners of the orchards they pick. But one of them violates more than the list of rules when he rapes his daughter, and Dr. Larch's protégé, an orphan called Homer Wells, understands why his mentor insisted he learn how to perform abortions when he helps the violated daughter of the migrant picker. Both the Cider House and the orphanage are provisional structures subject to changes that require their inhabitants to improvise. In both films, the chronotopic domestic spaces are closely connected to relationships and social networks in the public spaces that surround them.

Such ambiguous chronotopes also feature in some of Hallström's other films of the 1990s, most notably *What's Eating Gilbert Grape?* (1993), in which a morbidly obese woman who has been abandoned by the father of her children attempts to raise a mentally handicapped boy and his siblings in a small town. The domestic space—the dilapidated family farm—functions as a chronotope that is literally collapsing from the weight of a traumatic family history: the floorboards are caving in as the mother moves her weight around. As one commentator notes, it is a grotesque situation that is especially damaging for the children (Blocker 1996). Their liberation is signaled near the end of the film by two interrelated events, the death of the mother and the burning down of the house that had entrapped her and her children.

Chronotopes of Globalization and Multicultural Elsewheres

A preoccupation with place features in many of Hallström's other English-language films, including his 2000 foodie film, *Chocolat*, and his adaptation of Nicholas Sparks's 2010 novel, *Safe Haven* (2013), both of which lack the tensions and ambiguities of *The Cider House Rules*, *The Shipping News*, or *What's Eating Gilbert Grape?* Recently, however, Hallström's preoccupation with place has taken a cosmopolitan turn that confronts some of the cultural clashes that have arisen in the wake of globalization and mass migration.

Based on Paul Torday's epistolary novel by the same name, *Salmon Fishing in the Yemen* (2007) represents the absurd consequences of a wealthy sheikh's request that a British agency supply him with an employee capable of introducing salmon into Yemen, thus making it possible for the sheikh to pursue his passion for salmon fishing in his native country. Even when, after going to extreme lengths, the British functionary charged with the task is able to introduce some farmed salmon into a river in Yemen, the results are less than spectacular. Local inhabitants view the proceedings with suspicion and blow up the dam that might have made the enterprise successful. But some of the salmon do survive and the sheikh reflects on his lack of foresight in failing to discuss his plans with his subjects. Both he and his English assistants have learned something about the advantages and limits of their own cultural traditions. At the end of the film, the Englishman and his companion decide to remain in Yemen, which reveals itself to have hidden resources, such as cold streams coursing beneath its desert surfaces. It turns out to be a chronotope of a surprisingly safe place in a part of the world that is often dangerous and violent.

Similarly, in Hallström's second foodie film, *The Hundred-foot Journey* (2014), based on Richard C. Morais's 2010 novel, two restaurateurs, one Indian and one French, confront each other across the road separating their establishments in an out-of-the-way French village. Although initially hostile to each other, the owners of the two restaurants eventually learn to take advantage of their different styles of cooking and eventually to produce a new kind of "fusion cuisine" that wins the French restaurant an additional Michelin star. Their reconciliation and collaboration are unexpectedly sparked by racist attacks on the Indian newcomers, which prompt the owner of the French restaurant, Madame Mallory, to lend the Indians a hand. As in *Chocolat*, food and a fairy-tale setting make possible cultural rapprochements that might not have happened elsewhere, but in the later film, the cultural and political stakes are higher and the implications more far-reaching. Interestingly, the chronotope of this film, the two restaurants that face each other across a road that is both quite narrow and representative of the entire world, recalls Bakhtin's analysis of the Greek romance, in which the spatial journey at least one lover must make for the two lovers to be reunited at the end of the narrative is at once immense and subordinate to the representation of the lovers' relationship.

The chronotopes of these two recent films represent the interplay of Eastern or Middle Eastern and Western, rather than Swedish and American, traditions. The difference may not be as great as it at first might seem. Despite the American election of 2016 and the rise of populism throughout the West, many of us in Scandinavia and the USA believe that we are living in increasingly multicultural societies and that multiculturalism has much to offer. Even for viewers who fear immigration and the loss of cultural homogeneity, however, Lasse Hallström's fables of cultural reconciliation and even fusion may offer an alternative perspective on globalization and its discontents.

CONCLUSION

All the narrative films Hallström has made since 1991 have been adaptations. Such a practice, situates him in the tradition of the Swedish art film, which, we recall, harks back to the adaptations by Victor Sjöstöm and Mauritz Stiller of works by Selma Lagerlöf. Novels, however, also provide Hallström with the focus on character he prefers, and in addition, with insights into American and other cultures (see Jordahl and Lahger 1991, 47–8). For filmmakers such as Hallström, adaptations mediate between cultures and traditions. Directing films based on novels allows filmmakers from elsewhere to work with scripts that focus on character, while also representing American and other cultures from an insider's perspective. Such an approach eschews the greater control that European auteurs of the 1960s and later—most notably Ingmar Bergman, Federico Fellini, and Michelangelo Antonioni—exerted over their productions. Actors and crew members emphasize that Hallström's approach to filmmaking is collaborative, rather than all-controlling (Jordahl and Lahger 1991, 50–3; Hallström 2001).

Lasse Hallström is to date the most successful Scandinavian film director to work in the USA. His American adaptations of literary works focus on character, rather than action. He has directed many Hollywood stars, including Julia Roberts, Leonardo DiCaprio, Robert Redford, Michael Caine, Morgan Freeman, Julianne Moore, Judi Dench, Helen Mirren, and Richard Gere. Much like his Swedish wife, Lena Olin, however, Hallström has enjoyed a certain critical and financial success in the USA, but working steadily, if somewhat invisibly, inside and outside of the Hollywood mainstream.

REFERENCES

Bakhtin, M. M. 1981. "Forms of Time and the Chronotope in the Novel." In *The Dialogic Imagination: Four Essays*, ed. Michael Holquist. Trans. Caryl Emerson and Michael Holquist. Austin; London: University of Texas Press. 84–258.

Blocker, Jane. 1996. "Woman-House: architecture, gender, and hybridity in *What's Eating Gilbert Grape?*" *Camera Obscura: A Journal of Feminism, Culture, and Media Studies* 39: 126–50.

Cooke, Dervila. 2013. "Tradition, modernity, and the enmeshing of home and away: *The Shipping News* and Proulx's 1990s Newfoundland." *Studies in Canadian Literature/Études en Littérature Canadienne* 38(1): 90–209.

Elsaesser, Thomas. 2016. "The Global Author: Control, Creative Constraints, and Performative Self-Contradiction. In *The Global Auteur: The Politics of Authorship in 21st Century Cinema*, ed. Seung-hoon Jeong and Jeremi Szaniawski. London: Bloomsbury: 21–41.

Hallström, Lasse. 2001. *Dive Beneath the Surface of* The Shipping News: *The Film about the Making of* The Shipping News. Bonus material. *The Shipping News*. Directed by Lasse Hallström. Miramax DVD.

Irving, John. 1985. *The Cider House Rules*. New York: Morrow.

Jeong, Seung-hoon and Jeremy Szaniawski. 2016. Introduction. In *The Global Auteur: The Politics of Authorship in 21st Century Cinema*, ed. Seung-hoon Jeong and Jeremi Szaniawski. London: Bloomsbury: 1–19.

Jordahl, Anneli and Håkan Lahger. 1991. "Lasse Hallström: Nu vågar han fördjupning" [Lasse Hallstrom: now he dares to go beneath the surface]. *Chaplin* 33(2): 46–53.

Kepler, Lars. 2009. *Hypnotisören: Kriminalroman* [The Hypnotist: A Crime Novel]. Stockholm: Bonnier.

Lagerlöf, Selma. 1903. *Herr Arnes penningar* [*Sir Arne's Treasure*]. Stockholm: Idun.

Morais, Robert C. 2010. *The Hundred-Foot Journey: A Novel*. New York: Simon & Schuster.

Naficy, Hamid. 2001. *An Accented Cinema: Exilic and Diasporic Filmmaking*. Princeton: Princeton University Press.

Sparks, Nicholas. 2010. *Safe Haven*. New York: Grand Central.

Torday, Paul. 2007. *Salmon Fishing in the Yemen: A Novel*. New York: Harcourt.

Truffaut, François. 1954. "Une certaine tendance du cinéma français" [A Certain Tendency in French Cinema]. *Cahiers du cinéma* 31 (January): 15–30.

28. CRIMINAL UNDERTAKINGS: NICOLAS WINDING REFN, EUROPEAN FILM AESTHETICS, AND HOLLYWOOD GENRE CINEMA

Björn Nordfjörd

During the last two decades, Nordic cinema has shifted from the norms of European art cinema to those of Hollywood genre films. In this chapter I examine the extensive role played by Danish director Nicolas Winding Refn in this change. His debut film *Pusher* (Denmark, 1996) arguably ushered in the era of Nordic crime and gangster cinema. It was to spawn two Danish sequels and two English-language remakes before Refn traveled to the New World with *Valhalla Rising* (Denmark/UK, 2009). His subsequent three films, *Drive* (USA, 2011), *Only God Forgives* (Denmark/France/USA/Sweden, 2013), and *The Neon Demon* (Denmark/France/USA/UK, 2016), make up a set that could be called the American trilogy, considering their setting, characters, and subject matter.

Pusher played a key part in the shift toward Hollywood genre cinema in Scandinavia, of which the crime film was the first and remains the most visible example—although increasingly rivalled by horror films. Indeed, the *Pusher* trilogy is Andrew Nestingen's primary example in developing his influential definition of "medium concept" as a "combination of art film and genre film aimed at mainstream national and regional audiences" (2008, 53). It is worth noting that Nestingen distinguishes medium concept from the auteur cinema of directors such as Aki Kaurismäki and Lars von Trier (2008, 75), which is much more transnational in terms of financing, production, and distribution. And even though the latter director has made extensive use of Hollywood genres dating back to his first film, *The Element of Crime* (*Forbrydelsens element*, Denmark, 1984), they have been subjected to and defined by the norms of the art film. In other words, his films are first and foremost art films that make self-reflexive use of genre conventions. Conversely, Nordic directors like Renny Harlin and Baltasar Kormákur have made Hollywood genre films without the art cinema component. Refn differs in combining elements of both art and genre cinema in a precarious balance that does not privilege one over the other. And while he is not alone in doing so, he has arguably been the most conspicuous of Nordic directors working within the realm of medium concept. However, with the American trilogy Refn has in many ways converted to transnational auteur cinema. In looking at his career as a whole, we can see how he travels from addressing Scandinavian society through the register of Hollywood genre cinema to shedding light on and ultimately criticizing American culture and cinema by means of European film aesthetics—with a stopover or intermission in England as he makes the continental transition. As a director, Refn is constantly on the move and straddling both different locations and film traditions.

THE *PUSHER* TRILOGY

In the *Pusher* trilogy, Refn applies the generic norms of the American gangster film to address Danish society, in particular aggressive neoliberal individualism, with a national audience in mind (Nestingen 2008, 89–96). The original film, however, differs slightly from its American counterparts in focusing on the plight of two underdogs (played by Kim Bodnia and Mads Mikkelsen) who never amount to much in the criminal world. Aesthetically, realism is paramount in presenting the urban milieu of Copenhagen, and the stylistic excesses of Refn's later work are not yet evident—although an extended scene at a techno club toward the end of the film foreshadows some of his later work with color. As Mette Hjort has pointed out, *Pusher*, in its active engagement with immigration and ethnicity, especially the character of crime boss Milo (Zlatko Buric) who is of Serbian descent, helped give "rise to an ethnic turn in Danish filmmaking" (2005, 269). Interestingly, in the concluding chapter of the trilogy Milo becomes the main character and *Pusher III* (Denmark, 2005) allots him the same attention, with an emphasis on family life and personal struggles outside of crime, which in the earlier films was restricted to ethnic Danes, while also including characters of Albanian, Arab, and Polish origin. This emphasis on ethnicity and immigration is an essential part of the realism of the *Pusher* trilogy, which presents Copenhagen as a typical cosmopolitan metropolis characterized by remarkable cultural heterogeneity and fluidity where various ethnic groups interact. In Refn's Danish films the delimited national focus, long typical of Danish cinema, has given way to what could be called a multicultural or even a transnational outlook. Thus, even while he

Figure 28.1   In Nicolas Winding Refn's *Pusher III* (2005) Milo, played by Zlatko Buric, hosts a Serbian birthday party for his daughter in Copenhagen.

was still located in Denmark Refn was already working elsewhere in terms of aesthetics, genre, and subject matter.

Pusher also become a cult hit outside Denmark, where it was frequently compared to the cinema of Quentin Tarantino—*Pulp Fiction* (USA) had premiered two years earlier—no doubt because of moments of extreme violence (arguably the only consistent factor in Refn's oeuvre). It should be noted, though, that Refn's Danish work is never devoid of realism, unlike the films of Tarantino that always take place in a fully cinematic universe. However, these directors share a wide-ranging cinephilia with an emphasis on violent B-films. Notably, Refn's second feature, *Bleeder* (Denmark, 1998), is to a considerable extent set in a video rental store with an amazing variety of world cinema (too large a selection to sort out Refn's many influences) and it is well-known that Tarantino immersed himself in film history and genre from working in a video store in Los Angeles. Indeed, Refn's own film education is shaped to a great extent by growing up "in New York City between the ages of 8 and 17" (Lunde 2015, 237). This helps to account for the specificity of Refn within Nordic cinema; although Danish, he was already elsewhere as his film consciousness began to take shape. Ever since, he has had at least one foot outside the country.

Intermission, or a Stopover on the Way to the Promised Land

In between the *Pusher* trilogy and the American trilogy Refn makes heterogeneous attempts in terms of both subject matter and style at crossing the North Atlantic—initially the short distance to England, but ultimately to America. As Arne Lunde points out, Refn's first English-language film, *Fear X* (Denmark/UK/Canada/Brazil, 2003), was "an experimental departure from the realism of *Pusher*. *Fear X* is a down-a-rabbit-hole mystery story that withholds clarity or closure" (2015, 238). As such, the film prefigures elements from his most recent films, but *Fear X* turned out to be a box-office disaster and Refn returned to Denmark to complete the *Pusher* trilogy. His second attempt at English language cinema, *Bronson* (UK, 2008), was a playful biopic about legendary English prisoner Michael Gordon Peterson, who took up the name of Hollywood action star Charles Bronson. The title clearly emphasizes also the pull of Hollywood on Refn himself. Stylistically, the film spliced together a range of genres and modes, including animation and documentary. And while the film has plenty of violence, it now appears far removed from reality and lies closer to surrealism. Indeed, the film flaunts its self-reflexivity and becomes explicitly Brechtian as Bronson (Tom Hardy) directly addresses the audience with theatrical makeup on stage. Refn's next feature, *Valhalla Rising*, contains some of the now increasingly familiar traits of his work, including moments of extreme violence and a most striking use of the color red. In depicting the first voyage of Europeans to North America, which the seafarers believe to be the Promised Land, it additionally expresses an aesthetically nuanced portrayal of experiencing a new sublime world along the lines of films made by Werner Herzog and Terrence Malick on related subjects.

Overall, these English-language films are markedly much more experimental in both narrative structure and formal elements than the Danish ones. However, there is little consistency among them in how they go about being so, and it feels as if Refn is searching for and developing his English/American voice. But together they paved the way for Refn's biggest critical and commercial success, *Drive*, that returned him to the realm of the crime film.

The American Trilogy

With *Drive* Refn hit upon a rich vein that he has continued to mine in *Only God Forgives* and *The Neon Demon*, and it is one that flows directly out of America—especially its rich and violent mythology. It is for that reason that I propose we think of the films together in terms of an American trilogy.

Drive is the story of an unnamed Hollywood stuntman (Ryan Gosling) who drives a getaway car on the side. Having fallen for his neighbor Irene (Carey Mulligan), he decides to help her husband Standard (Oscar Isaac) out by participating in a heist that ends up going horribly wrong when Standard is shot dead. In the hope of saving Irene, the Driver sacrifices himself when killing crime bosses Nino (Ron Perlman) and Bernie (Albert Brooks). Stylistically, the realism of Refn's Danish work has gone out the window and we come face to face with the artifice of Hollywood—explicitly so in its Los Angeles setting and stuntman association—and its generic traditions and history.

If Iain Borden is correct in signaling out *Taxi Driver* as "the first movie to undertake a sustained exploration of city driving as both dynamic performance and alienating practice" (2012, 35) it would seem to be the obvious starting point in discussing *Drive*'s heritage. Refn, rarely shy of admitting to his influences, stated after receiving the prize for best director at Cannes from Robert De Niro: "So the guy that personified the type of character Ryan played ends up giving the award for best director" (Tobias 2011). Both De Niro's Travis Bickle and Gosling's Driver traverse the streets of their respective cities, accompanied by quite similar visuals: two loners who in following their own moral codes attempt to rescue innocent and endangered blondes and in doing so must also face Albert Brooks! However, Travis is suffering from great social angst and is dismayed by the society he finds himself suppressed by, while the angst of Driver is a private one. This is manifested by the different city scenes of the two films, as New York is crowded with people while Los Angeles appears deserted and desolate. Indeed, in terms of visuals Michael Mann's glossy images of Los Angeles are the more obvious influence, and his *Thief* (1981)—where Chicago makes way for LA in the finale—provides a similar plot outline. Other car heist films, such as *Bullitt* (Peter Yates, 1968) and *The Driver* (Walter Hill, 1978), loom large as well. All in all, *Drive* is a heterogeneous reworking of primarily certain American film traditions, appearing in a stylized form far removed from the realism of Refn's Danish work.

Drive's intertextual flaunting transcends the film's Hollywood generic constraints and helps align it with European film aesthetics. The same purpose is served by its stylized formal aesthetics in terms of mise-en-scène and cinematography, including slow motion, lighting, and an especially striking color palette, along with its narrative minimalism and ambiguity. As Miklós Kiss

Figure 28.2 A typical shot in Nicolas Winding Refn's *Drive* (2011), expressing the isolation of its hero, played by Ryan Gosling, in the vast urban landscape and using striking visuals.

and Anna Backman Rogers point out in their detailed analysis of the film, this is accomplished without preventing "intense emotional engagement on part of the viewer" along the lines of standard Hollywood genre films (Kiss and Rogers 2014, 44). In other words, *Drive* is in many ways an unusually balanced blend of Hollywood genre norms and art cinema aesthetics. Whether purposefully or not, it is this precarious balancing act which is undone in Refn's next two films and which no doubt helps to account for their disappointing reception.

The plot of *Only God Forgives* is akin to that of *Drive* as Gosling, now playing an American who runs a Thai boxing club in Bangkok, embarks upon a similar revenge mission. It lacks, however, the heroism of the original as his character Julian is avenging the death of his brother, who himself was guilty of brutally murdering a teenage prostitute. It is therefore much more difficult for the audience to identify with the new Gosling figure, which undermines the emotional engagement that Kiss and Rogers (2014) aptly define as part and parcel of *Drive*'s appeal. In a similar manner, the film's formal aesthetics also work against the immersion encouraged by Hollywood cinema. While some of the Bangkok scenes are filmed according to realist conventions, most of the film is characterized by extremely vibrant and stylized colors. They remind one of Seijun Suzuki, whose films were available at the *Bleeder* video rental store, and obsessively symmetrical head-on framings evoke the work of Stanley Kubrick. And although *Only God Forgives* is clearly indebted to Asian martial arts films, its extreme violence is countered with a slow pace more associated with art cinema than martial arts and action cinema. The film score is also more experimental and lacks the catchy songs of *Drive*. But perhaps the most noteworthy difference between the two films is that the charming romantic partner Irene makes way for a perplexing brutal mother figure played by Kristin Scott Thomas. She seems to be Julian's key opponent and the film's main villain—driving the revenge narrative and demanding blood for her firstborn. In this way she paves the way for Refn's next film, in which female characters take center stage and leave male characters at the margins.

In *The Neon Demon*, we return to Los Angeles where the world of advertising and fashion allows for a grim metacommentary on cinema and American culture more broadly. Refn leaves Gosling behind, and Elle Fanning takes over the main role as the sixteen-year-old Jesse, who moves to the city to embark upon a modeling career. It is a business and cultural realm that, to an even greater extent than the stuntman element in *Drive*, provides an avenue for an explicit critique of image production of all sorts. It begins with the very opening scene of Jesse "playing dead" in front of the camera (both a diegetic and non-diegetic one), her bloody makeup done by Ruby (Jena Malone), who also prepares the really dead before burial, and introduces her to established models Sarah (Abbey Lee) and Gigi (Bella Heathcote). Together they watch Jesse's rise in the model world with increasing envy before murdering and feasting on her, with Gigi even throwing up her eyeball in a gruesome follow-up scene. In this manner *The Neon Demon* emphasizes consumerism and visual culture gone astray—as the model/image is literally consumed. At this point, Sarah and Gigi have also begun to look and act almost like robots, and thus the film pushes the uncommunicative surface and "superficiality" of the silent and hollow but visually appealing Gosling figure to another and more troubling level.

The more subdued surrealism of the two prior films rises to the surface in *The Neon Demon* and in a genre framework that lies much closer to the horror film. Despite the consistency of gruesome violence throughout his career, now is the first time that the horror film takes center place. *The Neon Demon*, however, is no ordinary horror film, but a postmodern analysis of violence, consumerism, and images—evoking especially the work of David Cronenberg. Aesthetically, the film remains aurally and visually consistent with the two prior films, but the mise-en-scène and cinematography reach still another level of aesthetic distancing, including scenes with red light flashing in rhythm with music and single-colored backgrounds, like a plain white background during a photo shoot. Thus, *The Neon Demon* is not only the logical destination of Refn's aesthetic trajectory toward increased expressiveness and abstractness, his almost encyclopedic referentiality and reworking of major film auteurs and traditions, but it also offers a critical commentary on cinema and image production. *The Neon Demon*'s many mirrors ask us to consider the violent nature of the image—not least Refn's own work.

The three films I am grouping here under the rubric of the American trilogy certainly do not have the same narrative cohesion as the films making up the *Pusher* trilogy, and Refn has apparently not grouped them together as such. Indeed, it should be noted that Refn has worked with American genre parameters from the very beginning of his career and that the latter two films are in fact European-led co-productions rather than conventional Hollywood films. The three films are tied together by the recurring presence of Gosling and Los Angeles respectively, and offer a mutual commentary upon not only Hollywood film traditions but the USA more generally: its "superficiality" (that is, its obsession with the image—exteriors rather than interiors), its mythology, its ideology, its self-righteousness, and its violence (real and fictional). If, as Nestingen proposes, Refn used the American gangster film to comment upon Scandinavia in the *Pusher* trilogy, the director brings forth the conventions of the European art film to comment upon the USA in his second trilogy—justifying the American rubric.

All in all, Refn's trajectory from his debut *Pusher* to *The Neon Demon* is an unusual one, considering its transnational scope and its interplay of European film aesthetics and Hollywood genre cinema. Together, his films tell a most extraordinary story of heterogeneous image production, extreme stylistic endeavor, and wide-ranging, border-crossing intertextuality. No matter whether the films are set in Denmark, America or somewhere along the way, they are informed by a fascinating tension between here and elsewhere.

REFERENCES

Borden, Iain. 2012. *Drive: Journeys through Films, Cities and Landscapes*. London: Reaktion.
Hjort, Mette. 2005. *Small Nation, Global Cinema: The New Danish Cinema*. Minneapolis: University of Minnesota Press.
Lunde, Arne. 2015. "Going Hollywood: Nordic Directors in American Cinema." In *Nordic Genre Film: Small Nation Film Cultures in the Global Marketplace*, ed. Tommy Gustafsson and Pietari Kääpä. Edinburgh: Edinburgh University Press. 230–43.
Nestingen, Andrew. 2008. *Crime and Fantasy in Scandinavia: Fiction, Film and Social Change*. Seattle: University of Washington Press.
Kiss, Miklós and Anna Backman Rogers. 2014. "A Real Human Being and a Real Hero: Stylistic Excess, Dead Time and Intensified Continuity in Nicolas Winding Refn's *Drive*." *New Cinemas: Journal of Contemporary Film* 12 (1+2): 43–56.
Tobias, Scott. 2011. "Interview: Nicolas Winding Refn." *The A.V. Club*. September 15. <https://film.avclub.com/nicolas-winding-refn-1798227435> (last accessed November 15, 2017).

29. THE CINEMATIC KON-TIKI EXPEDITIONS: REALISM, SPECTACLE, AND THE MIGRATION OF NORDIC CINEMA

Benjamin Bigelow

In his essay "Cinema and Exploration," the renowned French film critic and theorist André Bazin famously praises Thor Heyerdahl's *Kon-Tiki* (1950) as one of the most compelling examples of the postwar turn toward authenticity in documentary cinema. After detailing the technical deficiencies of the footage that Heyerdahl and his editor, Olle Nordemar, had to work with, Bazin writes:

> *Kon Tiki* manages to be the most beautiful of films while not being a film at all. Like those moss-covered stones that, surviving, allow us to reconstruct buildings and statues that no longer exist, the pictures that are here presented are the remains of an unfinished creation about which one hardly dares to dream. (Bazin 2005, 160)

Bazin's architectural metaphor here points both to his enduring fixation on indexicality (since the moss-covered stone is a trace of a building that once was) and his conclusion that *Kon-Tiki* was ultimately something of an aesthetic failure. For Bazin, the holes in the documentary record of Heyerdahl's expedition were so numerous that "we can never feel truly satisfied with just the premature ruins of a film that was never completed" (Bazin 2005, 162). Despite this sense of inadequacy, however, Bazin still calls *Kon-Tiki* an "admirable and overwhelming film," since "the making of it is so totally identified with the action that it so imperfectly unfolds" and because "those fluid and trembling images are as it were the objectivized memory of the actors in the drama" (Bazin 2005, 161). Bazin's admiration for the film's ability to "objectify memory" goes hand in hand with his theoretical *idée fixe*, which was that film (as a photographic medium) "embalms time, rescuing it simply from its proper corruption" (Bazin 2005, 31).

In *Kon-Tiki*, this indexical connection to the real is most evident for Bazin in the moments of danger. Such moments are few, since, as Bazin points out, "whenever something of significance occurred, the onset of a storm for example, the crew were too busy to bother about running a camera," and since "when an exciting moment arrives, say a whale hurling itself at the raft, the footage is so short that you have to process it ten times over in the optical printer before you can even spot what is happening" (Bazin 2005, 161). For Bazin, even though the glaring holes in *Kon-Tiki* make it "the premature ruins of a film," they are also proof of the film's documentary authenticity. When we do see even a few frames of a killer whale approaching the boat, for instance, "it is not so much the photograph of the whale that interests us as the photograph of the *danger*" (Bazin 2005, 162). As incomplete and aesthetically deficient as these few scenes are in the film, they are compelling because they retain their status as photographic traces of *actual* peril.

It is instructive to compare Bazin's admiration for *Kon-Tiki* with his disdain for another film about a famous expedition, *Scott of the Antarctic* (1948). Directed by Charles Frend, the film depicts (in full Technicolor glory) the ill-fated Terra Nova expedition led by Robert Falcon Scott. Although the film's technical achievements are undeniable, the seamless visual effects are only proof of the film's "mastery of trick work and studio imitation" (Bazin 2005, 158). *Scott of the Antarctic* was based, among other things, on the original documentary footage of the Terra Nova expedition captured by Herbert Ponting and compiled in the 1924 documentary *The Great White Silence*. Comparing the two depictions of Scott's expedition, Bazin derides the latter's "shameless search after the spectacular and the sensational" (Bazin 2005, 155) and concludes that he has "never seen a more boring and ridiculous undertaking than *Scott of the Antarctic*" (Bazin 2005, 158). For Bazin, the latter film is proof "that the documentary-film-by-reconstruction is dead" (Bazin 2005, 156).

As a characterization of contemporary Nordic cinema, Bazin's prediction could hardly be further from the truth, since historical films (many of which are based on actual events) have accounted for a remarkable and unprecedented share of film productions in the Nordic countries. As Iversen (2015, 48) and Laine (2015, 22) each point out, changes in state film financing policies have made the production and international marketing of lavish historical dramas a major area of focus since roughly the beginning of the millennium. One of the most spectacularly large-scale historical film productions in recent years is *Kon-Tiki* (2012), a dramatization of Heyerdahl's expedition directed by Joachim Rønning and Espen Sandberg, which was at the time the most expensive film ever produced in Norway with a budget of 93 million NOK (Bryne 2012).

As a spectacle-driven cinematic dramatization of Heyerdahl's harrowing trans-Pacific journey, Rønning and Sandberg's film performs a similar cinematic reinterpretation of Heyerdahl's 1950 documentary to the one that *Scott of the Antarctic* had of Scott's expedition. Just as in the pair of films about the Terra Nova expedition, the latter *Kon-Tiki* takes an incomplete documentary record that (as a necessary consequence of its production conditions) elides the most exciting moments of the expedition, and mobilizes the latest visual effects technologies in order to make visually explicit the dangerous sequences so tantalizingly absent from the documentary original. Much of the early praise heaped on Rønning and Sandberg's *Kon-Tiki* by the Norwegian press centered on the dazzling visual effects that finally allowed us to see (in sometimes gory detail) the spectacular moments of danger on the expedition. Because of this strategy of foregrounding the spectacular and sensational moments of the journey in a depiction of historical events, we might follow Bazin's lead in asking—as he does of what he considers the superfluous visual effects in *Scott of the Antarctic*—"to what purpose?" (Bazin 2005, 158). By employing the most advanced digital effects used in a Norwegian film to that date to recreate precisely those moments that escaped Heyerdahl's lens in the original documentary, Rønning and Sandberg were aiming to fill gaps in the visual record left by Heyerdahl's documentary, as well as to rival the technical virtuosity of big-budget Hollywood productions. The purpose of such spectacle was thus to ensure that Rønning and Sandberg's film, despite its origin in a small national film culture, could traverse the globe as reliably as Heyerdahl's balsawood raft.

The Kon-Tiki expedition, Heyerdahl's documentary, and the 2012 film all center on the transnational migration of cultures, and a Nordic attempt to successfully re-enact such global journeys. Heyerdahl's documentary pitches the Kon-Tiki expedition not only as a daring feat of exploration, but as an effort on the part of a group of civilized Nordic men to mimic the "primitive" navigation techniques of a temporally and geographically remote Indigenous culture. Heyerdahl frames the journey as an effort to debunk the conventional wisdom of the scientific community, which took for granted that the Polynesian islands could not have been populated from the Americas, since the archeological record had already established that the only seafaring technology the Incas possessed was simple balsawood rafts. But the way Heyerdahl goes about testing his theory—by assembling a group of white Scandinavian men and having them mimic a hypothetical migration of Indigenous Americans to the islands of the South Pacific—frames the undertaking as one of cultural exchange or even (viewed less charitably) as cultural appropriation and parody. Despite the obviously culturally problematic aspects of the expedition, Heyerdahl was also driven by an intense fascination with (and celebration of) the freedom of movement between landscapes and cultures. Heyerdahl's utopian transnationalism posits that human populations since ancient times have ingeniously harnessed the powers of nature to migrate much more freely than scientific wisdom would have it. This emphasis has carried over to the Kon-Tiki Museum in Oslo, where a quotation widely attributed (without citation) to Heyerdahl is emblazoned prominently over a picture of a young Heyerdahl astride the mast of the Kon-Tiki: "Borders? I have never seen one. But I have heard they exist in the minds of some people." This quotation is displayed at the entrance of the museum, and thus seems designed to shape the visitor's understanding of Thor Heyerdahl's life and work. The vision Heyerdahl's statement lays out of being able to navigate the globe freely, uninhibited by borders (psychological or otherwise), is not only central to the actual expedition depicted in both Kon-Tiki films, but was also a main driving force behind the making of these films. In other words, both films sought not just to depict a successful journey across astounding physical expanses, but also to themselves be successfully transported and marketed throughout the world.

In the case of Rønning and Sandberg's dramatized version of the expedition, one of the main strategies the directors used to make the film appealing to a global audience was spectacle and visual effects, rather than framing the expedition through a dry, academic voiceover as Heyerdahl had done in his documentary. In describing their own aim in re-telling the story of the Kon-Tiki onscreen, Rønning and Sandberg reveal that one of their main goals was to restore the spectacle of danger that was necessarily absent from Heyerdahl's film. To do so, the directors returned to the book Heyerdahl had written about the expedition (Heyerdahl 1948), where he describes many of the sequences of danger that are only incompletely shown in the documentary. In a behind-the-scenes interview from the documentary *Seile sin egen sjø* (dir. Synnøve Macody Lund and Carl Christian Raabe, 2013), Joachim Rønning says:

> Our film is an adaptation of the book, not so much the documentary film, perhaps. When you watch the documentary film today, [you can see that] it is quite simple. I understand quite well that it fascinated the whole world at the time. It was an adventure, and they were out on the ocean. People hadn't seen that kind of thing before. It's clear that when exciting things happened, they had to put down the camera, of course, which we didn't have to do. That is the way in which we have really written a new Kon-Tiki chapter: we filmed those moments that Thor describes so well in the book.

Rønning stakes a claim here for authorial originality within the Kon-Tiki media canon by saying that they have achieved what Heyerdahl-authored Kon-Tiki documents could not: *showing* moments of danger onscreen, effectively spectacularizing what Heyerdahl had only been able to *describe* in words. Examining the scenes of danger in Rønning and Sandberg's film, it is evident that not only did the directors show more of the encounters with dangerous sea creatures than the original documentary could have; they also depicted the failure of young Heyerdahl to fully capture such moments on film. Such meta-cinematic gestures function as embedded justifications for Rønning and Sandberg's spectacle-driven aesthetic, since they make explicit just how much is missing from Heyerdahl's documentary.

    A case in point is the raft's encounter with a whale shark, a moment which is described in detail in Heyerdahl's book, and which Heyerdahl only manages to capture a few frames of in the documentary. In order to include the sequence, Heyerdahl had to rely almost entirely on voiceover description of the encounter. What we actually see onscreen is shaky, handheld footage of the ocean's surface, occasionally pierced by the whale shark's dorsal fin, with the crew gathered along the edge of the raft gazing out at the gargantuan creature. The only moment when the body of the shark is visible is when we see some telltale white spots just underneath the surface. The shot is frozen for several seconds so that Heyerdahl (in voiceover) can tell us about the physical dimensions and features of the whale shark. The narrative momentum in the scene is carried along entirely by the voiceover, which describes how the shark followed the raft for some time, before a member of the crew plunged a harpoon into the shark's head, which made the creature dive to the ocean's depths until the harpoon line snapped, leaving the raft alone for the rest of the journey.

    In Rønning and Sandberg's film, overhead and underwater shots are used to give us a fuller view of the giant fish, which was digitally rendered by the Swedish visual effects studio Important Looking Pirates. The shots also give us a sense of scale that is completely missing in the documentary, which must rely on narration to supply the dimensions of the beast. Besides the sense of nervousness the Kon-Tiki's crew feels about the possibility of being attacked by the shark, the scene focuses on both the spectacle of the giant shark (with the crew standing in awe, transfixed by the sight) and on Heyerdahl's struggles to capture the shark on film. As soon as he spots the fish in the distance, Heyerdahl is shown scrambling about the deck, yelling at crew member Bengt Danielsson to bring him the camera. When Bengt does finally manage to bring out the camera, Heyerdahl is momentarily prevented from using it when the shark knocks cross-boards up through the deck from below the raft, and Heyerdahl is occupied looking down to see whether the shark is going to attack the ship any further. It is not until the crew sees the splash of the shark's fin in the distance that Heyerdahl finally takes up the camera and starts recording. We see Heyerdahl filming for a few more seconds while the shark glides back toward the raft, but when Herman Watzinger (acting against Heyerdahl's instructions) plunges a harpoon into the shark's head, Heyerdahl drops the

Figure 29.1 Thor Heyerdahl (Pål Sverre Hagen) is shown trying to capture the *Kon-Tiki*'s encounter with a whale shark on film. By depicting how little of sequence Heyerdahl actually manages to record, Rønning and Sandberg make an implicit justification for their spectacle-driven narrative. From *Kon-Tiki* (Rønning and Sandberg, Norway, 2012). Courtesy of Nordisk Film.

camera again, so he can be ready to respond to the apparently imminent danger. Even though we never see the point-of-view shot from Heyerdahl's camera, the implications of this scene are clear: during any moments of real danger on the expedition, Heyerdahl and his crew were far too occupied with surviving to capture a sufficient visual record of the journey. Rønning and Sandberg's intervention was to recreate the spectacle of danger that was missing from Heyerdahl's original film, a strategy that they cannily justify by depicting how little of the action Heyerdahl actually captures on film. In the space of a brief scene, they have simultaneously demonstrated their own ability to provide visual coverage and stunning spectacle for the cinemagoer, while showing Heyerdahl's own failure to do the same.

The reliance of *Kon-Tiki* (1950) on voiceover narration to describe moments of danger during the journey is understandable, particularly given the sorry state of the raw footage that Heyerdahl brought back from his expedition, much of which had been destroyed by seawater. As Malin Wahlberg writes, the intervention of Swedish editor Olle Nordemar and his optical printer (one of the only such devices available in Europe at the time) allowed Heyerdahl to bracket damaged sections of film, and replace them with inserted stills (Wahlberg 2013, 145). But the extreme difference in narrative strategies between the two films—from Heyerdahl's reliance on verbal narration to Rønning and Sandberg's penchant for visual spectacle—again raises Bazin's question about the dazzling special effects in Charles Frend's dramatization of the Terra Nova expedition: to what purpose?

I have already suggested that Rønning and Sandberg justify their turn toward spectacle by depicting Heyerdahl *failing* to capture danger on film, an implicit historical and aesthetic argument about the insufficiency of the existing visual record of the expedition. But there is also an economic argument that has more to do with the way small-nation film cultures relate to an imagined Hollywood blockbuster aesthetic. One possible response is to rhetorically elevate the aesthetics of small-budget filmmaking, as Mette Hjort argues was the case with the Dogme 95 movement (Hjort 2005). Another possible response is one of imitating the aesthetics of Hollywood blockbuster filmmaking, which is what Rønning and Sandberg opted to do with *Kon-Tiki*, a big-budget (by Norwegian standards) historical film that largely succeeded in critical and commercial terms. In the predominantly glowing Norwegian critical reception of the film, there is an undercurrent of national pride that a domestic film production could so seamlessly achieve the look of a big-budget Hollywood film. Movie critic Birger Vestmo, for example, writes that *Kon-Tiki* is "impressively well filmed, with dazzling visual effects" and that the directors possess a "filmic virtuosity that goes beyond what we are used to seeing in domestic film" (Vestmo 2012). *Verdens gang* critic Jon Selås enthusiastically calls *Kon-Tiki* "a new national film," and praises the directors for their "well-applied international (read: Hollywoodesque) grasp of their film narrative" (Selås 2012). Even in these few representative quotations from critics, the curious combination of nationalist and internationalist ambitions at the heart of Rønning and Sandberg's film is clear. *Kon-Tiki* (2012), then, is a vivid, anti-Bazinian argument that in order to be viable in a global marketplace, and to thereby fulfill the Heyerdahl-esque dream of free movement through a borderless world, the cinema of small nations should adopt the aesthetics of spectacle that is central to Hollywood blockbuster filmmaking.

Note. All translations from Norwegian are my own.

References

Bazin, André. 2005. *What Is Cinema?* Vol. 1. Ed. and trans. Hugh Gray. Berkeley: University of California Press.
Bryne, Snorre. 2012. "Kon-Tiki er Norges dyreste film noen gang," *Dagbladet*, February 13. <https://www.dagbladet.no/kultur/kon-tiki-er-norges-dyreste-film-noen-gang/63372144> (last accessed November 1, 2017).
Heyerdahl, Thor. 1948. *Kon-Tiki ekspedisjonen*. Oslo: Gyldendal norsk forlag.
Hjort, Mette. 2005. *Small Nation, Global Cinema: The New Danish Cinema*. Minneapolis: University of Minnesota Press.
Iversen, Gunnar. 2015. "Voices from the Past—Recent Nordic Historical Films." In *Nordic Genre Film: Small Nation Film Cultures in the Global Marketplace*, ed. Tommy Gustafsson and Pietari Kääpä. Edinburgh: Edinburgh University Press. 47–58.
Laine, Kimmo. 2015. "*Sibelius* and the Re-emergence of the Great Man Biopic." In *Nordic Genre Film: Small Nation Film Cultures in the Global Marketplace*, ed. Tommy Gustafsson and Pietari Kääpä. Edinburgh: Edinburgh University Press. 21–32.

Selås, Jon. 2012. "Forventningene infridd!" *Verdens Gang* August 18. <https://www.vg.no/rampelys/film/filmanmeldelser/kon-tiki-anmeldelse-forventningene-innfridd/a/10067818/> (last accessed November 1, 2017).
Vestmo, Birger. "Kon-Tiki: Eventyrlysten tyter ut av filmruta!" *Filmpolitiet*, August 18. <http://p3.no/filmpolitiet/2012/08/kon-tiki/> (last accessed November 1, 2017).
Wahlberg, Malin. 2013. "Adventures in murky waters: the enactment and commemoration of Kon-Tiki." *Journal of Scandinavian Cinema* 3(2): 141–9.

INDEX

A City Called Copenhagen (Denmark, 1960), 145, 150–1
A Hard Day's Night (UK/USA, 1964), 76–8
A Taste of Honey (UK, 1961), 78
A Woman's Face (Sweden, 1938), 127
A Woman's Face (USA, 1941), 127
A World Not Ours (Lebanon, 2012), 299
Abortion (Norway, 1972), 86–92
accented cinema, 99–101, 245–6, 363
Act of Killing, The (Denmark, 2012), 271, 273–5
African Wildlife (Denmark, 1956), 108
All That Heaven Allows (USA, 1955), 117
Amazonas (Denmark, 1957), 108
Ambassador, The (Denmark, 2011), 270
Another Look at the Jungle People (Norway, 1950), 108
Antichrist (USA, 2009), 254–6
Arab Institute of Film, 289–301
Arcel, Nikolaj, 200–2
Around the World in 80 Minutes (Denmark, 1955), 108
art cinema, 208
Autumn Sonata (Sweden/West Germany, 1978), 138–9

Bakhtin, Mikhail, 174, 361–3, 368
Bali Everyday and in Holiday (Denmark, 1950), 108
Bazin, André, 137, 312–13, 378–80, 383–4
Beatles, The, 76–83
Bells of Saint Mary's, The (USA, 1945), 129
Bergfilme (mountain films), 58
Bergman, Ingmar, 78, 83, 109, 341–58
Bergman, Ingrid, 126–39
Berlin Alexanderplatz (West Germany, 1980), 349–52
Bihttoš (Canada/Norway, 2014), 279–85
Black Power Mixtape 1967–75, The (Sweden, 2011), 171–9
Blue Light, The (Germany, 1932), 58

Borgen (Denmark, 2010–13), 190, 195
Boy in the Tree, The (Sweden, 1961), 70
Brecht, Berthold, 87
Brechtianism, 244–6, 250–3, 343, 373
Brügger, Mads, 270, 275

Cab 519 (Denmark, 1909), 30
Cabaret (USA, 1972), 344–5, 347–8
Canudo, Ricciotto, 220
Carlsen, Jon Bang, 261–2, 267–9, 275
Casablanca (USA, 1942), 128–31
celebrity, 43–4, 128, 224–35
Chan, Charlie (Warner Oland), 42–50
Charlie Chan at the Race Track (USA, 1936), 47
Charlie Chan in Honolulu (USA, 1938), 47
Cider House Rules, The (USA, 1999), 366–7
cinefeminism, 88–90
Cinéma d'Essai, 305–16
Cinema Novo, 70–2
Cinémathèque Française, 207, 221, 310, 312
Cinephilia, 207–22, 305–16
Circus Girl, The (Denmark, 1911), 31–2
Cold Case Hammarskjöld (Denmark, 2019), 119
Concerning Violence (Sweden, 2014), 172–6, 180
Concrete Grandma (Sweden, 1986), 336–8
Count of the Old Town, The (Sweden, 1935), 127
Country Below the Equator, The (Sweden, 1950), 120
Crayons of Askalan (Lebanon, 2011), 298–9

D. . .for Design! (Denmark, 1955), 142, 152–5
Dahlin, Ture, 212

Dancer in the Dark (Denmark, 2000), 244–7
Dawn of Love, The (Sweden, 1919), 36
Dear Wendy (Denmark, 2004), 252–3
Delluc, Louis, 209–10, 214
Denmark Grows Up (Denmark, 1947), 143, 145, 148–9
Despair (West Germany/USA, 1979), 349
Dogville (Denmark, 2003), 252–4
Douglas, Mary, 117
Dr. Jekyll and Mr. Hyde (USA, 1941), 129
Dream of Sharazad, The, (South Africa, 2014), 99
Dreyer, Carl Th., 305–16
Drive (USA, 2011), 373–5
Dyer, Richard, 49, 128–29, 227–8

Eco, Umberto, 128–9
Ekberg, Anita, 224–35
Elsaesser, Thomas, 344–5, 352
Erotikon (Sweden, 1920), 37
Escape from Terror (Denmark/USA, 1955), 110
Eskimo (Norway, 1930), 113
Europe '51 (Italy, 1952), 136–7
Exit (Norway, 1970), 86
Expressionism, German, 341, 346, 350–2, 355–8

Fairy of Solbakken (Sweden, 1919), 37
Fear (Italy/West Germany, 1954), 136–7
film noir, 352–3
Firebird, The (Italy–Sweden, 1952), 109
Flame of Life, The (Sweden, 1919), 35–6
Flute and the Arrow, The (Sweden, 1957), 67–72
Fock-Göring, Carin, 53–64
Four Companions, The (Germany, 1938), 128

Fanon, Frantz, 172–6
FilmLab Palestine, 288–90, 296, 300–1
First Picture (Jordan, 2006), 297–8
French New Wave, 11, 70
French Suburbe—A No-go Zone? (Switzerland, 2017), 100
Frontiers of Dreams and Fears (Lebanon, 2001), 98
Full Bloom (Jordan, 2006), 298

Galapagos (Norway, 1955), 108
Gaumont Palace, 215, 221
Gilroy, Paul, 170, 176
Glass Dolls, The (Norway, 2014), 158, 166–7

globalization, 15–17, 245, 261–76, 363–4, 367–8
Goebbels, Josef, 53–8, 62–4
Goldmann, Peter, 76–83
Gorilla Safari (Sweden, 1956), 105
Göring, Hermann, 53–4, 60–2
Grierson, John, 264
Gulistan, Land of Roses (Canada/Germany, 2016), 100
Gypsies (Norway, 1973), 86

Hallström, Lasse, 360–8
Hell Ship, The (Sweden, 1923), 37
Help! (UK/USA, 1965), 76
Heyerdahl, Thor, 378–84
Hitler, Adolf, 53, 57–8, 63–4, 128
Holmberg, Folke, 211–12
Hundred-foot Journey, The (2014), 367–8

I Am Curious (Yellow) (Sweden, 1969), 319–25
I fetischmannens spår (Sweden, 1948), 120–3
I Hired a Contract Killer (1990), 183–4, 186–7
Imitation of Life (USA, 1959), 116
In the Hands of Imposters (Denmark, 1911), 30, 32
India: Matri Hhumi (Italy/ France, 1959), 68
Indian Village (Sweden, 1951), 68
Intermezzo (Sweden, 1936), 127, 129
Intermezzo: A Love Story (USA, 1939), 130
International Exile Film Festival, 94–101
It's All About Love (Denmark, 2003), 245–7, 249

Joan of Arc (USA, 1948), 130
Jordan, Jessica, 229
Jullier, Laurent, 306–9, 313–16
Jungle Dreams (India/Germany, 1996), 70

Kamilla (Norway, 1981), 86–7
Kaurismäki, Aki, 182–9
Kautokeino Rebellion, The (Norway, 2008), 158–9, 164–6
Killing, The (USA, 2007–12), 190, 195–6
Kingdom, The (Denmark, 1994), 194
Kitchen Sink films, 78, 86
Kon-Tiki (Sweden–Norway, 1950), 107, 378–84
Kon-Tiki (Norway, 2012), 379–84

La Tosca (France, 1909), 29
La Vie de Bohème (Finland, 1992), 183–5, 187–8

Le Havre (2011), 182–3, 185, 187–8
L'Herbier, Marcel, 216
Lagerlöf, Selma 37, 213–14, 362–3, 368
Laila (Sweden, 1958), 116–18
Langlois, Henri, 311
Laplanders, The (Norway, 1957), 108
Lapp Blood (Sweden, 1948), 116
Last King, The (Norway, 2016), 158, 164–6
Leningrad Cowboys Go America (Finland, 1989), 182, 184
Les Misérables (France, 1913), 29
Liv (Norway, 1967), 86
Lo Duca, 305–12, 316
Løkkeberg, Vibeke, 85–92
Look of Silence, The (2014), 273–5
Louisiana Story (USA, 1948), 113

Madsen, Ole Christian, 194, 198
Mahini, Hassan, 94, 101
Mahini, Hossein, 94, 101
Make Way for Lila (Sweden, 1958), 105, 117–18
Man of Aran (Ireland, 1934), 71
Manderlay (Denmark, 2005), 253–4
Mandingo (USA, 1975), 254
mapping film, 2, 34, 38
Melancholia (Denmark, 2001), 256–7
Miss Julie (Sweden, 1951), 108
Monika: The Story of a Bad Girl! (USA/Sweden 1955), 109, 231
Moonshiners, The (Finland, 1907), 27
Music Is the Weapon (Sweden, 1982), 173, 176
My Home Is Copacabana (Sweden, 1965), 67, 71–4
My Life as a Dog (Sweden, 1985), 365–6

Neon Demon (2016), 375–6
New German Cinema, 89, 341–58
New Hollywood, 354–7
Nichols, Bill, 68, 264–5, 270–2
Nine Lives (Norway, 1957), 109
Nordic Model, 106
Nordic Noir, 38, 190–202
Nordisk, 26–8, 30–1, 35–40, 111, 186–7, 211
Notorious (USA, 1946), 128–9
Nykvist, Sven, 118–23

Olsson, Göran Hugo, 169–80
Oland, Warner *see* Charlie Chan
On the Fateful Roads of Life (Sweden, 1913), 29
On the Other Side of the Earth (Sweden, 1972), 72

One Summer of Happiness (Sweden, 1951), 108, 231
Only God Forgives (2013), 373–5
Oppenheimer, Joshua, 270–5
Ordet (Denmark, 1955), 305
Our Wondrous World (Denmark, 1957), 108

Palestinian Cinema Association, 287–8, 291, 300
Passion of Joan of Arc, The (France, 1928), 305–16
Pathé Frères, 28–9
Pather Panchali (India, 1955), 68
Pathfinder (Norway, 1987), 157–67
"Penny Lane" (UK, 1967), 80–2
Persona (Sweden, 1966), 79, 346
Phantom Carriage, The (Sweden, 1921), 219–20
Phantom India (France, 1969), 68
Plantinga, Carl, 264–5
Prosperity Race, The (Sweden, 1962), 328, 331–2
Purity Beats Everything (Denmark, 2007), 267–9
Pusher (Denmark, 1996), 370–3

Qivitoq: The Mountain Wanderer (Denmark, 1956), 105, 111–12

Refn, Nicolas Winding, 370–7
Return of Ulysses, The (France, 1909), 29
Revelation, The (Norway, 1977)
Reverence of Life: A Short Film About Albert Schweitzer (Sweden, 1952), 120
Rhythm of a City (Sweden, 1947), 108
Riefenstahl, Leni, 53, 58–9, 64, 335
Rønning, Joachim, 380–4
Rossellini, Roberto, 68, 70, 126, 129, 134–8, 224, 356

Safari (Denmark, 1954), 108
Salminen, Carl H., 238–9
Salmon Fishing in the Yemen (USA, 2007), 367
Sandberg, Espen, 380–4
Scott of the Antarctic (UK, 1948), 379–80
Screen Institute Beirut, 289–91, 295–6, 299–301
Seagulls (Norway, 1991), 87
Selznick, David O., 127, 129–30
Serpent's Egg, The (West Germany/USA, 1977), 341–58
Seventh Age, The (Denmark, 1947) 143, 145–6, 148, 151

Sgt. Pepper's Lonely Hearts Club Band (1967), 78
Shipping News, The (2001), 360–2
Shipwrecked (1990), 157–61
Sieling, Charlotte, 191, 195–203
silent film, 25–40, 207–2, 305–16
Sjöman, Vilgot, 320–5
Sjöström, Victor, 37, 207–10, 214–21, 363–4
Smiles of a Summer Night (Sweden, 1955), 108
Snows of Destiny, The (Sweden, 1920), 36
Social Denmark film series (Denmark, 1947), 143–9
Some Like It Veiled (France, 2017), 98
Sontag, Susan, 54, 56
S.O.S. Eisberg (Germany/USA, 1933), 113
Space Invasion of Lapland/Terror in the Midnight Sun (USA/Sweden, 1959), 115–16
Spellbound (USA, 1945), 130, 132
stardom *see* celebrity
Stiller, Mauritz, 35–7, 39, 207–8, 210, 214–21, 362–3, 368
Storfilm, 108, 116, 121, 123
Stormy Petrel, The (Sweden, 1914), 29
"Strawberry Fields Forever" (UK, 1967), 77, 79–82
Stromboli (Italy/USA, 1950), 134–7
Studlar, Gaylyn, 225–6
Sucksdorff, Arne, 67–74, 122
Summer with Monika (Sweden, 1953), 109, 231
Suner, Asuman, 99
Suomi-Filmi, 237, 239–40
Swedes in America (USA, 1943), 132–4
Swedish Biograph, 26–9, 35–6
Swedishness, 43, 48–9, 53–5, 132–4, 212–13, 229–30

Tailfeathers, Elle-Máijá Apiniskim, 279–85
Tashunga (1996), 157–8, 161–4
Temptations of a Great City (Denmark, 1911), 30–5, 39
They Guide You Across (Denmark, 1949), 145, 147, 150
Thing from Another World, The (USA, 1951), 115
Third Cinema, 97–101
This Is Cinerama (USA, 1952), 107
This Sporting Life (UK, 1963), 78
Through a Glass Darkly (Sweden, 1961), 78, 118
Thy Soul Shall Bear Witness (Sweden, 1921), 37
Touch, The (Sweden, 1971), 354–5
Triumph of the Will (Germany, 1935), 58–9

Vikings, The (USA 1958), 110
Vilde, the Wild One (Norway, 1986), 87
Vinterberg, Thomas, 244–58
Visions of Eight (1973), 333–5
von Trier, Lars, 13, 192–4, 244–58, 283

Warren, Shilyh, 90–1
Warner, Oland *see* Charlie Chan
Wavelength (Canada, 1967), 79
Wedding of Palo (Denmark, 1934), 113
What's Eating Gilbert Grape? (USA, 1993), 366
Where Gods Are Dead (Norway, 1993), 87
Where Mountains Float (Denmark, 1955), 105, 111, 113–14
White Reindeer (Finland, 1952), 115
White Slave, The (Denmark, 1910), 30
Wild Strawberries (Sweden, 1957), 83
Wind and the River, The (Sweden, 1953), 68
Windjammer (USA, 1958), 110

Zetterling, Mai, 88, 327–39

EU representative:
Easy Access System Europe
Mustamäe tee 50, 10621 Tallinn, Estonia
Gpsr.requests@easproject.com

www.ingramcontent.com/pod-product-compliance
Lightning Source LLC
Chambersburg PA
CBHW051803230426
43672CB00012B/2609